D1236825

Nikolay Myaskovsky

Myaskovsky in 1923

Nikolay Myaskovsky:
A Composer and His Times

Patrick Zuk

THE BOYDELL PRESS

The right of Patrick Zuk to be identified as
the author of this work has been asserted in accordance with
sections 77 and 78 of the Copyright, Designs and Patents Act 1988

First published 2021
The Boydell Press, Woodbridge

ISBN 978-1-78327-575-5

The Boydell Press is an imprint of Boydell & Brewer Ltd
PO Box 9, Woodbridge, Suffolk IP12 3DF, UK
and of Boydell & Brewer Inc.
668 Mt Hope Avenue, Rochester, NY 14620-2731, USA
website: www.boydellandbrewer.com

A catalogue record of this publication is available
from the British Library

This publication is printed on acid-free paper

for Tatiana Fedorovskaya, Dmitry Gorbatov, Marianna Taymanova,
Ruth Fleischmann, Séamas de Barra
– and Ania Wasilewski in memoriam

Contents

Illustrations

MAPS

The author and publisher are grateful to all the institutions and individuals listed for permission to reproduce the materials in which they hold copyright. Every effort has been made to trace the copyright holders; apologies are offered for any omission, and the publisher will be pleased to add any necessary acknowledgement in subsequent editions.

Music Examples

Preface

Is minic a théann an bhréag níos faide ná an fhírinne (seanfhocal)

Falsehood often travels further than the truth (Irish proverb)

The present volume offers a critical reassessment of the career and achievement of Nikolay Myaskovsky (1881–1950), a Russian composer who was regarded in his native country as one of the major figures of his era, but whose work has only recently begun to emerge from the neglect into which it fell after his death. Such a reassessment is long overdue. Myaskovsky's œuvre contains superbly wrought music of compelling vividness and imaginative power: the quality of his finest contributions to the genres central to his creative preoccupations – the symphony, the string quartet, the piano sonata – has yet to be fully recognised.

Perhaps the most serious hindrance to a more extensive revival of interest in Myaskovsky has been the difficulty of finding out very much about him. Little has been published on the composer in any language other than Russian: until fairly recently, music lovers in the English-speaking world have had few sources of information at their disposal other than encyclopædia articles and the brief treatments accorded him in standard reference works on Russian music. These sketchy and often misleading accounts convey a very inadequate impression of a life that was unusually rich in interest – not least because of the single-mindedness with which Myaskovsky pursued his artistic vocation in the face of many difficulties throughout a turbulent era marked by dramatic political and social upheaval. Unlike Prokofiev and Shostakovich, whose exceptional gifts were apparent from childhood, Myaskovsky developed late and had to struggle long and hard to remedy the deficiencies of his haphazard early musical education: a military engineer by profession, he was twenty-five before he managed to extricate himself from the army and enrol to study composition at the St Petersburg Conservatoire. After completing his studies in 1911, he eked out a penurious existence while writing two symphonies and several other works that gave the first intimations of his potential stature as a creative artist. He was called up from the reserves immediately on the outbreak of the First World War and posted to Russia's western front, from which he was lucky to return alive; he remained in the armed forces throughout the grim aftermath of the October Revolution until the offer of a teaching post at the Moscow Conservatoire in 1921 enabled him to resign his commission. The premiere of his Sixth Symphony in 1923 was hailed as an artistic event comparable in importance to the premiere of Tchaikovsky's

Pathétique thirty years previously: by the end of the 1920s, he was regarded as the foremost Russian symphonist of his generation. Outside the USSR, his music attracted the attention of renowned conductors such as Leopold Stokowski, Frederick Stock, and Wilhelm Furtwängler. A highly respected composition teacher, whose many pupils included Vissarion Shebalin, Aram Khachaturian, and Dmitry Kabalevsky, he played an active role in revitalising the Moscow musical scene after the depredations of the Civil War years, especially in helping to create opportunities for new music to be heard. His circle of friends and acquaintances included notable musicians of the day, amongst them Sergey Prokofiev and Boris Asafiev. Despite his eminence, he experienced his share of the indignities to which artists and intellectuals were subject during the Stalinist era – especially his condemnation, together with other prominent composers, in a government decree promulgated in 1948 that criticised their work for its alleged decadence. A modest, shy man who shunned celebrity, Myaskovsky won his colleagues' respect for the personal and professional integrity that he displayed even in the most testing of circumstances.

Aside from being rich in human interest, Myaskovsky's career warrants closer study because of his important position in Soviet musical life: without exaggeration, it is impossible to understand that milieu adequately without some consideration of his place in it. His professional experiences tell us much about the conditions in which musicians had to operate during the first three decades of Soviet power and vividly illustrate the challenges confronting many members of the intelligentsia in their efforts to evolve a *modus vivendi* with the Bolshevik regime. In this respect, he constitutes an important test case when it comes to examining the validity of assumptions that have long shaped Western views of Soviet music and musicians. A reappraisal of his career also affords a useful opportunity to reflect on how our knowledge of both has been constructed. It is worth expanding on these points here, as the issues have considerable ramifications.

Prior to the dissolution of the USSR, such information as was available in the West about Soviet composers derived almost entirely from Soviet publications. Matters could scarcely have been otherwise. The practical difficulties attendant on conducting research on Soviet music in the USSR largely deterred foreigners from attempting it, and even if they did make the attempt, there were severe limits on what they could hope to find out at first-hand. They stood little chance of gaining access to materials such as composers' personal papers; furthermore, the Soviet musicians whom they encountered would have been understandably guarded when it came to discussing professional matters. The necessity to rely on Soviet publications created insuperable difficulties, as their trustworthiness was always open to question and their contents could seldom be independently verified. Censorship in the Soviet Union was notoriously strict and authors were expected to treat subjects from approved ideological standpoints.[1] At best, these writings offered a highly selective view of Soviet musical life and its leading figures; at worst, they could be seriously misleading.

This is certainly true of much of the literature on Myaskovsky, who wrote and spoke. about himself very little In part, this was a question of temperament, but it was also because his position was a vulnerable one. His father had held a high-ranking position in the tsarist army: given the discrimination to which 'class enemies' and their families were subjected after the October Revolution, Myaskovsky was understandably chary of drawing too much attention to himself. Uninterested in politics, he viewed with disdain the Bolsheviks' attempts to subordinate the arts to ideological ends. The resolutely apolitical nature of his output caused him to be regarded with suspicion, as did the perception that his music evinced decadent Western influences – although his private attitudes towards Western musical modernism were sceptical and ambivalent. When the climate of Soviet life grew increasingly repressive after Stalin's accession to supreme power, he came under pressure to display more overt political engagement. Myaskovsky's preferred strategy for dealing with these circumstances was to remain out of the public gaze and maintain a strict silence.

His sole substantial statement about his life and work was a brief essay titled 'Autobiographical notes about my creative path', which was published in the Composers' Union journal *Soviet Music* in 1936.[2] It is a curious production, to say the least. Most of it is taken up with a sketch of his early development as a musician: few details are given about his career after 1917. It concludes with a highly self-critical survey of his output that emphasised his dissatisfaction with his efforts to evolve a compositional approach consonant with Socialist Realism, the official Marxist-Leninist aesthetic philosophy introduced to guide Soviet artistic production. The unsuspecting reader might take Myaskovsky's account at face value, but a knowledge of the context is vital for its appraisal. As the composer's diary reveals, he did not write the piece on his own initiative: it was produced at the insistence of Nikolay Chelyapov, the government functionary in charge of the Moscow Composers' Union. The timing was significant: Chelyapov made his request shortly after the condemnation in *Pravda* of Shostakovich's opera *Lady Macbeth of the Mtsensk District*, an event that caused widespread alarm amongst the intelligentsia and signalled the government's intention to extirpate modernist tendencies in the arts. Under

1   For a discussion of pre-*glasnost'* scholarship on Soviet music, see the first four essays in Patrick Zuk and Marina Frolova-Walker (ed.), *Russian Music since 1917*, Proceedings of the British Academy (Oxford, 2017).

2   Nikolay Myaskovskiy, 'Avtobiograficheskiye zametki o tvorcheskom puti', *Sovetskaya muzika*, 6 (1936), 3–11.

the circumstances, Myaskovsky knew perfectly well what was expected of him – a statement confirming his artistic reform and his intention to comply with official directives. He duly 'concocted' something suitable (in his own phrase)[3], having evidently judged it inadvisable to demur – but the ritualised self-criticism expressed in his carefully crafted remarks was merely self-protective camouflage.[4]

Even during his lifetime, Myaskovsky's public silence did not prevent Soviet commentators from placing highly questionable constructions on his work. It was claimed that his outlook had transformed under the influence of Marxist-Leninist philosophy in the early 1930s, leading him to become a politically committed artist: his admiration for Stalin's ambitious schemes to modernise Soviet agriculture had supposedly prompted him in 1931 to write a programmatic Twelfth Symphony in celebration of them. His creative idiom was also said to have undergone radical change: he purportedly abandoned the esoteric style of his earlier music and evolved a more 'democratic' compositional language accessible to mass audiences. As shall be discussed in due course, all these claims are dubious: the so-called 'Collective Farm' Symphony was a fiction. Moreover, these assessments seriously misrepresent Myaskovsky's aesthetic stance and the course of his artistic development. Myaskovsky recorded in his diary his contempt for the 'rubbish' that was being written about him but did not contradict it, knowing that to object would be futile and counterproductive. Soviet critics and musicologists continued to fashion a narrative of his career that adhered to a standard plot of contemporary plays and novels: the representative of the pre-Revolutionary 'bourgeois intelligentsia' who 'reforged' his consciousness and overcame his alienation from Soviet society – like the protagonist of Alexander Afinogenov's popular drama *Fear* (1931).[5] It was not enough for Soviet art to imitate Soviet life: Soviet life also had to imitate Soviet art.

This narrative underwent further elaboration posthumously in the first major study of Myaskovsky's life and work, *Myaskovsky's Creative Path* by the musicologist Tamara Livanova, which appeared in 1953, three years after his death. Once again, a knowledge of the background circumstances is essential for appraising its contents. On the face of it, Livanova's decision to write about Myaskovsky seems puzzling: her principal area of specialism was eighteenth-century music, not modern music. She had no personal

---

3   Myaskovsky, 'Vïpiski iz dnevnikov' (hereafter: 'Vïpiski'), 9 April 1936, RGALI, 2040/1/65, l. 29.

4   Myaskovsky's essay is discussed more fully in chapter 9, pp. 346–8.

5   On narratives of the refashioning of the self under socialism, see Stephen Kotkin, *Magnetic Mountain: Stalinism as a Civilization* (Berkeley and Los Angeles, 1997); Oleg Kharkhordin, *The Collective and the Individual in Russia: A Study of Practices* (Berkeley, 1999); Jochen Hellbeck, *Revolution on My Mind: Writing a Diary under Stalin* (Cambridge, Masschusetts, and London, 2006).

connection with the composer and apparently only met him for the first time shortly before his death. There seems little doubt that her motivation was opportunistic and prompted by extraneous factors rather than by any genuine interest in Myaskovsky himself.

The sequence of events that led Livanova to undertake the project began in 1948, when Myaskovsky was publicly censured for his insufficient adherence to Socialist Realism. Later that year she published a piece in *Soviet Music* entitled 'Dispute about Myaskovsky', which takes the form of an imaginary debate between two musicians about the merits of his work.[6] One of the disputants expresses views that unmistakably echoed official strictures: Myaskovsky's output largely consisted of decadent, complex instrumental music that failed to appeal to a mass listenership; moreover, he had been insulated from corrective criticisms by fawning admirers, who praised him indiscriminately instead of prompting him to reconsider his position. The genre of the dialogue allowed Livanova to float these opinions without having to take personal responsibility for them (she coyly signed the piece 'taken down by T. Livanova'), but she shared and fully endorsed them. Her voluminous unpublished autobiography, written during the 1970s, reveals her to have been a zealous member of the Communist Party, to which she was admitted in 1948; she records her wholehearted approval of the Party edict condemning Myaskovsky and his colleagues in the same year, as well as her rapturously admiring responses to the speeches of Andrey Zhdanov, the government minister who presided over the concomitant official enquiry into the state of musical life. ('Zhdanov loved art, believed in its power, and passionately wanted to set it on the right path. . . . He was right, and remains right still . . .').[7] Highly ambitious, Livanova had evidently seized the opportunity to demonstrate her political loyalty, hoping the *Soviet Music* article might enhance her professional standing.

Her strategy backfired badly. She herself came under attack the following year in the course of a follow-up investigation of ideologically heterodox tendencies in Soviet musicology: Tikhon Khrennikov, the new head of the Composers' Union, upbraided her publicly for having overemphasised the importance of foreign influences on the development of eighteenth-century Russian musical culture. In the atmosphere of heightened xenophobia prevalent during the late Stalinist period, an accusation of this kind was potentially very serious and could have caused her to be dismissed from her institutional posts. Khrennikov was equally critical of her article on Myaskovsky, which he declared to evince an unduly 'obsequious' attitude

---

6   Tamara Livanova, 'Spor o Myaskovskom', *Sovetskaya muzïka*, 9 (1948), 23–7.

7   Tamara Livanova, 'Vospominaniya', RNMM, 194/1754a, ll. 500–501, 505.

to the proscribed composers rather than taking them properly to task for their errors.[8]

Livanova would not make the same mistake a second time. Though she was at pains to deny any careerist motives in her reminiscences[9], the biography of Myaskovsky that she wrote a few years later was not a disinterested scholarly endeavour but a piece of hackwork produced in order to redeem herself. Her book furnishes a telling demonstration of the degradation of Soviet musicology under ideological pressures. She undertook little new research; such factual information as contained was largely cobbled together from the composer's autobiography and articles that had appeared during his lifetime. By her own admission, she found it difficult to assess Myaskovsky's music from the scores alone in the virtual absence of any recordings[10]: it is doubtful how much of his work she actually knew, and her accounts of it are superficial and unilluminating. Her aim, however, was not to provide a technical appraisal of Myaskovsky's compositions or an objective account of his career based on a careful sifting of the available documentary evidence. In accordance with Party demands that ideological and political concerns should be paramount in all domains of scholarship, she presented Myaskovsky's life as an edifying morality tale of a decadent artist who reformed and realised his full creative potential under the redemptive influence of Marxism-Leninism. A short quotation from the preface will suffice to illustrate the book's tone and general tenor:

> Myaskovsky's creative destiny is of the utmost significance as an exemplar for our epoch and for our country. It can serve as an example of how a Soviet artist develops, of how he gradually reforges his consciousness in the new social conditions created under the wise guidance of the Communist Party. Myaskovsky's creative destiny can serve as a splendid example of the great transformative power of Marxist-Leninist ideas when they take possession of the complex and conflict-ridden consciousness of a great artist. [The young] Myaskovsky did not steer clear of the themes and images characteristic of modernism, or of its typical stylistic traits. This occurred because at that period Myaskovsky lacked a solid ideological foundation which would have enabled him to stand firm against decadent tendencies. . . . Myaskovsky sincerely strove to become an authentic Soviet artist and to make himself needed by the people, and at the same time express the ideas and feelings that were dear to him. This task turned out to be a most difficult one, for the images wrought by Myaskovsky's creative imagination had for a long time not corresponded or only partially corresponded to the Soviet people's progressive world-

---

8   Tikhon Khrennikov, 'O neterpimom otstavanii muzïkal'noy kritiki i muzïkovedeniya', *Sovetskaya muzïka*, 2 (1949), 14.

9   Livanova, 'Vospominaniya', RNMM, 194/1754a, l. 611.

10   Ibid., l. 608.

view. . . . At times it seemed that Myaskovsky had begun to grope his way towards the true path, at others that he had failed and fallen into error, more deeply, perhaps, than before. . . . But Myaskovsky lived and worked in the Soviet Union: he participated in the building of socialist culture, studied the classics of Marxism-Leninism, and came into contact with real life and with a broad spectrum of Soviet society. In the period around 1930–1934, when socialism triumphed in all sectors of life in our country, a decisive transformation occurred in Myaskovsky's psyche and creative consciousness.[11]

The creative climax of Myaskovsky's career, needless to say, came about in this scenario as a result of the Party's criticism of him in 1948: having at last repented wholly of his failings, he could depart this world in a state of ideological grace.

Livanova's monograph is tedious to the point of being unreadable – a tissue of questionable unsupported assertions and sententious observations larded with copious 'obligatory quotations' (*obyazatel'nïye tsitati*) from the writings of Lenin, Stalin, and other canonical Marxist authors, as had become customary practice in Soviet academic publications. Much space is devoted to stridently censorious discussions of Myaskovsky's artistic lapses and to descriptions of his supposed attempts to reform, punctuated by regrettable instances of recidivism. Widely regarded as a shameful production, the book elicited a scathing co-authored review from Shostakovich and Kabalevsky, in which they pointed out elementary howlers in its author's commentaries on Myaskovsky's compositions that were sufficiently egregious as to call her professional competence into question.[12] Nonetheless, it remained a standard reference work and continues to be cited as a supposedly authoritative source even today.

It will readily apparent that in composing accounts of this kind, factual evidence was largely redundant, if not downright inconvenient. From an ideological standpoint, the individuality of the artist was irrelevant: an artist's life and work only merited attention insofar as they conformed (or could be represented as conforming) to approved stereotypes. Like mediaeval hagiographies or *biographies moralisées*, Soviet biographies were fundamentally didactic in aim – portraits of exemplary lives offered as models for contemplation and emulation. The personalities of their subjects were characterised in terms of clichés: without exception, Soviet artists venerated the great Russian classics, were devoted to their motherland, and

11 Tamara Livanova, *N. Ya. Myaskovskiy: Tvorcheskiy put'* (Moscow, 1953), 4–6.

12 See Igor' Bélza, 'O T. I. Livanovoy – Uchyonom i cheloveke', in Devil' Arutyunov and Vladimir Protopopov (ed.), *T. I. Livanova: Stat'i, vospominaniya* (Moscow, 1989), 298; Dmitriy Kabalevskiy and Dmitriy Shostakovich, 'Kniga o N. Ya. Myaskovskom', *Sovetskaya muzïka*, 7 (1954), 99–108.

toiled industriously on its behalf. The reader generally learns little about their inner or private lives, and certainly not about any deviations from conventional notions of respectable behaviour. While it is readily understandable that Soviet biographers would have exercised discretion when writing about contemporary or recently deceased figures, their omissions and silences far exceed the dictates of tact. Delicate topics were studiously avoided, as was discussion of anything that might prompt critical reflection on Soviet society. Even when not studiedly mendacious, these narratives were heavily sanitised and idealising in tone; they bring to mind the Polish writer Tadeusz Boy-Żeleński's complaints about biographies of artists in which the subjects have been so 'pickled in virtue' as to make both them and their work seem insufferably dull.[13]

The second biography of Myaskovsky to appear, Alexey Ikonnikov's *Myaskovsky: An Artist of Our Time* (1966), is a case in point, even if it is a distinct improvement on Livanova's opus. Ikonnikov began to study Myaskovsky's music as a graduate student in the mid-1930s and had already produced several articles and a short book on the composer. He encountered Myaskovsky professionally and elicited information from him by correspondence and in interviews; he was also granted access to some of Myaskovsky's personal papers after the composer's death. It cannot be said that Ikonnikov made much of these advantages, however. His account of Myaskovsky's life, though more detailed in certain respects than Livanova's, is still pedestrian, especially so in dealing with Myaskovsky's Soviet career. And while it is not so blatantly tendentious, it adheres to the familiar narrative of the wayward artist's struggles to reform. Neither does Ikonnikov have anything particularly illuminating to say about Myaskovsky's compositions: as is usually the case with Soviet music criticism, he is principally concerned wherever possible to elucidate the ideological 'content' supposedly embodied in their musical imagery – in the case of the Twenty-Sixth Symphony, for example, 'the image of the Motherland, the patriotic spirit of the Soviet people'.[14] Myaskovsky privately opined that Ikonnikov's writings on his music contained 'frightful quantities of drivel'.[15] In an unpublished autobiography, his erstwhile pupil Yevgeny Golubev recounted that his teacher made ironic self-deprecating remarks about his work to Ikonnikov, only to discover to his dismay that the musicologist had reproduced them

---

13   Tadeusz Boy-Żeleński, *Ludzie żywi* (Warsaw, 1956), 236.

14   Aleksey Ikonnikov, *Khudozhnik nashikh dney: N. Ya. Myaskovskiy*, 2nd edn. (Moscow, 1982), 309.

15   Myaskovsky, 'Vïpiski', 11 November 1947, RGALI, 2040/1/65, l. 87.

verbatim in his text, not having the wit to realise that Myaskovsky did not intend them to be taken literally.[16]

As Golubev observed, the most fundamental problem with Ikonnikov's book and much other Soviet commentary on Myaskovsky is not simply that these publications are often unreliable and written from skewed perspectives. In most cases, their authors were writing about someone of whom they knew little and understood even less. Myaskovsky remained an enigma to his contemporaries. A deeply private and reserved man, he allowed few people to get close to him and was extremely cautious in his speech and actions. While his courteous, unassuming manner and personal modesty were undoubtedly authentic character traits, Golubev emphasises that they were also aspects of a social persona that Myaskovsky skilfully deployed for self-protective purposes, to minimise both the strains of dealing with his environment and his exposure to potential dangers. Most people never got to see behind that mask. Ikonnikov may have encountered Myaskovsky professionally – but as Golubev remarks, 'not everyone who came into contact with him understood him or knew what to make of him'. Authors 'who did not have the opportunity to know him were in a still more difficult position'. The comparatively small number of people who knew Myaskovsky well had to exercise discretion in writing about him: Soviet censorship would have made frank discussion of many aspects of his life impossible.

As is evident from the bibliography in the revised edition of Ikonnikov's biography, which came out in 1982, the Russian-language literature on Myaskovsky did not augment very much in the three decades after the composer's death. The most important additions were a two-volume collection of materials brought out in 1959 by Semyon Shlifshteyn, which comprised reminiscences of the composer, essays on his work, a small selection of his letters, and his complete musical journalism (most of the contents had already appeared in print)[17]; an edition of the Prokofiev-Myaskovsky correspondence, published in 1977 by Miralda Kozlova and Nina Yatsenko[18]; and Kozlova's subsequent publications of selections from the Myaskovsky-Asafiev correspondence.[19] (Soviet censors repeatedly blocked Kozlova's efforts to bring out a complete edition of the latter: the letters from the

---

16   Yevgeniy Golubev, 'Alogizmï' (unpublished memoir), RGALI, 2798/2/23, ll. 75–6. In an interview with the author on 30 April 2011, the late Grigory Frid characterised Ikonnikov as essentially benign, but 'not very bright'.

17   Semyon Shlifshteyn (ed.), *N. Ya. Myaskovskiy: Sobraniye materialov v dvukh tomakh*, 2 vols. (Moscow, 1959). A revised second edition was published in 1964.

18   Miral'da Kozlova and Nina Yatsenko (ed.), *S. S. Prokof'yev i N. Ya. Myaskovskiy: Perepiska* (Moscow, 1977) (hereafter cited as Kozlova and Yatsenko, *Perepiska*.)

19   Miral'da Kozlova (ed.), 'Iz perepiski B. V. Asaf'yeva i N. Ya. Myaskovskogo', *Sovetskaya muzika*, 11 (1979), 118–26 and 12 (1979), 95–105 (two-part article).

1920s and 1930s were deemed largely inappropriate for publication.) With few exceptions, the remaining items were fairly inconsequential and generally did not contribute much by way of new information. Livanova's and Ikonnikov's monographs remained the standard accounts of Myaskovsky's career, and the view that they presented was not significantly modified or challenged right up to the end of the Soviet period.[20]

Inevitably, this view shaped the reception of Myaskovsky outside his native country. The first, and for many years the only, publication of any substance on the composer in English was a translation of Ikonnikov's first book (in reality, not much longer than a pamphlet), which came out in the United States in 1946.[21] The timing of its appearance was not propitious: as relations with the USSR deteriorated with the onset of the Cold War, Western assessments of Soviet cultural life were growing increasingly hostile. Influential émigré commentators such as Nicolas Nabokov fostered perceptions of the Soviet Union as an artistic wasteland, drawing pointed contrasts between Western modernist art, which Nabokov extolled as the product of 'free minds in a free world', and the 'sad, grey, academic art' of Socialist Realism, which he summarily dismissed as 'thoroughly outmoded' and 'provincial'.[22] Given this climate, it is not difficult to imagine readers' likely responses to learning that a 'Collective Farm' Symphony written in the early 1930s had supposedly been an 'important landmark' in Myaskovsky's career and adumbrated his subsequent 'great successes . . . in the sphere of Socialist realism in art'.[23] They would have had no way of knowing that Myaskovsky never authorised this preposterous subtitle for the Twelfth Symphony or that the putative programme had been foisted on the score by others. They would also have been unaware that, far from being seen as having furnished successful models of Socialist Realist musical composition, Myaskovsky's work was regarded as distinctly problematic up to the very end of his life.

If in the USSR Myaskovsky's Twelfth Symphony was perceived as marking a significant advance in the struggle to liberate Soviet music from decadent Western stylistic and aesthetic influences (especially notions of *l'art*

20 The biography by Zoya Gulinskaya, *Nikolay Yakovlevich Myaskovskiy* (Moscow, 1981), which was aimed at a general readership, does not present any new research and is essentially a synthesis of information from previous publications.

21 Aleksey Ikonnikov, *N. Myaskovskiy* (Moscow, 1944).

22 Nicolas Nabokov, 'This Is Our Culture', *Counterpoint*, 17 (May 1952), 15; Nabokov's speech at the inaugural meeting of the Congress for Cultural Freedom, Berlin 1950, quoted in Ian Wellens, *Music on the Frontline: Nicolas Nabokov's Struggle against Communism and Middlebrow Culture* (Aldershot, 2002), 34.

23 Alexei Ikonnikov, *Myaskovsky: His Life and Work* (no translator credited: New York, 1946), 21, 22.

pour l'art), it was seen abroad as emblematic of the enforced abnegation of artistic freedom under totalitarianism. The 'top-down' models of Soviet cultural construction prevalent during the Cold War years encouraged the tendency to regard work by Soviet artists as contrived and ersatz, predominantly shaped by ideological and bureaucratic constraints rather than any authentic creative impulse.

This attitude was strongly in evidence in standard English-language accounts, such as Stanley Dale Krebs's *Soviet Composers and the Development of Soviet Music* (1970) and Boris Schwarz's *Music and Musical Life in Soviet Russia* (1972). Krebs's appraisals were almost uniformly dismissive and descend into crude invective: his book also exemplified the tiresome propensity to adopt a high moral tone when discussing Soviet composition. (Kabalevsky and Khachaturian are derided as 'the *canaille* of twentieth-century Art'; a score by Sviridov is held to exhibit 'the pathetic, mawkish prettiness of a Moscow prostitute'.[24]) Myaskovsky's music is deemed to show 'an almost total lack of feeling for originality'; the composer, Krebs avers, 'had always chosen a route of conformity'.[25] Schwarz's manner is more urbane, but he too leaves the reader in no doubt that he considered most music by Soviet composers to be unworthy of serious critical attention. He characterised the styles of Soviet composition from the early 1930s onwards as overwhelmingly 'conventional' and 'platitudinous' – deficiencies that he blamed on ideological 'regimentation' and the fact that Soviet music had become 'estranged and isolated from the musical mainstream of the West'.[26] Myaskovsky's work was held to typify the retreat into 'provincialism' and 'middle-of-the-road' blandness. Schwarz's account of Myaskovsky's career is based on the composer's autobiographical essay and Livanova's biography, both of which he cites. Neither source is interrogated critically: he simply reiterates the standard Soviet narrative. 'Like many of his fellow-artists, [Myaskovsky] felt compelled to be more responsive to the cultural appeals of the Party', the reader is informed: 'The non-political intellectual of the 1920s was *passé* – the so-called "fellow traveller" had to yield to the committed artist'. And in the best traditions of Soviet music criticism, Schwarz expounds the composer's purported expressive intentions and the supposed 'meanings' of various works ('Miaskovsky's obvious aim was to capture the mood of the Soviet people, the concern, sorrow and pride felt by his compatriots . . .'.)[27]

24 See Stanley Dale Krebs, *Soviet Composers and the Development of Soviet Music* (London, 1970), 184, 268.

25 Ibid., 112, 118.

26 Boris Schwarz, *Music and Musical Life in Soviet Russia, 1917–1981*, expanded ed. (Bloomington, 1983), 135.

27 Ibid., 165, 166.

It is unnecessary to labour the dubiousness of these judgements, but it is certainly worth emphasising the dubiousness of the bases on which they were made. Even though both Krebs and Schwarz undertook research in the Soviet Union in the 1960s, one wonders how much of Myaskovsky's music they actually had occasion to hear. (As Schwarz noted, it had 'faded out of the repertoire'[28] – which is not surprising, as a large proportion of Myaskovsky's output was seldom performed in his native country even during his lifetime.) One is also struck by the confidence with which both writers ascribed attitudes and motivations to someone of whom they knew little or nothing except what was mediated through Soviet publications. Despite the great emphasis that Krebs and Schwarz placed on the deleterious effects of Soviet censorship, neither acknowledged the problematic nature of the source materials at their disposal; nor did they express caution about their potential reliability. (In Schwarz's case, this is especially puzzling, as he devotes an entire chapter of his study to detailing the calamitous consequences for Soviet musical scholarship of the ideological campaigns of the late Stalinist period – and even instances Livanova as one of the musicologists who incurred public criticism.[29]) Both commentators approached Soviet music with preconceptions: both duly found 'evidence' in Soviet publications that they used to bolster a prevailing hegemonic Western assessment of Soviet cultural life. Ironically, as with Livanova and Ikonnikov, the lack of information at their disposal did not deter them from making categorical judgements. In Krebs's view, Myaskovsky's music evidently sufficed to furnish irrefragable evidence of his pusillanimous conformism – much as Tchaikovsky's music used to be adduced as supposedly incontrovertible proof of the character weaknesses arising from his homosexuality.

Even before the dissolution of the USSR, the validity of simplistic Cold War views of Soviet cultural life was increasingly questioned by a younger generation of historians. This revisionist trend intensified markedly with the advent of *glasnost'*, when the lifting of restrictions on access to information made available large quantities of institutional records and other documentation that had previously been classified. Researchers were afforded unprecedented opportunities to learn about the regime's inner workings and to discover what went on behind the scenes. Unsurprisingly, the picture that began to emerge was more complex and less amenable to reductive interpretations. In an article published in 1991, the notable German Soviet music specialist Detlef Gojowy reflected on the implications of these developments for work in his field: new information was already coming to light that challenged inherited views of notable Soviet composers and their outputs. 'How many supposedly reliable "facts" which have been copied

28   Ibid., 169.
29   Ibid., 249–58.

from book to book will now be called into question and have to be revised?', Gojowy wondered. 'Entire biographies will have to be written afresh'.[30]

Gojowy's rhetorical question touched on two issues of fundamental importance. The first was the epistemological status of what had hitherto been held to constitute 'knowledge' of Soviet music: the easy certitudes and pat judgements of the Cold War era had to yield to an attitude of radical agnosia. The second was the process by which that knowledge had been constructed and professionally validated. As the historian Richard F. Hamilton has demonstrated in a thought-provoking study, in spite of the presumed commitment of scholars to evidence-based enquiry, it is by no means uncommon for errors and erroneous interpretations to persist for decades – often, because the source texts in which they originated continue to be cited without being subjected to adequate critical scrutiny.[31] Students of Soviet music had to face the disquieting possibility that the accumulated 'knowledge' in the field might to a considerable extent have been compounded of misinformation, ignorance, and prejudice.

Gojowy's emphasis on the need for new biographical studies raised a further important issue which has not lost its pertinence three decades later. Although much valuable work has been done since then on various aspects of Soviet musical life, attempts at thoroughgoing reappraisals of individual figures remain few in number, even in Russian-language scholarship. We may be less inclined now to accept the assessments of Soviet compositional activity of the Stalinist period that Krebs and Schwarz present, but even after an elapse of five decades they have yet to be comprehensively superseded. And although the questionable features of Cold War accounts are far less in evidence in post-*glasnost'* publications (especially the sweeping generalisations, unsubstantiated assertions regarding composers' attitudes and outlooks, and the tendency to indulge in gratuitous sneering), they have not disappeared altogether. In a notable collection of essays on Russian music, Myaskovsky's last symphony, his Twenty-Seventh, is described as typifying the work of a 'hobbled, terrified geriatric generation' of Soviet composers in its 'servile affirmation': the same writer subsequently contended that a march-like theme in the symphony's finale was impossible to hear 'without a shuddering reminder of the last sentence – "He loved Big Brother" – in Orwell's *1984*'.[32]

30 Detlef Gojowy, 'Sinowi Borissowitsch im Keller entdeckt: Sowjetische Musikwissenschaft in der Perestrojka', *Das Orchester*, 11 (1991), 1244.

31 Richard F. Hamilton, *The Social Misconstruction of Reality: Validity and Verification in the Scholarly Community* (New Haven, 1996).

32 Richard Taruskin, *Defining Russia Musically: Historical and Hermeneutical Essays* (Princeton and Oxford, 1997), 96, 98; idem, *On Russian Music* (Berlekey and Los Angeles, 2009), 292.

In the cases of Shostakovich and Prokofiev, the composers who have benefitted most from the ongoing reassessment of the Soviet musical past, recent scholarship has dramatically enriched our view of both and complicated it considerably. This should also cause us to wonder how our inherited notions of Soviet musical life may yet be further transformed through investigations of the careers of their contemporaries who have yet to receive comparable attention – Glière, Shebalin, Khachaturian, and Kabalevsky, to mention only a few names, and, of course, Myaskovsky.[33] Knowledge and understanding of these composers, their music, and their milieu will only deepen if the effort is made to study them afresh, without preconceptions – and if Gojowy's challenge is taken up with the seriousness that it merits.

Such has been the task attempted in writing the present volume. Its aims are straightforward. The first and most fundamental is to provide an account of Myaskovsky's career based on a comprehensive critical examination of all the source materials, both published and unpublished, that the author managed to identify over the course of twelve years of research. Secondly, the book endeavours to give a sense of Myaskovsky's circumstances – his milieu and his circle of friends and colleagues; his living conditions; the professional opportunities that were open to him and the practicalities of how he made his livelihood; the institutions for which he worked; his dealings with authority. Thirdly, it seeks to cast light on his creative development, exploring how it was shaped by his background and education, his experiences, and his responses to the artistic and intellectual currents of his age. Finally, it sets out to bring into focus the nature of his creative achievement and establish a contextual framework that might enable it to be approached more sympathetically.

In spite of Myaskovsky's reticence, sources for a study of his life are quite abundant, especially when it comes to unpublished materials. These fall mostly into two categories – his personal papers and those of people with whom he came into contact; and institutional records of various kinds.

Myaskovsky left an extensive archive at the time of his death, which was subsequently transferred into two repositories in Moscow – the Russian State Archive of Literature and Art (RGALI) and the Russian National Museum of Music (RNMM), to use their present-day names. In addition to the autograph scores of Myaskovsky's compositions and the manuscripts of his writings, the materials donated comprised some 3,000 items of correspondence to and from over 150 identified correspondents, and much else besides – including financial records, contracts, concert programmes, newspaper cuttings, and photographs. The same institutions house a sizeable

---

33   Gregor Tassie's *Nikolay Myaskovsky: The Conscience of Russian Music* (Lanham, 2014) contains little original research and relies heavily on the standard Soviet publications on the composer.

quantity of pertinent documentation in additional collections – such as the diaries, correspondence, and unpublished memoirs of Myaskovsky's friends and associates. Smaller, but still significant holdings are preserved in other Russian and foreign archives. Although many items were evidently lost or destroyed, the materials are surprisingly informative – even those dating from the Soviet phase of Myaskovsky's life. Despite Soviet citizens' understandable caution in expressing their views on sensitive subjects (and especially in writing), Myaskovsky's correspondence with family members and trusted associates still reveals much about his and their attitudes, even if they generally avoid explicit discussion of political topics or their responses to the regime. But less intimate exchanges can also contain much that is illuminating and provide fascinating insights into everyday life and professional conditions.

This corpus of documents has never been explored systematically before, though some items have been published in whole or in part – principally, letters. These publications mostly predate *glasnost'*, and like all Soviet editions of primary source materials, their reliability cannot be taken on trust: even if the editors were conscientious, the exigencies of censorship often made it impossible to reproduce the texts in full. In consequence, the original manuscripts have been checked as a matter of consistent policy. Only one important collection remained inaccessible: Serge Prokofiev Jr refused permission to view the Prokofiev-Myaskovsky correspondence housed in RGALI. While it would have been desirable to consult these manuscripts for the sake of thoroughness, it is unlikely they contain anything that would alter our understanding very significantly. A comparison of the 1977 Soviet edition of the Prokofiev-Myaskovsky correspondence with a typewritten transcript prepared by Myaskovsky's sister Valentina Menshikova (which remains in the possession of her great-niece Tatiana Fedorovskaya) and with the carbon copies of a small portion of the letters now preserved in the Serge Prokofiev Archive at Columbia University suggests that the redactions are generally very minor – the omission of sharp remarks about people who were still alive, for example, and discussions of money matters.

One other document preserved amongst Myaskovsky's personal papers deserves mention here because of its importance: a compilation of extracts from his diaries that he prepared in the last year of his life prior to destroying them for reasons that are unknown.[34] It is difficult to tell how voluminous the originals may have been. The manuscript runs to just over two hundred handwritten pages and the entries span the period from 1906 to 1950. Most are very brief (sometimes comprising only a few words) and simply record his activities on a particular day – his progress in working on compositions, his responses to music that he had heard or was studying, details

---

34 'Vïpiski iz dnevnikov', RGALI, 2040/1/65 (see fn3 above).

of his professional commitments. Up to the second half of 1933 the entries are very sparse (in some years there are no entries at all), but thereafter they become much more frequent. They contain virtually nothing of a personal nature, although there are occasional revealing comments about colleagues or events. In spite of its fragmentariness, this manuscript is an exceedingly useful source.

A considerable amount of information about Myaskovsky's life and activities was yielded by materials from institutional archives – educational, military, and civic records, as well as those of the various establishments for which he worked or with which he had professional dealings. Further pertinent materials came to light in the files of Soviet government departments, such as the Committee for Artistic Affairs and the Department of Agitation and Propaganda. The holdings of these archives are often far from complete, however: what was preserved depended very much on the vagaries of circumstance. The Composers' Union archive is a case in point: much of it was apparently lost when the basement premises in which it was stored suffered a serious flood.[35] What remains of the archive of the union's Moscow branch is now housed in RGALI, but a large quantity of its institutional records for the 1930s and 1940s has seemingly disappeared without trace. The gaps for the 1930s at least are probably explained by the fact that the union's first chairman, the Party functionary Nikolay Chelyapov, was executed in 1938 after being convicted of fabricated charges of terrorist activity: destruction of archival documents was common during the Great Terror, especially if they contained allusions to 'enemies of the people'.[36] (Arlen Blyum, a noted historian of Soviet censorship, has described the wholesale 'bibliocide' carried out at the time for the same reasons, as librarians struggled to keep pace with the censorship bureau's directives to destroy printed materials mentioning victims of the purges.[37]) Many repositories suffered additional losses during the Second World War; further culls of archival holdings were carried out, it would appear, with the advent of *glasnost'*.[38] In general, secret police files are still not easily accessible

35   See Lyudmila Korabel'nikova, 'Nauchno-obshchestvennaya deyatel'nost' Yu. V. Keldïsha v kontekste razvitiya otechestvennogo muzïkoznaniya', in Nadezhda Teterina (ed.), *Yuriy Vsevolodovich Keldïsh: Vospominaniya, issledovaniya, materialï, dokumentï* (Moscow, 2015), 25.

36   See Tat'yana Goryayeva, 'Odna iz original'neyshikh i zamechatel'nïkh realizatsiy, osushchestvlennaya v SSSR. (K 70-letiyu RGALI)', *Otechestvennïye arkhivï*, 2 (2011), 28–9.

37   Arlen Blyum, *Sovetskaya tsenzura v épokhu total'nogo terrora, 1929–1953* (St Petersburg, 2000), 97–103.

38   See Arlen Blyum, *Za kulisami "Ministerstva Pravdï": Taynaya istoriya sovetskoy tsenzurï, 1917–1929* (St Peterburg, 1994), 7–10.

(a significant proportion of these have apparently also been destroyed)[39], although a small number of documents containing allusions to Myaskovsky have been published in reputable scholarly collections. Records pertaining to Myaskovsky's evacuation to Tbilisi during the Second World War are preserved in the National Archives of Georgia, but attempts to unearth materials concerning his subsequent transfer to Frunze (now Bishkek, in Kyrgyzstan) drew a blank.

Of published sources, the most useful are the reminiscences of the composer by family members, friends, and colleagues, several of which were included in the two-volume collection edited by Shlifshteyn. Special mention should also be made of the contributions to the literature on Myaskovsky and his circle by Olga Lamm (1908–97), the niece of Myaskovsky's close friend Pavel Lamm. In addition to writing informative essays about her uncle and his associates (amongst them, the conductor Konstantin Saradzhev and the composers Alexander Goedicke and Vissarion Shebalin), Lamm compiled a chronicle entitled *Stranitsï tvorcheskoy biografii Myaskovskogo* (Pages from Myaskovsky's creative biography), which was published in 1989. A labour of love to which she devoted years of painstaking work, her book tells the story of Myaskovsky's life through citations from his letters and other documents (principally, his diary extracts and his correspondence with Prokofiev, Asafiev, and the music critic Vladimir Derzhanovsky), which are presented without linking material and virtually without commentary. Although Lamm's examination of the available source materials was far from exhaustive and her book left important aspects of Myaskovsky's career unexplored, it laid a solid foundation for future research: I gratefully acknowledge my indebtedness to her pioneering endeavours. Lamm's desire to allow the source materials to speak for themselves is noteworthy – especially when one learns that she had been outraged by Livanova's biography.[40] Her pointed abstention from editorial intervention can be read as a tacit but forceful rebuke to those who had sought to place misleading constructions on the life and work of her uncle's friend, whom she admired deeply. Her book proved immensely helpful while I learned to decipher Myaskovsky's handwriting, which is sometimes very difficult to read, as well as the hands of several of his most frequent correspondents. Extensive use has also been made of Lamm's biography of her uncle, *Pavel Aleksandrovich Lamm: Opït biografii* (Pavel Aleksandrovich Lamm: A biographical sketch), which remained unfinished at the time of her death.[41]

---

39 See Theodore Karasik, *The Post-Soviet Archives: Organization, Access and Declassification* (Santa Monica, 1993), 21–2.

40 Livanova, 'Vospominaniya', RNMM, 194/1754a, l. 611.

41 The manuscript is preserved in the Russian National Museum of Music, RNMM, 192/361. Two extracts have been published: Martina Svetlanova (ed.),

Needless to say, important though letters and reminiscences potentially are as source materials, they cannot be relied on uncritically: their contents must be checked carefully for factual inaccuracies; allowance must be made for the personalities of the people concerned and the nature of their relationships with one another. Myaskovsky's interactions with friends and colleagues were often far from straightforward, and the circumstances of Soviet life made circumspection advisable in all social intercourse.

As will be apparent from the footnotes, the present volume draws widely on more recent publications on Soviet music, insofar as they either deal with Myaskovsky or illuminate the contexts in which he lived and worked. Major studies such as Yekaterina Vlasova's *1948 god v sovetskoy muzïke* (The year 1948 in Soviet music), Olesya Bobrik's *Venskoye izdatel'stvo 'Universal Edition' i muzïkantï iz sovetskoy Rossii* (The Viennese publisher 'Universal Edition' and musicians from Soviet Russia), Amy Nelson's *Music for the Revolution: Musicians and Power in Early Soviet Russia*, Kiril Tomoff's *Creative Union: The Professional Organization of Soviet Composers*, and Marina Frolova-Walker's *Stalin's Music Prize: Soviet Culture and Politics* – to mention only a very few titles – made my task incalculably easier.[42] I profited greatly not only from the information that these and other publications yielded but also from the intellectual stimulus they provided. I have benefitted similarly from post-*glasnost'* scholarship in other domains – ranging from studies in military history and the history of Russian education to work on aspects of Soviet social, economic, political, and cultural life.

My accounts of Myaskovsky's compositions are necessarily brief, given the size of his output. Adequate consideration of his twenty-seven symphonies alone would require another book.[43] I have concentrated on works

---

'Pavel Lamm v tyur'makh i ssïlkakh: Po stranitsam vospominaniy O. P. Lamm', in Marina Rakhmanova (ed.), *Al'manakh*, vol. 2, Trudï gosudarstvennogo tsentral'nogo muzeya muzïkal'noy kul'turï imeni M. I. Glinki (Moscow, 2003), 73–120; and Ol'ga Lamm, 'Vospominaniya (fragment: 1948–1951 godï)', in Marina Rakhmanova (ed.), *Sergey Prokof'yev: Vospominaniya, pis'ma, stat'i* (Moscow, 2004), 227–73.

42　Yekaterina Vlasova, *1948 god v sovetskoy muzïke* (Moscow, 2010); Olesya Bobrik, *Venskoye izdatel'stvo 'Universal Edition' i muzïkantï iz sovetskoy Rossii* (St Petersburg, 2011); Amy Nelson, *Music for the Revolution: Musicians and Power in Early Soviet Russia* (University Park, PA, 2004); Kiril Tomoff, *Creative Union: The Professional Organization of Soviet Composers, 1939–1953* (Ithaca, NY, 2006); Marina Frolova-Walker, *Stalin's Music Prize: Soviet Culture and Politics* (New Haven, 2016).

43　Interested readers are referred to George Calvin Foreman's doctoral thesis, 'The Symphonies of Nikolai Yakovlevich Miaskovsky' (University of Kansas, 1981) – a descriptive survey examining some of the symphonies in detail. Despite its undoubted importance as a pioneering study, its value is limited by its reliance on Soviet publications. The author's evaluations of Myaskovsky's symphonies, though not without insight, are sometimes rather questionable.

that I consider to be particularly noteworthy achievements and which either typify characteristic approaches or represent new points of creative departure. I have also deliberately eschewed detailed technical discussion and the jargonised terminology of music analysis in order to make the text more accessible to non-specialist readers. Comparatively restricted use has been made of Soviet-era publications on Myaskovsky's music – principally because many of them contain little of interest (though there are exceptions, such as Yelena Dolinskaya's insightful study of the piano works).[44] Much commentary on music by Soviet composers was concerned with explicating its putative 'ideological content'[45]: purely technical appraisals were regarded with suspicion as a manifestation of 'formalism'. The results often degenerated into little more than free association or the elucidation of 'phantom programmes', in Marina Frolova-Walker's apt phrase.[46] Insofar as these materials are cited, it has mostly been for the purposes of illustrating compositions' contemporary reception.

The present study, substantial though it is, makes no claims to definitiveness or exhaustiveness. Myaskovsky's career raises complex issues that merit much more detailed exploration: the account presented here will doubtless require modification and correction as research continues. In attempting to construct a narrative that is more objective and firmly grounded in fact than Soviet and Cold War–era accounts, I have been acutely aware of the difficulty of trying to capture something of the lived experience of a person whom one knows only through documents – and especially someone whose personality was as elusive as Myaskovsky's. It has been suggested, by Pierre Bourdieu, amongst others, that such attempts are inherently futile.[47] Perhaps so, but they are still worth making: we have no way to understand the past except through attempts to fashion narratives, including narratives of lives. Part of the inherent fascination of studying historical figures

44 Yelena Dolinskaya, *Fortepiannoye tvorchestvo N. Ya. Myaskovskogo* (Moscow, 1980).

45 For instances in point, see the discussions of Myaskovsky's work in two notable publications on Soviet symphonism – Genrikh Orlov, *Russkiy sovetskiy simfonizm* (Moscow, 1966) and Boris Yarustovskiy, *Simfonii o voyne i mire* (Moscow, 1966).

46 Marina Frolova-Walker, '"Music Is Obscure": Textless Soviet Works and Their Phantom Programmes', in Joshua S. Walden (ed.), *Representation in Western Music* (Cambridge, 2013), 47–63.

47 Pierre Bourdieu, 'L'illusion biographique', *Actes de la Recherche en sciences sociales*, 62–3 (1986), 69–72. For interesting discussions of the growing misprision of biography in the academy under the influence of structuralist and poststructuralist thought (especially in France) and the subsequent revival of interest in the genre, see Daniel Madelénat, *La biographie* (Paris, 1984) and François Dosse, *Le pari biographique* (Paris, 2011).

is the perspective that their circumstances afford on our own.[48] The choices that disclose a person's character, the actions that reveal their fundamental existential commitments, prompt us to reflect on our own values and our sense of what is important: as Myaskovsky's life shows, these choices and actions are especially interesting when the person feels profoundly at odds with their environment. Whatever its shortcomings, I hope that this book will be found to present him in an unexpected and thought-provoking light, and that it might win new listeners for a body of work that unquestionably deserves to be better known. At its finest, Myaskovsky's music is a moving testament to Russian artists' struggle to uphold civilised values in dark and destructive times.

Patrick Zuk
Cork, May 2020

---

48 Amongst the most stimulating considerations of these issues are books by two notable Brazilian writers which were published within a short time of each other during the Second World War – Edgard Cavalheiro, *Biografias e biógrafos* (São Paulo, 1943); and Luis Viana Filho, *A verdade na biografia* (Rio de Janeiro, 1945).

Acknowledgements

O ver the course of what proved to be a very protracted project, I had repeated cause to feel grateful for the kindness shown to me not only by friends and colleagues but also by people whom I had never met, yet who gave generously of their time to assist me. I offer cordial thanks to all of them and ask forgiveness of anyone I may have inadvertently overlooked.

In the early stages, postgraduates in the Music Department at Durham University provided invaluable help with various practical tasks – Chris Ferebee, Ivan Kolosov, David Mitchell, Jonathan Penny, Joseph Schultz, Daniel Tooke, and Bethan Winter. I retain happy memories of our work together and of our lively discussions of Russian music in seminars and supervisions.

The list of people who subsequently assisted and advised me soon lengthened considerably. It begins with Lidia Ader, Nataliya Braginskaya, Larisa Chirkova, Olga Digonskaya, Yelena Dolinskaya, Anna Fortunova, Levon Hakopian, Liudmila Kovnatskaya, Marina Rakhmanova, Nataliya Savkina, and Kiril Tomoff. Irakli Beridze helped me to locate materials in the Georgian-language catalogues of the National Archives of Georgia. I am indebted to Joris de Henau for many stimulating discussions of Marxist aesthetic philosophy and for directing me to Dutch-language accounts of Émile Verhaeren's contacts with Russia. Katja Kaiser granted access to Universal Edition's historical archive. George Malko kindly checked his mother's personal papers for references to Myaskovsky's half-sister, Varvara. Martin Maw explored Oxford University Press's records for information on Ivan Krïzhanovsky. Andrey Mikhaylkov provided expert guidance on the history of Russian military education. Oksana Oreshina undertook a search in the Russian state broadcasting archive (Gosradiotelefond) for the radio interview with Olga Lamm discussed in chapter 5. Avril Pyman shared her expertise on Silver Age writers, including Myaskovsky's friend Modeste Hofmann. Yekaterina Vlasova gave permission for me to consult manuscripts of letters from Myaskovsky to Asafiev to which access had been restricted during her work on an edition of their correspondence. It was my good fortune to have the opportunity in 2011 to interview Grigory Frid, one of the very few people still alive who knew Myaskovsky: at ninety-six years of age, his remarkable memory was undimmed. It was a strangely moving experience to hear his descriptions of the tense state of musical life after the public denunciation of Myaskovsky, Prokofiev, Shostakovich, and the country's other leading composers in 1948. I spent a very different, but no less absorbing, afternoon in 2015 with the late Nonna Shakhnazarova, who recounted her reminiscences of Aram Khachaturian and other Myaskovsky pupils.

Several colleagues provided source materials and information gleaned during research projects in which they were engaged. Philip Ross Bullock sent rare scores acquired in the course of his work on Russian song. Albrecht Gaub apprised me of his investigations into performances of Myaskovsky's work by Frederick Stock and the Chicago Symphony Orchestra. Aleksandr Komarov kindly shared typewritten transcripts of Myaskovsky's letter to Sofia Lamm quoted on p. 181 and chapters from Olga Lamm's unfinished biography of her stepfather, Pavel Lamm. Yekaterina Lebedenko supplied scanned reproductions of the programmes of musical evenings organised in 1921–2 by Pavel Lamm and her great-grandfather Maxim Gube, which she discovered in the Shebalin family archive. James Taylor permitted me to consult his transcript of a letter from Myaskovsky to Derzhanovsky. Maxim Truts alerted me to the existence of archival materials in the National Archives of Estonia and Finland relating to Myaskovsky's period of service at Peter the Great's Naval Fortress in Reval (Tallinn) and forwarded copies of some in his possession.

The research for this volume drew on documentation preserved in over two dozen archival repositories. Unfortunately, I did not always learn the names of the staff members who dealt with me during my visits but would like to record my appreciation of some who were especially helpful. At the Russian State Archive of Literature and Art (RGALI) in Moscow, Yekaterina Gunashvili, her predecessor Dmitry Neustroyev, and their colleagues were unfailingly obliging, as were Kseniya Yakovleva and Nina Lebed from RGALI's reproductions department. The pleasant surroundings and welcoming ambience of the reading room of the Russian National Museum of Music (formerly, the Glinka Museum of Musical Culture) more than compensated for the many long and tiring days that I spent there poring over documents. I gratefully acknowledge the consideration shown to me by Kira Ivanova, Yelena Fetisova, Olga Kuzina, Marina Abramova, and their colleagues, and their unstinting efforts to facilitate my work for over a decade: no request ever seemed to present a difficulty or be too much trouble. I similarly enjoyed working in the atmospheric reading room of the Russian Institute of Art History in St Petersburg, where I benefitted from the palaeographic skills and shrewd advice of Galina Kopïtova.

Vadim Vilinov allowed me to consult the unpublished diaries of Alexander Goldenweiser. Olga Kuznetsova guided my search for materials in the Vseroskomdram archive at the Gorky Institute of World Literature, and Eleonora Bolotina at the State Archive of the Russian Federation. At the Archive of the Bolshoi Theatre, I was ably assisted by Yekaterina Churakova and her colleagues, and by Raisa Trushkova at the Archive of the Moscow Conservatoire. Irina Garkusha at the Russian State Military

History Archive and Valentin Smirnov at the Russian State Naval Archive aided my investigation of Myaskovsky's military career. In St Petersburg, Tatyana Ivanova at the Russian State Historical Archive, Maria Perekalina at the Central State Historical Archive, and Yelena Rebriyeva at the Central State Archive for Literature and Art rendered similar service as I looked for documentation pertaining to Myaskovsky's family and his student years. Anastasiya Tsvetkova and Larisa Miller at the Archive of the St Petersburg Conservatoire tracked down institutional prospectuses which are now bibliographical rarities. Aleksey Shilenikov provided copies of documents about Myaskovsky's paternal grandfather, Konstantin, housed in the State Archive of Tula Oblast. Lyudmila Pril at the Centre for Documentation of Modern History of Tomsk Oblast found useful information and records relating to the wartime activities of the Committee for Artistic Affairs. I am obliged to Shakhim Shogenov at the Centre for Documentation of Modern History of the Kabardino-Balkar Republic and Dzhamilya Baybulatova at the Central State Archive of the Kyrgyz Republic for their responses to my enquiries about the archives of Soviet-era local government agencies.

Natalia Gladchenko expedited the necessary formalities to allow me examine materials at the National Archives of Georgia. Kyra Waldner in the manuscripts department of Vienna City Library assisted my exploration of Universal Edition's historical archive. Jennifer B. Lee, the curator of the performing arts collections in the Butler Library at Columbia University, sent exceptionally helpful responses to enquiries about the Serge Prokofiev Archive. I also thank Frank Villella, the director of the Rosenthal Archives of the Chicago Symphony Orchestra, for information about American performances of Myaskovsky's work.

My work required access not only to archival documents but also to rare published materials that were sometimes very difficult to obtain. Initially, one of my chief difficulties was to locate scores of all of Myaskovsky's compositions. Most of them were long out of print: I was unable to find a single copy of some works in any European or American library, and my enquiries of publishers were at first unavailing: not infrequently, items were reported as having been lost. On learning of my difficulties, Hervé Désarbre and Pascal Ianco at the French publishing firm Le chant du monde arranged for me to be sent complimentary copies of a number of scores that I lacked. I deeply appreciated their kind and supportive gesture, and it gives me much pleasure to acknowledge it here. The delightful Marina Savelyeva at the Composers' Union library in Moscow managed to unearth other scores and publications that I had all but despaired of finding: my visits were made memorable by her marvellous flow of talk and interesting anecdotes about people who figure in my narrative, quite a few of whom she knew professionally. I would also like to express my appreciation of the help provided by Riitta Tapanainen-Bukovski, Sari Virta, and Victoria Kurkina at the

Slavonic Library of the National Library of Finland, by Olga Perepelitsïna at the National Library of Russia, and by Yevgeniya Bakanova at the Russian State Library. The friendly staff of the Rare Books and Music reading room at the British Library came to the rescue on many occasions. Last, but by no means least, I offer sincere thanks to Judith Walton, Lynne Johnson, Barbara Parkinson, Alina Hyrniv, and other colleagues in the interlibrary loans section of Durham University's library for their seemingly inexhaustible patience in processing endless requests for obscure publications and for their resourcefulness in procuring them.

In undertaking the project, one of the greatest challenges was coming to grips with the large volume of handwritten source materials – which included almost 4,500 letters and much else besides. Myaskovsky's handwriting is sometimes very hard to read, as are the hands of some of his most frequent correspondents. Deciphering handwritten documents can be a slow and laborious task even for native speakers but is more taxing still for non-native speakers, testing their command of Russian to the utmost. The challenges were compounded by the deteriorated physical condition of a considerable proportion of the manuscripts (especially those dating from the early Soviet period and the Second World War years) and the extremely variable quality of the microfilm reproductions available for consultation. My St Petersburg colleague Irina Liutomskaia transcribed some folders of documents that presented especial difficulties – principally, Myaskovsky's early correspondence with family members and youthful acquaintances. I cannot thank her sufficiently: it is not an exaggeration to say that the project would have taken considerably longer without her help. I also wish to acknowledge the expert assistance of Irina Sinitsa at the Russian Institute for Art History, who transcribed Myaskovsky's letters to Maximilian Steinberg.

If the project entailed daunting challenges, it also brought many rewards – not least, occasions to make new friends and to benefit from enriching intellectual exchange. I offer my thanks to Konstantin Zenkin and Margarita Karatygina at the Moscow Conservatoire, not only for their assistance with Russian visa formalities but also for invitations to participate in several research colloquia at the conservatoire. Mikhail Epstein and his colleagues at the Department of Russian and East Asian Languages and Cultures at Emory University provided a warm welcome and lively stimulus during my visit in late 2016. It was my pleasure to receive several invitations to give talks on aspects of my work-in-progress at the Russian Institute of Art History in St Petersburg: my encounters with Liudmila Kovnatskaya, Zhanna Knyazeva, Galina Petrova, Dmitry Shumilin, and their colleagues were happy, festive events. I am indebted to Josephine Evetts-Secker and Ursula Wirtz for thought-provoking discussions of the phenomenon of trauma and the artistic representation of traumatic experience, which informed my account of Myaskovsky's Sixth Symphony in chapter 6: some of the ideas were initially developed in lectures given at the International School for Analytical Psychology in Zurich in May 2017. Irina Zolotova and Sophia Ghazaryan were welcoming hosts during my sojourn in Yerevan. For many years now, I have delighted in the hospitality of Yekaterina Lebedenko (*née* Shebalina) and her husband, Igor, on my visits to Nikolina Gora.

Kevin Bartig, Philip Ross Bullock, Pauline Fairclough, Ruth Fleischmann, Marina Frolova-Walker, Leah Goldman, and Harry White read the manuscript in whole or in part and made valuable suggestions for improvement. Their interest in the project has meant a great deal. I alone, of course, am responsible for whatever imperfections remain. In addition to reading the entire text, Garret Cahill, an old and dear friend, accompanied me on exploratory trips to Przemyśl and to various locations in and around Moscow: I thank him for the gift of his company and his stimulating conversation.

The costs of undertaking the fundamental research were principally covered by grants from the British Academy and the Wellcome Trust, with additional support from Durham University's Faculty of Arts and Humanities. The chairman of the Music Department, Tuomas Eerola, made available funds to purchase reproductions of photographic images.

Michael Middeke, my commissioning editor at Boydell and Brewer, deserves a special word of thanks. When he encouraged me to submit a proposal in 2013, I naively thought that I might be able to finish the project within two years. In the event, it took almost seven: I had grossly underestimated the amount of work that would be involved. He must privately have wondered whether he would ever receive a manuscript, but if so, he kept his doubts to himself and continued to treat me with unfailing kindness and tact. When the manuscript eventually did materialise, it turned out to be considerably more substantial than he had anticipated: to my immense relief, he did not baulk at the prospect of a longer book. I offer heartfelt thanks for his patient forbearance and also for his wise counsel and exemplary professionalism. His colleagues Elizabeth Howard and Julia Cook were a pleasure to deal with throughout the production process. I thank Irina du Quenoy for copy-editing the manuscript and Cath d'Alton for designing the maps.

The people to whom the book is dedicated have all played a vital role in assisting its completion. It was a privilege to get to know Myaskovsky's great-niece Tatiana Fedorovskaya, who has made Moscow feel like a second home over the years: her interest and enthusiasm have been unwavering. My visits to Myaskovsky's apartment, where she and her family still live, and to the dacha in Nikolina Gora where he spent his summers provided rich imaginative stimulus, as did our many conversations about her great-uncle and his milieu. Dmitry Gorbatov has aided me in ways that are far too numerous to detail: I will merely mention his illuminating explanations of Russian usage and of the social and cultural context. His 'lynx-like eye' (to recall Prokofiev's appreciative comment about Myaskovsky's skill as a proof-reader) has saved me from many errors. To Marianna Taymanova I largely owe whatever competence in Russian I possess. I hope this book might offer modest testimony to her pedagogical gifts and to the love of the Russian language that she imparted to the participants in her translation seminars. Ruth Fleischmann's friendship has been a source of joy and spiritual sustenance for almost three decades: her undeviating commitment to exacting standards and intellectual rigour inspire me still. My partner Séamas de Barra, the project's 'onlie begetter' (the suggestion that Myaskovsky's career and creative achievement merited reappraisal was his), has been a steadfast companion throughout this long adventure and shared fully in the excitement of discovery. In no small part, the book is a product of our many discussions of Myaskovsky's life and work and has been much improved by his critical acumen and attentive readings of my drafts. I am deeply grateful for his loving support.

I repeatedly turned to our friend Ania Wasilewski for advice on medical matters: she suggested modern English equivalents for obsolete Russian nosological terms and offered tentative diagnoses of some of Myaskovsky's more puzzling ailments. She died not long before the book was finished: her dignified stoicism in the face of terminal illness brought to mind his similarly courageous and uncomplaining acceptance of the inevitable.

Abbreviations

AMK	Archive of the Moscow Conservatoire
GABT	Archive of the Bolshoi Theatre, Moscow
GARF	State Archive of the Russian Federation, Moscow
GATO	State Archive of Tula Oblast, Tula
GMK	Alexander Goldenweiser Museum-Apartment, Moscow
GRI	Getty Research Institute, Los Angeles
IMLI	Gorky Institute of World Literature, Moscow
LC	Library of Congress, Washington
NAE	National Archives of Estonia, Tallinn
NAF	National Archives of Finland, Helsinki
NAG	National Archives of Georgia, Tbilisi
RBML	Rare Book & Manuscript Library, Butler Library, Columbia University, New York
RGALI	Russian State Archive of Literature and Art, Moscow
RGASPI	Russian State Archive of Socio-Political History, Moscow
RGAVMF	Russian State Naval Archive, St Petersburg
RGIA	Russian State Historical Archive, St Petersburg
RGVIA	Russian State Military History Archive, Moscow
RIII	Manuscript Room of the Russian Institute of Art History, St Petersburg
RNMM	Russian National Museum of Music, Moscow
RSL	Russian State Library, Moscow
TsDNI AS KBR	Centre for Documentation of Modern History of the Kabardino-Balkar Republic, Nalchik
TsDNI TO	Centre for Documentation of Modern History of Tomsk Oblast, Tomsk
TsGALI	Central State Archive for Literature and Art, St Petersburg
TsGIA	Central State Historical Archive, St Petersburg
WR	Wienbibliothek im Rathaus (Vienna City Library)

A Note on Transliteration
and Other Matters

The romanisation of names and terms from languages written in the Cyrillic script follows the transliteration system employed in the *New Grove Dictionary of Music and Musicians*. The customary exceptions are made: the Russian suffix -ский is rendered as -sky in masculine surnames such as 'Stravinsky'; and familiar transliterations of names have been retained, especially if these were the variants preferred by the individuals concerned (thus, 'Koussevitzky' rather than 'Kusevitskiy'; 'Glière' rather than 'Gliér'). When Russian-, Ukrainian-, and Bulgarian-language sources are cited in the notes, however, the *New Grove* conventions are adhered to strictly. Older Russian spellings predating the orthographical reform of December 1917 have been transliterated in accordance with modern usage.

All translations from Russian and other languages are my own, unless otherwise credited. Translating the citations from source materials at times presented formidable challenges – Myaskovsky's essays and letters, for instance, because of the sophistication and syntactical complexity of his prose; or at the opposite extreme, Soviet bureaucratic pronouncements, which are often stylistically crude and replete with rebarbative jargon. In many cases, a strictly literal translation would not only have sounded wooden, but paradoxically, would also have obscured the meaning or failed to convey it altogether. I have sought to strike a reasonable balance between maintaining literal fidelity to the originals and rendering them in a natural-sounding English that reproduces their linguistic register and preserves their authors' stylistic idiosyncrasies. I have also tried to capture something of the period flavour of the language: educated people of Myaskovsky's generation tended to express themselves rather more formally than we are wont to do, for example – especially in writing. As Park Honan pointed out, attention to these nuances is crucial if a biographer is to succeed in evoking the subject's presence and their milieu. 'Style is an integral "fact", as dates and events are, since it becomes part of the portrayed', he observes. 'Character-revealing or -suggesting elements of discourse cling to the person one writes about. If one is vulgar or sentimental in manner, [the subject] becomes so too, and one's authority is lost. . . . If a biography is to portray an individual closely, then its prose ought to suit the individual'.[1]

---

1   Park Honan, *Authors' Lives: On Literary Biography and the Arts of Language* (New York, 1990), 11.

In the interests of making the book as accessible as possible to readers who do not speak Russian, the titles of organisations and Russian-language publications are consistently translated in the main text (with the exception of well-known newspapers such as *Pravda* and *Izvestiya*), and the use of Soviet-era institutional acronyms has deliberately been kept to a minimum. For the same reason, I have permitted myself occasional latitude in the matter of Russian naming conventions. As anyone who has read a Tolstoy or Dostoyevsky novel will know, there is no real equivalent of the titles 'Mr' or 'Mrs' in Russian. If not on intimate terms, Russians address one another by their interlocutors' first names followed by their patronymics, middle names derived from their fathers' given names. Myaskovsky's father was Yakov (Jacob), so he would have been called 'Nikolay Yakovlevich' by his students and work colleagues. Very close friends and family members would simply have addressed him as 'Nikolay' – or, more frequently, by affection-ate pet names such as 'Kolya', 'Kolechka', or 'Kolenka'. Hypocorisms are used by English speakers too, of course ('Nick', 'Kate', 'Liz'), but in Russian they exist in far greater variety and are much more frequently employed. Rather than risk confusing the reader, I have generally omitted patronymics and diminutives when translating and referred to individuals either by their surname or the basic form of their first name, as best befits the context. Standard English spellings of names common to both languages are used for the sake of convenience (so, 'Alexander' rather than 'Aleksandr').

The names of many Russian cities changed several times in the course of the twentieth century: the successive renamings of St Petersburg rep-resent a well-known case in point (first Petrograd, then Leningrad, then a reversion to its original name shortly before the dissolution of the USSR). Myaskovsky's lengthy peregrinations during the two world wars took him to locations that were then situated within the territories of the Russian Empire and the Soviet Union but now lie outside the borders of the Russian Federation. He generally referred to them by their Russian and new Soviet names rather than those used by the local inhabitants in their own lan-guages. Some of these names changed once more in the post-Soviet era: the city of Pishpek, having been renamed Frunze in the early Soviet period, became Bishkek after the declaration of an independent Kyrgyz republic in 1991. Negotiating these complexities has not always been straightforward, but I have tried to assist the reader by consistently clarifying the coun-tries in which these places are now situated and using their modern names whenever feasible. The two maps on p. xlviii show the principal places in which Myaskovsky found himself during his wartime travels, as well as other towns and cities that feature in the narrative.

Giving the reader a meaningful sense of the comparative purchasing power of the Soviet rouble during Myaskovsky's lifetime is very difficult. Prices were fixed by the state and often bore little relation to commodities' real economic worth; the same was true of exchange rates for foreign currency. To complicate matters further, the value of the rouble was drastically altered by three currency reforms implemented in quick succession between 1922 and 1924, and then a fourth in 1947. Persistent chronic shortages of even basic necessities (let alone luxury goods) meant that Soviet citizens were often unable to obtain items that they wished to buy – unless, perhaps, they were prepared to pay exorbitant sums on the black market. For these reasons, I have not attempted to suggest equivalent prices for products and services in today's monetary terms but have simply given rough indications of the expenditure in proportion to Myaskovsky's monthly or yearly income.

Old Russian units of measurement such as the *versta*, the *sazhen'*, and the *pud* have been tacitly converted into their Imperial equivalents. The Gregorian calendar was not adopted in Russia until 14 February 1918. Unless otherwise indicated, all dates prior to the reform follow the Julian calendar; if necessary, the corresponding date according to the Gregorian calendar is given in brackets.

An explanation of the system used to reference Russian archival documents may be helpful for the non-specialist reader. In Russian archives, the materials in a documentary collection (*fond*) are generally divided into a number of sections. For each section, a separate numbered list (*opis'*) will be compiled of the files of documents (*dela*) that it contains. The volume of documents in a *delo* can range from a single leaf (*list*) of paper to several hundred leaves: the leaves are numbered consecutively (reverse sides with the Russian equivalent of *verso* – 'ob.', for *oborot lista*), though a file may contain multiple documents. Footnote references to documents start with the acronym of the archive in which it is housed, followed by the numbers of the *fond*, *opis'*, and *delo* – and then the leaf number. Thus, 'RGALI, 2040/1/65, l. 7' means that the document in question is housed in the Russian State Archive of Literature and Art in *fond* 2040 (the collection of Myaskovsky materials) and is in file number 65 listed on *opis'* number 1: the *recto* side of the seventh leaf has been cited. A somewhat simpler cataloguing system is used at the Russian National Museum of Music: there, collections are inventoried as a single list, rather than several – so the *opis'* number is omitted, and merely the numbers of the *fond* and *delo* are given (e.g. 'RNMM, 71/485'). Moreover, files usually only contain a single document.

English speakers who do not know Russian may be unsure how to pronounce Myaskovsky's surname. It comprises three rather than four syllables and is stressed on the second: Myas-kov-sky. The 'ya' in the first syllable is pronounced approximately as in the word 'yak': the 'y' glides swiftly into the 'a', rather than sounding like the diphthong in the possessive pronoun 'my'.

MAP 1. Myaskovsky's locations during the First World War.

MAP 2. Myaskovsky's locations in evacuation during the
Second World War. (The route of his journey from Tbilisi
to Frunze by train and ferry is indicated with a broken line.)

1

Beginnings: 1881–1902

Myaskovsky's birthplace had a curious symbolic aptness, for a man who spent much of his life feeling spiritually besieged and contending with environments that he experienced as profoundly alien. Modlin Fortress's picturesque location at the confluence of the Narew River with the majestic Vistula, some twenty-five miles northwest of Warsaw, does little to offset its dour dominance of the surrounding countryside. The idea of constructing a fort here originated with Napoleon, who was quick to grasp the area's strategic importance as he set about strengthening the border between Russia and the Duchy of Warsaw, the client state that he created from ceded Prussian territory in 1807. By the time of its completion in 1810, Napoleon was planning actively for a future Russian campaign: he now envisioned Modlin as the principal supply depot and defensive bulwark behind the front lines. A second, more ambitious programme of works was instituted to surround the citadel with an outer ring of defences, and by 1812, over twenty thousand labourers were toiling on the site. The project was never completed: after the Grande Armée's retreat from Moscow, the fortress was captured by Russian forces in December 1813. The Duchy of Warsaw effectively became absorbed into the Russian Empire after the Congress of Vienna and Russian control of the region intensified in the wake of the Polish uprising of 1830–1, which prompted a massive expansion of Modlin between 1832 and 1841 to accommodate a large Russian garrison. The principal additions were an enormous granary and a tall, fortified barracks capable of billeting twenty thousand soldiers, which at almost one and a half miles in length remains one of the longest buildings in Europe. Predictably, the fortress was given a new Russian name –Novogeorgievsk. Its enlargement also served to strengthen the Russian Empire's western frontier, as Novogeorgievsk formed part of a chain of fortifications commenced in the 1830s that extended southward to Warsaw and Ivangorod (Dęblin) and thence eastward to Brest. This costly investment in military infrastructure yielded a poor return, for the fortresses proved to be little more than white elephants: interest in them only revived after the Franco-Prussian War, which afforded a dramatic demonstration of the potential of new technologies to transform traditional warfare. Plans to modernise Novogeorgievsk were mooted in 1872, but their realisation would be mired in delays for over a decade. The deteriorating international situation and the formation of the Triple Alliance between the German and Austro-Hungarian Empires and the Kingdom of Italy eventually roused the government to action: renovation works commenced in 1883, overseen by Myaskovsky's father, Captain Yakov Myaskovsky.[1]

Yakov (1847–1918) had been assigned to Novogeorgievsk in 1875, four years after graduating from Russia's most prestigious training institute for military engineers, the Tsar Nicholas I Engineering Academy in St Petersburg. He evidently impressed his superiors as capable and conscientious, and this assignment inaugurated his rise to prominence as a notable expert on military fortifications.[2] One learns little about Yakov's distinguished career, however, from the guarded brief reminiscences published by his son in 1936 under the title 'Autobiographical notes about my creative path'.[3] The essay's opening declaration – 'My biography is of no particular interest' – was not merely a modest disclaimer, but a deliberate ploy to deflect curiosity about Myaskovsky's family background. His reticence on the subject of his father is explained by three considerations: Yakov came from the nobility, ultimately held the very senior rank of engineer-general in the tsarist army, and died in mysterious circumstances, apparently as a result of violence, shortly after the October Revolution of 1917. It would have been unwise to draw attention to these inconvenient facts under Bolshevik rule, during which the offspring of former tsarist army officers and officials experienced widespread discrimination on account of their social origins.

Such scant information as has come down to us about Myaskovsky's forebears is mostly to be gleaned from a folder of documents preserved amongst his personal papers in the Russian State Archive of Literature and Art, which detail the births, deaths, and marriages of various relatives and include a family tree together with some fragmentary genealogical notes.[4] As the unidentified compiler of the latter noted, the family's surname was of Polish origin ('Miaskowski'), and can be traced in historical records of the Polish nobility back as far as the fifteenth century.[5] Yakov's

---

1   On the history of Modlin Fortress, see Ryszard Bochenek, *Twierdza Modlin* (Warsaw, 2003); Andrzej Aksamitowski (ed.), *200 lat Twierdzy Modlin (1806–2006)* (Modlin, 2006).

2   See Dmitriy Ivkov, *Istoricheskiy ocherk Glavnogo inzhenerskogo upravleniya* (Petrograd, 1915), 292–3; Sergey Volkov, *Generalitet Rossiyskoy Imperii: Ėntsiklopedicheskiy slovar' generalov i admiralov ot Petra I do Nikolaya II*, vol. 2 (Moscow, 2009), 184.

3   Myaskovskiy, 'Avtobiograficheskiye zametki', 3–11.

4   RGALI, 2040/4/47. The documents are in German, Polish, and Russian. The oldest dates from 1843; the latest in date comprise the family tree and genealogical notes, compiled around 1910.

5   Hipolit Stupnicki, *Herbarz Polski i imionospis zasłużonych w Polsce ludzi wszystkich stanów i czasów*, vol. 1 (Lwów, 1855), 84; Emilian Żernicki-Szeliga, *Der polnische Adel und die demselben hinzugetretenen andersländischen Adelsfamilien*, vol. 2 (Hamburg, 1900), 78.

grandfather August Myaskovsky (1772–1847),[6] hailed from Uman, now in central Ukraine, but migrated around 1800 to Arensburg, or Kuressaare, to give it its present-day name – the westernmost town in modern Estonia, situated on the island of Saaremaa. At the time, Arensburg was located in Livonian territory that had been ceded to Russia by the Swedes in 1721: August served as dragoon officer and later paymaster at the Russian army fortress there. Between 1803 and 1820, August's wife bore him eight children, several of whom married into the German-speaking Baltic nobility that constituted Livonia's social élite. Baltic Germans were prominently represented in high-ranking military and administrative posts throughout the Russian Empire, but especially in St Petersburg, to where the more ambitious family members gravitated.[7] Two of August's sons became figures of some note: Karl (1810–?) was appointed the capital's postmaster general and rose to the rank of state counsellor[8], while his younger brother, also called August (1815–1908), had a distinguished career in the army. Both were conferred with Russian patents of nobility, and no less a personage than Tsar Alexander II stood as godfather for August junior's granddaughter Maria on the occasion of her baptism in May 1871.[9] The Russian genealogist Leonid Savyolov, who knew August junior and his family well, remembered him as being 'completely Germanised': he spoke German at home, and his daughter associated almost exclusively with other Germans.[10] He and his siblings were raised as Lutherans.

6   These dates are inscribed on his gravestone in Kudjape Cemetery in Kuressaare. I would like to thank Tatiana Fedorovskaya for providing this information.

7   On the Baltic Germans, see Anders Henriksson, *The Tsar's Loyal Germans. The Riga German Community: Social Change and the Nationality Question, 1855–1905* (New York, 1983); Henning von Wistinghausen, *Zwischen Reval und St Petersburg: Erinnerungen von Estländern aus zwei Jahrhunderten* (Weissenhorn, 1993). By the early 1800s, German speakers in St Petersburg dominated professions ranging from medicine and the army to salami manufacture, construction, and wig-making: see Igor' Arkhangel'skiy, *Annenshule. Skvoz' tri stoletiya* (St Petersburg, 2004), 17.

8   Karl's son August von Miaskowski (1838–99) became a distinguished jurist and economist who held university posts at Basel, Vienna, and Leipzig. His family befriended Friedrich Nietzsche. See Karl Bücher, 'Nekrolog auf August von Miaskowski', *Berichte über die Verhandlungen der Königliche Sächsischen Akademie der Wissenschaft zu Leipzig, philologisch-historische Klasse* 52 (1900), 351–8; Kurt von Miaskowski, 'Basler Jugenderinnerungen', *Basler Jahrbuch*, 1929, 86–7.

9   Letters patent issued to August junior and his granddaughter's baptismal record RGALI, 2040/4/47, ll. 16 and 21–2. Records pertaining to August senior and his descendants are preserved in the archive of the St Petersburg Assembly of the Nobility (Dvoryanskoye sobraniye), TsGIA, 536/6/3210.

10 Leonid Savyolov, *Vospominaniya* (Moscow, 2015), 136–7.

Little is known about August's brother Konstantin (1813–76), Yakov's father, beyond the fact that he too pursued a military career, rising to the rank of major general[11], and that he taught at the military school in the city of Oryol, 230 miles south of Moscow.[12] He chose to assimilate more fully than his siblings: he converted to the Orthodox faith in 1839[13] and married a Russian wife. Yakov's early life is sparsely documented, apart from a few facts concerning his education. Myaskovsky informed his Soviet biographer Alexey Ikonnikov that his mother, Vera Petrakova, also came from a military family and that her father oversaw the running of military educational establishments in Nizhny Novgorod, but virtually nothing else is known about her – not even the year in which she was born or when she and Yakov married. Their eldest child Sergey was born in 1877, after Yakov

FIGURE 1.1. Myaskovsky's father, Yakov Myaskovsky (1882)

11   Myaskovsky family tree, RGALI, 2040/4/47, l. 81.

12   Ikonnikov, *Khudozhnik nashikh dney*, 11.

13   'Delo o prinyatii pravoslaviya lyuteraninom Konstantinom Ivanovichem Myaskovskim', GATO, 3/5/42, ll. 1–30b.

FIGURE 1.2. Myaskovsky's mother, Vera Myaskovskaya

was transferred to Novogeorgievsk; Nikolay came into the world four years later, on 8 April 1881 (20 April New Style) and was baptised on 20 May.[14]

At Novogeorgievsk Yakov and his family lived in one of the small houses built for officers and their families on land adjacent to the barracks. It had a spacious garden, and Myaskovsky recalled that he and his siblings enjoyed considerable freedom, being largely left to their own devices.[15] Two years after his birth the surrounding area became a vast construction site. The fortress complex, already the size of a town, swelled further as a result of the programme of modernisation implemented by Yakov: between 1883 and 1888 the citadel was encircled by eight forts of a standard design approved by the Russian war ministry. As Yakov would have been well aware, the invention of powerful new explosives such as melinite (a compound of picric acid and guncotton) which could withstand the shock of being fired from conventional artillery meant that these forts were obsolete even before

14 'Svidetel'stvo o rozhdenii N. Ya. Myaskovskogo v 1881g.', RGALI, 2040/1/165, ll. 1–10b.

15 Aleksey Ikonnikov, 'N. Ya. Myaskovskiy (biograficheskiy ocherk)', *Sovetskaya muzïka*, 4 (1941), 21.

they were built: only six years after their completion, the brick used in their construction had to be replaced or overlaid with four-foot thick slabs of concrete.[16] By then, Yakov had been transferred elsewhere – initially, in 1888, to Orenburg, seventeen hundred miles to the east near Russia's present-day border with Kazakhstan, an important military outpost, trading station, and gateway to the empire's Central Asian territories. But the challenge of constructing bomb-resistant fortifications would become one of his central professional preoccupations: in 1889, he published an important essay proposing the adoption of a new design of casemate, a vaulted chamber used to link fortress structures, which would enhance defensive capacity and afford greater protection to men and equipment.[17] His career advanced rapidly: within a year he was reassigned to Kazan, five hundred miles east of Moscow, and put in charge of engineering operations in the Kazan military district – a responsible administrative post.

Myaskovsky's reminiscences do not describe the lengthy, gruelling journeys necessitated by his father's transfers, merely a few impressions of the new locations in which he found himself – the novel sights of camels and maize in Orenburg and the city's swirling dust clouds and stupefying heat; travels with his father on the Volga and Kama Rivers after they moved to Kazan. By then, two younger sisters had made their appearance, Vera in 1885 and Valentina in 1886. A third daughter, Yevgeniya, was born in December 1889, but Myaskovsky's mother died soon afterwards.[18] Yakov's unmarried younger sister Yelikonida, who had been close to his wife since their schooldays (both attended the Yekaterininsky Institute for young noblewomen in St Petersburg), moved to Kazan to care for the stricken widower's children, the eldest of whom, Sergey, was only fourteen. In later life, Myaskovsky's sisters remembered Yelikonida as a fundamentally good-natured woman who looked after them to the best of her ability, but who suffered from a 'severe nervous illness that left its melancholy mark on every aspect of our daily life'. Her 'illness' manifested itself in bouts of depression, agoraphobic anxiety attacks, and a tendency to morbid religiosity. The relaxed existence that the children had previously enjoyed came to an abrupt end. Religious observance was punctiliously enforced: games, music, and other

16   Stefan Fuglewicz, 'Rozbudowa Twierdzy Modlin w XIX i XX wieku', in *200 lat Twierdzy Modlin*, 53.

17   Yakov Myaskovskiy, 'Vopros o sovremennom znachenii krepostnogo forta', *Inzhenernïy zhurnal*, 12 (1889), 1351–80. On Yakov's contribution to fort design, see Viktor Yakovlev, *Istoriya krepostey: Evolyutsiya dolgovremennoy fortifikatsii* (Moscow, 1931), 175.

18   The family tree referred to above records the date of Yevgeniya's birth as 24 December 1889 (old style), but gives the date of her mother's death as '31 January 1889' – '1889' presumably being a slip of the pen for '1890'. RGALI, 2040/4/47, l. 81.

entertainments were forbidden on Sundays and holy days; the family kept the Orthodox Lenten fast. She instituted a ritual that the children came to dread: on Saturdays, they would be assembled and subjected to a lengthy sermon – often lasting several hours – about their lapses in good behaviour during the week. If Yelikonida considered an infraction sufficiently serious, her usual punishment was to refuse to speak to the miscreant, sometimes for weeks on end. Myaskovsky recalled that the tense, oppressive atmosphere at home caused him to become withdrawn and uncommunicative. His sisters similarly remembered a dominant mood of dreariness and unhappiness, which their father, immersed in his grief, seems to have done little to alleviate.

Yelikonida was by no means without positive qualities, though she was clearly a troubled soul. As the family correspondence abundantly attests, she was fond of her charges and cared about their welfare. She was also intelligent and possessed considerable musical ability: in her youth, her fine voice had gained her a place in the Mariinsky Theatre chorus. When in the mood, she would play the piano and sing songs and arias for the children. She was the first person to notice Nikolay's interest in music, and at his request, started to give him piano lessons, though her instruction, as he later realised, was hopelessly unsystematic: rather than learning to read musical notation properly, he assimilated pieces by ear. Yelikonida supplemented his musical diet of Hünten's *Méthode pour le piano-forte* and Bertini études with occasional visits to the theatre when touring companies brought productions of operas and operettas – amongst others, they attended *Die Fledermaus*, *Prince Igor*, and *A Life for the Tsar*.[19]

The boy was initially sent for two years to the local *real'noye uchilishche*, the Russian equivalent of a German *Realschule*, at which pupils were taught technical and scientific subjects instead of Greek and Latin, the core of the traditional gymnasium curriculum.[20] When it came to his children's schooling beyond an elementary level, however, Yakov had few options open to him. As late as the 1890s, educational opportunities in Russia were still largely restricted to those who could afford to pay for them: it is indicative that almost four-fifths of the population, even in European Russia,

19 This description of Yelikonida's personality draws on Ikonnikov, 'N. Ya. Myaskovskiy', 22; Valentina Men'shikova, Vera Yakovleva, and Yevgeniya Fedorovskaya, 'Pamyati brata', in Semyon Shlifshteyn (ed.), *N. Ya. Myaskovskiy: Sobraniye materialov* vol. 1, 163–4; Myaskovskiy, 'Avtobiograficheskiye zametki', 3.

20 Ikonnikov, *Khudozhnik nashikh dney*, 12. On Russian *Realschulen*, see Vasiliy Rudakov, 'Real'nïye uchilishcha', in Konstantin Arsen'yev and Fyodor Petrushevskiy (ed.), *Èntsiklopedicheskiy slovar' Brokgauza i Yefrona* (St Petersburg, 1899), 410–13.

was illiterate.[21] The numbers of scholarships that schools could offer were fixed at low levels by ministerial decree. Gymnasium fees rose sharply due to reactionary policies implemented by Alexander III's Minister of Public Education Ivan Delyanov, who declared gymnasium schooling unsuitable for the offspring of 'coachmen, lackeys, cooks, laundresses' and other representatives of the lower classes and deliberately sought to hinder their access to it.[22] As an army officer, Yakov had a fairly elevated social status, but even after promotion to the rank of colonel in 1893 it was a struggle to raise five children on his salary. Low pay that failed to keep pace with inflation was a long-standing complaint in the army, and the situation did not improve significantly until the turn of the century.[23] One of the few privileges that more senior officers enjoyed was the right to have their children educated at state expense – in the case of their sons, at military boarding schools known as 'cadet corps' (*kadetskiye korpusa*).[24] Nikolay's older brother Sergey had already been sent to the cadet corps in Nizhny Novgorod, and on turning twelve in 1893 Nikolay joined him there.

Like gymnasiums and *Realschulen*, the cadet corps were modelled on German educational institutions – in this instance, Prussian military schools for the children of the nobility, the first of which, the Royal Prussian Cadet Corps in Berlin, had been established by Friedrich Wilhelm I in 1716 as a 'nursery' for the Prussian officer corps.[25] The earliest Russian equivalent, initially styled 'The Academy of Knights' (*Rïtsarskaya akademiya*) and eventually renamed the First St Petersburg Cadet Corps, was founded in 1731 by Empress Anna as a reward for aristocrats who had supported her contentious accession to the throne – the idea being that the new institution would prepare their younger sons for a career in the army to compensate for their lack of patrimony.[26] Only a handful of other cadet corps were founded in Russia during the later eighteenth century, but the number multiplied considerably during the nineteenth and early twentieth centuries: on the eve of the First World War, the total stood at thirty. In 1893, when

21   Arcadius Kahan, *Russian Economic History: The Nineteenth Century*, ed. Roger Weiss (Chicago and London, 1989), 171.

22   Nina Gurkina, *Istoriya obrazovaniya v Rossii (X–XX veka)* (St Petersburg, 2001), 24–6.

23   See Sergey Volkov, *Russkiy ofitserskiy korpus* (Moscow, 2003), 236–62.

24   The relevant entitlements are detailed in 'Polozheniye o kadetskikh korpusakh, vïsochayshe utverzhdyonnoye 14 fevralya 1886g.', *Polnoye sobraniye zakonov Rossiyskoy Imperii*, series 3, vol. 6 (St Petersburg, 1888), 54–77.

25   Adolf Friedrich Johannes von Crousaz, *Geschichte des Königlich Preussischen Kadetten-Corps, nach seiner Entstehung, seinem Entwickelungsgange und seinen Resultaten* (Berlin, 1857), 14.

26   Nikolay Petrukhintsev, *Tsarstvovaniye Annï Ioannovnï: Formirovaniye vnutripoliticheskogo kursa i sud'bï armii i flota, 1730–1735g.* (St Petersburg, 2001), 117–19.

Myaskovsky was sent to Nizhny Novgorod, over eight thousand pupils were enrolled in cadet corps nationally.[27]

By then, they had become rather controversial establishments. From the 1850s onwards, articles appeared regularly in the liberal press questioning the appropriateness of sending children to boarding school at such a young age and subjecting them to strictly regimented training.[28] The ethos of the cadet corps was thoroughly militarised, seeking to instil unhesitating obedience to authority and devotion to tsar and fatherland: boys wore army-style uniforms and were even assigned to 'companies' of a student 'battalion' under the command of staff members. Bullying of younger pupils by older ones was ubiquitous, but teachers largely turned a blind eye, believing that it helped to toughen boys up and develop character.[29] Unsurprisingly, many children found enforced separation from their families deeply traumatic. Cadet corps accepted pupils as young as ten, and one former inmate recalled teachers doing little else at the start of the new school year but wiping the 'rivers of tears' and running noses of new arrivals – and this as late as the early twentieth century.[30] Not a few boys developed serious psychological difficulties, exacerbated, in some cases, through being abandoned altogether by their relatives and not even being allowed home during the holidays.

Yakov was hardly unaware of cadet corps' shortcomings, but as his later correspondence with his son confirms, he could not afford the alternatives: there was no other way to provide him with a good education. Within military families, moreover, the tradition of sending male children to military schools was very strong and largely unquestioned.[31] The Nizhny Novgorod Cadet Corps was considered an élite school, being one of the oldest and most prestigious, and numbered the sons of notable aristocratic families amongst its pupils.[32] It had an excellent reputation: Count Dmitry Milyutin, Alexander II's long-serving war minister entrusted with reforming the Russian army after its humiliating defeat in the Crimean campaign, judged it to be amongst the best institutions of its kind when he visited in

27   Andrey Mikhaylov, *Rukovodstvo voyennïm obrazovaniyem v Rossii vo vtoroy polovine XIX – nachale XX veka* (Pskov, 1999), 444.

28   Mikhaylov, *Rukovodstvo*, 214–17; Aleksandr Belyayev, *Kadetskiye korpusa Rossii: Istoriya i sovremennost'* (Stavropol, 2008), 112–13.

29   Mikhaylov, *Rukovodstvo*, 383–6; Belyayev, *Kadetskiye korpusa*, 86.

30   Anatoliy Markov, *Kadetï i yunkera* (San Francisco, 1961), 34.

31   See Belyayev, *Kadetskiye korpusa*, 95.

32   See Pavel Kartsov, *Istoricheskiy ocherk Novgorodskogo grafa Arakcheyeva kadetskogo korpusa i Nizhegorodskoy voyennoy gimnazii* (St Petersburg, 1884); Valeriy Krïlov, *Kadetskiye korpusa i rossiyskiye kadetï* (St Petersburg, 1998), 44–5.

May 1875.[33] Yakov's sons would have been considered fortunate to secure
places there, as the government imposed strict admissions quotas for state-
funded pupils and they had to sit competitive entrance examinations.[34] Both
boys were evidently bright. The school's location was a further advantage:
Nizhny Novgorod was reasonably close to Kazan, by Russian reckonings at
least (roughly 250 miles by ferry on the Volga), and the family had relatives
living in the city.

As it transpired, Myaskovsky remained there for only two years. In April
1894 Yakov was selected to be amongst the staff officers reporting to the War
Ministry's Military Engineering Directorate (*Glavnoye inzhenernoye upravleniye*), and in December 1895, he was appointed to an administrative position within the Directorate itself – significant promotions which resulted in
his transfer back to St Petersburg.[35] The move was timely, as 1895 brought
fresh misfortune. Yakov's oldest son Sergey had contracted tuberculosis and
was sent to live with friends in the Caucasus in the hope that a warmer climate would prove beneficial. His health quickly deteriorated, and he died
there, aged only eighteen. He seems to have been a young man of considerable potential, which made his premature death all the more poignant:
Myaskovsky recalled his brother possessing 'great artistic gifts'. These circumstances heightened the family's relief at the opportunity to leave behind
a 'boring provincial life' in Kazan and make a fresh start in the capital.[36]

Yakov arranged Nikolay's transfer from Nizhny Novgorod to the Second
Cadet Corps in St Petersburg, which enabled him to see much more of
his family: though it was also a boarding school, he was allowed to spend
Sundays, holy days, and vacations at home. If anything, his new school was
an even more select establishment: it was one of the oldest, having been
founded in 1756, and many of its alumni went on to have careers as officers
in the artillery and engineering corps. Situated in the historic Petrogradsky
district, it occupied an imposing complex of buildings which in addition to
offices, classrooms, and living quarters also housed Lutheran and Catholic
chapels, a museum, and even a ballroom.[37]

33 Dmitriy Milyutin, *Dnevnik General-Fel'dmarshala Grafa Dmitriya
    Alekseyevicha Milyutina, 1873–1875*, ed. Larisa Zakharova, 2nd ed. (Moscow,
    2008), 180.

34 Mikhaylov, *Rukovodstvo*, 257–8, 264.

35 Ivkov, *Istoricheskiy ocherk*, 392.

36 Men'shikova *et al.*, 'Pamyati brata', 163–4; Myaskovskiy, 'Avtobiograficheskiye
    zametki', 3.

37 Aleksandr Lindeberg (ed.), *Istoricheskiy ocherk 2-go Kadetskogo Korpusa,
    1712–1912* (St Petersburg, 1912) relates the institution's history up to the mid-
    nineteenth century (a projected second volume covering later developments
    seems never to have been completed). See also Krïlov, *Kadetskiye korpusa*,
    27–32. The premises now houses the A. F. Mozhaysky Military-Space
    Academy.

At this remove, it is difficult to appraise the general standard of instruction at nineteenth-century Russian cadet corps or judge how conscientiously staff members discharged their duty of care towards their pupils *in loco parentis*: both, no doubt, varied considerably. The memoir literature suggests that some boys, at least, did not find the environment unduly oppressive. Alexander Spiridovich, who wrote a well-known account of his time at the Nizhny Novgorod Cadet Corps in the 1880s, not long before Myaskovsky went there, describes an atmosphere of camaraderie and experiences of good teaching, as well as his schoolmates' resourcefulness in perpetrating the usual adolescent misdemeanours: discipline does not seem to have been excessively harsh.[38] By the 1890s the cadet school curriculum largely resembled that of the *Realschulen*, the principal focus being on mathematics and scientific subjects, supplemented with religious instruction and tuition in Russian, foreign languages, history, and geography. Its design was a product of Milyutin's overhaul of military education, undertaken as part of his wider programme of reforms during the 1860s and 1870s and his drive to raise professional standards. The aim was to provide a solid foundation for subsequent specialised training at a military academy, thereby ensuring the maintenance of a highly skilled officer corps.[39]

A typical school day began at 6 a.m. with morning ablutions, sprucing up of uniforms, and polishing of boots, followed by prayers and a small collation of a bread roll and tea before inspection and drill practice from 7 to 8 a.m. The period between 8 a.m. and 2.40 p.m. was taken up with classes, with an hour's break between 10.50 and 11.50 a.m. for a more substantial breakfast at which hot dishes were provided, followed by a morning constitutional. Lunch was served at 3 p.m., and the period from 4 to 6 p.m. was given over to extracurricular activities. The boys did their homework between 6 and 8 p.m. and went to bed at 9 p.m. after an evening snack.[40] Compulsory physical education formed an intrinsic part of the curriculum, and older pupils were expected to engage in field training exercises

---

38   Aleksandr Spiridovich, *Zapiski zhandarma* (Kharkov, 1928), 13–22. Andrey Mikhaylov, a noted historian of Russian military education, suggests that the use of corporal punishment at cadet corps declined in the later nineteenth century: Mikhaylov, *Rukovodstvo*, 372–3.

39   Andrey Zayonchkovskiy, *Voyennïye reformï 1860–1870 godov v Rossii* (Moscow, 1952), 221–53, remains a foundational account of Milyutin's educational reforms. See also Robert F. Baumann, 'Universal Service Reform: Conception to Implementation, 1873–1883', in David Schimmelpennick van der Oye and Bruce W. Menning (ed.), *Reforming the Tsar's Army* (Cambridge, 2004), 12–13 and 19–24; John W. Steinberg, *All the Tsar's Men: Russia's General Staff and the Fate of the Empire, 1898–1914* (Baltimore and Washington, 2010), 16–20.

40   See F. B. Grekov, *Kratkiy istoricheskiy ocherk voyenno-uchebnïkh zavedeniy, 1700–1910* (Moscow, 1910), 31; Vladimir Danchenko and Gleb Kalashnikov, *Kadetskiy korpus: Shkola russkoy voennoy elitï* (Moscow, 2007), 325–7.

at specially organised camps during the holidays. The range of extracurricular activities in which the boys could participate was wide, especially
at the better-resourced schools: they could avail themselves of coaching in
fencing and gymnastics, learn practical skills such as woodwork, play chess,
attend dancing lessons, take part in plays, or perform in a school choir or
orchestra.[41] Many cadet corps had strong musical traditions and hired notable professional musicians to provide instrumental and vocal tuition.[42] The
cellist Konstantin Poprzhedzinsky (Poprzedziński), who taught for many
years at Nizhny Novgorod Cadet Corps, was held in high regard by Nikolay
Rubinstein and appeared in concerts with him and with other eminent virtuosi when they visited the city.[43]

Myaskovsky's muted account of his school years in his 'Autobiographical
Notes' suggests that they held few happy memories for him, although he was
an able student who never came lower than second in his class. He passes
over most aspects of the experience in silence: the reader learns nothing
about his fellow pupils, his teachers, or his impressions of the school environment, apart from the extent to which it hindered his development as a
musician. Instead, he dwells on the two abiding frustrations of his adoles-
cence – haphazard piano tuition and the constant struggle to find an instrument on which to practice. Looking back from late middle age, he admitted
to lingering feelings of bitterness – his own word – at having missed out
on a systematic musical training during a crucial formative phase, and the
difficulties that this created for him subsequently.

His sisters' portrayal of him as a teenager – 'very quiet, intense, rather
sombre, and very reserved' – suggests someone temperamentally ill-suited
to the rough-and-tumble of boarding school.[44] Fastidious in his dress,
impeccably well-mannered, but remote, he gave the impression of inhabit-
ing a closely-guarded inner world from which he emerged with reluctance.
His love of nature and proclivity for disappearing on long solitary hikes in
the countryside were already in evidence, as were a strong artistic streak
and an active imagination: they remembered him remodelling a stuffed doll
to a more pleasing shape and painstakingly sewing clothes to make an elegant fashionable outfit for it; and his construction of a toy theatre in which
he put on 'operas' and 'ballets' with a cast of cardboard cut-out figures.
(He varied the stage lighting by placing translucent confectionary wrap-
pings of different colours in front of a lamp.) The family's move to a large

41   Belyayev, *Kadetskiye korpusa*, 88–9.
42   Valeriy Krïlov and Vitaliy Semichev, *Zvan'ye skromnoye i gordoye kadet:*
     Istoricheskiye i kul'turnïye traditsii kadetskikh korpusov Rossii (St Petersburg,
     2004), 104–9 and 116–20.
43   Belyayev, *Kadetskiye korpusa*, 138–9.
44   Men'shikova *et al.*, 'Pamyati brata', 165.

state-owned apartment on Znamenskaya Street (now Vosstaniya Street) near Nevsky Prospekt facilitated the resumption of domestic music-making. From 1896, Yakov was able to earn supplementary income by lecturing at his alma mater, the Tsar Nicholas I Engineering Academy[45]: his finances improved sufficiently to permit the acquisition of a grand piano and paying for Nikolay to have piano lessons at home on Sundays. The composer César Cui, a fellow expert on fortifications and a colleague of Yakov's at the academy[46], recommended a tutor by the name of Stuneyev, who boasted of being a relative of Glinka's wife but proved a fairly mediocre pianist and an ineffectual teacher. Myaskovsky's progress was further hampered by the fact that he had limited access to an instrument during term-time. On discovering that he was taking lessons privately, the management forbade him to play the school pianos, although the practice rooms were often empty: when he tried to do so surreptitiously, they would eject him. Even after an elapse of forty years, he had not forgotten the feelings of 'burning hatred' that this used to arouse.[47]

He increasingly devoted all his spare time to music. In spite of his defective piano technique, he had considerable natural facility and was an excellent sight-reader: he made sufficient progress as to be able to play four-hand arrangements of standard orchestral repertoire with Stuneyev – symphonies and overtures by Haydn, Mozart, and Beethoven, and works by the early Romantics. He took up the violin in order to join the school orchestra, which was conducted by Nikolay Kazanli, a composition student of Rimsky-Korsakov. Its standard was evidently not very high (the irascible Kazanli often beat time with the leg of a chair, as he regularly broke his baton when he flew into a rage), but it provided some experience of ensemble playing. He acquired additional chamber music partners when Karl Myaskovsky's granddaughter Shura (Alexandra) and her husband Yury Gvozdinsky came to live with the family. Myaskovsky's sisters remembered Shura, then in her mid-thirties, as 'a good musician who sang charmingly and was a very cultured person in general'.[48] She not only encouraged Nikolay's musical interests but exerted a beneficent influence on the entire household, especially on Yelikonida. Yury played the violin ('enthusiastically, but very out of tune', in Myaskovsky's recollection) and performed with one of the numerous 'German' amateur orchestras in the city – ethnic Germans were as prominent in the capital's musical community as they were in other domains. He brought Nikolay to its rehearsals and concerts, as well as

---

45　Ivkov, *Istoricheskiy ocherk*, 392–3.

46　Cui was appointed to a professorship at the Academy in 1880: see Aleksandr Nazarov, *Tsezar' Antonovich Kyui* (Moscow, 1989), 110.

47　Myaskovskiy, 'Avtobiograficheskiye zametki', 4.

48　Men'shikova *et al.*, 'Pamyati brata', 167.

professional symphony orchestra concerts organised by the Russian Musical Society. Hearing a superb performance of Tchaikovsky's *Pathétique* conducted by Arthur Nikisch in 1896 proved a powerful formative experience for the fifteen-year-old boy, initiating a lifelong love of Tchaikovsky's music and prompting his first attempts at composition. He asked Kazanli to give him harmony lessons but found them of little benefit. He persevered nonetheless in his efforts to get his ideas down on paper and completed about a dozen or so piano preludes in the style of Chopin, the manuscripts of which have been lost.[49]

This intense absorption in music provided an escape not only from an uncongenial school environment but also, it seems likely, from difficulties at home. Like all families of their social position, the Myaskovskys hired servants as well as a *bonne* to help look after the smaller children. After their move to St Petersburg, a woman of Baltic German descent by the name of Alida Reksting was employed in the latter capacity. She and Yakov became intimate and in 1897 she gave birth to their daughter, Varvara. As it turned out, the relationship was not a transient affair but lasted until Yakov's death in 1918. Nothing is known about how the couple managed matters during its earlier phases, but the situation was clearly very awkward. Although there was no legal impediment to formalising their union, there were significant social impediments, as a marriage between a nobleman and a nursery maid would have been viewed as a *mésalliance*. It seems significant that they only formalised their relationship in 1907, a year after Yakov was appointed to the Chief Engineering Directorate: he may have feared damaging his career prospects had he married Alida sooner. (He would be promoted to the very senior rank of lieutenant-general in 1908.) The social conventions of the period made it virtually impossible for Alida to live with Yakov's family, even after marriage: it would have been considered unthinkable for a former servant to assume the role of mistress of the household. The annual editions of *Ves' Peterburg* ('The Complete St Petersburg'), the contemporary directory of the city's residential and business addresses, reveal that she and Yakov maintained separate domiciles after their marriage until Yakov retired in 1914, and they presumably also dwelt apart during the decade preceding their marriage. Records survive pertaining to Varvara's schooling between 1911 and 1914 at the Prince Oldenburg Shelter in St Petersburg, an educational establishment that mostly cared for orphans and foundlings; she may have been enrolled at similar institutions previously.[50]

---

49 Ikonnikov, 'N. Ya. Myaskovskiy (biograficheskiy ocherk)', 23; idem, *Khudozhnik nashikh dney*, 15.

50 'Delo Popechitel'nogo soveta Priyuta Printsa Petra Georgiyevicha Ol'denburgskogo: Ob opredelenii vospitanitsï Varvarï Myaskovskoy', TsGIA, 394/1/7089, ll. 1–10.

One imagines that Yakov and Alida's relationship and the birth of their daughter must have engendered domestic tensions, but there is no record of Myaskovsky's reaction to these events. For understandable reasons, the family evidently preferred to avoid discussion of Yakov's second marriage. No materials relating to Alida or Varvara have been preserved amongst Myaskovsky's personal papers, and the few terse allusions to Alida in the family correspondence (all occurring in letters written between 1914 and 1917) suggest that her stepchildren's relationship with her was strained and distant. Only the chance discovery amongst St Petersburg church records of a set of papers documenting Alida's efforts to legitimise Varvara in 1908–9 has made it possible to establish the few facts presented here.[51]

Myaskovsky finished his studies at the cadet corps in 1899, having achieved excellent results in his final-year examinations.[52] The brightest students generally went on to enrol at either the Engineering or Artillery Academies[53], as their admission requirements were the most stringent and their courses considered the most intellectually demanding. It was taken for granted that Myaskovsky would train as a military engineer, following in his father's footsteps: the possibility of an alternative career does not seem to have arisen for discussion. In his reminiscences, he recalled acquiescing in this plan because of 'family and social traditions' and opting to attend an engineering institute because he thought it would be 'the least military in nature'. As the son of a senior officer, he was able to continue his education at state expense and was duly admitted to the Tsar Nicholas I Engineering Academy, where his father taught. Like the cadet corps at which he had studied, this too was regarded as an élite institution, and had notable experts on its staff. A similar militarised ethos prevailed: students lived in barracks and were grouped into army divisions. Apart from instruction in the different aspects of military engineering, such as the construction of field defences, roads, bridges, and fortifications, the curriculum included classes on tactics, strategy, military topography, and weaponry, as well as foreign languages and other subjects. The course lasted three years, a year longer than at most other military academies, and trainees were conferred

51 'Po prosheniyu zhenï general-mayora Alidï Nikolayevnï Myaskovskoy ob ispravlenii metrich[eskikh] zapisey o kreshchenii yeyo docheri Varvarï', TsGIA, 19/114/3417. The date of Yakov and Alida's marriage is stated as 12 November 1907 on l. 2, and Yakov's paternity of Varvara is confirmed in Alida's submission of 28 June 1908, l. 5. The fact that Alida was the family *bonne* was recorded by Ikonnikov, who presumably obtained this information from Myaskovsky himself: *Khudozhnik nashikh dney*, 12.

52 His graduation certificate, dated 1 August 1899, is preserved in RGALI, 2040/1/166, l. 1.

53 See Boris Bazilev, 'Pamyati odnogo iz nemnogikh', *Pedagogicheskiy sbornik*, 6 (1906), 509.

Figure 1.3. The young cadet (1899)

with the rank of sub-lieutenant on successful completion of their studies.[54] About one hundred students graduated annually.[55]

Of the military educational establishments that he attended, Myaskovsky described the academy as the one for which he felt 'the least loathing' – hardly an enthusiastic commendation. Nonetheless, it was an improvement on the cadet corps: although his engineering studies were demanding, he had more free time to devote to musical pursuits than heretofore. And as the academy recruited the best students, he found that 'it served as a refuge for young men of a markedly intellectual bent', which made it easier to find congenial companions.[56] Chief amongst these were Vadim Modzalevsky (1882–1920) and Vsevolod Hofmann [Gofman] (1879–?), whose backgrounds were similar to his own: both had previously attended cadet corps and came from families with strong traditions of military service. Modzalevsky, who like

---

54 For an account of Russian higher military education at the period, see Mikhaylov, *Rukovodstvo*, 322–87.

55 Lyubomir Beskrovnïy, *Armiya i flot Rossii v nachale XX veka: Ocherki voyenno-èkonomicheskogo potentsiala* (Moscow, 1986), 34.

56 Myaskovskiy, 'Avtobiograficheskiye zametki', 5.

Myaskovsky was of Polish extraction, ultimately left the army to pursue a career as a historian of seventeenth- and eighteenth-century Ukrainian culture.[57] Hofmann's family had strong artistic interests: his elder sister Nadezhda was a pianist and his younger brother Modeste (1887–1959) later came to prominence as a writer and Pushkin scholar.[58] Myaskovsky made the acquaintance of both siblings and began to attend the soirées that the Hofmanns hosted in their home. In addition to arousing his enthusiasm for the music of Balakirev, Borodin, Musorgsky, and Rimsky-Korsakov, they also introduced him to the work of contemporary figures on the St Petersburg literary scene, several of whom they knew personally. Over the next decade, these new acquaintances not only provided intellectual stimulus but were strongly supportive of his creative ambitions.

Myaskovsky continued taking piano lessons during his time at the engineering academy, after finding a more methodical teacher who helped to remedy his deficient technique.[59] The demands on his time made it infeasible to take composition lessons, but he also continued to compose. The manuscripts have survived of six piano preludes written between 1899 and 1901, comprising the first of eight sets of pieces composed between then and 1919 to which Myaskovsky gave the collective title *Flofion*. This whimsical epithet derived from the French *flonflon*, a pejorative term for a tawdry vaudeville song – the refrains of which often featured the nonsense syllables *flon, flon, flon*.[60] The atmosphere of Myaskovsky's piano miniatures is in no way redolent of the theatre, so the title was evidently a private joke. The pieces in this first set are mostly very short, no longer than a page. They demonstrate a fairly assured grasp of common-practice harmony but have limited textural interest: they are beginner's work and not in any way remarkable.[61] Myaskovsky's first known attempt at a vocal composition also dates from 1901 – the song 'Tak i rvyotsya dusha' (And thus yearns the soul), a setting of a lyric by Pushkin's contemporary Aleksey Kol'tsov (1809–42) that had previously been set by Balakirev and Cui, amongst others. Unlike

57   On Modzalevsky, see Valeriy Tomozov, 'K yubileyu V. L. Modzalevskogo', *Izvestiya Russkogo genealogicheskogo obshchestva*, 4 (1995), 45–51; idem, 'Modzalevs'kyy, Vadim L'vovich', in Valeriy Smoliy *et al.*, *Entsiklopediya istorii Ukraïni*, vol. 7 (Kyiv, 2010), 20–1.

58   The most detailed summary available of Hofmann's career is given in Tat'yana Krasnoborod'ko, 'Pis'ma M. L. Gofmana k B. L. Modzalevskomu: Chast' 1 (1904–1921)', in *Ezhegodnik Rukopisnogo otdela Pushkinskogo Doma na 2000 god* (St Petersburg, 2004), 180–238.

59   Myaskovskiy, 'Avtobiograficheskiye zametki', 5.

60   See Sergey Prokofiev to Myaskovsky, 5 October 1923, in Kozlova and Yatsenko, *Perepiska*, 171.

61   'Shest' preludiy' [Six Preludes], RGALI, 2040/2/30.

the piano preludes, he thought sufficiently highly of this youthful effort to revise it for publication in February 1950, only six months before his death.[62]

It was perhaps no accident that Kol'tsov's poem evokes a young person's ardent longing for the freedom to live life differently – an increasingly urgent concern for Myaskovsky as his studies at the engineering academy drew to a close in spring 1902. On graduation, he would be required by law to serve for four and a half years in a sapper battalion – eighteen months for every year of his tertiary education at the state's expense.[63] Myaskovsky's reminiscences do not recount the events of this year in any detail, but it was clearly an unhappy time: he felt trapped in a profession that he found wholly uncongenial.

In April, he wrote to Vsevolod Hofmann (who had graduated the previous year and had been posted to Moscow), confiding in him that he aspired to be a composer. This letter, like virtually all of Myaskovsky's letters from this period, has been lost, but Hofmann's reply, which has been preserved, indicates that it had the nature of an intimate confession, revealing anguished uncertainty about his abilities and anxiety for the future. The relationship between the two men was close, and Hofmann responded with sensitivity and warmth. He affirmed his belief in his friend's talent ('If any of us will amount to anything, it will be you'), urging him to 'cast off sloth and apathy' and apply himself seriously to his musical studies.[64] Myaskovsky's self-doubt and hesitancy are not difficult to understand: he had been a late starter, was keenly aware of his patchy musical education, and had yet to demonstrate any noteworthy creative ability. He had no choice but to remain in the army for the foreseeable future, so it was far from clear how his ambition could be realised, assuming it was not completely misguided.

After stepping out of the academy's 'hateful walls' for the last time (in his own vehement phrase), Myaskovsky was assigned on 10 August to the Second Reserve Sapper Battalion and travelled to Moscow to await his impending dispatch to an army base in Zaraysk, a small town situated a hundred miles to the south-east. Eager to resume his musical studies, he made enquiries about composition teachers, feeling in need of more expert guidance. As he recalled in later life: 'My general musical development had advanced apace, and I found my compositional efforts to date manifestly unsatisfactory'. He sent 'a naive letter' to Nikolay Rimsky-Korsakov asking him to recommend someone suitable and was surprised to receive a

62   Myaskovskiy, 'Vïpiski', entry for 7 February 1950, RGALI, 2040/1/65, l. 1010b.

63   For a discussion of this standard requirement, see Volkov, *Russkiy ofitserskiy korpus*, 154. Myaskovsky's obligation to remain in the army for a further four and a half years is stipulated in his Eighteenth Sapper Battalion service record: RGVIA, 5399/1/332, l. 200b.

64   Vsevolod Hofmann to Myaskovsky, 17 April 1902. RGALI, 2040/2/135, ll. 12–140b.

gracious reply suggesting that he approach Sergey Taneyev. It would appear that he managed to arrange a meeting with Taneyev before departing for Zaraysk on 13 September.[65]

A few days later, Yakov wrote expressing concern that something was amiss: he admitted having wanted to enquire before now, but their mutual reserve and his own awkwardness about broaching the topic had 'bound his clumsy tongue'. After telling his son that he missed him and hoped they would not be separated for long, he continued: 'I would be very grateful if, in your spare time or at a moment of spiritual need, you would put your trust in me and describe to me those innermost thoughts that are upsetting you'.[66] This communication initiated an intensive correspondence over the next few months, of which only Yakov's side survives. In addition to shedding light on Myaskovsky's state of mind at an important turning point in his life, Yakov's letters are richly revealing of the two men's personalities and their relationship. Far from conforming to stereotypes of the gruff and authoritarian military paterfamilias, Yakov emerges as a kind, loving father who was concerned to see his son so unhappy and anxious to do what he could to help.

At first, Nikolay spoke merely of feeling isolated in Zaraysk, a small provincial town with few amenities, especially after discovering that he had little in common with his fellow officers. Yakov responded sympathetically:

> I understand completely what a cheerless and unpleasant impression everything that you've encountered in Zaraysk must have produced at first. Only one thing reconciles me to the situation – the thought that experiencing such setbacks and misfortunes when one is just starting to live independently can be useful for a decent, upright fellow of sound and prudent character, and will only strengthen it, instilling greater circumspection and teaching him to cope with any situation. I have confidence in you: I know your thoughtful nature, your capacity to remain in control of situations and circumstances in which you find yourself. I am not fearful for you and am convinced that living in the provinces without any intellectual or spiritual outlets will not drag you down.

Exhorting Nikolay to preserve his 'purity of mind and body' and avoid the unwholesome pursuits of his companions ('drinking, cards, and chasing

---

65 This chronology of events is reconstructed from the following: 'Avtobiograficheskiye zametki', 6; Myaskovsky's service record ('Posluzhnoy spisok, 26 iyunya 1923'), RGALI, 2040/1/168, l. 3; August Myaskovsky junior to Myaskovsky, 22 September 1902, RGALI, 2040/1/196, ll. 1–10b; Vsevolod Hofmann to Myaskovsky, 2 October 1902, RGALI, 2040/1/135, ll. 38–40.

66 Yakov Myaskovsky to Myaskovsky, 18 September 1902, RGALI, 2040/1/134, ll. 1–40b.

after women'), he counselled patience and raised the prospect of arranging a transfer to another regiment if the situation proved intolerable.[67]

Nikolay answered almost by return of post: he confessed his loathing of the army and declared that he would find his life unbearable if he could not devote himself to music. He went on to outline the first steps of a long-term plan to achieve that aim. As he would soon be assigned to the Seventeenth Sapper Battalion in Moscow, he proposed to live as economically as he could on the outskirts of the city, eating only once a day if necessary, to enable him to afford the cost of private tuition from Taneyev.

Yakov's response to this dramatic confession was greatly to his credit: notwithstanding the conventionality of his outlook in certain respects, his letter was not only empathic and insightful but free of cant. 'Don't think that I am going to be issuing advice or admonishments of some kind – because I'm not', he wrote, explaining that he intended merely to offer his opinion and leave his son to decide matters as he saw best. Yakov opened with the surprising admission that he shared Nikolay's dislike of the army and had only joined it out of necessity: 'I needed to find my feet quickly and help my parents, who were poor'. He had no illusions about military service, though he acknowledged the importance of the army's defensive role; at bottom, it was 'a preparation for destroying one's fellow human beings in the easiest and most effective manner possible'. He had chosen to become a military engineer because he regarded it as the 'noblest branch' of military service, which sought to save lives rather than to take them. Like Nikolay, he had a deep love of nature and would have preferred a profession based in the countryside, but 'now that I am an old man . . . it is too late to start all over again'.

> You think that I am devoted to the army and consider it the be-all and end-all. . . . I would willingly give it up if there was any possibility of doing so. If I still put my energies into it, it is not because I love it and not because of my reputation (as you seem to think): it is because my con-science will not allow me act otherwise. I derive moral satisfaction from doing honestly and conscientiously that which I am compelled to do by force of circumstances and the will of God.

He observed that the 'petty tyranny' of which Nikolay complained in the army was equally prevalent in civilian life, where superiors often treated their underlings in unjust and humiliating ways; even artists were subject to the 'petty tyranny of the mob and of fashion'.

Nikolay could hardly have hoped for a more supportive reaction to his revelation of his artistic ambitions. 'Your aspiration to become a musician not only does not trouble me, but I wholeheartedly welcome it', Yakov

67 Ibid.

wrote, adding that it was perhaps not so incompatible with military service as Nikolay seemed to imagine: he adduced Borodin and Cui as notable examples of composers who had pursued dual careers. Uppermost in Yakov's mind was undoubtedly the question of how realistic this aspiration was, especially as his son admitted to being tormented by doubts about whether he had any talent. He sensibly observed that the only way for Nikolay to find out was to start applying himself seriously:

> With regard to your acknowledgement of lacking a divine spark, . . . if you have not been aware of it up to the present, that does not necessarily mean that it is not there. In music, there are so many places, so many hearths where this spark could smoulder unseen, awaiting only a libation of holy oil to make it flare up brightly. . . . If this is so, then it is up to you to ensure that you eliminate opportunities to waste your time and occupy yourself usefully in order to realise your potential.

Yakov concluded by proposing that Nikolay should move back to St Petersburg and look for a composition teacher there, as it would be easier to help him financially: using his army connections, he would seek to have him transferred to the Eighteenth Sapper Battalion, which was based in the capital.[68]

His son evidently acquiesced in this plan, but in the event it took over a year to effect the transfer, rather than a few weeks as Yakov had hoped: demand for vacant places was intense.[69] By mid-October, Myaskovsky had returned to Moscow to join the Seventeenth Sapper Battalion. His mood plummeted. As his sisters recalled:

> Torn away from his family, to which he was deeply attached, deprived of his habitual conditions of household music-making, being at the same time extremely shy and, in consequence, unsociable, he was unable to acclimatise himself quickly to an unfamiliar milieu. Moreover, he loathed military service and his extremely limited means meant that he was unable to attend concerts and the theatre as much as he would have liked. As a result, he completely lost heart.[70]

His letters to friends and family were increasingly taken up with morbid self-analyses of his putative vices, declarations of his own worthlessness, and despairing reiterations of the conviction that he would never amount to anything as a musician – as though re-enacting the Saturday ritual of his childhood. He admitted to Vsevolod Hofmann that he was drinking to

---

68 Yakov Myaskovsky to Myaskovsky, 25 September 1902, RGALI, 2040/1/134, 8–13ob.

69 Yakov explained the delays in his letters of 8, 19, and 24 October, 11 November, and 29 December 1902: RGALI, 2040/1/134, ll. 15–23ob, 41–2.

70 Men'shikova *et al.*, 'Pamyati brata', 168.

excess and had got himself into debt in the officers' mess. Hofmann tried to talk sense into him, suggesting his friend had lost perspective ('It's a pity I'm not in Moscow, or I'd unbutton your pants, pull them down, and give you a good hiding for all your sins', he jested), as did Modzalevsky, who told him that he needed to stop feeling sorry for himself and do something productive by devoting himself seriously to his musical studies.[71] These admonitions temporarily fell on deaf ears: Myaskovsky may well have been close to a nervous breakdown.

Yelikonida and Yakov were dismayed to receive disturbing letters in which he accused himself of being cold, egotistical, and wholly lacking in feelings for others – a 'bad character', a fantasist and a dreamer who was incapable of applying himself to anything worthwhile.[72] These communications must have made for difficult, even painful reading, but both did their utmost to respond in a caring and reassuring way, sending lengthy, thoughtful replies.

Yelikonida diagnosed his self-dissatisfaction as a sign that he had yet to realise himself fully: she declared his nature to be formed of 'good material' and urged him to work on himself to bring his 'spiritual chaos into a more ordered state'. To this end, she encouraged him to read intellectually nourishing literature as an aid to understanding his inner struggles, since his development as an artist was bound up with the growth of his entire personality. In response to his claim that he lacked the willpower and inclination to overcome his difficulties, she countered that this attitude was unworthy of him – it not only betokened self-indulgence and sloth but showed a lack of imagination. She spoke with remarkable honesty about her own psychological difficulties and her strivings to overcome them, emphasising that this had demanded a sustained effort of will which he too needed to make. 'Stop slandering yourself, my dear', she concluded, 'bestir yourself, and remember that there are people in this world who love you deeply and boundlessly'.[73]

Yakov was distressed to receive a letter in which his son complained of having been sent to military educational establishments where he had learnt nothing worthwhile and which had left him with no choice but to serve in the army. 'If I had my way', Nikolay wrote, 'I would do everything possible to get out of the army, but unfortunately it would displease you and

71   Vsevolod Hofmann to Myaskovsky, 27 October 1902, RGALI, 2040/2/135, ll. 29–310b; Modzalevsky to Myaskovsky, 3 November 1902, RGALI, 2040/2/192, ll. 16–20.

72   Yelikonida Myaskovskaya to Myaskovsky, 2 and 7 November 1902, RGALI, 2040/2/197, ll. 11–130b, 15–220b.

73   Yelikonida Myaskovskaya to Myaskovsky, 26 November 1902, RGALI, 2040/2/197, ll. 27–360b.

I am tied to it by material necessity'.[74] Yakov's reply, which runs to several thousand words, shows that he was deeply worried but found it difficult to know what to do. He dealt firmly, but not defensively, with Nikolay's accusations, pointing out that he had tried to provide him with the best education he could, and that the alternatives, even had he been able to afford them, would not necessarily have been any better. He was evidently concerned that Nikolay had a rather starry-eyed view of what life as a musician would be like and felt obliged to confront him with the reality of what might lie in store should he not succeed in establishing himself professionally – if not penury, then a lifetime trapped in a soul-destroying and poorly paid clerical post. Nonetheless, he told Nikolay that he would not stand in his way if he decided to leave the army and undertook to help him as best he could: 'I am your father and I will never leave you without support'.[75]

Neither did Yakov and Yelikonida react censoriously to his disclosure that he had been drinking too much and owed money: they paid his debts without reproach.[76] Their demonstration of love and concern succeeded in alleviating his psychological crisis, and Yakov's support of his decision to resign his commission proved of crucial importance. By the New Year, Myaskovsky was able to consider his next steps with a clearer head.

---

74 Yakov quotes this phrase from his son's letter verbatim.

75 Yakov Myaskovsky to Myaskovsky, 1–4 December 1902, RGALI, 2040/1/134, ll. 30–40ob.

76 Yelikonida Myaskovskaya to Myaskovsky, 24 January 1903 and undated communication, January 1903, RGALI, 2040/2/197, ll. 39–43ob.

2

Apprenticeship: 1903–11

Having resigned himself to the fact that his return to St Petersburg would take longer than anticipated, Myaskovsky resolved to make the most of his time in Moscow. In late 1902 he began to study privately with Taneyev. By his own admission, he probably made 'a rather strange impression', because he was too shy to show the eminent composer any of the music that he was writing. As the lessons proved unproductive, Taneyev suggested that Myaskovsky transfer to his former student Reinhold Glière, with whom he started in January 1903.[1] The twenty-seven-year-old Glière, who had graduated from the Moscow Conservatoire two years previously and been awarded the institution's coveted gold medal, already had a symphony and several substantial chamber works to his credit. Taneyev held him in high regard and regularly sent him private pupils[2]: earlier that year, he had recommended him as a tutor for the precocious Sergey Prokofiev, with whom Glière spent the summer at the Prokofiev family's estate in Sontsovka (now Sontsivka, in Ukraine's Donetsk Oblast).[3] Myaskovsky established a better rapport with his new teacher: within six months he had consolidated his knowledge of music theory sufficiently to tackle chorale harmonisations and advanced exercises in chromatic harmony.[4] His rapid progress bolstered his self-confidence and lifted his spirits. He reported to his sister Vera that the tormenting doubts of the previous year had dissipated:

> I am quite calm: it is all the same to me whether I will ever amount to anything or not, I have chosen my path and I will stick to it for the simple reason that, out of all the things that exist for me, this and nothing else arouses the greatest appetite for work, meaning that it is my strongest inclination – in other words, my vocation. Having made this decision, I set to work and quietly got on with things. It has often happened that my efforts are unsuccessful and that work progresses slowly – but it has been progressing nonetheless; and when I get down to it and persevere unremittingly, my work has turned out well; and not only has the piece progressed, but working on it stimulated new ideas and yielded material for other compositions.[5]

1   Myaskovskiy, 'Avtobiograficheskiye zametki', 6.

2   Valerian Bogdanov-Berezovskiy (ed.), *Reyngol'd Moritsevich Glièr: Stat'i, vospominaniya, materialï*, vol. 1 (Moscow, 1965), 14–15, 318.

3   See Sergey Prokof'yev, *Avtobiografiya*, 2nd ed. (Moscow, 1982), 79–91.

4   The exercises that Myaskovsky completed for Glière are preserved in RGALI, 2040/2/63.

5   Myaskovsky to Vera Myaskovskaya, undated letter of early 1903, RNMM, 204/974.

FIGURE 2.1. Reinhold Glière

His family was naturally relieved that circumstances had taken a marked turn for the better, although Yakov expressed concern that his son seemed to be leading a very solitary existence and urged him not to cut himself off from all social intercourse – perhaps fearing that his depression might return.[6]

Myaskovsky was not entirely isolated. Vadim Modzalevsky and Vsevolod Hofmann continued to send long chatty letters from Kiev and Novgorod, where they had respectively been posted, and he struck up a new acquaintance with a friend of Hofmann's, Vasiliy Yakovlev. Yakovlev, who was a year older than Myaskovsky, had also studied at Tsar Nicholas I Engineering Academy in St Petersburg (he finished there in 1899, the year in which Myaskovsky started). After graduating, he served for two years in a sapper unit in the Russian Far East before being transferred back to his native Moscow in 1902. In common with Myaskovsky's other army friends, he had strong artistic interests and eventually left the army to pursue a career as a music historian and critic: in later life, he became a notable authority on nineteenth-century Russian music.[7] The two men's association proved a durable one: Yakovlev married Myaskovsky's sister Vera in 1908, and they came into regular professional contact subsequently.

In 1956, a year before his death, Yakovlev published a brief but vivid memoir of this early phase of their friendship.[8] They first met in November 1902 at the opening night of a new production of Rimsky-Korsakov's opera *The Snow Maiden* (the first in almost twenty years), with a fine cast that featured the outstanding soprano Nadezhda Zabela-Vrubel in the title role. The pair took to attending operas and symphony concerts together as much as their limited means allowed. For both, the period afforded some powerful formative experiences, amongst them, hearing Rachmaninoff give one of the first performances of his still unpublished Second Piano Concerto under the baton of Alexander Siloti; and the premiere of Rimsky-Korsakov's opera *Kashchey the Immortal*, with the composer in attendance. Yakovlev spent many evenings in Myaskovsky's spartan lodgings near Ryazansky (now Kazansky) railway station, which were furnished with little more than a bed, a small table, an upright piano. The room was always spotlessly clean, but much of the free space was occupied by piles of sheet music, purchased with whatever money Myaskovsky could spare from his modest wages. (He told his father: 'If I pass Jurgenson's and have money in my pocket, I almost go crazy out of a desire to loot the shop'.[9]) Yakovlev was struck by the intensity of his absorption in music: little else seemed to interest him. 'During my visit the hospitality consisted of a quick cup of tea and a bread roll – and music', he recalled:

> I do not remember that we ever even drank a glass of wine. We never discussed quotidian or work-related matters, nor did we have 'philosophical' or aesthetic disputes – I merely listened to whatever Nikolay played. He could carry on playing through music without cease, and our exchange of impressions was usually very brief. ... The programmes typically consisted of Rachmaninoff's recently published songs or piano pieces and works by Skryabin. ... It used to surprise me how meaningfully Nikolay conveyed the sense of the music he played, as he was not a pianist. He was an excellent sight-reader, so he easily came to grips with a new composition and could give a sufficiently polished account of it. ... How Nikolay managed to combine his military service with the serious

7   For an account of Yakovlev's career, see Daniėl' Zhitomirskiy, 'Vasiliy Vasil'yevich Yakovlev: Ocherk zhizni i deyatel'nosti', in Yelena Grosheva *et al.* (ed.), *Vasiliy Yakovlev: Izbrannïye trudï o muzïke*, vol. 1 (Moscow, 1964), 7–36.

8   Vasiliy Yakovlev, 'V yunïye godï', in Shlifshteyn (ed.), *N. Ya. Myaskovskiy: Sobraniye materialov*, vol. 1, 194–200 (originally published in *Sovetskaya muzïka*, 5 [1956], 109–13).

9   Myaskovsky to Yakov Myaskovsky, 30 January 1903, RNMM, 204/972.

study of music and comparatively frequent attendance at concerts, I can scarcely begin to imagine.[10]

Yakovlev subsequently discovered that his friend often studied and composed late into the night, playing the piano as quietly as possible so as not to disturb the neighbours. In spite of this gruelling regime, Myaskovsky did not neglect his army duties: his colleagues found him capable and efficient, and he was widely liked.

Myaskovsky's application and desire to learn also impressed Glière, who remembered him in old age as being amongst the best students he had ever taught.[11] Their lessons ceased for the summer, when Myaskovsky's unit participated in military festivities near Nizhny Novgorod and subsequently in field exercises in the Kaluga district, some hundred miles south-west of Moscow. For a time, it seemed that he might have to remain in the provinces indefinitely, and he wrote anxiously to Glière to seek advice on how he could best continue his studies if that proved to be the case. Glière sent a kind and encouraging reply, telling him that there was still much he could do on his own. He offered to look at any work that Myaskovsky might wish to send him by post, and in the event that Myaskovsky returned to Moscow, he undertook to teach him free of charge if he were unable to afford payment. He also promised to put him in contact with a suitable teacher in St Petersburg if his transfer came through in the meantime. 'I wish you would stop worrying and have confidence in your abilities', his letter concluded.[12]

Fortunately, the matter was swiftly resolved, and by September Myaskovsky was back in St Petersburg, having transferred to the Eighteenth Sapper Battalion.[13] His family's joy at his homecoming was muted by grief at the loss of their cousin Shura, who had died in the Caucasian spa resort of Zheleznovodsk on 9 June, two days after undergoing surgery.[14] Yakov was deeply distressed by her death, and his sisters sorely missed Shura's soothing influence on Yelikonida: a gloomy and oppressive atmosphere reigned once more in the apartment.[15]

Myaskovsky lost no time in finding another teacher – Glière's friend Ivan Krïzhanovsky (1867–1924)[16], a fellow native of Kiev who trained as a doctor

10   Yakovlev, 'V yunïye godï', 196, 199.

11   Reyngol'd Glièr, 'O professii kompozitora i vospitanii molodyozhi', *Sovetskaya muzïka*, 8 (1954), 9.

12   Glière to Myaskovsky, 19 August 1903, RGALI, 2040/2/127, ll. 1–20b.

13   Myaskovsky's Eighteenth Sapper Battalion service record states that the transfer took effect on 30 September 1903: RGVIA, 5399/1/147, l. 210b.

14   Yakov Myaskovsky to Myaskovsky, 17 June 1903, RGALI, 2040/1/134, ll. 61–2.

15   Men'shikova *et al.*, 'Pamyati brata', 174.

16   On Glière's relationship with Krïzhanovsky, see Bogdanov-Berezovskiy (ed.), *Reyngol'd Moritsevich Glièr*, vol. 1, 189–92.

but subsequently studied composition under Rimsky-Korsakov at the St Petersburg Conservatoire, graduating in 1900. Although he succeeded in having a few works published, material necessity soon forced his return to the practice of medicine: from 1901 he worked as an anatomist at the St Petersburg Medical Institute, a position he held until his premature demise from a heart condition. He continued to compose (chamber music, principally), but his work met with scant recognition and his personal circumstances were not the most fortunate. A man of wide interests and considerable ability (he was also a violinist and painter), he was widely liked and respected in Petersburg musical circles and assumed an active role in efforts to enliven the city's concert life.[17] Myaskovsky took lessons from Krïzhanovsky for almost three years, until the spring of 1906, studying counterpoint, fugue, form, and orchestration. Their relationship is sparsely documented. Krïzhanovsky does not seem to have been the most methodical of teachers (Myaskovsky's Soviet biographer Alexey Ikonnikov suggests that he imparted 'general musical knowledge rather than the requisite technical skills'[18]), but Myaskovsky liked him personally and found his contact with him beneficial. To judge from stray remarks about Krïzhanovsky in his letters and diary, the older man became a supportive mentor on whom he could rely to provide constructive criticism.

The relationship helped to broaden Myaskovsky's artistic horizons in other respects. Krïzhanovsky avidly kept abreast of new trends in musical composition (though, curiously, his own work did not evince pronounced innovative tendencies – his contemporaries detected a strong Tchaikovskian influence) and was one of the organisers of the 'Modern Music Evenings' (*Vechera sovremennoy muzïki*), a concert series of seminal importance for the subsequent development of Russian and early Soviet musical life. It had been founded in 1901 by two members of Sergey Diaghilev's entourage, Walter Nouvel and Alfred Nurok, both keen amateur musicians who served on the editorial board of *Mir iskusstva* (The world of art), a notable periodical of the era.[19] The periodical's ethos also animated this offshoot venture, which aimed to introduce St Petersburg audiences to noteworthy recent works by Russian and foreign composers that they would otherwise have no opportunity to hear, given the generally unenterprising nature of concert

---

17   Little is known about Krïzhanovsky's life: a posthumous tribute by Viktor Belyayev and Yuliya Veysberg, 'I. I. Krïzhanovskiy', *Sovremennaya muzïka*, 13–14 (1926), 97–100, seems to be virtually the only source of biographical information.

18   Ikonnikov, 'N. Ya. Myaskovskiy (biograficheskiy ocherk)', 24.

19   On Nouvel and Nurok, and their involvement with *Mir iskusstva*, see Sjeng Scheijen, *Diaghilev: A Life*, trans. Jane Hedley-Prôle and S. J. Leinbach (Oxford, 2009), 97ff.

programming in the capital.[20] Nouvel and Nurok were subsequently assisted by others, including Krïzhanovsky and Vyacheslav Karatïgin, a young scientist who later became one of the country's leading music critics.[21]

It has been asserted that the repertoire performed at these concerts was not as adventurous or wide-ranging as the organisers liked to believe[22], but the series was actually quite a remarkable enterprise, especially when one considers that it was run on a shoestring and the performers were rarely remunerated for their services. The 'Evenings' have yet to be researched adequately and it is unclear how much pertinent documentation survives[23], but a set of programmes preserved amongst Myaskovsky's personal papers amply bears out this contention.[24] Myaskovsky seems to have attended at least thirty-four 'Evenings' between February 1904 and March 1912, just over two-thirds of an apparent total of fifty-five. At these thirty-four concerts alone, music by eighty-seven composers was performed, almost all of it by living figures, foreign as well as Russian, and much of it of recent date. A large proportion of the performances were Russian premieres. Amongst the French composers, for example, were Debussy and Ravel (featured in five and four programmes respectively), as well as Chausson, d'Indy, de Séverac, Duparc, Fauré, Février, Ingelbrecht, Ladmirault, Roger-Ducasse, Ropartz, Roussel, Saint-Saëns, Schmitt, and Vuillermoz. Of figures from the German-speaking world, we find familiar names such as Reger, Mahler, and Strauss as well as those of Korngold, Scheinpflug, Schillings, and Schreker. Scandinavian composers (Stenhammar, Sinding, and Nielsen), Spanish composers (Albéniz, Falla), and British composers (Bantock, Dale,

---

20   In an article published in *Mir iskusstva* in 1902, Nurok teasingly contrasted the repertory promoted in the new series with that performed at the concerts of the rival Chamber Music Society, claiming that the latter mostly comprised dull 'classics' and music by composers who had given a solemn undertaking 'not to say anything in their work that has not been said before': 'A. N.' [Al'fred Nurok], 'O nekotorïkh muzïkal'nïkh novinkakh', *Mir iskusstva*, 11 (1902), 51–2.

21   For an account of Karatïgin's career, see Yuriy Verkhovskiy, 'Ocherk zhizni i deyatel'nosti V. G. Karatïgina', in Andrey Rimskiy-Korsakov *et al.* (ed.), *V. G. Karatïgin: zhizn', deyatel'nost', stat'i, materialï* (Leningrad, 1927), 11–35. See also: Aleksandr Ossovskiy, 'V.G. Karatïgin', *Muzïkal'naya letopis'* 3 (1926), 161–4.

22   Richard Taruskin dismissively describes the series as 'no hotbed of radicalism' (*Stravinsky and the Russian Traditions: A Biography of the Works through Mavra*, vol. 1 [Oxford, 1996], 376), but his account is both misleading and inaccurate in some details.

23   The most comprehensive account of the 'Evenings' is Izrail Nest'yev, 'Muzïkal'nïye kruzhki', in Aleksandr Alekseyev (ed.), *Russkaya khudozhestvannaya kul'tura kontsa XIX-nachala XX veka*, vol. 3: 1908–19 (Moscow, 1977), 474–82. Nest'yev does not indicate the sources of much of the information provided, however, so it is difficult to judge its reliability.

24   RGALI, 2040/3/96.

Hurlstone, and Scott) also featured. Few recital series offer such varied and unusual fare even today; and assembling these programmes must have required extensive research and planning. To help them select repertoire, the organisers arranged private play-throughs of potentially suitable scores for interested friends and prospective performers (in later years, these gatherings took place at Karatïgin's apartment); the final choice of pieces was often decided by a vote.[25]

No doubt the quality of the performances was variable, and not all the music programmed was equally interesting, but the fact remains that the series significantly enriched the city's musical life and provided valuable artistic stimulus, especially to younger musicians. Igor Stravinsky stressed the importance of these concerts for his early development, and he was not alone.[26] Myaskovsky, too, acknowledged that they assisted his artistic maturation, though his terse remarks about the 'Evenings' in his autobiographical reminiscences indicate that he found his encounters with Krïzhanovsky's associates a rather unsettling experience.[27] He did not elaborate on the subject, but it emerges from other accounts that the concert organisers could be quite intimidating: Prokofiev described the circle's members as 'having tart tastes and equally tart tongues'.[28] They had a generally low opinion of the music being written by young Russian composers, finding it stylistically *passé* and reflective of a provincial mentality. In a letter of 1907, Nouvel informed his friend Alexandre Benois that he and his associates despaired of finding suitable Russian works to perform at the concerts: 'In music there is nothing new, not even a single talent that would give cause for hope'.[29] Nor did they trouble to conceal these opinions. The young Mikhail Gnesin (1883–1957) was disconcerted when Karatïgin and Nouvel not only criticised his compositions as old-fashioned but declared bluntly that the sooner his teacher Rimsky-Korsakov died, 'the better it would be for Russian music', because Rimsky was preventing young composers from striking out on new paths.[30]

Myaskovsky recalled that the *habitués* of the 'Evenings' were overwhelmingly preoccupied with technical and stylistic innovation, deeming these

---

25 Nest'yev, 'Muzïkal'nïye kruzhki', 474–5.

26 Igor Stravinsky, *Chroniques de ma vie* (Paris, 1935), 39.

27 Myaskovskiy, 'Avtobiograficheskiye zametki', 6. According to Ikonnikov, Krïzhanovsky introduced Myaskovsky to the other members of the circle in 1905: 'N. Ya. Myaskovskiy (biograficheskiy ocherk)', 24.

28 Sergey Prokof'yev, ['Kratkaya avtobiografiya'], in Semyon Shlifshteyn (ed.), *S. S. Prokof'yev: Materialï, dokumentï, vospominaniya*, 2nd ed. (Moscow, 1961), 139.

29 Nouvel to Benois, 31 January 1907, quoted in Nest'yev, 'Muzïkal'nïye kruzhki', 477.

30 Raisa Glezer (ed.), *M. F. Gnesin: Stat'i, vospominaniya, materialï* (Moscow, 1961), 140–1.

the paramount criteria of artistic value. In this respect, the circle's aesthetic outlook was very much of its time: by the late nineteenth century, notions of artistic 'progress' influenced by Hegelian philosophy and Darwinism were pervasive in narratives of music history and routinely invoked by critics to validate or to discredit contemporary musical developments.[31] After the Revolution, Krïzhanovsky would write a book that exemplifies this tendency, *The Biological Bases of the Evolution of Music*, which attempts to demonstrate that the art of music is 'subject to the same biological laws as the whole of organic, living nature'[32] – with the result it 'evolves' over time, manifesting an ever-increasing complexity of harmonic language and formal organisation. And just as lifeforms of previous epochs became extinct because they proved incapable of adapting to changed environmental conditions, so too, he warned, would contemporary composers be doomed to oblivion if they failed to align themselves with the most 'progressive' stylistic trends of their age. Krïzhanovsky's book contains a great deal of windy nonsense and does little more than reformulate Romantic envisionings of the artist-hero in quasi-Darwinian terms – but it nonetheless encapsulates understandings characteristic of the early modernist period and illustrates the kinds of views that Myaskovsky might have heard aired.

Inevitably, such an atmosphere tended to induce anxiety about whether one's work sounded sufficiently sophisticated and respectably up to date. A heightened self-consciousness about style and technique was by no means unique to Russian composers of this era; this was, indeed, a ubiquitous phenomenon in artistic circles across Europe. Myaskovsky admitted half-apologetically to being 'infected' by it at the time and experiencing the painful realisation that he was 'still a dilettante'.[33] Whatever his subsequent reservations about the circle's aesthetic outlook, the 'Evenings' emboldened him to experiment and prompted what he described as his first 'serious' compositions – a status affirmed by the assignment of opus numbers.

The compositions in question were songs – settings of verse by the symbolist poet Zinaida Hippius (1869–1945), a prominent figure on the St Petersburg literary scene. Myaskovsky informed Aleksey Ikonnikov that his interest in contemporary literature was stimulated by attending soirées

31 For an illuminating discussion of the origins of this tendency, see Golan Gur, 'Music and "Weltanschauung": Franz Brendel and the Claims of Universal History', *Music and Letters*, 3 (2012), 350–73.

32 Ivan Kryzhanovsky, *The Biological Bases of the Evolution of Music*, trans. Samuel Pring (London, 1928), 36. I have been unable to establish whether the manuscript of the original Russian text is still extant, or how Krïzhanovsky's book came to be translated into English and issued by Oxford University Press. A copy of the editorial file has not been preserved in the press's archive (Communication from OUP archivist Dr Martin Maw to author, 13 September 2010).

33 Myaskovskiy, 'Avtobiograficheskiye zametki', 7.

hosted by the Modzalevsky and Hofmann families at which new Russian writing was read and discussed. Much of it appeared in literary journals associated with the symbolist movement, such as *Vesï* (*Libra*) and *Zolotoye runo* (The golden fleece), or the collections issued by Znaniye (Knowledge), the left-leaning publishing house run by Maxim Gorky.[34] It is not surprising that he was reticent on the subject in his reminiscences, or that Ikonnikov dealt with it so briefly: the writings of the symbolists were mostly banned in the USSR and remained unavailable until the late 1980s. Soviet literary histories and reference works largely passed over them in silence: if mentioned at all, it was in disparaging terms. Hippius was the object of especially intense disapproval because she emigrated after the Revolution and openly proclaimed her hostility to the Bolshevik regime.[35] Myaskovsky's settings of her work incurred an opprobrium by association, which strengthened as a result of the campaigns against Western cultural influences during the late Stalinist period. The songs were instanced as evidence of Myaskovsky's long-standing decadent tendencies and could not be performed in public.[36]

Myaskovsky never seems to have come into personal contact with Hippius, but he was repeatedly drawn to her poetry. Between 1904 and 1914 he composed no fewer than twenty-seven songs to her verse – the largest number of settings that he made of any poet's work.[37] Eighteen were written during the period when he was studying with Krïzhanovsky. The earliest songs set texts from Hippius's first major collection, published in

---

34 Ikonnikov, *Khudozhnik nashikh dney*, 17. See also the fragment of an unpublished memoir by Vera Yakovleva [*née* Myaskovskaya] cited in Iosif Kunin (ed.), *N. Ya. Myaskovskiy: Zhizn' i tvorchestvo v pis'makh, vospominaniyakh, kriticheskikh otzïvakh*, 2nd ed. (Moscow, 1981), 27.

35 See Temira Pachmuss, *Zinaida Hippius: An Intellectual Profile* (Carbondale, 1971), 408.

36 Tikhon Khrennikov alluded critically to Myaskovsky's Hippius settings in his keynote address at the First All-Union Composers' Union Congress, convened after the notorious Central Committee decree 'On the opera *The Great Friendship* by V. Muradeli' of February 1948: Viktor Gorodinskiy *et al.* (ed.), *Pervïy vsesoyuznïy s'ezd sovetskikh kompozitorov: Stenograficheskiy otchyot* (Moscow, 1948), 31. See also Tamara Livanova's censorious remarks about Myaskovsky's settings of Hippius's 'anti-artistic, decadent, and malodorous [*smerdyashchiye*]' poems in her *N. Ya. Myaskovskiy: Tvorcheskiy put'*, 28–30. A report submitted to the Communist Party Central Committee in August 1940 records that the censor forbade a proposed radio broadcast of a group of these songs because the texts were by Hippius: GARF, 9425/2/25, l. 30.

37 For a discussion of these songs, see Zuk, 'Romansï N. Myaskovskogo na slova Z. Gippius', in Natal'ya Degtyaryova and Nataliya Braginskaya (ed.), *Sankt-Peterburgskaya Konservatoriya v mirovom muzïkal'nom prostranstve: Kompozitorskiye, ispolnitel'skiye, nauchnïye shkolï, 1862–2012* (St Petersburg, 2013), 218–23. Myaskovsky reworked many of the songs subsequently (in some cases, more than once) and they were eventually published in three sets as Opp. 4, 5, and 16.

1903, which, like the remainder of her slender poetic output, is largely concerned with two themes – the experience of profound alienation from one's fellow human beings and the struggle to find meaning in existence in spite of its seeming banality and futility.[38] The poems repeatedly explore a state of anguished spiritual desolation fraught with nameless terrors from which there is no prospect of escape: love and joy seem but chimerical illusions; moments of consolation and hope are fleeting. Some of Hippius's most striking expressive effects arise from the tension between her sparse diction – with its simple, everyday language and conversational cadences – and her startling imagery. In the first poem set by Myaskovsky, for example, she likens her despair to sinister black leeches battening on her soul:

Там, где заводь тихая, где молчит река,	Where the backwater is still, where the river is silent,
Липнут пьявки чёрные к корню тростника.	There, black leeches cleave to the reed's root.
В страшный час прозрения, на закате дней,	In the dread hour of illumination, at the decline of day,
Вижу пьявок, липнущих и к душе моей.	I see leeches cleaving also to my soul.
Но душа усталая мертвенно тиха.	But the weary soul is deathly still.
Пьявки, пьявки чёрные жадного греха!	Leeches, black leeches of ravening sin!
	('Leeches' ['P'yavki'], 1902)

Lines such as these were scornfully derided by not a few contemporary commentators, and Hippius's weaker poems can lapse into a hollow portentousness that was fatally easy to parody.[39] Nonetheless, her best verse not only demonstrates an impressive technical subtlety, but is deeply felt and moving.

Hippius's explorations of alienation and of struggles with a hostile fate clearly had a strong personal resonance for Myaskovsky and inspired him to write some remarkable music. His setting of 'Leeches' memorably amplifies the poem's expressive import and its mood of lassitude and ennui with the simplest of musical means – an oscillating accompaniment figure underpinned by the ominous reiterated peal of a low pedal-note G sharp, enveloping a slow-moving vocal line that seems to be pulled inexorably into the texture's turbid depths, as though drowning in the stagnant backwater evoked in the poem's opening line (ex. 2.1). The agitated central section struggles to break free of the ostinato's hypnotic spell, only to revert

---

38 *Sobraniye stikhov 1889–1903*, issued by Skorpion [Scorpio], a Moscow publisher closely associated with the Russian symbolists.

39 See Avril Pyman, *A History of Russian Symbolism* (Cambridge, 1994), 40, 47.

resignedly to the music of the opening after a despairing climactic out-burst. The song is surprisingly remote in style and sensibility from other Russian art songs of its period. Even more unconventional are 'In the draw-ing room' ('V gostinoy') and 'Spiders' ('Pauki'), composed respectively in October and November 1904. 'Spiders' conjures up a nightmarish halluci-nation of being incarcerated in a noisome cellar and watching helplessly as monstrous spiders encroach to swathe one's head in suffocating cobwebs. Myaskovsky responded with aptly analogous musical imagery: the piano progressively shrouds the vocal line in a dissonant web of close imitative polyphony. 'In the drawing room' is remarkable in two respects. First, the setting is startlingly austere, being in two-part counterpart and proceeding at subdued dynamic levels throughout: the writhing piano countermelody coils around the vocal line, spanning an expanse of over four octaves as it arches agonisingly towards the central climax (ex. 2.2). Secondly, the song must be amongst the first examples of atonality in Russian composition. (In 1904, the most radical harmonic experiments of Alexander Skryabin and Vladimir Rebikov still lay in the future.) Tonal references are not altogether absent (the opening and closing bars could respectively be interpreted as suggesting the regions of C-sharp minor and B-flat minor, for example) but are highly attenuated, as is any sense of functional harmonic progression.

EXAMPLE 2.1. 'Leeches': opening.

EXAMPLE 2.2. 'In the drawing room': opening.

(continued)

EXAMPLE 2.2.—*(concluded)*

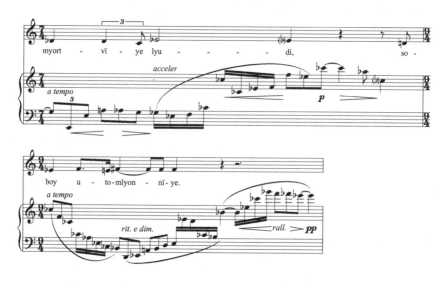

A grey room. Unhurried conversations, / not dreadful even or sinful even, /
not moving, not aggrieved, / dead people, weary of themselves.

It is difficult to find obvious precedents for these and some of the other
Hippius settings, even in Musorgsky at his strangest. Their closest stylistic
kinship is with Austro-German Expressionism in their evocations of psychological disturbance and recourse to extremes of dissonance, although
Schoenberg and Berg had yet to write the works that exemplify such tendencies. Not all the songs are so stark and intense, and they exhibit considerable variety of mood. The best are undoubtedly amongst the neglected
masterpieces of the Russian vocal repertoire and will amply reward the
attention of performers capable of mastering their formidable technical and
interpretative challenges.

Between 1903 and the autumn of 1906, when he enrolled at the St
Petersburg Conservatoire, Myaskovsky composed twenty-one additional
songs to texts by other authors, including twelve settings of another symbolist poet, Konstantin Balmont[40], as well as piano miniatures and two
piano sonatas (the manuscripts of some of these works have been lost). On
the whole, these scores are more conventional than the Hippius songs, and
less distinguished – although a few of the Balmont settings rise above the
commonplace, especially the atmospheric 'I constantly dream of the sea'

---

40   Myaskovsky revised the twelve Balmont settings in 1945, designating them his
     op. 2. Eight were published posthumously in volume 9 of the Selected Works
     in 1956. The remainder were not published until 1981.

('Vsyo mne grezitsya more'), op. 2/8. Notwithstanding the variable quality of his output during this period, Myaskovsky's consistent productivity suggests a growing self-confidence and fluency – even if he was still in the process of finding his own creative voice.

His exploration of a modernist idiom may have partly been prompted by internal pressures of creative necessity and partly by external pressures of fashion, but it did not prevent him from also writing music that evinced strong continuities with nineteenth-century traditions. Myaskovsky's reactions to contemporary manifestations of musical modernism were by no means uniformly enthusiastic. When he wrote in his autobiographical reminiscences that he never felt wholly part of the 'Modern Music Evenings' circle because 'even at that time the striving to "have the last word" in musical technique and invention did not have a self-sufficient value for me'[41], this remark should not be interpreted merely as a timid disavowal of his youthful modernist sympathies. Myaskovsky did not share the circle's misprision of Tchaikovsky and Rimsky-Korsakov, and of younger figures of a traditionalist bent such as Rachmaninoff; he felt no need to effect a radical breach with the past and was genuinely drawn to developing approaches initiated by previous generations of Russian composers. One of his earliest surviving diary entries records his pleasure in studying Anatoly Lyadov's recently published orchestral suite *Eight Russian Folksongs*, op. 58, which he held to demonstrate 'the strength of the foundation' that 'the folk music of one's own nation' furnished for Russian composition.[42]

This ambivalence about artistic modernism was not confined to music but extended to literature. His admiration for Hippius, Balmont, and other contemporary authors was far from unalloyed. When Yakovlev wrote to express concern in May 1904 that he might be succumbing to their unhealthy influence, Myaskovsky retorted ironically that the stolidity of character fostered by his upbringing was ample proof against decadence.[43] Bohemianism never held any attraction for him. Through Vsevolod Hofmann's younger brother Modeste, who had ambitions to become a writer, Myaskovsky was introduced to at least three prominent symbolist poets – Vyacheslav Ivanov, Sergey Gorodetsky, and Mikhail Kuzmin, all of whom Modeste Hofmann knew well.[44] (Hofmann published a pioneering study of the Russian symbolists in 1908, when he was only

---

41 Myaskovskiy, 'Avtobiograficheskiye zametki', 6.

42 'Vïpiski', 28 April 1906, RGALI, 2040/1/65, l. 2.

43 Yakovlev to Myaskovsky, undated letter [early May 1904], RGALI, 2040/2/289, ll. 7–100b; Myaskovsky to Yakovlev, 9 May 1904, RNMM, 204/769.

44 See Modest Gofman, 'Peterburgskiye vospominaniya', in Vadim Kreyd (ed.), *Vospominaniya o Serebryanom veke* (Moscow, 1993), 367–78.

FIGURE 2.2. Modest Hofmann.

twenty-one.[45]) In spite of having a ready *entrée* to literary circles and even to the select Wednesday gatherings at Ivanov's 'Tower' (the poet's seventh-floor apartment overlooking the Tauride Palace gardens)[46], Myaskovsky seems to have made little effort to cultivate these new acquaintances: no records of his encounters with them have come to light other than a few passing allusions in Kuzmin's voluminous diaries. (Hofmann introduced his friend to Kuzmin in October 1906: Kuzmin found him pleasant, but very shy and reserved.[47]) He preferred to remain at the margins of the St Petersburg literary scene rather than seek to involve himself more actively.

The symbolists' religious and philosophical preoccupations held scant interest for him, to judge from comments in Modeste Hofmann's letters. The Bloody Sunday massacre of 9 January 1905 and the widespread social unrest and violence that convulsed Russia in its wake plunged the literary movement into crisis, causing its leading representatives to question their long-held

45   Modest Gofman, *Poèti simvolizma* (St Petersburg, 1908).

46   On Ivanov's salon, see Carin Tschöpl, *Vjačeslav Ivanov: Dichtung und Dichtungstheorie* (Munich, 1968), 25–48.

47   See Nikolay Bogomolov and Sergey Shumikhin (ed.), *M. Kuzmin. Dnevnik 1905–1907* (St Petersburg, 2000), 237–8 and 275–6.

belief that artists should hold themselves aloof from politics.[48] Much vaporous theorising ensued on how the divisions in Russian society could best be healed. Hofmann's idol Ivanov promulgated the doctrine of 'mystic anarchism'[49], which diagnosed a hypertrophied individualism as the root cause of the present evils. Their cure, Ivanov believed, would require nothing less than a comprehensive renunciation of bourgeois values and a national spiritual renewal catalysed by art and love, which afforded mystical intimations of the underlying unity of all that exists. ('In the formation of the new soul', he proclaimed in an essay of 1907, 'ethics will become erotics'.[50]) Hofmann not only became an enthusiastic advocate of Ivanov's teachings[51], but underwent an intense personal crisis of his own which brought him close to a nervous breakdown. In summer 1906 he sent Myaskovsky several rather incoherent missives hinting darkly at struggles with his sexuality and agonising at length over his religious doubts: the letters bristle with allusions to the writings of Hippius's husband Dmitry Merezhkovsky and other Russian authors of the era on the subjects of sex and religion and are strongly redolent of the hothouse atmosphere that enveloped Ivanov and his circle. Myaskovsky's side of the correspondence has not been preserved, but from Hofmann's discussion of his responses, it emerges that he found his friend's mystical and theological ruminations rather trying and eventually urged Hofmann to desist, refusing to discuss them with him any further. Interestingly, Hofmann notes that Myaskovsky had become an atheist – in reaction, perhaps, to his oppressively strict religious upbringing.[52] Their relationship survived this episode, and perhaps by way of atonement, Hofmann began to make efforts to promote Myaskovsky's work: he sought to interest Ivanov in it and approached the city's music publishers on his friend's behalf.[53] His efforts bore fruit later that year, when Zimmermann [Tsimmerman] agreed to bring out an album

48   See Pyman, *A History of Russian Symbolism*, 245–84.

49   For a lucid account, see Bernice Glatzer Rosenthal, 'The Transmutation of the Symbolist Ethos: Mystical Anarchism and the Revolution of 1905', *Slavic Review*, 4 (1977), 608–27.

50   Vyacheslav Ivanov, 'O lyubvi derzayushchey', in Dmitriy Ivanov and Ol'ga Deschartes (ed.), *Vyacheslav Ivanov: Sobraniye sochineniy*, vol. 3 (Brussels, 1979), 133.

51   Hofmann's first book, *Sborniy individualizm* (Communitarian individualism), published in 1907, was written in support of Ivanov at the height of the polemics over mystical anarchism.

52   Hofmann to Myaskovsky, 21 and 26 June 1906, RGALI 2040/2/136, ll. 88–91ob and 93–99ob. Some fifty-two letters and postcards from Hofmann to Myaskovsky survive. Hofmann did not preserve his correspondence or personal papers: see Krasnoborod'ko, 'Pis'ma M. L. Gofmana k B. L. Modzalevskomu: chast' 1 (1904–1921)', 181, fn4.

53   Hofmann to Myaskovsky, 20 and 30 July 1906, RGALI 2040/2/136, ll. 103 and 105–80ob.

of six Hippius settings at Myaskovsky's expense, with a cover design by Sergey Gorodetsky.[54]

Throughout this period, Myaskovsky remained firmly focussed on achieving his aim of being admitted to the composition course at the St Petersburg Conservatoire – as a part-time student, if necessary, until he was able to leave the army. His friends admired his single-mindedness but were somewhat puzzled by his unsociability and complete indifference to the pursuits typically enjoyed by young men of his age. When Yakovlev suggested it would do him good to mix with people who were not musicians and 'maybe even go dancing, . . . go courting, fall in love', Myaskovsky replied that such activities held no appeal for him and that he regarded them as time-wasting distractions.[55] As he later recalled, he displayed considerable ingenuity at finding legitimate ways of evading his military duties to free up time for composition. He even feigned interest in taking a course at the Academy of Jurisprudence and persuaded his superiors to grant him extended leave over the summer of 1905 to allow him to prepare for the entrance examinations. In the event, he never sat them, pleading illness.[56] Fortunately, his battalion was not placed on active service after the outbreak of hostilities with Japan in February 1904, though his father was dispatched to the front the following December. (Yakov, who had since risen to the senior rank of major-general and been appointed to the position of deputy engineer inspector-general in the army high command, witnessed at first-hand the ineptitude that bedevilled the Russian forces' conduct of this ill-fated campaign.[57]) So too was Vsevolod Hofmann, who was posted to an army base near Mukden (now Shenyang in China, a city situated near the border with North Korea, but then in Manchurian territory that had effectively been annexed by Russia). Reading Hofmann's letters, which described his tedious and isolated existence working in difficult conditions, Myaskovsky must have felt grateful to have been spared a prolonged interruption of his musical studies.[58] When sent on summer field exercises in the countryside, he still managed to find time to practise solfège even if he could not compose.[59]

Neither does he appear to have had any direct involvement in political activity during 1905–6, unlike some of his associates. (Vadim Modzalevsky

54 *Shest' stikhotvoreniy Z. Gippius dlya peniya i royalya* (Six poems of Z. Hippius for voice and piano) (St Petersburg, 1906).

55 Yakovlev to Myaskovsky, undated letter (early May 1904), RGALI, 2040/2/289, ll. 90b; Myaskovsky to Yakovlev, 9 May 1904, RNMM, 204/769.

56 Myaskovskiy, 'Avtobiograficheskiye zametki', 7.

57 See Pyotr Duz', *Istoriya vozdukhoplavaniya i aviatsii v Rossii*, 2nd ed. (Moscow, 1981), 143.

58 See, for example, Vsevolod Hofmann to Myaskovsky, 9 June 1904, RGALI, 2040/2/135 ll. 95–100.

59 Myaskovsky to Yakovlev, 2 June 1904, RNMM, 204/771.

was arrested in Kiev for distributing seditious literature, but charges were not pressed and he was transferred shortly afterwards back to St Petersburg, where he took a teaching post at the First Cadet Corps.[60]) Events impinged on him indirectly, however, forcing the postponement of his admission to the St Petersburg Conservatoire by a year.[61] As at other higher educational institutions, the conservatoire's student body organised strikes and demanded reforms: in March 1905 its board of directors expelled a hundred of the protestors and unceremoniously sacked Rimsky-Korsakov when he criticised its handling of events. Much to the board members' chagrin, his dismissal became a *cause celèbre*: three hundred students and other eminent staff members, including Lyadov and Alexander Glazunov, left the conservatoire in a show of solidarity. Rimsky found himself hailed a national hero, rather to his bewilderment: the St Petersburg premiere of his opera *Kashchey the Immortal* later that month acquired the character of a public demonstration against Nicholas II's repressive rule. Eventually the board was forced to make a humiliating climb-down. In August the government acceded to demands from the universities for greater institutional autonomy and in November extended it to conservatoires. Glazunov was invited to take over as director of the St Petersburg Conservatoire and Rimsky-Korsakov was reinstated in his post.[62] The institution's functioning only returned to normal in the 1906–7 academic year, when tuition, examinations, and entrance auditions resumed.

As it transpired, the year's delay probably worked out for the best. In his father's absence, Myaskovsky had to deal with time-consuming domestic responsibilities, including overseeing the family's move to another apartment during the summer of 1905 and planning for his sister Valentina's wedding in the autumn.[63] Throughout the winter and spring, he continued to devote what little free time he had to preparing for the conservatoire entrance examinations and to assembling a portfolio of compositions to show at his interview. (This included a three-movement sonata in C minor, the score of which has been lost.[64]) In the summer of 1906 he was ill for

60   Tomozov, 'K yubileyu V. L. Modzalevskogo', 47.

61   See Prokof'yev, *Avtobiografiya*, 279.

62   For an informative analysis of how the conservatoire was affected by events, see Lynn Sargeant, 'Kashchei the Immortal: Liberal Politics, Cultural Memory, and the Rimsky-Korsakov Scandal of 1905', *Russian Review*, 1 (2005), 22–43. See also Rimsky's account of this episode in his memoirs: Nikolay Rimskiy-Korsakov, *Letopis' moey muzïkal'noy zhizni*, ed. Nadezhda Rimskaya-Korsakova (St Petersburg, 1909), 353–9.

63   Men'shikova *et al.*, 'Pamyati brata', 174–5; Yelikonida Myaskovskaya to Myaskovsky, 29 June, 19 and 29 July, and 4 August 1905, RGALI, 2040/2/197, ll. 55–62.

64   'Vïpiski', 3 August 1906, RGALI, 2040/1/65, l. 2.

four months with 'intestinal catarrh' – presumably enteritis, inflammation of the small intestine, an ailment commonly caused by food poisoning.[65] Nonetheless, he made a sufficiently good recovery to proceed in August with his application to be admitted to the conservatoire.[66]

The entrance examination proved something of an ordeal. His understandable nervousness was aggravated by an additional anxiety: his application to the conservatoire was in breach of army regulations, which forbade military personnel from studying at civilian institutions. He almost failed the chorale harmonisation task but managed to redeem himself by writing a good modulating prelude on a theme set by Glazunov.[67] (He presumably also had to pass *solfège* and sight-reading tests, though he made no mention of these, or of the panel's assessment of his compositions.[68]) To his relief, he was offered a place, and no-one thought to enquire about his eligibility to accept it. He duly commenced his studies on 1 September 1906 and hoped that his anomalous status would remain undetected until he could leave the army on completion of his period of compulsory military service at the beginning of 1907.[69]

The course in which he enrolled, 'Theory of Composition', had been devised by Rimsky-Korsakov in 1901 but was not fully implemented until 1908. It was divided into two parts, and as its title indicates, the primary emphasis was on the acquisition of technical competence – something that Rimsky regarded as being of paramount importance. (This will come as no surprise to anyone who has read Rimsky's autobiography, in which he describes with disarming candour his youthful feelings of professional inadequacy and the strenuous efforts he made subsequently to remedy his haphazard musical education.[70]) The first part of the course comprised four years of technical studies in harmony, counterpoint, fugue, musical form, and orchestration, supplemented by obligatory piano lessons and classes in score-reading as well as lectures on music history and aesthetics. It was intended to provide a foundation for undertaking original creative work in the second part, which lasted two further years. Students could conclude their studies on completion of the first part and graduate with a diploma conferring on them the title of Free Artist (*Svobodnïy khudozhnik*). Rimsky

---

65   Myaskovskiy, 'Avtobiograficheskiye zametki', 6.

66   Myaskovsky's application letter, dated 21 August 1906, is preserved in TsGIA, 361/1/2794, l. 1.

67   Myaskovskiy, 'Avtobiograficheskiye zametki', 6–7.

68   See Prokofiev's account of his own entrance examination two years previously: *Avtobiografiya*, 156–62.

69   'Vïpiski', 1 September 1906, RGALI, 2040/1/65, l. 2; Myaskovskiy, 'Avtobiograficheskiye zametki', 7.

70   Rimskiy-Korsakov, *Letopis'*, 102–8.

FIGURE 2.3. Myaskovsky in 1906, the year in which
he enrolled at the St Petersburg Conservatoire.

intended that only students who displayed genuine creative talent should
progress past that point. Those permitted to do so were expected to produce a portfolio of original compositions and substantial graduation exercise (a large-scale orchestral work, perhaps, or a cantata), but received the
same qualification.[71]

Together with three other applicants, Myaskovsky was admitted directly
into the second year of the course – in compensation for the fact that they
had hoped to start the previous year but had been unable to do so because
of the disrupted circumstances. They were required nonetheless to take the
first-year harmony course, because Lyadov and Glazunov considered their
previous instruction in the subject to have been insufficiently thorough (it

---

71   The course content is detailed in a conservatoire prospectus published in
1909, *Programmï spetsialnïkh i obyazatel'nïkh muzïkal'nïkh predmetov i
nauchnïkh klassov S.-Peterburgskoy konservatorii* (St Peterburg, 1909), 40–1.
On the conservatoire's composition courses, see Leonid Bobïlyov, *Istoriya i
printsipï kompozitorskogo obrazovaniya v pervïkh russkikh konservatoriyakh*
(Moscow, 1992), 96–137; and idem, *Russkaya kompozitorskaya pedagogika:
Traditsii, lichnosti, shkolï* (Moscow, 2013). The second section of Prokofiev's
posthumously published autobiography describes his studies on this
course in considerable detail (*Avtobiografiya*, 150ff.). His account is
usefully supplemented by Aleksandra Akhonen's monograph *Prokof'yev v
Peterburgskoy konservatorii* (St Petersburg, 2016).

ceased to be taught after first year: second-year students moved on to study counterpoint and orchestration).[72] As Myaskovsky later recalled, his first year at the Conservatoire required 'phenomenal resourcefulness' in juggling his military duties and academic commitments. At the start of 1907, he applied for discharge to the reserves – much to the disappointment of his father, who had not given up hope that he might remain in the army. His application was approved and he was allowed to take unpaid leave of absence until his discharge formally took effect the following year.[73] His decision demonstrates the seriousness of his commitment to his musical studies, as it left him without any source of income in the short term. For the time being, he could continue to stay in the family apartment at 43 Suvorovsky Prospect, not far from the Tauride Gardens. (Musorgsky died in 1881 in a hospital further along the same street.) He took on private students at the first opportunity, but his finances would remain very straitened. He economised in every way possible, making the four-mile trek to and from the conservatoire on foot even in the depths of winter.[74] He evidently regarded these inconveniences as a price worth paying for his freedom.

Several of the students in Myaskovsky's class went on to have distinguished careers – most notably, Sergey Prokofiev, then aged fifteen, whose remarkable talent had led Glazunov and Rimsky-Korsakov to admit him to the course while still a schoolboy. His classmates also included Boris Asafiev (1884– 1949), who achieved renown as a writer about music and a composer for the ballet; Lazare Saminsky (1882–1959), who emigrated after the 1917 Revolution to the United States, where he made a name as a composer, conductor, and expert on Jewish folk and liturgical music; and Yakiv Akimenko (1883–1921), or 'Yakiv Stepovy' as he later styled himself, an important figure in Ukrainian composition whose career was cut short by his death from typhus during the Russian Civil War. Myaskovsky found their company congenial and took to attending concerts and socialising with them.[75]

He grew especially close to Asafiev. Asafiev came from a poor background and experienced considerable hardship when young. His father, a low-ranking functionary, was an alcoholic and feckless, given to resigning from jobs on impulse: his mother was reduced to taking in sewing to make ends meet. As the family's circumstances deteriorated, they had to fall back on charity. Their son was bright, and at the age of twelve had the good

---

72   Prokof'yev, *Avtobiografiya*, 279.

73   Myaskovsky's military service record states that it took effect on 25 March 1908: RGALI, 2040/1/168, l. 3.

74   Myaskovskiy, 'Avtobiograficheskiye zametki', 7; Men'shikova *et al.*, 'Pamyati brata', 175; 'Vïpiski', 19 September 1907, RGALI, 2040/1/65, l. 20b.

75   Men'shikova *et al.*, 'Pamyati brata', 175; Myaskovskiy, 'Avtobiograficheskiye zametki', 7.

fortune to be offered a scholarship to a gymnasium in Kronstadt, a large town situated twenty miles west of St Petersburg on Kotlin Island, which served as the capital's principal sea port and the main base of the Russian navy.[76] He did sufficiently well at school to be admitted to the Historical and Philological Faculty of St Petersburg University in 1903, where he attended lectures on classical languages, Russian language and literature, and general history.[77] Music was at the centre of his interests, however. His musical education had been rather patchy, but he possessed considerable natural pianistic facility, had a highly retentive memory, and was an excellent sight-reader. He had also tried his hand at composing. He applied to the conservatoire in 1904, was accepted, and proceeded to study composition while reading for his university degree. In the same year, he was introduced to Vladimir Stasov (1824–1906), chiefly remembered now for his advocacy of Russian nationalist compositional styles and his championship of music by Balakirev and his circle. The eminent critic was sufficiently impressed with Asafiev's abilities as to adopt him as a protégé: the young man visited him regularly on Sundays to participate in domestic music-making until Stasov's death two years later.[78] Stasov encouraged Asafiev's creative aspirations and even helped to devise the libretto for *Zolushka* [*Cinderella*], an opera for children, on which Asafiev was working when he and Myaskovsky became acquainted.[79] Asafiev had difficult sides to his personality: his timid, diffident manner concealed enormous ambition; he was highly-strung and quick to take offence at imagined slights. He got on well with Myaskovsky, however, and they started meeting to play through music together.[80]

An amicable relationship also formed between Myaskovsky and Prokofiev, but on a much more superficial level; as Prokofiev noted in his diary, the ten-year difference in their ages remained a barrier to intimacy even as

76 The information given here draws on Asafiev's autobiographical reminiscences, eight chapters of which were published under the title 'O sebe' ('About myself') in Andrey Kryukov (ed.), *Vospominaniya o B. V. Asaf'yeve* (Leningrad, 1974), 317–508; and Yelena Orlova and Andrey Kryukov, *Akademik Boris Vladimirovich Asaf'yev: Monografiya* (Leningrad, 1984), 18–33.

77 These subjects are listed on Asafiev's student record for 1907, TsGIA, 14/3/40771, l. 23.

78 See Vladimir Stasov to Dmitry Stasov, 24 August 1904, in Yelena Stasova (ed.), *V. V. Stasov: Pis'ma k rodnim*, vol. 3, part 2 (Moscow, 1962), 235.

79 In an unpublished autobiographical memoir, Asafiev stated that the opera was written 'at Stasov's urging': 'Moya muzïka', RGALI, 2658/1/415, l. 3. See also the entry on *Zolushka* in the *catalogue raisonné* of Asafiev's compositions published in Dmitriy Kabalevskiy *et al.* (ed.), *Akademik B. V. Asaf'yev: Izbrannïye trudï*, vol. 5 (Moscow, 1957), 353.

80 'O sebe', 441.

he matured into adulthood.[81] Nonetheless, his interest was aroused by the handsome young lieutenant who initially turned up to classes in uniform, feeling at once attracted and held at a distance by his courteous reserve. He was particularly intrigued by Myaskovsky's seemingly casual declaration that he had 'no matrimonial tendencies' when another student enquired about his domestic arrangements.[82] Prokofiev alludes to Myaskovsky's lack of interest in women elsewhere in his autobiography and evidently wondered whether he might be homosexual.[83] (He was apprised of the existence of homosexuality by his mother as a teenager.[84]) St Petersburg had an active gay subculture and Myaskovsky moved in circles where attitudes were relaxed.[85] Several members of the 'Modern Music Evenings' circle were gay, and although Karatïgin was not, he had no difficulty hosting a private gathering in his apartment at which Mikhail Kuzmin read extracts from his novella *Kril'ya* (*Wings*), which caused a scandal when published in 1906 because of its frank treatment of same-sex relationships.[86] Of Myaskovsky's acquaintances, at least one, Modeste Hofmann, was drawn sexually to other men (he became infatuated with Kuzmin, who found himself in the embarrassing position of having to fend off his unwanted advances).[87] If Myaskovsky were gay, he could hardly have inhabited a more accepting milieu – by the standards of the period, at least. Whatever the nature of his sexual inclinations, however, they remain a mystery – much like those of Maurice Ravel. There is no evidence to indicate that he ever had intimate congress with a member of either sex or formed an attachment to someone whom he regarded as a partner. His relationship with Prokofiev was of irreproachable propriety. Prokofiev recalled that they only discussed music: the conversation never strayed to more personal matters.[88] 'Myaskovsky does not exist apart from music', he concluded: 'He's a strange fellow'.[89]

If Myaskovsky and Prokofiev gravitated towards one another, it was not in search of friendship in the usual sense of the word, but of an intelligent companion with whom to discuss the music that they were writing. This

81 Entry for 10 September 1909, Sergey Prokof'yev, *Dnevnik 1907–1918*, ed. Svyatoslav Prokof'yev (Paris, 2002), 87.

82 Prokof'yev, *Avtobiografiya*, 279, 281.

83 Ibid., 343, 421.

84 Ibid., 405–7.

85 For an overview of gay subculture in late imperial Russia, see Dan Healey, *Homosexual Desire in Revolutionary Russia* (Chicago and London, 2001), 21–49.

86 John E. Malmstad and Nikolay Bogomolov, *Mikhail Kuzmin: A Life in Art* (Cambridge, Masschusetts and London, 1999), 93.

87 Bogomolov and Shumikhin (ed.), *M. Kuzmin. Dnevnik 1905–1907*, 432–3.

88 Prokof'yev, *Avtobiografiya*, 298.

89 Prokofiev, *Dnevnik 1907–1918*, entry for 12 August 1910, 131.

mutual need was rendered more acute by their disillusioning experiences of studying at the conservatoire. Reading the reminiscences of Prokofiev and other students, it comes as a surprise to learn how dull and unstimulating they found it, and how little encouragement they received for their youthful creative efforts.

Myaskovsky's cohort had very limited contact with the most eminent composers on the staff, Glazunov and Rimsky-Korsakov. As director, Glazunov's duties were predominantly administrative, and Rimsky-Korsakov reduced his workload considerably after being reinstated in his post, retaining only his second-year orchestration course. He discharged his responsibilities conscientiously, but his methods were ill-suited to the large classes with which he had to deal. His preferred procedure was to discuss each student's exercise in turn at the piano – which would have worked well if the group were small and the other students could sit close enough to see the score and follow the discussion. Prokofiev recalled Rimsky's course being so heavily subscribed in 1906–7 that some attendees had to perch on the classroom windowsills, as there was not enough space to accommodate everyone on the benches. Unless one sat in the front two rows, one could neither see nor hear very much, and Prokofiev often had to endure a long and tedious wait to be summoned up to the podium.[90] He learned little, and to judge from the conservatoire orchestration exercises preserved amongst Myaskovsky's papers, the standard expected was not very high.[91]

Apart from a fourth-year course on pastiche composition in small forms, which was given by Latvian composer Jāzeps Vītols (1863–1948)[92], the other so-called 'special' subjects – harmony, counterpoint, and fugue – were taught by Lyadov, the staff member that they encountered most. Lyadov was a highly competent and knowledgeable musician but had serious shortcomings as a teacher. Accounts by former students repeatedly allude to his disagreeable manner and professional negligence (he was chronically unpunctual and frequently cancelled classes without warning).[93] His attitude towards his charges was openly contemptuous, intimating that they were so talentless as to be unworthy of his attention. 'If I had money, do you imagine I would be teaching the likes of you?', he would snap at them

---

90 Prokof'yev, *Avtobiografiya*, 281–2. See also his account of these classes in 'Kratkaya avtobiografiya', 138.

91 RGALI, 2040/2/61 and 2040/2/62.

92 The Russian form of his name is Iosif Vitol'.

93 See Prokof'yev, *Avtobiografiya*, 162, 165, 175, 368, and elsewhere; and also the reminiscences of the conductor Nicolai Malko in Ol'ga Dansker (ed.), *N. A. Mal'ko: Vospominaniya, stat'i, pis'ma* (Moscow, 1972), 46. A note from Saminsky to Myaskovsky dated 26 September 1906 records that their progress on the course had already been retarded significantly by Lyadov's frequent absences: RGALI, 2040/2/239, l. 2.

in his more irascible moods.[94] He struck Lazare Saminsky, who likened his appearance to a 'huge block of livid fat', as being consumed with self-loathing: '[He] hated his own inertia, his Homeric laziness and drinking that made him disappear for weeks on end; his composing – only once in a blue moon – trifling and pretty water colours for orchestra. He hated his own bloated, unwieldy body'.[95] Saminsky's inferences about Lyadov's personal difficulties may well have been correct: he was undoubtedly a deeply unhappy man and had strong depressive tendencies.[96] But understanding this did not make it any easier to deal with him. Asafiev dreaded Lyadov's classes[97], and Myaskovsky admitted to remembering his former teacher 'with horror', while acknowledging that he had helped to develop his technique and feeling for style.[98]

At this stage of the theory of composition course, there was no opportunity for the students to show their attempts at original composition to their teachers –except, perhaps, informally, outside of class. It would have been pointless to ask Lyadov to look at their efforts, and not merely because he was so condescending and unapproachable. By the time Myaskovsky and Prokofiev enrolled at the institution, the ethos of the composition faculty had become deeply conservative. The dominant influence was that of Rimsky-Korsakov, who had long since abjured the iconoclastic attitudes of his former mentor Balakirev. He was intolerant of new music that did not conform to his rather narrow tastes, and scornful of modernists such as Richard Strauss, Mahler, and Debussy, whom he regarded as decadent.[99] The conductor Nicolai Malko witnessed his outraged reaction when a fellow student praised Paul Dukas's *L'apprenti sorcier*, hardly the most *outré* score of the period: it provoked a pedantic disquisition on contemporary composers' disregard for 'correct' voice leading.[100] Unsurprisingly, Rimsky-Korsakov viewed the 'Modern Music Evenings' with deep suspicion. By

94   Prokof'yev, *Avtobiografiya*, 284, 333. See also Aleksandra Akhonen, 'Prokof'yev v klasse Lyadova', in Tat'yana Zaytseva (ed.), *Nepoznanniy A. K. Lyadov* (Chelyabinsk, 2009), 279–80.

95   Albert Weisser, 'Lazare Saminsky's Years in Russia and Palestine: Excerpts from an Unpublished Autobiography', *Musica Judaica*, 1 (1977–8), 2–3.

96   See Mikhail Mikhaylov, *A. K. Lyadov: Ocherk zhizni i tvorchestva*, 2nd ed. (Leningrad, 1985), 114, 120.

97   Asafiev to Myaskovsky, 14 August 1907, in Kozlova, 'Iz perepiski B. V. Asaf'yeva i N. Ya. Myaskovskogo', *Sovetskaya muzïka*, 11 (1979), 121.

98   Myaskovskiy, 'Avtobiograficheskiye zametki', 7. Myaskovsky's exercises for Lyadov, which are preserved in RGALI, 2040/2/59, suggest that he applied himself diligently to his contrapuntal studies.

99   See, for example, Rimsky's dismissive remarks about Strauss and Mahler recorded by his amanuensis: Vasiliy Yastrebtsev, *Nikolay Andreyevich Rimsky-Korsakov: Vospominaniya 1886–1908*, vol. 2 (Leningrad, 1960), 34–5 and 439.

100 Dansker, *N. A. Mal'ko*, 56.

FIGURE 2.4. Anatoly Lyadov.

the end of his life, the conservatoire's composition course amply justified Balakirev's strictures on the harmful effects of institutional education, as it encouraged and rewarded conformity to a bland academicism. It would be unfair to dismiss the music written by the conservatoire's graduates at the period *en masse*, for some of them, such as Gnesin and Maximillian Steinberg, were very talented. Nonetheless, the fact remains that the conservatoire training perpetuated an unthinking adherence to compositional approaches which felt increasingly stale and routine.

Like Glazunov, Lyadov wholly concurred with his former teacher's views. Composition students soon learned to be circumspect about displaying interest in modernist developments and to refrain from essaying anything unorthodox in their coursework. Lyadov was known to stamp his feet in rage when presented with an exercise that he considered too harmonically complex or dissonant. 'If you want to write music like that, why are you in my class?', he would explode. 'Go to Debussy, take yourself off to Richard Strauss!' Prokofiev recalled that this injunction conveyed the unmistakeable subtext: 'And go to hell!'[101] The students were consequently thrown back entirely on their own resources when it came to original composition – the

101 Prokof'yev, *Avtobiografiya*, 368.

very activity that the theory of composition course supposedly existed to foster. As Myaskovsky later observed:

> [Lyadov's] relationship with the class was so odd that we did not risk showing him the things we were writing 'for ourselves', all the more so because he knew we had been infected by modernism (especially Prokofiev and myself). I must admit that the abnormality of this relationship meant that one had to expend too much effort trying to develop on one's own in various areas, when timely advice from an experienced teacher and outstanding composer would have naturally saved one a lot of energy and I would not have been forced to waste time 'rediscovering America'.[102]

When Myaskovsky expressed interest in seeing what Prokofiev was writing, Prokofiev seized the opportunity to establish a connection and invited him home to play though some music together. From his autobiography, it is evident that he was eager to impress, having discovered that his classmate was someone of discerning judgement. He succeeded. Myaskovsky immediately registered the younger man's unusual ability and inventiveness. Not being given to effusiveness, he merely remarked drily after examining Prokofiev's piano pieces: 'What a viper we have been nursing in our bosom!' – but his curiosity had been aroused.[103] Thereafter, they took to meeting from time to time outside class and kept in touch by letter during the summer months when Prokofiev returned to the family estate in Ukraine. The correspondence affords glimpses of sides to Myaskovsky's personality that tended to remain concealed beneath his shy and reserved manner – most notably, an arch humour and fondness for whimsical wordplay. The more substantial letters are almost exclusively taken up with discussions of compositions in progress and relaying reactions to one another's latest work. Their relationship was sufficiently relaxed, in the beginning at least, to permit amicable mutual criticism: in later life, Prokofiev remarked that he derived far greater benefit from these exchanges than from Lyadov's 'dry and curmudgeonly lessons'.[104]

Whatever the limitations of the conservatoire course, Myaskovsky made the most of his new-found freedom. He worked hard to improve his piano technique and score-reading skills and sought to broaden his general knowledge by reading works on history, philosophy, and other subjects.[105] His creative productivity also surged: during the first year of his studies, he composed two dozen or so piano miniatures (comprising the

---

102 Myaskovskiy, 'Avtobiograficheskiye zametki', 7.

103 Prokof'yev, *Avtobiografiya*, 292–3.

104 Ibid., 307, 315.

105 These activities are mentioned in his diary entries of 20 June and 3 July 1907, 'Vïpiski', RGALI, 2040/1/65, l. 20b.

second, third, and fourth sets of the *Flofion* series), four piano sonatas, and songs, and made his first attempt at writing a string quartet. He withheld almost all of this music at the time, regarding only two works as suitable for public performance – *Razmïshleniya* (*Meditations*), a group of seven songs to texts by the early nineteenth-century poet Yevgeny Baratïnsky (1800–1844), which became his op. 1; and a piano sonata in D minor, which was issued by Jurgenson in 1913 as Piano Sonata no. 1, op. 6. (Another of these early sonatas, in B major, was eventually published in a revised form in 1946 as Piano Sonata no. 5, op. 64/1; and some of the *Flofion* miniatures were reworked for inclusion in sets of piano pieces that Myaskovsky composed in the 1920s and 1930s.) Nonetheless, he could take a justified pride in his increasing technical command and growing confidence in tackling more complex compositional challenges, despite having no-one to guide his efforts but Krïzhanovsky, whom he continued to consult occasionally.[106] Looking back in middle age, he remembered feeling for the first time 'almost like a professional'.[107]

The Baratïnsky settings and the D minor Piano Sonata demonstrate a level of professionalism far transcending student work and testify to a remarkably swift artistic maturation. The sonata is a particularly striking achievement – a highly cogent experiment in cyclical form that displays considerable originality in handling the traditional four-movement design. Its first movement comprises an elaborate fugal treatment of a solemn angular theme (ex. 2.3) that rises to a powerful culmination over an extended dominant pedal and leads directly into the agitated sonata-form second movement, to which it is effectively a prelude. The slow movement, a ternary structure with a developmental middle section based on the first movement's fugue theme, is excellently sustained, its mood of ardent intensity heighted by a canonic presentation of the opening melodic idea on its final appearance. The finale, which is again in sonata form, maintains a powerful forward sweep and effectively integrates the contrasts and tensions of the preceding movements, climaxing in an impassioned apotheosis of the opening fugue theme. The sonata is a completely viable work, displaying not only an impressive formal coherence but also a strongly individual personality. Myaskovsky's writing for the medium is resourceful and effective, and while the finale does not eschew the overblown rhetoric of much late-Romantic keyboard music, elsewhere the textures are far sparer, being often contrapuntally organised. Of Russian composers active at the period,

106 Amongst the few items of correspondence from Krïzhanovsky preserved amongst Myaskovsky's papers is a message dated 15 April 1907 inviting him to call – 'with manuscripts, of course': RGALI, 2040/2/168, l. 3. On this occasion, Myaskovsky showed him two of the recently completed piano sonatas: 'Vïpiski', 28 April 1907, RGALI, 2040/1/65, l. 20b.

107 Myaskovskiy, 'Avtobiograficheskiye zametki', 7.

EXAMPLE 2.3. Piano Sonata no. 1, first movement: opening.

in many respects, the sonata evinces the strongest stylistic kinship to the music of Taneyev.

Myaskovsky maintained this level of productivity during the following academic year, despite being taken ill for over two months with appendicitis, for which he underwent surgery in October 1907.[108] In addition to writing songs (including three new Hippius settings), short piano pieces, and another piano sonata in A-flat (published in a revised form in 1946 as Piano Sonata no. 6, op. 64/2), he began to contemplate more ambitious undertakings. A diary entry for January 1908 alludes to plans for a programmatic symphony entitled *Cosmos* or *Cosmogony* (*Kosmos, Kosmogoniya*)[109], apparently based on Edgar Allen Poe's prose poem *Eureka* (1848) – an eccentric account of the origins of the universe which the American writer regarded as his masterpiece, deeming it of greater significance than Newton's theory of universal gravitation.[110] This rather odd choice of subject was undoubtedly influenced by the contemporaneous vogue for Poe amongst the symbolists: his writings were enthusiastically promoted by Balmont and Valery Bryusov.[111] Myaskovsky mulled over the idea for several years but eventually abandoned it. A later diary entry for 1908 alludes to plans for an opera based on Dostoyevsky's novel *The Idiot*, another unusual choice, but this project would also remain unrealised, even though he continued to work on it as late as 1918.

108 'Vïpiski', 28 January 1908, RGALI, 2040/1/65, l. 20b; Prokof'yev, *Avtobiografiya*, 343–4.

109 'Vïpiski', 28 January and 3 October 1908, RGALI, 2040/1/65, l. 20b; 28 April 1914, l. 4.

110 See Jeffrey Myers, *Edgar Allan Poe: His Life and Legacy* (New York, 1992), 219–20.

111 See Joan Delaney Grossman, *Edgar Allan Poe in Russia: A Study in Legend and Literary Influence* (Würzburg, 1973).

In February 1908, however, he began to make sketches for a symphony 'without a programme' which became his Symphony no. 1 in C minor, op. 3, completed the following September after intensive labour over the summer. His determination to finish the score seems to have been spurred by material necessity as much as creative aspiration. His money had run out and he was unable to pay his tuition fees. He evidently did not feel he could ask his father for help: if, as seems likely, Yakov was contributing to Alida's upkeep, he probably had little money to spare. His only hope of continuing his studies was to obtain a scholarship; having a substantial achievement to show would strengthen his application. Sensibly bypassing Lyadov, he took his score to Glazunov, who was sufficiently impressed by its 'maturity of thought' as to provide Myaskovsky with some badly needed financial assistance in the form of a fee waiver and a stipend.[112] (According to Maximilian Steinberg, Glazunov often paid for these scholarships himself: being well-off, he chose not to draw his director's salary and diverted it into a student hardship fund.[113]) Prokofiev, who had made a pact with Myaskovsky to write a symphony of his own over the summer[114], was greatly displeased to learn on his return to St Petersburg that Myaskovsky had already shown his score to Glazunov: he had wanted them to meet the director together and was apprehensive about losing out on an opportunity to have his symphony performed at a student concert.[115] It did not occur to him that Myaskovsky might have had private reasons for wanting to see Glazunov alone, rather than merely wishing to steal an advantage on him. His diary entries about this incident shed light on the underlying tensions in their relationship caused by Prokofiev's unrelenting competitiveness, which was so intense that he kept detailed track not only of fellow students' examination results but also of the number of solecisms that Lyadov detected in their exercises.[116] Fearing that his own symphony might impress Glazunov less favourably than Myaskovsky's, he admitted to feeling envy but quickly consoled himself: 'All the same, I am convinced that [Myaskovsky] will not become a great composer: he writes learnedly, often beautifully; he writes a lot; but there is nothing vivid, engaging, and original about his music'.[117] Prokofiev's condescending attitude to his classmate's work would strengthen over time.

112 'Vïpiski', 29 September and 19 October 1908, RGALI, 2040/1/65, ll. 20b, 3; Myaskovskiy, 'Avtobiograficheskiye zametki', 7.

113 Maksimilian Shteynberg, 'A. K. Glazunov. Vospominaniya o nyom i yevo pis'ma', in Yuriy Keldïsh *et al.* (ed.), *Glazunov: Issledovaniya, materialï, publikatsii, pis'ma*, vol. 2 (Leningrad, 1960), 22.

114 Prokof'yev, *Avtobiografiya*, 384; *Dnevnik 1907–1918*, 52.

115 See Prokofiev to Myaskovsky, 12 August and 15 September 1908, in Kozlova and Yatsenko, *Perepiska*, 58, 61; Prokof'yev, *Dnevnik 1907–1918*, 55.

116 Prokof'yev, *Avtobiografiya*, 196–7.

117 Prokof'yev, *Dnevnik 1907–1918*, 57.

Myaskovsky was understandably proud of his accomplishment (his jubilant diary entry for 27 July 1908 reads: 'Finished the symphony . . . No. 1!'[118]) and dedicated the work to Krïzhanovsky in gratitude for his former teacher's support and encouragement. While the symphony's compositional idiom is to some extent derivative, as one would expect with an early work, many characteristic traits of Myaskovsky's mature manner are nonetheless in evidence: the general seriousness of tone, the prevalence of contrapuntal textures and tendency to concentrated motivic working, and a certain austerity of sound-world. Interestingly, its closest stylistic kinship is once again with the music of Taneyev rather than Rimsky-Korsakov and his school. The symphony is cast in three movements, a design for which there was no obvious Russian precedent: like Cesar Franck's Symphony in D minor, it comprises two quick outer movements flanking a central one in a slow tempo. The decision to omit a scherzo is noteworthy, when one considers that Russian symphonists had traditionally revelled in the opportunity to compose piquant *Charakterstücke* featuring inventive displays of orchestral colour (such as the scherzi in, say, Borodin's Second Symphony, Tchaikovsky's Fourth or Glazunov's Third). If it departs from convention in this particular respect, the symphony is firmly traditional in others. Apart from a few striking passages of octatonic and whole-tone sonorities in the finale, its harmonic language is notably less adventurous than that of the Hippius settings or the First Piano Sonata. A comparable conservatism is manifest in the approach to structural organisation: the outer movements are both in orthodox sonata forms and the slow movement in a spacious ternary form. All are conceived on a generous scale and have a combined duration of about forty-five minutes. Myaskovsky demonstrates an ability to fill these expanses with continuously interesting music and a natural capacity to think in symphonic terms. As is often the case in his earlier work, the thematic material was fashioned primarily with a view to what it could yield when subjected to processes of development, rather than any intrinsic sensuous appeal. The principal themes of the first movement are an excellent case in point. Both are adumbrated in a lengthy slow introduction – a procedure perhaps influenced by the opening of Tchakovsky's Sixth Symphony. The first theme, a solemn idea outlining a diminished seventh, is readily amenable to contrapuntal treatment and is initially presented in a sombre fugato; the second, introduced at the fugato's climax, is constructed from a simple rising scalic figure (exxs. 2.4 and 2.5). The introduction leads seamlessly into the exposition by means of an *accelerando*, whereupon these ideas are successively restated in a modified guise as the first and second subjects, with the latter presented in the orthodox key of the relative major. The influence of Tchaikovsky is also manifest in

118 'Vïpiski', RGALI, 2040/1/65, l. 20b.

the handling of the second subject group, which is slower in tempo and has the character of a self-contained lyrical episode rounded off by a group of ancillary themes. As in the *Pathétique*, the development section breaks in harshly on its dying fall, subjecting the first subject to vigorous imitative elaboration before building to a climax based on a minor mode variant of the second subject. The recapitulation presents the principal themes of the exposition in the expected tonic minor and major with only small alterations, returning to a quick tempo for a stormy coda which is largely taken up with further development of the second subject.

The spacious *Larghetto* provides an effective contrast to the preceding turbulence, being predominantly serene in mood, though rising at times to peaks of ardent intensity. Its opening long-breathed viola cantilena is shown in example 2.6; its initial outline of a descending sixth also features prominently in the movement's other themes, establishing a subtle connexion between them. Like the material of the first movement, this melody has been designed to allow for contrapuntal working – a possibility exploited later when its initial phrase is imitated in canon at the octave at the rhythmic intervals of a bar and, later, a single crotchet beat. The thematic material of the radiant central section is also susceptible to canonic treatment: it unfolds in the unusually remote tonality of G major, the key of the leading note; and Myaskovsky achieves a telling dramatic effect by having the material of the A section return climactically in that key for a few bars before moving swiftly to A-flat via C minor for a majestic restatement. The

EXAMPLE 2.4. Symphony no. 1, first movement: opening.

EXAMPLE 2.5. Symphony no. 1, first movement:
subsidiary idea in introduction (bars 41–8).

[string figurations omitted]

EXAMPLE 2.6. Symphony no. 1, second movement: opening.

remainder of the section proceeds much as previously, concluding with a rapt coda. In many respects, this is the symphony's most impressive movement: it is admirably well-sustained and has passages of affecting nobility.

The finale, *Allegro assai e molto risoluto*, while not marring the symphony irretrievably, is less successful. All the material presented in the exposition – the first and second subjects, one of the transition themes and the codetta theme – can be presented in quadruple invertible counterpoint if the second subject is rendered in diminution. This *tour de force*, an idea inspired by the finale of Mozart's *Jupiter* Symphony[119], is reserved for a climactic build-up in the coda (a brief extract is shown in example 2.7). While ingenious, the necessity of devising themes capable of combining in such fashion vitiated their intrinsic melodic interest – as Prokofiev pointed out. ('Your combination of themes in the finale made me see red', he told Myaskovsky with characteristic bluntness. 'Who's that for? Lyadov, by any chance? And I guarantee you that it's detracted fatally from the beauty of each theme on its own, which is much more important than four bars that no-one will understand or appreciate'.[120]) The opening phrase of the first subject, for example, has a poor continuation that extends it mechanically though sequential repetitions; and the later strains of the second subject are equally undistinguished. The polyphonic treatment of these ideas in the development section sounds laboured, and most seriously, the calamitous dénouement of the closing pages seems insufficiently justified by what has preceded it.

The shortcomings of the First Symphony are readily apparent: a tendency to overwork ideas, an overreliance on sequences as a means of development, excessively foursquare phrase structure, and insufficiently varied restatements of musical material. It also strikes one as being a rather self-conscious score that strives too effortfully to make a monumental statement and to demonstrate technical mastery, though this is perhaps unsurprising

119 Myaskovsky to Vladimir Derzhanovsky, 16 July 1914, RNMM, 3/341.

120 Prokofiev to Myaskovsky, 11 July 1908, in Kozlova and Yatsenko, *Perepiska*, 55.

EXAMPLE 2.7. Symphony no. 1, third movement: bars 278–81.

given the circumstances under which it was written: Myaskovsky was understandably anxious to impress Glazunov as being worthy of a scholarship. The First Symphony was a creditable achievement nonetheless, if not on the same level as the First Piano Sonata. Myaskovsky habitually referred to it as an immature work, but did not suppress it – though he revised the score extensively in 1914, 1917–18, and again in 1921–2 to eliminate *longueurs* and improve the orchestration before he eventually allowed it to be published in 1929.

If he entertained hopes that Glazunov might arrange a performance of the symphony, they came to nothing. (Glazunov did, however, arrange for a private play-through of Prokofiev's symphony with the court orchestra under its principal conductor Hugo Wahrlich in February 1909: with characteristic selflessness, Myaskovsky helped to correct the score and parts when Prokofiev fell ill beforehand.[121]) He did not show the symphony subsequently to Lyadov, having evidently decided that it would be pointless.[122] If Asafiev is to be believed, Lyadov thought that Myaskovsky had no future as a composer and Glazunov found his work desiccated and cerebral – though these reports must be treated with caution, as Asafiev's view of Myaskovsky in middle age was heavily coloured by professional jealousy.[123] The fact remains, however, that neither showed any interest in helping him to establish himself professionally: Lyadov's efforts on his behalf amounted merely to sending him a few private students.[124]

121 Prokof'yev, *Avtobiografiya*, 435–8; Prokof'yev, *Dnevnik 1907–1918*, 67–70; Myaskovsky to Prokofiev, 16 February 1909, in Kozlova and Yatsenko, *Perepiska*, 63.

122 Myaskovskiy, 'Avtobiograficheskiye zametki', 7.

123 Prokof'yev, *Avtobiografiya*, 370; Boris Asaf'yev, 'Nikolay Yakovlevich Myaskovskiy', in *Izbrannïye trudï*, vol. 5, 123.

124 Myaskovskiy, 'Avtobiograficheskiye zametki', 9; Myaskovsky to Prokofiev, 12 July 1907, in Kozlova and Yatsenko, *Perepiska*, 41.

A lack of opportunities to hear work performed represents a serious hindrance to a composer's development, especially when it comes to gaining experience in writing for the orchestra. The only performance of Myaskovsky's compositions that took place throughout his entire time at the conservatoire was organised wholly independently of the institution. On 18 December 1908, three of his Hippius settings were performed at one of the 'Modern Music Evenings' by the soprano Sof'ya Demidova, with Karatïgin as accompanist – probably at the instigation of Krïzhanovsky. Prokofiev made his debut as pianist-composer on the same occasion, playing several miniatures that he subsequently included in the two sets of piano pieces published as op. 3 and op. 4.[125] Myaskovsky did not attend, pleading illness. Prokofiev privately suspected that he was too nervous to come and noted with satisfaction in his diary that his own piano pieces made far more of an impression than Myaskovsky's songs, which were coolly received by the audience and regarded as disappointingly old-fashioned, he thought, by Karatïgin.[126] Although Karatïgin played excellently, Demidova disliked the Hippius settings: Prokofiev reported her waspish verdict that they were written 'for a machine rather than a singer'.[127] The critical notices were equally unenthusiastic, drawing unflattering comparisons with other songs in the programme by Nikolai Tcherepnin, a former pupil of Rimsky-Korsakov.[128]

The remainder of Myaskovsky's third year at the conservatoire seemed as though it would prove otherwise uneventful. Apart from the symphony, he composed two sets of songs, the lovely cycle *Madrigal* (op. 7), five settings of Konstantin Balmont's poetry; and the atmospheric *Three Sketches to Words by Vyacheslav Ivanov*, op. 8. Both opuses reveal new sides to Myaskovsky's creative personality – including a capacity for charm and elegant lyricism. The Ivanov settings in particular suggest a creatively fruitful encounter with the music of Debussy, whose influence is perceptible in the treatment of harmony and pianistic sonority. The academic year came to an unexpectedly dramatic close, however, with the final examinations in April 1909. As Myaskovsky was now in the fourth year of the course, these were an important hurdle to surmount successfully if he wished to stay on to study 'practical composition'. When Lyadov saw the coursework that he and his classmates had produced for Vïtols's class on pastiche composition

125 'Vïpiski', 22 December 1908, RGALI, 2040/1/65, l. 3; Prokof'yev, *Avtobiografiya*, 375, 404–5, 416–19.

126 *Dnevnik 1907–1918*, 52.

127 Prokofiev to Myaskovsky, 19 December 1908, in Kozlova and Yatsenko, *Perepiska*, 62.

128 See 'G. T.' [Georgiy Timofeyev], 'XLV vecher sovremennoy muzïki', *Rech'*, 22 December 1908; 'Vecher sovremennoy muzïki' (unsigned review), *Peterburgskiy listok*, 24 December 1908.

in small forms, he was outraged: Prokofiev overheard him complaining indignantly to the other members of the jury that the students 'all wanted to be Skryabins'. Initially he refused point-blank to teach any of them but eventually relented and accepted a few students into his class, including Myaskovsky.[129] Clearly, he was a far from ideal choice of composition teacher, but there was no-one else suitable or available. Lyadov's difficult character traits seem to have become more exaggerated after Rimsky-Korsakov's death the previous year in June 1908, an event that affected him deeply and exacerbated his tendency to misanthropy and depression.[130] It is indicative that Asafiev dropped out of the theory of composition course without sitting the fourth-year examinations or taking his diploma: he found Rimsky-Korsakov's and Lyadov's reactions to his early stage works deeply humiliating and held an enduring grudge against the institution because he believed his teachers had failed to recognise his talent.[131]

As it transpired, Lyadov acted as Myaskovsky's teacher in little more than name, and Myaskovsky seems to have made few demands on his time. To judge from his remark in a letter of June 1909 to Prokofiev that he was 'writing nothing for Lyadov'[132], he is unlikely to have shown him the ambitious project on which he worked over the summer – the symphonic poem *Silence* (*Molchaniye*), op. 9, based on Edgar Allen Poe's 'Silence: A Fable', a short prose work that Myaskovsky had read in a translation by Konstantin Balmont. One of Poe's most enigmatic texts, it has a strange dreamlike atmosphere. Set in an imaginary exotic wilderness, it depicts the Devil's attempts to disrupt the lonely meditations of a hermit whose expression bespeaks 'sorrow, and weariness, and disgust with mankind, and a longing after solitude'. The Devil rouses a horde of wild beasts which surround the rock on which the anchorite sits and roar 'loudly and fearfully beneath the moon' – but the man is unperturbed. He then unleashes a 'frightful tempest' which shakes the hermit's resting place 'to its foundation': 'the man trembled in the solitude; – but the night waned and he sat upon the rock'. Enraged at not being able to disturb the hermit's composure, the Devil blasts the wilderness with the 'curse of silence', suppressing 'any shadow of

129 Prokof'yev, *Dnevnik 1907–1918*, 73–4.

130 Mikhaylov, *A. K. Lyadov*, 113–14.

131 Orlova and Kryukov, *Akademik Boris Vladimirovich Asaf'yev*, 59–60; Asafiev to Myaskovsky, 4 February 1910, in Kozlova, 'Iz perepiski B. V. Asaf'yeva i N. Ya. Myaskovskogo', *Sovetskaya muzïka*, 11 (1979), 124; Myaskovsky to Maximilian Steinberg, 4 February 1926, RIII, 28/3/487, l. 29–290b. This did not prevent Asafiev subsequently from indulging in wholesale reinvention of the past: in later life, he took to presenting himself as 'one of Lyadov's favourite students'. See, for example, Asafiev to Platon Kerzhentsev, 22 September 1937, RGALI, 962/3/331, l. 102.

132 Myaskovsky to Prokofiev, 25 June 1909, in Kozlova and Yatsenko, *Perepiska*, 68.

sound throughout the vast illimitable desert'. At this, the hermit's countenance turns 'wan with terror': he flees 'afar off in haste' and is seen no more.

Perhaps the most illuminating suggestion about the possible meaning of
this curious tale was made by the editor of Poe's *Collected Works*, Thomas
Mabbett: 'Man clings to the rock of reality, however terrible; the true silence,
cessation of being, terrifies even a brave man'.[133] The text's evocation of solitude and despair at the apparent meaninglessness of existence touch on
concerns that are central to the poetry of Hippius, and the sound-world of
Myaskovsky's new symphonic poem was clearly adumbrated in his Hippius
settings. The idea of writing a programmatic orchestral work inspired by
Poe's fable had occurred to him in the summer of 1908. He began to sketch
it a year later in mid-June 1909, prompted by a flash of inspiration while
walking by the famous St Petersburg landmark, the Church of the Saviour
on the Spilled Blood – a rather incongruous location to be thinking about
the Devil, as he wryly remarked to Asafiev.[134] Although he complained of
finding *Silence* difficult to compose, it was finished in draft just over a month
later. The orchestration caused him the most labour and anxiety – understandably, given his inexperience – as the work was scored for large forces
(including quadruple woodwind and eight horns) and was texturally intricate. He eventually drew the final double-bar line the following February.[135]

Lasting just under twenty minutes in performance, *Silence* comprises a
large-scale bi-partite structure, the second section of which develops material presented in the first, rounded off by a brief coda. Myaskovsky's programme note[136] indicates that two of the themes heard in the slow opening
section are associated respectively with the hostile forces that assail the Man
(a sinister motif enunciated by the bass clarinet and lower strings) and with
the figure of the Man himself. The developmental second section loosely follows the events of the fable, culminating in a vivid depiction of the tempest
and the eerie silence that descends in its wake, while the coda portrays the
Man's despair and terrified flight. *Silence* represented another remarkable
leap in Myaskovsky's artistic maturation and is on a much higher plane of
accomplishment than the First Symphony. It is not only a more individual

133 Thomas Ollive Mabbett (ed.), *The Collected Works of Edgar Allan Poe. Volume
     II: Tales and Sketches, 1831–1842* (Cambridge, Masschusetts, 1978), 192.

134 Myaskovsky to Asafiev, 22 June 1909, RGALI, 2658/1/645, l. 21.

135 Myaskovsky to Asafiev, 11 July 1909, RGALI, 2658/1/645, ll. 25–250b;
     Myaskovsky to Prokofiev, 20 July and 4 August 1909, in Kozlova and Yatsenko,
     Perepiska, 73, 77. Myaskovsky's diary records his completion of the sketch on
     20 July 1909 and of the orchestral score on 7 February 1910: 'Vïpiski', RGALI,
     2040/1/65, l. 3.

136 First published under the title 'K ispolneniyu "Skazki" N. Ya. Myaskovskogo' in
     Muzïka, 22 May 1911; reprinted in *N. Ya. Myaskovskiy: Sobraniye materialov*,
     vol. 2, 239–41.

utterance, but demonstrates far greater formal cogency, despite its resolute eschewal of textbook models. Its sound-world is quite unlike anything else that was being written in Russia at the period, least of all by the composers attached to the St Petersburg Conservatoire. Although the musical rhetoric and gestures in a few passages recall Tchaikovsky, the idiom is essentially post-Wagnerian. It is noteworthy that Myaskovsky listed the *Ring* cycle as being amongst the works which made the strongest impression on him at this period.[137] The dark-hued orchestration and highly chromatic musical language of *Silence* suggest an unmistakable kinship to *Götterdämmerung* and the spacious unfolding of the musical material undoubtedly owes much to Wagnerian procedures more generally. Nonetheless, the Wagnerian influences are thoroughly assimilated, and the score defines a psychological realm very different to the voluptuous, erotically charged sound-world of middle- and late-period Skryabin, the Russian contemporary whose style owed most to Wagner. *Silence* requires meticulous attention to phrasing, tone colour, and textural balance if it is to make its proper effect in performance (in these respects, the published commercial recordings of *Silence* are very inadequate), but in a well-considered reading it makes a powerful impression, rising towards the close to a splendidly calculated climax imbued with a searing intensity of tragic feeling.

Little is known about Myaskovsky's day-to-day existence during his final year at the conservatoire. In the summer of 1910, he began to compose a string quartet in D minor while holidaying in Batovo, a village located some fifty miles south of St Petersburg. This was the third quartet that he wrote at this period[138]: two others, respectively in F major and F minor, also seem to have been composed around 1909–10. In the event, none of the three quartets would be premiered for many years. This may have been simply due to lack of suitable performance opportunities, or perhaps Myaskovsky withheld them because he regarded them as student work. The D-minor and F-minor quartets were written as contributions to the portfolio of compositions that he produced for Lyadov. In the first movement of the D-minor quartet, he allowed himself a private joke at his teacher's expense: the opening phrase of the second subject outlines the pitches B-flat-D-G-sharp-A-C-F (ex. 2.8) – in Russian nomenclature ('be-re-gis-lya-do-fa'), a sequence of syllables that sounds like the words 'Beware of Lyadov!' (*Beregis' Lyadova!*). Both quartets are very accomplished, displaying an excellent feeling for the medium and expert contrapuntal skill. Myaskovsky was pleasantly surprised when he

137 Myaskovskiy, 'Avtobiograficheskiye zametki', 8.

138 See Myaskovsky to Asafiev, 1 July 1910, RGALI, 2658/1/635, l. 32; Myaskovsky to Prokofiev, 13 August and 4 September 1910, in Kozlova and Yatsenko, *Perepiska*, 85, 88.

EXAMPLE 2.8. String Quartet in F (op. 33/3), first movement: bars 50–5.

eventually heard the D-minor quartet performed in 1926.[139] After his interest in writing chamber music revived in 1930, when he composed two new quartets (opp. 33/1 and 33/2), he revised and published it in 1931 as op. 33/3. The F-minor quartet was revised in 1937 and issued as op. 33/4 the following year, while the F-major was reworked in 1945 and published as op. 67/1.

Having completed the two quartets, Myaskovsky started to make sketches for a number of other compositions, including the Sinfonietta, op. 10, which he completed the following year. His studies at the conservatoire concluded without much ceremony in May 1911. He never sat the final examination in practical composition[140], but simply claimed his diploma, having shown Lyadov the two quartets and *Madrigal*.[141] His graduation certificate records that his coursework for the fugue and orchestration classes was judged 'excellent', his portfolio of exercises for the Musical Form (pastiche composition) class 'very good'. A handwritten addition in the margin states that 'St[uden]t Myaskovsky studied practical composition under the supervision of Prof[essor] Lyadov, which is attested both by a signature and the affixing of a seal'.[142] Myaskovsky's terse account of these events in his reminiscences conveys that he found the closing stage of his studies to be a disappointing anticlimax, even if he could take legitimate pride in what he had achieved over the previous five years.

He was now thirty years old and had no reputation to speak of. His prospects did not look very promising, but a new professional acquaintance formed early in 1911 proved of far-reaching importance for the next stages of his career.

---

139 Myaskovsky to Asafiev, 27 March 1926, RGALI, 2040/1/641, ll. 11–110b.

140 Myaskovsky is not recorded on the student register as having sat the examination: see Akhonen, 'Prokof'yev v klasse Lyadova', 290.

141 Myaskovskiy, 'Avtobiograficheskiye zametki', 8.

142 RGALI, 2040/1/166, l. 2.

3

Emergence: 1911–14

Within a fortnight of being awarded his conservatoire diploma, Myaskovsky travelled to Moscow to attend rehearsals for the premiere of *Silence* – the first performance of one of his larger-scale works. Once more, Krïzhanovsky had played a central role in events. Earlier in the year, he had been contacted by Konstantin Saradzhev, an Armenian violinist friendly with Glière since their student days at the Moscow Conservatoire.[1] A pupil of the renowned virtuoso Jan Hřímalý, Saradzhev (1877–1954) graduated with a silver medal in 1898 and continued his training under Otakar Ševčík in Prague, but his interests increasingly turned to conducting. Between 1904 and 1908 he studied in Leipzig under Arthur Nikisch (1855–1922), one of the outstanding *maestri* of his generation. (Nikisch had strong professional ties to Russia and was a notable advocate of the music of Tchaikovsky.[2]) On returning to Moscow, Saradzhev set out to establish himself as a prominent figure in the city's musical life. He made regular appearances as a soloist and chamber musician and won widespread respect for his efforts as chairman of the Orchestral Players' Mutual Aid Society to improve musicians' working conditions.[3] In the same year, he was invited to form an orchestra and present a season of open-air summer concerts in Sokolniki, a district to the north-east of the city boasting an extensive municipal park that was a popular location for leisure outings.[4] Although the venue was far from ideal[5], Saradzhev was determined to make the most of the opportunity: the concerts received complimentary notices and were well attended. A dapper man of diminutive stature, with a swarthy complexion and a shock of jet-black hair, Saradzhev's dandyish appearance belied a phenomenal capacity for hard work. When the invi-

---

1 Glière's String Quartet no. 1 in A major, op. 2 was dedicated to Saradzhev. Krïzhanovsky and Saradzhev participated in a performance of Glière's String Octet, op. 5 in Kiev in 1903: see Bogdanov-Berezovskiy (ed.), *Glièr: Stat'i, vospominaniya, materialï*, vol. 1, 188–92.

2 See Larisa Kutateladze (ed.), *Artur Nikish i russkaya muzïkal'naya kul'tura* (Leningrad, 1975), 15–22 and *passim*.

3 This account of Saradzhev's early career draws on an autobiographical résumé of 1935, 'Moya avtobiografiya', RNMM, 4/2; and Georgiy Tigranov's biographical sketch in Georgiy Tigranov (ed.), *K. S. Saradzhev: Stat'i, vospominaniya* (Moscow, 1962), 7–55.

4 See Konstantin Aver'yanov (ed.), *Istoriya moskovskikh rayonov: Èntsiklopediya* (Moscow, 2005), 538–55.

5 See Grigoriy Prokof'yev, 'Letniy sezon v Moskve', *Russkaya muzïkal'naya gazeta*, 25 September 1911.

FIGURE 3.1. Konstantin Saradzhev (1914).

tation was renewed in 1910, he planned an ambitious series of thirty-one concerts over four months, in which he presented some fifty large-scale works and seventy-five shorter ones. Thirteen of these performances were premieres, reflecting his keen interest in modern music.[6]

In preparation for a further season in 1911, he made a special trip to St Petersburg early in the New Year to consult Krïzhanovsky about works by younger local composers that he could consider programming.[7] Krïzhanovsky introduced him to Myaskovsky[8], and he was sufficiently impressed by *Silence* as to give an undertaking to perform it at Sokolniki in May. Having perhaps gathered that Myaskovsky had little money to spare, Saradzhev invited him to stay in his Moscow apartment when he travelled down for the performance.[9] The three-week trip proved surprisingly

6   Georgiy Konyus, 'K zakrïtiyu sezona simfonicheskikh kontsertov', *Utro Rossii*, 3 October 1910.

7   Yekaterina Koposova-Derzhanovskaya, 'V. V. Derzhanovskiy po vospominaniyam zhenï i druga', RNMM, 3/3365, l. 30.

8   Myaskovskiy, 'Avtobiograficheskiye zametki', 8. The date of the meeting is unrecorded, but it had taken place by 25 February 1911, to judge from an allusion to the forthcoming premiere of *Silence* in a letter from Yakovlev to Myaskovsky of that date: RGALI, 2040/2/290, l. 2.

9   Saradzhev to Myaskovsky, 31 March 1911, RGALI 2040/2/240, l. 1.

pleasant. Saradzhev was out much of the day, which enabled Myaskovsky to spend time alone composing, without interruptions and distractions – a welcome respite from his family's increasingly crowded apartment, as Valentina and Yevgeniya were still living there with their husbands, and children had started to make their appearance.[10] The performance was originally scheduled for 27 May but had to be postponed until 31 May because of a delay in preparing the instrumental parts. Apart from this minor hitch, everything went smoothly. Myaskovsky reported to Prokofiev that Saradzhev was 'a wonderfully accomplished musician': 'He has a fine technique, a strong artistic personality and superlative musicianship. . . . His orchestra is splendid and his relationship with it is excellent'.[11] The responses to his tone poem were encouraging, on the whole, the exception being a rather condescending review by Skryabin's acolyte Leonid Sabaneyev, soon to become Myaskovsky and Prokofiev's principal bugbear amongst Moscow's music critics.[12] The most consistently expressed reservation concerned some passages of ineffective orchestration, a shortcoming correctly attributed to inexperience. (*Silence*, like Myaskovsky's other early orchestral works, was extensively revised before publication.) After the stultifying atmosphere of the St Petersburg Conservatoire, Myaskovsky found this experience of professional validation liberating. He was particularly heartened by Saradzhev's enthusiasm for his score after Alexander Siloti's imperious rejection of it the previous year when he had enquired whether the renowned pianist would be prepared to programme it during the annual cycle of symphony concerts that he conducted in the capital.[13] It was also gratifying to be able to 'wipe Lyadov's eye', as he told another Conservatoire acquaintance, Viktor Belyayev.[14] Writing to Prokofiev afterwards, he described feeling as though he had been relieved of a great psychological burden.[15] Prokofiev was grateful to learn that Myaskovsky had succeeded in arousing Saradzhev's interest in his work too, which led to a performance of his 'symphonic tableau' *Dreams*, op. 6 in the autumn.[16]

---

10 Myaskovsky to Asafiev, 24 June 1911, in RGALI, 2658/1/645, l. 350b.

11 Myaskovsky to Prokofiev, 26 May 1911, in Kozlova and Yatsenko, *Perepiska*, 89.

12 The concert was reviewed in *Russkiye vedomosti, Moskovskiye vedomosti*, and *Utro Rossii* on 2 June 1911. Sabaneyev's review appeared in *Golos Moskvï* on 3 June 1911. On Sabaneyev (1881–1968), see Aleksandr Stupel', *Russkaya mïsl' o muzïke 1895–1917: Ocherk istorii russkoy muzïkal'noy kritiki* (Leningrad, 1980), 207–13; Larry Sitsky, *Music of the Repressed Russian Avant-Garde, 1900–1929* (Westport, Connecticut, 1994), 291–302.

13 Siloti to Myaskovsky, 22 July 1910, RGALI, 2040/2/150, ll. 1–2.

14 Belyayev to Myaskovsky, 23 June 1911, RGALI, 2040/1/99, l. 7.

15 Myaskovsky to Prokofiev, 23 June 1911, in Kozlova and Yatsenko, *Perepiska*, 93.

16 Prokof'yev, *Dnevnik 1907–1918*, 157.

FIGURE 3.2. The three sisters: Vera, Valentina, and Yevgeniya in Batovo (1911).

FIGURE 3.3. Sergey Prokofiev (1911).

While in Moscow, Myaskovsky also made the acquaintance of Saradzhev's administrative assistant Vladimir Derzhanovsky and his wife, Yekaterina Koposova-Derzhanovskaya, another encounter that would decisively shape his future. Derzhanovsky's important position in musical life of the late imperial and early Soviet periods has yet to be adequately appraised: his enthusiastic advocacy of Western musical modernism made it a problematic subject for discussion in the USSR. The Derzhanovskys were an interesting and colourful couple.[17] Born in Tiflis in 1881, Derzhanovsky trained as a horn player and percussionist at the city's music academy, where his contemporaries included Samuil Samosud, subsequently one of the USSR's foremost conductors, and the composers Grigory and Alexander Kreyn. He enrolled at the Moscow Conservatoire in 1902 but was forced to leave when the director Vasily Safonov discovered that he was supporting himself by working as a music critic. From 1904, he reviewed for the leading liberal newspaper *The Russian Gazette* (*Russkiye vedomosti*) and various literary periodicals. He became increasingly drawn to Marxist revolutionary politics and joined the Russian Social-Democratic Labour Party, the precursor of the Communist Party of the Soviet Union.

Yekaterina and Derzhanovsky met in 1904. From an affluent and cultured family, Yekaterina studied at the Moscow Conservatoire, graduating in 1901, and embarked on a professional singing career, performing in concerts and appearing with the Private Opera Company founded by the industrialist Savva Mamontov, which premiered several of Rimsky-Korsakov's later operas. Derzhanovsky courted her eagerly: as she toured the provinces, he sent her ardent letters that presented his participation in revolutionary activity during the unrest of 1905 in a thoroughly romantic light. They became engaged in 1906 but lived together without marrying for two years. Yekaterina also became involved in underground activity, helping to distribute subversive literature. After experiencing vocal strain, she decided to retire from the operatic stage and concentrate on giving recitals, specialising in new music – a predilection she shared with Derzhanovsky, who regarded progressive art and progressive politics as related spheres of activity. In an article of 1905 entitled 'Art and the Proletariat', which strikingly adumbrated the rhetoric of Soviet music criticism, he declared: 'Bourgeois art is decaying and will not regenerate, because the class to which it caters has already had its historical say and its day is done. The

---

17 The information presented here draws on two unpublished sets of reminiscences by Derzhanovskaya, both probably written in the late 1940s and early 1950s: 'V. V. Derzhanovskiy po vospominaniyam zhenï i druga' (see fn7), RNMM, 3/3365, ll. 1–26; and 'Stranitsï proshlogo', RNMM, 3/1641, ll. 1–17 and 82–135.

youthful [proletarian] class, which is inspired by lofty aims, does not care for the dreary, boring songs of the old world'.[18]

In 1906, Derzhanovsky mooted the idea of setting up a Moscow analogue of the St Petersburg 'Modern Music Evenings', but it only became feasible to realise his ambition when he met Saradzhev two years later. By this time, Derzhanovsky was working for the Russian Musical Society, helping the conductor and composer Sergey Vasilenko to run its recently inaugurated 'Historical Concerts'.[19] Saradzhev invited him to oversee the organisation and promotion of the Sokolniki series also, and Derzhanovsky accepted. The two initially took an intense dislike to one another, but their mutual antipathy quickly thawed, and they became close friends. Saradzhev was equally keen about the idea of instigating a concert series devoted to new music and readily lent his assistance. Derzhanovsky scraped together sufficient funds to hire the Small Hall of the Moscow Conservatory and they presented their first 'Modern Music Evening' on 18 January 1909. Saradzhev roped in colleagues to play the Ravel String Quartet. The young pianist Yelena Bekman-Shcherbina (1882–1951), a pioneering exponent of early twentieth-century French keyboard music, performed Debussy's *Estampes* and accompanied Derzhanovskaya in the same composer's *Ariettes oubliées* and in *mélodies* by Déodat de Séverac. Not content with supplying the audience with literal Russian prose renditions of the French texts, Derzhanovsky asked the poets Lev Kobïlinsky ('Ellis') and Fyodor Sologub to make verse translations. The remainder of the booklet was prepared with similar care, down to the detailed programme notes and a cover designed by the artist Nikolay Feofilaktov featuring a rather risqué illustration of a scantily clad maiden playing a harp. The critics' reactions to the music performed were almost uniformly hostile (the Ravel quartet was found 'anarchic' and the Debussy songs 'oppressive and long-winded'), but this was probably to be expected. As Grigory Kreyn's son Julian observed when discussing the 'Evenings' in an unpublished memoir, very little new music was performed in Moscow at the time – even Ravel was virtually unknown.[20] The large audience, however, was warmly appreciative and the event could be accounted a modest triumph.

A second evening, presenting compositions by Skryabin, Rebikov, the Kreyn brothers, and Gyorgy Catoire [Katuar], took place on 11 March 1909, but a considerable hiatus ensued before the third, which was not held until 6 April the following year – a programme of songs and keyboard works by Debussy and Ravel, once again performed by Derzhanovskaya and

18   'Iskusstvo i proletariat', *Bor'ba*, 6 December 1905.

19   See Sergey Vasilenko, *Vospominaniya*, ed. Tamara Livanova (Moscow, 1979), 196–210.

20   Yulian Kreyn, 'Grigoriy Kreyn. Materialï dlya issledovaniya', RNMM, 482/178, ll. 17–18.

Bekman-Shcherbina, and Vincent d'Indy's Second String Quartet, played by Saradzhev and colleagues. As it transpired, Derzhanovsky's plan to run a regular series of concerts was hindered by his inability to place it on a financially secure footing, although the performers only received token honoraria or gave their services for nothing. (Almost four years elapsed before a fourth evening, which proved to be the final one, was held on 23 January 1914.)[21] Nonetheless, he gained valuable experience from the venture and made professional contacts that would be useful in the future: in the early 1920s Saradzhev, Myaskovsky, and Derzhanovsky were centrally involved in setting up the Association for Modern Music, which organised performances of new music on a more ambitious scale.

The Derzhanovskys recognised in Myaskovsky a kindred spirit, although as with Saradzhev, they did not establish an immediate rapport. Derzhanovskaya recalled not being quite sure what to make of him when he called to introduce himself while in Moscow for the premiere of *Silence*:

> I looked out the window and saw a gentleman with a little beard ringing the doorbell at the entrance. He wore a straw boater, which, from the way he kept poised it on his head, might have been a vessel filled with some precious liquid... It turned out to be Myaskovsky, whom we had been expecting. All of his movements were slow; he spoke quietly, in a reserved way, without smiling. At that period Myaskovsky rarely laughed and then only soundlessly – covering his eyes with his hand and shaking slightly. Vladimir and I made light ironic fun of what we took to be his air of self-importance, but the lingering impression of our first encounter was nonetheless a pleasant one.[22]

Their puzzlement probably deepened when a package arrived shortly afterwards containing *Madrigal* and some of his Ivanov and Hippius settings, in which they had expressed interest. 'I am sending on my vocal trash', his covering note opened rather startlingly. It continued in remorselessly self-deprecating fashion, explaining that he had refrained from sending other songs because he thought them 'worthless', 'naive', 'weak', 'utterly dilettantish', and 'clumsy'. (When Derzhanovsky had previously requested information for the concert programme booklet, Myaskovsky declined to supply a list of his other compositions on the grounds that they were 'not of the slightest value'.)[23] As they later came to realise, their new acquaint-

21 A selection of documentation pertaining to the Moscow Modern Music Evenings, including programmes, reviews, and correspondence, is compiled in Yuliya Deklerk *et al.* (ed.), *Dernier cri, ili posledniy krik modï v iskusstve nachala XX veka: Moskva, Parizh, Peterburg*, vol. 1: *Vladimir Derzhanovskiy i vechera sovremennoy muzïki v Moskve* (Moscow, 2012).

22 Yekaterina Koposova-Derzhanovskaya, 'Pamyati druga', in Shlifshteyn (ed.), *N. Ya. Myaskovskiy: Sobraniye materialov*, vol. 1, 202.

23 Myaskovsky to Derzhanovsky, 15 May and 9 June 1911, RNMM 3/325 and 3/326.

ance's odd behaviour was not a pose but resulted from a chronic lack of self-confidence.

There matters rested for the time being: Myaskovsky returned to St Petersburg and spent the remainder of the summer completing the first draft of a second symphony, commenced the previous year. In August he left for the countryside, basing himself some fifty miles south of the capital in the village of Batovo, where he orchestrated a three-movement Sinfonietta, op. 10, composed the previous December, and sketched a sonata for cello and piano.[24] In letters to friends, he complained of 'nervous fatigue' and exhaustion.[25] One suspects that his overwrought state was caused as much by personal circumstances as overwork. Myaskovsky's finances were still very straitened, and even though he found living in the family apartment increasingly trying, he could not afford to move out. His income from composing was negligible: his efforts to interest publishers in his compositions had led only to the acceptance of a single song, 'Sonnet of Michelangelo', by Éditions Russes de Musique, the publishing house founded by Serge Koussevitzky and his wife Natalie in 1909.[26] And while the Moscow premiere of *Silence* had been an encouraging start, further performance opportunities had yet to present themselves. Apart from Saradzhev, he had no professional contacts who were prepared to exert themselves on his behalf: there was certainly little prospect of any help from Lyadov, and he was temperamentally incapable of acting on his brother-in-law Vasiliy Yakovlev's advice to try to ingratiate himself with Sabaneyev and the circle of musicians running the Moscow branch of the Russian Musical Society.[27]

He was by no means the only conservatoire composition graduate in this position: Asafiev was so discouraged by his unpromising career prospects that he considered giving up composing altogether and took a post as rehearsal pianist for the Mariinsky ballet company in order to have a reliable source of income.[28] When it came to earning money, Myaskovsky had fewer options open to him than his classmates, as he was neither a proficient instrumentalist nor a conductor. He taught students at home and at a

24 'Vïpiski', 21 October 1910, 22 June and 16 August 1911, RGALI, 2040/1/65, l. 30b.

25 Yakiv Akimenko to Myaskovsky, 19 June 1911, RGALI, 2040/1/89, l. 22; Myaskovsky to Asafiev, 24 July 1911, RGALI, 2658/1/645, l. 37ob.

26 Notwithstanding the title, the song is not a setting of a sonnet, but of Michelangelo's celebrated epigram about his sculpture *Night* ('Caro m'è 'l sonno, e più l'esser di sasso') in a translation by the Romantic poet Fyodor Tyutchev (1803–73). It was subsequently republished as op. 87/10 in the collection *Za mnogiye godï*.

27 Yakovlev to Myaskovsky, 8 August 1911, RGALI 2040/2/290 ll. 7–7ob.

28 Asafiev to Myaskovsky, 12 July 1911, in Kozlova, 'Iz perepiski B. V. Asaf'yeva i N. Ya. Myaskovskogo [Part 2]', *Sovetskaya muzïka*, 12 (1979), 95–7; Asaf'yev, 'O sebe', 466.

private music school[29], but found his earnings insufficient. In October 1908, he applied for a supernumerary clerical post at the Imperial Chancellery.[30] As was customary, supernumeraries did not receive a salary but could apply for a salaried position once a suitable vacancy arose: this exploitative system required one to take an unpaid job in the hope of eventually securing a paid one. (In the event, Myaskovsky had to wait almost five years.) He presumably saw a civil service post as the best way to ensure a modicum of financial security while he sought to establish himself as a professional composer. The problem, however, was that his duties were not only tedious but also time-consuming. He increasingly resented having to divert his best energies from composition – especially as ideas for other projects were pressing on his attention. In February 1911 he noted in his diary plans for a symphonic poem based on Percy Bysshe Shelley's *Alastor* and three further symphonies to follow the Second – a 'tragic' Third Symphony, the projected *Cosmogony* Symphony as the Fourth, and a 'light' Fifth Symphony.[31] For the foreseeable future, however, composing would have to be fitted into whatever spare time remained at his disposal.

Mounting frustration with the professional circumstances in which young composers had to operate (and, indeed, with the state of St Petersburg's musical life more generally) was undoubtedly the primary motivation for Myaskovsky's foray into journalism between 1911 and 1914 – an unexpected development which came about through his contact with Derzhanovsky. In 1910, Derzhanovsky realised a long-standing ambition to found an independent music periodical, having finally managed to accumulate sufficient capital for the venture and secured the backing of the liberal newspaper *Russian Morning News* (*Utro Rossii*), which allowed him to use its printing press. (Derzhanovsky was the paper's chief music critic and its founder, the merchant Pavel Ryabushinsky, was very supportive of him.[32]) The first issue of *Music* (*Muzïka*) came out on 27 November 1910. In his editorial, Derzhanovsky was at pains to emphasise the new journal's seriousness of intent:

> Seeing in music, as in the other arts, one of the highest manifestations of cultural life, the editors of this weekly periodical will aim to show support for everything that promotes the growth and wider dissemina-

29   The music school in question remains unidentified. Ikonnikov records Myaskovsky's employment as commencing in the autumn of 1911 ('N. Ya. Myaskovskiy: Biograficheskiy ocherk', 26), but Myaskovsky recalled starting in 1908: Myaskovskiy, 'Avtobiograficheskiye zametki', 8.

30   Myaskovsky's application, dated 24 October 1908, is preserved in RGIA, 1409/11/33, l. 7.

31   'Vïpiski', 8 February 1911, RGALI, 2040/1/65, l. 30b.

32   Koposova-Derzhanovskaya, 'V. V. Derzhanovskiy po vospominaniyam zhenï i druga', RNMM, 3/3365, ll. 26.

tion of musical culture in society. And conversely, the editors will seek to combat whatever is inimical to the free development of musical art. Holding the concept of culture to be inextricably bound up with the notion of continuity, *Music*'s editors will combine their quest for the new with a love and respect for the past.[33]

Keeping *Music* going proved a constant challenge, even for someone of Derzhanovsky's practical resourcefulness and remarkable verbal fluency: the enterprise relied largely on the good will and idealism of a small circle of enthusiasts. His wife provided secretarial assistance and helped with translations; the contributors, with few exceptions, were unpaid. Printing and engraving costs absorbed most of the revenue generated by sales and advertising. In spite of its modest circulation, *Music* quickly gained a reputation for its interesting content and impressive breadth of coverage. In addition to reviews of concerts and new books on music, it featured lengthy opinion pieces, extended articles on Russian and foreign composers and their work, analytical and theoretical essays, and even verse by contemporary poets (amongst them Valery Bryusov and Fyodor Sologub) that was potentially suitable for musical setting. It was also a visually pleasing publication, being handsomely brought out. Over the five-and-a-half years of its existence, it significantly enriched contemporary Russian writing on music and did much to support younger native composers – though this was only grudgingly acknowledged in Soviet reference works, which as late as the 1970s continued to criticise *Music* for publishing 'modernist attacks on progressive realistic art'.[34]

Derzhanovsky was always on the lookout for new contributors and after meeting Myaskovsky invited him to write a report on the St Petersburg musical scene. Myaskovsky responded with a review of the annual summer concerts at Pavlovsk, a town located about twenty miles south of the city which grew up around Pavlovsk Palace, one of the most important imperial residences. Pavlovsk had been a fashionable summer retreat for the wealthy and a popular destination for day trips since the advent of rail travel: the line between Pavlovsk and St Petersburg was the first to be laid in Russia, opening in 1838. The spacious hall constructed adjacent to the station in the same year was the first permanent custom-built venue for orchestral performances in the country; the concerts held there had considerable cachet, being the principal focus of the capital's musical life during the summer months, and regularly featured internationally renowned soloists of the calibre of Sophie Menter and Eugène Ysaÿe.[35] Myaskovsky's article,

33   'Ot redaktsii', *Muzïka*, 27 November 1910, 5.

34   'Derzhanovskiy, V. V.', in Yuriy Keldïsh *et al.* (ed.), *Muzïkal'naya èntsiklopediya*, vol. 1 (Moscow, 1973), 201.

35   See Aleksandr Rozanov, *Muzïkal'nïy Pavlovsk* (Leningrad, 1978).

which appeared in the issue of 20 August 1911 under the heavily ironic title 'Provincial Chronicle', must have raised quite a few eyebrows: his scathing account of the mediocre performance standards and meretricious nature of some of the music programmed made for bracing reading. His comments about the concert's musical director Alexander Aslanov[36], a junior staff conductor at the Mariinsky Theatre, bordered on the libellous, characterising him as a talentless nonentity who owed his success to obsequious toadying and an obliging readiness to feature the amateur compositional efforts of the city's music critics and various influential patrons.[37] Amongst these modest talents was the secretary of state in charge of the Imperial Chancellery, Alexander Taneyev, second cousin once removed of the more famous Sergey – a circumstance that may have imparted an additional asperity to the review's tone. As was the practice at the period, the reviewer's identity was not disclosed: the piece was signed merely 'N. Ya.', which was just as well, since it would have been found highly offensive.[38]

Its principled stance certainly made an impression on Derzhanovsky, who discovered that Myaskovsky's reserved and shy manner concealed a passionate nature, capable of being roused to strong emotions over matters which concerned him deeply. Although his criticisms of the Pavlovsk concerts could have been expressed in a more temperate fashion, he was not merely indulging in gratuitous invective: his review reflected an idealistic young man's indignation at Aslanov's cynical careerism and abdication of his responsibility to uphold artistic standards. His writing, moreover, was lively and engaging, showing a talent for the arresting turn of phrase – precisely the kind of thing that could help to boost *Music*'s reputation and readership. When Myaskovsky contacted him again in the late autumn to report on progress with orchestrating the Second Symphony (which he hoped that Saradzhev might agree to perform) and to relay the news that Prokofiev had sketched a one-act opera entitled *Maddalena*, Derzhanovsky seized the opportunity to ask if he would become a regular contributor. 'I absolutely beg you not to refuse my plea', he wrote. 'Write about whatever you want, however you want'.[39] In his characteristically diffident reply, Myaskovsky promised to help as best he could but expressed doubt that he had sufficient aptitude for the task. He enclosed a piece on Stravinsky's ballet *The Firebird*, based on his perusal of the recently published piano

36   On Aslanov, see 'Aleksandr Petrovich Aslanov', *Novoye russkoye slovo*, 10 October 1954.

37   'Letopis' provintsii', *Muzika*, 20 August 1911, 778–81.

38   Myaskovsky's authorship is confirmed by Derzhanovskaya: see 'Pamyati druga', 203.

39   Myaskovsky to Derzhanovsky, 26 September 1911, RNMM, 3/237; Derzhanovsky to Myaskovsky, 27 September 1911, RNMM, 71/98.

reduction, telling Derzhanovsky that he could do with it as he saw fit: 'cut it, chop and change it, print it, or tear it up'. He went on to warn that he would only continue writing for *Music* if Derzhanovsky did not try to force him to accept payment.[40] Expressing his 'boundless happiness' that Myaskovsky had acquiesced, Derzhanovsky frankly admitted to feeling relief on learning Myaskovsky's terms: much as he wished matters were otherwise, he could not afford to remunerate contributors. He did, however, offer to pay Myaskovsky an allowance of ten to fifteen roubles a month to cover the cost of buying tickets when no complimentary ones were provided, and stipulated that he could keep most of the scores sent to him for review. He concluded with some succinct advice on how to approach writing contributions: 'Avoid long phrases and sentences: readers dislike them. As far as everything else is concerned, just be yourself, and may Allah deliver you from the deadly sins of reviewers' clichés and the urge to write like a seasoned professional'.[41]

Myaskovsky's appreciative review of *The Firebird*, which appeared in the 8 October issue[42], elaborated his admiring comments about the work in letters to Prokofiev and Asafiev.[43] He had high praise for Stravinsky's 'inexhaustible inventiveness' and his technical mastery (especially of orchestration), though he found the score somewhat derivative and lacking 'a vividly expressed individuality' – an observation which was by no means unjust. The two men were not acquainted, so Myaskovsky's generous appraisal was entirely dispassionate: it certainly suggests not the slightest hint of jealousy of Stravinsky's sudden fame, which had been further boosted by the triumphant premiere of *Petrushka* in Paris the previous June.

From November 1911, Myaskovsky began to write regularly for *Music* and would continue to do so until late 1914, although his contributions became more intermittent from 1913. All told, they comprised eighteen substantial reports on concert activity in the capital (mostly published under the title 'Letters from St Petersburg'), six essays, and over eight dozen reviews of recently published scores, ranging in length from a sentence or two to pieces of five hundred words or more.[44] As Myaskovsky was already complaining of overwork, the question arises why he decided to assume such a burdensome commitment. He was evidently not motivated by financial considerations

40 Myaskovsky to Derzhanovsky, 1 October 1911, RNMM, 3/238.

41 Derzhanovsky to Myaskovsky, 2 November 1911, RNMM, 71/99

42 'Ig. Stravinskiy "Zhar-ptitsa", skazka-balet dlya fortepiano v dve ruki', *Muzïka*, 8 October 1911, 970–2.

43 Myaskovsky to Prokofiev, 23 June 1911, in Kozlova and Yatsenko, *Perepiska*, 93; Myaskovsky to Asafiev, 24 June 1911, RGALI, 2658/1/645, ll. 37–370b.

44 Myaskovsky's contributions to *Muzïka* were collected in Shlifshteyn (ed.), *N. Ya. Myaskovskiy: Sobraniye materialov*, vol. 2, 21–203.

and had little interest in journalism or music criticism per se. The most plausible explanation, to judge from the contributions themselves, is that he saw writing for *Music* as an opportunity to raise important issues about the current state of musical life and to champion the work of young Russian composers. His choice of pseudonym, 'Misanthrope', most likely a private allusion to his father's characterisation of his nature as 'misanthropic'[45], was of itself indicative of his markedly negative attitude towards many aspects of his professional environment. It could more aptly be described as a *nom de guerre* than a *nom de plume*, given the combative tone of many of his articles. (Derzhanovsky was enjoined to strict secrecy about Misanthrope's identity, as Myaskovsky feared that its public disclosure could damage his job prospects in the Chancellery.[46])

Aside from its value as an account of contemporary musical activity, Myaskovsky's journalism reveals much about his artistic outlook and aesthetic orientation, as well as his tastes and sympathies during a formative period.[47] It also sheds light on his own creative preoccupations, which even at this early stage focussed almost exclusively on orchestral and chamber music: he declined to review stage works, telling Derzhanovsky that they did not interest him.[48] The 'Letters from St Petersburg' mostly deal with the three main series of professional orchestral concerts in the capital – those organised by the local branch of the Russian Musical Society, for which Vasiliy Safonov acted as principal conductor between 1910 and 1913; the Alexander Siloti concerts; and the concerts given by the double-bass virtuoso turned conductor Serge Koussevitzky, with the orchestra that he had founded in 1909.[49] Although Myaskovsky was never niggardly with praise when it was justified, much of what he heard clearly irked him. He had high

45 Yakov referred to his son's 'inclination to misanthropic solitude' in a letter to him of 27 March 1903: RGALI, 2040/1/134, l. 54.

46 Myaskovsky to Derzhanovsky, 14 November 1911, RNMM, 3/239.

47 For Russian-language discussions of Myaskovsky's musical journalism, see particularly: Semyon Shlifshteyn, 'Myaskovskiy-kritik', in Shlifshteyn (ed.), *Myaskovskiy: Sobraniye materialov*, vol. 1, 103–27; Oleg Belogrudov, *N. Ya. Myaskovskiy – Kritik* (Moscow, 1989). Both offer useful overviews, but neither, in the opinion of the present writer, brings Myaskovsky's dominant concerns and aesthetic standpoint into sufficiently clear focus.

48 Myaskovsky to Derzhanovsky, 14 November 1911, RNMM, 3/239.

49 For a useful overview of orchestral concert activity in St Petersburg at this period, see Lev Raaben, 'Kontsertnaya zhizn'', in Aleksandr Alekseyev *et al.* (ed.), *Russkaya khudozhestvennaya kul'tura kontsa XIX-nachala XX veka (1908–1917). Kniga tret'ya: Zrelishchnïye iskusstva, muzïka* (Moscow, 1977), 449–55. On the Siloti concerts, see Lev Raaben (ed.), *Aleksandr Il'ich Ziloti, 1863–1945: Vospominaniya i pis'ma* (Leningrad, 1963), 20–5; Charles F. Barber, *Lost in the Stars: The Forgotten Musical Life of Alexander Siloti* (Lanham, Maryland, 2002), 109–63. On the Koussevitzky Orchestra concerts, see Viktor Yuzefovich, *Sergey Kusevitskiy*, vol. 1, *Russkiye godï* (Moscow, 2004), 215–76.

regard for Siloti as a pianist but thought him an ineffectual conductor and was very critical of the sloppiness and lack of rhythmic precision of the orchestral playing under his direction. Koussevitzky struck him as a poseur and he found his interpretations often superficial and ill-considered.[50] He faulted the concert programmes of all three series (and especially those of the Russian Musical Society concerts, which were very conservative) for their lack of enterprise and for including music of questionable value by contemporary foreign composers while largely ignoring work by Russians. As he pointed out, the dearth of opportunities for younger composers to hear their orchestral scores performed presented a significant impediment to their professional development.[51]

Throughout his time writing for *Music*, one of his principal aims was to highlight significant creative achievements by native composers and to combat the widespread tendency 'to make a big fuss about everything foreign, but with typical Russian vandalism to reject everything home-grown', as he remarked in a letter to Derzhanovsky.[52] This statement is revealing, and confirms the marked divergence in his outlook from that of the organisers of the St Petersburg 'Modern Music Evenings'. Stravinsky was by no means the only Russian composer to earn his praise. Of figures active at the period, he not only deemed Skryabin to be the most gifted but regarded him for a time as the greatest of all living composers: reviewing a performance of the *Poem of Ecstasy* in 1912, he asked rhetorically whether anyone else could bear comparison with 'such a whirlwind of titanic creative power'.[53] He wrote respectfully and insightfully about other contemporaries, from established figures such as Balakirev, Glazunov, Taneyev, and Rachmaninoff to those of a younger generation such as Maximilian Steinberg, Grigory and Alexander Kreyn, Mikhail Gnesin, and Nikolai Tcherepnin. His responses were by no means blandly uncritical, but his desire to be supportive was never in doubt: when works aroused his interest, he took pains to write lengthy, carefully considered accounts of them. They evinced an open-minded attitude not only in matters of style and compositional approach, but in other respects too – as demonstrated by his complimentary reviews of music by the St Petersburg composer Julia Weissberg (1879–1942), which appraised it entirely on its own terms, without reference to her gender.[54]

50 See, for example, 'Peterburgskiye pis'ma', *Muzïka*, 27 October 1912, 907–11; and 16 November 1913, 773–8.

51 'Peterburgskiye pis'ma', *Muzïka*, 5 November 1911, 1080–1; and 3 December 1911, 1197–9.

52 Myaskovsky to Derzhanovsky, 14 November 1911, RNMM, 3/239.

53 'Peterburgskiye pis'ma', *Muzïka*, 10 November 1912, 973.

54 See, for example, 'Peterburgskiye pis'ma', *Muzïka*, 27 October 1912, 907–11. Myaskovsky remained supportive of Weissberg subsequently: see Marina

He was open to innovation and keenly appreciative of work that struck him as fresh and original: an excellent case in point is his essay on *Petrushka*, which energetically defended Stravinsky against accusations of vulgarity for employing popular urban songs and emphasised the score's inventiveness and sparkling humour.[55] At the same time, he was no advocate of novelty for novelty's sake. Reviewing a group of Ivanov settings by Gnesin, he praised Gnesin's renunciation of his previously 'convulsed' harmonic language in favour of a more diatonic idiom which was piquant and even astringent, but without sounding contrived.[56]

He had little patience with pretentiousness, technical ineptitude, or routine academicism, which elicited his sharpest critical comments. In a blistering review of a Russian Musical Society concert of music by Alexander Vishnegradsky (the father of Ivan Wyschnegradsky, the pioneer of microtonal composition), Rimsky-Korsakov's student Witold Maliszewski, and Balakirev's protégé Sergei Lyapunov, he remarked caustically that 'if one were not aware of the background factors shaping the programmes of these concerts, one would imagine that musical creativity in St Petersburg was in short supply'.[57] Why perform dull assemblages of conservatoire clichés by Rimsky-Korsakov epigones such as Vasily Kalafati, he wondered, when you could play interesting music by Stravinsky, Tcherepnin, or Steinberg?[58] Of Mikhail Ippolitov-Ivanov's recently completed First Symphony in E minor (1908), he wrote: 'Forty years ago, this symphony's appearance would have surprised no-one: only the complacency of an inveterate graphomaniac can explain its emergence now. . . . Its draughtsmanship is simple and straightforward, making the score suitable for performance on open-air stages at summer spa resorts, but in the interests of the spa-frequenting public – heaven forbid. The symphony is designated 'No. 1'. Are there really going to be more?!'[59]

In general, however, he displayed greater forbearance towards the shortcomings of music by native composers than by foreign ones. While it would be unfair to describe Myaskovsky as a chauvinist in musical matters, when it came to contemporary composition from the West his outlook had more in common with that of Rimsky-Korsakov than he might have cared to admit. Reading through his contributions to *Music*, it is interesting to note just

Mazur, 'Perepiska Yu. Veyzberg s N. Myaskovskim', *Vestnik Akademii russkogo baleta imeni A. Ya. Vaganovoy*, 2 (2018), 104–12.

55 '*Petrushka*, balet Ig. Stravinskogo', *Muzïka*, 14 January 1912, 72–5.

56 'M. Gnesin. Soch. 10. *Posvyashcheniya*', *Muzïka*, 16 February 1913, 127.

57 'Peterburgskiye pis'ma', *Muzïka*, 11 February 1912, 180–1.

58 'Peterburgskiye pis'ma', *Muzïka*, 14 April 1913, 267–70.

59 'M. Ippolitov-Ivanov. Op. 46. Simfoniya No. 1 e-moll dlya orkestra', *Muzïka*, 16 February 1913, 127.

how few foreign composers excited his wholehearted admiration. His attitude to most French music, for example, was at best equivocal – he thought
Ravel an overrated minor talent and generally had scant praise for the work
of prominent figures such as Jean Roger-Ducasse and Florent Schmitt (he
dismissed the latter's *La tragédie de Salomé* as 'insipid and boring beyond
belief').[60] Reger's work received short shift and he suggested that it would
be better if Mahler's 'talentless windbaggery' remained behind the Austrian
frontier.[61] A concert of 'prattle' (*lepet*) by Albéniz and other Spanish composers provoked a particularly irate review, in which he again lamented the
neglect of music by young composers from Russia and neighbouring Slav
countries.[62] Privately, he complained to Derzhanovsky about the damage
that Siloti's promotion of 'foreign muck' (*zagranichnaya dryan'*) was doing
to Russian music.[63] It is important to contextualise these pronouncements,
while not ignoring their flagrant bias: one would have little difficulty finding abundant examples of negative critical responses to foreign music elsewhere in Europe at this period. (One thinks of the hostility towards German
music voiced by a range of French composers, from Saint-Saëns to Milhaud,
for example.) Myaskovsky's verdicts suggest a strong influence of Slavophile
intellectual traditions, which viewed Western culture with ambivalence and
held that Russia's development should proceed independently of Europe,
following a path shaped by its distinctive national character and history.
Antagonistic appraisals of foreign music which impugned it for its supposed decadence and nugatory artistic value originated long before Soviet
cultural propaganda.

   And it was precisely on these grounds that Myaskovsky's objections
rested. Although he never formulated his opinions on the subject in systematic fashion, it is readily evident from his reviews that he held a very
exalted view of the nature and purpose of artistic creation, shaped to some
extent by the ethos of the symbolist movement and ultimately derived from
German Romanticism. He had stringent expectations not only in regard
of the technical competence that musical works should exhibit, but also
their content. There were strict limits to the kinds of emotional experience
that he considered worthy of musical embodiment: these were predominantly serious in nature and demanded a correspondingly elevated style. If
a work's content struck him as vacuous, it would elicit severe censure for

---

60   See 'Peterburgskiye pis'ma', *Muzïka*, 19 November 1911, 1147–9, and 1 March
     1914, 192–6; 'Florent Schmitt. Op. 50bis. *La tragédie de Salomé*, version
     choréographique', *Muzïka*, 9 November 1913, 755–6.

61   'Peterburgskiye pis'ma', *Muzïka*, 28 January 1912, 131–3, and 23 February 1913,
     137–40.

62   'Peterburgskiye pis'ma', *Muzïka*, 3 December 1911, 1197–9.

63   Myaskovsky to Derzhanovsky, 30 December 1913, RNMM, 3/331.

its 'vulgarity', 'banality', or 'triviality'. (For this reason, he was highly critical of Mahler's employment of intentionally banal musical material, which he considered inappropriate in a symphonic context.[64]) His frequent recourse to such epithets echoes the prose style of Vyacheslav Karatïgin[65], whose writings exerted a strong influence on his outlook.

Myaskovsky judged contemporary music from the West against these lofty standards and found most of it wanting. The stridency with which he expressed his views is explained by his desire to counter assumptions that foreign music was inherently superior solely by virtue of being foreign. Only two foreign composers received his unstinting respect. One was Debussy, whom he described as 'one of the most subtle and profound poets of modernity', deeming his work 'the quintessence of refinement'.[66] His love of Debussy's music endured: a diary entry from 1934 records his pleasure in hearing a performance of *La mer*, which he deemed 'the finest score in the world'.[67] He was equally admiring of the music of Schoenberg, a composer about whom Viktor Belyayev had aroused his curiosity[68] and whose work was starting to come to attention in Russia around this time.[69] (The first known Russian performance of a score by Schoenberg was given by Prokofiev, who played the *Drei Klavierstücke*, op. 11, at one of the St Petersburg 'Evenings' in 1911.[70]) On becoming acquainted with his compositions, he declared Schoenberg 'an amazing artist' and hailed his resolute eschewal of creative compromise. Reviewing a performance of *Pelleas und Melisande* in 1913, he wrote approvingly: 'This is music in which one does not sense the slightest attempt to ingratiate itself with either commoners (the *demos*) or connoisseurs', and went on to praise the 'iron logic' of the

---

64 See, for example, his review of Mahler's Seventh Symphony, a score that 'incensed' him, as he admitted to Derzhanovsky: 'Peterburgskiye pis'ma', *Muzïka*, 19 January 1913, 54–8; Myaskovsky to Derzhanovsky, 10 January 1913, RNMM, 3/274.

65 See Ol'ga Dansker (ed.), *V. G. Karatïgin: Izbrannïye stat'i* (Moscow and Leningrad, 1965), 16.

66 'Peterburgskiye pis'ma', 16 November 1913, 776.

67 Entry for 24 November 1934, 'Vïpiski', RGALI, 2040/1/65, l. 19.

68 Belyayev discussed Schoenberg's work in two letters to Myaskovsky dated 21 August 1912 and 13 July 1913: RGALI, 2040/1/100, ll. 27–80b and 44–440b.

69 On the early history of Schoenberg reception in Russia, see Arkadiy Klimovitskiy, '"Lyudi dolzhnï znat', chtó ya khochu skazat'!!": Arnol'd Shyonberg v Peterburge', *Muzïkal'naya akademiya*, 4–5 (1995), 166–74 and 1 (1996), 217–21 (two-part article); and Natal'ya Vlasova, 'A. Shyonberg v Rossii: Iz istorii vospriyatiya', in Yekaterina Vlasova and Yelena Sorokina (ed.) *Naslediye: Russkaya muzïka – Mirovaya kul'tura* (Moscow, 2009), 56–96.

70 Prokofiev discussed the concert in his diary, but did not record the date: it appears to have taken place in March or April 1911. *Dnevnik 1907–1918*, 158–9.

score's structural organisation, its 'nobility in all particulars' and 'stupendously virtuosic' technical command.[71]

The music of Schoenberg and Debussy represented an artistic ideal for Myaskovsky and his discussions of it shed much light on his own aspirations. In this respect, perhaps the most revealing of his contributions to *Music* was an essay entitled 'Tchaikovsky and Beethoven', which he wrote in 1912 at Derzhanovsky's repeated urging.[72] In this piece, he challenged the condescending views of Tchaikovsky that were then commonplace[73], which he declared a regrettable result of 'indiscriminate, servile adulation of everything foreign', and offered a radical reappraisal of Tchaikovsky's significance, making the remarkable claim that he had been responsible for the instauration of the Western symphonic tradition after a protracted decline following Beethoven's death. Employing rhetoric unmistakably influenced by Slavophile convictions of Russia's predestined mission to revitalise a degenerating Western culture, he contended that Tchaikovsky's achievement not only demonstrated Russia's centrality to the future evolution of the genre but also adumbrated his homeland's impending pre-eminence in international musical life. As the genre of the symphony already dominated Myaskovsky's compositional preoccupations, his ambition to lead this development is readily apparent – especially as he published the article under his own name.

Also evident is the extent of his personal identification with Tchaikovsky, to whom he ascribed character traits decidedly reminiscent of his own – a 'melancholic temperament' caused by mysterious factors to which he makes veiled allusion but refrains from discussing (presumably Tchaikovsky's sexuality); disdain for the crowd and a craving for solitude 'bordering on misanthropy'; impatience with quotidian concerns as a vexing distraction from artistic creation. The music composed by artists of this kind, he averred, was imbued with an 'incandescent spirituality' that lent it exceptional communicative potency: 'For people with a wonderfully developed sensitivity of thought and feeling, who are responsive to the most varied external impressions of an aesthetic as well as of a speculative and ethical order, given their aforementioned inclination to solitude, isolation, and self-absorption,

---

71   'Peterburgskiye pis'ma', *Muzïka*, 19 January 1913, 57–8.

72   'Chaykovskiy i Betkhoven', *Muzïka*, 16 May 1912, 431–40. Myaskovsky's plan to write an essay portraying Tchaikovsky as a 'Russian Beethoven' is discussed in Derzhanovsky to Myaskovsky, 12 and 16 March 1912, RNMM, 71/105 and 71/106; Myaskovsky to Derzhanovsky, 14 and 19 March 1912, RNMM, 3/246 and 3/247.

73   On this subject, see Iosif Rayskin's informative essay 'Artisticheskiy vostorg i issledovatel'skaya glubina: N. Myaskovskiy o Chaykovskom-simfoniste, ' in Oleg Kolovskiy (ed.), *Kritika i muzïkoznaniye: Sbornik statey*, vyp. 2 (Leningrad, 1980), 207–16.

it is natural that they should accumulate in their souls reserves of the most profound emotions, the artistic manifestation of which cannot but prove infectious'. At its most highly developed, Myaskovsky held the symphony to constitute a 'living revelation of the inner emotional experiences' of such exceptional beings – their joys and sorrows; their will to persist in the face of indifference, incomprehension or hostility; their struggles with an ineluctable Fate.

In another remarkable passage, he discusses Skryabin as an artist of a comparable greatness whose work offered profound insights into the nature of existence and intimated ultimate truths:

> By means of a completely new and unprecedented [musical] language, he opens up for us such extraordinary emotional perspectives which are not yet even capable of being brought into consciousness, such heights of spiritual enlightenment, that he grows in our eyes to a phenomenon of world importance in comparison with which Beethoven seems almost of local significance. ... Skryabin's music is completely devoid of any local colouring; accordingly, as time goes on, his work becomes more spiritually inspired to the point of being almost metaphysical, and in consequence, it inevitably becomes universal.

Myaskovsky evidently considered 'local colouring' to limit the wider significance of musical creativity and regarded its absence from the compositions of Skryabin as a crucial determinant of their universality. His own work from this period has no recourse either to folk music or the exotic coloration that had long since become a conventional signifier of 'Russianness', which suggests that he aspired to a comparable universality of utterance and internationalism of style. Although his encounter with Skryabin's music was undeniably important in shaping his aesthetic outlook, there is little evidence of direct stylistic influence: Myaskovsky's youthful compositions inhabit a sound-world far removed from the voluptuousness of the older man's mature scores and explore very different realms of emotional experience. In view of Myaskovsky's austere treatment of instrumental sonority in much of his work at this period, it is interesting that he praised elsewhere the music of Nikolay Medtner precisely for its lack of vivid colouring or picturesque qualities.[74] Unlike his admiration for Tchaikovsky, however, his enthusiasm for Skryabin quickly cooled, yielding to an attitude of detachment and scepticism.

Despite its hyperbole, 'Tchaikovsky and Beethoven' is of considerable interest – and not merely from a biographical perspective but also for what it reveals about contemporary Russian imaginings of the composer and musical creativity. Myaskovsky's view has much in common with

---

74 'N. Metner. Vpechatleniya ot yego tvorcheskogo oblika', *Muzïka*, 2 March 1913, 148–57.

Schoenberg's heroic self-envisioning as well as that of Skryabin. Once more, it demonstrates that characteristic tropes of Soviet music criticism, and especially forceful assertions of the artistic supremacy of Russian musical traditions, were already current in the pre-Revolutionary period. And last, but not least, Myaskovsky's essay is an important document in the history of Russian Tchaikovsky reception: his courageous defence of Tchaikovsky at a time when the latter's critical standing was low caused quite a stir, as he informed Asafiev.[75]

Reactions of this kind did much to enhance *Music*'s reputation as a journal with lively and thought-provoking content. Derzhanovsky was keenly appreciative of Myaskovsky's efforts and the two men's growing frequency of professional contact led to a rapid deepening of intimacy. Before long, they were exchanging letters at least once a week.[76] Derzhanovsky increasingly assumed the role of a confidant with whom Myaskovsky discussed his creative work and day-to-day concerns. He had a shrewd understanding of his friend's anxieties and vulnerabilities, many of them caused by setting himself standards of achievement so stringent as to be paralysing. On reading their correspondence, one is repeatedly struck by Myaskovsky's self-deprecating comments about his compositions. In letters from late 1911, for example, he dismissed his recently composed cello sonata as 'sugary water' and wrote apologetically about its 'retrograde' musical idiom; he was equally disparaging about his songs, which he described as being 'of null significance'.[77] Needless to say, such remarks should not be taken at face value. Derzhanovsky evidently understood what prompted Myaskovsky to make them – an uncertainty about his own abilities which was so inhibiting as to prevent him from making any attempt to promote his compositions. Even though he was desperately short of money, as he admitted to Derzhanovsky in a letter of early 1912 (he had given up his private students but his chancellery work was still unpaid, though consuming increasing amounts of his time), he hesitated to submit his scores to publishers because he feared committing to print anything that might be less than perfect.[78] Derzhanovsky did his best to talk sense into him, urging him to compromise and overcome his scruples. He gave useful practical advice on how to approach negotiations and sought to smooth Myaskovsky's path

75   Myaskovsky to Asafiev, 21 May 1912, RGALI, 2658/1/636, ll. 20b–3.

76   Over six hundred items of correspondence are preserved in their respective
     personal archives in the Russian National Museum of Music, mostly dating
     from the period between 1911 and 1918. An additional twelve letters from
     Derzhanovsky to Myaskovsky are preserved in RGALI, 2040/1/114.

77   Myaskovsky to Derzhanovsky, 1 October, 5 December, and 11 December 1911,
     RNMM, 3/238, 240, and 241.

78   Myaskovsky to Derzhanovsky, 31 January and 5 February 1912, RNMM, 3/243
     and 244.

by writing a recommendation to the Moscow branch of the Zimmermann firm.[79] Nonetheless, Myaskovsky found dealing with publishers an ordeal and his fragile self-confidence made it more difficult to overcome setbacks. When Zimmermann declined to issue his piano works and dithered about accepting the Second Symphony, which had been completed in December 1911[80], Myaskovsky withdrew from the discussions in high dudgeon. Although he claimed to have swiftly put the incident behind him, he declined to send on the manuscript of the Sinfonietta, op. 10, and told Derzhanovsky that he preferred to 'hide it away in a drawer', having decided that its first movement's main theme was 'too frivolous' and even 'vulgar'.[81] This highly attractive score would only be published posthumously.

There were a few signs of interest in his work, however, despite his self-defeating and impractical attitude. Éditions Russes de Musique agreed to bring out a new set of three Hippius settings[82] and *Three Sketches to Words by Vyacheslav Ivanov*, though their progress through the press proved very dilatory.[83] At the suggestion of Karatïgin, Aslanov agreed to conduct *Silence* at one of the forthcoming Pavlovsk concerts (he was presumably unaware of Myaskovsky's authorship of the scathing review of the 1911 season), but the performance eventually fell through for practical reasons to do with the very large orchestra required.[84] Saradzhev undertook to give the premiere of the Second Symphony in Moscow during the summer, though this concert too came close to being cancelled due to lack of funds. The symphony was also scored for augmented forces and Saradzhev had to assume liability for paying the additional personnel.[85]

In spite of his increasingly onerous workload, Myaskovsky managed to find time during the spring of 1912 to bring the cello sonata he had composed the previous summer into a final state and to complete another substantial keyboard work, Piano Sonata no. 2 in F-sharp minor, op. 13. The two sonatas are very different in character. Sonata no. 1 in D major for Cello and Piano, op. 12, has earned a place in the regular repertoire because

79　Derzhanovsky to Myaskovsky, 29 November 1911 and 4 March 1912, RNMM, 71/100 and 104.

80　Myaskovsky's diary records the date of completion as 9 December 1911: 'Vïpiski', RGALI, 2040/1/65, l. 30b.

81　Myaskovsky to Derzhanovsky, 22, 27, and 31 March and 23 April, RNMM, 3/248, 249, 250, and 252.

82　'Iz Z. N. Gippius', op. 5.

83　Myaskovsky to Derzhanovsky, 31 August and 19 December 1912, RNMM, 3/261 and 271. Both opuses were eventually published in 1913.

84　Myaskovsky to Derzhanovsky, 11 April and 8 August 1912, RNMM, 3/251 and 259.

85　Koposova-Derzhanovskaya, 'V. V. Derzhanovskiy po vospominaniyam zhenï i druga', RNMM, 3/3365, l. 31.

of its attractive lyricism and grateful writing for the stringed instrument. Myaskovsky described it to Derzhanovsky as an uncharacteristic work composed in a more conventional idiom as a gift for the Hofmann family, but this characterisation by no means does it justice. Its two-movement design is skilfully unified by the reintroduction of material from the slow ternary-form opening movement as a coda to the sonata-form second movement, effectively resolving the tensions generated through the interplay of the latter's sharply contrasted themes. Viewed in the context of Myaskovsky's output as a whole, it clearly adumbrates stylistic traits of his later music, especially in its piquant blending of chromaticism and diatonic modality. Piano Sonata no. 2, on the other hand, demonstrates little concern for surface appeal, compacting a turbulent drama into a terse single movement lasting twelve minutes – a sonata-form structure with a development section largely based on the opening phrase of the famous plainchant setting of the *Dies irae*.[86] Myaskovsky's treatment of this familiar melody is in no way redolent of hackneyed Romantic *diablerie* but creates a powerfully compelling oppressive and doom-laden atmosphere. It is subjected to further intensive development in the coda during a magnificently virtuosic contrapuntal build-up to the frenzied final climax. In a detailed and appreciative review published in 1916, Karatïgin rightly singled it out as being as 'one of the most interesting and substantial of all new Russian sonatas'.[87]

Few details of Myaskovsky's daily life at this period emerge from sources other than his correspondence with Derzhanovsky, and his diary entries virtually ceased for several years after 1911. The next significant event on his horizon was the premiere of the Second Symphony, for which he travelled down to Moscow in mid-June[88], spending a month there. Once again, he stayed with Saradzhev. As he reported back to Prokofiev, who was busy preparing for the Moscow premiere of his First Piano Concerto under Saradzhev's baton on 25 July, much of his time was taken up correcting the orchestral parts, which turned out to be in very poor order.[89] Nonetheless, the rehearsals went well, as did the premiere on 11 July, despite the concert venue's difficult acoustics. Myaskovsky presented Saradzhev afterwards with the manuscript of the symphony, which he inscribed with a dedication thanking him for his 'exceptionally insightful' rendering of the score.[90]

---

86   For a more detailed discussion of the sonata's formal organisation, see Yelena Dolinskaya, *Fortepiannoye tvorchestvo N. Ya. Myaskovskogo* (Moscow, 1980), 34–52.

87   Vyacheslav Karatïgin, 'N. Myaskovskiy. Sonata No. 2 fis-moll, dlya f[orte] p[iano]', *Muzïkal'nïy sovremennik*, vol. 2 (1916), 120.

88   Myaskovsky to Derzhanovsky, 1 June 1912, RNMM, 3/256.

89   Prokofiev to Myaskovsky, 15 June 1912 and Myaskovsky to Prokofiev, 6 July 1912, in Kozlova and Yatsenko, *Perepiska*, 101.

90   Tigranov, *Saradzhev*, 22.

In an article on Myaskovsky published in 1915, Asafiev aptly described Symphony no. 2 in C-sharp minor, op. 11 as exploring 'a desolate spiritual world, charged with impulsive outbursts, shudders, turmoil, and spasmodic urges to self-determination'.[91]. He hinted at an underlying conception very close to Myaskovsky's description in 'Tchaikovsky and Beethoven' of the symphony as a symbolic analogue to psychic processes, evoking the artist-hero's struggle for self-realisation:

> It is as if the composer wishes to grasp hold of something, looks for a basis on which to proceed, but everything around is unstable and precarious! Themes [in the first movement] signifying flight or transport inevitably encounter in their course a malicious, baleful motif which burgeons during the development into a powerful antagonistic force that suppresses the free unfolding of personality. The struggle yields at times to oblivion or doubt, or to contemplative immersion in nature (the pastoral theme in the slow movement), but never to rapture or self-content.

The Second Symphony defines a much more individual realm of psychological experience than its predecessor, even if its indebtedness to Tchaikovsky is readily discernible. (The opening six-eight theme of the first movement, shown in example 3.1, is clearly modelled on the analogous theme in Tchaikovsky's Fifth; and the employment of bass ostinati in the movement's coda also derives from the same source.) Once again, it is cast in a three-movement design of slightly more generous proportions than the First and is scored for a large orchestra with triple woodwind and an enlarged brass section. All of the movements are in sonata form, though featuring significant departures from textbook norms. The management of tonal relationships is considerably more imaginative than in the First Symphony: Myaskovsky experiments not only with presenting second subject groups in remote tonal areas but also with recapitulating themes in unexpected regions. Thus, the second subject of the slow movement is first heard in E-flat major, at the remove of a tritone from A minor, the principal tonality; and he obtains a powerful effect by commencing the recapitulation with a *fortissimo* statement of the first subject in E-flat minor on brass before switching abruptly to A minor for a *piano* restatement on divided strings accompanied by poignant new figurations in the woodwind. The formal organisation of all three movements is less than ideal, however. As in the First Symphony, Myaskovsky follows Tchaikovskian precedents: the second subject groups in the outer movements are in significantly slower tempi and are also quite lengthy. The satisfactory integration of such quasi-independent episodes into a sonata structure presents considerable technical challenges, especially with regard to the maintenance of

---

91   Igor' Glebov [Boris Asaf'yev], 'O tvorcheskom puti N. Myaskovskogo', *Muzïka*, 18 April 1915, 257–62.

EXAMPLE 3.1. Symphony no. 2, first movement: bars 3–9.

a taut symphonic argument. In the opening movements of his Fourth and Sixth Symphonies, Tchaikovsky solves the problem brilliantly through his management of the development sections, which not only comprise substantial unbroken spans of music in a quick tempo but also rise to violent climaxes that make the subsequent slowing down for the presentation of the second subjects in the recapitulation seem psychologically justified and necessary. Myaskovsky attempts a similar solution in his first movement, but the development section is insufficiently long to balance the expanse of the second subject group. The finale is even more problematic, because the development section never picks up speed. As a result, in a movement lasting over a quarter of an hour, some three-fifths of it unfolds at a slow pace – and this after a slow movement of comparable proportions. In consequence, the balance of slow to fast music over the work as a whole is disproportionate – a miscalculation that Tchaikovsky never perpetrates (the lengthy slow finale of the Sixth Symphony, for example, is preceded by two movements in unremittingly quick tempi).

This shortcoming is regrettable, because the symphony contains music of great distinction – especially in the powerful central movement, which rises to high points of searing intensity. Myaskovsky also demonstrates an impressive ability to integrate a wide range of contrasts over the work's course. Here, for the first time, he experiments with a device that is employed repeatedly in the later symphonies – generating dramatic tension from the interaction of highly disparate musical material. The opening theme of the finale is lent a restless, disruptive character by angular dissonant intervals, nervous syncopations, and a tonally elusive harmonisation[92]

92 The Soviet musicologist Vladimir Protopopov suggested that Myaskovsky's predilection for thematic material of this nature reflected the influence of Taneyev: see his essay 'O tematizme i melodike S. I. Taneyeva', *Sovetskaya muzïka*, 7 (1940), 49–60.

EXAMPLE 3.2. Symphony no. 2, finale: opening.

EXAMPLE 3.3. Symphony no. 2, finale: bars 107–12.

(ex. 3.2), for which the lyrical, predominantly diatonic second subject (ex. 3.3) acts as an effective foil. Its mood of muted resignation is not allowed to prevail when it returns in the tonic major in the recapitulation, being swept away by the impetuous coda, a passage of which Myaskovsky was particularly proud[93]: this brings the first subject and transition material to a new pitch of malevolent fury and culminates in a strident seven-note dissonance constructed of superimposed fourths that is brutally cut short at the movement's close, transcendence of the preceding conflicts having proved impossible. Writing to Asafiev a few days after the premiere, Myaskovsky informed him that the finale was received by the audience in baffled silence – which was perhaps unsurprising in view of its strange atmosphere and unexpected conclusion, but he found it a rather disconcerting experience. He acknowledged that the second and third movements were excessively long and that the orchestration was unsatisfactory in places, defects which

---

93   Myaskovsky to Asafiev, 24 June 1911, RGALI, 2658/1/635, l. 36.

he sought to remedy, though not altogether successfully, when he revised the score later in the year. Despite its shortcomings, the symphony marked an important stage in the crystallisation of his mature style.

Whatever Myaskovsky's private reservations, the work received laudatory reviews which spoke of him respectfully as a young composer of promise.[94] On the eve of his departure on 16 July, Derzhanovsky and Saradzhev arranged a farewell dinner at a local Caucasian restaurant – an enjoyable and high-spirited evening that left the attendees feeling decidedly the worse for wear the following day.[95] (Saradzhev could be very amusing company and was an excellent raconteur.[96]) Myaskovsky evidently felt at ease with both and valued their support – especially as he felt unable 'to count on receiving any in St Petersburg', as he told Derzhanovsky.[97] Saradzhev would remain a staunch champion of his work and subsequently premiered five more of his symphonies.

Soon after returning home, however, his sombre mood returned. He tried to rouse himself to purposeful activity by revising the Second Symphony, but in his letters to Derzhanovsky he repeatedly alluded to feeling in low spirits and even spoke of giving up composing altogether.[98] It is difficult to be certain of the underlying causes of his malaise, but it is evident that he was prone to depression and would periodically experience similar episodes throughout the remainder of his life. His crippling self-doubt and self-tormenting perfectionism were undoubtedly important factors (Myaskovsky's evaluations of his own work were generally far harsher than his verdicts about the work of others), and ones which probably explain a rather surprising development during his visit to Moscow – his decision to undertake further technical studies in composition.

While in Moscow, Myaskovsky was introduced to Boleslav Yavorsky, an acquaintance of the Derzhanovskys who had expressed interest in meeting him after reading about his work in *Music*. A native of Kharkov, Yavorsky (1877–1942) studied composition at the Moscow Conservatoire under Taneyev, to whom he became very close. After graduating in 1903, he continued to compose but chiefly gained renown as a music theorist and pianist. While still a student, Yavorsky began to develop on the basis of Taneyev's teachings an elaborate theory of the nature of music and the

94 Reproduced in Ol'ga Milovanova, *Ranneye tvorchestvo N. Ya. Myaskovskogo: Vzglyad sovremennikov. Materialï. Stat'i. Personalii.* (Moscow, 2017), 54–60.

95 Koposova-Derzhanovskaya, 'V. V. Derzhanovskiy po vospominaniyam zhenï i druga', RNMM, 3/3365, ll. 31–2.

96 See Yekaterina Koposova-Derzhanovskaya, 'Vospominaniya o druge i khudozhnike', in Tigranov, *Saradzhev*, 68–9.

97 Myaskovsky to Derzhanovsky, 11 December 1911, RNMM, 3/241.

98 Myaskovsky to Derzhanovsky, 26 July and 8 August 1912, RNMM, 3/258 and 259.

underlying universal 'laws' that supposedly governed melodic, harmonic, and formal organisation. This so-called theory of 'modal rhythm' (or 'musical thinking', to use the term Yavorsky preferred later in life) was intended to furnish an alternative to the work of German theorists such as Hugo Riemann, which he derided as arid scholasticism. Although he published little and displayed lifelong reluctance to present his thought in a systematic fashion, he attracted an admiring coterie of disciples. He was unquestionably an erudite man and his writings contain interesting insights, but his theory had many dubious aspects and some of his notions were downright eccentric: he claimed, for example, that Beethoven, Chopin, and other major figures had notated compositions with incorrect key signatures and inappropriate barring and note values due to their defective comprehension of modal rhythm.[99] Nonetheless, despite proving controversial, Yavorsky's ideas subsequently exerted an important influence on Soviet music analysis and aesthetics – especially his conception of music as a mode of speech.[100]

Myaskovsky's curiosity about Yavorsky's theory had been aroused by his own study of Taneyev's writings on counterpoint[101] and by his discussions with Viktor Belyayev of Yavorsky's first published formulation of his ideas – *The Construction of Musical Speech*, issued as a series of pamphlets in 1908. (Unsurprisingly, Belyayev complained of finding the text difficult to understand[102], as Yavorsky's elliptical exposition is at times highly obscure.) When they met, Myaskovsky showed Yavorsky the score of the Second Symphony and was sufficiently impressed by the acuity of his observations that he asked Yavorsky to initiate him into the principles of modal rhythm, hoping to derive some technical benefit from his instruction. For the next eighteen months, Myaskovsky kept in contact with him by post, sending exercises in voice leading and form that Yavorsky returned with corrections and

99   See Boleslav Yavorskiy, *Stroyeniye muzïkal'noy rechi. Materialï i zametki.* Chast' 3, otdel 2 (Moscow, 1908), 4–12.

100 Yavorsky is regarded as a major figure in Russia to this day, but his life and thought still await comprehensive critical reappraisal: a significant proportion of his writings remain unpublished and his extensive personal archive has yet to be systematically explored. For introductions to Yavorsky in English, see Gordon D. McQuere, 'The Theories of Boleslav Yavorsky', in idem (ed.), *Russian Theoretical Thought in Music* (Ann Arbor, Michigan, 1983), 109–64; Ellon DeGrief Carpenter, 'The Theory of Music in Russia and the Soviet Union, ca. 1650–1950' (unpublished dissertation, University of Pennsylvania, 1988), 450–519.

101 Myaskovsky alludes to studying Taneyev's *Moveable Counterpoint in the Strict Style* in a letter to Prokofiev of 12 August 1911 (Kozlova and Yatsenko, *Perepiska*, 98–9) and a diary entry of 16 August 1911, 'Vïpiski', RGALI, 2040/1/65, l. 30b.

102 Belyayev to Myaskovsky, RGALI 2040/1/99, ll. 24–90b.

comments.[103] None of this material has been preserved, so it is difficult to assess the extent to which his compositional approach may have changed under Yavorsky's tutelage. On the whole, his influence was probably not very significant. Myaskovsky grew increasingly sceptical of all theorising about music, and it is noteworthy that he disclaimed any detailed knowledge of Yavorsky's work when he wrote a statement in 1940 in support of a proposal to confer Yavorsky with a doctorate, while professing admiration for him as a musician.[104] To judge from what survives of their correspondence[105], the most valuable service that Yavorsky performed for Myaskovsky was to provide badly needed encouragement at a difficult time. He urged him to ignore unhelpful adverse comment about his work, pointing out that the standard of Russian music criticism was generally low, and exhorted him not to take rejection to heart: 'If Siloti wants to perform all kinds of insect-buzzings, that does not diminish the value of your compositions in the slightest'.[106] Two of his letters address one of the chief causes of Myaskovsky's creative inhibitions – an anxiety that his work was still immature. Yavorsky sensibly pointed out that composers learn from experience and that a premature striving for artistic maturity would only succeed in engendering stunted compositions like 'dwarves – with the stature of a child and the face of an old man'. He stressed the importance of accepting that aspects of the compositional process proceeded independently of conscious control and of not underestimating the value of youthful spontaneity.[107] Yavorsky also sought to be supportive in a practical way: the following spring, he gave the first performance of the Cello Sonata with the cellist Mikhail Bukinik at a concert of the Chamber Music Society in Moscow on 3 March.

Despite his talk of giving up composing, Myaskovsky remained steadily productive, though his letters to Derzhanovsky reiterated familiar complaints – money worries, persistently low spirits, and insufficient free

103 See Myaskovsky to Sergey Protopopov, 3 May 1944, reproduced in Izrail' Rabinovich (ed.), *B. Yavorskiy: Vospominaniya, stat'i i pis'ma* (Moscow, 1964), 488–9.

104 Ibid., 665–6.

105 Fifteen items of correspondence (twelve from Yavorsky, three from Myaskovsky) are preserved in Yavorsky's personal archive in RNMM and were published in the 1964 edition of Rabinovich, *Yavorskiy: Vospominaniya, stat'i i pis'ma*. (Three of these letters were omitted from the revised 1972 edition: all subsequent references, unless otherwise stated, are to the first edition.) A further three communications from Yavorsky are preserved in RGALI, 2040/2/287.

106 See Yavorsky to Myaskovsky, 29 July and 5 and 14 August 1912, in Rabinovich, *Yavorskiy: Vospominaniya, stat'i i pis'ma*, 491–7.

107 Yavorsky to Myaskovsky, 14 August and 7 September 1912, ibid., 495–501.

time.[108] He continued to contribute to *Music*, though with diminishing eagerness (in his lone diary entry for 1912, he grumbled about finding it a 'torture'[109]). Matters were not helped by the gloomy atmosphere at home: his sister Yevgenia's husband Yury Sakharov was seriously ill with tuberculosis[110] and died before the year was out at the age of twenty-two, having been married less than a year. In late August, he got down in earnest to work on the tone poem *Alastor*, which became his op. 14, making detailed contrapuntal sketches for the development of the thematic material.[111] The score was completed in draft in mid-November and orchestrated by late January 1913.[112] As in the case of *Silence*, the literary work on which it was based had unmistakable autobiographical resonances. Shelley's *Alastor, or the Spirit of Solitude*, which was completed in 1815 and is one of the first of his major poems, relates the fate of a young poet who rejects earthly love and withdraws from all human contact into a solipsistic pursuit of ultimate wisdom, symbolised by a veiled woman of surpassing beauty who appears to him in a dream: his quest to be reunited with her proves futile and self-destructive. Myaskovsky became acquainted with the text in a translation by Balmont.[113] The poem is prefaced by a quotation from the *Confessions* of St Augustine, *Nondum amabam, et amare amabam, quaerebam quid amarem, amans amare*[114], 'I loved not yet, yet loved to love; I sought what I might love, in love with loving'. Its title refers not to the hero, but to the alluring 'vèilèd maid', a classic Jungian *anima* figure who turns out to be a manifestation of the demonic: αλάστωρ was a Greek epithet for an avenging demon.[115] Interestingly, while Shelley's poem is perfused with an atmosphere of heady eroticism[116], Myaskovsky completely desexualised the object of the hero's longing in the brief summary of the poem given in his

108 Myaskovsky to Derzhanovsky, 31 August 1912 and 2 October 1912, RNMM, 3/261 and 262.

109 'Vïpiski', entry for 1 December 1912, RGALI, 2040/1/65, l. 30b.

110 Myaskovsky to Derzhanovsky, 27 November 1912, RNMM, 3/268.

111 Myaskovsky to Prokofiev, 20 August 1912, in Kozlova and Yatsenko, *Perepiska*, 103.

112 Myaskovsky to Derzhanovsky, 15 November 1912 and 23 January 1913, RNMM, 3/267 and 277.

113 'Alastor, ili Dukh uyedineniya', *Shelli. Polnoye sobraniye sochineniy v perevode K. D. Bal'monta*, vol. 1 (Moscow, 1908), 427–56.

114 From Liber tertius: Augustine, *Confessions*, ed. James J. O'Donnell (Oxford, 1992), 23.

115 Henry George Liddell and Robert Scott, *A Greek-English Lexicon*, new edition, rev. Henry Stuart Jones *et al.* (Oxford, 1940), 60–1.

116 For a discussion, see Richard Holmes, *Shelley: The Pursuit* (London, 1994), 300–306.

programme note[117], which alludes merely to an 'image' (*obraz*) of unspecified gender. Lasting about twenty-five minutes in performance, *Alastor* is a less persuasively realised score than *Silence*, though it has stretches of powerful and vivid music. Its principal interest resides in its adumbration of future creative explorations (especially the Tenth and Thirteenth Symphonies) – especially in its intermittent employment of a densely dissonant harmonic idiom evocative of extreme psychological states.

At the end of 1912, Myaskovsky's supernumerary post at the Imperial Chancellery was converted into a salaried position: on 6 December he was raised to the rank of court chancellor (*nadvornïy sovetnik*) and from 1 January 1913 received the very modest salary of nine hundred roubles a year.[118] This improvement in his circumstances happened just in the nick of time: he was so hard up that he had been sorely tempted to accept an offer made two months previously to appoint him director of a music school in Voronezh, 320 miles south of Moscow.[119] He immediately acquired a fine new piano, an item of expenditure that says much about his sense of priorities.[120] While he was glad to have a regular income, he was soon complaining of having even less free time than before and of being so busy that he had to bring paperwork home at night.[121] Nonetheless, he started to sketch a new symphony while orchestrating *Alastor*, and in spite of his claim that he had come to feel 'loathing' for criticism, he informed Derzhanovsky of his plan to write an essay on Nikolay Medtner – a composer who aroused his increasing interest.[122] In a letter to Prokofiev, he described Medtner as a 'colossal talent' and declared his Piano Sonata op. 25/2 ('Night Wind') to be 'one of the most substantial and outstanding of modern compositions' – a verdict reiterated shortly afterwards in his review of a concert at which Medtner gave the St Petersburg premiere of the same sonata.[123] Derzhanovsky eagerly seized on Myaskovsky's suggestion: he was evidently anxious not to lose him as a contributor and sought

---

117 '*Alastor* (poéma Shelli) N. Myaskovskogo', *Muzïka*, 25 October 1914, 488–91.

118 Myaskovsky's Chancellery service record, RGIA, 1409/11/33, l. 22.
     Interestingly, Myaskovsky made no allusion to his Chancellery post in the official questionnaires eliciting information about employees' personal, family, and employment histories (*lichnïye listki po uchyotu kadrov*) that became mandatory in all Soviet workplaces – presumably because of the widespread attitude of hostility towards former tsarist government officials under the Bolshevik regime.

119 Myaskovsky to Derzhanovsky, 21 October 1912, RNMM, 3/264.

120 Entry for 24 December 1912, Prokof'yev, *Dnevnik 1907–1918*, 199.

121 Myaskovsky to Derzhanovsky, 5 February 1913, RNMM, 3/279.

122 Myaskovsky to Derzhanovsky, 1, 11, and 16 January 1913, RNMM, 3/273, 275 and 278; Myaskovsky to Prokofiev, 26 January 1913, in Kozlova and Yatsenko, *Perepiska*, 104.

123 'Peterburgskiye pis'ma', *Muzïka*, 23 February 1913, 137–40.

repeatedly to impress on him how much he valued his services, describing him as the journal's 'conscience'.[124] 'Medtner: Impressions of his Creative Personality', which was published in *Music* in early March[125], is not only an insightful appraisal of Medtner's work but also contains some highly interesting observations on musical form. Forms, Myaskovsky points out, are not merely abstract constructive schemes: in the work of a great composer, there is always an intimate correlation between what he termed its 'inner form', the succession of emotional states that it evokes, and its 'external form', its structural organisation. Medtner's music, he contended, demonstrated this correlation to a high degree, unlike the music of Glazunov, in which the treatment of form often seemed formulaic, Glazunov's undeniable technical mastery notwithstanding. As with 'Tchaikovsky and Beethoven', one of Myaskovsky's primary reasons for writing the article was to defend a composer whom he believed to have been misunderstood and unfairly criticised – in Medtner's case, by Sabaneyev and Karatïgin, who dismissed his work as arid, cerebral, and colourless.[126] Medtner's brother Emil was delighted with the essay and repeatedly pressed Myaskovsky to write a more extended article for the journal *Works and Days* (*Trudï i dni*), of which he was editor – but the idea never came to fruition.[127] In other quarters, the essay met with a much cooler reception: the conservatoire set predictably took umbrage at his comments about Glazunov.[128] (They were even more irritated when he published an article a month later criticising the dullness of the Belyayev Symphony Concerts, established by 1885 by Rimsky-Korsakov and Glazunov's patron Mitrofan Belyayev, and the organisers' failure to represent work by promising young composers such as Prokofiev.[129]) Viktor Belyayev wrote to inform him that Julia Weissberg and her St Petersburg colleagues had guessed the identity of 'Misanthrope', so his authorship of the 'Letters from St Petersburg' was now an open secret.[130]

---

124 Derzhanovsky to Myaskovsky, 29 January and 22 February 1913, RNMM, 71/139 and 142.

125 *vide* fn74.

126 See, for example, Leonid Sabaneyev, 'Nikolay Metner', *Muzïka*, 11 February 1912, 169–72; Vyacheslav Karatïgin, 'Tretiy kamernïy kontsert Ziloti. Kontsert iz sochineniy Metnera', *Rech'*, 23 January 1913, reproduced in *Karatïgin: Izbrannïye stat'i*, 67–9.

127 Myaskovsky and Emil Medtner's correspondence about the proposal is preserved in RSL, 190/71/12 and 190/71/13. See also Shlifshteyn (ed.), *N. Ya. Myaskovskiy: Sobraniye materialov*, vol. 2, 507–9.

128 Myaskovsky to Derzhanovsky, 8 March 1913, RNMM, 3/284.

129 'Peterburgskiye pis'ma', *Muzïka*, 14 April 1913, 267–70; Prokof'yev, *Dnevnik 1907–1918*, 263, 268.

130 Belyayev to Myaskovsky, 26 March 1913, RGALI 2040/1/100, ll. 40–1.

Work on the Third Symphony progressed in halting fashion: he hinted to Derzhanovsky that its structure 'would not be uninteresting', but his ideas were slow to crystallise. As state employees were allowed to take six weeks' annual leave during the summer, he planned to accompany his sister Vera and her children for a month to the popular Estonian seaside resort of Shmetsk (now Auga), where he hoped to have sufficient time alone to think out the details.[131] Before his departure on 25 May, he received word that Aslanov intended to programme the Second Symphony in one of the Pavlovsk summer concerts on 28 June.[132] The date was subsequently changed to 25 June, which meant he had to cut his holiday short. His break was not as restful or productive as anticipated: he found Vera's children rather a trial and made little headway with the new symphony.[133] The performance of the Second Symphony proved a dispiriting occasion, as Aslanov had not learned the score properly and the orchestral playing was excruciatingly out of tune. To his surprise, it met with a warmer response from the audience than in Moscow the previous year.[134]

As Myaskovsky still had some unused annual leave, he availed of the opportunity to spend ten days with Derzhanovsky in the first half of August while his wife was visiting relatives in the Crimea.[135] It was a more relaxing trip than his Estonian holiday: the two men spent much of their time chatting, reading, and playing through music together.[136] Derzhanovsky remained steadfastly supportive. He encouraged his friend to think about writing an opera and renewed his efforts to get him to send works to publishers, though Myaskovsky was palpably reluctant to submit the scores of the First Symphony and *Alastor*, as he had not had a chance to judge the effectiveness of their orchestration in performance.[137] Derzhanovsky also mooted plans to revive the 'Evenings' and put on a chamber music concert featuring works by Myaskovsky and Prokofiev.[138] His good intentions

---

131 Myaskovsky to Derzhanovsky, 3 and *circa* 20 April 1913, RNMM, 3/286 and 288.

132 Myaskovsky to Derzhanovsky, 16 May 1913, RNMM, 3/289.

133 Myaskovsky to Derzhanovsky, 4 and 20 June 1913, RNMM, 3/292 and 293.

134 Myaskovsky to Derzhanovsky, 2 July 1913, RNMM, 3/295; Myaskovsky to Prokofiev, undated letter [early July 1913], in Kozlova and Yatsenko, *Perepiska*, 108–9.

135 Myaskovsky to Derzhanovsky, 27 July 1913, RNMM, 3/299.

136 Koposova-Derzhanovskaya, 'V. V. Derzhanovskiy po vospominaniyam zhenï i druga', RNMM, 3/3365, l. 33.

137 Derzhanovsky to Myaskovsky, 18 June 1913, RNMM, 71/157; Myaskovsky to Derzhanovsky, 20 June 1913, RNMM, 3/293.

138 Prokof'yev, *Dnevnik 1907–1918*, 327; Prokofiev to Myaskovsky, 26 July 1913, in Kozlova and Yatsenko, *Perepiska*, 109–10.

inadvertently gave rise to an unpleasant contretemps with Prokofiev, which followed hard on the heels of another involving Stravinsky.

Derzhanovsky shared Myaskovsky's admiration for Stravinsky's work and, in the lead-up to the premiere of the *Rite of Spring* in Paris on 29 May, wrote to express interest in preparing a substantial article on the new ballet for *Music*.[139] He had recently published a letter from Ravel responding to the criticisms by Andrey Rimsky-Korsakov and others of the newly orchestrated version of Musorgsky's *Khovanshchina* that Ravel and Stravinsky had prepared for Diaghilev's forthcoming production at the Théâtre Champs-Elysées, and sought to capitalise on this contact, hoping that Stravinsky and his Parisian associates might agree to contribute to his periodical. *Music* had already published a number of substantial articles on Stravinsky's work (including another by Myaskovsky, on the Symphony in E-flat[140]) and Stravinsky was keenly aware of the value of this publicity in his homeland. Nothing came of Derzhanovsky's suggestion that Ravel might write the article, so he proposed to Stravinsky that Myaskovsky could write it instead, being one of the few people who could be relied on to produce a competent appraisal of such a complex new composition. As the full score had yet to be printed, Derzhanovsky enquired if Stravinsky could supply a set of prepublication proofs, since Myaskovsky had yet to hear the work and could only consult a piano duet arrangement.[141] Stravinsky duly sent on the proofs of part I (the remainder was still in preparation), which Myaskovsky received not long before he left for Moscow.[142]

Myaskovsky's examination of the piano duet score of the *Rite* earlier in the summer had left him feeling bewildered – as did his perusal of the recently published *Three Japanese Lyrics* (he thought Stravinsky's text-setting perverse and privately wondered whether he had 'taken leave of his senses').[143] Nevertheless, he was intrigued and decided to suspend judgement until he had time to familiarise himself with the score: he opined to Asafiev that the *Rite* was definitely 'not contrived, because it is too organic'.[144] His subsequent responses to the *Rite* vacillated: he joked with Prokofiev about its 'cacophony' and expressed reservations to Derzhanovsky about its 'primitivism', but after examining the full score of part I and playing through the

---

139 Derzhanovsky to Stravinsky, 30 April [13 May] 1913, in Viktor Varunts (ed.), *I. F. Stravinskiy: Perepiska s russkimi korrespondentami. Materialï k biografii*, vol. 2, (Moscow, 2000), 72–4.

140 'Simfoniya I. Stravinskogo', *Muzïka*, 22 August 1912, 685–703.

141 Derzhanovsky to Stravinsky, 8 [21] July 1913, in Varunts (ed.), *Stravinskiy: Perepiska*, vol. 2, 109–11.

142 Stravinsky to Derzhanovsky, 11 [24] July 1913, and Myaskovsky to Stravinsky, 25 July [7 August] 1913, ibid., 113, 120.

143 Myaskovsky to Derzhanovsky, 25 May 1913, RNMM, 3/291.

144 Myaskovsky to Asafiev, 26 May 1913, RGALI, 2658/1/636, l. 15.

piano duet transcription with Asafiev at the end of July, he claimed that he 'had started to like it enormously' and informed Derzhanovsky of his firm intention to write an essay about it.[145]

His attitude changed sharply when Stravinsky contacted him shortly afterwards to ask whether Myaskovsky would be prepared to come to his family estate in Ustilug (now Ustyluh, in Ukraine) to work as his amanuensis and correct the proofs of the *Rite*, *The Nightingale*, and other scores, as he was too busy to deal with them himself. Myaskovsky did not reply, which obliged Stravinsky to ask Derzhanovsky to act as an intermediary in a letter of 12 [25] August.[146] It arrived on 16 August, while Myaskovsky was still in Moscow, and to judge from Derzhanovsky's response dated the same day, he reacted badly to Stravinsky's proposal. Derzhanovsky was clearly anxious not to alienate Stravinsky and sent an evasive diplomatic explanation of Myaskovsky's unwillingness to go to Ustilug, attributing it to his shyness and solitary disposition. On 20 August, two days after Myaskovsky's departure, Stravinsky wrote again to ask if he could at least undertake some of the proofreading – a request that Derzhanovsky duly relayed and which met with a categorical refusal.[147]

Myaskovsky's disinclination to help was prompted by what he regarded as the insensitivity of Stravinsky's request and the attitude of self-importance that it betrayed, rather than an aversion to the task itself. He was obliging by nature and, despite his heavy workload, regularly found time to assist colleagues with routine professional chores: the previous month, he had helped to prepare the piano transcription of Asafiev's new ballet *The White Lily*[148], and he had just curtailed his visit to Moscow and returned to St Petersburg at Prokofiev's urgent request to help check the orchestral parts of his Second Piano Concerto in advance of its premiere at Pavlovsk on 23 August.[149] As he subsequently elaborated in two further letters, he took exception to being viewed not as a fellow composer with projects of his own in hand, but as a lackey who could be expected to drop everything to facilitate what he disdainfully described as Stravinsky's 'commercial

145 Prokof'yev, *Dnevnik 1907–1918*, 323; Myaskovsky to Derzhanovsky, 2 and 31 July 1913, RNMM, 3/295 and 300.

146 Stravinsky to Derzhanovsky, 12 [25] August 1913, in Varunts (ed.), *Stravinskiy: Perepiska*, vol. 2, 127–8. As Stravinsky explained, he had sent Myaskovsky a telegram, but this communication has not been preserved.

147 Stravinsky to Derzhanovsky, 20 August [2 September] 1913, ibid., 134–5; Derzhanovsky to Myaskovsky, 26 August 1913, and Myaskovsky to Derzhanovsky, 31 August and 2 September 1913, RNMM, 71/175, 3/305 and 306.

148 Myaskovsky to Derzhanovsky, 20 July 1913, RNMM, 3/298.

149 Prokofiev to Myaskovsky, 14 August 1913, in Kozlova and Yatsenko, *Perepiska*, 112; Prokof'yev, *Dnevnik 1907–1918*, 338.

operations'. 'He should cease his haste', he told Derzhanovsky, adding waspishly: 'It could only be good for him, as he might return to writing real music'.[150] It was one thing to put himself out for Prokofiev and Asafiev, both of whom were still trying to establish themselves professionally. It was quite another to do the same for Stravinsky, who was now an international celebrity in receipt of lucrative commissions and, as Yavorsky had discovered, in a position to secure highly preferential terms from Éditions Russes de Musique, which had recently rejected his own and Prokofiev's work once more.[151] In spite of his irritation at Stravinsky's behaviour, Myaskovsky kept his promise to write an essay about the *Rite*, which he completed in January 1914.[152] Though somewhat more muted in tone that his previous articles on *The Firebird* and *Petrushka*, his account of the work is informative and insightful, and he had generous praise for its vividness of invention. Nonetheless, he informed Derzhanovsky that he had no desire to come into further contact with Stravinsky and that his interest in his music had waned.[153] (Derzhanovsky's own relationship with Stravinsky foundered not long afterwards, in part because of Stravinsky's antipathy to Sabaneyev, one of *Music*'s regular contributors.[154])

Myaskovsky's letters to Derzhanovsky in the autumn of 1913 indicate the persistence of his depressed mood, which may account in part for the severity of his reaction to Stravinsky. By early September he was back to work in his 'loathsome office job' and once again struggling to find time for composition, though he had at last managed to complete the sketch of the Third Symphony. He next turned to revising his early Hippius songs, with 'nightmarishly grey', but 'satisfying' results.[155] Feeling unable to tackle a larger project for the time being[156], he composed five new Hippius settings in October, including the splendid 'Zaklinaniye' ('Incantation'), which he collected into a new set, together with revised versions of three earlier settings, under the title *From Z. I. Hippius. Eight Sketches for Voice and Piano*, op. 16. His low spirits stubbornly refused to lift. 'I have been suffering from such hypochondria for the last while, that if it hadn't been for the work on the Hippius songs, I would have hanged myself', he confided

150 Myaskovsky to Derzhanovsky, 12 September 1913, RNMM, 3/307.

151 Myaskovsky to Yavorsky, 3 June 1913, and Yavorsky to Myaskovsky, 15 June 1913, in Rabinovich, *Yavorskiy: Vospominaniya, stat'i i pis'ma*, 504–7.

152 'O *Vesne svyashchennoy* I. Stravinskogo', *Muzïka*, 1 February 1914, 106–12.

153 Myaskovsky to Derzhanovsky, 9 January 1914, RNMM, 3/472.

154 See Stravinsky to Derzhanovsky, 13 [26] December 1913, and Derzhanovsky to Stravinsky 2 [15] May 1914, in Varunts (ed.), *Stravinskiy: Perepiska*, vol. 2, 187–8 and 247–50.

155 Myaskovsky to Derzhanovsky, 2, 8, and 12 September 1913, RNMM, 3/306, 334, and 307.

156 Myaskovsky to Derzhanovsky, 28 September 1913, RNMM, 3/310

to Derzhanovsky.[157] Although he initially declared himself pleased with the songs, only a few days later he wrote to tell Derzhanovsky that he now thought they were 'trash' and had only 'reluctantly' sent them on to him.[158]

He dedicated the new opus to Derzhanovskaya, who had expressed interest in performing some of his songs at the chamber music concert that Derzhanovsky wanted to organise. Plans for the projected fourth 'Modern Music Evening' were beset by unexpected difficulties and delays. Derzhanovsky proposed a programme comprising vocal works by Myaskovsky and Stravinsky, Myaskovsky's Cello Sonata and Prokofiev's *Ballade* for cello and piano, and solo piano works by Prokofiev and Myaskovsky, including the latter's Piano Sonata no. 1. He hoped that Prokofiev would play Myaskovsky's piano sonata as well as his own solo keyboard works[159], as he had already studied the sonata and promised to include it in his concert repertoire, though he had yet to perform it. The sonata, moreover, had been dedicated to him.[160] Prokofiev was reluctant to commit himself to taking part, however, pleading the pressure of other work – he evidently regarded the concert as a matter of minor importance. (He was in his final year at the conservatoire, having stayed on to continue his studies of piano and conducting). His attitude exasperated Derzhanovsky, as he seemed completely unappreciative of the efforts that were being made on his behalf.[161]

At some point during the summer Prokofiev informed Myaskovsky that he did not intend to perform his piano sonata. The circumstances are not entirely clear, but he communicated his decision in a manner that Myaskovsky found offensive and led him to withdraw the work's dedication.[162] Myaskovsky downplayed the incident in his letters to Derzhanovsky, but it is evident that he was hurt by it.[163] Derzhanovsky hoped that Prokofiev might reconsider his decision, but Myaskovsky refused to raise the matter with him. His reply to Derzhanovsky shows a remarkably clear-sighted understanding of Prokofiev's personality and the limitations of his relationship with his former classmate:

> My relationship with him can essentially be described as follows. He shows me his compositions and every now and then will indulge me by

157 Myaskovsky to Derzhanovsky, 21 October 1913, RNMM, 3/316

158 Myaskovsky to Derzhanovsky, 25 and 30 October 1913, RNMM, 3/317 and 318.

159 Derzhanovsky to Myaskovsky, 12 September 1913, RNMM, 71/181.

160 See Prokofiev to Myaskovsky, 7 and 20 August 1911, in Kozlova and Yatsenko, *Perepiska*, 94–7, 99.

161 Derzhanovsky to Myaskovsky, 23 September 1913, RNMM, 71/182.

162 Prokof'yev, *Dnevnik 1907–1918*, 375.

163 Myaskovsky to Derzhanovsky, 3 August and 14 September 1913, RNMM, 3/301 and 470.

agreeing with my comments about them. I show him my compositions only if he asks insistently. I will always be more than willing to help him in any way that I can, but I expect nothing in return: I never ask for anything and I do not even want to ask. On the whole, the link between us is his music and, perhaps, personal affinity.[164]

At bottom, Myaskovsky knew that Prokofiev had little interest in his work and did not think much of it. He was also under no illusions that he should expect much gratitude for the services he had rendered him, which in the past year had included making a piano reduction of *Dreams*[165] as well as correcting the score and parts of the Second Piano Concerto. He had even offered to help orchestrate *Maddalena*[166] in the hope that a production could be put on at the recently opened Free Theatre in Moscow, where Saradzhev had been appointed principal conductor.[167] Prokofiev seems to have regarded this attention as no more than his due and did not feel under any obligation to reciprocate. When Prokofiev called to see Myaskovsky on 27 September, he made no allusion to Myaskovsky's sonata and was evasive about what he would play at the concert.[168] He ignored Derzhanovsky's urgent requests for clarification until the latter eventually sent him an ultimatum a few days later[169], whereupon he announced that he would only play his own compositions and refused to perform anything else.[170] Derzhanovsky's attempts to find another pianist to play Myaskovsky's sonata were unavailing, but Myaskovsky was philosophical: he told Derzhanovsky that he did not bear a grudge, adding 'Prokofiev is not free of knavery, but his music is good all the same!'[171] Throughout this episode, he showed a remarkable detachment: at the end of September he wrote a laudatory review for *Music* of Prokofiev's *Four Pieces for Piano*, op. 4 and the *Toccata*, op. 11, which had

164 Myaskovsky to Derzhanovsky, 24 September 1913, RNMM, 3/308. Emphasis in original.

165 Prokof'yev, *Dnevnik 1907–1918*, 242, 246.

166 Ibid., 325. The project is also discussed in Derzhanovsky to Myaskovsky, 19 July 1913, and Myaskovsky to Derzhanovsky, 21 August 1913, RNMM, 71/165 and 3/302.

167 See Tigranov (ed.), *Saradzhev*, 29.

168 Myaskovsky to Derzhanovsky, 28 September and 1 October 1913, RNMM, 3/310 and 311.

169 Derzhanovsky to Myaskovsky, 28 September 1913, RNMM, 71/184; Derzhanovsky to Prokofiev, 24 October and 1 November 1913, in Deklerk *et al.* (ed.), *Dernier cri*, vol. 1, 89–92.

170 Prokof'yev, *Dnevnik 1907–1918*, 361.

171 Myaskovsky to Derzhanovsky, 1 October 1913, RNMM, 3/311 and 312 (two communications).

recently been published by Jurgenson.[172] (Jurgenson also agreed to publish Myaskovsky's two piano sonatas around this time.)

The 19 October issue of *Music* carried an announcement that the concert would take place in the Small Hall of the Moscow Conservatoire on 24 November. Apart from Derzhanovskaya and Prokofiev, the other performers were to include the cellist Yevsey Belousov, a notable young virtuoso, and the pianist Pavel Lamm, with whom Myaskovsky subsequently formed a close friendship. Various circumstances forced a deferral until January – amongst them, insufficient funds.[173] Myaskovsky spent the intervening months elaborating his sketch of the Third Symphony into a short score with indications of the orchestration, a task that he found more than usually challenging. He increasingly resented the constraints that his Chancellery post imposed his creativity. Ideas for a Fourth and a Fifth Symphony has started to germinate: it cost him all he could do not to 'do a bunk and open a symphony factory', as he wrote to Derzhanovsky.[174] His friend must have found his moods rather trying at times. He talked about withdrawing his Hippius songs from the forthcoming concert because the audience might think the texts 'crazy' and refused to provide an analytical programme note about the Cello Sonata because the 'disgusting' nature of the themes and their 'banal' treatment would be more apparent if they were written down.[175] He also reproached Derzhanovsky for not appreciating the effort it cost him to review for *Music*, telling him that he found it a 'scourge' and was reluctant to continue.[176]

Derzhanovsky dealt patiently with these outbursts, although he had worries of his own: he was in acute financial difficulties and his wife was seriously ill.[177] Fortunately she recovered in time for the concert, as a considerable portion of the programme depended on her participation – Stravinsky's *Two Poems of Konstantin Balmont* and *Three Japanese Lyrics* (the latter accompanied by an instrumental ensemble conducted by Saradzhev); two Prokofiev Balmont settings; and two of Myaskovsky's Ivanov *Sketches* and five Hippius settings. Prokofiev partnered Belousov in his *Ballade* and played his Second Piano Sonata and a selection of shorter pieces; Lamm played the piano part of the Myaskovsky's Cello Sonata in

172 'Sergey Prokof'yev. Op. 4. [. . .] Op. 11. Tokkata dlya f-p', *Muzïka*, 12 October 1913, 667–8.

173 Prokof'yev, *Dnevnik 1907–1918*, 378.

174 Myaskovsky to Derzhanovsky, 8 November 1913, RNMM, 3/320.

175 Myaskovsky to Derzhanovsky, 10 November and 31 December 1913, RNMM, 3/321 and 3/332.

176 Myaskovsky to Derzhanovsky, 11 and 30 November 1913, RNMM, 3/322 and 327.

177 Derzhanovsky to Myaskovsky, 29 December 1913, RNMM, 71/203.

addition to accompanying Derzhanovskaya. Prokofiev recorded in his diary that the event was reasonably well attended and went successfully on the whole.[178] Myaskovsky's songs were warmly received. Recalling the concert over twenty years later in his 'Autobiographical Notes', Myaskovsky had high praise for Derzhanovskaya's interpretations.[179] (He was by no means alone in his estimate of her abilities: Bekman-Shcherbina, who had previously accompanied Derzhanovskaya in performances of French *mélodies*, thought her very musical; her voice, though not powerful, was attractive in timbre, and her intonation and diction were excellent.[180])

The reviews of the concert were at best lukewarm, however, and in some cases, decidedly unenthusiastic: Derzhanovsky reprinted them in three successive issues of *Music*, flaunting the unfavourable ones as a badge of honour.[181] Myaskovsky was particularly indignant on reading the notice penned by Sabaneyev, although his own work received the most laudatory comment (not the Cello Sonata, however, which was dismissed as 'unoriginal' and 'vapid'). He upbraided Derzhanovsky for reproducing Sabaneyev's 'vulgar, indecent, impudent, and obtuse vituperations' and urged him to stop using him as a reviewer.[182] His ire was intensified by Sabaneyev's condescending appraisal of his work as dull and lacking in originality in another article surveying recent musical developments, which evidently cut him to the quick – so much so that he spoke once more of 'closing up shop'.[183] It would be unjust to construe such remarks as self-indulgent histrionics: his letters unmistakably suggest that he was in the grip of a serious personal crisis.

His mental state was not helped by domestic tensions. Myaskovsky had continued to postpone moving out largely from concern about the effects that it might have on the emotionally unstable Yelikonida, whom he treated with great kindness: his sisters recalled that he grew closer to her during these years and made a considerable effort to spend time with her.[184] The family's circumstances were complicated considerably when Myaskovsky's father retired, which meant that they were obliged to relinquish their state-owned apartment. Yakov decided that he would go to live separately with Alida, leaving the other family members to find separate accommodation.

---

178 Prokof'yev, *Dnevnik 1907–1918*, 404–6.

179 Myaskovskiy, 'Avtobiograficheskiye zametki', 9.

180 Yelena Bekman-Shcherbina, *Moi vospominaniya* (Moscow, 1982), 93.

181 'Vechera sovremennoy muzïki. Otzïvï moskovskoy pechati', *Muzïka*, 1 February 1914, 112–16; 8 February 1914, 138–42; and 22 February 1914, 171–2.

182 Myaskovsky to Derzhanovsky, 4 and 22 February 1914, RNMM, 3/474 and 477.

183 Leonid Sabaneyev, 'Obzor muzïkal'noy zhizni za 1913 god', in G. Angert and Ye. Shor (ed.), *Muzïkal'nïy al'manakh* (Moscow, 1914), 19; Myaskovsky to Derzhanovsky, 16 February 1914, RNMM, 3/476.

184 Men'shikova *et al.*, 'Pamyati brata', 176–7.

Myaskovsky seems to have been particularly upset by this development. Between his Chancellery post, his frustration at his slow progress on the Third Symphony, his discouragement at recent critical responses to his work, and the tense atmosphere at home, he felt under great strain, telling Derzhanovsky that he feared 'ending up in the madhouse' because he was 'completely losing equilibrium' at times.[185] By mid-March, he had succumbed to 'black melancholy' on account of his own and his family's 'uncertain future'.[186] A fortnight later, he told his friend that felt unable to continue working on the Third Symphony because 'the spark had gone out', though he had nearly finished elaborating his draft into a short score. Having played through it with Asafiev, he concluded that it was 'rubbish' and lost faith in himself to the point where he contemplated giving up composing altogether: 'I'm in the grip of despair . . . complete apathy, indifference to any kind of music, whether it's good, bad, my own or other people's; and apathy of such a kind and to such a degree that no pangs of conscience or any kind of ethics have any effect on me . . .. You'll have to give me up as a bad job – both as a composer and as a 'musician'.[187]

The prospect of performances of *Alastor* and the First Symphony lifted his spirits somewhat, as did the news that conductor of the Moscow Russian Musical Society concerts Emil Kuper had expressed interest in giving the premiere of the Third.[188] He suffered a further setback, however, when Éditions Russes de Musique refused to publish the Second Symphony because its readers deemed its musical language too conservative and excessively reminiscent of Tchaikovsky. Myaskovsky reacted with consternation to this verdict but was even more outraged to hear that Siloti had returned the manuscript of Prokofiev's Second Piano Concerto with a patronising covering note informing him that he would consider performing his work when Prokofiev 'eventually found himself'.[189] He took up the cudgels on Prokofiev's behalf in an article for *Music*, ironically entitled 'Petersburg Fogs', in which he excoriated Siloti for his attitude, pointing out that in his reminiscences of studying with Liszt, Siloti had quoted his teacher's remarks on the need for Russians to support their own composers.[190] His confrontational tactics proved surprisingly effective: a week later, Siloti contacted Prokofiev to inform him that he intended to perform his

---

185 Myaskovsky to Derzhanovsky, 6 February 1914, RNMM, 3/475.

186 Myaskovsky to Derzhanovsky, 18 March 1914, RNMM, 3/479.

187 Myaskovsky to Derzhanovsky, 4 April 1914, RNMM, 3/480.

188 Myaskovsky to Derzhanovsky, 5 and 9 April 1914 and Derzhanovsky to Myaskovsky, 12 April 1914, RNMM, 3/481 and 482, 71/215.

189 Myaskovsky to Prokofiev, 9 April 1914 and Prokofiev to Myaskovsky, 10 April 1914, Kozlova and Yatsenko, *Perepiska*, 113–14.

190 'Peterburgskiye tumanï', *Muzïka*, 19 April 1914, 334–6.

Sinfonietta.[191] By this point, however, Myaskovsky felt that the time had come for him to stop reviewing – a feeling that was confirmed by the hostile reaction to his highly critical account of Glazunov's incidental music for the Grand Duke Konstantin Konstantinovich's mawkish religious drama *The King of the Jews* which he published in the same issue as the article on Siloti.[192] As he told Derzhanovsky, he felt that he was in danger of repeating himself and that his contributions were becoming 'bilious'.[193]

Finding somewhere for himself, his sisters, and his aunt to live occupied much of April, and in May they moved into an apartment in the Vasilevsky Island district. On 20 May, Myaskovsky attended the premiere of his First Symphony in Pavlovsk – which proved to be just as depressing an affair as Aslanov's performance of the Second Symphony the previous year. Writing to Asafiev, who was on holiday in Italy, he described his dismay at discovering that even after two rehearsals Aslanov was still unable to identify the symphony's principal thematic elements and had to ask his assistance. 'He's not a musician at all', he observed wearily. 'When you give him your composition, it feels as though you have allowed yourself to be clutched by filthy, sticky paws'.[194] He continued to work on the Third Symphony as best he could amidst the disruption, and on completion of a piano transcription, started to write out the full score – a task that he finished on 7 July while on holiday in Shmetsk, where he had returned with his sister. His First Symphony was given in Moscow by the young conductor Alexander Yurasovsky on 10 July, but he did not attend.[195] As the Third Symphony approached completion, Derzhanovsky urged him to consider realising his long-standing plan to write an opera based on Dostoyevsky's *Idiot*, but he struggled to envisage how a viable libretto could be fashioned from the novel.[196] 'My head is empty', he told Derzhanovsky, 'and my life is so beset by tiresome trivialities that I have no perspective on things'.[197]

A week later, on 19 July (1 August according to the Gregorian calendar) came the ominous news that Germany had declared war on Russia. Asafiev wrote anxiously from Moscow, where he had travelled to hear the performance of the First Symphony, to enquire whether Myaskovsky would be

191 Prokof'yev, *Dnevnik 1907–1918*, 453, 455.

192 'Peterburgskiye pis'ma', *Muzïka*, 19 April 1914.

193 Myaskovsky to Derzhanovsky, 28 April 1914, RNMM, 3/487.

194 Myaskovsky to Asafiev, 19 June 1914, RGALI, 2658/1/636, l. 21.

195 Myaskovsky to Derzhanovsky, 27 June and 7 July 1914, RNMM, 3/338 and 491.

196 Myaskovsky to Derzhanovsky, 6 June and 23 July 1914; and Derzhanovsky to Myaskovsky, 8 July 1914, RNMM 3/336 and 342, 71/227

197 Myaskovsky to Derzhanovsky, 11 July 1914, RNMM, 3/339.

affected.[198] The answer to this question was as yet uncertain: Myaskovsky had been discharged from the reserves earlier that year[199], but was still potentially liable to be called up for active service in the militia. He returned to St Petersburg, waiting for the situation to clarify.[200] Yelikonida and his sisters were aghast: to pacify them, he spent several exhausting, nerve-wracking days 'running from one back street to another', as he related to Yakiv Akimenko, petitioning to be allowed remain in St Petersburg.[201] His efforts were fruitless. On 1 August, he received his mobilisation papers. Although he can have had no inkling of the fact at the time, life in his native country was poised to undergo profound change, with consequences that would bring about a far-reaching transformation in his circumstances.

198 Asafiev to Myaskovsky, 23 July 1914, in Kozlova (ed.), 'Iz perepiski B. V. Asaf'yeva i N. Ya. Myaskovskogo [Part 2]', 103.

199 Myaskovsky's army service record ('Posluzhnoy spisok'), RGALI, 2040/2/168, l. 20b.

200 Myaskovsky to Asafiev, 25 July 1914, RGALI, 2658/1/636, l. 27.

201 Myaskovsky to Akimenko, 19 August 1914, in Tamara Bulat, 'Pis'ma N. Ya. Myaskovskogo k Ya. S. Stepovomu', *Sovetskaya muzïka*, 12 (1979), 109.

4

War and Revolution: 1914–17

Myaskovsky had yet to learn where he would be assigned, knowing only that his departure was imminent. He hoped to be sent to Moscow, but on 4 August received instructions to report three days later to an army base in Borovichi, a town situated 210 miles southeast of St Petersburg. He spent his last few days of freedom finalising the fair copy of the Third Symphony.[1] As usual after completing a major project, he was immediately wracked with agonies of self-doubt despite his friends' enthusiastic responses when he played the score to them – Krïzhanovsky went so far as to invoke comparisons with Tchaikovsky's *Pathétique*.[2]

Their enthusiasm was merited: in every respect, Symphony no. 3 in A minor, op. 15, represents a notable advance on its predecessors. It not only surpasses them in technical sophistication and expressive force but is also more novel in conception, as its design constitutes a radical rethinking of traditional formal approaches. The symphony is cast in two movements – a predominantly quick sonata-allegro lasting about twenty minutes followed by a rondo which is also in a fast tempo but culminates in a slow epilogue with the character of a funeral march. Two-movement symphonies are surprisingly uncommon, principally, one suspects, because of the inherent problem of attaining overall unity: the chief difficulty is to ensure that the second movement will provide a persuasive ending to the work as a whole and not leave an impression of incompleteness. To accomplish this, it must convey a sense that it brings unfinished business from the first movement to a satisfactory conclusion. Furthermore, the problem of integrating slow and fast music in a two-movement symphony is particularly acute. Myaskovsky's solution to these challenges is as original as it is ingenious. As in his previous symphonies, the second subject group in his turbulent first movement is much slower in tempo. When it returns in the recapitulation, one of its component ideas is subjected to further development in an ethereal slow coda that follows without a break; and although the movement ends in the tonic major, its stability is precarious, undermined up to the last by excursions to remote harmonic regions and a strangely indeterminate final cadence. The relief from conflict is short-lived: the restless A section of the rondo is pervaded with a sense of anxious disquiet; and although the episodes provide some respite (especially the lyrical C

---

1   Myaskovsky to Derzhanovsky, 2, 4, and 7 August, RNMM, 3/985, 3/343, and 3/344.
2   Myaskovsky to Asafiev, 19 June 1914, RGALI, 2658/1/636, l. 22.

section), the circularity of the A section's successive returns engenders a sense of growing menace and entrapment. The rondo design is truncated before the anticipated final recurrence of the A section (A^3): instead, the B^1 section is extended until it has issue in a strenuous climax that collapses catastrophically. After ominous recitative-like interjections punctuated by tense pauses, a funeral march ensues, which rises to a culminating paroxysm of disconsolate grief before subsiding into numbed silence.

The symphony's magnificent closing pages are charged with a concentrated intensity of tragic feeling. Although Myaskovsky acknowledged that the work had been prompted by reflections on the phenomenon of death after the premature demise of his brother-in-law Sakharov, he denied that it had any extra-musical import.[3] And yet, the work's musical symbolism seemed to cry out for interpretation: as Asafiev observed in an essay written in 1915, the imposing heroic motto theme heard at the very opening (ex. 4.1) seemed to permit no doubt that it would ultimately prevail over adversity in the course of subsequent struggles, but this expectation was deceptive: the motto's final transformation in the funeral march prompted thoughts of 'lamentation over blighted hopes . . . and the mournful realisation of powerlessness', suggesting that 'the composer has not solved the riddle of his existence because hostile forces, lurking perhaps externally or perhaps in the depths of his own soul, hindered the flowering and full revelation of his personality'.[4] However, for all its depth of feeling, Asafiev rightly pointed out that the music was devoid of self-indulgence and that its emotional impact was heightened by the austerity of its sound-world. This, together with the absence of any impulse to affirmation, he suggested, was likely to prove the greatest barrier to understanding:

> [Myaskovsky] stubbornly declines to mask the intensity of his emotional experiences and torments with beautiful self-sufficient forms and sound for the sake of sound, and in his keen search for means of embodying the aural images that occur to him, he never makes these means a self-sufficient end in itself. Because of this nakedness of content, because of this utter disdain for sensuous pleasure as such, because of this eschewal of any aims other than those with which his powerful 'ego' demands to be confronted in its craving for self-discovery, Myaskovsky's work is little understood both by the public, which has become used to having its pills sugared, and by musicians, for the latter are either self-absorbed or not interested in complex conceptions, preferring something ephemeral and impressionistic, or else because they are mired in conventionality and have no feeling for anything vital.[5]

3   Myaskovsky to Derzhanovsky, 30 June 1916, RNMM, 3/414.
4   Glebov [Asaf'yev], 'O tvorcheskom puti Myaskovskogo', 259.
5   Ibid., 259, 260.

EXAMPLE 4.1. Symphony no. 3, first movement: bars 5–10.

EXAMPLE 4.2. Symphony no. 3, first movement: bars 17–19.

From a technical point of view, the symphony is notable for its remarkable closeness of motivic working. Its musical material largely derives from the motto theme and an ancillary idea (ex. 4.2), characterised by Asafiev as a malign counteragency, which imperiously interrupts it. (Myaskovsky once again has recourse to the device of pitting extremely contrasted diatonic and chromatic musical material against one another; and it is notable that the motto theme is first heard in the key of E flat, establishing a tritonal opposition to A minor, the principal key of the work). These reappear in various guises – example 4.1 forms the basis of a constituent theme of the second subject group, for example – and also recur in the finale. The concluding funeral march brings many of these ideas together in a fresh synthesis, endowing them with new meaning after the preceding dénouement. (In a particularly subtle touch, the eerie final sonority, a diatonic major seventh chord heard on muted horns, constitutes a last faint echo of the initial motto theme, superimposing its opening four notes.)

The Third Symphony amply justified Myaskovsky's decision to pursue a vocation as a creative artist: it was not only an impressive achievement on a personal level but was also one of the most original symphonic works of its period. It would make a superb impression in a live performance, provided sufficient time could be devoted to it in rehearsal to make the phrase structure coherent and ensure satisfactory balance in the texturally complex passages.

After leaving St Petersburg on 7 August, Myaskovsky had to readjust rapidly to being back in the army. He was not alone amongst his acquaintances in being called up: Saradzhev and Akimenko were also conscripted.[6] Derzhanovsky was declared unfit for service on health grounds[7], while

---

6 Tigranov (ed.), *Saradzhev*, 30–31; Akimenko to Myaskovsky, 12 August 1914, RGALI, 2040/1/89, ll. 40–400b.

7 Derzhanovsky, 'Lichnaya kartochka', GARF, 2306/44/127, l. 4.

Asafiev and Belyayev were able to secure exemptions because they worked respectively at the Mariinsky Theatre and the St Petersburg Conservatoire.[8] Being the only son of a widow, Prokofiev was also exempt, though he took the additional precaution in 1915 of re-enrolling at the Conservatoire as an organ student.[9] On hearing that Myaskovsky had been drafted, he wondered privately how 'helpless Nick' would cope. ('Some warrior he'd make!', he remarked condescendingly in his diary.)[10] For all his loathing of military service, Myaskovsky was far from helpless: he proved a highly competent officer and would display much courage and resilience.

His attitude to being called up was stoical: he told Derzhanovsky that he was 'not downhearted and even somewhat glad to be disappearing from St Petersburg'.[11] He served initially as a junior officer (*mladshiy ofitser*), a rank roughly equivalent to lieutenant, in the Second Militia Sapper Half-Company.[12] (A company of soldiers typically comprised about 250 men in the tsarist army at this period.[13]) His role was to act as assistant to the half-company commander, helping to drill and train the men in preparation for active service in the field. He arrived in Borovichi to discover that disorder and confusion reigned: it was unclear who was in charge and the half-company was not fully constituted. In letters to family and friends, he complained of a lack of information and sufficiently precise instructions, and even that wages were not being paid.[14] He had to learn quickly on the job, never having held a position of comparable responsibility before: he found himself putting in long days, with much of his time consumed by tedious administrative chores. He discharged his duties conscientiously but could muster no enthusiasm for the war itself. Writing to Asafiev, he admitted to feeling disturbed by the widespread re-emergence of humankind's 'animalistic, savage instincts' and to bewilderment at the thought that any 'sane, intelligent person' could 'countenance war between

---

8   Belyayev to Myaskovsky, 5 October and 24 November 1914, RGALI, 2040/1/100, l. 54, 60.

9   Izrail' Nest'yev, *Zhizn' Sergeya Prokof'yeva* (Moscow, 1973), 128; Akhonen, *Prokof'yev v Peterburgskoy Konservatorii*, 248–52.

10 Prokof'yev, *Dnevnik 1907–1918*, 485, 493.

11 Myaskovsky to Derzhanovsky, 4 August 1914, RNMM, 3/344.

12 Myaskovsky's service record ('Posluzhnoy spisok'), 23 June 1923, RGALI, 2040/1/168, l. 3.

13 On the organisation of sapper forces in the tsarist army, see Konstantin Velichko *et al.*, *Voyenno-inzhenerniy sbornik: Materialï po istorii voyni, 1914–1918 gg.*, vol. 1 (Moscow, 1918).

14 Myaskovsky to Derzhanovsky, 9 August 1914, RNMM, 3/345; Myaskovsky to Asafiev, 17 August 1914, RGALI, 2658/1/636, l. 28; Myaskovsky to Akimenko, 19 August 1914, in 'Pis'ma N. Ya. Myaskovogo k Ya. S. Stepovomu', 109; Myaskovsky to Vera Yakovleva (*née* Myaskovskaya), 25 August 1915, RGALI, 2040/1/82, l. 3.

European peoples'.[15] Nor, as he told Derzhanovsky, did he experience any upsurge of patriotism – merely 'detachment from everything that is going on, as though all these stupid, brutal, bestial shenanigans are taking place on a different plane'. He had become convinced, he added, that 'art, and music especially' was 'definitely devoid of nationality, and even of the nationalistic. When all is said and done, only the colouration changes, and the essence that endures far transcends Germany, France, Russia, and so forth'.[16] These conclusions were perhaps unsurprising, given his conviction that truly great art was supranational in character and universal in relevance – but they demonstrate how little he was influenced by the prevailing atmosphere of chauvinism. On 18 August, the name of Russia's capital was officially changed to Petrograd to make it sound less German, and before long calls were heard to ban the performance of German music.[17]

In the midst of this whirl of activity, he learned that Lyadov had died on 15 (28) August at his country estate, situated only a short distance from the Borovichi army camp. Despite his ambivalent attitude to his former teacher, he was saddened by the news, remarking that the conservatoire's standing would be significantly diminished by his loss.[18] Towards the end of the month, he was sent to Petrograd for supplies only to be informed on arrival that he need not return to Borovichi, as his platoon was being transferred to Krasnoye Selo, a picturesque village southwest of the city where Nicholas II presided annually over military manoeuvres.[19] In the event, his platoon ended up in the far less glamourous hamlet of Kapitolovo, twenty miles north-east of Petrograd, where Myaskovsky spent the next month overseeing the construction of defences to protect the capital.[20] His workload became very onerous: although militia units, being composed of civilian personnel, were supposed to function as an emergency supplement to the regular army, this distinction was not observed in practice. The field forces made increasing demands on him, and he had to be constantly vigilant to prevent his inexperienced troops from slacking or making mistakes. The attractive countryside compensated somewhat for the hard work and squalid accommodation (a filthy peasant hut lacking even the most basic

15   Myaskovsky to Asafiev, 26 August 1914, RGALI, 2658/1/636, l. 300b.

16   Myaskovsky to Derzhanovsky, 19 August 1914, RNMM, 3/349.

17   See Vladimir Derzhanovsky, 'Stranitsï "gorestnïkh" zamet: O nashem germanofobstve i prakticheskikh rezultatakh onago', *Muzïka*, 30 January 1916, 67–72.

18   Myaskovsky to Prokofiev, 17 August 1914, in Kozlova and Yatsenko, *Perepiska*, 120; Myaskovsky to Asafiev, 26 August 1914, RGALI, 2658/1/636, ll. 30–300b.

19   Myaskovsky to Derzhanovsky, 1 September 1914, RNMM, 3/353.

20   Prokof'yev, *Dnevnik 1907–1918*, 514.

amenities).[21] In a letter to Derzhanovsky, he lyrically evoked an early morning scene: 'snow passing in front of the sun, a blue lake in the background, green-gold hills – a real Japanese landscape painting'.[22]

Derzhanovsky loyally stayed in regular contact and persisted in his efforts to promote his friend's work. To Myaskovsky's surprise, he managed to interest Koussevitzky in performing *Alastor* in Moscow and St Petersburg in November, and Emil Kuper gave a firm undertaking to conduct the premiere of the Third Symphony at a Moscow Russian Musical Society concert the following January.[23] Anxious that his friend should not cease composing altogether, he urged him to think about his plan to compose an opera based on Dostoyevsky's *Idiot*, and spoke of trying to persuade a prominent writer such as Hippius or Andrey Bely to write the libretto.[24] As Myaskovsky had to remind him, his present living conditions and exhausting daily routine were scarcely conducive to creative work or to writing for *Music*, as Derzhanovsky also pressed him to continue doing. 'I am not thinking about music and do not want to think about it because I sense that it will only irritate me', he replied: 'I will have to put music aside for at least a year'.[25] He was not sanguine about a swift end to hostilities, given Germany's implacable drive to dominate Europe, and correctly foretold that the war would only end when the Germany army was 'completely and decisively' defeated.[26] For the time being, his energies would have to be directed elsewhere.

Asafiev also corresponded frequently, keeping him informed of news and gossip from the capital. On learning of the impending premieres of *Alastor* and the Third Symphony, he sent a note expressing his pleasure at these signs of growing recognition.[27] Myaskovsky responded with touching modesty:

> I am always boundlessly glad when you like something I've written ... I always suppose what I write to be just dabbling and not real art, so your comments seem to me exaggerated in the extreme... If I had not lost hope of writing a real and thoroughly artistic work one day, I would

21 Myaskovsky to Derzhanovsky, 11 September 1914, RNMM, 3/354

22 Myaskovsky to Derzhanovsky, 27 September 1914, RNMM, 3/355.

23 Derzhanovsky to Myaskovsky, 14 September and 3 October 1914, RNMM, 71/245 and 71/253; Myaskovsky to Asafiev, 3 October 1914, RGALI, 2658/1/636, l. 330b.

24 Derzhanovsky to Myaskovsky, 3 and 12 October 1914, RNMM, 71/253 and 71/257.

25 Myaskovsky to Derzhanovsky, 23 October 1914, RNMM, 3/360.

26 Myaskovsky to Derzhanovsky, 16 October 1914, RNMM, 3/359.

27 Asafiev to Myaskovsky, 6 October 1914, in Miral'da Kozlova (ed.), '"Chuvstvuya polnotu oshchushcheniya i rost soznaniya": Iz perepiski Asaf'yeva s Myaskovskim 1914–1916gg.' [part 1], *Sovetskaya muzïka*, 9 (1984), 49–50.

not take a single step to hear my compositions in a decent performance. While this hope is not extinguished, I must not let slip the opportunity to learn something. Prokofiev is another matter . . . his creativity is genuine, of divine provenance, so to speak.[28]

He managed to spend an evening with Asafiev when he returned to Petrograd in mid-October while waiting to hear where his platoon would be sent next. They were joined by Prokofiev, who had been away for the summer and much of the autumn – first on holiday to London in June (a present from his mother to mark his graduation from the conservatoire) and then in the spa resort of Kislovodsk in the North Caucasus. Prokofiev's sojourn in London coincided with the Diaghilev company's touring productions of opera and ballet at the Theatre Royal in Drury Lane, which afforded an opportunity to meet the famous impresario. Diaghilev was sufficiently impressed by the compositions that Prokofiev performed for him as to express interest in commissioning him. Prokofiev was now hard at work on *Ala and Lolly*, a ballet score based on a scenario by Sergey Gorodetsky that was conspicuously indebted to the *Rite of Spring* in its evocation of the barbarous Scythians, a tribe of nomadic warriors which controlled extensive territories along the Black Sea coast between 600 BC and 300 AD. Only a few days previously, he had received a telegram from Diaghilev inviting him to Rome for further discussions of the project. Prokofiev was understandably eager to go, although the long journey would be far from straightforward in wartime.[29]

A summons of a very different nature awaited Myaskovsky. Instead of being assigned to construct defences at another location near Petrograd, as he had expected, his militia half-company was absorbed into the regular army to form the 26th Sapper Battalion and was being dispatched to the front in Galicia[30], a province of the Austro-Hungarian Empire straddling south-eastern Poland and western Ukraine which had been overrun by Russian forces in the early months of the war. Its occupation was a cause of considerable concern to the Central Powers, as it raised the possibility of Russian incursions into Hungary and other territories of the empire.

Myaskovsky's battalion was to be stationed in the vicinity of Przemyśl, a small city just inside the present-day Polish border with Ukraine. It is difficult for the modern visitor to this picturesque region of Poland, with its rich pastureland and winding country lanes lined with fruit and walnut trees, to imagine that it witnessed some of the fiercest fighting of the war: an account of events by a Hungarian historian is aptly entitled 'The Great

28 Myaskovsky to Asafiev, 12 October 1914, RGALI, 2658/1/636, ll. 34–34ob.

29 Prokof'yev, *Dnevnik 1907–1918*, 478–81, 512–14.

30 Myaskovsky's 'Posluzhnoy spisok' (service record), RGAVMF, 406/9/2791M, ll. 30ob.

Graveyard'.[31] Przemyśl and its environs were of major strategic importance, being the site of a massive fortress (the third-largest in Europe after Antwerp and Verdun) surrounded by forty-four forts disposed in two rings, the outer of which extended over a circumference of twenty-eight miles. The fortress was constructed to strengthen the northern-eastern frontier of the Austro-Hungarian Empire when relations with Russia deteriorated as a result of the Crimean War. It safeguarded not only an important land route over the Carpathian Mountains between Poland and Hungary but also road and rail links between Vienna and L'viv.[32] At the outbreak of hostilities, over 130,000 soldiers were garrisoned there. Although the fortress was now deep behind enemy lines, it had resisted capture by the Russian army which laid siege to it between 4 (17) and 27 September (10 October), an engagement that left ten thousand Russian troops dead or wounded. A second siege was instituted on 23 October (5 November), which sought to starve the garrison into submission by encircling it completely and blocking its supply lines.[33]

Myaskovsky left for the front on 2 November.[34] Two weeks previously, a sapper captain with whom the family had a connection, Ivan Avgustovsky, had offered to arrange a transfer to his regiment in Reval (now Tallinn, the capital of Estonia). Avgustovsky and his wife pressed him to accept, promising pleasant living conditions and even proposing that he should live with them.[35] He evidently declined this proposal, as he similarly declined a proposal to appoint him commander of a company when the 26th Sapper Battalion was formed, because he felt he would be abandoning the men in the platoon that he had led previously.[36] These decisions testify to the seriousness with which he took his responsibilities and his duty of care as an officer.

The lengthy journey to Galicia followed a circuitous route via Kiev, which he passed through on 6 November, and by 16 November he was in L'viv, sixty miles east of Przemyśl.[37] In the meantime, Koussevitzky had performed *Alastor* twice, in Moscow on 5 November and in Petrograd on 12 November. The orchestra's playing in Moscow impressed Derzhanovsky as

31 László Szabó, *A nagy temető (Przemysl ostroma 1914–1915)* (Budapest, 1982).

32 For an account of the history and design of the Przemyśl complex, see Tomasz Idzikowski, *Twierdza Przemyśl: Powstanie, rozwój, technologia* (Krosno, 2014).

33 For a useful overview of events, see Graydon A. Tunstall, *Written in Blood: The Battles for Fortress Przemyśl in WWI* (Bloomington, 2016).

34 Myaskovsky to Asafiev, 1 November 1914, RGALI, 2658/1/636, l. 38.

35 Yakovlev to Myaskovsky, 11 October 1914, RGALI, 2040/2/290, l. 26.

36 Myaskovsky to Asafiev, 2 February 1915, RGALI, 2658/1/637, l. 20b.

37 Myaskovsky to Yelikonida Myaskovskaya, 6 November 1914, RGALI, 2040/1/75, l. 1; Myaskovsky to Derzhanovsky, 15 November 1914, RNMM, 3/365.

'anaemic' and 'lifeless': he wondered whether Koussevitzky had been nervous about conducting the piece.[38] Asafiev and Prokofiev furnished similar reports of its rendition at the Petrograd concert, faulting the conductor for his excessively cautious tempi. Despite the inadequacies of the performance, they judged *Alastor* to be very good on the whole, though with some reservations. Prokofiev found it overlong and thought that the orchestration needed to be revised in places, while Asafiev was disappointed by the music portraying the mysterious maiden of Alastor's dream-vision.[39] In a characteristic overreaction, Myaskovsky decided that the work was seriously flawed and supplemented his friends criticisms' with a lengthy list of his own, telling Asafiev that he was incapable of evoking 'the eternal and un-eternal feminine' because they were temperamentally alien to him.[40]

He had little time to dwell on these gloomy reflections, as he was swept up in a further round of hectic activity immediately on arrival in L'viv. Five days later, on 22 November, he was put in sole change of a half-company of one hundred men and tasked with the construction of defence works near Sokilnyky, a small town five miles to the south. His lodgings were more salubrious than previously (he was able to occupy a house abandoned by an Austrian officer, which was still in reasonably good condition), but his days were long and gruelling.[41] The defences were to extend over a five-mile stretch of terrain and much of what had been proposed proved impracticable. To complicate matters, he experienced considerable difficulty hiring local labourers to assist with the task. Galicia was one of the poorest and most backward regions of the Austrian empire, and the occupying Russian forces were viewed with considerable suspicion by the native population. Myaskovsky found himself trying to supervise a workforce of half-starved Polish and Ruthenian peasants who regularly deserted. The weather quickly deteriorated, and before long he and his men were toiling knee-deep in mud and slushy snow.[42] Writing to his father, he described the disorganisation with which he had to contend:

> They promised to send at least 1,000 workers to help. . ., they promised to provide rations for these workers – and the end result? I have only 250 workers at hand, but the rations didn't arrive in time, which means that they're going to desert. So now, they want our regiment to do all the

38　Derzhanovsky to Myaskovsky, 11 November 1914, RNMM, 71/262.

39　Asafiev to Myaskovsky, 13 November 1914, in Kozlova (ed.), '"Chuvstvuya polnotu oshchushcheniya"' [part 1], 50; Prokofiev to Myaskovsky, 20 and 21 November 1914, in Kozlova and Yatsenko, *Perepiska*, 126–7.

40　Myaskovsky to Asafiev, 5 December 1914, RGALI, 2658/1/636, l. 41.

41　Myaskovsky to Vera Yakovleva, 27 November 1914, RGALI, 2040/1/82, ll. 5–7ob.

42　Myaskovsky to Derzhanovsky, 3 December 1914, RNMM, 3/366.

work on our own; and on top of that, man our position all day . . ., look after the equipment, and find workers, and find food for them and money to pay them; and they can't even fulfil the simplest of requests, such as deliver the equipment that we need punctually. At times, I find it almost impossible to keep going.

Later in the letter, he highlighted the incongruity of the activity in which he was engaged amidst such lovely surroundings: '[It's] a gorgeous, picturesque place . . .. The air is fresh, and when the sun shines it's almost like springtime . . .. Rooks and skylarks dart over the fields; and when there was snow in the trenches, you could see baby stoats running about and wild goats in the woods. And the woods look beautiful – beeches, oaks, and spruces now and then'.[43] One day merged swiftly into the next and it was often difficult even to find an hour to attend to his personal correspondence. 'Time flies so quickly that weeks flit by as in a kaleidoscope', he wrote to his sister Vera: 'You end up losing all sense of time'.[44]

On the whole, Myaskovsky coped surprisingly well with the physical and mental demands of his role – far better than his friends might have expected, given his shyness and introversion. He acknowledged that the experience was not without its beneficial aspects: he told Derzhanovsky that he felt it had developed his character and helped to toughen him up, enabling him to respond with greater equanimity to professional setbacks and criticisms of his music.[45] He was also fortunate to remain in good health in spite of the challenging working conditions during the bitterly cold winter of 1914–15 – unlike Saradzhev, who developed streptococcal quinsy with potentially life-threatening complications and had to be invalided out for an extended period.[46]

The coming months would tax his resilience to the utmost. In November and December, the forces garrisoned at Przemyśl made several unsuccessful sorties in an attempt to break the siege and rejoin the main body of the Austro-Hungarian army, which had launched an offensive in the vicinity of Sanok – a town forty miles to the southwest in the foothills of the Carpathian Mountains. The Russians responded by intensifying the siege and assaulting outlying fortified positions to the north. By mid-January, Myaskovsky's battalion was moved nearer to the conflict zone. It is difficult to track his movements during this period, as the strict censorship imposed

---

43 Myaskovsky to Yakov Myaskovsky, 7 December 1914, RGALI, 2040/1/76, ll. 1–3.

44 Myaskovsky to Vera Yakovleva, 19 December 1914, RGALI, 2040/1/82, l. 8.

45 Myaskovsky to Derzhanovsky, 10 December 1914, RNMM, 3/367.

46 Saradzhev to Myaskovsky, 2 January 1915, RGALI, 2040/2/240, l. 3; Tigranov (ed.), *Saradzhev*, 74.

FIGURE 4.1. Myaskovsky (second from left) in Przemyśl (spring 1915).

on letters from the front prevented him from disclosing his precise location.[47] However, it emerges that he was sufficiently close to the enemy lines
as to be in genuine danger. His half-company was tasked with constructing
trenches near a village that had been virtually destroyed by artillery fire.
He recounted to Derzhanovsky how they were forced to spend a sleepless
night in the freezing cold, as there was nowhere to shelter. The following morning, their position was shelled by the enemy. One of his men was
wounded and another killed outright, his arm and chest ripped away by the
force of the blast. Both had been standing only a short distance from him.
Shells continued to explode overhead, and the air was thick with the acrid
stench of burning and gunpowder smoke. Witnessing scenes of this kind
was difficult enough, but if anything, he was even more troubled by his psychological reactions to the circumstances in which he found himself. 'My
peaceable nature notwithstanding, I can feel destructive instincts developing', he wrote. 'When there's rifle-fire going on under your nose (recon-
naissance patrols often bump into one another), I long to grab someone's
gun and try to pick off an Austrian myself. And here I am writing about this
beastliness and I really don't feel the slightest pang of conscience'.[48]

Although he spared his family such gruesome accounts, he was evidently
deeply perturbed by the brutalisation of human nature wrought by war,
which felt like wholesale regression to savagery. He returned to the subject
in a letter to Asafiev, describing his numbed reactions to the horrific deaths

---

47   The censors routinely excised information from letters that might potentially
     be useful to the enemy, as well as soldiers' criticisms of the army or of the
     conduct of the war: see Vladimir Chernyayev, 'K izucheniyu èpistolyarnïkh
     istochnikov nachala XX v. (kontrol' pochtovoy perepiski)', in Arkadiy Man'kov
     et al. (ed.), *Problemï otechestvennoy istorii*, vol. 1 (Moscow and Leningrad,
     1976), 148–50.
48   Myaskovsky to Derzhanovsky, 14 January 1915, RNMM, 3/370.

and injuries suffered by his sappers, and his sense of being party to a monstrous crime against the natural order:

> The absence of even minimal constraints on human nature turns people into some sort of primitive savages: one's inner life doesn't receive the slightest nourishment . . .. I have formed the view that war is the most appalling, ruthless, and obscenely cunning manhunt, on the one hand, and a pitiful and often impotent attempt at self-defence, on the other. Individual instances of heroism, nobility, and such like – which I've never had occasion to witness, incidentally – would hardly change my view of the matter. And when you see the wonderful natural surroundings here, the glorious woods, mountain streams, and valleys, and so forth, then you feel all the enormity of human folly. . . . In war, man is stripped almost completely of his personality. All in all, war is one of the greatest sacrileges against man and nature.[49]

And yet, life carried on: even in the midst of such devastation, the ruined village's inhabitants did not deviate from their usual routine – he watched men digging up potatoes and women washing clothes in the stream, while children ran about playing nearby.

On 22 January 1915, Myaskovsky was awarded the Order of St Anna, Third Class, one of four decorations for valour and distinguished service that he received during his army career.[50] It is noteworthy that Myaskovsky did not draw attention to these awards either at the time or subsequently, and never sought to present his wartime activities in a glamorous or heroic light. When Derzhanovsky asked him again to contribute to *Music* and proposed publishing his articles under the caption 'From Our Musical Correspondent in the Field Army', Myaskovsky balked at the idea, and had to point out once more the infeasibility of the request.[51] He was also discomfited when Derzhanovsky subsequently published photographs of him in two successive issues of *Music* in February 1915 and ironically upbraided his friend for 'trying to cash in on the war'.[52]

The two issues in question carried an article on the Third Symphony and reproduced a laudatory review of its premiere, which was given by the orchestra of the Moscow branch of the Russian Musical Society under Emil

---

49 Myaskovsky to Asafiev, 2 February 1915, RGALI, 2658/1/637, ll. 1–10b, 20b–3.

50 'Posluzhnoy spisok', RGAVMF, 406/9/2791M, l. 30b. Another service record preserved amongst Myaskovsky's personal papers, written in his own hand and dating from 1923, records the award of being of Fourth Class, and lists three others: the Order of St Anna, Second Class; and the Order of St Stanislav, Second and Third Class: RGALI, 2040/1/168, l. 20b.

51 Myaskovsky to Derzhanovsky, 14 January 1915, RNMM, 3/370.

52 Myaskovsky to Derzhanovsky, 1 March 1915, RNMM, 3/372.

Kuper on 14 February.[53] (Practical circumstances had forced the concert to be postponed by a month.[54]) Derzhanovsky attended the rehearsals as well as the concert and was highly enthusiastic, telling his friend that the work had been warmly received and made a 'stunning' impression in places. 'I absolutely loved the symphony', he continued, 'and so will everyone else in time, especially when you make some changes to the orchestration'.[55] Hypersensitive as usual, Myaskovsky inferred from the latter remark that his writing for the orchestra sounded incompetent, and responded with a list of anxious queries about the effectiveness of the scoring in various passages.[56] Derzhanovsky hastened to reassure him that his impression was mistaken, as did Asafiev, who sent a lengthy letter in which he sought to allay his friend's anxieties.[57] Myaskovsky's frustration at being unable to attend the premieres of *Alastor* and the Third Symphony is readily understandable, as is his uncertainty about how to interpret the reports of his friends, whom he suspected of trying to spare his feelings. His uncertainty was heightened by the reviewers' responses to both scores. Though generally respectful (with one or two exceptions), they were not very perceptive: his music's complexity and its deliberate eschewal of sensuous appeal were found rather forbidding.

For this reason, Myaskovsky keenly appreciated Asafiev's efforts on his behalf in his new métier as music critic – a development for which he had been responsible, having recommended Asafiev to Derzhanovsky as a potential contributor to *Music*.[58] After the outbreak of war, Asafiev effectively took over from him as the periodical's Petrograd correspondent. Under the pen name of 'Igor Glebov', he published a lengthy review of *Alastor* which gave a detailed account of its literary basis and formal organisation.[59] After the premiere of the Third Symphony, which was dedicated to him, he followed up with 'Myaskovsky's Creative Path'[60], a substantial article that aimed to promote sympathetic understanding of his friend's recent work. Myaskovsky was very supportive in turn of Asafiev's journalistic activities and repeatedly praised his contributions to *Music* for their perceptiveness

53 'Simfoniya a-moll (No. 3) N. Myaskovskogo', *Muzïka*, 14 February 1915, 104–9; 'Yu. É (v *Russkikh vedomostyakh*) o III simfonii Myaskovskogo', *Muzïka*, 21 February 1915, 133–4.

54 Derzhanovsky to Myaskovsky, 31 December 1914, RNMM, 71/280.

55 Derzhanovsky to Myaskovsky, 15 February 1915, RNMM, 71/287.

56 Myaskovsky to Derzhanovsky, 1 March 1915, RNMM, 3/372.

57 Derzhanovsky to Myaskovsky, 14 March 1915, RNMM, 71/291; Asafiev to Myaskovsky, 2–12 March 1915, in Kozlova, '"Chuvstvuya polnotu oshchushcheniya"' [part 1], 52–3.

58 Asaf'yev, 'O sebe', 472. Asafiev's first contribution, a review of the 1913–14 St Petersburg season of opera, was published in the issue of 15 March 1914.

59 '*Alastor* Myaskovskogo', *Muzïka*, 22 November 1915, 547–54.

60 See chapter 3, fn91.

and interesting content.[61] In spite of the cordiality of their relationship, however, it was not altogether free of tension. By this point, Asafiev had virtually given up composing after suffering a crisis of confidence in his talent.[62] It cannot have been easy for him to observe the growing professional recognition accorded Prokofiev and Myaskovsky by influential commentators such as Karatïgin, who referred to them in an article published in early 1915 as being amongst the most gifted figures of their generation.[63] Myaskovsky was sensitive to this circumstance and displayed both modesty and tact when discussing his own work with him. Matters were complicated by the fact that he found it difficult to be reciprocally complimentary about Asafiev's compositions. Asafiev was phenomenally fluent and could turn out a substantial ballet score in a fortnight, but Myaskovsky could muster little enthusiasm for the results: he was severely critical of his friend's 'primitive harmonies and naïve melodies' and thought that he had an unrealistic view of his capabilities.[64] Anxious to avoid hurting Asafiev's feelings, he did his utmost to find positive things to say without sounding insincere: in a letter of October 1914, for example, he expressed regret that Asafiev was composing so little and encouraged him to try his hand at writing instrumental works.[65] It was easier to be complimentary about his journalism, but Asafiev can hardly have failed to register Myaskovsky's muted response to his music. In time, these circumstances would place a serious strain on their friendship.

Asafiev apparent inability to bring the critical acumen that he evinced in his reviews to bear on his own compositional efforts puzzled Myaskovsky, for whom acute self-dissatisfaction was a habitual state of mind. 'If the Austrians' monstrous toys spare me, then maybe I will manage to bring less dishevelled offspring into the world', he remarked to Derzhanovsky after the premiere of the Third Symphony.[66] Writing to Vera, he voiced anxiety that the protracted enforced suspension of creative work would have detrimental consequences: 'I have formed the firm and unshakeable conviction that all distractions from music are harmful: art demands that you dedicate yourself to it entirely, and not allow your work to be interrupted. Otherwise,

---

61　See, for example, Myaskovsky to Asafiev, 21 December 1914 and 21 February 1915, RGALI, 2658/1/636, l. 44 and 2658/1/637, l. 6.

62　In a letter to Myaskovsky of 5 July 1914, Asafiev once more discussed his doubts about his abilities and mentioned that he had written very little for some time: Kozlova, '"Chuvstvuya polnotu oshchushcheniya"', [part 2], 102–3.

63　Vyacheslav Karatïgin, 'Noveyshiye tendentsii v russkoy muzïke', *Severnïye zapiski*, 2 (1915), 99–109.

64　Myaskovsky to Prokofiev, 26 July 1907, in Kozlova and Yatsenko, *Perepiska*, 43; Myaskovsky to Derzhanovsky, 14 March 1912, RNMM, 3/246.

65　Myaskovsky to Asafiev, 12 October 1914, RGALI, 2658/1/636, l. 35.

66　Myaskovsky to Derzhanovsky, 1 March 1915, RNMM, 3/372.

your brain starts to rust and stop functioning properly, and your ear loses its sensitivity. If I ever return from this, I'm afraid that I'm almost going to have to start all over again'.[67]

Returning to the peace and quiet of his study was as yet a remote prospect, however. Throughout February and early March, the Russian army subjected Przemyśl Fortress to continuous bombardment and succeeded in capturing outlying strongholds to the north. The position of the besieged occupants became increasingly desperate: food supplies were running out and the hospitals could no longer deal with the numbers of sick and wounded. Weakened by severe malnutrition, the garrison troops became easy prey to disease. Fearing that morale and discipline might break down altogether, the fortress commander ordered a further sortie in an attempt to break the siege, which commenced at dawn on 6 (19) March. After several hours of fierce fighting, the sortie troops were forced to withdraw back into the fortress. On 9 (22) March, the garrison of over 2,500 officers and 117,000 solders surrendered, having first destroyed anything that might be of use to the enemy. The siege had lasted 133 days.[68]

In the lead-up to the sortie, other Austro-Hungarian army divisions mounted feint attacks to the south and south-west as a diversionary tactic. Myaskovsky's company was caught up in one of these engagements: he described to Derzhanovsky the eerie sensation that he experienced on seeing the huge craters made by 12-inch shells near his dugout. He was present at the surrender of Fort VII, 'Prałkowce', four miles west of the city. Three days later, he returned to a position nearer the front lines to oversee the repair of transport routes along a thirty-mile stretch extending south-eastward from the railway junction of Zagórz towards the Volovets Pass in the Carpathian Mountains. The weather remained unremittingly foul; it was unusually cold, and his company laboured in blizzards and driving rain, trying to patch roads that were in such a poor state as to be almost beyond remedy. Heavy fighting continued to the south-west around Medzilaborce, a town now situated five miles over the Polish-Slovakian border, and the Russian army sustained serious losses. Of the sixteen thousand men in the 81st Infantry Division, with which Myaskovsky's company had worked near Przemyśl, less than a quarter remained after an engagement on 22–23 March (4–5 April): the rest were killed or taken captive. He detected worrying indications of declining morale amongst the Russian troops, who had fought throughout the long, harsh winter in exceptionally challenging conditions. As he remarked to Derzhanovsky, his company's

67 Myaskovsky to Vera Yakovleva, 1–14 March 1915, RGALI, 2040/2/82, ll. 11–120b.
68 Tunstall, *Written in Blood*, 268–94.

task was not made any easier by the 'scandalous confusion, inadequate oversight, poor communication, and other such delights as prevail here'.[69]

A feeling of futility became increasingly pervasive. 'I'm sick of roads, I'm sick of bridges, I'm sick of filthy villages, bovine offal, and horse carcases', he wrote to Derzhanovsky on 7 April. He was billeted in a succession of peasant huts: their foetid interiors reeked of smoke and crawled with bedbugs, fleas, and lice. His legs broke out in boils, one of which was so painful that he was temporarily unable to ride his horse and carry out his round of inspections on the worksite. His battalion continued to be transferred closer to the front and by 20 April he was in the village of Radoszyce, only ten miles from Medzilaborce.[70] While in transit, he received a letter from Asafiev inform-ing him that the Court Orchestra had given fine performances of *Silence* and the Second Symphony under Hugo Wahrlich at a concert in Petrograd on 6 April.[71] The upsurge of interest in his work showed no signs of abating: even Siloti was now talking about conducting one of his compositions and had asked to see the score of the Third Symphony.[72]

In his letters home, Myaskovsky played down the hazards to which he was exposed, not wishing to worry his family. Nonetheless, they were suf-ficiently alarmed by reports received from other sources as to press him to accept Avgustovsky's renewed offer to arrange a transfer – a proposal to which he consented.[73] Processing the request would take some time, how-ever; until it was granted, they had to be content with doing what little they could to care for him at a distance and endure the anxious waits to hear from him. Postal deliveries to and from the front had become increasingly erratic: not infrequently, letters went astray or were held up for weeks while awaiting inspection by the censors, so Myaskovsky increasingly resorted to asking colleagues to act as couriers when they went home on leave. His

---

69   Myaskovsky to Derzhanovsky, 1 April 1915, RNMM, 3/375. The general accuracy of Myaskovsky's tally of the losses sustained by the 81st Infantry Division is confirmed by army records: see Aleksandr Kollerov and Andrey Samoylov, *Nezabïtaya voyna – Nezabïtïye sud'bï. Kovrovskiy, Gorbatovskiy, Klyaz'minskiy pekhotnïye polki: Boyevoy put', lyudi i podvigi* (Vladimir, 2014), 209.

70   Myaskovsky to Asafiev, 7 April 1915, RGALI, 2658/1/637, l. 8; Myaskovsky to Derzhanovsky, 7 April 1915, RNMM, 3/376; Myaskovsky to Yelikonida Myaskovskaya, 20 April 1915, RGALI, 2040/1/75, ll.2–30b; Myaskovsky to Valentina Menshikova [*née* Myaskovskaya], 17 May 1915, RGALI, 2040/1/74, ll. 1–20b.

71   Asafiev to Myaskovsky, 7 April 1915, in Kozlova, '"Chuvstvuya polnotu oshchushcheniya"' [part 2], 89.

72   Myaskovsky to Vera Myaskovskaya, 7 April 1915, RGALI, 2040/1/82, ll. 130b–14.

73   Vera Yakovleva to Myaskovsky, 27 March and 7 April 1915, RGALI, 2040/2/293, ll. 28, 380b.

sisters did their best to keep him supplied with necessities – socks and undergarments, soap, delousing preparations of camphor and sabadilla – as well as reading material and small luxuries such as chocolate. In return, he regularly sent money from his wages to help offset the rapidly rising cost of living in Petrograd.

Just as conditions started to become more tolerable with the arrival of spring, the Russian army's fortunes suffered a dramatic reversal. On 18 April (1 May), the Central Powers launched a major offensive along a thirty-mile front extending southwards from Tarnów, roughly fifty miles east of Kraków, to Gorlice.[74] By this point, the Russian forces were critically short of men and munitions, and although they initially offered heavy resistance, they were soon forced to cede their positions. The enemy troops pressed relentlessly forward and by 3 (16) May had reached Przemyśl. From 23 April (6 May) Myaskovsky's company was swept up in a nerve-wracking, hastily improvised retreat north-eastward to Jarosław, twenty miles north of Przemyśl, and thence onward in the direction of Oleszyce – a journey of over one hundred miles.[75] By 17 (29) May, it halted near Lubaczów, a town located about eight miles from the modern border with Ukraine, and he finally managed to send word to family and friends. 'I don't think you could imagine what we've been through', he told Valentina:

> What a terrible rout and frantic retreat: we literally fled pell-mell for a week and only stopped on 1 May when we reached the outskirts of Jarosław, where dreadfully fierce fighting broke out. In the noise of the artillery fire, you couldn't distinguish a single individual shot: it was like some kind of fiendish hellish pounding, which, if it died down, was replaced by the sound of a ferocious deluge – of machine gun and rifle fire. It was like something out of a nightmare and continued for three days without let-up. .... During those engagements we slept no more than two or three hours a day, and then only after a fashion – on the ground, virtually on top of a dunghill. Once I was leading the company on horseback and dozed off to sleep until I heard a shout, 'Nikolay Yakovlevich, wake up, you're falling off your horse!' . ... We're still in a very overwrought state: although I've slept soundly for two nights now, I have yet to catch up properly on sleep – my nerves are shot.[76]

74　On this campaign, see Juliusz Bator, *Wojna galicyjska: Działania armii austro-węgierskiej na froncie północnym (galicyjskim) w latach 1914–1915* (Kraków, 2005), 216–77; Richard L. DiNardo, *Breakthrough: The Gorlice-Tarnow Campaign, 1915* (Santa Barbara, 2010).

75　For a classic account of the Russian army's retreat, see Norman Stone, *The Eastern Front: 1914–1917* (London, 1975), 165–93.

76　Myaskovsky to Valentina Menshikova, 17 May 1915, RGALI, 2040/1/74, ll. 1–20b.

He elaborated more fully on the causes of his persistent state of exhaustion to Derzhanovsky. The Russians had suffered such severe losses that regiments were now at less than two-fifths of their former strength: from the Third Army alone, the number of dead, wounded, and captured came to over two hundred thousand.[77] No reinforcements had been sent. By sheer luck, his sapper battalion managed to survive more or less intact but was still in a perilously exposed position. In a passage that would undoubtedly have raised eyebrows in the censorship bureau, he excoriated the Grand Duke Nicholas Nikolayevich, Radko Dimitriev, and the other 'scandalously mediocre' Russian commanders on the Eastern front for their incompetence and failure to take seriously the threat of a German counteroffensive in Galicia.[78] 'We have no plan of campaign, no weapons, no supply organisation, no troops', he wrote. 'There are no surgical dressings or medications in the field hospitals!'[79] As he had recently been appointed acting company commander, his burden of responsibility increased considerably.

He was by no means out of danger. A week later, he was in the nearby village of Maczugi overseeing the construction of defences and trenches. Enemy troops were positioned a mere two hundred yards away and he could have come under fire at any moment. The news that the Germans had recaptured Przemyśl only reinforced his conviction of the campaign's pointlessness. He was due a period of leave but learned that it had been postponed until further notice. 'In all forces, it's only natural that the high command should get especially fatigued, so they require leave as a matter of priority', he remarked sarcastically to Derzhanovsky.[80] When a recent issue of the *Russian Musical Gazette* arrived in the post and he opened it to see a review of the Court Orchestra's performance of his Second Symphony[81], he told Asafiev that it felt strangely unreal – as though he were being written about posthumously.[82] Composing was rapidly coming to seem like an activity that he had undertaken in a former life. His sense that the war marked the passing of an era was heightened by the news of Skryabin's premature demise on 14 (27 April) from sepsis, a fatal complication from a carbuncular infection of his upper lip, and Taneyev's death not long afterwards on 6 (19) June as an indirect result of attending Skryabin's funeral. (Taneyev

---

77   Tunstall, *Written in Blood*, 313.

78   The Russian military high command received reliable intelligence that a German counteroffensive was imminent but failed to make any preparations – with catastrophic consequences. See Stone, *The Eastern Front*, 136–40; Ivan Drenski, *General Radko Dimitriev: Biografichen ocherk* (Sofia, 1962), 168–72.

79   Myaskovsky to Derzhanovsky, 17 May 1915, RNMM, 3/379.

80   Myaskovsky to Derzhanovsky, 24 May 1915, RNMM, 3/381.

81   ['Bertram'], 'Khronika', *Russkaya muzïkal'naya gazeta*, 19 April 1915, 308–10.

82   Myaskovsky to Asafiev, 24 May 1915, RGALI, 2658/1/637, l. 140b.

developed pneumonia after standing outside the church for several hours in torrential rain, waiting patiently amongst the very large crowd of mourners in the mistaken expectation that someone would deliver a graveside oration.)[83] Over the previous few years, Myaskovsky's admiration for Skryabin had cooled considerably: he confessed to Derzhanovsky that he had never taken Skryabin's messianic posturing seriously, though he continued to profess appreciation for his music.[84] His high regard for Taneyev, however, remained unchanged.

Amongst the other correspondents to whom Myaskovsky owed a letter was Prokofiev, who had recently returned from a six-week sojourn in Italy made possible by Diaghilev's largesse.[85] In addition to organising a performance of the Second Piano Concerto in Rome and introducing him to wealthy patrons, Diaghilev laid on sightseeing excursions to Naples, Pompeii, and Capri. His principal motivation for inviting Prokofiev to Italy, however, was to find out how the commissioned ballet score was progressing. When Prokofiev played his sketch, Diaghilev was unenthusiastic: he insisted on an entirely new scenario and that much of the music be jettisoned. Prokofiev was uncharacteristically pliant in the face of these demands – not least because Diaghilev held out the tantalising prospect of a dazzling Parisian success comparable to those that Stravinsky had enjoyed. The impresario's argument was straightforward: Paris, rather than provincial Petrograd, was the international arbiter of artistic fashion, so if Prokofiev wished to be famous, he should consciously craft his work to appeal to Parisian tastes. Towards the end of his stay, Diaghilev introduced him to Stravinsky in Milan. The encounter with his eminent compatriot decisively shaped Prokofiev's professional ambitions and sparked his determination to achieve comparable renown. As he reported to Myaskovsky, Stravinsky and Diaghilev encouraged him to capitalise on the continuing Parisian vogue for everything Russian because 'internationalism' was out of favour there; so too, they informed him, was Romantic emotionality and pathos. He also relayed Diaghilev's expression of interest in hearing some of Myaskovsky's music.[86]

Myaskovsky's response highlights the marked disparity between the two men's temperaments. 'Since my work exhibits both pathos and emotionality as well as all the other characteristics that are currently unfashionable, I see no point in showing it to him', he wrote. Having previously expressed

83   Yuriy Éngel', 'A. N. Skryabin: biograficheskiy ocherk', *Muzikal'nïy sovremennik*, 4–5 (1916), 90–5.

84   Myaskovsky to Derzhanovsky, 24 May 1915, RNMM, 3/380.

85   See Prokofiev's account in *Dnevnik: 1907–1918*, 543–57.

86   Prokofiev to Myaskovsky, 10 April 1915, in Kozlova and Yatsenko, *Perepiska*, 133.

surprise that Prokofiev had consented 'to mangle' his score at the impresario's behest[87], he did not conceal his disappointment that he would continue
to expend energy on mere 'applied music'[88] for a ballet, rather than something more worthwhile.[89] Another composer would have eagerly seized the
opportunity to establish a connection with Diaghilev, but Myaskovsky did
not: he had no interest in writing a ballet score and felt that working with
Diaghilev would entail unacceptable compromises of artistic autonomy and
integrity. He was evidently horrified at the idea that he might not have complete control over the musical conception or come under pressure to adapt
his style in conformity with Parisian fashions to make his work a more mar-
ketable commodity. The matter was not pursued any further.

Prokofiev was a notably less regular correspondent than Asafiev and
Derzhanovsky, and as the war wore on, his letters became increasingly
intermittent. He spoke occasionally of performing one of Myaskovsky's
piano sonatas in concert, assuring him that they 'still adorned' his music
stand – but never did so.[90] Derzhanovsky, by contrast, tirelessly promoted
his friend's work and effectively became his agent, acting as intermediary
with conductors and dealing with enquiries about performing materials.
The Derzhanovskys became increasingly concerned by their friend's communications, which conveyed that he was under great stress.[91] 'I've continued to do my utmost to discharge my duties conscientiously up to now', he
wrote, 'but it costs me an unbelievable expenditure of nervous energy and
demands far too great an effort. I'm not only forced to do something that I
loathe, but must banish all thoughts of the only work that matters to me. . .
I so badly want to return to it, that I sometimes lose all self-possession and
am reduced to a state of complete mental and physical prostration'.[92]

The large-scale Russian retreat from Galicia continued apace. His position as acting company commander was made permanent and he was still
unable to take leave. Avgustovsky persisted in his efforts to arrange a transfer, but the shortage of officers at the front presented a serious obstacle:

---

87 Myaskovsky to Prokofiev, 7 April 1915, ibid., 132–3.

88 *Prikladnaya muzïka* – the customary Russian term for music serving an
    ancillary purpose, such as incidental music or film music.

89 Myaskovsky to Prokofiev, 17 May 1915, in Kozlova and Yatsenko, *Perepiska*,
    135.

90 Prokofiev to Myaskovsky, 29 April and 15 June 1915, ibid., 133–4, 136. Prokofiev
    began to learn Myaskovsky's Second Sonata in February 1920 with the
    intention of performing it, but found it very difficult and did not include it in
    his repertoire. Prokof'yev, *Dnevnik 1919–1933*, ed. Svyatoslav Prokof'yev (Paris,
    2002), 79–80.

91 Koposova-Derzhanovskaya, 'V. V. Derzhanovskiy po vospominaniyam zhenï i
    druga', RNMM, 3/3365, l. 42.

92 Myaskovsky to Derzhanovsky, 28 May 1915, RNMM, 3/381.

the battalion commander Nikolay Totleben refused his consent.[93] By 21 June, Myaskovsky's company had moved seventy miles further north-east to Hrubieszów. Conditions there were initially quieter, if still chaotic, but did not remain so for long.[94] 'We've been under non-stop bombardment for three days now', he wrote to Yevgeniya on 3 July. 'They keep attacking at night, but fortunately we've been able to fend them off (they attacked six times last night) – machine guns and rifles sputtering, bombs crashing, shrapnel shells whining and wailing. By day, the artillery fire sounds as though enormous elephants are cavorting about wildly on gigantic corrugated iron roofs'. Totleben had to be treated for shellshock and there was no-one sufficiently experienced to replace him during his absence, which only compounded the prevailing disorganisation. Myaskovsky found himself trying to manage construction works over an impracticably wide area (some of his troops were ten miles away) with a much reduced contingent and inadequate communications. The forces stationed in the vicinity had little notion of how the wider campaign was progressing: when newspapers reached them, they were up to ten days old. He did not lose all hope of being transferred to Reval, but it would evidently require pressure to be brought to bear by someone higher up the chain of command. The protracted physical and mental strain was taking its toll: he found it difficult to sleep because his skin was still erupting in painful boils.[95]

Mercifully, he was granted leave sooner than expected. By 19 July he was in Petrograd and spent just over a week there seeing family and friends.[96] On the evening of 28 July he caught the overnight train to Moscow[97], where he stayed with the Derzhanovskys until 10 August. His hosts tactfully avoided discussing the war, as the subject visibly agitated him, but concentrated on making his stay as restful and pleasant as possible.[98] He spent much of the time at the piano accompanying Derzhanovskaya in songs by Debussy and Russian composers. His brief holiday passed all too quickly. On the day of his departure, he maintained a stoical reserve as they accompanied him to the train station; anxious to avoid any emotional scenes, he took leave of them abruptly and hastened into his carriage. As they waited

93 Myaskovsky to Derzhanovsky, 10 June 1915, RNMM, 3/382; Valentina Menshikova to Myaskovsky, 21 June 1915, RGALI, 2040/2/189, ll. 7–80b; Myaskovsky to Valentina Menshikova, 21 June 1915, RGALI, 2040/1/74, ll. 5–60b.

94 Myaskovsky to Derzhanovsky, 29 June 1915, RNMM, 3/384.

95 Myaskovsky to Yevgeniya Sakharova (*née* Myaskovskaya), 3 July 1915, RGALI, 2040/1/80, ll. 1–20b.

96 Myaskovsky to Prokofiev, 19 July 1915, in Kozlova and Yatsenko, *Perepiska*, 138.

97 Myaskovsky to Derzhanovsky, 23 July 1915, RNMM, 3/387.

98 Koposova-Derzhanovskaya, 'Pamyati druga', 216.

FIGURE 4.2. Myaskovsky on leave in summer 1915, with
Yekaterina Koposova-Derzhanovskaya and Vladimir Derzhanovsky.

on the platform for the train to depart, they could see that his face was wet
with tears.[99]

The Central Powers armies forced the Russians relentlessly eastward over
the summer, and when Myaskovsky rejoined his company on 15 August it
had retreated 120 miles further north to the outskirts of Kobryn, a town
situated thirty miles east of Brest. The region was thronged with refugees
who had either fled the advancing German forces or been displaced by the
Russian army, which instituted a 'scorched earth' strategy as its retreated,
burning towns and villages to the ground.[100] 'I can hardly describe what's
going on', he wrote to Derzhanovsky. 'The highway is littered with carrion,
and along the edges – graves, and often also stiffening corpses and groups
of dying people. All are refugees. 1,300,000 of them have passed this way in
the last four days! . . . What's happening is appalling. And we're still being

---

99 Koposova-Derzhanovskaya, 'V. V. Derzhanovskiy po vospominaniyam zhenï i
    druga', RNMM, 3/3365, l. 45.

100 Peter Gatrell, *A Whole Empire Walking: Refugees in Russia during World War I*
    (Bloomington, 1999), 21.

pounded and pounded and pounded'.[101] The pace of the retreat accelerated. On 1 September he was close to Baranovichi and by 9 September in
Minsk, 220 miles further north-east.[102] Over the next six weeks, his company proceeded by a circuitous route towards Dvinsk (now Daugavpils in
south-eastern Latvia), another 190 miles to the north. Along the way, he
once more supervised work in positions close to enemy lines: he was busier
than ever, he told Derzhanovsky, as he had to use inexperienced volunteer
labourers and the tasks to be performed were unusually complex and challenging. His working day commenced at six or seven in the morning and
often did not finish until eleven at night – and even then he could not rest:
the staff members with whom he was billeted turned out to be a boorish and
disorderly lot, partial to gambling and drunken brawling.[103]

An end to this arduous nomadic existence was in sight, however. His
father took up the matter of his transfer directly with Totleben, and although
Yakov had retired, his former position in the military high command evidently still carried weight. (He had been promoted to the honorary rank of
engineer-general on his retirement.) On 21 August, he wrote to inform his
son that Totleben had consented and would attend to the necessary formalities.[104] Yakov's eagerness to remove him from danger was intensified
by concerns connected with his own declining health.[105] Though only in
their twenties, two of Myaskovsky's sisters were now widows (Valentina's
husband Vladimir Menshikov committed suicide before the war[106], leaving
her with a daughter who turned nine in 1915): as the only remaining son, he
had to assume the role of family breadwinner. Valentina had a clerical post
in the Imperial Chancellery, but like many other Russians, she struggled
to make ends meet due to the soaring cost of living. As she informed her
brother in June, staples such as eggs, flour, sugar, and meat were becoming
prohibitively expensive, when available at all.[107] Myaskovsky continued to
send his sisters money and, as commodities became scarcer, provisions to
supplement their diet. Their letters vividly illustrate the strategies to which

101 Myaskovsky to Derzhanovsky, 23 August 1915, RNMM, 3/389.

102 Myaskovsky to Derzhanovsky, 1 and 9 September 1915, RNMM, 3/390 and
　　　3/391.

103 Myaskovsky to Derzhanovsky, 26 September 1915, RNMM, 3/392.

104 Yakov Myaskovsky to Myaskovsky, undated letter [*circa* 21 August 1915],
　　　RGALI, 2040/1/134, l. 113–113ob.

105 Men'shikova *et al.*, 'Pamyati brata', 178.

106 Myaskovsky informed Prokofiev that Menshikov had shot himself because
　　　'he got mixed up in some financial dealings' – a euphemism, perhaps, for bad
　　　gambling debts (Prokof'yev, *Dnevnik 1919–1933*, 478). The family tree preserved
　　　in Myaskovsky's personal archive records the date of Menshikov's death as 12
　　　October 1909: RGALI, 2040/4/47, l. 81.

107 Valentina Menshikova, 19 June 1915, RGALI, 2040/2/189, ll. 7–80ob.

many had recourse to cope with wartime hardships: by 1917, food supply networks of family members and friends could mean the difference between life and death.[108] One of the first packages his sisters received contained twenty pounds of sugar tied up in a shirt (for want of anything else suitable), which a colleague returning home on leave brought in his luggage.[109]

After a month working on defences near Dvinsk under the command of a particularly cantankerous general, Myaskovsky's transfer finally came through. In mid-November he travelled to Reval via Petrograd – a journey of almost six hundred miles.[110] As 1915 drew to a close, the German advance halted and the eastern front stabilised along a line that curved south-eastwards from Riga to Dvinsk (roughly following the contour of the modern Lithuanian-Latvian border) and thence ran more or less directly south though Belorussia to Ternopil in Galicia. The front subsequently altered little until 1917. As Reval was almost two hundred miles north of Riga, Myaskovsky was well away from the conflict zone. On 1 January 1916 he was formally reassigned to the navy and appointed to the Construction Division at Peter the Great's Naval Fortress, part of a complex of fortifications erected along the northern and southern shores of the Gulf of Finland to protect St Petersburg after the disastrous rout of the Russian fleet in the Russo-Japanese War. Building works were still in progress when he arrived.[111]

Myaskovsky would remain in Reval for almost two years. This period of his life is more sparsely documented, and such correspondence as survives is comparatively uninformative about his day-to-day life, but it emerges that he was kept very busy in his new role. In April 1916 he was promoted to *Shtabs-kapitan*, a rank intermediate between captain and lieutenant; the following month he was seconded to the fortress sapper battalion and on 1 September took over as commander of its Second Company.[112] His

---

108 For a summary account of Russian food shortages during the war, see Peter Gatrell, *Russia's First World War: A Social and Economic History* (Abingdon and New York, 2014), 154–74.

109 Myaskovsky to Vera Yakovleva, 6 October 1915, RGALI, 2040/1/82, ll. 18–19.

110 Myaskovsky to Derzhanovsky, 25 October and 10 November 1915, RNMM, 3/395 and 3/397.

111 On the history of the fortress, see Leonid Amirkhanov, *Morskaya krepost' Imperatora Petra Velikogo* (St Petersburg, 1995).

112 'Prikazï Komendanta Morskoy kreposti Imperatora Petra Velikogo, 26-ogo aprelya 1916 goda. No. 827', NAE, 218/1/2, l. 147ob; 'Prikaz po Upravleniyu Stroitelya Morskoy kreposti Imperatora Petra Velikogo. 25-go maya 1916g., g. Revel'. No. 128', NAF, VeSa 8008; 'Vïpiska iz prikaza po Krepostnomu Sapyornomu batal'onu Morskoy kreposti Imperatora Petra Velikogo. No. 20. 1 sentyabrya 1916 goda', NAE, 4699/1/85, l. 89. There are minor discrepancies between these records and the details that Myaskovsky furnished in his 1923 service record, 'Posluzhnoy spisok', RGALI, 2040/1/168, l. 3.

duties appear to have been primarily administrative: he complained to Derzhanovsky of being worn out from dealing with 'cascades of paperwork' showered on him by his superiors. 'I've been spending days on end dashing about', he told his friend in May 1916, 'collating information, drawing up accounts and reports, and writing and writing'.[113] Other letters indicate that he remained under severe psychological strain and experienced considerable difficulty adjusting to his changed circumstances:

> When I was at the front, I was often weary, but only from physical and nervous fatigue. The main reason I managed to maintain some degree of psychic equilibrium was because I was kept constantly busy, sometimes to the point of complete self-oblivion, which prevented me from dwelling on the past and on personal matters and so on. I'm not busy now in the strict sense but have to deal with endless boring problems. . . . I curse my own weakness, which forced me to agree to a transfer here because of nervous exhaustion. I find being here dreadfully difficult – to the point of feeling mentally unbalanced.[114]

In a diary entry for 1918, Myaskovsky recorded that he suffered shellshock (*kontuziya*[115]) during the Przemyśl campaign.[116] No documentary confirmation of this diagnosis has so far come to light, but it would not be surprising if his experiences of the previous year had induced post-traumatic stress disorder.[117] It is also evident that the transfer produced strong feelings of guilt, which intensified when he learnt in late June 1916 that his former battalion had endured serious losses. 'Once more, I felt I was in the completely wrong place', he told Derzhanovsky: 'It's really dreadful to feel that I'm not where I'm needed'.[118]

Nonetheless, he was fortunate to be alive and living in conditions of relative comfort and safety (the Avgustovskys put him up, as promised). And although he had little free time, he could start to think about music again. Shortly after moving to Reval, he asked Derzhanovsky to send him the scores of the Third Symphony and other works so that he could revise them, and

113 Myaskovsky to Derzhanovsky, 29 May 1916, RNMM, 3/411.

114 Myaskovsky to Derzhanovsky, 2 June 1916, RNMM, 3/412.

115 Although *kontuziya* can also mean 'concussion', the definitions of the term in older Russian medical reference works indicate that it was primarily used to designate shellshock: see, for example, 'Kontuziya', in Boris Petrovskiy (ed.), *Bol'shaya meditsinskaya éntsiklopediya*, 3rd ed., vol. 11 (Moscow, 1979), 339–40.

116 'Vïpiski', 27 April 1918, RGALI, 2040/1/65, l. 4.

117 For an informative overview of historical debates on the causes of shellshock and a discussion of the syndrome's relation to post-traumatic stress disorder, see Edgar Jones and Simon Wessely, *Shell Shock to PTSD: Military Psychiatry from 1900 to the Gulf War*, Maudsley Monographs (Hove and New York, 2015).

118 Myaskovsky to Derzhanovsky, 24 June 1916, RNMM, 3/413.

was soon talking about trying to buy a piano.[119] Moreover, Reval's comparative proximity to Petrograd enabled him to return to the capital occasionally to attend concerts (the 230-mile journey could be made by train). His first excursion was to hear *Silence*, which was included in the programme of a Russian Musical Society symphony concert conducted by Nicolai Malko on 12 December 1915. Although conductor and composer initially had reservations about one another (Myaskovsky found Malko's reading of his score pedestrian; Malko thought *Silence* poorly orchestrated[120]), Malko would subsequently become a steadfast champion of Myaskovsky's work. He returned a few weeks later to hear Prokofiev conduct his *Scythian Suite* (based on music from the discarded ballet *Ala and Lolly*) with Siloti's orchestra on 9 January. Glazunov walked out in disgust, to Prokofiev's delight, and other members of the Rimsky-Korsakov circle such as Maximilian Sternberg were equally appalled, but the score only confirmed Myaskovsky's estimate of his former classmate's talent.[121] 'That our Serge is a genius, I have no doubt', he wrote afterwards to Derzhanovsky, adding that he thought the work 'stunning both in content and in sonority'.[122]

Derzhanovsky repeatedly encouraged him to return to composing and even hoped that he would resume writing for *Music*. Although Myaskovsky admired Derzhanovsky's determination to keep the periodical going, he had become convinced that music criticism was a largely futile occupation – especially if one engaged in it, as he had done, in the hope of advancing worthy causes and reforming taste. As he explained to his friend, he had concluded that the philistinism of the general public was invincible:

> One can value and love individuals, but the masses – I was going to say that one can only despise them, but that's not so; for the masses, from a purely quotidian perspective, one can only feel indifference, neither more nor less. I would put it this way: one must be demanding towards oneself, but there's nothing one can do about the crowd; it is as it ought to be, and getting indignant with it, raging at it, hurling thunderbolts and lightning at it is a waste of time at best. ... Will upbraiding people really make them mend their ways and become less base?[123]

As with some of the opinions expressed in his *Music* articles, it is important to contextualise this passage. Professions of disdain for the masses and

119 Myaskovsky to Derzhanovsky, 16 December 1915, 31 January and 8 April 1916, RNMM, 3/399, 3/402, and 3/408.

120 Myaskovsky to Derzhanovsky, 16 December 1915, RNMM, 3/399; Dansker, *N. A. Mal'ko*, 19.

121 Prokof'yev, 'Kratkaya avtobiografiya', 153–4; Belyayev to Myaskovsky, 16 January 1916, RGALI, 2040/1/101, l. 21.

122 Myaskovsky to Derzhanovsky, 21 January 1916, RNMM, 3/401.

123 Myaskovsky to Derzhanovsky, 26 February 1916, RNMM, 3/405.

popular taste had been commonplace since the dawn of Romanticism and were a frequent trope in *fin-de-siècle* cultural discourse. Here, as in many other instances, they were essentially an expression of disillusion with the apparent failure of contemporary society at large to comprehend or appreciate significant artistic achievements. Under Soviet rule, however, such sentiments not only came to be regarded as ideologically objectionable but marked one out as a 'class enemy': Myaskovsky would not be the only artist to find that his pre-Revolutionary outlook was at variance with the temper of the new era.

The question of his continuing involvement with *Music* soon resolved itself, as the periodical ceased publication in April 1916 when its financial difficulties finally became insurmountable.[124] (Notwithstanding Myaskovsky's pessimism, it had achieved more than he acknowledged – not least in helping to establish several composers' reputations, including his own.) As far as composing was concerned, he needed no prompting to return to his desk: the problem was finding the time. Derzhanovsky tried to redirect his attention to his stalled operatic project, but Myaskovsky was eager to make a start on a long-planned Fourth Symphony and had ideas for an orchestral work inspired by poems from Rabindranath Tagore's collection *Gitanjali*.[125] He continued to think about an operatic adaptation of *The Idiot*, but without with much enthusiasm: as he subsequently confessed to Derzhanovsky, he did not feel attracted to writing for the stage and doubted that the plan would ever be realised.[126] So it eventually proved, and in the shorter term, he did not succeed in writing either of the new orchestral works during his time at Reval.

His lack of productivity may not have been entirely due to lack of time, however, even if this was undoubtedly the most important factor. Several comments in his letters suggest a dissatisfaction with his output to date and a crisis of confidence. After hearing a performance of his Third Symphony under Aslanov at Pavlovsk on 14 July, he told Asafiev that he found it 'scholastic', 'un-organic', and 'contrived': he wanted his future work to become 'a natural development of musical thinking in moods and feelings . . . a song of the soul, rather than a game of the mind'.[127] Shortly afterwards, we find him extolling Verdi's melodic gifts to Derzhanovsky after hearing gramophone recordings of arias from *Il Trovatore*, and criticising his own Second Symphony as 'dull', 'prosaic', and 'ponderous'.[128] As always, these self-dep-

124 The final issue, No. 255, came out on 23 April 1916.

125 Myaskovsky to Derzhanovsky, 14 February 1916, RNMM, 3/404.

126 Myaskovsky to Derzhanovsky, 4 September 1916, RNMM, 3/425, l. 1–10b.

127 Myaskovsky to Asafiev, 17 July 1916, RGALI, 2658/1/637, l. 300b.

128 Myaskovsky to Derzhanovsky, 27 July and 24 August 1916, RNMM, 3/417 (l. 20b) and 3/422.

recating evaluations should not be taken at face value. Nonetheless, he had evidently come to feel his music lacked spontaneity and immediacy, but did not yet sense how these elusive qualities could be attained. It is likely that this renewed bout of self-questioning was prompted by hearing Prokofiev's recent work: in his account of his impressions of the *Scythian Suite*, adjectives such as 'fresh', 'vivid', and 'captivating' feature prominently, and he was deeply impressed when Prokofiev played for him the recently completed piano score of *The Gambler* in April 1916.[129] He had a clear enough idea of the tendencies that he wished to avoid – first and foremost, the sterile academicism of the Rimsky-Korsakov school, which was being perpetuated merely 'through inertia' as he observed to Derzhanovsky[130] – but had as yet to achieve a decisive breakthrough in his quest for creative self-renewal.

Despite his reiterated laments in the pages of *Music* about the failure to support younger composers, he could not complain of any lack of interest in his own work throughout the war. Aslanov conducted the Second Symphony at Pavlovsk in August 1916, two months after performing the Third.[131] On 26 November, the Third was given again, this time by Siloti's orchestra in Petrograd: Siloti honoured his undertaking to programme the symphony, though he declined to conduct it himself, knowing Myaskovsky's reservations about his abilities. (Myaskovsky hoped that Saradzhev might conduct, but this proved infeasible; in the end it was entrusted to Kuper once more.)[132] The following month, the Second Piano Sonata was premiered in Petrograd by its dedicatee Boris Zakharov at a chamber music concert that also included the Cello Sonata and four of the Hippius settings.[133] His reservations about *Silence* notwithstanding, Malko expressed interest in conducting the Second Symphony: he met Myaskovsky in October 1916 to go through the score with him, and although the performance never materialised, he premiered the Sinfonietta, op. 10, in Petrograd the following July.[134] But while these continuing signs of attention were encouraging, they intensified his frustration with the enforced diversion of his best energies from composing: he described himself to Derzhanovsky as suffering 'the torments of Tantalus'.

129   Myaskovsky to Prokofiev, 31 January 1916, in Kozlova and Yatsenko, *Perepiska*, 141; Myaskovsky to Derzhanovsky, 21 April 1916, RNMM, 3/409.

130   Myaskovsky to Derzhanovsky, 26 February 1916, RNMM, 3/405.

131   Asafiev to Myaskovsky, 24 August 1916, in Ol'ga Lamm, *Stranitsï tvorcheskoy biografii Myaskovskogo* (Moscow, 1989), 123.

132   Derzhanovsky to Myaskovsky, 13 June and 17 July 1915, RNMM, 71/313 and 71/325.

133   'Khronika. Kontsertï v Petrograde', *Russkaya muzïkal'naya gazeta*, 1 January 1917, 20–3.

134   Myaskovsky to Derzhanovsky, 5 October 1916, RNMM, 3/427; Asafiev to Myaskovsky, 6 August 1917, in Lamm, *Stranitsï*, 128.

The tedium of his duties and the seeming interminability of the war weighed heavily on his spirits: he had come to loathe military service more than ever – 'with every fibre of my being', as he told Vera.[135] It was also impossible to remain unaffected by the increasingly sombre national mood. The war had become deeply unpopular in the wake of the ignominious defeats on Russia's western front and army desertion rates rose sharply. The country's economy and transport infrastructure were on the verge of collapse. A major crisis was clearly imminent, yet Nicholas II obdurately ignored warnings that far-reaching reforms would be necessary to avert the growing threat of violent revolution. In Petrograd, soaring prices and intensifying shortages of basic commodities exacerbated conditions of widespread hardship after an unusually severe winter. By the last week of February 1917, the city was paralysed by strikes and its streets thronged with demonstrators calling for the cessation of hostilities. The protests escalated into rioting, and then into open rebellion when troops in the municipal garrison mutinied on being ordered to quell the unrest by force. Within a few days the government had effectively lost control of the capital. His authority fatally undermined, Nicholas abdicated on the advice of his ministers and the military high command, who were fearful that the mutiny would spread to the armies at the front. His brother, the Grand Duke Michael, declined to succeed him to the throne, bringing three hundred years of Romanov rule to an abrupt end.

Myaskovsky's family were deeply concerned for his safety once more after the outbreaks of insubordination in the armed forces. On 4 March, the day on which Nicholas's abdication was announced, Valentina sent him an anxious note to enquire how matters stood in Reval: as newspapers had ceased production, Petrograd's inhabitants lacked reliable sources of news. His relatives were all safe, she reported, though she had been unable to make contact with Yakov. The disturbances had abated for now, but the atmosphere in the city remained tense. An uncanny stillness reigned: the shops were mostly closed, and public transport had yet to resume.[136]

Her brother's reaction to events is difficult to assess due to the dearth of documentary evidence. As Valentina subsequently heard from Avgustovsky's wife, 'complete anarchy' reigned in the Reval fortress during the February Revolution[137], but Myaskovsky does not seem to have experienced any hostility either then or subsequently. In their respective memoirs, Yekaterina Derzhanovskaya and his sisters recorded hearing from Myaskovsky's colleagues that he was liked and respected by his men. He was clearly

135 Myaskovsky to Vera Yakovleva, 15 September 1916, RGALI, 2040/1/82, l. 27.

136 Valentina Menshikova to Myaskovsky, 4 March 1917, RGALI, 2040/2/189, l. 39.

137 Valentina Menshikova to Myaskovsky, 30 March 1917, RGALI, 2040/2/189, l. 40.

conscientious and competent, and had a reputation for being strict, but fair.[138] Ikonnikov (apparently drawing on Yakovlev's oral reminiscences) states that he invariably addressed his subordinates courteously in the second person plural and, unlike other officers, never resorted to demeaning punishments.[139] One of his letters to Derzhanovskaya from Reval certainly suggests a benevolent attitude: he enlisted her help in purchasing a set of balalaikas for his men out of his own funds.[140] A subsequent communication to her of March 1917 indicates that, in common with many of his contemporaries, he initially viewed the February Revolution in a positive light:

> Everything that has occurred has pleased me greatly of itself, both in a general sense and in relation to military life. The moral cleansing of this swamp is a matter of vital importance. It is not difficult for me, for, as you know, I was never a vain, self-important person and I judged people not by their class or how they were dressed, but by their intellectual and spiritual qualities. I did not judge them in other respects. Consequently, I do not experience the present great commotion, such as always takes place at times of change, as a rupture either.[141]

Writing to Asafiev, he remarked that 'after the downfall of a monarchy such as Russia's, monarchism as a principle is becoming something akin to the appendix to the intestine'. He also expressed impatience with the seeming inability of affluent left-leaning members of the intelligentsia to understand that more radical reforms would be required to address the country's social problems than the adjustments to taxation demanded by the Menshevik faction of the Russian Social Democratic Labour Party – measures that he evidently regarded as merely palliative: 'How pitiful our intelligentsia is: they run around after one another, unable to break out of a vicious circle of people and ideas. I prefer "Leninism" in all branches of life. I've had my fill of these Social Democrats, who pay thousands in taxes and filter their ideology through thick window curtains. To hell with them!'[142]

It would be unwarranted to interpret this surprising outburst as betokening his ideological radicalisation, however, let alone advocacy of violence to secure political ends. To the best of the author's knowledge, this allusion to Lenin is unique in his correspondence. It is important to be mindful of the context in which it occurs: a diatribe about the discussions of a new national anthem in *The Musical Contemporary*, which struck Myaskovsky

138 Men'shikova *et al.*, 'Pamyati brata', 178–9; Koposova-Derzhanovskaya, 'Pamyati druga', 218.

139 Ikonnikov, *Khudozhnik nashikh dney*, 76–7.

140 Myaskovsky to Derzhanovskaya, 28 December 1916, RNMM, 3/3286, ll. 20b–3.

141 Myaskovsky to Derzhanovskaya, 19 March 1917, RNMM, 3/3289, l. 1.

142 Myaskovsky to Asafiev, 16 April 1917, RGALI, 2658/1/638, l. 10.

as patronising and out of touch. His declaration is more plausibly read as a rhetorical overstatement indicative of his exasperation with the country's 'chattering classes' rather than of support for the Bolsheviks. In his biography, Ikonnikov claimed (once again citing Yakovlev as his source) that the composer had been strongly influenced by an army doctor named Alexander Revidtsev who supposedly brought him closer to 'a correct understanding of the political events then taking place in Russia'.[143] There is no evidence to corroborate this claim: there are a few fleeting allusions to Revidtsev in Myaskovsky's correspondence, but nothing to suggest that he played a decisive role in transforming his outlook or that the relationship was particularly significant. Myaskovsky's brief summary of his responses to contemporary events in his 'Autobiographical Notes' is vague and equivocal: he stated that his 'democratic tendencies' had been strengthened by the February Revolution and subsequent developments, which drew him towards 'the most radical positions, though to a significant extent, merely instinctually'[144] – a convoluted formulation that did not commit him to very much and was far from being an explicit endorsement of the Bolshevik political programme. The documentary evidence suggests that Myaskovsky consciously held himself aloof from politics, much as the symbolists had done before 1905. Throughout his life, he avoided discussing political questions or political leaders in his letters and rarely referred to current events unless they impinged on him directly, as in wartime. Even then, his references to them tended to be brief and oblique. The period around 1917 was no exception: insofar as he commented on circumstances at all, he was chiefly concerned with the day-to-day difficulties that they engendered for him and his family.

If he initially entertained hopes that the February Revolution might act as a catalyst for long-overdue social and political reforms, remarks in subsequent letters suggest growing disillusion and well-grounded fears of the disorder likely to result from social upheaval. 'I have begun to lose faith everything', he wrote to Asafiev in May 1917: 'in Russian life, in the Russian mind, in Russian decency – and consequently about the fate of Russia and all that; and at closer hand, I am starting to despair about myself. I cannot adapt to a new way of life: I am already too old for that, too passive; and aside from everything else, I am constitutionally incapable of dealing with disorder, confusion, and chaos'.[145] He had no inclination to engage in political activism, unlike his sister Vera, who was enthusiastically helping to organise meetings and demonstrations, much to Valentina's disdain.[146]

143 Ikonnikov, *Khudozhnik nashikh dney*, 76.

144 Myaskovskiy, 'Avtobiograficheskiye zametki', 9.

145 Myaskovsky to Asafiev, 17 May 1917, RGALI, 2658/1/638, l. 13.

146 Valentina Menshikova to Myaskovsky, 4 April 1917, RGALI, 2040/2/189, l. 430b.

As he acknowledged with self-deprecating irony to Asafiev, he was by temperament 'ultra-bourgeois', fond of refined middle-class domesticity and its trappings – French scent, fine table linen, comfortable chairs; he desired nothing more than for the war to end as quickly as possible so that he could be left undisturbed to write music 'morning, noon, and night'.[147]

As a first step towards attaining that objective, in March 1917 he sought a transfer back to Petrograd. His brother-in-law Yakovlev was now attached to the naval General Staff and undertook to make enquiries about prospective vacancies. As previously, however, the transfer was beset by lengthy delays and complicated by ongoing restructuring of the personnel manning naval fortresses.[148] His decision to move was also prompted by anxiety about his family. There was growing fear that the Central Powers might attempt to attack Petrograd from the sea and Valentina's descriptions of the worsening food shortages had become increasingly alarming. In spite of the fact that her job entitled her to receive rations, by June she was subsisting on a diet of bread, porridge, and cocoa. Meat, eggs, dairy produce, and fresh fruit and vegetables had become unobtainable luxuries and she feared that the situation would deteriorate further by the winter.[149] Myaskovsky did what he could to help, but the increasingly unreliable postal service and public transport hindered both communication and his efforts to send supplies.

In the early months of 1917, Myaskovsky appears to have been based away from Reval for a time in the nearby town of Kiisa, but returned to the city at the start of June.[150] By this point, he had been reassigned from the fortress's construction division to its financial division, of which he was appointed acting head.[151] The work was dull and his days were long, but he nonetheless found time to revise the First Symphony and then to compose eighteen piano miniatures in June and July, having finally managed to hire a piano for his lodgings.[152] (Many of these pieces were subsequently revised and included in collections that he published in the 1920s.) Derzhanovsky hoped to revive *Music* and asked him once more to return as a contributor, but Myaskovsky was reluctant. He also declined an invitation to write for a

---

147 Myaskovsky to Asafiev, 15 August 1917, RGALI, 2658/1/638, ll. 25–25ob.

148 Valentina Menshikova to Myaskovsky, 30 March and 4 April 1917, RGALI, 2040/2/189, ll. 40–10ob and 43–40ob.

149 Valentina Menshikova to Myaskovsky, 15 June 1917, RGALI, 2040/2/189, ll. 46–70ob.

150 Myaskovsky to Derzhanovsky, 31 May 1917, RNMM, 3/438.

151 I have been unable to establish the date on which Myaskovsky commenced in this new role, but he was evidently in post by 15 May 1917, to judge from the fortress's records: 'Trebovatel'naya vedomost'', NAE, 4699/1/84, l. 218–180ob.

152 Myaskovsky to Derzhanovsky, 31 May and 12 June 1917, RNMM, 3/438 and 3/439; Myaskovsky to Vera Yakovleva, 12 June 1917, RGALI, 2040/2/293, l. 33; Myaskovsky to Asafiev, 15 August 1917, RGALI, 2658/1/638, l. 240ob.

new journal that Asafiev planned to found, having recently resigned in acrimonious circumstances from *The Musical Contemporary*.[153] (Its editor-in-chief Andrey Rimsky-Korsakov had refused to publish Asafiev's laudatory review of works by Stravinsky, Prokofiev, and Myaskovsky because he had a low opinion of all three.[154]) He was unwilling to devote his limited free time to anything else but composition.

As the delay with his transfer dragged on, his impatience to leave the navy mounted. The question was still undecided at the start of October, despite Yakovlev's efforts to progress matters. The political situation had continued to deteriorate throughout the autumn and the country was affected by renewed waves of strikes, demonstrations, and social unrest. Discipline amongst the troops at Reval had broken down and he was eager to move.[155] In the middle of October, he received the surprising news that he might soon be allowed to apply for discharge.[156] A few days later, a telegram arrived informing him that his transfer had finally been approved.[157] Myaskovsky was torn by indecision. Much as he longed to return to civilian life and no longer have to concern himself with overseeing supplies of 'boots, berets, cabbages, and meal', as he wryly remarked to Derzhanovsky, it was far from clear how he could earn a living, especially in the prevailing circumstances.[158] The Chancellery had closed down, so it was impossible to return to his former job. He had some savings, but there was no knowing long they might last at a time of runaway inflation. Derzhanovsky proposed that he move to Moscow, suggesting it would afford a convenient base to resume his professional activities, and offered him a room in his apartment.[159]

On 25 October (7 November), three days after Derzhanovsky sent his letter, the Bolsheviks led an armed insurrection in Petrograd and deposed the Provisional Government. By 30 October, the insurgents had gained control of Moscow. Myaskovsky's blunt comments on events in his reply to Derzhanovsky were never reproduced in any Soviet publication: 'Whoever invented such an idiotic country as our godforsaken fatherland! How did such overwhelming vulgarity and such bestial nonentities triumph? What

153 Myaskovsky to Asafiev, 17 May 1917, RGALI, 2658/1/638, ll. 140b–15.

154 For an account of the controversy, see Miral'da Kozlova, '"Teper vse troye – opredelivshiyesya velichinï". . . Iz nenapechatannogo', *Sovetskaya muzïka*, 5 (1977), 93–9; and also Andrey Rimskiy-Korsakov, 'Ot redaktora', in *Muzïkal'nïy sovremennik*, kniga 4, 1914, 9–13.

155 Myaskovsky to Vera Yakovleva, RGALI, 2040/1/82, ll. 35–60b.

156 Myaskovsky to Derzhanovsky, 15 October 1917, RNMM, 3/443.

157 Myaskovsky to Vera Yakovleva, 20 October 1917, RGALI, 2040/1/82, l. 37.

158 Myaskovsky to Derzhanovsky, 18 October 1917, RNMM, 3/444.

159 Derzhanovsky to Myaskovsky, 22 October 1917, RNMM, 71/343.

do these apes care about the [Socialist] International?'[160] The Bolshevik coup compounded his uncertainty about what to do. He appreciated the Derzhanovskys' generous offer but was doubtful that living with them would prove conducive to creative work. Valentina sent a note imploring him not to make a hasty decision about leaving the navy, which she followed up with a longer letter later the same day.[161] Concerned that he would struggle to survive financially, she counselled him to accept the transfer and wait to see how it worked out, adding that he would enjoy significantly better conditions than in Reval.

Valentina deliberately postponed discussing her reactions to the recent 'sickening' occurrences until they met, but evidently found them very alarming. So too did Yakov and his wife, who concluded that it was no longer safe to remain in Petrograd and were in the process of selling their belongings in preparation for moving permanently to Ukraine. Their decision was not made entirely on impulse: Yakov had a long-standing plan to move to the Crimea when Varvara finished secondary school, hoping that the warmer climate might benefit his health.[162] In the summer of 1915, the couple spent several weeks at a spa resort near Odessa before travelling to Golta, a town 120 miles to the north, to stay with Alida's relatives.[163] They returned again the following year.[164] Valentina suspected Alida of having seized the opportunity to distance Yakov from his first family. She went to the station to see her father off on 11 November. It was a sad occasion: Valentina thought he looked old and frail, and Alida's overbearing bossiness grated on her.[165]

Myaskovsky does not appear to have seen Yakov before he left. In a letter of 4 October, he told Derzhanovsky that it was virtually impossible for him to travel or get time off, so it may well have been infeasible for him to make the journey to Petrograd.[166] Taking Valentia's advice, he deferred making a decision about leaving the navy. On 8 November he sent Yevgeniya a food parcel with a covering note telling her that he hoped to join his sisters soon

160 Myaskovsky to Derzhanovsky, 9 November 1917, RNMM, 3/445.

161 Valentina Menshikova to Myaskovsky, 6 November 1917, RGALI, 2040/2/189, ll. 52–30b and l. 55.

162 Valentina Menshikova to Myaskovsky, 8 November 1916, RGALI, 2040/2/189, ll. 28–280b; Vera Yakovleva to Myaskovsky, RGALI 2040/2/294, l. 140b.

163 Yakov's letters to Yelikonida during this trip have been preserved amongst Myaskovsky's papers: RGALI, 2040/4/41.

164 Vera Yakovleva to Myaskovsky, undated letter [December 1915], RGALI, 2040/2/293, l. 81

165 Valentina Menshikova to Myaskovsky, 11 November 1917, RGALI, 2040/2/189, l. 56.

166 Myaskovsky to Derzhanovsky, 4 October 1917 and 1, RNMM, 3/442.

in their 'proletarian Holy Land'.[167] A week later, he was suddenly taken ill and collapsed: he passed fifteen hours in an unconscious state, having suffered a sharp blow to his head when he fell. The infirmary doctor diagnosed severe anaemia, a likely underlying cause of his persistent skin infections. On waking, he experienced sharp pains and numbness in his right arm and leg[168] – symptoms possibly indicative of a minor stroke, and which took some time to abate. He recovered sufficiently to travel to Petrograd and was confirmed in post on 10 December as an aide-de-camp attached to the Naval General Staff.[169] It was as though the strain of the last three-and-a-half years had finally overwhelmed him: he felt weary in body and mind. 'I long to do nothing, at least for a while', he told Derzhanovsky, but there was no prospect of respite just yet. He reluctantly recognised that he had little choice but to remain in service for the time being. His savings would not last long and it would be virtually impossible to find an alternative reliable source of income in the 'disgraceful shambles' that currently obtained. As the institutions at which Valentina and Vera worked were both on strike, the extended family depended on him to supplement Yakovlev's earnings.[170]

There was one consolation: he was at least back in familiar surroundings and could escape periodically into the seclusion of his study. On 20 December he commenced work on a long-postponed project, a Fourth Symphony.[171]

---

167 Myaskovsky to Yevgeniya Sakharova, 8 November 1917, RGALI, 2040/1/80, l. 7.

168 Myaskovsky to Derzhanovsky, 1 December 1917, RNMM, 3/446.

169 'Posluzhnoy spisok', RGALI, 2040/1/168, l. 3.

170 Myaskovsky to Derzhanovsky, 12 December 1917 and 1 January 1918, RNMM, 3/447 and 3/449.

171 Viktor Vinogradov, *Spravochnik-putevoditel' po simfoniyam N. Ya. Myaskovskogo* (Moscow, 1954), vii.

5

Aftermath: 1918–21

If Myaskovsky hoped that conditions might improve sufficiently to permit his return to civilian life before too long, he was to be disappointed. As it transpired, he would have to remain in the armed forces for three further years – a period that proved the most turbulent in the country's history.

In the months following the October Revolution, Lenin's grip on power remained tenuous. The Bolshevik faction of the Russian Social-Democratic Workers' Party (renamed the Russian Communist Party [Bolsheviks] in 1918) had at most two hundred thousand members and its support was essentially confined to the major industrial centres of European Russia. Having seized power, it refused to share it with other socialist parties, but won less than a quarter of the votes in the national elections to the new Constituent Assembly held in November 1917. Lenin responded by dissolving the assembly after its first session, effectively instituting single-party rule. Although he promptly sued for peace with the Central Powers, the conclusion of the Treaty of Brest-Litovsk on 3 March 1918 exacerbated rather than alleviated domestic tensions. The punitive terms imposed by the Germans, which forced Russia to cede a quarter of the former territories of its empire (including the Baltic states, Belorussia, and Ukraine – populous regions with fertile agricultural land and important concentrations of industry and natural resources) were widely regarded as unacceptably humiliating. Members of the army high command objected to Russia's withdrawal from the war as a dishonourable betrayal of its commitments to the Allies. General Mikhail Alekseyev, who had been instrumental in persuading Nicholas II to abdicate, set up a volunteer army in the southern Don region with the aim of resuming hostilities against Germany: it quickly grew into a formidable fighting force. Disparate factions antagonistic to the Bolsheviks – including monarchists, local separatist movements, and other left-wing parties – formed similar forces in Siberia and elsewhere. These so-called 'White' armies initially received significant supplies of men and *matériel* from the Allied powers, which were eager for conflict to resume on the eastern front and divert German troops from the western one. In the face of hardening opposition, the Bolsheviks resorted to repression to consolidate their dominance. Russia swiftly descended into a chaotic civil war during which millions met violent deaths or perished from starvation and disease.

Amongst the earliest victims of the conflict may have been Yakov Myaskovsky. Alexey Ikonnikov, presumably drawing on information provided by Myaskovsky himself, stated that the composer's father died soon after moving to Ukraine and that the family's contact with his second wife came to an abrupt end.[1] Though never mentioned in Soviet publications, stories circulated for many years that Yakov was murdered by Bolshevik supporters during the Civil War. This claim could well be true, but corroborating evidence is almost entirely lacking. Confirmation that there was something untoward about Yakov's death is furnished by only a single documentary source – an unfinished biography of Myaskovsky's friend Pavel Lamm by his niece (and adopted daughter) Olga Lamm (1908–97), in which she stated that Yakov died 'in tragic circumstances', but does not elaborate further.[2] There is no reason to doubt Lamm's testimony. Her uncle became one of Myaskovsky's closest associates and was one of the very few people whom he trusted without reservation: Myaskovsky could well have confided the story of Yakov's death to him, knowing him to be someone of like mind. (As his niece's account of his life reveals, Pavel Lamm regarded the Bolshevik regime with such deep antipathy that he repeatedly considered emigrating during the 1920s.) It is interesting to note Lamm's reference to Yakov's demise in her book *Pages from Myaskovsky's Creative Biography*, a compendium of quotations from the composer's letters and what survives of his diaries, arranged in chronological sequence. In the section for 1918, she reproduces an entry from one of Myaskovsky's service books in which he recorded his father's death as having occurred in that year.[3] Although he did not indicate the precise date, Lamm interpolated the reference between quotations from letters dated 10 and 15 January. This positioning is unlikely to have been arbitrary and suggests that she had definite information. Her reticence about revealing what she knew is unsurprising: if Yakov died as a result of Bolshevik violence, Soviet censorship would have made public discussion of the matter impossible. The musicologist Valida Kelle has claimed that Lamm disclosed what happened when Kelle interviewed her towards the end of her life for a radio programme made in 1992. In an essay published in 2006, she quoted what purported to be Lamm's verbatim account of events:

> When we got to know Nikolay Yakovlevich in 1919, he was very morose. When I asked why, my father Pavel Aleksandrovich Lamm replied: 'You know, Nikolay Yakovlevich's father died during the Civil War. He was in the countryside, he was a general, he put on his general's greatcoat, most likely because it was cold. . . . And then he was torn apart [*rasterzan*] by a mob when they saw a general'.[4]

1　Ikonnikov, *Khudozhnik nashikh dney*, 12.

2　Ol'ga Lamm, 'Pavel Aleksandrovich Lamm: Opït biografii', RNMM, 192/361, l. 155. For a discussion of this manuscript, see the Introduction.

3　'Posluzhnoy spisok', RGALI, 2040/1/168, l. 50b; *Stranitsï*, 133.

4　Valida Kelle, 'Ob otdel'nïkh faktakh tvorcheskoy biografii N. Myaskovskogo', in Yelena Dolinskaya (ed.), *Neizvestnïy Nikolay Myaskovskiy: Vzglyad iz XXI veka*

FIGURE 5.1. Yakov Myaskovsky (1913).

A recording of the programme has not been conserved in the Russian national broadcasting archive, however, so her report of Lamm's statement cannot be independently verified.[5] Kelle did not clarify who the members of the mob were or offer any explanation of their motive for killing Yakov.

Even if the story's reliability is open to question, it is nonetheless plausible. In a letter of 26 November 1917, Vera told her brother that Yakov had written to inform her of his safe arrival in Golta: Yakov managed to travel as far as Ukraine, though it is unknown whether he attempted to proceed onward to the Crimea.[6] (Yakov's letter was not preserved, or any subsequent communications from him.) He and Alida could hardly have chosen a worse time to travel, as Ukraine was plunged into turmoil in the wake of the October Revolution. After the declaration of an autonomous Ukrainian People's Republic on 20 November 1917, forces loyal to the

---

(Moscow, 2006), 44. According to Kelle, the programme was entitled 'Slovo o Myaskovskom' ('A word about Myaskovsky') and broadcast on 22 November 1992.

5   Oksana Oreshina (Gosteleradiofond) to author, 27 March 2019. Dr Kelle did not respond to the author's requests for information about the interview.

6   RGALI, 2040/2/294, l. 18.

Bolsheviks invaded the region and Bolshevik uprisings were successfully staged in Kharkiv, Odessa, and other major cities in late December and January.[7] The situation in the Crimea was even more volatile: the Crimean People's Republic, declared in December 1917, was quickly overthrown by a Bolshevik coup d'état and the peninsula was the scene of fierce fighting and atrocities throughout the winter.[8] It is by no means impossible that Yakov met with misfortune during his journey, especially if his military attire made him conspicuous. There were numerous instances of attacks on former tsarist officers by Bolshevik supporters, the most notorious case being that of the last commander-in-chief of the Russian Imperial Army, General Nikolay Dukhonin, who was lynched by a mob in December 1917.[9]

The present author's investigations have not yielded any information that sheds further light on events. Attempts to obtain confirmation of Yakov's fate from other sources have drawn a blank, though this is probably to be expected given the fragmentariness of records for the Civil War years. More surprising is the absence of materials pertaining to Yakov's death amongst Myaskovsky's personal papers: if such documents existed, they have been lost or destroyed. It is not even clear how the family was informed of the event: no communications from Alida or Varvara have been preserved, or any notification from another source. Nor have any allusions to Yakov's demise been found in the composer's surviving correspondence – not even an expression of condolence from a friend. He evidently avoided discussing the subject subsequently – except, it would seem, with Pavel Lamm. Taken together, these circumstances are undeniably odd and call for explanation.

There is no evidence that father and son were estranged, as has been claimed[10]: the family letters indicate that they remained on affectionate terms. Myaskovsky's silence on the subject of his father can be readily explained by other considerations. Irrespective of how Yakov died, his provenance from the nobility and his position in the high command of the tsarist army became a serious liability for his offspring after the October Revolution. The constitution of the Russian Soviet Federative Socialist Republic, promulgated on 10 July 1918, proclaimed the new state to be 'a dictatorship of the urban and rural proletariat and the poorest peasantry'; it called for the 'merciless suppression of exploiters', who were summarily

7   Serhy Yekelchyk, *Ukraine: Birth of a Modern Nation* (Oxford, 2007), 71–3; Ivan Hoshulyak, 'Pro prychynu porazky Tsentral'noï Rady', *Ukraïn'skiy istorychnyy zhurnal*, 1 (1994), 35–7.

8   See Tetyana Bykova, *Stvorennya Kryms'koï ASRR (1917–1921 rr.)* (Kyiv, 2011), 60–4.

9   Irina Mikhutina, *Ukrainskiy Brestkiy mir* (Moscow, 2007), 45–6.

10 See, for example, Tat'yana Sidorina and Igor' Karpinskiy, 'Revolyutsiya i yeyo virazheniye v simfonicheskoy muzïke: N. Myaskovskiy i D. Shostakovich', *Voprosï filosofii*, 12 (2017), 55–63.

disenfranchised and their property declared subject to expropriation. Members of the 'exploiting classes' included aristocrats, clergy, landowners, and anyone who engaged in private business or profited from hired labour. At a stroke, the regime created a new underclass of 'former people' (*bivshiye lyudi*) who were stripped of their previous social status.[11] Amongst them were senior tsarist officials and army officers. 'Former people' were vilified, harassed, and murdered with impunity during the mass repressions instituted in August 1918 to break resistance to Bolshevik rule. The announcement of Nicholas II's execution the previous month forcefully underlined the regime's ruthless intent: the national newspapers *Pravda* and *Izvestiya* exhorted the populace to 'crush the hydra of counterrevolution' and 'purge our cities of bourgeois rottenness'.[12] Long afterwards, 'former people' continued to experience discrimination: they were shunned by employers and disadvantaged in many aspects of everyday life such as housing, ration allowances, or educational opportunities for their children. Many were reduced to abject poverty.[13]

Given this situation, it is not difficult to understand why Myaskovsky would have avoided discussing his father – especially if Yakov were a victim of Bolshevik violence. Like many others in a similar position, he prudently chose to be economical with the truth when filling out the obligatory questionnaires required by Soviet officialdom, which routinely enquired about citizens' social origins and the professions of their parents.[14] In the service record cited by Olga Lamm, Myaskovsky gave his father's occupation merely as 'military engineer'. He designated Yakov's profession in similar fashion in his 'Autographical Notes' and described him to Ikonnikov as a 'professor in a military academy', without even mentioning that he had served in the army.[15] It cannot have escaped him that his father's departure for Ukraine and his swift demise were fortuitous in one respect, as it made it easier to deflect attention from his family background. Had Yakov remained alive, his children's lives could have been complicated considerably.

11   For a detailed study, see Tat'yana Smirnova, *"Bivshiye lyudi" Sovetskoy Rossii: Strategii vizhivaniya i puti integratsii, 1917–1936 godï* (Moscow, 2003).

12   *Pravda*, 31 August 1918; 'K rabochemu klassu', *Izvestiya*, 3 September 1918.

13   See Sheila Fitzpatrick, 'The Problem of Class Identity in NEP Society', in Sheila Fitzpatrick *et al.* (ed.), *Russia in the Era of NEP: Explorations in Soviet Society and Culture* (Bloomington, 1991), 12–33; Golfo Alexopoulos, *Stalin's Outcasts: Aliens, Citizens, and the Soviet State, 1926–1936* (Ithaca and London, 2003).

14   See Yury Zaretskiy, 'Confessing to Leviathan: The Mass Practice of Writing Autobiographies in the USSR', *Slavic Review*, 4 (2017), 1027–47.

15   See Ikonnikov, 'N. Ya. Myaskovskiy (biograficheskiy ocherk)', 21. Tamara Livanova similarly described Yakov as a professor of military engineering in her 1953 biography of Myaskovsky. The fact that Yakov had risen to the rank of army general was only disclosed in the first edition of Ikonnikov's *Khudozhnik nashikh dney*, published in 1966.

If Myaskovsky were notified of Yakov's death between 10 and 15 January 1918, it might explain his cryptic comment in a letter to Derzhanovsky on the latter date that he wanted to leave the country because he found the atmosphere so oppressive.[16] Whatever his apprehensions, he evidently decided that emigrating was not a feasible option – unlike Prokofiev, who left for America in May 1918 because conditions in Russia looked so unpromising for his career.[17] (Myaskovsky met him shortly before his departure, but had heard little from him since late 1916.[18]) The two men's personal circumstances were very different, however, as were their temperaments. Prokofiev had few close ties apart from his mother, who joined him abroad in 1920. His exceptional capabilities as a performer gave him a significant advantage when it came to establishing himself professionally in a new environment; he spoke French and quickly applied himself to learning English; he had abundant self-confidence and relished adventure. He already had a number of useful contacts abroad. Myaskovsky, by contrast, was not a skilled instrumentalist and did not speak any foreign language well, so would have found it much harder to make a living in exile. He disliked travelling, was shy and reclusive, and had no connections outside Russia. His aunt and sisters depended on his financial support. Abandoning them at such an anxious and uncertain time was unthinkable. For better or worse, he had no choice but to adapt as best he could to the changed conditions.

Though he remained undecided whether to seek discharge from the navy, it soon became apparent that it would be ill-advised. Finding alternative adequately remunerated work would be difficult, and his naval post entitled him to receive special rations – a vital supplement to his family's diet at a time of dire food shortages. His duties were not very onerous at first, as the Naval General Staff's functioning was initially impeded by strikes at other institutions.[19] Myaskovsky availed of the opportunity to commit ideas for new works to paper: in the thirteen weeks between 20 December 1917 and 5 April 1918, he sketched not only a Fourth but also a Fifth Symphony.[20]

After this intense bout of creativity, he returned to his plan to write an opera based on Dostoyevsky's *The Idiot*, which had originated almost ten years previously.[21] Pyotr Suvchinsky, a young music critic friendly

---

16   Myaskovsky to Derzhanovsky, 15 January 1918, RNMM, 3/450.

17   Prokof'yev, *Dnevnik 1907–1918*, 678.

18   Their last recorded meeting was after a recital that Prokofiev gave in Petrograd on 17 April 1918: Prokof'yev, *Dnevnik 1907–1918*, 695.

19   Myaskovsky to Derzhanovsky, 1 January 1918, RNMM, 3/449.

20   'Vïpiski', 27 April 1918, RGALI, 2040/1/65, l. 4. The Gregorian calendar was introduced in Russia on 14 February 1918: the latter date immediately succeeded 31 January, skipping the preceding 13 days of the old Julian calendar.

21   For a summary of what little is known about the project, see Semyon Shlifshteyn, 'Myaskovskiy i opernoye tvorchestvo', *Sovetskaya muzïka*, 5 (1959),

with Asafiev, agreed to fashion a libretto. Myaskovsky had high praise for Suvchinsky's abilities[22], but quickly lost interest in the project again. Suvchinsky got as far as completing a draft which reduced the literary original to nine scenes[23], but even with such drastic compression, its viability for musical setting was doubtful. Dostoyevsky's novel, completed in 1869, narrates the ordeals suffered by the unworldly Prince Myshkin, an idealised embodiment of Christian virtue, on encountering the depravity of contemporary Russian society. He ends his days in an asylum, having lost both his innocence and his sanity through involvement in a destructive love triangle that concludes sordidly in murder. *The Idiot*'s intricate plot and its complex philosophical and theological concerns would seem to make it an intractable subject for operatic treatment. If Myaskovsky sketched any of the music, the drafts have not survived. Work came to a halt when Suvchinsky left Petrograd at the start of the summer and never resumed.[24] As the composer acknowledged long afterwards in his 'Autobiographical Notes', the theatre 'never held any attractions' for him: before 1918, as subsequently, his creative interests lay almost exclusively in the domain of instrumental music.[25]

The composition of the Fourth and Fifth symphonies would be followed by a long fallow period that lasted until the end of 1920. A striking passage in a letter to Derzhanovsky vividly evokes his state of mind during the early months of 1918:

> Even the coming of spring has had no effect on me. I constantly feel split somehow in body and mind. I am experiencing overwhelming depression, apathy, and mental exhaustion, almost to the point of losing my wits and being muddled in my thought and actions; but at the same time, I feel somewhere inside a kind of elation and sense a deeply hidden source of potential inspiration. It's a dreadfully strange and inexpressibly pleasant condition, but at the same time, it feels like an illness, or rather, as though I were recovering from an illness. In general, though, I'm feeling awful.[26]

He was evidently at very low ebb mentally and physically, which was scarcely surprising after all that he had been through; and his father's death, if it occurred earlier in the year, would have come as a serious blow. Under the circumstances, it seems remarkable that he managed to write two symphonies in such a short space of time. Directly after finishing the Fifth, he

41–6.

22   Myaskovsky to Derzhanovsky, 3 May 1918, RNMM, 3/457.

23   RGALI, 2040/3/15. The draft libretto is undated, but Myaskovsky's discussion of it in a letter to Derzhanovsky of 30 May 1918 indicates that it was complete by that point: RNMM, 3/458.

24   Myaskovsky to Derzhanovsky, 6 June 1918, RNMM, 3/459.

25   Myaskovskiy, 'Avtobiograficheskiye zametki', 7–8.

26   Myaskovsky to Derzhanovsky, 3 May 1918, RNMM, 3/457.

began to elaborate his sketches for the Fourth into a full score – a task he completed by 11 July.

Concert life was severely disrupted during the Civil War years and it was virtually impossible for composers to secure performances of large-scale works. As a result, the premiere of the Fourth Symphony in E minor, op. 17, was delayed for over six years, until February 1925. It has seldom been performed since, though its neglect is undeserved: it is not only amongst the best of Myaskovsky's symphonies but inaugurates a highly individual approach to the genre that he would subsequently explore further. In essence, that approach evolved from nineteenth-century envisionings of the symphony as a large-scale working-out of contrasts and their integration. Its novelty resides in the unusual intensity of those contrasts and Myaskovsky's handling of them. In essence, the Fourth enacts a process in which the disruptive effects of tonally indeterminate, highly dissonant material are gradually contained through interaction with diatonic material. It culminates in the consolidation of a tonal centre that had been asserted at the work's opening, but initially remained highly precarious. The process is not a straightforward reattainment of a tonal region that functioned throughout as a stable point of reference: stability has to be achieved through struggle. As one might expect, there is a close correlation between the work's 'external form' and its psychological content, or 'internal form', to use Myaskovsky's idiosyncratic terminology. The symphony's musical imagery of tonal and thematic conflict is evocative of a struggle to master psychic conflicts. The states of high tension and disturbance evoked by the dissonant musical material are transformed and ultimately transcended: tonal resolution mirrors emotional resolution.

The symphony is cast in three movements, with a combined duration of approximately forty minutes. The first is prefaced by a lengthy introduction which commences with a four-bar idea repeated three times by a solo flute, very softly and initially unaccompanied. It is of the utmost simplicity, outlining a series of slurred stepwise ascents rising from the tonic to the dominant (ex. 5.1), yet creates a strangely powerful mood of desolation. It is restated in a loosely inverted form by the clarinet and then by the strings; the texture gradually becomes fuller, building steadily towards a climax. The paragraph is striking in two respects. The first is Myaskovsky's skilful management of increasingly insistent repetition and the unvarying crotchet movement to potent expressive effect, suggestive of a slow, pain-filled awakening from a state of numbed exhaustion. The second is his handling of tonality. Although the opening idea is entirely diatonic and unambiguously establishes E minor, its stability is immediately undermined when other instruments enter in the fifth bar, harmonising the phrase with plangent dissonances: the lower voices slip chromatically downward, countering its upward striving.

EXAMPLE 5.1. Symphony no. 4, first movement: opening.

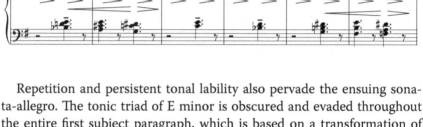

Repetition and persistent tonal lability also pervade the ensuing sonata-allegro. The tonic triad of E minor is obscured and evaded throughout the entire first subject paragraph, which is based on a transformation of the opening flute idea (ex. 5.2): the music quickly moves to remote tonal regions, and the insistent reiterations of the basic motif lend it an oppressive character, as if unable to break free of an obsessive preoccupation. The mutedly lyrical second subject (which was also adumbrated in the introduction) affords brief respite, though it too is tonally restless. The two ideas interact throughout the turbulent development section, but its tonal argument has no decisive issue: while the first subject returns at the expected pitch in the recapitulation, its harmonisation is even more ambiguous and dissonant than before. E minor is eventually reasserted at the close of the stormy coda, though there is no sense of a definitive outcome.

The achievement of tonal stability becomes the task of the slow movement. The opening section of this three-part structure presents a fugato on a subject comprising ten of the twelve notes of the chromatic scale. Its contrapuntal elaboration is so dissonant as to render the prevailing key signature of four flats entirely notional. Once again, the mood is strained and claustrophobic: the movement rises to the first of two searing climaxes, which ushers in the central section. This develops a lyrical idea in A-flat presented by the piccolo and flutes to the ethereal accompaniment of *tremolando* strings. Its unfolding is brusquely cut short by a forceful resumption of the opening material, but it returns in an extended developmental coda, re-establishing A-flat major via G major, the key of its leading note. As it develops, this theme incorporates the dissonant contours of the fugato subject: its disruptive chromaticism is neutralised, enabling the movement to close serenely in A-flat major. This tonicisation of A-flat, alias G-sharp, the major third of E major, prepares for the attainment of the latter key at

EXAMPLE 5.2. Symphony no. 4, first movement: bars 62–73.

the close of the finale. Chromatic and diatonic musical material continue to vie for ascendency in the latter, but E major decisively prevails in the coda, an energetic development of a resolute modal theme against an airborne texture of pulsating triplet figurations in the woodwinds. The score's final pages are deeply impressive, conveying an exhilarating emotional uplift and sense of release – the first of Myaskovsky's symphonies to close in a mood of affirmation. It is tempting to posit a connection between the Fourth's musical imagery of struggle and Myaskovsky's wartime experiences, but he expressly repudiated any such link (as he also did in the case of the Fifth).[27]

Shortly after completing the full score of the Fourth, Myaskovsky was transferred from Petrograd, a development he had anticipated for some time. Throughout the winter of 1917–18, there was a very real threat that the city would be the site of an invasion by German forces if they extended their control over the entire Baltic region. As a precaution, the seat of government was moved to Moscow; the headquarters of the armed forces relocated there together with other government institutions. The evacuation of personnel from the Naval General Staff took place over several months, starting in late March.[28] It was initially unclear whether Myaskovsky would be kept on, but in the event he was appointed aide-de-camp to the head of

---

27 Myaskovsky dealt with this issue in a handwritten response of 2 October 1936 to questions that Ikonnikov had posed about the Fifth Symphony: RGALI, 2040/4/9, ll. 4–40b.

28 For an account of the restructuring of the navy after the October Revolution, see Kirill Nazarenko, *Flot, revolyutsiya i vlast' v Rossii, 1917–1921* (Moscow, 2011), 183–279.

the Organisational Division.[29] After vacillating for some time, he decided
to accept a transfer, though Asafiev and other acquaintances counselled
against it because they considered Moscow provincial and culturally stagnant.[30] It is not entirely clear what prompted him to overcome his reluctance. He told Derzhanovsky that he was looking forward to the change of
scene because his nerves 'were in tatters'.[31] Whether he had specific cause
for anxiety or just felt generally under strain, it is impossible to say.

After repeated delays, he eventually arrived in Moscow in mid-August.[32] He had hoped to live with his sister Valentina, who had also been
evacuated with her institution, but as this proved infeasible, he accepted
the Derzhanovskys' offer of a room in their apartment. The arrangement
turned out to be far from ideal. Although the apartment was large (it comprised five rooms and a kitchen), there were already six other people living
there – including Derzhanovskaya's mother and a married couple with two
children.[33] The location was noisy because the building was situated at a
junction. Myaskovsky's 'room' turned out to be a dark passageway, which
was uncomfortable and afforded scant privacy. He had little alternative but
to remain there for the time being: as he discovered, accommodation in
Moscow was in short supply and becoming increasingly expensive.[34] The
city council had instituted a policy of 'concentrating' occupancy (*uplot-
neniye*) in the wake of recent measures to nationalise private property. Each
adult occupant was permitted no more than a single small room and those
who had previously rented or owned spacious apartments were forced to
share their living quarters, which were turned into so-called *kommunalki*
('communal flats').[35] As in other respects, manual workers received preferential treatment; 'former people' were often evicted as 'parasitic and harmful elements' and ordered to live outside the city boundaries.[36]

29   Myaskovsky to Derzhanovsky, 22 February and 10 March 1918, RNMM, 3/453
     and 3/452; 'Posluzhnoy spisok', RGALI, 2040/1/168, l. 30b.

30   Myaskovsky to Derzhanovsky, 30 May 1918, RNMM, 3/458.

31   Myaskovsky to Derzhanovsky, 25 July 1918, RNMM, 3/463.

32   Derzhanovsky to Myaskovsky, 16 August 1918, RNMM, 71/472.

33   Derzhanovsky's Narkompros employment file ('lichnoye delo'), GARF,
     2306/44/127, l. 9.

34   Myaskovsky to Asafiev, 12 September 1918, RGALI, 2658/1/639, ll. 20b–3;
     Myaskovsky to Vera Yakovleva, 26 September 1918 and 2 January 1919, RGALI,
     2040/1/82, ll. 410b and 44–440b.

35   See Tat'yana Kuznetsova, 'K voprosu o putyakh resheniya zhilishchnoy
     problemï v SSSR (revolyutsionnïy zhilishchnïy peredel v Moskve, 1918–
     1921gg.)', *Istoriya SSSR*, 5 (1963), 140–7.

36   Aleksandr Il'yukhov, *Zhizn' v èpokhu peremen: Material'noye polozheniye
     gorodskikh zhiteley v godï revolyutsii i grazhdanskoy voynï* (Moscow, 2007),
     150–1.

In spite of his unsatisfactory lodgings, the move to Moscow was well-timed: his connection with Derzhanovsky enabled Myaskovsky to take the first steps towards returning to civilian life and resuming his musical career. A few weeks before his arrival, Derzhanovsky had accepted a post as Head of Periodical Publications in the Music Division of the People's Commissariat of Enlightenment, the new Soviet ministry responsible for education, the arts and sciences, and cultural heritage.[37] (The old tsarist ministries and departments of the civil service were reorganised and restyled 'commissariats' pursuant to a government decree promulgated on 26 October 1917.[38]) 'Narkompros', to use the acronym by which the commissariat was generally known[39], originally comprised a bewildering plethora of departments, sub-departments, committees, and subsections with an equally bewildering plethora of responsibilities – ranging from education and oversight of theatres, museums, galleries, and libraries to support of scientific bodies and learned societies, publishing, and specialist projects that included the eradication of tuberculosis, care for children with mental and physical disabilities, and the promotion of Esperanto and other constructed languages. All seemed to function in 'chaotic independence' of one another, as a notable historian has observed.[40] Recruitment to posts was managed on a very casual basis at first. Arthur Lourié, a twenty-five-year-old composer with little reputation to speak of, was appointed director of the Music Section (MUZO) after a chance conversation with the commissariat's chief Anatoly Lunacharsky, whom he went to see one day in late 1917 to seek permission to put on a play.[41] Lunacharsky's willingness to appoint inexperienced people to senior positions attests to his difficulties in finding suitably qualified staff to replace the former tsarist officials. Disdain for the Bolsheviks was widespread amongst the intelligentsia and few of its representatives were initially willing to work for the new government.

There were exceptions, however – amongst them, the Derzhanovskys, who both began to work for MUZO in 1918. Derzhanovsky's long involvement in radical politics naturally predisposed him to view the Bolsheviks favourably, but it was not the most important factor that influenced his decision. As he explained to Myaskovsky in a lengthy letter, the Revolution

37 GARF, 2306/44/127, l. 4.

38 'Dekret II Vserossiyskogo s"ezda Sovetov ob obrazovanii Rabochego i Krest'yanskogo pravitel'stva, 26 oktyabrya (8 noyabrya) 1917g.', *Dekretï sovetskoy vlasti*, vol. 1 (Moscow, 1957), 20–1.

39 A contraction of 'Narodnïy komissariat prosveshcheniya'.

40 Sheila Fitzpatrick, *The Commissariat of Enlightenment: Soviet Organization of Education and the Arts under Lunacharsky, October 1917–1921* (Cambridge, 1970), 22–3.

41 Nikolay Punin, 'V dni Krasnogo Oktyabrya (otrïvki iz vospominaniy)', *Zhizn' iskusstva*, 8 November 1921.

made it possible to wrest control from the cabal of conservative musicians who had previously dominated musical life and stifled innovation. It had also struck a blow at 'vulgarity and the foundations of the musical *ancien régime*, at the buying and selling of things of [cultural] value and also of the very people who produce them'. It consequently made possible a thoroughgoing renovation of national musical culture on a radically different basis. The advent of socialism promised to liberate artists from their humiliating subservience to the market, since the state would now act as their patron; and with the disappearance of the bourgeoisie as a class, the meretricious commodities produced to gratify its vulgar tastes would disappear also, to be replaced with artworks of genuine value. Such beliefs may have been naïve, but Derzhanovsky was nothing if not idealistic. He hoped that working for the Music Division's publications section would allow him to revive *Music* – this time with government funding. Knowing Myaskovsky's eagerness to leave the armed forces, he suggested that he too should consider joining the staff of MUZO. Plans were afoot to set up a state music publisher which would promote the work of young composers and reprint Russian musical classics in cheap editions. He could also contribute to MUZO's music journals.[42]

In the absence of any overt statement, it is difficult to assess Myaskovsky's attitudes to working for Narkompros or to the government's plans for the administration of cultural life. There is certainly no indication that he greeted the Revolution with 'joy and hope', as Derzhanovskaya recalled of her husband.[43] Asafiev, by contrast, published numerous opinion pieces which were manifestly sympathetic to the new regime.[44] Myaskovsky regarded Asafiev's journalistic activity as a waste of time ('He's only fooling himself if he thinks that he's playing a cultural role', he remarked to Derzhanovsky[45]) and had no impulse to active political or social involvement. His previously cited comments about the Bolshevik takeover unequivocally suggest that he was repelled by the vulgarity of the new administration. At the same time, he did not lament the passing of tsarism: his wartime experiences had strengthened his left-wing tendencies, though he saw no reason to proclaim his political views openly, as he told Derzhanovsky.[46] It is not difficult to understand how someone of his high-minded outlook might have taken a broadly favourable

42   Derzhanovsky to Myaskovsky, 21–4 July 1918, RNMM, 71/471.

43   Koposova-Derzhanovskaya, 'V. V. Derzhanovskiy po vospominaniyam zhenï i druga', RNMM, 3/3365, l. 46.

44   For a discussion of Asafiev's attitude to the new regime and his professional activities in 1918–19, see Orlova and Kryukov, *Akademik Boris Vladimirovich Asaf'yev*, 92–6.

45   Myaskovsky to Derzhanovsky, 4 October 1917, RNMM, 3/442.

46   Myaskovsky to Derzhanovsky, 31 July 1918, RNMM, 3/465.

view of the developments that his friend had outlined. He had been fiercely critical of many aspects of contemporary musical life in his writings for *Music*. He also deplored what he saw as the corrupting effects of the marketplace on artistic creativity, as artists came under increasing pressure to follow fashion and consciously craft their work with an eye to commercial success – a temptation to which he believed Stravinsky had succumbed. A passage in a letter of late 1916 to Derzhanovskaya makes these concerns explicit in language of an almost religious fervour: 'Why has the art of composition declined amongst us, and even more so, the art of performance? Why is this? What is needed to restore an authentic attitude to art? In my view, art demands first and foremost a love 'stronger than death' and true 'service'. Now they have all run off to the market. How do we return from there?'[47]

In a similar vein, he had fantasised about publishing his work at his own expense after the war to spare himself the indignity of having to haggle with publishers.[48] The prospect of state support for the arts overseen by like-minded associates such as Derzhanovsky may consequently have seemed attractive. The reality, of course, would prove very different – but the oppressive bureaucratic controls of the Stalinist era could not have been foreseen in 1918.

He had already entered the pay of the Bolsheviks – so working for Narkompros hardly required any further sacrifices of principle. Since there was no possibility that he could support himself solely by composing, he would require a supplementary source of income for the foreseeable future, such as he had previously obtained from the State Chancellery. He did not take long to make up his mind: he submitted an application to MUZO on 21 August, almost immediately after his arrival in Moscow. The following day, Lourié put him in charge of the division's new journal *Concord* (*Lad*) on a salary of 650 roubles a month. As a government employee, he was supplied with a certificate declaring that he should not be evicted from his lodgings and that his clothes, books, and other items of personal property were exempt from requisitioning.[49] Lourié was evidently prepared to agree to flexible working conditions, since Myaskovsky was able to take on the job while remaining in his naval post. However, his position at MUZO was initially rather precarious. *Concord* ceased production after its first issue and his salary was stopped in consequence.[50] This did not reflect any neg-

47   Myaskovsky to Koposova-Derzhanovskaya, 28 December 1916, RNMM, 3/3286, l. 4.

48   Myaskovsky to Prokofiev, 28 June 1915, in Kozlova and Yatsenko, *Perepiska*, 137–8.

49   Myaskovsky's Narkompros employment file, GARF, 2306/51/804, ll. 2–5.

50   Myaskovsky to Vera Yakovleva, 26 September 1918, RGALI, 2040/1/82, ll. 41–41ob.

ative judgement of his competence. Narkompros was chronically under-funded throughout the early years of its existence: given the dire economic situation, the government did not see its activities as a priority. The commissariat struggled to pay employees' salaries and heat its premises, let alone fund music periodicals. This did not mark the end of Myaskovsky's association with MUZO. He was also offered work in the Music Publishing subdivision in 1918, but it too terminated on 1 January 1919 when the music division underwent internal reorganisation. Later that year, however, he began to work for MUZO on a more-or-less regular basis as further openings presented themselves – in spite of the fact that the division was coming under increasing pressure to let staff go.[51]

MUZO's charter declared it to be responsible for 'directing, controlling, and administering the entire musical life of the Soviet republic'[52] – music education, orchestras and opera houses, the activities of composers and performers, and much else besides. Fulfilling this remit was an enormous challenge during the Civil War years, especially when one considers the size of the country, its chaotic state, and the general dearth of resources. Matters were not helped by Lourié's incompetence and disorganisation, which were the subject of persistent complaints: he was eventually sacked in January 1921.[53] The programmatic statement of MUZO's aims, which he wrote in consultation with Asafiev and others, disdained all discussion of mundane practical matters, its extravagant rhetoric being more reminiscent of an artistic manifesto:

> In these heroic times the spirit of music reveals itself in the seething rhythms of worldwide revolt – avenging itself for having been forgotten and dissolving the accretions of fossilised educational systems currently imposed by a fearfully quaking, deaf humanity which has wilfully and blindly fettered its life-creating power.... The Music Division DECLARES music to be liberated henceforth from all the spurious canons that have prevailed heretofore and from the rules of musical scholasticism in all its manifestations, in the domain of creativity as in the domain of music pedagogy – affirming that cultured music, being a reflection of the spirit

---

51 Asafiev, who acted as deputy director of the Petrograd section of MUZO, reported in May 1919 that 27 of its 153 staff had been let go, and that further redundancies would follow in accordance with government directives: GARF, 2306/25/86, l. 43.

52 'Polozheniye o muzïkal'nom otdele', GARF, 2306/25/6, l. 34.

53 See Izrail' Nest'yev, 'Iz istorii russkogo muzïkal'nogo avangarda', *Sovetskaya muzïka*, 1 (1991), 83; Olesya Bobrik, 'Arthur Lourié: A Biographical Sketch', in Klára Móricz and Simon Morrison (ed.), *Funeral Games in Honor of Arthur Vincent Lourié* (New York, 2014), 43–6.

of music, is subject only to the laws of nature in its sensuous apprehension and embodiment, both in individuals and collectively.[54]

In spite of Lourié's shortcomings, MUZO was not an entirely ineffectual institution. From 1919, it comprised six subdivisions that administered a range of activities, including music education, music publishing, concert life, and musical scholarship[55], employing over two hundred staff members in full-time and part-time capacities.[56] Amongst them were noted musicians with wide experience as organisers and administrators – including Koussevitzky, Glière, the choral conductor and composer Alexander Kastalsky, and the pianist Alexander Goldenweiser. Not all would remain in the country, but the fact that MUZO had begun to attract personnel of this calibre meant that some aspects of its activities at least were in capable hands.

Working at MUZO thus placed Myaskovsky at the centre of national musical life and brought him into contact with some of its leading figures, which helped to consolidate his own professional standing. Establishing his subsequent employment history and the precise nature of his responsibilities is difficult, as much documentation in the division's archive appears to have been lost or destroyed, and a considerable proportion of what survives is illegible due to its deterioration with age. The minutes of meetings of the Concert Subdivision, which took place five or six times a month, record his attendance between November 1919 and April 1921.[57] Items on the agenda included concert planning and programming, artists' fees, and the distribution of requisitioned instruments. He also became a member of the Concert Subdivision's Artistic Council.[58] A register of MUZO employees potentially eligible for so-called 'academic rations', drawn up in February 1921 as a result of an initiative to improve the living conditions of the country's scientists and other specialists, lists additional responsibilities: by then, he had also been appointed deputy director of the Academic Subdivision

---

54   'Deklaratsiya', *Lad*, 1919, 3.

55   'Polozheniye o muzïkal'nom otdele NKP', GARF, 2306/25/6, ll. 46–9.

56   An undated list of MUZO personnel, seemingly compiled in 1919, lists 215 employees: 'Polnïy spisok sotrudnikov Muzïkal'nogo otdela Narodnogo komissariata po prosveshcheniyu', GARF, 2306/25/6, ll. 50–3. The music historian Svetlana Stepanova estimated MUZO's staff in 1920 at 798 (inclusive of performing groups and instrument manufacturers), but did not explain how she arrived at this figure: *Muzïkal'naya zhizn' Moskvï v pervïye godï posle Oktyabrya* (Moscow, 1972), 16. A comprehensive study of MUZO has yet to be written.

57   GARF, 2306/25/140.

58   The minutes of the council's meetings record his attendance between December 1919 and May 1920, but the documentation is very incomplete: GARF, 2306/25/108.

(which oversaw musical scholarship, music libraries, and archives) and was a member of the Publications Committee that reviewed submissions to the state music publishing house.[59]

At this remove, it is impossible to judge the extent of the commitment that these roles required, but each of itself cannot have been very time-consuming, when one considers that Myaskovsky remained in his naval post throughout this period. To judge from one of his letters to Asafiev, he generally attended MUZO meetings after work or during his lunchbreak.[60] (The Naval General Staff headquarters was conveniently situated nearby.) One assumes that such arrangements were common, as many of MUZO's employees had positions at other institutions. The minutes of meetings indicate that he attended conscientiously, but rarely raised items of business or contributed to discussions. Such reserve would have been characteristic of him, but he may also have felt it prudent to keep his own counsel. Even at this early stage, there were already disquieting signs of the growing politicisation of artistic affairs. A network of left-wing cultural and educational organisations known as 'Proletkult'[61] was brought under the jurisdiction of Narkompros in May 1919: some of its representatives advocated jettisoning the entire bourgeois cultural heritage as worthless lumber and attempting to create a new proletarian culture afresh. Amongst the matters discussed at the Concert Subdivision meetings were proposals to organise lectures on music history from a Marxist perspective and the need to programme repertoire that would appeal to audiences with little prior experience of classical music.[62] On the latter occasion, a meeting held in April 1920, Koussevitzky voiced concern that the nationalisation of musical life would lead to a calamitous drop in artistic standards. Two months later he emigrated.[63]

If MUZO was prepared to employ Myaskovsky in multiple capacities, the question arises why he did not relinquish his job with the Naval General Staff. Although records of his service in the latter role are also very incomplete, the post was by no means a sinecure: his assignments included sitting on a commission to revise field service regulations,[64] and he complained

59   GARF, 2306/25/397, l. 8.

60   Myaskovsky to Asafiev, 18 August 1920, in RGALI, 2658/1/639, l. 230b.

61   A contraction of 'The All-Russian Committee of Proletarian Cultural-Educational Organisations'. On Proletkult, see Fitzpatrick, *Commissariat of Enlightenment*, 89–109; Lynn Mally, *Culture of the Future: The Proletkult Movement in Revolutionary Russia* (Berkeley, 1990).

62   GARF, 2306/25/140, ll. 13, 34.

63   For a discussion of the factors that influenced Koussevitzky's decision to emigrate, see Yuzefovich, *Sergey Kusevitskiy. Tom pervïy: Russkiye godï*, 391–405.

64   RGAVMF, 342/1/452, ll. 32–3.

to Asafiev and others of being kept very busy. The explanation is almost certainly to be found in the dramatic worsening of the economic situation in late 1918.

The causes of this deterioration were complex and are still a subject of debate.[65] The Civil War placed additional strain on a parlously fragile economy. Industrial and agricultural outputs, already depressed, declined further after the nationalisation of private businesses and the introduction of *razvyorstka*, the confiscation of agricultural surplus to feed urban workers, which gave peasant farmers no incentive to produce food beyond subsistence levels. Tax revenues were low and foreign borrowing became infeasible after the Bolshevik regime defaulted on international loans. The government resorted to printing money, sparking off hyperinflation which stubbornly resisted attempts to bring it under control for several years. By 1922, banknotes were being printed in denominations of hundreds of millions of roubles.[66]

Throughout the Civil War years, a large sector of the population suffered great hardship. As the economic historian Aleksandr Il'yukhov has observed in his harrowing account of contemporary living conditions, the most serious difficulty faced by Soviet citizens was not merely the soaring cost of essential commodities, but that these commodities were largely unavailable on open sale.[67] Money becomes useless if there is nothing to buy. Food and firewood were in chronically short supply; clothing, footwear, and everyday necessities such as soap, kerosene, and matches all but disappeared from shops. To mitigate the situation, the state sought to centralise control of distribution and introduced a new system of rationing in October 1918, with allocations fixed according to social class. In the cities especially, entitlement to rations became a crucial determinant of physical survival. Manual workers received the largest allowances, followed by white-collar employees of Soviet institutions. 'Bourgeois elements' were the most meagrely provided for, if at all, and were often reduced to bartering their clothes and furniture for food. Members of the intelligentsia fared particularly badly: many perished from malnutrition and disease.[68] By 1920,

---

65 For a discussion, see Andrey Markevich and Mark Harrison, 'Great War, Civil War, and Recovery: Russia's National Income, 1913 to 1928', *Journal of Economic History*, 3 (2011), 672–703. Silvana Malle, *The Economic Organization of War Communism 1918–1921* (Cambridge, 1985) remains a foundational study of the Russian economy during the Civil War years.

66 See Stephen Marks, 'The Russian Experience of Money, 1914–1924', in Murray Frame *et al.* (ed.), *Russian Culture in War and Revolution, 1914–22: Book 2* (Bloomington, 2014), 121–48.

67 Il'yukhov, *Zhizn' v épokhu peremen*, 89.

68 On the early Soviet rationing system, see Il'yukhov, *Zhizn' v épokhu peremen*, 68–122. For an overview of difficulties with food production and supply during

the country had largely reverted to a primitive exchange economy. Many employees were paid partially in goods, rather than money (manual workers saw the proportion of their wages paid in kind rise to 93 percent) – on the understanding that they could trade these for items that they needed.[69]

Although Narkompros personnel were technically eligible to obtain rations, the level of material support that the commissariat received in this respect, as in all others, was grossly inadequate. It struggled to retain its staff, as employees continually sought transfers to other government departments where conditions were better. Derzhanovskaya recalled that neither she nor her husband received any rations and had to make do with exiguous lunches in the Narkompros canteen.[70] By December 1919, the situation was described as 'catastrophic': there were reports of deaths of Narkompros staff members from inanition.[71] The writer Ilya Ehrenburg, who worked in the Theatre Section, remembered the general dismay when he and his colleagues were presented with tins of shoe polish rather than food as part payment around this time, and wondering what on earth he was going to do with it.[72]

Given these circumstances, it is not difficult to understand why Myaskovsky remained in the navy, though he was clearly anxious to maintain his connection with MUZO – presumably wishing to keep open the possibility of obtaining full-time employment there in the future. His responsibilities towards his family also had an important bearing on his decision. Conditions in Petrograd deteriorated very quickly after his departure in August 1918: he was sufficiently concerned as to propose in early January 1919 that Yelikonida, Yevgeniya, and Vera and her children should move to Moscow. (Vera had remained behind in Petrograd when her husband Yakovlev transferred to the capital with the Naval General Staff.) Writing to Vera, he explained that although food supplies were also poor in Moscow, the family could be fed adequately with the help of his and Yakovlev's naval rations. Finding somewhere suitable for them to live was more of a challenge, however, as he could attest from recent experience. The previous month he had moved out of the Derzhanovskys' into a room in a communal flat, unable to endure any longer the spouses' constant bickering. In some of the apartments he had viewed, the central heating was not operating because no firewood could be obtained for the stoves. Living in such

this period, see Lars T. Lih, *Bread and Authority in Russia, 1914–1921* (Berlekey and Los Angeles, 1990), 105ff.

69   Vladimir Dmitrenko, *Torgovaya politika sovetskogo gosudarstva posle perekhoda k NEPu: 1921–1924gg.* (Moscow, 1971), 142.

70   Koposova-Derzhanovskaya, 'Pamyati druga', 219.

71   Fitzpatrick, *Commissariat of Enlightenment*, 163.

72   Il'ya Èrenburg, *Lyudi, godï, zhizn'*, vol. 1 (Moscow, 1990), 339.

conditions presented a real danger to health, as the winter of 1918–19 was exceptionally severe. He counted himself fortunate that the temperature in his new lodgings had so far been maintained at around 17°C (62°F).[73] With the exception of Yevgeniya, his other close relatives came to Moscow later in the year – the surviving family correspondence does not reveal when, but it would appear to have been during the summer.[74] The move was probably postponed because of his elderly aunt's state of health: already frail, by April her body was swollen from malnutrition. Although Myaskovsky did what he could to send supplies and money, Vera was reduced to selling items of furniture to make ends meet.[75]

He had hoped to return to Petrograd as he found it difficult to settle in Moscow, but was forced to abandon the idea. Belyayev offered to look for work for him in Petrograd and mooted ambitious plans to found a new Academy of Musicology and Music Theory, of which he proposed to make Myaskovsky a member, but nothing came of his efforts. Early in 1919, Myaskovsky considered taking a post at the conservatoire in Saratov, a city five hundred miles south-east of Moscow, where Saradzhev was now based, but ultimately declined the offer.[76] Despite his impatience to leave the armed forces, his decision to remain in Moscow: however bad living conditions were in the capital, they were even worse elsewhere.

Contemporary diaries and memoirs are replete with distressing accounts of lives lived amidst unimaginable squalor. The sociologist Pitirim Sorokin, who was among a group of eminent intellectuals forced into exile by the Bolsheviks in 1922, vividly evoked scenes that were ubiquitous. The Petrograd apartment building in which he lived was unheated and had neither running water nor functioning toilets on the upper floors; the pipes had burst in the freezing cold and there was no-one to repair them. Washing oneself or laundering clothes were virtually impossible. The electricity supply operated only for an hour or two in the evening: in the depth of the Northern winter, one spent most of the day in darkness. Water had to be boiled before it was safe to drink because it was contaminated by typhus and other pathogens. Citizens spent hours standing in queues for meagre portions of

73   Myaskovsky to Vera Yakovleva, 2 January 1918, RGALI, 2040/1/82, ll. 43–40b.

74   The last letter of Myaskovsky's to Vera that has been preserved, dated 3 May 1919, indicates that they had yet to move by that point: RGALI, 2040/1/82, ll. 51–20b. In her memoir of Myaskovsky, Vera's daughter Tatyana confirms that the family moved to Moscow in 1919: Tat'yana Yakovleva, 'Moi vospominaniya o dyade Nikolaye Yakovleviche Myaskovskom', RGALI, 2040/4/28, l. 3.

75   Myaskovsky to Vera Yakovleva, 12 and 15 April 1919, RGALI, 2040/1/82, l. 48 and 49–500b.

76   Belyayev to Myaskovsky, 11 November 1918 and 13 February 1919, RGALI, 2040/1/102, ll. 1–4 and 90b.

inferior-quality foodstuffs.[77] Public transport ceased to function in Moscow and Petrograd, which made getting around difficult, especially in wintertime. Streets were littered with uncollected rubbish and streamed with raw sewage.[78] Vyacheslav Ivanov's daughter Lydia recalled a decomposing horse carcass lying for weeks by the entrance to MUZO's premises and being devoured by starving dogs. The interiors of buildings were almost as filthy as their exteriors: rooms teemed with cockroaches and fleas.[79] In such insanitary surroundings, outbreaks of typhus, cholera, and other potentially fatal diseases were inevitable. Many of those infected were insufficiently resilient to recover, being too weakened by malnutrition and exhaustion. Amongst those who died were Myaskovsky's school friend Vadim Modzalevsky, who succumbed to dysentery in 1920, and Yakiv Akimenko, who perished of typhus in 1921.[80] As the crisis escalated, inhabitants of the cities fled to the countryside in droves. Emigration soared. Modeste Hofmann and Lazare Saminsky were amongst Myaskovsky's acquaintances to leave Russia during the Civil War years, never to return.[81] Myaskovsky continued to wonder whether he too should leave: in January 1919 he wrote to Derzhanovsky in a mood of deep dejection to tell him that he wanted to emigrate to America, but as before, he did not act on this plan.[82]

Musical life in Moscow continued after a fashion even in such grim circumstances, though it is difficult to assess how much Myaskovsky and his colleagues in MUZO's Concerts Subdivision managed to accomplish. Performing activity during the early post-Revolutionary period still awaits detailed critical appraisal.[83] Soviet-era accounts gloss over the disruptive effects of contemporary social and economic conditions and are decidedly rose-tinted, claiming a dramatic upsurge of interest in music on the part of the new proletarian audiences. (One Soviet music historian assured readers that an atmosphere of 'festive animation and joyous excitement' prevailed, 'created as much by the new democratic listenership's sensitive appreciation of what it was hearing and getting to know for the first time as

77   Pitirim Sorokin, *A Long Journey: The Autobiography of Pitirim A. Sorokin* (New Haven, 1963), 176–7.

78   Il'yukhov, *Zhizn' v épokhu peremen*, 160–1.

79   Lidiya Ivanova, *Vospominaniya: Kniga ob otse* (Paris, 1990), 81.

80   Tomozov, 'K yubileyu V. L. Modzalevskogo', 50; Bulat, 'Pis'ma N. Ya. Myaskovkogo k Ya. S. Stepovomu', 107.

81   Krasnoborod'ko, 'Pis'ma M. L. Gofmana k B. L. Modzalevskomu: chast' 1', 198; Weisser, 'Lazare Saminsky's Years in Russia and Palestine', 14.

82   Derzhanovsky to Myaskovsky, 25 January 1919, RNMM, 71/473, l. 1. The letter from Myaskovsky that prompted this response has not been preserved.

83   Stepanova's *Muzïkal'naya zhizn' Moskvï v pervïye godï posle Oktyabrya* (see fn56 above), a chronicle of Moscow concert life between 1917 and 1920, is one of the few attempts of its kind.

by the general political situation in the country'.[84]) Notwithstanding these dubious portrayals, the government regarded music as a matter of very minor concern. Lenin moved to shut down the Bolshoi Theatre because he deemed its subsidy an unjustifiable waste of money: it only survived because of Lunacharsky's dogged persistence in raising objections.[85] Much of the music-making in the capital, as elsewhere, seems to have consisted of concerts of folk music and light classical music in workers' clubs, factories, and schools, often with amateur participants. Recitals and chamber music performances by professional musicians continued to be held in more conventional venues, and there were even occasional symphony concerts – but the conditions in which they took place can well be imagined. The composer Alexander Gretchaninov remembered developing frostbite while giving recitals in Moscow and being robbed on several occasions when he performed in Petrograd. His fee was often paid in flour or groats.[86]

All things considered, it is hardly surprising that Myaskovsky composed virtually nothing for two and a half years, especially at a time when one could not even rely on having light to read by in the evenings. Aside from completing the orchestration of the Fifth Symphony in December 1918, he wrote only a single short piano piece. Nor is it surprising that there are no records of any performances of his music in 1918 or 1919, though this was demonstrably not due to any lack of interest. Hermann Scherchen, who had been interned as an enemy alien in Russia during the war[87], expressed a desire to perform the Third when Myaskovsky played it for him in April 1918; Grzegorz Fitelberg planned to conduct several of his orchestral works later in the same year; and Koussevitzky had offered to give the premiere of the Fourth.[88] None of these performances materialised, but all three conductors would renew their contact with him in the future. His creative inactivity was a source of deep frustration, as was the fact that circumstances had forced him to remain in Moscow. He seems initially to have felt very

84 Yuriy Keldïsh, 'Sovetskoye muzïkal'noye stroitel'stvo v pervïye godï posle Oktyabrya', in Yuriy Keldïsh *et al.* (ed.), *Istoriya muzïki narodov SSSR. Tom I: 1917–1932* (Moscow, 1970), 33. For another account in a similar vein, see Izrail' Gusin, 'Sovetskoye gosudarstvennoye muzïkal'noye stroitel'stvo', in Valerian Bogdanov-Berezovskiy and Izrail' Gusin (ed.), *V pervïye godï sovetskogo muzïkal'nogo stroitel'stva: Stat'i, vospominaniya, materialï* (Leningrad, 1959), 62–157.

85 See the official communiqués reproduced in Leonid Maksimenkov (ed.), *Muzïka vmesto sumbura: Kompozitorï i muzïkantï v Strane Sovetov* (Moscow, 2013), 34–44; and Fitzpatrick, *Commissariat of Enlightenment*, 268–9.

86 Aleksandr Grechaninov, *Moya zhizn'* (New York, 1952), 118–19.

87 See Hermann Scherchen, *Aus meinem Leben. Rußland in jenen Jahren* (Berlin, 1984), 69–125.

88 Myaskovsky to Derzhanovsky, 17 April, 3 May, and 10 July 1918, RNMM, 3/456, 457, and 460.

isolated there and keenly missed the stimulus of Asafiev and Prokofiev's company.

Fortunately, his work for MUZO brought him into contact with several musicians whom he found congenial companions, including one, Pavel Lamm, with whom he formed one of the closest friendships of his life. Myaskovsky and Lamm had met before the war: Lamm had accompanied Derzhanovskaya in performances of Myaskovsky's songs in the 'Modern Music Evening' that Derzhanovsky organised in January 1914. Lamm's friend and piano-duet partner Sergey Popov brought Myaskovsky with him when visiting Lamm at home one day during the summer of 1919. The two men struck up an immediate rapport, being in many ways alike in temperament.

Slim, of medium height, with blond hair and pale-grey eyes that lent his face a kindly, but rather sad expression, Lamm was an engaging man, and in his own quiet way, an unconventional one.[89] Myaskovsky's junior by a year (he turned thirty-seven in 1919), he was one of six children born to a Russian mother and a German migrant labourer who settled in Moscow in the 1860s and subsequently had a reasonably prosperous career in business. Shy and sickly as a boy, Lamm turned to books and music as an escape from the unhappy domestic atmosphere created by his brutal authoritarian father. His musical education was haphazard, but his talent was spotted by Gretchaninov, who was a friend of his elder brother. With Gretchaninov's help and encouragement, Lamm became a sufficiently proficient pianist to be accepted onto the Moscow Conservatoire's diploma course, from which he graduated in 1912. He made a considerable reputation as a chamber musician and for a time regularly appeared in recitals with Maria Olenina-d'Alheim, a much-admired singer of the period who was instrumental in assisting the growth of Musorgsky's posthumous reputation outside Russia.[90] At the outbreak of the October Revolution, Lamm was working for Éditions Russes de Musique. When music publishers and music shops were nationalised by government decree in December 1918[91], he transferred to MUZO's Publications Subdivision, which took over their functions and became the new state music publisher, Gozmuzizdat.[92] On 1 February 1919, Lamm was appointed as manager of Gozmuzizdat's Technical Section:

---

89 The biographical information presented in this and the following three paragraphs about the Lamm family draws on Lamm, 'Pavel Aleksandrovich Lamm: Opït biografii', RNMM, 192/361, ll. 1–171.

90 On Olenina-d'Alheim, see Alexander Tumanov, *The Life and Artistry of Maria Olenina-d'Alheim*, trans. Christopher Barnes (Edmonton, 2000).

91 See Maksimenkov (ed.), *Muzïka vmesto sumbura*, 29.

92 A contraction of 'Gosudarstvennoye muzïkal'noye izdatel'stvo' – State Music Publisher.

thanks to his efforts, much of the stock and equipment of the pre-Revolutionary music publishing firms was preserved.

Like Myaskovsky, Lamm appears never to have entered into any sexually intimate personal relationships. He lived with his sister Sofia, who kept house for him. This arrangement had come about under unusual circumstances. An intelligent and independent-minded woman, Sofia had hoped to enrol at the University of Zurich in 1906 but was diagnosed with tuberculosis shortly after arriving in the city. She had to abandon her studies and was sent for treatment to a sanatorium in Arosa. Alone and deeply unhappy, she had an affair with a fellow patient, a Russian man who was also seriously ill, hoping to hasten her death. When she discovered that she was pregnant, he offered to divorce his wife, from whom he was estranged, but she refused to marry him. Remarkably, she recovered her health and gave birth in March 1908 to a daughter, Olga. Her elder brother Vladimir, now head of the family after their father's death, reacted very censoriously, but Pavel came to the rescue. He not only undertook to support Sofia but formally adopted Olga to remove the stigma of illegitimacy.

The Lamms had had their own share of difficulties during the war. As neither had ever applied for Russian citizenship, they were categorised as enemy aliens on account of their father's German nationality and exiled to Birsk, a provincial town eight hundred miles east of Moscow. They experienced considerable hardship on their return in late 1917. Their apartment was inconveniently situated in a distant suburb and they could seldom heat it in winter due to the scarcity of fuel. Pavel had a heart condition and was unable to chop wood or perform any other physically strenuous tasks, which placed a considerable additional burden on Sofia. Olga remembered that their ration cards entitled them to little more than a few ounces of bread each per day and some frozen potatoes and carrots. In desperation, her mother bartered her toys and the family's clothes for additional foodstuffs, but despite Sofia's best efforts, Olga became seriously malnourished and nearly died of Spanish influenza during the epidemic of 1918–19.

One of the few solaces of those bleak years had been the musical evenings held in their home. The programmes largely comprised transcriptions of orchestral music for two pianos, eight hands – an ensemble of which Lamm was especially fond. When Myaskovsky and Lamm renewed their acquaintance, these gatherings had recently ceased due to the demise of two of the regular participants during the influenza epidemic. Lamm's insatiable appetite for music rivalled Myaskovsky's own, as they discovered to their mutual pleasure during Myaskovsky's first visit. When Lamm broached the subject of his recent compositions, Myaskovsky produced his piano-duet arrangements of the Fourth and Fifth Symphonies. They went to the piano and played both works twice. Lamm thought the symphonies very fine and was most taken with his guest: Myaskovsky's charm and refinement of manner made a strong impression, in spite of his shyness. They remained in contact thereafter, though in the absence of public transport, it was infeasible for Myaskovsky to call to Lamm's home very often. They saw more of each other when the musical evenings resumed in 1920. At first, these were held in the apartment of Lamm's friend Maxim Gube, because it was heated to some extent and in a more central location. Gube had only one piano, but Myaskovsky acquired a second, making it possible to revive the two-piano ensemble, of which he became a regular member. By this point, Lamm had been offered part-time hours teaching piano as a second instrument at the Moscow Conservatoire. Several of his new colleagues began to attend the musical evenings, including the composers Alexander Goedicke and Anatoly Aleksandrov, both of whom were fine instrumentalists. Gube, an economist by training, was a keen amateur singer and used to perform *Lieder* and other song repertory. A touching note from Myaskovsky to Gube, sent in July 1920, makes clear just how much these gatherings meant to him. 'The musical circle formed by you and Pavel is for me personally a real spiritual oasis, thanks to the attitude of artistic and loving devotion to music *an und für sich* which reigns in it', he wrote: it represented a haven of civilisation into which he could escape, if only for a few hours, from the harshness and dreariness of everyday life.[93]

Myaskovsky did not think of them in utilitarian terms, but these social encounters with prominent musicians significantly assisted the growth of his reputation in the capital. So too did the premiere of the Fifth Symphony in D major, op. 18, which was given by Nicolai Malko on 18 August 1920 with an orchestra formed from members of the recently founded Russian National Professional Union of Arts Workers (RABIS).[94] Although his songs and chamber music were featured in concerts that Belyayev organised in Petrograd a few months previously, this was the first time that any of his orchestral works had been given in over three years.[95] The fact that Malko managed to arrange a performance of the Fifth is significant: it seems to have been the only new Russian symphony premiered between 1917 and 1922, as concert programmes throughout this period consisted almost exclusively of popular classics that would appeal to proletarian audiences.[96] Gratifyingly, the performance was not only very good, but a resounding

93 Myaskovsky to Maxim Gube, 16 July 1920, RGALI, 2012/2/208, l. 2.

94 Concert programme, RNMM, 71/485. The RABIS orchestra seems essentially to have consisted of players from the Bolshoi Theatre: see Lev Grigor'yev and Yakov Platek, *Moskovskaya gosudarstvennaya filarmoniya* (Moscow, 1973), 51.

95 The concerts took place on 16 April and 19 June 1920. The programme of the first included the premiere of the F minor quartet of 1909–10. Belyayev to Myaskovsky, 17 April and 9 June 1920, RGALI, 2040/1/102, ll. 11–14 and 17–18.

96 See David Fanning, 'The Symphony in the Soviet Union (1917–91)', in Robert Layton (ed.), *A Companion to the Symphony* (London, 1993), 318–19.

FIGURE 5.2. Pavel Lamm, Sergey Popov, Maxim Gube, and Myaskovsky (1923).

success: the scherzo had to be encored and Myaskovsky was summoned onto the stage to acknowledge the applause afterwards.[97] A second performance the following month was equally successful – to a degree unprecedented in his experience, as he reported to Yevgeniya.[98]

The enthusiastic reception of the Fifth is readily understandable, as it is one of Myaskovsky's most immediately appealing compositions. Like the Fourth, it is a key work for understanding his later creative development. The four-movement Fifth explores a very different psychological world to its predecessors: though by no means without its passages of disturbance, these are contextualised and contained to a far greater extent. The sonata-form first movement is predominantly pastoral and lyrical; the Scherzo, the third movement, is instinct with a quirky playfulness; and the finale closes in a mood of radiant solemnity and confidence. Much of the music has a fundamentally diatonic basis, though the harmonic language is strikingly fresh and piquant, adumbrating Myaskovsky's increasingly extensive exploration of modality from the 1930s onwards. The highly chromatic, densely dissonant sonorities characteristic of much of his previous work

97 Myaskovsky to Asafiev, 18 August 1920, RGALI, 2658/1/639, l. 26.
98 Myaskovsky to Yevgeniya Sakharova, 14 September 1920, RGALI, 2040/1/80, l. 100b.

are also in evidence, but largely confined to the slow movement, which constitutes the symphony's centre of gravity. Here, Myaskovsky juxtaposes strikingly disparate musical material to powerful dramatic effect – a plaintive modal melody, heard at the opening, and an agitated idea in triplets that is subjected to intense contrapuntal development and rises to a searing culmination.

The symphony merits a much more detailed discussion of its formal organisation and compositional approach than is feasible here, but a few points of a general nature should be made. The first is that the symphony represents a significant creative breakthrough, both in terms of technical command and a broadening of expressive range. Although Myaskovsky's earlier work included some very impressive achievements, it also had limitations that he recognised and sought to overcome. The dissonant post-Wagnerian musical language of much of his early music was entirely apt for exploring certain kinds of psychological states but presented considerable challenges when it came to writing large-scale works. Unless very carefully handled, densely dissonant chromaticism can militate against the attainment of sustained fast momentum, vitally necessary for contrast. The intense emotional charge characteristic of such sonorities can also pall, especially if accompanied by a tendency to unrelieved textural density. For the most part, Myaskovsky dealt successfully with these challenges, but like other composers who started out writing in post-Wagnerian idioms – Szymanowski and Bartók being cases in point – he clearly began to find them limiting.

In Myaskovsky's case, creative renewal came from re-engagement with the work of his Russian predecessors. The Fifth's indebtedness to Borodin, Tchaikovsky, and even Glazunov is readily apparent, though these influences were completely assimilated by his own strong and independent musical personality. Perhaps the biggest gain was in spontaneity and directness of expression. In conversation with Derzhanovsky in 1915, Yavorsky shrewdly observed that the greatest obstacle to Myaskovsky's artistic development was his excessive self-consciousness: he needed to be bolder in his approach. This shortcoming was particularly evident, Yakovsky felt, in his thematic material, which was seldom notable for its vividness of melodic invention; it sometimes produced an impression of contrivance, being fashioned primarily for what it could yield when subjected to contrapuntal treatment.[99] Yavorsky's diagnosis was perspicacious. Myaskovsky's early creativity was indubitably beset by insecurities and anxieties – especially the fear, frequently expressed in his letters, of being too obvious, of lapsing into banality and vulgarity. But as Yakovsky had previously cautioned, artistic maturity and profundity are not qualities that can be forced or willed, and

99   Derzhanovsky to Myaskovsky, 18 March 1915, RNMM, 71/292.

EXAMPLE 5.3. Symphony no. 5, first movement: opening.

an excessive preoccupation with their attainment can become paralysing. The score of the Fifth suggests a marked relaxation of such inhibitions: one of its most immediately striking features is its warm lyricism, exemplified by the long-breathed opening theme of the first movement (ex. 5.3). And although the symphony demonstrates a highly sophisticated compositional technique, it never draws attention to itself. The expert contrapuntal writing sounds deft and natural, and the orchestration is much more assured, evincing a new transparency and feeling for instrumental colour.

The fact that Myaskovsky's active creative engagement with Russian musical traditions commenced at this comparatively early stage of his career, long before the advent of Socialist Realism, is crucial for understanding his later work. He has often been instanced as an example of a modernist who 'regressed' stylistically in the face of the ideological pressures of the Stalinist era, but his artistic development was far more complex

EXAMPLE 5.4. Piano Sonata no. 3: conclusion.

– and interesting – than the stereotype would suggest. Throughout the 1920s, this engagement proceeded simultaneously with a continued exploration of approaches adumbrated in his early Expressionist scores. His next composition after the Fifth Symphony, the single-movement Piano Sonata no. 3 in C minor, op. 19, which was completed in December 1920, reverts to a dark, oppressive realm of experience, taking the dissonance of his harmonic language to new extremes. The gestural violence of the closing bars (ex. 5.4) with their vertiginous successions of quartal sonorities (superbly realised in Sviatoslav Richter's recorded performance of 1974) was unprecedented in Myaskovsky's output to date. The fact that the Fifth Symphony and the Third Piano Sonata could be composed in succession vividly illustrates the range of expression that his style could now encompass.

The warm reception accorded the performances of the Fifth Symphony in the autumn of 1920 brightened an otherwise cheerless period. In September, his sister Valentina was subjected to a distressing ordeal which demonstrated the extent of the siblings' vulnerability on account of their social origins. After the State Chancellery was abolished, Valentina had found work in the People's Commissariat of State Control,[100] whose functions included administration of the national finances. Her superiors were sufficiently impressed by her competence as to promote her in January 1920 to the position of senior financial controller in the new state bank. In September, both she and her daughter fell seriously ill – Valentina with a heart condition, Marianna from malnutrition. When she took sick leave, her newly appointed superior, a zealous Party member, seized the opportunity to denounce her on trumped-up charges that she was deliberately obstructing the functioning of her unit and had absented herself without permission. He demanded that she be sacked in the interests of 'cleansing' the workforce of alien class elements and banned from ever working in a government department again. An undated handwritten note in her personnel file confirms that the attack was politically motivated: it instructs the recipient to phone another ministry 'to find out when the personnel purge [*chistka*] will take place'. Fortunately, Valentina's senior colleagues defended her against the allegations, pointing to her exemplary employment record: her dismissal was overturned, and she was transferred to People's Commissariat of Foreign Affairs. Nonetheless, the experience can only have been a deeply unsettling one: the loss of her job and her ration allowance could have had disastrous consequences.[101]

The few items that survive of Myaskovsky's correspondence from late 1920 indicate his mounting impatience to resign from his naval post and a

---

100 Narodnïy komissariat gosudarstvennogo kontrolya RSFSR.

101 The relevant documents are preserved in Valentina's Narkomgoskont personnel file, GARF, 406/24b/850, ll. 1–24.

renewed desire to move back to Petrograd. Writing to Asafiev in December, he complained of being in persistently low spirits, worn out by tedious administrative duties that robbed him of the time and mental energy to compose.[102] Yelikonida was also eager to return home, but that was out of the question, given Yevgeniya's accounts of the worsening food shortages in Petrograd and the withdrawal of her own ration entitlement. 'Nothing's available apart from vegetables', she reported, 'and when they're gone, I don't know what will happen'.[103] Even in Moscow, the highest ration categories available provided just over one thousand calories a day by October 1920.[104] If Myaskovsky were to find another job, it would be vital to procure a ration allowance: the importance of this practical necessity was underlined when he fell so ill from malnutrition and exhaustion that he had to be admitted to a Narkompros sanatorium towards the end of the year. Pavel Lamm was also hospitalised around the same time, having developed a stomach ulcer because of his poor diet.[105] Olga Lamm recalled the family's relief when her uncle was declared eligible to receive 'academic rations' after being appointed director of the state musical publishing house that winter. Every month he obtained a half *pud* (about eighteen pounds) of herring, a leg of lamb, a bottle of sunflower oil, flour, millet, and a bar of laundry soap – a rare luxury at the period. She and her mother used to collect the allowance on his behalf and drag it home on a sleigh.[106]

The circumstances are unclear, but there appears to have been ongoing discussion throughout 1920 and early 1921 of appointing Myaskovsky to a senior post either in MUZO or in a major musical institution. A gnomic comment in one of his letters to Yevgeniya in the spring of 1920 suggests that he came under considerable pressure to accept the directorship of the Moscow Conservatoire – an offer that he evidently declined.[107] Matters came to a head after Lourié's sacking as director of MUZO in January 1921 and his replacement by the composer and political activist Boris Krasin, brother of the senior Bolshevik functionary and diplomat Leonid Krasin. In April 1921, it was proposed to make Myaskovsky Krasin's deputy – a position that would entitle him to receive academic rations. Around the same time, Myaskovsky was notified that the Naval General Staff was being transferred back to Petrograd. He consequently had to make a choice either

102 Myaskovsky to Asafiev, 27 December 1920, RGALI, 2658/1/639, l. 40.

103 Yevgeniya Sakharova to Myaskovsky, undated letter [autumn 1920?], RGALI, 2040/2/259, l. 30.

104 Il'yukhov, *Zhizn' v ėpokhu peremen*, 110, 247.

105 Lamm, 'Pavel Aleksandrovich Lamm: Opït biografii', RNMM, 192/361, l. 175.

106 Ibid, l. 153.

107 Myaskovsky to Yevgeniya Sakharova, n.d. [May 1920?], RGALI, 2040/1/80, l. 110b.

to accept the MUZO position and stay in Moscow, or to remain in his naval post and return to the northern capital. He was torn by indecision, and promptly wrote to Yevgeniya to enquire about regaining occupancy of his former rooms in the family apartment (which had since been turned into a communal flat), adding that he was still unsure what would happen.[108] Matters quickly resolved themselves. On 21 April, a day after his fortieth birthday, Myaskovsky's duties were officially reassigned from the Naval General Staff to Narkompros and he accepted the deputy directorship of MUZO.[109] After almost seven years, he could at last devote himself to music once more.

108 Myaskovsky to Yevgeniya Sakharova, 15 April 1921, RGALI, 2040/1/80, ll. 15–150b.

109 'Posluzhnoy spisok', RGALI, 2040/1/168, l. 4

6

Expanding Horizons: 1921–3

Myaskovsky's appointment to the deputy directorship of MUZO was not a particularly surprising development: by this point, he had a considerable reputation as a composer and had acquired extensive administrative experience. He had no interest in becoming a career bureaucrat, however, and regarded the post as a stopgap until he found more suitable employment, preferably in Petrograd. Belyayev and his other acquaintances in the city repeatedly urged him to return, holding out alluring prospects of better working conditions.[1] In the event, Myaskovsky remained in Moscow – a decision almost certainly influenced by developments over the summer of 1921. Although the Civil War had effectively concluded by the spring of the previous year, the population's sufferings were far from over. Food supplies remained critically low, and by July the government was forced to acknowledge what had long been evident – that the country was in the grip of a catastrophic famine. Faced with growing unrest, Lenin abandoned the practice of confiscating agricultural produce from the peasantry and allowed private enterprise to resume to some extent in the hope of reviving the economy. Since the benefits of this so-called 'New Economic Policy' would not be felt immediately, the government continued to print money to cover budgetary deficits in the interim. The inevitable result was a new phase of hyperinflation which caused prices of food and fuel to soar further. As usual, the crisis was particularly acute in Petrograd: by the late autumn, Belyayev was sending Myaskovsky grim accounts of his experiences of hunger and cold: his 'academic rations' had been cut by two-thirds and he was no longer able to heat his apartment.[2] Asafiev was reduced to such a weakened state by malnutrition that his memory and general psychological functioning were severely affected: he was saved only by the arrival of food parcels provided as humanitarian aid to Soviet Russia by the American Relief Administration.[3] Given these circumstances, it would clearly have been highly inadvisable for Myaskovsky to move back. Conscious of the

---

1   Viktor Belyayev to Myaskovsky, 10 June 1921, RGALI, 2040/1/103, ll. 4–40b.

2   Belyayev to Myaskovsky, 17 September and 10 October 1921, RGALI, 2040/1/103, ll. 19 and 21.

3   Asafiev to Pavel Lamm, 10 June 1922, RGALI, 2743/1/76, l. 90b. On the ARA's famine relief efforts, see Benjamin M. Weissman, *Herbert Hoover and Famine Relief to Soviet Russia 1921–23* (Stanford, 1974); Bertrand M. Patenaude, *The Big Show in Bololand: The American Relief Expedition to Soviet Russia in the Famine of 1921* (Stanford, 2002).

plight of friends and family members in Petrograd, he did what he could to help by sending money and provisions spared from his own rations.

His decision was also influenced by further job offers.[4] In October, he was appointed to a part-time position as professor of composition at the Moscow Conservatoire. As a result, he was able to resign from his MUZO post the following January when, thanks to the efforts of Pavel Lamm, he was hired by the state music publishing house Gosmuzizdat as a consultant, with the responsibility of assessing submissions and approving them for publication.[5] Within a comparatively short period, his circumstances had altered dramatically: his new employment was not only more congenial but also made it easier to find time to compose.

There were welcome changes in his personal life too. In the autumn of 1921, his sister Valentina secured an additional room in the communal apartment where she lived with her daughter Marianna, which enabled Myaskovsky to move in with them. The apartment was in a building (since demolished) on Denezhnïy Lane in the central Arbat district, conveniently located not far from the conservatoire. Valentina and he would remain there until 1930, when Myaskovsky eventually managed to buy an apartment of his own. They lived very simply and such furnishings as they possessed were unremarkable, except for the grand piano in Myaskovsky's study-cum-bedroom and his heavily laden bookshelves, which barely left room for an armchair and the couch-bed on which he slept at night.[6] The impression of monastic austerity was offset only by a vase of fresh flowers; and although Myaskovsky had a keen appreciation of elegant china and beautiful things, he preferred to spend whatever spare money he had on books and scores. Spartan though these surroundings were, they afforded a modicum of domestic comfort. At a time when adults were permitted a mere ten square metres of living space (an allocation reduced to eight square metres in 1924), having a room to oneself, no matter how small, was a luxury, and one that was unattainable for many.[7]

One further development made Moscow begin to feel more like home. In May 1921, Pavel Lamm and his family were allocated rooms in one of the apartments in the east wing of the conservatoire, which had served as residences for the institution's teaching staff since Vasiliy Safonov's time as rector. This supportive gesture lifted Lamm's spirits and led him to abandon

---

4   Myaskovsky to Asafiev, 23 October 1921, RGALI, 2658/1/639, ll. 48–480b.

5   Myaskovsky's Moscow Conservatoire personnel file, AMK, 1/23/84, l. 8.

6   Vladmir Fere, 'Nash uchitel' Nikolay Yakovlevich Myaskovskiy (stranitsï vospominaniy)', in Yekaterina Alekseyeva *et al.* (ed.), *Vospominaniya o Moskovskoy konservatorii* (Moscow, 1966), 423.

7   See Anna Chernïkh, 'Zhilishchnïy peredel: Politika 20-kh godov v sfere zhil'ya', *Sotsiologicheskiye issledovaniya*, 10 (1998), 71–8.

his plan to emigrate.[8] His new accommodation also served as an office for Gosmuzizdat, so he could conveniently conduct meetings there rather than having to go out.[9] He taught his conservatoire students at home too, as did other many staff members at this time.[10] The depredations of the immediate post-Revolutionary period had left the building in a poor state, and for some years funds were insufficient to pay for heating and essential repairs.[11]

The apartment was situated on the ground floor overlooking the courtyard in front of the conservatoire: in the early 1920s, poultry belonging to the institution's domestic staff still roamed freely over the cobblestones. (Vera Mukhina's imposing Tchaikovsky monument, which currently occupies much of the area, was not erected until 1954.) The Lamms had two rooms at their disposal. One served as a sitting room-cum-dining room, and, at night, as a bedroom for Lamm's sister Sofia and her daughter Olga, then thirteen years of age. A connecting door led into Lamm's study, which contained his two grand pianos, both excellent instruments, and his enormous writing desk; its walls were lined with bookcases laden with the holdings of his extensive library. Although the rooms were far from unattractive, the apartment presented many inconveniences. The kitchen had been claimed by the other occupants, so Sofia cooked meals on a cast-iron stove in the cramped entrance hallway, which also housed their supply of firewood and the wardrobe containing their clothes.[12] They had their own lavatory, situated behind the door-curtain in the study, but a single cold-water tap and sink had to suffice for all personal and domestic needs.[13]

Lamm's move meant that he and Myaskovsky could meet more regularly and led to a rapid deepening of their friendship. The two men had much in common: a tendency to melancholy and introspection, a love of literature and stimulating conversation, and a similar gentleness and refinement of manner. Olga Lamm recalled that her uncle admired Myaskovsky not only as 'a composer of genius' but also for 'the honesty and sensitivity of his feelings, the depth and nobility of his thought, his goodness and the generous outlook on life that arose from it'.[14] It would be easy to dismiss

8   Lamm, 'Pavel Aleksandrovich Lamm: Opït biografii', RNMM, 192/361, l. 182.

9   Martina Svetlanova (ed.), 'Pavel Lamm v tyur'makh i ssïlkakh: Po stranitsam vospominaniy O. P. Lamm', in Rakhmanova (ed.), *Al'manakh*, vol. 2, 85.

10   Fere, 'Nash uchitel'', 423.

11   See Lev Ginzburg (ed.), *Moskovskaya konservatoriya 1866–1966* (Moscow, 1966), 291.

12   Svetlanova (ed.), 'Pavel Lamm v tyur'makh i ssïlkakh', 85–6.

13   Viktor Lamm, 'P. A. i O. P. Lamm v moikh vospominaniyakh', in Rakhmanova (ed.), *Al'manakh*, vol. 4 (Moscow, 2013), 538.

14   Ol'ga Lamm, 'Druz'ya Pavla Aleksandrovicha Lamma i uchastniki muzïkal'nikh vecherov v yego dome (20-ye godï XX veka)', in Tamara Livanova (ed.), *Iz proshlogo sovetskoy muzïkal'noy kul'turï*, vol. 1 (Moscow, 1975), 76.

such high-flown expressions of regard as indicative of uncritical hero-worship, but this would be to overlook the fact that such attitudes were widely shared. Notwithstanding his reserve, Myaskovsky seems to have had an unusual capacity to inspire affection and devotion in others. In assessing such responses, one must bear in mind the enduring influence throughout the Soviet period of distinctively Russian envisionings of the artist – understandings, as Isaiah Berlin observed, that derived from German Romanticism but became prevalent in Russia in a much intensified form. Intrinsic to them was a conception of the artist as a being apart, devoted to a higher spiritual cause, and for whom personal integrity and artistic integrity were at bottom one and the same.[15] Yet, for all the respect in which Myaskovsky was held, he seems to have been free of vanity or self-importance. His friendship with Lamm was one of the closest he ever formed, and he would prove an unfailing source of support to the family in times of difficulty.

Lamm's move made it easier to meet for domestic music-making, whether at the Lamms' apartment or that of their mutual friend Maxim Gube, who lived a short distance away. The summer of 1921 saw the inauguration of weekly musical evenings which continued for many years and became legendary in the annals of Soviet musical life. Initially, they took place at both venues, but by the following year were mostly held at Lamm's apartment.[16] The small circle of musicians which had previously met in 1919–20 grew considerably in size. The most frequent habitués were Alexander Goedicke, Grigory Catoire, Anatoly Aleksandrov, and Samuil Feinberg, accompanied by their spouses and family members. As the 1920s progressed, they were joined by the conductors Konstantin Saradzhev and Nicolai Malko, and younger composers such as Myaskovsky's student Vissarion Shebalin. The occasional visitors included Asafiev and Belyayev, and the pianists Konstantin Igumnov, Heinrich Neuhaus, and Lev Oborin, who tried out new programmes before performing them in public. Later in the decade, Prokofiev would put in appearances during his visits to the USSR, as would Shostakovich when business brought him to Moscow.

Many of the participants held posts at the conservatoire and at MUZO. Personal and professional relationships became closely intertwined – a circumstance that soon engendered hostile perceptions of the Myaskovsky-Lamm circle as a powerful clique controlling key positions in national musical life. Such views were unjust, but it was perhaps inevitable that the circle would arouse envy and resentment, particularly at a time when competition for publication and performance opportunities was intense. There

15   Isaiah Berlin, *Russian Thinkers*, ed. Henry Hardy and Aileen Kelly (London, 1978), 127–31.

16   Lamm, *Stranitsï*, 9

can be no doubt that the primary bond uniting its members was a shared love of music. In the early years, their appreciation of these evenings was all the more keen because opportunities to hear music were so few, concert life having virtually ceased.

Pavel Lamm envisioned the musical evenings as a kind of 'creative laboratory'[17], through which he could support the activities of composers and performers.[18] This support went to remarkable lengths: he made numerous arrangements for two pianos of new orchestral scores by the circle's composers (and much other music besides), which became staple items in the musical evenings' programmes. For the composers concerned, this activity was invaluable at a time when it was virtually impossible to arrange orchestral performances. All of the symphonies that Myaskovsky would write subsequently – from the Sixth to the Twenty-Seventh – would be 'premiered' in this fashion.[19]

Maxim Gube's records of the music played at the first twenty-eight of these evenings have recently come to light in the Shebalin family archive.[20] They testify eloquently to its members' commitment to the maintenance of cultural and intellectual life during these grim years. The bulk of the music performed consisted of eight-hand arrangements of orchestral works, usually with Aleksandrov and Lamm at the first piano and Sergey Popov and Myaskovsky at the second. A considerable quantity of vocal music featured, sung either by Gube or Aleksandrov's wife, Nina, whose fine soprano voice was allied to the rarer gifts of intelligence and good taste.[21] Chamber music for other combinations was included occasionally.

Entire evenings were devoted to the work of Schumann, Borodin, Musorgsky, Tchaikovsky, Liszt, Brahms, and Wagner, as well as Myaskovsky, Feinberg, Medtner, Goedicke, and Aleksandrov. Some programmes were very substantial: at a Schumann evening held on 2 March 1922, for example, the Second and Fourth Symphonies were performed, in addition to *Dichterliebe* and twelve assorted *Lieder*.[22] Learning so much music required

---

17   Lamm, *Stranitsï*, 10.

18   Lamm, 'Druz'ya', 75.

19   Ol'ga Lamm, 'Vospominaniya o N. Ya. Myaskovskom', in Semyon Shlifshteyn (ed.), *N. Ya. Myaskovskiy: Sobraniye materialov*, 238–9.

20   The manuscript, which is entitled 'Pyatnitsï 1921/22 gg.: Programmï', runs to thirty typewritten pages. I would like to thank Vissarion Shebalin's granddaughter Yekaterina Lebedenko for making this document available for consultation.

21   A student of Jacques Dalcroze, Nina Aleksandrova had a distinguished career in her own right as a teacher of 'musical gymnastics': see Vera Rossikhina, 'N. G. Aleksandrova i ritmika Dal'kroza v nashey strane', in Tamara Livanova (ed.), *Iz proshlogo sovetskoy muzïkal'noy kul'turï*, vol. 3 (Moscow, 1982), 238–70 and Lamm, 'Druz'ya', 97.

22   'Pyatnitsï', l. 21.

a serious commitment from the group's members, notwithstanding the fact that it included accomplished instrumentalists, some of whom, like Feinberg and Goedicke, were virtuosi of the first rank. Though an excellent sight-reader, Myaskovsky was the least technically proficient, so preferred to take the less demanding *secondo* parts.[23] The group's repertoire subsequently expanded to comprise much of the standard orchestral literature from the Classical period up to the early twentieth-century, including scores by Debussy, Strauss, and Mahler. Needless to say, Russian composers were strongly represented.[24]

As the decade wore on, the musical evenings provided useful opportunities to play new orchestral works by the circle's members for Soviet or visiting foreign conductors: on such occasions, they assumed a more formal character.[25] But for the most part they were relaxed and intimate events. Tea and home-made cake or biscuits were served once the guests assembled at eight o'clock, after which music would be performed until around midnight. Afterwards, the guests would again be provided with food and refreshments to fortify them before going home. The participants would often linger over the table into the small hours, chatting and exchanging stories. In spite of his shyness, Myaskovsky clearly felt relaxed in this company. After many years spent working in comparative isolation, becoming part of an artistic community meant a great deal.

The eventful spring and summer of 1921 culminated in a flurry of activity in September. At the start of the month he travelled to Petrograd with his aunt Yelikonida and returned her to the care of his sister Yevgeniya: notwithstanding the difficult conditions in her native city, she was anxious to return home. The next few weeks were taken up with moving flats and settling into his new job at the conservatoire, after which he managed to snatch a fortnight's holiday in the countryside outside Moscow. In spite of the inclement weather, contact with nature had its usual restorative effect. He reported to Asafiev that his 'nerves felt less frayed' and that he had been revising the First Symphony in an effort to get himself back into a frame of mind conducive to composing.[26] In a diary entry of 17 October, his first in almost three years, he recorded the meagre creative harvest of the intervening period – the Third Piano Sonata and *Six Poems of Alexander Blok*, op. 20, which he had composed for Maxim Gube the previous winter. Ideas had occurred to him for a Sixth Symphony some six months beforehand, but

23 Ol'ga Lamm, 'Vospominaniya ob A. F. Gedike', in Konstantin Adzhemov (ed.), *A. F. Gedike: Sbornik statey i vospominaniy* (Moscow, 1960), 127; and Lamm, 'Vospominaniya o N. Ya. Myaskovskom', 236, 238, 240.

24 Lamm, 'Vospominaniya o N. Ya. Myaskovskom', 237–8.

25 Ibid., 233.

26 Myaskovsky to Asafiev, 23 October 1921, RGALI, 2658/1/639, l. 48.

then dried up. Nor had he made much progress with three settings of texts by the nineteenth-century poet Fyodor Tyutchev, intended for Yekaterina Koposova-Derzhanovskaya. In early November, he started to plan another symphony in B minor 'of a somewhat capricious character'[27], but the end of the month brought further disruption and fresh sorrows. On 22 November Yevgeniya sent a telegram informing him that Yelikonida had suffered a serious stroke.[28] He did not manage to reach Petrograd before she died three days later: the unusually severe winter compounded the already chaotic state of public transport and turned the lengthy train journey into a gruelling ordeal.[29] On arrival, his former family home made an impression of eerie desolation: the shrill nocturnal ululation of the wind in the empty stoves echoed forlornly through the icy-cold apartment as though intoning a lament for the deceased. The experience left an indelible impression, prompting musical imagery for the slowly gestating Sixth Symphony. Of necessity, the funeral had to be conducted without much ceremony: in the absence of any other form of transport, his aunt's body was borne on a sleigh through the frozen streets to the graveyard.[30]

Yelikonida's sudden passing affected Myaskovsky deeply. In spite of the shadow that her morbid religiosity and 'nervous illness' had cast over his upbringing, he had been fond of her: he retained a deep gratitude for her care of him and his siblings after their mother's early death, and for her encouragement of his musical interests. Her demise added to the misfortunes that war and revolution had brought in their wake. As often happened at times when he was under strain, Myaskovsky fell ill. On his return from Petrograd, he came down with a heavy cold which stubbornly lingered into the New Year. By February, his condition had deteriorated sufficiently to warrant admission to a sanatorium for a month. He developed a mysterious swelling of the lymphatic glands on his head and neck which turned out to be of tubercular origin. Thereafter, he succumbed to a serious bout of influenza, and it was only towards the beginning of June that his health eventually began to improve.[31] His correspondence suggests that he suffered as much mentally as physically. On returning to Moscow, he complained to Yevgeniya of feeling depressed and unable to rouse himself to activity[32]

27 'Vïpiski', RGALI, 2040/1/65, l. 4

28 Myaskovsky to Yakovlev, 23 November 1921, RGALI 2040/1/80, ll. 2–20b.

29 For the state of the country's railways at the period, see Nikolay Aksyonenko *et al.* (ed.), *Istoriya zheleznodorozhnogo transporta Rossii i Sovetskogo Soyuza*, vol. 2: 1917–45 (St Petersburg, 1997), 12–21.

30 'Vïpiski', RGALI, 2040/1/65, l. 4.

31 Myaskovsky to Asafiev, 5 June 1922, RGALI, 2658/1/640, l. 60b.

32 Myaskovsky to Yevgeniya Sakharova, 10 December 1921, RGALI, 2040/1/80, 16–160b.

– complaints reiterated a month later in a letter to Asafiev. 'Since coming back from Petersburg I've been in a state of complete mental and emotional disarray – and am in absolutely no state to do work of any kind, let alone compose.... Sometimes I think I'm finished not only as an artist... but also as a living human being'.[33]

In an attempt to distract himself, he undertook a further extensive revision of the First Symphony, bringing it into what proved to be its definitive version. By mid-April, there were encouraging signs that his protracted creative block was easing. Between 14 and 16 April, he managed to complete the Tyutchev settings *Na sklone dnya*, op. 21, as an Easter gift for Derzhanovskaya. The allusive title, which might be translated (echoing Byron) as 'At the Decline of Day', aptly indicates the subject matter of the poems, sombre meditations on the themes of transience, loss, and mortality. The saturnine sound-world of Myaskovsky's settings, with their viscous chromaticism and leadenly monotonous rhythmic movement, evokes a benumbed state of *accidie*: the dynamic level of the first two songs scarcely rises above a tensely suppressed *piano*. Both evoke the sense of horror at the prospect of extinction and the ineluctable loss of everything one holds dear. In the light of his recent experiences, Myaskovsky may have found the text of the second poem especially resonant:

Как ни тяжёл последний час –	However distressing the final hour –
Та непонятная для нас	And incomprehensible to us
Истома смертного страданья, –	That agonised weariness unto death –
Но для души еще страшней	For the soul it is even more dreadful
Следить, как вымирают в ней	To witness the expiration
Все лучшие воспоминанья...	Of all her happiest memories...

Only the last poem ends on a faint Schopenhauerian note of consolation, suggesting that, faced with the prospect of annihilation, we can nonetheless derive comfort from emphatic mutual understanding of our shared plight.

Death would also prove to be central preoccupation of the slowly gestating Sixth Symphony, on which he began at last to make significant progress. Writing to Asafiev on 5 June, he reported that he had finished over half the score in draft, commenting cryptically that it was becoming 'stranger and stranger' as it progressed. The remainder was sketched in the early autumn, after Myaskovsky had returned from a six-week sojourn in the Tchaikovsky House-Museum in Klin, a small village some sixty miles to the north-west of Moscow where the famous composer resided for the last eighteen months of his life. This holiday was made possible by Pavel Lamm,

---

33 Myaskovsky to Asafiev, 15 January 1922, RGALI, 2658/1/640, 20b.

who had been closely involved with the museum since 1920.[34] Together with Sergey Popov and Viktor Belyayev (Belyayev moved to Moscow in 1923), Lamm volunteered to assist with cataloguing the museum's extensive collection of musical manuscripts, letters, and other documentation, and was invited by the house-museum's director Nikolay Zhegin to spend the summer at Klin for this purpose, accompanied by his family.[35] In accordance with stipulations made in Modeste Tchaikovsky's will, four rooms in the house continued to be set aside for the use of visiting scholars and performers. Zhegin regularly had friends and colleagues to stay for extended periods, and Lamm managed to secure additional invitations for Goedicke and Myaskovsky.

In comparison with the grim conditions of urban daily life in the early 1920s, Klin was a veritable idyll. The museum's grounds opened out onto rolling pastures and woodland. Geese, goats, and cattle grazed in the laneway, and the house itself had changed little since Tchaikovsky's death in 1893. A sign reading 'Pyotr Il'ich is not at home' still hung by the entrance, as though the composer were only temporarily absent and would shortly return. The furnishings had not yet been cordoned off, nor had items been placed in protective display cabinets, but none of the museum's new proletarian visitors seemed tempted even to touch, let alone steal anything: they maintained a respectful silence as Zhegin showed them around, listening attentively to his explanations and musical illustrations at the piano.[36] For Myaskovsky, who revered Tchaikovsky, staying at Klin must have been a fascinating experience, especially as Zhegin allowed his guests unrestricted access to the composer's sketch books, letters, and diaries, which were stored in the museum's office. (The same room also contained a memento of a more macabre nature – the couch on which Tchaikovsky's beloved nephew Vladimir Davïdov had been sitting when he committed suicide at the age of thirty-five by shooting himself in the head.)[37] The countryside afforded abundant opportunities for extended solitary walks, one of Myaskovsky's favourite recreations.

Lamm's invitation to spend the summer vacation together testified to Myaskovsky's growing closeness to the Lamm family, who were still discovering hitherto unsuspected qualities in their friend: his excellent orienteering skills, which enabled him to guide skilfully them out of danger when a

34   Lamm, 'Pavel Aleksandrovich Lamm: Opït biografii', RNMM, 192/361, l. 172. On the history of the Tchaikovsky House-Museum, see Kseniya Davïdova *et al.*, *Gosudarstvennïy dom-muzey P. I. Chaykovskogo v Klinu: Putevoditel'*, 4th ed. (Moscow, 1980).

35   Lamm, *Stranitsï*, 15.

36   Lamm, 'Druz'ya', 93.

37   For an account of life at the house-museum in the 1920s, see Il'ya Bondarenko, 'V gostyakh u P. I. Chaykovskogo', *Moskovskiy zhurnal*, 10 (2005), 24–9.

large-scale forest fire broke out; or his surprising physical agility, demonstrated when he shinned up the front of the house onto a first-floor balcony
to retrieve Goedicke's walking stick. Another incident revealed the extent
to which he preferred to discommode himself rather than put anyone to
trouble – in this case, Sofia Lamm, who did the cooking. At mealtimes, he
dutifully downed the raw milk that she served every day – though as they
later discovered, he loathed milk and suffered considerable discomfort from
having to drink it. Good manners, he explained, dictated that guests should
adapt to the household routine and not discommode their hosts.[38]

Myaskovsky's response to Sofia may have been influenced by other factors, however. Earlier that year, a difficult situation had arisen on account
of Sofia's increasing attraction to her brother's friend. The fact that women
were drawn to Myaskovsky was scarcely surprising: he was a man of great
charm and retained his striking good looks well into middle age. Matters
came to a head when Sofia wrote to him making passionate asseverations
of love and admiration. Myaskovsky's lengthy reply was not only sensitive
and considerate of her feelings, but surprising in its candour:

> The longer I have cause to scrutinise myself and to think about myself, I
> am more and more firmly persuaded that I am a solitary person. . . . I am
> not the mating kind. This strange (if you wish) quality of mine shapes all
> of the relationships in my life: I form everyday acquaintanceships with a
> great many people, experience feelings of friendship towards a very few
> of them, but there has never been, and to all appearances there will never
> be a person whom I would find organically indispensable – I repeat, I
> do not understand such a necessity; to me it is a realm closed off behind
> seven seals. . . . I cannot imagine a time when my inner nature might so
> alter as to feel a need to avoid solitude. This is not something contrived
> or an affectation: for as long as I can remember, it has been characteristic
> of me – a mental, emotional, and physical trait that is organic in the full
> sense of the word.[39]

Sofia's reaction to this remarkable confession is not known. It required
considerable courage for him to reveal more or less unequivocally that he
had never entered into a relationship of an emotionally or sexually intimate nature and could not ever envisage doing do. So far as is known, he
remained celibate for the rest of his life. There is no reason to regard this
as aberrant: it might be closer to the truth to think of Myaskovsky as a
secular contemplative, similar in temperament to those who join confined
religious orders because they lead particularly intense inner lives, prefer a
solitary existence, and are innately disposed to celibacy.

---

38 Lamm, 'Vospominaniya o N. Ya. Myaskovskom', 246.
39 Myaskovsky to Sofia Lamm, 31 March 1922, RGALI, 2743/1/399, ll. 1–7.

This episode evidently did not damage his relationships with the Lamms or spoil their holiday in Klin. To judge from his letter of 9 August to Asafiev, the tranquil surroundings had not only assisted his convalescence but stimulated his creativity:

> I've just returned this week from Klin, where I spent almost a month and a half – walking, picking berries and mushrooms, eating, and doing absolutely nothing. Apparently, idling can also bear unexpected fruits, because on my return I quickly delivered myself of my Sixth wanton child, admittedly in a crude and slapdash state, but down to the last bar nonetheless. . . . The first movement is stormy and in the minor, with a despairing conclusion; the second – impetuous and fantastical; the third – an *Andante* in the major mode; and the fourth is a wild and gaudy riotous mix of the *Carmagnole*, *Ça ira*, *Dies irae*, and finally a Russian sacred chant . . . . There will be a (church) choir in the finale . . . . It ends in the major, very peacefully, E-flat minor going to E-flat major.[40]

It would take him another year to elaborate his draft into a full score, in part because he found it a particularly challenging task but also because he broke off work on it to orchestrate the Seventh Symphony, sketched during this unusually intense bout of creativity and completed about ten days after the Sixth on 21 August. His summer of 'idling' had certainly not been misspent.

The two symphonies are very different: the Sixth is a monumental fresco of over an hour's duration, while the highly compressed Seventh is one of the shortest of the twenty-seven, lasting only twenty minutes. The Sixth is unquestionably one of Myaskovsky's finest achievements and deserves to be much better known, although live performances are likely to remain infrequent on account of its technical difficulty and its requirement of a choir that sings for only a few minutes towards the end. (Although the choir is marked *ad libitum*, its entry in the finale is integral to the symphony's dramaturgy.) It is also a work of considerable historical importance, as the first major Soviet musical composition to engage, albeit indirectly, with the October Revolution.

Even if nothing were known about Myaskovsky's reactions to the Revolution, on the basis of this score alone one could safely infer that they were anything but enthusiastic. There is none of the dutiful pious celebration that would later become de rigueur with the advent of Socialist Realism: the emphasis throughout is on its tragic aspects. When discussing with his Soviet biographer Alexey Ikonnikov the ways in which the symphony reflected his experiences of the Revolution, the only specific event to which Myaskovsky alluded was hearing the Bolshevik leader Nikolay Krïlenko deliver in Petrograd an incendiary public speech concluding with

40 Myaskovsky to Asafiev, 9 August 1922, RGALI, 2658/1/640, ll. 120b–13.

the exhortation 'Death, death, death to the enemies of the Revolution!', which he described as making an 'indelible impression'.[41] Krïlenko was an enthusiastic advocate of terror to quell dissent and became notorious for his bloodthirsty public oratory. (He subsequently became a leading theorist of the infamous concept of 'socialist legality' and served as chief prose-cutor in the Moscow show trials of the late 1920s and early 1930s, exhib-iting a degree of fanatical zeal that was regarded as exceptional even by Stalinist norms.[42]) If Yakov Myaskovsky met his death as an 'enemy of the Revolution', it is difficult to imagine that his son's reaction to Krïlenko's speech can have been anything but horrified revulsion.

In his 'Autobiographical Notes', Myaskovsky alluded to two other impor-tant stimuli. The first was a chance meeting in 1919 with the Derzhanovskys' Narkompros colleague Boris Lopatinsky, a painter and illustrator who had resided in France for some years. On this occasion, Lopatinsky gave a rousing rendition of two well-known songs associated with the French Revolution, *Ça ira* and *La carmagnole*, as he had heard them sung in work-ing-class districts in Paris. Myaskovsky was sufficiently struck by these ver-sions as to write them down, because they differed from any with which he was familiar. However, it was only in 1922 when he reread the play *Les aubes* (The dawn) by the Belgian symbolist poet Émile Verhaeren that the idea occurred to him of making use of both songs in the Sixth's finale.[43] *Les aubes*, which was written in 1898, embodies its author's radical polit-ical views: it portrays a revolutionary uprising in the imaginary town of Oppidomagne in which the local workers and peasantry unite to overthrow

41 Ikonnikov, *Khudozhnik nashikh dney*, 109.

42 For Krïlenko, see Yuri Feofanov and Donald D. Barry, *Politics and Justice in Russia: Major Trials of the Post-Stalin Era* (New York, 1996), 228ff; and Donald D. Barry, 'Nikolai Vasil'evich Krylenko: A Re-Evaluation', *Review of Socialist Law* 15 (1989), 131–47.

43 Myaskovskiy, 'Avtobiograficheskiye zametki', 8–9; and Derzhanovskaya-Koposova, 'Pamyati druga', 220–1. Lopatinsky worked under Osip Mandelstam at Narkompros, and in 1921 arranged for the poet and his wife Nadezhda to accompany him to Tbilisi: see Nadezhda Mandel'shtam, *Vtoraya kniga* (Moscow, 1999), 38–9. Although he was a figure of considerable standing, Lopatinsky's name is conspicuously absent from standard Soviet reference works: he had the misfortune to be arrested during the so-called 'Kremlin affair' of 1935, a large-scale purge of Kremlin staff and people compromised by association with them who were supposedly conspiring to murder Stalin. This circumstance may well explain why Myaskovsky referred to him in 'Autobiographical Notes' merely as 'an artist' whose name he claimed to have forgotten: his identity was revealed by Koposova-Derzhanovskaya in the essay cited above. Lopatinsky was initially sentenced to three years' exile from Moscow (see 'O tak nazïvayemom "Kremlyovskom dele"', *Izvestiya TsK KPSS*, 7 [1989], 89), but records held by the Krasnoyarsk branch of Memorial indicate that he was subsequently re-arrested and sent to a labour camp, from which he was released in poor health in 1946. Nothing is known of his subsequent fate.

their capitalist oppressors. It concludes with an imposing crowd scene in which they lament the assassination of their charismatic leader Jacques Hérénien and give grandiloquent expression to their faith in a bright utopian future:

> [The nations] will understand one day what immortal deed was accomplished here in illustrious Oppidomagne, whence the loftiest human ideas have taken flight, one after another, throughout the ages. . . . The entire earth had to shake, all blood, all sap had to surge back towards the heart of things. Concord and harmony have triumphed over hatred. [*Cheers*] Human strife, in its bloody form, has been repudiated. A new beacon burns henceforth on the horizon of future tempests. Its steadiness shall dazzle eyes, obsess minds, conjure forth desires.[44]

Although *Les aubes*, like the rest of Verhaeren's dramatic output, never established itself in the regular theatrical repertory in the French-speaking world[45], it became widely known in Russia. In 1913 Valery Bryusov arranged for Verhaeren to visit Moscow and St Petersburg, where his public appearances were received with great enthusiasm.[46] Interest in Verhaeren grew even stronger in the post-Revolutionary period and he came to be viewed as a proletarian writer *avant la lettre*.[47] When the director Vsevolod Meyerhold sought a suitable play for the inaugural production of his new theatre company to mark the third anniversary of the October Revolution in 1920, his choice fell on *Les aubes*, which he and his assistant hastily adapted to heighten its relevance to contemporary events.[48] Myaskovsky had been familiar with the play for at least a decade and had even discussed with his friend Modeste Hofmann the possibility of an operatic adaptation.[49] As it transpired, this plan came to nothing, but the subject matter evidently acquired a new resonance for him while working on the Sixth. He

44 *Les aubes*, Act IV Scene 2, translation mine. Émile Verhaeren, *Hélène de Sparte – Les aubes*, 2nd ed. (Paris, 1920), 241–2.

45 See Jacques Marx, *Verhaeren: Biographie d'une œuvre* (Brussels, 1996), 359–63.

46 See ibid., 482–90; Paul Servaes, *Emile Verhaeren: Vlaams dichter voor Europa* (Berchem-Antwerpen, 2013), 813–29; Bart Salu (ed.), *Emile Verhaeren en Rusland* (Sint-Amands aan de Schelde, 1990).

47 Yakov Frid, *Èmil' Verkharn: Tvorcheskiy put' poèta* (Moscow, 1985), 6–7. Anatoliy Lunacharsky averred: 'If we cannot regard Verhaeren as a fully proletarian poet who can be admitted without reservation into our pantheon of great writers, then we must nonetheless regard him as standing on the threshold of that pantheon'. Anatoliy Lunacharskiy, 'Verkharn, Èmil'', in Vladimir Friche (ed.), *Literaturnaya èntsiklopediya*, vol. 2 (Moscow, 1929), 193.

48 Vsevolod Meyerhold, *Meyerhold on Theatre*, ed. and trans. with a commentary by Edward Braun (London, 1978), 163.

49 Modeste Hofmann to Myaskovsky, n.d. [1912?], RGALI, 2040/2/136, l. 133.

can only have been struck by the disparity between Verhaeren's utopian vision and the reality of revolution as a lived experience.

Beyond these hints, Myaskovsky offered no further insights into his creative intentions, but it seems clear that in his imagination the Revolution was inextricably linked with images of uncontrollable destruction. The work constitutes a symphonic requiem meditating on personal and collective experiences of upheaval and calamitous loss. An essay by Myaskovsky's friend Viktor Belyayev makes this link explicit: he describes the symphony as being 'dedicated to the memory of two people close to him' – presumably his father and his 'second mother' Yelikonida – 'whose passage into eternity against the backdrop of the Revolution affected him profoundly'. Furthermore, Belyayev draws a comparison between the Sixth and Alexander Blok's celebrated poem 'The Twelve' [*Dvenadtsat'*], a powerful evocation of the October Revolution pervaded by imagery of an implacable winter blizzard that violently disperses everything in its path and is blindly indifferent to human suffering.[50]

The Sixth Symphony displays notable originality in its rethinking of the dynamics of symphonic organisation. Myaskovsky's handling of tonal and thematic processes evokes unmistakable symbolic parallels with the struggle to transcend a traumatised psychological state caused by an experience so overwhelming as to shatter one's sense of ontological security. The phenomenology of trauma has long been an important focus of study for psychiatry and various branches of psychotherapy, and although the explanations of the phenomena involved vary considerably, there is a broad consensus on one point. As a self-protective measure, our minds employ powerful defence mechanisms to prevent us experiencing fully the unbearably distressing emotions aroused by the traumatising event, both at the time of its occurrence and subsequently. But these mechanisms are only partially successful and the relief from immediate distress comes at a price: the post-traumatic state is typically characterised by emotional numbing and other marked disturbances of psychological functioning. The psyche remains in a state of violently fractured disunity; and it is only when the unassimilated memories and emotions are fully experienced and brought into conscious awareness that healing of the trauma can commence. Integral to this process are the development of a capacity to mourn the traumatic occurrence and its effects, and the external acknowledgement and validation by an emphatic witness of the suffering that has been experienced.[51] The Sixth enacts this psychic transformation musically.

50 Viktor Belyayev, *Nikolay Yakovlevich Myaskovskiy* (Moscow, 1927), 13.

51 For a useful introduction see Bessel A. van der Kolk, Alexander C. McFarlane, and Lars Weisaeth (ed.), *Traumatic Stress: The Effects of Overwhelming Experience on Mind, Body, and Society* (New York, 2007).

The symphony's argument unfolds as a fiercely conflicted dialectic between two sharply contrasted categories of musical material – one turbulent, highly dissonant, and tonally indeterminate; the other lyrical and diatonic, making extensive use of the Dorian mode. Throughout the work, the second category of material attempts to stabilise various tonal regions but is repeatedly thwarted by the first. As the symphony proceeds, it comes evident that its ultimate goal is to establish E-flat minor, the symphony's ostensible home key, as a stable region in which the modal musical material can ultimately prevail, culminating in the introduction of a traditional Russian folk lament for the dead. A higher synthesis is effected at this point between the two contending categories of material by means of their covert motivic interrelatedness, which makes possible a serene close in E-flat major signalling a transcendence of the preceding conflicts. Myaskovsky's management of this long-range tonal trajectory from tonic minor to major develops the approach adumbrated in the Fourth Symphony. The first movement is nominally in E-flat minor, but a close examination of the score reveals that this tonal region is never securely established, and its stability remains precarious even at the concluding cadence. The Scherzo and slow movement are also tonally elusive, though the latter eventually affirms the region of B major. The finale opens in E-flat major, but this attempted resolution of the preceding tensions proves premature: E-flat minor must be unambiguously attained first by dint of protracted conflict. The symphony's central tonal struggle, therefore, is not merely for tonic major to displace tonic minor: it is the struggle to establish a central tonality *at all*, and to wrest tonal order from ceaseless chromatic flux.

These processes are highly complex in detail, and only the briefest summary can be given here. The arresting introduction to the first movement presents a stentorian idea shown in example 6.1 (henceforth called *x*) outlining descending arpeggiations of the triads of E-flat minor and C-flat major triads harmonised with grating dissonances. This idea, which Myaskovsky apparently associated with Krïlenko's exhortation[52], plays a prominent role throughout the work, often functioning as an agent of harmonic disruption at important junctures; and as previously mentioned, the tonality of C-flat major, enharmonically respelled as B major, subsequently assumes a role of central significance. For the moment, however, there is little sense of any prevailing key: the impetuous first subject, with its vaulting angular leaps (ex. 6.2), ventures restlessly from region to region, merging seamlessly into an agitated transition theme to the second subject group. Although the latter has an initial key signature of F-sharp major, this tonality is largely notional and only established fleetingly in the codetta. Much of the second subject area develops a subsidiary lyrical idea that modulates constantly.

52 Ikonnikov, *Khudozhnik nashikh dney*, 109.

EXAMPLE 6.1. Symphony no. 6, first movement: motto theme *x*.

EXAMPLE 6.2. Symphony no. 6, first movement: bars 6–9.

EXAMPLE 6.3. Symphony no. 6, first movement: bars 104–12.

Harmonic repose is briefly afforded by the first idea of the second subject group, a solemn theme opening in a Dorian G-sharp minor (ex. 6.3) which subtly adumbrates the modality of the Russian chant in the finale. But this moment of repose is brief, and when this idea is restated towards the close of the exposition, its harmonic stability is lost: the dissonant sonorities of *x* encroach on it.

The subsequent treatment of this Dorian material is striking. Throughout the development, it attempts to establish stable tonal regions, but its unfolding is cut short on each occasion by *x*, which assumes increasingly menacing and extended forms. The conflict eventuates in a violent climax which is so dissonant as to be virtually atonal. The recapitulation is even more tonally unstable than the exposition. Although it initially seems as though Myaskovsky intends to restate the second subject group material a fifth lower (to judge from the key signature of five sharps at this point), B major is never attained, unlike F-sharp major in the exposition. Instead, the codetta remains tonally ambiguous. One further notable detail: in the coda, Myaskovsky unexpectedly interpolates a short passage of ethereal beauty that clearly suggests the tonality of E flat major, even though the tonic triad itself is withheld. The ultimate tonal goal of the work is revealed fleetingly as a possibility, but the music soon reverts to a sombre E-flat minor, transforming the Dorian second subject idea into a funeral march. The stability of this key is undermined up to the last by a highly ambiguous cadence, and the movement ends as though in suspension, with the unaccompanied pitch of the dominant B flat sounded by the first and second horns and fading into silence. The failure of the first movement to effect any reconciliation of the opposing tensions means that these are then projected forward into the remaining movements.

The furious Scherzo, *Presto tenebroso*, is a magnificent tour de force of sustained momentum. Its mood of unrelenting malevolent fury undoubtedly owes something to Tchaikovsky's depiction in *Francesca da Rimini* of the *contrari venti* that torment the lovers in hell, as does its vertiginous tonal lability. It is nominally in F minor, but as in the first movement, incessant abrupt shirts of tonal centre obscure the centrality of this key: the tonic triad is scarcely sounded. The only passage of tonal stability occurs in the Trio, in which we once again hear material in the Dorian mode – the opening of the plainchant setting of the *Dies irae* sequence from the Latin Requiem mass (ex. 6.4). Not only does this borrowed material feature motivic cells common to the first movement's Dorian second subject idea, but it establishes a semantic association of that modal material with the idea of mourning. It is noteworthy, however, that the diaphanous scoring of this episode, pervaded by the glacial tintinnabulation of the celesta, lends it a disembodied quality: it is far from being a passionate outpouring of grief, as though mourning is as yet but an abstract idea. The *Dies irae* is swept aside by the reappearance of the Scherzo material which rises to a fresh pitch of delirium; and after a final frenzied onslaught, the movement ceases abruptly, its tensions unresolved.

The slow movement continues to be dominated by conflict between these opposing categories of musical material. Its sombre opening does not establish a tonal centre – but a stable tonal region gradually consolidates as the movement unfolds: B major, the enharmonic equivalent of the C-flat major adumbrated in the symphony's opening idea x, which had been

EXAMPLE 6.4. Symphony no. 6, second movement: bars 160–6.

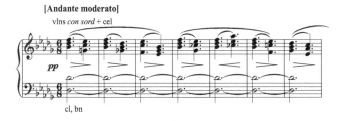

EXAMPLE 6.5. Symphony no. 6, third movement: bars 52–5.

withheld in the recapitulation of first movement. In this key, Myaskovsky introduces a serene, long-breathed melody (ex. 6.5) which is heard three times, interspersed with episodes of a darkly turbulent character. It is intensely moving in its effect, not least because this is the first time that any tonal region has been established securely. The melody is soon presented together with the *Dies irae*, heard over a mediant pedal on B in G-sharp minor, again, strengthening the semantic association between the secure attainment of a tonal region and the possibility of mourning. One other telling detail: the continuation of this lyrical idea closes with a succession of rising scalic ascents that prominently emphasise the pitch D-sharp. E-flat, as its enharmonic equivalent of D-sharp, is at last affirmed securely, but for the time being as the third scale degree of another tonal region. Although the slow movement ends in B major, the symphony's tensions are by no means resolved – which means that the finale must constitute the work's dramatic centre of gravity.

After the deeply poetic conclusion of the preceding movement, the finale opens with brash statements of the two French Revolutionary songs, starting with a *fortissimo* presentation of *La carmagnole* blared out on six horns in unison against an orchestral texture evocative of a military band (ex. 6.6). The effect is jarring and strikes an incongruous note of banality. This is by no means a gross miscalculation on Myaskovsky's part, however, as might first appear. The obvious question arises why Myaskovsky chose to use songs associated with the French rather than the Russian Revolution:

indeed, he was much criticised by Soviet commentators for doing so.[53] One possible answer may be that the French Revolution was perceived as the archetype of all modern revolutions and that Myaskovsky wished to emphasise the universality of the suffering caused by such events. But a more likely explanation suggests itself: the associations prompted by the songs' texts and their musical character. Both songs embody a simplistic view of revolutionary violence, especially the demotic variants that entered French folklore. The *sans culottes* version of *Ça ira*, which Lopatinsky may well have heard sung in Paris, details with relish how the aristocracy will be strung up from the city's lampposts. Similarly, *La carmagnole* gloatingly describes the humiliations visited on Marie Antoinette and her supporters, and is reputed to have regularly accompanied dancing around the guillotine.[54] Whichever versions of these songs Myaskovsky heard, he can have been in no doubt of their sinister import. As Constant Pierre, a leading French authority on this repertory, observed, both songs evoke associations with 'wild public disorder and murder'.[55] Neither acknowledges the suffering that the Revolution has caused and both are set to trite, mindlessly jolly tunes which are startlingly at variance with their sanguinary sentiments: they suggest a state of consciousness that is profoundly dissociated from the consequences of violence. And as their subsequent treatment reveals, it is precisely such a one-sided view of revolutionary violence that the Sixth Symphony emphatically repudiates.

These melodies twice seek to impose E-flat major by fiat and force an artificial, premature transcendence of the preceding conflicts. Neither attempt is successful: on both occasions the contours of the closing phrases of *La carmagnole* are soon liquidated into chain of thirds recalling the baleful idea x, and the tonal stability of E-flat major undermined by its disruptive harmonies (exxs. 6.7a and 6.7b). The symbolic import of these passages is unmistakable. On the first occasion, the *Dies irae* reappears, and its associations with mourning are reinforced by a new theme – a traditional chant 'The parting of the soul from the body' (ex. 6.8) presented by the clarinet in a modal B-flat minor. (Myaskovsky came across this melody in a volume of folksongs collected by the eminent ethnographer

---

53   A representative example: 'It is noteworthy that the finale dealing with the revolutionary theme contains no Russian melody, with the exception of the chant, and that the Russian people fighting for the revolution are symbolized conventionally, in accordance with an abstract "bookish" tradition, by melodies of songs associated with the French Revolution'. Lyudmila Polyakova, *Soviet Music* (Moscow, n.d. [?*circa* 1960]), 42–3.

54   Both songs exist in numerous variants. See Constant Pierre, *Hymnes et chansons de la Révolution* (Paris, 1904), 477–93 and 554–60; and Laura Mason, *Singing the French Revolution: Popular Culture and Politics, 1787–1799* (Ithaca and London, 1996), 42–6.

55   Pierre, *Hymnes et chansons*, 554, 557.

EXAMPLE 6.6. Symphony no. 6, finale: opening.

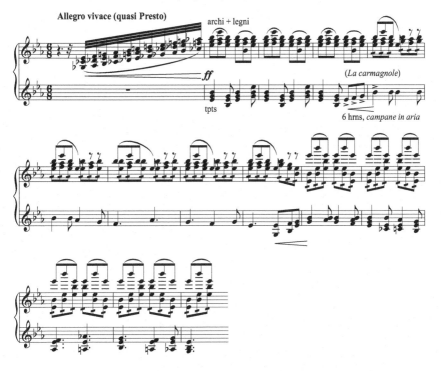

Mitrofan Pyatnitsky.[56]) The French revolutionary songs seek to reassert themselves, but they are rejected with even greater vehemence and never return. Instead, Myaskovsky reintroduces some of the most strenuously dissonant passages from the first movement, but this time resolves them into E-flat minor at the apex of an overwhelmingly powerful climax. In a superb dramatic stroke, the choir enters with piercingly dissonant cries of anguish reminiscent of the Yurodivy's lament for the fate of Russia in Musorgsky's *Boris Godunov* – a reference unlikely to have escaped the notice of a Russian audience. (The stepwise descent of these slurred two-note figures also relates them to the opening of the *Dies irae*). Now, at last, mourning can become a lived, embodied experience rather than an abstract possibility: the choir proceeds to intone 'The parting of the soul from the body' in a modal E-flat minor – a possibility prepared by the modal component of the first movement's second subject group and the subsequent recurrences of modal musical material. In spite of the severe restraint with which the chant is handled, it furnishes a deeply moving culmination to the work as a whole and is all the more powerful for sounding as the inevitable

56 Mitrofan Pyatnitskiy *et al.*, *Kontsertï M. Ye. Pyatnitskogo s krest'yanami* (Moscow, 1914).

outcome of a carefully planned symphonic argument. In the context, the chant text is most apt, with its emphasis on the necessity of the act of 'seeing' and bearing witness to realities that are seldom acknowledged in official narratives of revolutions:

Что мы видели?	What have we seen?
Диву дивыную,	Marvel of marvels
Диву дивную,	Marvel of marvels,
Телу мёртвую.	A dead body.
Как душа-та с телом	How that soul
Расставалася,	Parted from the body,
Да прощалася.	Yea, bade it farewell.
Как тебе-та, душа,	You, soul, to go
На суд Божий идить	To God's judgement;
А тебе-та, тело,	And you, body,
Во сыру мать землю.[57]	To damp mother earth.

The sense that the suffering caused by the Revolution can at last be mourned is underlined not only by the long-delayed stabilisation of the symphony's ostensible home key of E-flat minor but also by the employment of a Russian chant setting the Russian language (in contrast to the Latin *Dies irae*) and the unexpected introduction of voices, signalling both a crucial moment of *Anerkennung* and an assertion of our common humanity in the face of inhumanity.[58] The emotional realisation 'strikes home' in every sense. Only when this is accomplished can the tonality move to E-flat major and the serene lyrical theme of the slow movement return in the radiant coda, now that the conflicts have at last been transcended.

The Sixth represents an exceptional achievement and reveals Myaskovsky's full stature as a powerful and original musical thinker. In some respects, such as its introduction of voices into the symphony and its allusion to contemporary events, it remained an isolated experiment in his output. In other respects, however, it represented a summation of tendencies that had long been in evidence, especially in its exploration of an embattled subjectivity and of a profoundly tragic sense of life. More

---

57   Apart from making emendations to comply with the 1917 spelling reforms, Myaskovsky otherwise retained the nonstandard lexical, orthographical, and grammatical features of the chant text as reproduced in Pyatnitskiy *et al.*, *Kontsertï M. Ye. Pyatnitskogo s krest'yanami*.

58   This point was not lost on contemporary listeners: in a review of the first performance, Anatoly Aleksandrov noted that the impression produced by the chant was enormously heightened by its juxtaposition with the French Revolutionary songs: 'O 6-y simfonii N. Ya. Myaskovskogo', *Muzïkal'naya kul'tura*, 1 (1924), 62–3.

EXAMPLE 6.7a. Motivic relationship between *La carmagnole* and *x*.

EXAMPLE 6.7b. Symphony no. 6, finale: bars 139–51
(liquidation of *La carmagnole* into *x*).

EXAMPLE 6.8. Old Believer chant 'The parting of the soul from the body'.

than perhaps any other of his works, it eloquently evokes the struggle to affirm existence despite anguished awareness of the 'fragile ordinance of the world' (*die gebrechliche Einrichtung der Welt*), in Heinrich von Kleist's memorable phrase. In an insightful performance, such as the magnificent reading recorded by the Moscow State Philharmonic Choir and Orchestra under Kirill Kondrashin in 1978, it makes for compelling listening.

The Seventh Symphony, which was dedicated to Pavel Lamm, is so unlike its predecessor as to suggest that Myaskovsky deliberately set out to essay a very different kind of work. Like the Third, the Seventh is cast in two movements, but is much more compact. The opening sonata-form movement is prefaced by a slow introduction: its curious tempo marking *Allegro minaccioso, poco stravagante* ('quick, menacing, a tad whimsical') evokes an atmosphere akin to some of Myaskovsky's early piano miniatures – an unsettling blend of the sinister and quirkily playful. Its conclusion leads seamlessly into the opening of the second movement, which commences by restating and elaborating the introduction to the first. The remainder of the movement comprises two sections of unequal length. The first of these, the longer of the two, has a ternary structure with slow outer components enclosing a quick scherzo-like central episode. The second section reprises material from the *Allegro minaccioso*, bringing the symphony to a close in a fast tempo. Myaskovsky evidently envisioned the second movement as a conflation of slow movement, scherzo, and finale. In principle, such a plan could constitute an elegant solution to the difficulties inherent in devising a viable two-movement symphonic design, especially when it came to achieving a satisfactory distribution of fast and slow music and ensuring that the second movement would furnish a persuasive conclusion to the work as a whole.

Its successful accomplishment, however, would depend on having a compelling rationale to reintroduce material from the first movement – ideally, by creating the impression that its treatment of the thematic ideas was somehow insufficient and that further working-out was required to effect a definitive resolution of their tensions. Myaskovsky's realisation of his concept is far from ideal. Although the first movement works well in itself, it does not produce a feeling of incompleteness, which makes the recurrence of its material in the second movement seem psychologically unmotivated rather than a dramatically necessary recrudescence of postponed conflict. Moreover, this section is too brief and fragmentary, and does not build to a sufficiently intense or sustained climax furnishing an adequate culmination to the work as a whole. Matters are not helped by the inconsistent quality of the thematic invention: the introductory idea (which Myaskovsky apparently described to Ikonnikov as evoking 'the voice of nature'[59]) is undistinguished, while the *Lento* section of the second movement is marred by its unrelievedly foursquare phrase structure. These shortcomings are a pity, because the symphony contains some vivid stretches of music, especially in the waltz-like first movement, which is unlike anything else that he wrote in its alternations of sensuous languor and delirious transport.

---

59   Ikonnikov, *Khudozhnik nashikh dney*, 141. The introduction features a motif that Myaskovsky heard played on a shepherd's horn in 1912 near Batovo, a village located to the south of St Petersburg: 'Vipiski', 21 August 1922, RGALI, 2040/1/65, l. 40b.

The Seventh also testifies to his desire to explore more fully the capabilities of the modern virtuoso symphony orchestra. He was keenly aware of his need to overcome certain shortcomings in his handling of the medium, such as his overuse of low-lying legato basses and a tendency to muddiness[60], and to a considerable extent he succeeded. A new delicacy is in evidence, and a few passages suggest that he had been studying the orchestral works of Ravel. (The spectacular cadential flourish that concludes the *Feria* of Ravel's *Rhapsodie espagnole* is recalled at figure 127, for example.) Of all the aspects of the compositional process, however, orchestration continued to cause him the greatest uncertainty, as of old. He confessed to Asafiev that scoring the Sixth had cost him 'six months of agonising labour',[61] and he subsequently made extensive revisions to his original version. He would do the same with the Seventh after its premiere in 1925, having found it to be 'textually monotonous', 'full of completely unforgiveable naiveties and impracticalities ... redundant figurations, wild howls and snarls from the brass'.[62] It must be borne in mind, however, that Myaskovsky had had few opportunities to date to hear his orchestral compositions and was still comparatively inexperienced. Moreover, the mediocre performances that his work generally received did little to boost his confidence.[63] In 1927 he was fortunate to hear a superb account of the Seventh by the visiting German conductor Hermann Scherchen, which revealed how inadequate the previous ones had been. As he told Asafiev: 'People scarcely recognised my Seventh: it sounded so natural, flexible, expressive – and fast. I could previously only have dreamt of such tempi and would never have imagined them to be possible. It turned out that the first movement can be played 'wildly' (for the first time it didn't irritate me!) and the coda impetuously. And it all made sense'.[64]

In the autumn of 1922, when he completed both symphonies in draft, the prospect of securing performances of either was remote. The only regularly functioning orchestra in Moscow was that of the Bolshoi Theatre, and the programmes of its occasional symphony concerts did not venture beyond standard classics. For the time being, Myaskovsky had to content himself

---

60 Writing to Prokofiev on 12 August 1923, he expressed particular satisfaction with the Seventh's 'eschewal ... of solidly filled-in bass lines and backgrounds in general – the music sometimes seems to hang very pleasantly in mid-air'. Kozlova and Yatsenko, *Perepiska*, 167.

61 Myaskovsky to Asafiev, 2 July 1923, RGALI, 2658/2/50, l. 40b.

62 Myaskovsky to Prokofiev, 16 March 1925, in Kozlova and Yatsenko, *Perepiska*, 212.

63 The paucity of competent Soviet conductors was openly acknowledged at the period: see, for example, Arnol'd Tsukker, *Pyat' let Persimfansa* (Moscow, 1927), 30.

64 Myaskovsky to Asafiev, 24 October 1927, RGALI, 2658/2/50, l. 48.

with 'christenings' (as Lamm humorously described them) of both symphonies in piano arrangements. It is indicative of the state of musical life at the
period that musical evenings organised by friends had provided virtually
the only opportunities to hear his own work over the previous two years.

In these dispiriting circumstances, a brave initiative by Myaskovsky's
colleague Lev Tseytlin, professor of violin at the Moscow Conservatoire,
was especially welcome. One of Auer's most talented pupils, Tseytlin was a
superb musician of wide experience: as a young man, he had played under
Colonne in Paris and after his return to Russia led Koussevitzky's orchestra
from 1908, transferring to the orchestra of the Bolshoi Theatre from 1917.
After the Revolution, he threw himself actively into the reconstruction of
the country's musical life and set about realising his aspiration to found a
conductorless orchestra which would give performances reflecting 'the collective interpretation of all the players, and not merely of one person'.[65] The
new ensemble, which styled itself 'Persimfans' (an acronym formed from its
official title 'Pervïy simfonicheskiy ansambl' Mossoveta', First Symphonic
Ensemble of the Moscow Soviet of People's Deputies), made its debut on
13 February 1922, with players largely drawn from the Bolshoi orchestra.
Although Tseytlin's experiment initially met with scepticism, the venture
proved a success: the orchestra remained in existence for over ten years and
attracted a loyal public following. Its wide repertoire included a considerable quantity of music by living Russian composers – notably Prokofiev
and Stravinsky.[66] Myaskovsky's Fifth Symphony was the first contemporary
score to be included in Persimfans's programmes and was performed on 25
September 1922. Although the standard of the ensemble's playing was variable, at its best it could be very good, as Myaskovsky discovered when he
attended a rehearsal. He reported to Asafiev: 'In truth, I don't know whether
conductors are actually necessary. Aside from some wholly understandable
hesitations over tempo changes . . . and some difficult entries (after lengthy
pauses and long-held chords), which all got sorted out quickly and went
smoothly thereafter, the orchestra played so uninhibitedly, flexibly, and
with such conviction, that I thought the symphony would come off really
well'.[67] In the event, the performance did indeed go well and Myaskovsky
was given a rousing ovation.[68]

65   Tsukker, *Pyat' let Persimfansa*, 155. The Artistic Council of MUZO's Concerts
     Subdivision considered Tseytlin's proposal to found a conductorless orchestra
     at a meeting on 10 May 1920: GARF, 2306/25/108, l. 7.

66   See Stanislav Ponyatovskiy, *Persimfans – Orkestr bez dirizhyora* (Moscow,
     2003).

67   Myaskovsky to Asafiev, 30 August 1922, RGALI, 2658/1/640, ll. 15–16.

68   Pavel Lamm, diary entry for 25 September 1922, quoted in Lamm, *Stranitsï*,
     151–2.

After his productive summer of 1922, Myaskovsky resumed teaching in the conservatoire and his work for Gosmuzizdat, settling into a professional routine that would scarcely alter for the rest of his life. His workload at the conservatoire was comparatively light: he had started with only three students in his class the previous year[69] (a number that would soon augment considerably), though he was also required to fulfil other duties such as presiding at examinations and auditions. The surviving documentation in his personal archive suggests that discharged his duties as 'consultant' conscientiously: even Prokofiev would be impressed in due course by his 'phenomenal, lynx-like eye' for errors and his meticulous attention to detail.[70] Nonetheless, his role was not without its pressures, as the state publishing house was operating in challenging times.

Pavel Lamm approached his work for Gosmuzizdat in an idealistic spirit, seeing it primarily as a means of supporting a high musical culture. One of his principal concerns was to secure more favourable rates of payment for composers, many of whom were in parlous material circumstances, but soaring inflation set severe limits on what he could hope to accomplish, at least in the shorter term.[71] Plans were mooted to reorganise the state publishing house and to run Gosmuzizdat as an independent self-financing entity on a profit-and-loss basis. This opened up enticing prospects of greater autonomy and the possibility of promoting music by Soviet composers abroad by entering into reciprocal arrangements with Western publishers, but it also brought the press's economic viability under close scrutiny. Lamm's job became increasingly stressful. As the monetary crisis escalated, he faced a constant struggle to retain staff and to cover regular expenditure.[72] Although the press had managed to publish 323 new compositions since 1919, this total mostly comprised songs and piano pieces, as it was impracticable to bring out larger works in any quantity.[73] This situation would persist for some years due to the lack of skilled engravers and ongoing chronic paper shortages.[74] (Catoire's son recalled his father's Solovyov

69 'Vïpiski', 17 May 1921, RGALI, 2040/1/65, l. 4.

70 Prokofiev to Myaskovsky, 9 November 1931, in Kozlova and Yatsenko, *Perepiska*, 367.

71 Lamm, 'Pervïye godï rabotï', 199–201.

72 Lamm, 'Pavel Aleksandrovich Lamm: opït biografii', RNMM, 192/361, ll. 199, 209, 216–23.

73 Lamm, 'Pervïye godï rabotï', 201.

74 These problems were encountered in all areas of Soviet publishing: see Yevgeniy Nemirovskiy *et al.*, *Istoriya knigi v SSSR: 1917–1921*, vol. 1 (Moscow, 1983), 64ff.

settings being printed in 1922 on low-grade wrapping paper of the kind used by fishmongers.[75])

Composers found themselves competing for scarce resources, a circumstance that readily fomented suspicions and resentments. In the winter of 1922–3, a contretemps occurred with Alexander Kreyn which had unfortunate consequences.[76] In November 1922, Kreyn signed a contract allowing Gosmuzizdat to publish the bulk of his output. By his own admission, he had not troubled to read it properly, and on examining it subsequently became persuaded that Lamm had deliberately set out to defraud him. The suspicion was unjustified: the contract was perfectly in order. Its terms were not particularly generous, but they were nonetheless standard.

The situation quickly deteriorated. Kreyn stopped turning up for work at Gosmuzizdat and Lamm terminated his contract. Prompted by contacts in Rabis, the Russian Trade Union of Arts Workers, Kreyn reported the dispute to *Pravda*, and on 17 January an article appeared accusing Lamm of wholesale fraud in his dealings with composers, making specific allusion to Kreyn's contract.[77] An investigation the following month found unequivocally in Lamm's favour.[78] With this, the matter should have been at an end, but events took an unexpected turn. On 26 March, Lamm was arrested and taken into custody by secret police agents of the OGPU[79] (a precursor of the KGB). No explanation was given, but it emerged that the OGPU had acted on the basis of a denunciation submitted by Kreyn accusing Lamm of anti-Semitism, counterrevolutionary activity, and theft of scores and manuscripts belonging to the state. Lamm was not alone in suffering harassment: writing to Pyotr Suvchinsky in Paris, Belyayev informed him that other musicians close to Lamm had their apartments searched.[80] Shortly afterwards, Belyayev was himself arrested and imprisoned.

For some weeks, the outcome remained uncertain. Lamm was humanely treated but felt the injustice of what had befallen him very keenly. He was anxious about how his dependents would fare in his absence: they not only

---

75 Anna Zassimova, *Georges Catoire: Seine Musik, sein Leben, seine Ausstrahlung* (Berlin, 2011), 57.

76 The account of events given here draws on Lamm, 'Pavel Aleksandrovich Lamm: Opït biografii', RNMM, 192/361, and documents preserved in Alexander Kreyn's personal archive in RGALI, 2435/2/247.

77 'Muzizdatel'stvo i kompozitorï', *Pravda*, 17 January 1923.

78 'Protokol zasedaniya komissii kollektiva kompozitorov ot 11 fevralya 1923', RGALI, 2435/2/247, l. 13.

79 'Ob"yedinyonnoye gosudarstvennoye politicheskoye upravleniye pri SNK SSSR' (Joint State Political Directorate).

80 Belyayev to Suvchinsky, 21 May 1923, in Yuliya Deklerk, '"Dolgaya doroga v rodnïye kraya". Iz perepiski S. S. Prokof'yeva s rossiyskimi druz'yami', in Marina Rakhmanova (ed.), *Sergey Prokof'yev. K 110-letiyu so dnya rozhdeniya. Pis'ma, vospominaniya, stat'i*, 2nd ed. (Moscow, 2006), 102–3.

faced being left penniless, as his salary ceased to be paid on his arrest, but were also threatened with eviction from their apartment. Myaskovsky and Lamm's other colleagues at Gosmuzizdat concealed the true state of affairs from Sofia and paid her Pavel's 'wages' out of their own pockets. Fortunately, Lamm was not without influential advocates. Kreyn's imputation of anti-Semitic motives aroused the indignation of prominent Jewish members of the Moscow musical community who rallied to Lamm's defence – amongst them the pianist Alexander Goldenweiser, who seems to have been instrumental in securing his release at the end of May.[81] Myaskovsky reported to his sister Yevgeniya:

> At least the business with Lamm and Belyayev has become less complicated since it was handed over to the Public Prosecutor: Lamm was arraigned on seven absolutely absurd charges and all of them were dropped except one – dereliction of duty; and even that might be dropped for lack of evidence. In any case, he has been released from prison. Belyayev was let out much earlier – they kept him for a week and a half, and all to absolutely no purpose.[82]

In the end, no charges were pressed. An official investigation into the press's affairs failed to discover any signs of counterrevolutionary activity and Lamm was able to demonstrate his legitimate ownership of the contents of his library. His name was cleared and he was notified that he would not be obliged to disclose information about his imprisonment – a matter of great practical importance, as Soviet citizens were required to fill out increasingly intrusive questionnaires when seeking employment. He was not, however, reinstated in post, but was replaced by Alexander Yurovsky, a former student of Goldenweiser whose brother was an influential member of the Communist Party. Since Lamm had not been found guilty of any wrongdoing, this prompted suspicions that Kreyn's denunciation had served as a convenient pretext to oust him and to appoint someone more politically orthodox in his stead. Fortunately, Goldenweiser came to Lamm's rescue and offered him additional teaching duties at the conservatoire. In a final twist to this strange saga, Kreyn was overcome with remorse for his actions and contacted Lamm through intermediaries to ask if he could meet him to offer a formal apology. Lamm responded with remarkable generosity of spirit to this overture, having concluded that Kreyn was

81 Goldenweiser wrote on of 4 April 1923 to Nikolay Zhegin: 'I have been greatly affected by the arrest of Pavel Lamm . . .. Everything that has happened is as absurd as if they arrested Sergey Popov and myself for saving Taneyev's library, manuscripts, and correspondence. Life is becoming completely unbearable!' Aleksandr Skryabin *et al.* (ed.), *Nastavnik: Aleksandr Gol'denveyzer glazami sovremennikov* (Moscow and St Petersburg, 2014), 202–3.

82 Myaskovsky to Yevgeniya Sakharova, n.d. [May 1921?], RGALI, 2040/1/80, ll. 220b–3.

psychologically unstable. A meeting duly took place, and the proffered apology was accepted – but, unsurprisingly, their relationship remained distant.

Lamm and his associates were understandably shaken by the episode, which can have left them in little doubt about the realities of the circumstances in which they were operating. Goedicke was so distressed by Lamm's arrest and the police searches of their lodgings that he suffered a nervous breakdown.[83] Myaskovsky confided in Asafiev that the episode had left him feeling so 'mentally polluted' as to render creative work impossible: the mere thought of returning to the 'cloaca' of the state publishing house filled him with revulsion.[84] It also caused him to become the subject of unsavoury rumours – as is illustrated by the correspondence of the Ukrainian composer Pavel Kovalyov[85], who encountered Kreyn and members of the Myaskovsky-Lamm circle around the time of the conflict and regaled his friend the musicologist Boris Tyuneyev with luridly embellished accounts of events. He depicts Myaskovsky as the 'cold, evil, and vindictive' *éminence grise* at the centre of an influential clique of musicians who abused their privileged positions to further their own interests and ruthlessly stymied the careers of others. All of this supposedly went on with the active connivance of Pavel Lamm as director of Gozmuzizdat, at whose expense Myaskovsky and his cronies wined and dined. Kovalyov believed that the press had declined to publish his own compositions because the Myaskovsky-Lamm circle considered them insufficiently adventurous in style; he also held that Kreyn had been ill-treated because Myaskovsky was jealous of him.[86]

That Kovalyov's lurid characterisation was largely compounded of garbled gossip and his own unbridled imaginings goes without saying; but such views of Myaskovsky as a maleficent bogy proved stubbornly durable throughout his career and would be articulated in almost identical form in secret denunciations in 1948. His taciturnity and reserve presented a blank that invited projections. The insinuation that Myaskovsky regarded other composers as rivals and sought to hinder their careers is demonstrably untrue, as his supportive treatment of colleagues would repeatedly show. Equally absurd was the notion that he received preferential treatment from Gosmuzizdat. The press had so far only published a handful of

83 Lamm, 'Pavel Aleksandrovich Lamm: opït biografii', RNMM, 192/361, l. 256.

84 Myaskovsky to Asafiev, 2 July 1923, RGALI, 2658/2/50, l. 30b.

85 Kovalyov (1889 [1890]–1951) emigrated in 1926 and from 1929 lived in Paris. See Lev Mnukhin *et al.* (ed.), *Rossiyskoye zarubezh'ye vo Frantsii 1919–2000: Biograficheskiy slovar'*, vol. 1 (Moscow, 2008), 702.

86 Svetlana Stepanova, 'Novïy Rastin'yak, ili Kak Kovalyov zavoyovïval Moskvu', *Muzïkal'naya akademiya*, 3–4 (1998), 306–15.

his compositions (the Third Piano Sonata, *Alastor*, some songs); all of his symphonies remained in manuscript.

From Kovalyov's letters, it is clear that Myaskovsky had come to be perceived as the leading representative of a younger generation of composers of a modernist stylistic orientation. The accuracy of this view was questionable because his responses to modernist compositional trends were growing more ambivalent and sceptical. However, the fact remains that he was regarded as holding an aesthetic outlook against which other composers increasingly felt obliged to define themselves at a time when sharply divergent visions of the future of Soviet musical culture were beginning to take shape. Kovalyov spoke of allying himself with an opposing faction headed by Kreyn and noted the formation of another around the composer David Chernomordikov, an Old Bolshevik who founded the Association of Proletarian Musicians in March 1923, the month of Lamm's arrest. This organisation would play a fateful role in the history of Soviet music until its liquidation in 1932 and, as the decade progressed, it launched increasingly strident attacks on musicians who did not subscribe to its platform. Chernomordikov, who had mysteriously turned up with the OGPU agents at Lamm's apartment, assumed a key position at Gosmuzizdat shortly afterwards. It consequently seems likely that Lamm's deposition was contrived to bring the press under firmer ideological control. With hindsight, the episode can be understood as inaugurating a power struggle to shape national cultural policy on music that would intensify as the decade progressed.

Myaskovsky continued to work for the publishing house and was appointed to its reconstituted board in September 1923.[87] However, with Lamm's departure, the circumstances confronting composers of serious music looked set to deteriorate further. Under its new management, the press published little other than agitprop and educational works. Plans to enter into a partnership with a foreign publisher were shelved, as was the proposal to establish Gosmuzizdat on an independent footing from the state publishing house.[88] In addition to being disadvantaged by the dearth of performance and publication opportunities, composers were more or less completely cut off from the outside world.

Two developments in the winter of 1922–3 helped to alleviate Myaskovsky's sense of isolation. The first was the establishment of the joint-stock company International Books (Mezhdunarodnaya kniga) which imported foreign books and exported Soviet publications. Vladimir Derzhanovsky was put in charge of its music section, which had its premises on Kuznetsky Bridge, an

---

87 'Trudovoy spisok', RGALI, 2040/1/167, ll. 280b–9.

88 Lamm, 'Pavel Aleksandrovich Lamm: Opït biografii', RNMM, 192/361, 261.

upmarket street not far from the Bolshoi Theatre.[89] For the first time in several years, it became possible to obtain scores from the West, and Myaskovsky could acquaint himself with the latest works of Schoenberg, Webern, Bartók, Casella, Hindemith, Milhaud, and other prominent contemporary figures. Enterprising as ever, Derzhanovsky was quick to spot an opportunity and used the bookshop as a venue for concerts later in the year. In effect, this series revived the Modern Music Evenings that he had run before the war. It furnished a basis on which to set up a new organisation, the Association for Modern Music (Assotsiatsiya sovremennoy muzïki), which would play an important role in Moscow musical life during the 1920s.

The second development was the resumption of epistolary contact with Prokofiev in early January 1923 after an elapse of nearly five years. Having recently moved back to Europe from the United States, Prokofiev resided initially in the picturesque village of Ettal in the Bavarian Alps. He had obtained Myaskovsky's address from Derzhanovsky, with whom he had been in correspondence since September 1922.[90] Since leaving Russia in 1918, Prokofiev had tried to keep in touch with his Russian friends and acquaintances, though the unreliable postal service made this difficult. He persistently made enquiries about Myaskovsky in letters to Russian correspondents ('I beg you forty-five thousand times to tell me Myaskovsky's address', he implored Eleanora Damskaya, an old friend from his conservatoire days, in June 1922[91]) and whenever he encountered Russian émigrés likely to have news of mutual acquaintances, but succeeded in finding out little more than the fact that he was still alive. His occasional references to his former classmate in his diaries during the intervening years express continued concern for his welfare.[92] Myaskovsky apparently made no effort to re-establish contact from his side, however, which seems curious – especially as he would have been aware that Asafiev had resumed correspondence with Prokofiev in the autumn of 1920.[93] Derzhanovsky showed him Prokofiev's letters, in which he repeatedly sent his regards and even enquired whether Myaskovsky had composed any short piano pieces suitable for him to record on a reproducing piano for commercial release.[94]

89   Koposova-Derzhanovskaya, 'V. V. Derzhanovskiy po vospominaniyam zhenï i druga', RNMM, 3/3365, l. 48.

90   Prokofiev's letters to Derzhanovsky in 1922–3 are published in Deklerk, '"Dolgaya doroga v rodnïye kraya"'.

91   Prokofiev to Eleanora Damskaya, 18 June 1922, ibid., 34.

92   Prokof'yev, *Dnevnik 1919–1933*, 106, 116, 180.

93   See Miral'da Kozlova, 'Pis'ma S. S. Prokof'yeva – B. V. Asaf'yevu (1920–1944)', in Tamara Livanova (ed.), *Iz proshlogo sovetskoy muzïkal'noy kulturï*, vol. 2 (Moscow, n.d.), 5.

94   Prokofiev to Derzhanovsky, 1 and 20 October in Deklerk, '"Dolgaya doroga v rodnïye kraya"', 45–6.

(Prokofiev had entered into a contract with the Aeolian Company in 1919 to make five piano-rolls every year using its Duo-Art system.[95]) Myaskovsky still did not write to him, though he duly revised six piano miniatures that he had composed in 1917–19 and sent them on through Derzhanovsky.[96] (This attractive set of pieces was published under the title *Prichudï* [Caprices], op. 25.) Prokofiev eventually had recourse to what he described to their mutual acquaintance Pyotr Suvchinsky as 'drastic measures'[97] and wrote to Myaskovsky directly early in the New Year: he was eventually rewarded by a response a few weeks later.

Myaskovsky's behaviour suggests a certain awkwardness – an impression that is reinforced by his reply to Prokofiev's letter. He blamed his failure to write sooner on pressure of work, which strikes one as disingenuous. And while Prokofiev at first used affectionate diminutive forms of his first name (Kolechka, Kolenka), Myaskovsky addressed the younger man formally by his first name and patronymic (Sergey Sergeyevich), leaving him little choice but to follow suit. The studied courtesy of his first communication unmistakably conveyed a desire to establish a certain distance – a fact that did not go unnoticed by Prokofiev, in spite of Myaskovsky's assurance that he was 'exceedingly pleased' to hear from him.[98] Both men were glad that the ice had been broken at last, but seemed initially rather unsure of how to behave towards one another.

Although hymned by Dmitry Kabalevsky as an example of a 'wonderful friendship' between two great artists in his preface to the Soviet edition of their correspondence, the two men's relationship was far more complex than Kabalevsky's saccharine characterisation would suggest, and marked by a considerable ambivalence on both sides. They had never been intimate and never would be: it is indicative that up to the very end of Myaskovsky's life in 1950 they continued to employ the formal second person plural with one another. (Asafiev and Prokofiev, by contrast, had progressed to using the informal second person singular by the early 1920s.) Although they would exchange close on two hundred and fifty letters over the following thirteen years, the correspondence reveals little about their personal or inner lives: they confined themselves almost entirely to discussing business

95 David Nice, *Prokofiev: From Russia to the West, 1891–1935* (New Haven and London, 2003), 157.

96 They were selected from the set of nineteen *Nabroski i otrïvki* (Sketches and fragments) composed between 1899 and 1919. The manuscripts are preserved in RGALI, 2040/2/30.

97 Prokofiev to Suvchinsky, 4 April 1923, in Anatoliy Kuznetsov, '"Dorogoy Pyotr Petrovich. . . ": Dva pis'ma S. S. Prokof'yeva k P. P. Suvchinskomu', *Muzïkal'naya zhizn'* 15–16 (1991), 24.

98 Myaskovsky to Prokofiev, 15 January 1923 and Prokofiev to Myaskovsky, 6 February 1923, Kozlova and Yatsenko, *Perepiska*, 150–3.

matters or compositions in progress. This reticence cannot be attributed merely to their awareness of the routine perlustration of foreign post by Soviet security organs: Prokofiev's letters to other Russian correspondents such as Eleanora Damskaya and Asafiev are notably chattier and more informal. Rather, it bespeaks a strong sense of mutual reserve. The ten-year difference in their ages had been an impediment to intimacy from the outset, as had Prokofiev's self-absorption, which placed severe limits on his interest in the activities of others. They had seen little of one another during the war and met only a few times between Myaskovsky's return to Petrograd in late 1917 and Prokofiev's emigration in May 1918. Since then, the former child prodigy had matured into an exceptionally talented young musician of growing international renown. By 1923, Prokofiev had a busy schedule of engagements as a pianist and his compositions were receiving high-profile performances in Europe and America. Myaskovsky was rather in awe of the younger man's remarkable gifts and felt insecure about Prokofiev's estimate of his own abilities, suspecting, not without good reason, that he did not rate them very highly.

Prokofiev's comments about his Blok settings and Third Piano Sonata, which Derzhanovsky had sent on to gratify his curiosity, can have done little to reassure him, and may well have been responsible for his procrastination in putting pen to paper. Although professing to find the sonata 'superb', Prokofiev nonetheless impugned its Tchaikovskian 'hysterics' and employment of 'trashy' sequences. He was even more scathing about the Blok cycle: he singled out the first song for praise as being 'stunningly beautiful' in places but was witheringly dismissive of its conclusion, which reminded him of 'Glière in the grip of his very feeblest inspiration': 'When the voice falls to that damned F-sharp, you want to flee from the room and hide yourself in a dark corner somewhere out of shame. How dare Myaskovsky write a page like that?!'[99] Clearly, he considered both works to be embarrassingly old-fashioned and marred by seriously lapses of taste. (In his diaries and letters to others, he stated this opinion more explicitly.[100]) It would hardly have been surprising if Myaskovsky found these comments hurtful and insulting. In this instance, Prokofiev had asked Derzhanovsky not to show him the letter – but he did not refrain subsequently from voicing

99 Prokofiev to Derzhanovsky, 23 November 1922, RNMM, 3/871, l. 2.

100 Writing to Suvchinsky on 1 December 1922, Prokofiev compared the Blok settings to the vocal music of Rubinstein and Rimsky-Korsakov – scarcely a compliment, since he derided the latter in a parenthesis as 'the ghastliest stuff ever written' – and declared that some passages 'plunged into a dark pit of vulgarity'. Yelena Pol'dyayeva, "'Ya chasto s nim ne soglashalsya. . .": Iz perepiski S. S. Prokof'yeva i P. P. Suvchinskogo', in Alla Bretanitskaya (ed.), *Pyotr Suvchinskiy i yego vremya* (Moscow, 1999), 79–80.

harsh criticisms to Myaskovsky directly. Sensitivity to the feelings of others had never been a notable trait of Prokofiev's character.

Prokofiev's reaction to Myaskovsky's recent work inaugurated a new dynamic in their relationship. If, in the past, Myaskovsky had acted as a mentor, Prokofiev now assumed the dominant role. Despite his eagerness to maintain personal and professional ties to his homeland, his attitude toward his Russian colleagues was ambivalent. He desired their respect and regard, but ultimately did not take them very seriously. Some of the less attractive sides to Prokofiev's character are in evidence in his correspondence with Myaskovsky, especially his complacent assumption of superiority and his condescension towards those whose talents he deemed inferior to his own. He voiced his opinions with the seemingly unassailable self-confidence of someone who believed himself to have 'arrived' and consequently entitled to pontificate on artistic matters from a position of international eminence. At times, he writes as though he regarded himself as an exiled artistic leader with a self-imposed mission to introduce a breath of bracing cosmopolitan fresh air into the stagnant fug of Moscow's parochial musical life.

The interesting question, of course, is why Myaskovsky not only put up with being treated *de haut en bas* but endured without protest Prokofiev's harsh comments about his music. In part, it was because Prokofiev was not altogether devoid of redeeming traits: when minded, he could be helpful, offering practical advice and occasionally acting as intermediary with foreign conductors and publishers. He also made limited efforts to promote Myaskovsky's music by programming three of the *Prichudï* in his piano recitals. Myaskovsky's loyalty to Prokofiev cannot be attributed merely to self-interest, however. The most important reason was his conviction that Prokofiev was not only a genius but displayed an order of ability surpassing that of any other contemporary composer. Though by no means wholly uncritical, Myaskovsky's admiration for Prokofiev was of an intensity bordering on hero-worship.

His encounter in 1922–3 with the music that the younger man had written since 1917 constituted a defining moment in his artistic development. He repeatedly expressed delighted appreciation on familiarising himself with scores such as the First Violin Concerto and the Third Piano Concerto, and was fulsome in his praise of Prokofiev's imaginative fecundity and technical skill. In a letter to Prokofiev of 15 September 1923, he wrote:

The score of *Chout* hasn't been taken off the piano – I've been feasting on it constantly. It's a magnificent piece – colourful, ingenious, and cohesive, with unbelievably vivid and memorable basic elements – but it can only be taken in small doses – it's too concentrated. I must confess that I even use your music for hygienic purposes: when one has had one's fill of all these Bartóks, Welleszes, Křeneks, Poulencs, Groszes, Hindemiths, and so on, one simply has to go outside to breathe the pure and healthy air of your estates. Somehow, apart from the venerable Schoenberg and some Honegger, I don't particularly care for any music from the West at all.[101]

For all its extravagance of expression, the sentiment was sincere. Myaskovsky's admiration remained unwavering; and as his disillusionment with the state of new music in the West deepened during the 1920s, so too did his certitude that Prokofiev was one of the very few composers whose work represented a genuinely significant contribution to contemporary musical culture. As he explained to Asafiev: 'In my opinion, the whole lot of them over there [in Europe] have got stuck in a dead-end, and are trying to extricate themselves from the mire of chaos by walking on stilts. Serge is following the truest path. If he doesn't "know" what needs to be done, he certainly senses it – and does so with the certitude of genius'.[102]

This conviction not only enabled him to make allowances for the more unpleasant sides to Prokofiev's personality but caused him to become a devoted propagandist for his music. The first manifestations of this impulse were two pseudonymous reviews that he contributed to the short-lived journal *Towards New Musical Shores* [*K novïm beregam muzïkal'nogo iskusstva*], which had been set up by Pavel Lamm early in 1923. In the first, which discussed the recently published *Visions fugitives*, op. 22, he noted signs of an 'organic deepening and enrichment' of Prokofiev's art and suggested that this modest set of piano pieces alone furnished sufficient justification for regarding Prokofiev as 'the rightful heir to the pleiad of musical geniuses who have recently passed into the history of our youthful [national] music'.[103] Myaskovsky did what he could to arrange performances of Prokofiev's compositions, which became increasingly feasible as concert life revived. Transcriptions of orchestral works such as the Third Piano Concerto (with Feinberg playing the solo part) and the Scythian Suite began to feature in the programmes of the musical evenings held in Lamm's apartment, which enabled Moscow musicians to become acquainted with them and led to performances by Persimfans. Prokofiev's music was also prominently represented in the series of chamber recitals held at the International Books premises in October 1923. These ventures were instrumental in assisting the growth of Prokofiev's reputation in his native country and helped prepare the way for his triumphantly successful visit to the USSR in 1927.

In spite of the undoubted excitement occasioned by his discovery of Prokofiev's recent work, Myaskovsky's encounter with it also proved a

101 Kozlova and Yatsenko, *Perepiska*, 169.

102 Myaskovsky to Asafiev, 19 December 1924, RGALI, 2658/2/50, l. 13.

103 'S. Prokof'yev. Mimolyotnosti, Op. 22', *K novïm beregam*, 1 (1923), 60–1.

rather traumatic experience, as its immediate effect was to reawaken doubts about his own stylistic trajectory. For Myaskovsky, for whom composing was an arduous process accompanied by constant uncertainty, it must have been difficult not to feel daunted when confronted by overwhelming evidence of Prokofiev's seemingly effortless fluency and inventiveness, as well as the freshness and originality of his musical language. His fragile self-confidence shattered, precipitating a major creative crisis that would last for several years. Anyone reading the Myaskovsky-Prokofiev correspondence will be struck immediately by the disparaging manner in which Myaskovsky habitually spoke of his own work, almost as if to anticipate the harshest criticisms that Prokofiev might level at it. He dismissed his Blok songs as 'boringly written', his Fifth Symphony as 'very primitive and somewhat vulgar', his Sixth as a 'kind of intensely emotional and rather academic music' that he should give up writing 'once and for all'; and even spoke of withdrawing his first six symphonies and restarting the numbering with the Seventh.[104] Similarly negative verdicts would be pronounced about many of the works that he completed subsequently. Myaskovsky's student Yevgeny Golubev records that the composer's sister Yevgeniya was reluctant to allow his letters to Prokofiev to be published, as she feared her brother's self-deprecatory comments about his music would do his reputation an active disservice.[105] They are often so manifestly unbalanced that they cannot and should not be taken at face value: read in conjunction with Myaskovsky's fairly frequent allusions to being in low spirits, they are a clear indication of strong depressive tendencies. Myaskovsky's mood was not helped by the dispiriting developments in the wake of Lamm's arrest. As he explained to Prokofiev:

> Now that everyone's obsessed with the profitability of businesses, and orchestras prefer to play without conductors, there can be no question of such luxuries as the publication or performance of even a miniscule symphony such as my Seventh. Even my Fourth Symphony has remained unperformed so far. Thanks to a combination of a lucky opportunity and Malko's persistence, my Fifth dame has gone into circulation and is now in great demand. The rest of my wares will probably remain in a heap under my piano.[106]

Another correspondent might have felt sympathy for these difficulties. Prokofiev had little understanding of the older man's emotional vulnerability and of how different conditions in Moscow were from those obtaining in

104 Myaskovsky to Prokofiev, 15 January, 18 June, and 25 July 1923, Kozlova and Yatsenko, *Perepiska*, 150, 159, 163.

105 Golubev, *Alogizmï*, RGALI, 2798/2/23, l. 75.

106 Myaskovsky to Prokofiev, 12 August 1923, Kozlova and Yatsenko, *Perepiska*, 168.

Paris, Prokofiev's artistic Mecca. Ignoring the fact that it had been impossible even to obtain scores of Western new music in Russia, for six or seven years, let alone hear performances of it, Prokofiev nonetheless proceeded to judge Myaskovsky's work by the standards of Parisian taste and found it wanting. It struck him as stylistically passé and dull, displaying little of the striving after sensational effect and novelty prized by Parisian critics. In its continued cultivation of a style manifestly indebted to nineteenth-century Russian traditions, Prokofiev saw only evidence of an incorrigibly provincial outlook that was hopelessly out of touch with contemporary developments. His condescending view of Myaskovsky's music had more complex causes that might first appear, however: the question of stylistic legitimacy was a very sensitive one for him at this particular juncture. Only a few months previously, he had had a blazing row with Diaghilev and Stravinsky during which they bluntly told him that he had taken the 'wrong path' in his recent work.[107] Disquietingly, their views were echoed by Suvchinsky, who criticised as outmoded his plan to write an opera based on Valery Bryusov's symbolist novel *The Fiery Angel*.[108] In raising this subject with Myaskovsky, Prokofiev was also dealing with undeclared anxieties of his own.

Matters came to a head when Koussevitzky expressed interest in seeing a score of Myaskovsky's Fifth Symphony. Prokofiev volunteered to play it for him and asked Myaskovsky to send a four-hand arrangement. When he received the score, Prokofiev's response was predictable: he told Suvchinsky that he felt 'embarrassed', adding, 'this kind of rustic merrymaking [*narodnoye gulyan'ye*] is hardly going to help Myaskovsky make his mark in Paris'.[109] A fortnight later, Myaskovsky sent him a dejected letter in which he complained of finding it difficult to compose because of an inhibiting self-consciousness and expressed fear that the kind of music he wished to write would soon become redundant in an environment where it increasingly looked as though there would only be a market for simplistic agitprop songs and marches:

> I must tell you frankly that I feel I've completely lost my talent and have had the ground swept away from underneath me. Writing out of that philosophy [i.e., his former aesthetic outlook] – that is, literally not thinking of anything at all – I can no longer do, since it is evident that no-one wants that kind of trumpery anymore. It's difficult to write the kind of stuff that would be considered worthwhile here, since I'd have to simplify my style to the point of Edenic innocence, and I've long left that unclouded and

107 Prokof'yev, *Dnevnik 1919–1933*, 205.

108 Prokofiev to Suvchinsky, 12 December 1922, in Pol'dyayeva, '"Ya chasto s nim ne soglashalsya. . .'", 81–2.

109 Prokofiev to Suvchinsky, 10 December 1923, ibid., 94.

unclothed state behind. In a word – I'm falling between two stools, and needless to add, am in a state of complete creative impotence.[110]

Prokofiev seized the opportunity to give him a stern lecture on the need to overhaul his compositional idiom radically if he were to stand any chance of making a reputation outside the USSR. (In his diary, he recorded his resolve to 'rouse Myaskovsky from his sluggishness and clumsy old-fashioned approaches, otherwise no-one will want to listen to him'.[111]) He reported that Koussevitzky reacted very negatively to the symphony, continuing:

I must also come down hard on you, for, to be blunt, not only I am not in raptures over [the symphony], but I am absolutely horrified by much of it. Yes! This symphony reveals the clumsy, deadly influence of Glazunov. How can one explain the influence of this cadaver? ... When you breed a horse and a donkey, you get a mule – but a mule is sterile. ... [Glazunov's] influence is similarly sterile, and only brings forth decay. ... Take, for example, [the passages at] rehearsal numbers 5 or 6 ... they're pale, clumsy, outdated, without the slightest feeling for timbre, without the slightest love for the orchestra; there's no attempt to conjure it into colour, life and sonorousness. ... And the start of the finale – God almighty, what hopeless Glazunov! What lack of regard for orchestration! As if Stravinsky or Ravel had never existed. [...] And the closing pages – couldn't you at least have wound up with some kind of a colourful *tutti*, instead of simplistic clumps of minims and semibreves? ... I implore you, douse your head with some cold water. Glazunov is a cumbersome decaying corpse . . ..

I am glad to read in your last letter that you feel you have lost the ground from under your feet: that means that in your heart of hearts, you are experiencing something like what I felt when I looked at the Fifth Symphony. Where do you go from here? Here's where: you should compose, not thinking about the music for the time being . . ., but seeking to create new approaches, a new technique, and novel orchestration. You should rack your brains to this end, sharpen your ingenuity, and strive for colourful and fresh sonorities at any cost. You should shun the compositional schools of St Petersburg and Moscow as you would a sullen devil – and you will immediately feel not only the ground under your feet, but wings on your back and most important of all – the way forward. I don't doubt that Aleksandrov, Feinberg, and the rest are all fine fellows, but these chips off the old Metner block [*metnerovskiye oskolki*] are hanging around your neck like a stone and are invisibly dragging you down into a warm and cosy bog. To a bog dweller, a bog is paradise; but an original fellow like you gives a shout of horror as you sink down: 'Save me, there's

110 Myaskovsky to Prokofiev, 23 December 1923, in Kozlova and Yatsenko, *Perepiska*, 179–80.

111 Prokof'yev, *Dnevnik 1919–1933*, 231.

no firm ground underfoot!' You bet, for where will you find firm ground
in a bog? Only at the very bottom.[112]

One wonders how Myaskovsky reacted on reading this diatribe, which not
only characterised Moscow in insulting terms as an artistically stagnant
backwater but described his symphony as a typical manifestation of its
provincial mentality. His response was dignified: he acknowledged that
the symphony had shortcomings but demurred to Prokofiev's overwhelmingly negative appraisal. He also gently pointed out that his correspondent
seemed to have little sense of the conditions confronting Soviet composers
and of how isolated from European musical life they had been until very
recently. His letter concluded forlornly: 'I'll probably continue to compose – and compose in a different way than I've done up to now – but
the 'firm ground' that you recommend seems almost as if it's on another
planet. Although the sketches that I'm currently making for the Eighth
[Symphony] give me some hope, whether or not I'll be successful, I don't
know'.[113]

The two men's relationship survived this incident, but it had been deeply
damaging to Myaskovsky's sense of self. He would spend the next decade
struggling to work out his artistic salvation, negotiating the contending
claims of Russian musical traditions and European modernism, as well as
the increasingly insistent demands of the state.

---

112 Prokofiev to Myaskovsky, 3 January 1924, RBML, SPA2483. The grossest of
     Prokofiev's derogatory comments about Glazunov were excised from the text
     of the letter as reproduced in Kozlova and Yatsenko, *Perepiska*, 181–3.

113 Myaskovsky to Prokofiev, 12–16 January 1924, in Kozlova and Yatsenko,
     Perepiska, 183.

7

Cross-Currents: 1924–6

On 21 January 1924 Lenin died of a massive stroke, having spent the last year of his life as a chronic invalid. His death prompted a nationwide outpouring of grief – in no small part, a displaced catharsis for a traumatised population that had endured almost a decade of armed conflicts and social upheaval, and the protracted ravages of hunger and disease. For several days, hundreds of thousands of mourners gathered outside the House of Unions in Moscow where his body lay in state, braving blizzards and temperatures as low as -40°C as they patiently waited their turn to process past the scarlet catafalque. Theatres closed; newspapers were wholly given over to coverage of reactions to the leader's demise. On 26 January, the day of his funeral, Petrograd was renamed Leningrad by official decree. At countless meetings convened in workplaces and institutions around the country, citizens made solemn vows to cherish Lenin's memory and devote themselves to building socialism.[1]

How best to accomplish that aim remained a moot issue. Marxist theory held that its successful realisation depended on transforming the new state into a major industrial power – but that would require a substantial investment in infrastructure, and capital was in short supply. Grain exports were one of the few viable means of accumulating sufficient hard currency to purchase the necessary equipment abroad. But as Lenin himself acknowledged in a speech of 31 October 1921, the Bolsheviks' attempt to remodel the economic basis of the state by 'storm tactics' had failed, causing a precipitous drop in agricultural outputs.[2] The government was consequently left with little choice, he argued, but to attempt to rebuild the shattered economy by abandoning the draconian requisitioning of foodstuffs and partially revoking the enforced nationalisation of private enterprise. If the state re-incentivised the peasantry to produce a surplus by permitting them to retain a portion in which they could trade, it would allow grain exports to resume and create disposable income that farmers could spend on goods. This would in turn help to revive the re-privatised domestic manufacturing and services sectors, causing money to circulate around the economy and generate badly needed tax revenues for the exchequer. In effect, this had begun to happen by the time of his death. Lenin presented the New

---

1   See Nina Tumarkin, *Lenin Lives! The Lenin Cult in Soviet Russia*, enlarged ed. (Cambridge, Masschusetts and London, 1997), 134–64.

2   'Rech' tov. Lenina na Moskovskoy gubpartkonferentsii', *Pravda*, 3 November 1921.

Economic Policy as a regrettable temporary concession to circumstances – a strategy of *reculer pour mieux sauter* – but his arguments failed to persuade some senior Party members, who regarded it as a flagrant betrayal of principle. The policy came close to being reversed in 1924 and remained contentious[3], becoming an issue central to the power struggles within the Soviet leadership that ultimately culminated in Stalin's accession as de facto dictator in 1929.

Ideological reservations notwithstanding, the policy proved effective. The economy recovered; goods and foodstuffs became more abundant. Although many of the country's inhabitants continued to suffer hardship, a significant proportion experienced a modest improvement in living standards. Not a few entrepreneurs grew rich: luxurious shops, restaurants, and places of entertainment opened to cater to their tastes, arousing the ire of Party members and workers. The young virtuoso violinist Nathan Milstein vividly recalled the sudden reappearance of viands that had long been a distant memory, such as the pastries filled with fresh cream that he and Vladimir Horowitz relished together one day in a chic Moscow café – a welcome contrast to the coarse fare served in the capital's more downmarket establishments, which was sometimes so revolting as to be inedible.[4]

In old age, Nadezhda Mandelstam noted a tendency amongst her contemporaries to idealise the NEP years as a time of freedom which allowed the arts and intellectual life to flourish.[5] As she rightly pointed out, such views were decidedly rose-tinted: the liberalisation of the economy was accompanied by a progressive tightening of state controls in other domains. The same period witnessed the expulsion of eminent intellectuals from the country, the elimination of rival political parties, the construction of a network of forced labour camps, the rapid expansion of a secret police force, growing persecution of the Russian Orthodox Church, and increasingly draconian censorship. If artists were generally left to their own devices (provided they were not openly antagonistic to the regime), it was because the government had more pressing concerns. A comprehensive state policy on the arts had yet to be formulated, but there were already disquieting intimations of its future general tendency. Lenin's wife Nadezhda Krupskaya, who acted as Lunacharsky's deputy in Narkompros, expressed a widely shared view in a front-page *Pravda* article in February 1921: state agencies should oblige creative artists to produce work in forms 'most accessible

---

3   See Alan M. Ball, *Russia's Last Capitalists: The Nepmen, 1921–1929* (Berlekey and Los Angeles, 1987), 38–55; Yefim Gimpel'son, *NÉP i sovetskaya politicheskaya sistema v 20-ye godï* (Moscow, 2000), 75–121.

4   Nathan Milstein and Solomon Volkov, *From Russia to the West: The Musical Memoirs and Reminiscences of Nathan Milstein*, trans. Antonina W. Bouis (London, 1990), 49, 61.

5   Nadezhda Mandel'shtam, *Vospominaniya*, vol. 1 (Moscow, 1999), 196–97.

and comprehensible to the masses' which served 'to convey, strengthen, and deepen communist sentiments'.[6] The prevalence of such instrumentalised understandings was unsurprising: the members of the early Bolshevik administration were not conspicuous for their breadth of culture. When Lenin posed for a portrait by Yury Annenkov in 1921, he told the renowned avant-garde painter that he regarded art 'as being something akin to the intelligentsia's appendix': 'When it's fulfilled its necessary propagandistic role – snip, snip! – and we'll excise it as something superfluous'.[7]

The only notable exception was Lunacharsky, who not only wrote plays and several works of literary criticism but had an informed appreciation of music and the visual arts. He responded open-mindedly to the diverse artistic trends of the early Soviet period, actively seeking to foster co-operation with the new regime.[8] But while he was undoubtedly well-meaning, initially, at least, he could do little to better the lot of creative and performing artists. Unemployment levels across the sector were high in the early 1920s and the meagre national arts budget was mostly absorbed by the country's major theatres and galleries. State patronage did not develop significantly until the end of the decade; and although the government allowed so-called 'spontaneously formed' (*samoproizvol'nïye*) arts organisations and artists' co-operatives to come into being during the NEP years, most received meagre state support, if any at all.[9]

As Myaskovsky had described to Prokofiev, the state of musical life at the end of 1923 gave little cause for cheer. Pavel Lamm's removal from the state publishing house had been a serious blow. The new management showed little interest in contemporary classical music and quickly closed down *Towards New Musical Shores*, the journal that Lamm had helped to set up earlier in the year. And although concert activity in the capital revived somewhat after the creation in 1921 of 'Moscow Philharmonic' (Mosfil), an administrative structure attached to Narkompros which functioned as a centralised concert agency, few works by living Russian or foreign composers were performed. Myaskovsky was involved in Mosfil from its inception and advised on programming, but his efforts to increase representation of contemporary music met with scant success.[10] By 1922 Mosfil was already

6   'Glavlitprosvet v iskusstvo', *Pravda*, 13 February 1921.

7   Yuriy Annenkov, *Dnevnik moikh vstrech: Tsikl tragedii*, vol. 2 (Moscow, 1991), 269.

8   On Lunacharsky's attitudes and approach, see Fitzpatrick, *Commissariat of Enlightenment*, 110–61.

9   See, for example, the discussion of state funding for the visual arts during the 1920s in Vitaliy Manin, *Iskusstvo v rezervatsii: Khudozhestvennaya zhizn' Rossii 1917–1941gg.* (Moscow, 1999), 84–120, *passim*.

10 His programming recommendations for Mosfil's chamber and piano recitals between January and May 1922 included music by Schoenberg, Debussy, and

seriously in debt, as its meagre state subsidy barely covered half of its operating costs. The situation in regard to new music remained unchanged when
it was reorganised and renamed 'Russian Philharmonic' (Rosfil) the following year: Rosfil's concert programmes were designed to appeal to mass
audiences and consisted almost exclusively of popular classics, a policy dictated as much by financial considerations as ideological ones.[11] Attempts
had been made to set up organisations to support contemporary music,
but they had either petered out or were not very active.[12] Myaskovsky and
his associates evidently concluded that matters were unlikely to improve
unless they took them into their own hands. Their collective initiative led
to the foundation of the Association for Modern Music (ASM)[13] in late
1923. In effect, ASM and its journal *Modern Music* (*Sovremennaya muzïka*)
were a continuation of Derzhanovsky's pre-war activities as organiser of
the 'Modern Music Evenings' and editor of *Music*, but on a more ambitious
scale: similar personnel were involved in both. Derzhanovsky was once
again at the centre of things, together with Lamm, Viktor Belyayev, and
other members of Myaskovsky's circle.[14]

In setting up ASM, the founders made effective use of their professional connections. Several of them, including Belyayev and Lamm[15], were
attached to the Music Section of the Russian Academy of Arts Studies
(RAKhN), an interdisciplinary research institute formed in 1921 to develop
scientific approaches to the study of the arts and serve as a state advisory
body on cultural policy.[16] RAKhN's charter made provision for 'arts asso-

---

Ravel: RNNM, 71/539.

11   On Mosfil and Rosfil, see Lev Grigor'yev and Yakov Platek, *Moskovskaya
     gosudarstvennaya filarmoniya* (Moscow, 1973), 48–64.

12   Lamm, 'Pavel Aleksandrovich Lamm: Opït biografii', RNMM, 192/361, l. 269.

13   Assotsiatsiya sovremennoy muzïki.

14   While an 'Association for Modern Music' was founded under the auspices of
     Narkompros in 1919, in practice it had little more than a paper existence: see
     'Assotsiatsiya sovremennoy muzïki', *Lad*, 1 (1919), 23–4. A Moscow-based
     'Union of Composers' formed around the same time still functioned and held
     occasional chamber recitals: see Myaskovsky to Asafiev, 12 March 1919 in
     RGALI, 2658/1/639, ll. 13–16 (Myaskovsky forwarded the organisation's draft
     charter, ll. 15–16); 'Moskovskiye kontserti', *Sovremennaya muzïka*, 1 (1924),
     22–3.

15   'Soobshcheniya', *Sovremennaya muzïka*, 2 (1924), 51; Lamm, 'Pavel
     Aleksandrovich Lamm: Opït biografii', RNMM, 192/361, l. 270.

16   Rossiyskaya (from 1925, *Gosudarstvennaya* – 'State') akademiya
     khudozhestvennïkh nauk. On RAKhN/GAKhN, see Nikolay Plotnikov
     and Nadezhda Podzemskaya (ed.), *Iskusstvo kak yazïk – yazïki iskusstva:
     Gosudarstvennaya akademiya khudozhestvennïkh nauk i ėsteticheskaya teoriya
     1920-kh godov*, 2 vols. (Moscow, 2017).

ciations and societies' to be formed under its jurisdiction.[17] ASM's connection with RAKhN was essentially nominal, but convenient – not least because it allowed the association to use RAKhN's premises free of charge. Being affiliated to a state institution also made it easier to surmount the bureaucratic obstacles that censorship laws increasingly placed in the way of publishing journals and organising public events.[18] On 6 June 1922, a government decree made it a criminal offence to print anything – including musical compositions – without first obtaining clearance from Glavlit, the newly created state censorship apparatus. (Within three years, even seemingly innocuous materials such as stationery, concert posters, and admission tickets would have to undergo such scrutiny.) A subsidiary of Glavlit, Glavrepertkom, formed in February 1923, imposed similar 'prophylactic censorship' on theatre productions and shows, which was quickly extended to concerts and public lectures. These measures were not so much concerned with safeguarding public decency as with control of the public sphere and access to information: their principal aim was to suppress anything deemed to 'hinder the construction of socialism' – a rubric that was interpreted with steadily growing latitude and would block much musical repertoire from being performed.[19]

Although its importance in early Soviet musical life is routinely acknowledged in historical accounts, information about ASM is surprisingly sketchy: it is not even clear how much documentation of its activities survives apart from its journal.[20] The founders initially hoped to set up branches in other cities, but its operations remained confined to Moscow: a cognate organisation in Leningrad, LASM, was not formed until January 1926 and functioned entirely independently.[21] It would be inaccurate to imagine ASM merely as a bureau that arranged performances of contemporary music and

17 'Ustav Rossiyskoy akademii khudozhestvennïkh nauk', GRI, Wassily Kandinsky Papers, Series III, box 4, folder 1; 'Assotsiatsii pri gosudarstevnnoy akademii khudozhestvennïkh nauk', *Byulleteni GAKhN*, 1 (1925), 44.

18 Myaskovsky to Steinberg, 4 April 1925, RIII, 28/1/487, l. 8.

19 'Glavlit' and 'Glavrepertkom' were respectively acronyms for Glavnoye upravleniye po delam literaturï i izdatel'stv (Chief Directorate of Matters Pertaining to Literature and Publishers) and Glavnïy repertuarnïy komitet (Chief Repertoire Committee). On both, see Blyum, *Za kulisami "Ministerstva pravdï"*, 82–96, 161–76. Glavlit would become the model for censorship bureaux across the Eastern bloc after the Second World War: see, for example, Liliana Corobca, *Controlul cărții: Cenzura literaturii în regimul comunist din România* (Bucharest, 2014), 85–99.

20 A comprehensive study of ASM has yet to be written. The opprobrium that the association subsequently incurred lingered for decades, effectively making it an off-limits topic for Soviet musicologists.

21 See Valerian Bogdanov-Berezovskiy, 'Leningradskaya assotsiatsiya sovremennoy muzïki', in Igor' Glebov [Boris Asaf'yev] and Semyon Ginzburg (ed.), *Pyat' let novoy muzïki: Stat'i i materialï* [*Novaya muzïka*, god 1, vïp.

issued a promotional periodical: it was set up as an association of musicians who were professionally involved with new music, and administered on behalf of its members by an executive committee of volunteers.[22] ASM's charter declared two principal aims – first, to foster the study of modern music 'in all its manifestations'; and secondly, to 'assist its dissemination by organising concerts and lectures'.[23] This wording suggests that the founders envisioned ASM as a learned society which engaged in public outreach activities. The size of its membership is not known, but it is unlikely to have been large: it probably consisted mostly of conservatoire staff members and students.

ASM's activities were managed by two 'commissions' – one of which oversaw the production of its journal, and the other, its concert series. *Modern Music* was initially edited by Derzhanovsky and two former writers for *Music*, Sabaneyev and Belyayev. It came out irregularly, according to the state of ASM's finances (thirty-two issues in total appeared between 1924 and 1929), and was generally similar to *Music* in format – slim volumes of thirty to forty pages containing a mixture of articles on composers and notable new works (the first issue, for example, contained essays on Hindemith and his chamber music), news items, reports on recent and forthcoming performances, opinion pieces, and reviews. Much of the content was initially written by the editors, supplemented by pieces elicited from Asafiev and others. The contributors were probably unpaid.[24]

The personnel in charge of the concert series also performed their roles on a voluntary basis. Myaskovsky effectively acted as artistic director, though he preferred to remain in the background, leaving the organisational practicalities to Derzhanovsky. Potentially suitable repertoire was played and discussed at musical evenings hosted by Pavel Lamm or the Derzhanovskys.[25] Myaskovsky was well-suited to his role. The composer Anatoly Aleksandrov remembered him as being discerning, but open-minded. Although his choices of non-Russian repertoire tended to favour the work of notable modernist figures (presumably, to enable the association's members to keep abreast of developments abroad), he sought to be as representative as

1] (Leningrad, 1926), 37–41; Mikhail Druskin, *Issledovaniya, vospominaniya* (Leningrad, 1977), 202–5.

22 See 'Assotsiatsiya sovremennoy muzïki', *Sovremennaya muzïka*, 1 (1924), 19.

23 'Assotsiatsiya sovremennoy muzïki', *Byulleteni GAKhN*, 1 (1925), 48. The original version of ASM's charter was lost (Myaskovsky to Maximilian Steinberg, 4 April 1925, RIII, 28/1/487, l. 8).

24 In a letter of 30 April 1927, Derzhanovsky informed Asafiev that he hoped to be able to pay contributors in future – which suggests that they had not received an honorarium previously. RGALI, 2658/1/542, l. 12.

25 Koposova-Derzhanovskaya, 'Pamyati druga', 222; Lamm, 'Pavel Aleksandrovich Lamm: Opït biografii', RNMM, 192/361, l. 270.

possible when it came to the music of his Russian colleagues[26] – in keeping with the stance articulated in Sabaneyev's editorial in *Modern Music*'s first issue, which advocated taking an inclusive view of 'musical modernity'.[27] The association's ethos was thus quite different to that of the pre-war 'Modern Music Evenings' in St Petersburg. Looking back in later life on his involvement with ASM, Myaskovsky's student Vissarion Shebalin emphasised the organisation's 'non-programmatic' stance: it did not espouse any stylistic tendencies or compositional approaches in particular and simply sought to provide opportunities to hear new music of all kinds.[28] A perusal of the lists of works performed at ASM's events confirms the accuracy of Aleksandrov and Shebalin's observations: Goedicke, Catoire, and other composers of a traditionalist orientation featured alongside those of a more iconoclastic cast, such as Nikolay Roslavets and Alexander Mosolov. A considerable effort was also made to perform music by young composers to help them gain experience – something that Myaskovsky had repeatedly advocated in his articles for *Music*.

ASM's activities were necessarily modest in scale. In the first four years of its existence, it received an annual stipend of around 2000 roubles[29] – not a large sum, when one considers that the average yearly salary of a skilled industrial operative was roughly 1150 roubles in late 1924.[30] These funds had to cover the production costs of ASM's journal and other expenses: its concert series had to be financed from whatever remained. Its opening season comprised six chamber recitals held between February and May 1924.[31] All took place in a hall in RAKhN's premises on Kropotinskaya Street, which had formerly housed a secondary school.[32] The performers were mostly attached to the Moscow Conservatoire and probably only received a token honorarium, if they were paid at all: in April 1925, Myaskovsky apologetically informed Maximilian Steinberg that the association's 'poverty' prevented it from inviting Leningrad colleagues to participate. He went on to explain that its first season of concerts had been 'virtually closed' to the public, which suggests that one had to be a member of ASM to attend and

---

26 Vladimir Blok and Yelena Polenova (ed.), *Anatoliy Nikolayevich Aleksandrov: Stranitsï zhizni i tvorchestva* (Moscow, 1990), 124.

27 'Sovremennaya muzïka', *Sovremennaya muzïka*, 1 (1924), 1–3.

28 Vissarion Shebalin, 'O proydennom puti', *Sovetskaya muzïka*, 2 (1959), 76.

29 'Assotsiatsiya sovremennoy muzïki', *Sovremennaya muzïka*, 23 (1927), 5.

30 See Aleksandr Il'yukhov, *Kak platili bol'sheviki: Politika sovetskoy vlasti v sfere oplatï truda v 1917–1941gg.* (Moscow, 2010), 88.

31 Details of ASM's first three concert series are summarised in *Sovremennaya muzïka*, 15–16 (1926), 166–75.

32 Lamm, 'Pavel Aleksandrovich Lamm: Opït biografii', RNMM, 192/361, l. 269.

that the audiences were presumably small.[33] It is not clear why the initial recitals were run as private events – a policy that seems curiously at variance with ASM's mission to promote new music. ASM's journal described them as 'performance meetings' (*ispolnitel'nïye sobraniya*) rather than concerts, which may provide a clue. The term suggests that they were meetings of the association's members at which music was not only performed but also discussed – in other words, that they were akin to seminars convened by a study group.[34] If so, the exclusion of the general public would be understandable, especially if the performances were for demonstration purposes and somewhat rough-and-ready. ASM continued to convene 'performance meetings' during its 1924–5 and 1925–6 seasons but started to hold a small number of public events which were billed as 'concerts' in the customary sense.

ASM's 'performance meetings' were thus not dissimilar to the musical evenings held in Pavel Lamm's apartment, except that chamber music was played instead of piano transcriptions of orchestral works, the attendance was presumably larger, and their institutional setting lent them a more formal character. The private nature of these events meant that initially, at least, ASM had the character of a club for composers and new music enthusiasts. Before 1917, an association of this kind would have been considered unremarkable. By 1924, however, it was inherently problematic: not only were artists and arts organisations increasingly expected to engage with proletarian audiences but notions of the self-sufficient value of the arts were under attack. ASM's apolitical stance is noteworthy and reflects the desire of most of its founder members, Myaskovsky and Pavel Lamm amongst them, to remain aloof from politics. When helping to set up ASM, it is doubtful that Myaskovsky gave much thought to the social relevance of its activities – or of his own as a composer. It would not be long before both started to be questioned insistently, and not merely by people external to ASM but also by some of his close associates.

Myaskovsky's growing prominence made it inevitable that he would be drawn into the artistic controversies of the period. The mere fact of

33 Myaskovsky to Steinberg, 4 April 1925, RIII, 28/1/487, l. 8.

34 Compare, for example, the writer Vladislav Khodasevich's reference in his memoirs to participating in a 'performance meeting' of writers attached to a Proletkult studio in 1918, at which 'the students read poetry and then discussed what had been read': Vladislav Khodasevich, *Sobraniye sochineniy v chetïryokh tomakh. Tom chetvyortïy: Nekropol', vospominaniya, pis'ma*, ed. Inna Andreyeva *et al.* (Moscow, 1996), 226. In a report on LASM's activities in Leningrad, the musicologist Mikhail Druskin similarly referred to plans to hold 'closed performance meetings': the context suggests that these events had the character of lecture-recitals. See 'Deyatel'nost' LASM', in Igor' Glebov [Boris Asaf'yev] and Semyon Ginzburg (ed.), *Oktyabr' i novaya muzïka* [*Novaya muzïka*, god 2, vïp. 1] (Leningrad, 1927), 54.

being virtually the only composer to have any large-scale works performed during the early 1920s of itself placed him at the centre of attention. The premiere of the Sixth Symphony by the orchestra and choir of the Bolshoi Theatre under the young conductor Nikolay Golovanov on 4 May 1924[35] was regarded as a major artistic event. Despite the technical inadequacies of the performance, the symphony made an overwhelming impression. By the close, many members of the audience were in tears: older musicians such as Catoire and Igumnov invoked comparisons with the premiere of Tchaikovsky's *Pathétique*.[36] The composer was brought onstage seven times to acknowledge the applause.[37] His colleagues went to considerable lengths to publicise the concert: a booklet about the symphony was brought out in advance, and the April issue of *Modern Music* included a substantial programme note with musical examples as well as two essays on Myaskovsky and his work by Asafiev and Belyayev. These initiatives clearly demonstrate the high regard in which he was held: the anonymous author of the booklet spoke of him as figure of central importance in Russian musical life and a successor to Glazunov and Skryabin.[38] Myaskovsky wore his growing renown lightly: even someone like Alexander Goldenweiser, who was not particularly well-disposed towards him and disliked his music, had to acknowledge his modesty and lack of self-importance.[39] But that of itself did not forestall criticisms, some of them from unexpectedly close quarters. The premiere of the Sixth Symphony brought to the surface submerged tensions in his relationships with Asafiev and Derzhanovsky. As their correspondence reveals, both men felt ambivalent about Myaskovsky's recent work and his artistic orientation.

In Derzhanovsky's case, the causes of his dissatisfaction were straightforward: a fervent supporter of the new regime, he believed that artists should be politically engaged and was impatient with Myaskovsky's unwillingness to write works on overtly political subjects. He also held that the new times demanded a new artistic outlook and creative approaches which broke decisively with the past. Writing to Asafiev in June 1923, he lamented that 'the fire of the Revolution' had yet to revitalise Russia's 'moribund' musical life; 'counterrevolution' was still everywhere in evidence, so the critic's most pressing task, as he saw it, was 'to drag' musicians of 'conservative,

35 The concert programme is preserved in RGALI, 2040/2/359, ll. 118–19.

36 Lamm, 'Pavel Aleksandrovich Lamm: Opït biografii', RNMM, 192/361, l. 272.

37 Viktor Belyayev to Viktor Uspensky, 5 May 1924, quoted in Ikonnikov, *Khudozhnik nashikh dney*, 110–11.

38 *N. Ya. Myaskovskiy. K ispolneniyu yego simfoniy v Bol'shom Teatre v Moskve* (Moscow, 1924), 8.

39 Aleksandr Gol'denveyzer, 'O Myaskovskom-cheloveke', in Shlifshteyn (ed.), *N. Ya. Myaskovskiy: Sobraniye materialov*, vol. 1, 254–5.

retrograde' tendencies into the new era by whatever means necessary[40] –
Myaskovsky included.

The reasons for Asafiev's negative reactions were more complex. Envy
played an important part. By 1924, Asafiev had given up composing to
pursue an increasingly busy career as a researcher, teacher, consultant, and
writer. He still longed to compose, as he confessed to Derzhanovsky, but felt
that it was now too late.[41] Myaskovsky's steadily rising critical stock did not
exactly please him. On the surface, their relations remained cordial (they
seldom met, as Asafiev remained in Leningrad), but Asafiev's asseverations
of affection and regard in his letters to Myaskovsky cannot be taken at face
value. He was perfectly capable of telling him that he 'loved and cherished
him as a friend and as the foremost composer in Russia', only to dispar-
age him to another correspondent soon afterwards ('Myaskovsky's growing more "academic" by the day. For he's a *maître* now!') and make snide
remarks about his Moscow associates.[42] Myaskovsky's standing amongst
the members of the Lamm circle particularly irked him.

It is indicative that when Derzhanovsky asked him to contribute an article on Myaskovsky to *Modern Music* in February 1924[43], Asafiev was at first
inclined to refuse: he offered a lengthy litany of excuses and complained that
Myaskovsky seemed to have dropped him, as he had not heard from him
in some time.[44] (As Myaskovsky later explained, his silence was caused by a
protracted bout of depression after Lamm's imprisonment, which left him
feeling like 'the living dead' (*polutrup*): he had evidently found the episode
highly disturbing.[45]) Asafiev changed his mind, but the essay 'Myaskovsky as
Symphonist' that he dashed off and sent on three days later[46] unmistakably
indicates his lack of enthusiasm for the task – notwithstanding its opening
description of Myaskovsky as 'one of the outstanding Russian musicians of
our time'.[47] Like much of Asafiev's writing, the piece says little but at disproportionate length: instead of discussing Myaskovsky's symphonic output, as
its title would lead one to expect, it largely consists of vague impressionistic
description of his creative personality. While he does not articulate criticisms explicitly, they are clearly implied between the lines of his account,
which presents a decidedly equivocal assessment. Myaskovsky's music is

40 Derzhanovsky to Asafiev, 30 June 1923, GABT, R-2263, KP 3500/611, ll. 1–20b.

41 Asafiev to Derzhanovsky, 15 February 1924, RNNM, 3/732.

42 Asafiev to Myaskovsky, 17 January 1926, in Lamm, *Stranitsï*, 174; Asafiev to
    Alexander Vaulin [Waulin], 13 July 1926, RNNM, 171/148, ll. 7–70b.

43 Derzhanovsky to Asafiev, 1 February 1924, GABT, R-2263, KP 3500/612, l. 10b.

44 Asafiev to Derzhanovsky, 7 March 1924, RNNM, 3/733, ll. 1–10b.

45 Myaskovsky to Asafiev, 11 March 1924, RGALI, 2658/1/640, ll. 21, 22.

46 Asafiev to Derzhanovsky, 10 March 1924, RNNM, 3/734.

47 Asafiev, 'Myaskovsky kak simfonist', *Sovremennaya muzïka*, 3 (1924), 66–77.

Figure 7.1. Boris Asafiev (late 1920s).

characterised as sombre and agitated in mood, cerebral, and lacking in sensuous appeal: 'Its dominant colouration is gloom [*mgla*]: grey, sinister autumnal gloom under lowering dense clouds ... shading into pitch darkness'. These traits supposedly reflected Myaskovsky's 'stubbornly closed', hypersensitive nature, which shunned human contact, reacted in 'nervous, convulsive' fashion to external stimuli, and remained in a constant state of 'agonised instability'. The reader is left with the unmistakable impression of a neurotic composer who wrote neurotic music. (Despite his warm praise for the essay, Derzhanovsky thought Asafiev's portrayal of Myaskovsky's 'solitariness' and 'isolation' exaggerated.[48]) Asafiev's characterisation is demonstrably tendentious: he makes no allusion to the affirmative conclusion of the Fourth Symphony or to the warm lyricism of the Fifth, as they do not suit his purpose. And though he praises Myaskovsky's mastery of counterpoint (he describes him as a 'faithful student of Lyadov') and of 'European' musical forms, these were very back-handed compliments – especially as Asafiev spent much of the 1920s railing against the 'academicism' of the St Petersburg Conservatoire's pedagogical traditions and the 'scholastic' German music theory on which they were based.[49]

48 Derzhanovsky to Asafiev, 25 April 1924, GABT, KP-3500/614, l. 1.
49 In the first volume of his treatise *Musical Form as Process* (*Muzïkal'naya forma kak protsess*), published in 1930, Asafiev attempted to offer an

'Myaskovsky as Symphonist' none too subtly attempts to cut its subject down to size. Asafiev's motives were not merely personal, however. His essay also reflects his awareness that much of Myaskovsky's work to date would be construed as reflecting an outlook fundamentally at variance with the Bolshevik worldview. Myaskovsky's conception of the symphony as a symbolic representation of the isolated artist's embattled subjectivity (as outlined in his essay 'Tchaikovsky and Beethoven') was deeply problematic in a context where the traditional notions of the value of the individual and of individual autonomy were under sustained attack.[50] Modernist envisionings of the alienated artist were forcefully challenged by prominent supporters and representatives of the regime: now that the Revolution had supposedly swept away the causes of that alienation along with the old bourgeois world order, artists were expected to affirm rather than criticise the new society of which they were a part. In 1918, Maxim Gorky republished his polemical essay 'The Destruction of Personality', a blistering critique of the 'bourgeois individualism' of contemporary artists who failed to offer an optimistic vision of life, preferring to wallow in 'neurasthenia', 'vulgarity', and 'despair'. ('Each of them considers their "ego" to be deserving of special attention and high esteem', Gorky wrote, 'but the proletariat which is renewing the life of the world does not want to bestow the charity of its attention on these "aristocrats of the spirit" . . . which is why they hate it'.)[51] Lunacharsky's collection of essays *Philistinism and Individualism*, brought out in 1923, contained several pieces in a similar vein: one in particular, 'August Strindberg: the "Great Martyr of Individualism"', directly influenced Asafiev's portrayal of Myaskovsky, to judge from some striking textual similarities.[52]

---

alternative approach to the study of voice leading and musical form based on his view of music as a quasi-organic entity imbued with a 'life force': it was conceived in express contradistinction to what he regarded as the 'lifeless' and 'mechanical' understandings of music fostered by Riemann and other German theorists.

50 For a classic contemporary account, see René Fülöp-Miller, *Geist und Gesicht des Bolschewismus: Darstellung und Kritik des kulturellen Lebens in Sowjet-Russland* (Vienna, 1926), 1–35.

51 Maksim Gor'kiy, 'Razrusheniye lichnosti', in *Stat'i. 1905–1916gg.*, 2nd ed. (Petrograd, 1918), 19.

52 Anatoliy Lunacharskiy, '"Velikomuchenik individualizma" Avgust Strindberg', in Lunacharsky, *Meshchanstvo i individualizm* (Moscow, 1923), 224–9. Lunacharsky describes how Strindberg's tormented 'hyperindividualism' and his 'mimosa-like sensitivity to every contact' made him solitary and misanthropic, though he craved companionship; echoing his unusual metaphor, Asafiev speaks of Myaskovsky's 'vivid individual reactions' to the outside world and his 'mimosa-like nature' causing him to 'recoil from unwanted contact' into solitude, yet yearn for 'affection'.

Asafiev was acquainted with Lunacharsky and carefully cultivated contact with him, mindful of the importance of official patronage. An enthusiastic adherent of the new regime (his memoirs profess effusive admiration for Lenin[53]), he had been swift to avail of the professional opportunities that opened up at a time when Lunacharsky could not afford to be too fussy about whom he appointed. He soon levered himself out of his lowly post as *répétiteur* at the Mariinsky Theatre into more elevated positions, amongst them the directorship of the Institute of Arts History's Music Division – a post for which he could hardly have been described as ostentatiously qualified. Lunacharsky remained supportive: Asafiev was even allowed to have direct personal access to him. In early 1924, for example, Asafiev met him to seek official backing for proposals to expand the division and to set up a New Music Association that would run concerts for proletarian audiences (though not merely of 'modern music').[54] Having the ear of a government minister was professionally advantageous and Asafiev was clearly anxious to make the most of this privileged position. It is no accident that his writings started to echo official pronouncements more consistently around this time, or that he grew more chary of endorsing anything that might be found ideologically suspect.

As Asafiev recognised, the Sixth was a highly problematic score in this respect. Though he claimed to have 'fallen in love' with it when Myaskovsky showed him the symphony in draft[55], he was unwilling to discuss it in print, notwithstanding its importance as a major new work about to receive a high-profile premiere. When Derzhanovsky invited him in April 1924 to write about it for *Musical Culture*, a new journal edited by Nikolay Roslavets, Asafiev replied that Roslavets himself should write an article 'defending' the symphony – a telling choice of verb.[56] He declined again when Derzhanovsky renewed the invitation in June, urging Asafiev to counter the 'idiotic' reviews that the symphony had received and the rumours that were circulating about its supposed secret programme depicting victims of the Revolution.[57] Seemingly uncomprehending of the work's import, Derzhanovsky was eager for the score to be regarded as a foundational contribution to a new Soviet canon of 'revolutionary music', hoping that it might instigate a new phase in Myaskovsky's development. Asafiev – rightly – believed Derzhanovsky to be indulging in wishful thinking. As he eventually admitted, he had deliberately avoided writing about the Sixth because

53 'O sebe', 505–6.
54 See Andrey Kryukov (ed.), *Materiali k biografii B. Asaf'yeva* (Leningrad, 1981), 15–17, 108.
55 Asafiev to Myaskovsky, 23 January 1923, in Lamm, *Stranitsï*, 154.
56 Asafiev to Derzhanovsky, 9 April 1924, RNNM, 3/747.
57 Derzhanovsky to Asafiev, 19 July 1924, RGALI, 2658/2/44, ll. 12–120b.

his reservations were so serious. At bottom, he averred, Myaskovsky's artistic response to the Revolution interpreted events from a 'mystical' (that is, religious) standpoint, viewing them through the prism of traditional Christian imagery of the Apocalypse – a claim presumably prompted by Myaskovsky's use of the *Dies irae* plainchant and its reappearance during the cataclysmic climax of the finale. This called the future viability of his creative path fundamentally into question, as it suggested an inability to 'shift his work onto the plane of collective consciousness' – in other words, to overcome his 'bourgeois individualism' and embrace the Marxist-Leninist worldview.[58]

The basis of this negative verdict was wholly in line with official thinking, and Asafiev's strictures adumbrated an appraisal of the symphony that became more or less standard in Soviet publications. In an atmosphere of intensifying anti-religious sentiment, Myaskovsky's employment of sacred chants would inevitably be viewed with suspicion. More seriously, the score suggested an interpretation of the Bolshevik coup that did not conform to approved stereotypes: the depiction of the Revolution was already a matter of such sensitivity that censors routinely suppressed publications deemed to represent it in a 'distorted' fashion. (Amongst them was the symbolist poet Maximilian Voloshin's powerful collection *The Burning Bush* (1922), which portrayed the violent upheavals of the Revolution and Civil War as a latter-day Armageddon.[59])

Asafiev's strictures about the Sixth touched on issues with significant implications not merely for Myaskovsky but for all Soviet composers – chief amongst them the extent to which their work should be informed by Marxist-Leninist ideology. And although he shrank from criticising Myaskovsky directly, he nonetheless decided that the time had come to raise these issues for public discussion and to fire an opening salvo in the campaign against musical 'counterrevolution' that Derzhanovsky longed to initiate. The interesting question is why Asafiev chose to force matters. His letters to Derzhanovsky suggest that he was motivated by personal ambition – a desire to establish himself as a leading musical commentator (much as his mentor Stasov had been for a previous era) and play an active role in shaping official cultural policy on music. Between September and December 1924, he wrote a series of essays on contemporary Soviet composition that he intended to publish initially as articles and subsequently assemble into a projected volume entitled *The Conditions of Russian Musical Life*. He attached great importance to the project and spoke of sending some of the essays to Lunacharsky. All return to the same theme – that Soviet composition was in the grip of a serious crisis caused by composers' failure to

58   Asafiev to Derzhanovsky, 28 January 1925, RNNM, 3/772, ll. 1–10b.

59   See Blyum, *Za kulisami "Ministerstva pravdi"*, 61–3, 99–100.

recognise that the Revolution necessitated radical changes of outlook and approach. Derzhanovsky readily helped him to place the essays in Moscow journals.

Asafiev described the first of them, 'The Crisis of Personal Creativity' as 'an alarm bell': when he sent on the manuscript to Derzhanovsky, he asked him to circulate it to any musicians in administrative positions 'to whom it might be useful' – a clear indication that he hoped to influence official thinking.[60] Derzhanovsky had elicited it as a contribution to *Musical Culture*, but Roslavets refused to point-blank to publish it, so he took an executive decision, without consulting his fellow editors, to feature it as the lead article in the November 1924 issue of *Modern Music*.[61] The reasons for Roslavets' refusal are not difficult to guess. In essence, Asafiev suggested that the contemporary classical music currently being written in Russia was mostly incomprehensible and irrelevant to proletarian audiences. Instead of producing complex 'individualistic" compositions' (as Asafiev explicitly characterised them – echoing the disapprobatory epithet employed by Gorky and Lunacharsky) such as sonatas and symphonies, he declared that composers should instead focus on mass songs, stage works and music for popular festivities, and aspire to write music comparable in popular appeal to the Verdi operas.[62] He returned to the attack on 'individualists' the following month in 'Composers, Hurry Up!', deriding the musical 'high priests' who feared 'the street' and preferred to shut themselves away in their studies, clinging to the illusion that they could continue to write for a select few and adhere to an aesthetic of 'art for art's sake'. He warned that 'life would begin to dispense with' such composers if they did not 'advance with modernity' and renounce their 'proud state of alienation'; he exhorted them to 'create music for the sake of the life that surrounds us [. . .] and not for the sake of insubstantial dreams'.[63]

These pieces were written with a deliberate intention to provoke: Asafiev told Derzhanovsky that he wanted 'Composers, Hurry Up!' to 'put the wind up the hypocrites'. There can be no doubt that Myaskovsky was the principal intended target amongst the 'hypocrites', being by far the most conspicuous example of the composers whom Asafiev deemed to have caused the alleged crisis because of their 'obstinate persistence in writing symphonies and sonatas'.[64] He was, after all, the only contemporary Russian composer

60 Asafiev to Derzhanovsky, 21 September 1924, RNNM, 3/750.

61 Derzhanovsky to Asafiev, 22 November 1924, RGALI, 2658/2/45, l. 1–2.

62 'Krizis lichnogo tvorchestva', *Sovremennaya muzïka*, 4 (1924), 99–106.

63 'Kompozitorï, pospeshite!', *Sovremennaya muzïka*, 6 (1924), 146–9.

64 Igor' Glebov [Boris Asaf'yev], 'Krizis muzïki (nabroski nablyudatelya leningradskoy muzïkal'noy deystvitel'nosti)', *Muzïkal'naya kul'tura*, 2 (1924), 106.

of note to write several new symphonies between 1917 and 1924, and one of the very few whose symphonic works were performed.[65] There is similarly no doubt that he formed the basis for Asafiev's caricatures of the 'individualistic' composers and stubbornly conservative 'aesthetes' who wrote 'academic' music according to 'petrified rationalistic [formal] schemes' for the 'closed circle [of the] salon (in the broadest sense of the word)' – to quote another essay that he wrote around this time.[66] (One notes the unmistakable swipe at Lamm's musical evenings.) In a letter to a former student, Asafiev made caustic comments about Myaskovsky that echo formulations in 'Composers, Hurry Up!': '[Myaskovsky] flees from life, he fears the street, and "inside" him – it's dark, he's afraid'.[67]

Myaskovsky appears to have had no inkling of Asafiev's hostile attitude towards him or of his collusion with Derzhanovsky: the articles in *Modern Music* came like a bolt from the blue and caused consternation amongst his ASM associates. Pavel Lamm was furious and wrote to Asafiev accusing him of opportunism. Myaskovsky's reaction, by contrast, was surprisingly calm and measured. He acknowledged that the essays raised important questions, especially in regard of the relationship between the composer and the new proletarian listenership, but took issue with Asafiev's analysis and his proposed remedy: 'I fear that you are rushing into an excessively simplistic solution of the problem – by taking the line of least resistance. Your consumer is a yokel, so you must write yokel-music. . . . If so, the same conclusion should be drawn for literature etc. (down with the novel, the poem and so on). But why? Are there really only "yokels" left, and no intelligentsia? And there never will be?'[68]

His comments went to the heart of the issues. Talk of a 'crisis' was wholly premature: as yet, composers had scant opportunity to encounter their new audience or gauge its reactions to their work. It was unwarranted to assume that there would be no place for music of a more sophisticated nature: the recent performances of his own Fifth and Sixth Symphonies in Moscow had been very warmly received. Asafiev imagined 'the masses' as a monolith with uniform musical tastes and interests. He did not allow for

---

65 A grand total of ten symphonies by Moscow and Leningrad composers are known to have been completed between 1917 and 1924. Of these, only four were performed during this period: Andrey Pashchenko's Second Symphony (1922), Goedike's Third (1923) and Myaskovsky's Fifth and Sixth. See David Fanning, 'The Symphony in the Soviet Union (1917–91)', in Robert Layton (ed.), *A Companion to the Symphony* (London, 1993), 318–19.

66 Igor' Glebov [Boris Asaf'yev], 'Dvi techiï – dvi otsinky', *Muzika*, 11–12 (1925), 381–2.

67 Asafiev to Alexander Waulin [Vaulin], 13 September 1925, RNNM, 171/144, l. 27.

68 Myaskovsky to Asafiev, 5 December 1924, RGALI, 2658/1/140, ll. 26–260b.

the possibility that different musical repertories might evolve for different kinds of audience or that working-class listeners might develop an appreciation of contemporary classical music in time, as they gained experience of attending concerts and as educational opportunities improved. His position was not only poorly thought-out but demonstrated little capacity to offer an imaginative vision of how Soviet composition might develop.

Myaskovsky's letter to Asafiev was friendly in tone: he made his disagreement clear but was evidently anxious to keep the peace. His affection for his old acquaintance and understanding of his excitable, highly strung disposition inclined him to take a forbearing attitude. (As he remarked to Nicolai Malko a few years later, he believed Asafiev to be fundamentally sincere, but someone who 'easily gets carried away, so readily hurtles to extremes of ecstasy and indignation'.[69]) He might have reacted rather differently if he had known of the disparaging manner in which Asafiev spoke about him to others. Although Asafiev sent an emollient reply, claiming rather implausibly that he had been misunderstood ('Just because there are thoughts that are comprehensible to the masses, must we burn Kant? Nowhere do I say that'), he did not retract his opinions. Two days later he penned a melodramatic letter to Lamm in which he declared himself to have been so wounded by the accusation of opportunism that he was considering giving up writing altogether: he claimed that he had simply been trying to confront composers with some unpalatable truths.[70]

In the meantime, he had been in discussions with Derzhanovsky about publishing further articles in a similar vein and his plan to send some of them (including 'Composers, Hurry Up!') to Lunacharsky.[71] Derzhanovsky responded enthusiastically, telling Asafiev that the time was ripe to enlist Lunacharsky's support for their efforts to institute a thoroughgoing reform of musical life:

> I am completely willing to aid and abet you. We need to conduct a theoretical propaganda campaign (through publications) as well as a practical one (by acting as nanny to suitably disposed composers). . . . We need to gain power and influence in official circles and push the same policy there. . . . Why don't you press Lunacharsky more strongly if he's that amenable to your influence? Why don't you drive home that you'll only be able to get things moving if he gives you the necessary authority?

The best way to change composers' attitudes, he argued, was to start by working on Myaskovsky. If he could be brought round, other composers would follow suit because of his prestige. He outlined a strategy to

69 Myaskovsky to Nicolai Malko, 30 May 1930, RNNM, 71/783, l. 10b.
70 Asafiev to Lamm, 10 December 1924, RGALI, 2743/1/76, ll. 20–2.
71 Asafiev to Derzhanovsky, 2 December 1924, RNNM, 3/761, 10b.

coax Myaskovsky into becoming a 'revolutionary' composer: he would first encourage him to resume work on his abandoned opera *The Idiot* and then arrange to commission another on an explicitly ideological topic. He also hoped that Lunacharsky would agree to institute 'strong Party control' in theatres and concert organisations to ensure that suitable repertoire would be performed – and install Asafiev, Saradzhev, and himself in key positions.[72]

Derzhanovsky's fantasies suggest not only a less than astute understanding of Myaskovsky's temperament but also a remarkable political naivety. Myaskovsky was not so easily manipulated as Derzhanovsky seemed to think; and even in the unlikely event that he could be persuaded to complete *The Idiot*, it was inconceivable that an opera on such a subject would be performed. (Soviet censors repeatedly blocked theatrical adaptations of Dostoyevsky's novels from being staged during the 1920s.[73]) 'Strong Party control' of musical organisations was already being implemented, but its effects on musical life would be far from beneficent. Derzhanovsky's scheming came to nothing: he had completely overestimated Asafiev's influence in government circles. He duly sent a selection of Asafiev's essays to Lunacharsky, together with a document outlining proposals of his own, only to receive a courteous, but wholly predictable response – a vague undertaking to consider the contents when time permitted. The minister was disinclined to be too proscriptive in matters of cultural policy for fear of alienating the intelligentsia: he refrained from demanding overt political engagement from artists, preferring to maintain his gradualist approach.[74]

Asafiev's journalistic campaign promptly ground to a halt. Roslavets categorically refused to accept any more of his articles because of their 'demagoguery'.[75] (As it transpired, *Musical Culture* was shut down at the end of the year, so they would not have been published in any case.) Belyayev and Lamm similarly objected to further contributions of this kind appearing in *Modern Music*. They not only took exception to the essays' content and tone, which were uncomfortably reminiscent of the attitudes and rhetoric characteristic of the Association of Proletarian Musicians[76], but were even

---

72　Derzhanovsky to Asafiev, 5 December 1924, RGALI, 2658/2/45, ll. 5–8ob.

73　Blyum, *Za kulisami "Ministerstva pravdi"*, 181.

74　Derzhanovsky sent Asafiev a handwritten copy of Lunacharsky's letter, which is dated 29 December 1924: RGALI, 2658/2/45, ll. 300b–1.

75　Derzhanovsky to Asafiev, 16–17 December 1924, RGALI, 2658/1/542, ll. 70b–8. Two of the unpublished essays appeared in the Ukrainian-language journal *Muzika* the following year (see fn66 above).

76　Asafiev's sneering references to artistic 'high priests' (*zhretsi*), for example, echo a derogatory term commonly used by musicians associated with APM: see, for example, 'Obrashcheniye gruppï professorov Moskovskoy gosudarstvennoy konservatorii', *Muzikal'naya nov'*, 4 (1924), 21–2.

more outraged by Derzhanovsky's attempt to compromise ASM's apolitical stance and his complicity in publishing polemics directed against his ASM colleagues in the association's own journal. Derzhanovsky was summoned to a very tense meeting of ASM's executive committee, at which Lamm challenged him about his behaviour: having upbraided Derzhanovsky at a previous meeting for publishing the 'Crisis of Personal Creativity' without consulting anyone, he was deeply angered when 'Composers, Hurry Up!' appeared. Derzhanovsky was unrepentant and declined to give an undertaking not to publish similar polemical pieces by Asafiev again. Myaskovsky attempted to act as peacemaker but found himself in a difficult position. Although he objected to Asafiev's views, he also objected as a matter of principle to censoring their expression: accordingly, he proposed that any further contributions of this kind should be printed as a supplement to the journal, as a way of indicating that Asafiev was writing in a purely personal capacity rather than on behalf of ASM. Derzhanovsky scorned this suggestion and the meeting broke up inconclusively. Nonetheless, it soon became clear to him that his position in ASM had become untenable.[77] His actions brought the organisation close to splitting – several members of the executive committee, including Pavel Lamm, were minded to resign.

In the end, it was Derzhanovsky who resigned, though he remained long enough to oversee a series of four symphony concerts that the association managed to put on in February and March 1925, thanks to the willingness of a Moscow theatre orchestra to lend its services on the basis that it would receive all the proceeds from ticket sales.[78] The orchestra (from the Theatre of the Revolution) was mediocre[79], but it was better than nothing. Under Saradzhev's direction, it gave the long-delayed premieres of Myaskovsky's Fourth and Seventh Symphonies on 8 February; the programmes for the second and third concerts comprised works by Goedicke, Aleksandrov, Dmitry Melkikh (an *habitué* of Lamm's musical evenings), and Lev Knipper (ASM's Secretary); the fourth, on 29 March, featured the Soviet premiere of Prokofiev's Third Piano Concerto, with Samuil Feinberg as soloist. His task completed, Derzhanovsky left the editorial board of *Modern Music* and distanced himself from ASM for almost two years.[80] The difficulties with Asafiev were smoothed over sufficiently to make it possible for him to contribute a

77 Koposova-Derzhanovskaya, 'V. V. Derzhanovskiy po vospominaniyam zhenï i druga', RNMM, 3/3365, ll. 49–50.

78 Myaskovsky to Steinberg, 4 April 1925, RIII, 28/1/487, l. 8.

79 Myaskovsky to Prokofiev, 3 February 1925, in Kozlova and Yatsenko, *Perepiska*, 209.

80 In a letter to Asafiev of 21 October 1925, Derzhanovsky explained that the unwillingness of Belyayev, Myaskovsky, and others to appoint his wife to ASM's committee of founder-members had been an additional reason for his departure: GABT, KP-3500/621, ll. 1–3.

short article, 'The Construction of the Modern Symphony', to the first issue of *Modern Music* for 1925, the concluding paragraphs of which were devoted to Myaskovsky. He took pains to characterise Myaskovsky's recent work in more positive terms, averring that it suggested a move away from 'egotistical preoccupation with personal experiences'. (The editors elicited a second piece on the Fourth and Seventh Symphonies for the next issue, but ironically, the censor refused to pass it for publication, objecting to Asafiev's 'excessive praise' of a 'White-Guardist composer' – in other words, one hostile to the regime.[81]) On the face of it, harmony had been restored, but the underlying strains in his relationship with Myaskovsky persisted.

For the time being, Myaskovsky's creative autonomy was not seriously threatened, despite the first signs of peer pressure from colleagues: he could continue to compose as he wished. The authorities kept a watchful eye on literature and the other arts, but as yet refrained from direct interference. Trotsky's book *Literature and Revolution*, published in 1923 to rapturous acclaim, argued for tolerance of so-called 'fellow travellers', provided these non-communist members of the artistic community did not pursue 'overtly noxious, debauched tendencies'.[82] Notwithstanding Trotsky's increasingly beleaguered position, Party edicts took a similar line in the face of considerable pressure from self-styled 'proletarian' artistic organisations. A resolution passed at the Party's Thirteenth Congress in May 1924 expressed support for the 'most gifted' fellow travellers, emphasising that no one 'tendency, school, or group' was entitled to claim that it 'speaks in the Party's name'.[83] Even more pointedly, a Central Committee resolution 'On Party Policy in the Domain of Literature' promulgated in July of the following year advocated a 'considerate' and 'patient' attitude towards fellow travellers and the 'free competition of different [artistic] groups and tendencies', while reaffirming the Party's desire to foster a committedly socialist literature.[84] Reassuring as this was, there was no telling how long the policy might continue.

Unlike Asafiev, Myaskovsky took no part in the debates about the future of Soviet musical culture at this period. Nor was he tempted to resume his pre-war journalistic activity: after contributing a handful of reviews of new scores to *Musical Culture* and *Modern Music*, he ceased reviewing for good. He kept a low profile and avoided involvement in controversy, a strategy that he would maintain until the end of his life. His temperament demonstrated a remarkable self-containment. He was not professionally ambitious

81   Derzhanovsky to Asafiev, 16 March 1925, RGALI, 2658/2/45, l. 74.

82   Lev Trotskiy, *Literatura i revolyutsiya* (Moscow, 1991), 24.

83   *Trinadtsatïy s"ezd RKP(b): Stenografichskiy otchyot* (Moscow, 1963), 653.

84   'O politike partii v oblasti khudozhestvennoy literaturï (Rezolyutsiya TsK RKP(b))', *Pravda*, 1 July 1925.

and did not actively seek celebrity or positions of power. But while he could limit his contact with his environment, he could not avoid contact altogether or the frictions that contact engendered – not least, because of the necessity to make a living.

Notwithstanding the stabilisation of the Soviet economy during the NEP years, the circumstances for composers of serious music remained challenging.[85] Much as Myaskovsky would have liked to devote himself entirely to composition, he was unable to do so – even after becoming one of the small number of musicians deemed eligible in 1925 to receive a so-called 'academic maintenance grant' from the Central Commission for the Improvement of Specialists' Living Conditions (TsEKUBU[86]), a body established four years previously to alleviate the dire hardship experienced by the country's scientific and scholarly community. As a specialist ranked in the second-highest category of eminence he was awarded a monthly subsidy of sixty roubles.[87] This sum was insufficient for his needs, modest though they were, as his sisters and their children remained partially dependent on his financial support.

His earnings from composition were not only meagre but also too erratic to constitute a dependable regular source of income. State schemes to commission musical compositions did not yet exist. New legislation was being developed to protect copyright and regulate payment of royalties[88], but his work was performed too infrequently during the first half of the 1920s to generate much revenue. (His royalty statement for 1925, for example, records a payment of ten roubles and thirty-seven kopeks for the performances of his Fourth and Seventh Symphonies at the ASM concert on 8 February.[89] A kilogramme of beef typically cost just under a rouble in

---

85 A detailed study of Soviet composers' material circumstances is as yet lacking, as are comprehensive studies of the economics of music publishing and the performance and promotion of contemporary classical music during the first decades of Soviet power.

86 For details of TsEKUBU's maintenance grants, see *Pyat' let raboti Tsentral'noy komissii po uluchsheniyu bïta uchyonïkh pri Sovete narodnïkh komissarov RSFSR (TsEKUBU), 1921–1926* (Moscow, 1927), 17–18.

87 'Kratkaya spravka TsKUBU po vïdache akademicheskogo obespecheniya, posibiy i po premirovaniyu akademicheskikh trudov' [undated, 1926], GARF, 4737/1/197, ll. 22–220b, 24. The other musicians listed included Glière and Goldenweiser.

88 Valentin Melik-Khaspabov, *Sbornik zakonov i postanovleniy (partiynïkh, profsoyuznïkh i sovetskikh) o trude rabotnikov iskusstv i khudozhestvennom proizvodstve* (Moscow, 1925), 46–7, 91–4.

89 Royalty statement from Moscow Society of Dramatists and Composers (MODPiK) for April–October 1925, RGALI, 2040/2/325, l. 1.

Moscow in 1926; a litre of sunflower oil – around fifty kopeks.[90]) Revenues from publication of his work were similarly small. The private music publishers that operated before the Revolution had all been absorbed into the Music Section of the state publishing house (now renamed Muzsektor), giving it a monopoly. Although it had resumed publishing serious music by the spring of 1924 after issuing little but agitprop songs and marches since Lamm's departure, the engravers had to work their way through a large backlog of accumulated submissions. Myaskovsky informed Steinberg in December 1924 that Vasilenko's Second Symphony had just been brought out after a delay of six years.[91] The press's sluggish production tempo picked up somewhat, but letters to Myaskovsky from colleagues suggest that its efficiency left much to be desired: they complained of poor communication, long unexplained hold-ups, and shoddy production standards.[92]

In circumstances such as these, it is readily understandable why all composers had to find other ways of supporting themselves – in Myaskovsky's case, by part-time posts teaching at the conservatoire and working for Muzsektor as a reader, with responsibility for selecting music by living composers and deciding on the order of production. (Ironically, his employment by Muzsektor further limited opportunities to publish his own work: as he explained to Prokofiev, he felt that it placed him in an invidious position and was anxious to avoid perceptions of a conflict of interest.[93] After the press brought out his Fifth Symphony at the end of 1923, he withdrew the Third from the production schedule and had nothing else published by Muzsektor for over two years.[94]) Remarks in his correspondence indicate that Myaskovsky found aspects of both jobs rather trying – not so much on account of the work itself, but because of increasing bureaucratic interference and ideological pressures. Even before the Revolution, his high-minded artistic outlook had often caused him to feel at odds with his professional milieu: the circumstances of Soviet life rendered that tension even more acute. Soviet power began to demand an increasing degree of behavioural accommodation in the workplace and to punish nonconformity. Individuals' freedom of manoeuvre did not necessarily disappear

90　*Moskva i moskovskaya oblast' 1926/27–1928/29. Statistiko-èkonomicheskiy spravochnik po okrugam* (Moscow, 1930), 374–5.

91　Myaskovsky to Steinberg, 25 December 1924, RIII, 28/1/487, ll. 4–40b.

92　In November 1925, for example, the young Ukrainian composer Boris Lyatoshinsky informed Myaskovsky that he had just received the proofs of a piano sonata after an eighteen-month delay, only to discover they were riddled with mistakes: Lyatoshinsky to Myaskovsky, 5 and 8 November 1925, RGALI, 2040/1/132, ll. 7–80b and 10–11.

93　Myaskovsky to Prokofiev, 11 May 1924, in Kozlova and Yatsenko, *Perepiska*, 193.

94　Myaskovsky to Steinberg, 25 December 1924, RIII, 28/1/487, l. 40b.

altogether, but the choices available to them were not always very palatable. For Myaskovsky, as for other fellow-traveller artists and intellectuals, evolving a *modus vivendi* with Soviet power demanded a strenuous effort of adjustment, especially when it came to their work in institutional contexts.

This is illustrated by his responses to unsettling developments at the Moscow Conservatoire during the summer of 1924, in which he became involved after being appointed to the State Academic Council (GUS[95]) in May of that year.[96] The Council, which had been established under the aegis of Narkompros in 1919, was responsible for directing state policy in the domains of the arts and sciences, and for overseeing higher education in these areas. Myaskovsky found himself in distinguished company, as the council's members included leading intellectual and artistic figures. His motivation for accepting the invitation is not clear, but it was probably because of the potential benefit to ASM. The responsibilities defined in GUS's charter gave it significant influence over musical institutions and organisations even if they were not technically within its jurisdiction, and his membership afforded an opportunity to represent the association's interests.[97] (Amongst other things, GUS's support would prove valuable when ASM began to organise promotional activities abroad.) The Music Subdivision of GUS's Artistic Division was chaired by Yavorsky. Over the previous two years, a major focus of its attention had been the implementation of the latter's proposals to overhaul the structure of the country's conservatoires and their curricula.[98] Soon after Myaskovsky joined, it was presented with an additional task – considering the outcome of an 'academic review' of Moscow Conservatoire staff members, undertaken as part of a nationwide appraisal of teaching personnel and students at higher educational establishments initiated by the government earlier that year. The ostensible purpose of the exercise was to raise academic standards and to ease the financial strains on institutions by reducing student numbers: during the Civil War years they had been placed under pressure to accept more applicants from peasant and proletarian backgrounds, many of whom turned out to be inadequately equipped for third-level study. An equally

95 *Gosudarstvennïy uchyonïy sovet.*

96 'Posluzhnoy spisok', RGALI, 2040/1/168, l. 7ob.

97 On GUS's role in musical life at this period and the background to the events described here, see Amy Nelson, *Music for the Revolution: Musicians and Power in Early Soviet Russia* (University Park, Pennsylvania, 2004), 130–49.

98 The proposed reforms are detailed in Viktor Belyayev (ed.), *Uchebnïye planï muzïkal'no-uchebnïkh zavedeniy RSFSR* (Moscow, 1924). See also: Ginzburg (ed.), *Moskovskaya konservatoriya 1866–1966*, 294–7; Lev Barenboim (ed.), *Iz istorii sovetskogo muzïkal'nogo obrazovaniya: Sbornik materialov i dokumentov, 1917–1927* (Leningrad, 1969), 226–33.

important motivation, however, was to purge them of 'counterrevolutionary elements'.[99]

At the Moscow Conservatoire, a list of staff members proposed for dismissal had been drawn up by representatives of the so-called 'Faction of Red
Professors', based on recommendations from student Party activists. After
being considered by the conservatoire's Board of Studies and Narkompros's
Central Directorate of Professional Education (Glavprofobr), the list was
tabled for discussion at a meeting of GUS's Music Subdivision on 15 July, as
the responsibility for confirming and terminating staff appointments ultimately lay with the council.[100] In addition to Yavorsky and Myaskovsky,
the meeting was attended by Goldenweiser, present in his capacity as the
conservatoire's rector, and two of the principal organisers of the purge –
Nadezhda Bryusova, sister of the symbolist poet and a prominent figure
in adult music education, and Pyotr Smilga, a violinist on the conservatoire's diploma course.[101] Goldenweiser protested at the manner in which
the list had been compiled and abstained from the proceedings: although
the finalised version may well have included teachers of dubious quality, previous ones had featured the names of prominent musicians such
as Saradzhev and the pianist Yelena Bekman-Shcherbina – a clear indication of the purge's political motivation. Bryusova and Smilga peremp-
torily dismissed Goldenweiser's objections and pushed for the list to be
approved. Yavorsky's position was complicated by his close professional
relationship to Bryusova, who was a long-standing disciple and enthusiastic
proponent of his theories. Myaskovsky's position was also delicate, as the
conservatoire activists were plainly hostile towards him. Nonetheless, he
too raised objections. Yavorsky told Derzhanovsky afterwards that he had
been impressed by Myaskovsky's 'calm and dignified tone': his self-possession unsettled Bryusova, who became visibly flustered.[102] Although the
meeting was merely an exercise in rubber-stamping and Myaskovsky was
powerless to influence the outcome, he found it a disturbing experience.

99 On the 1924 student purges, see Sheila Fitzpatrick, *Education and Social
    Mobility in the Soviet Union 1921–1934* (Cambridge, 1979), 97–105; Peter
    Konecny, 'Chaos on Campus: The 1924 Student *Proverka* in Leningrad',
    Europe-Asia Studies 4 (1994), 617–35.

100 See 'Polozheniye o Gosudarstvennom uchyonom sovete, 15 marta 1923g.',
    in Konstantin Ostrovityanov *et al.* (ed.), *Organizatsiya nauki v pervïye godï
    sovetskoy vlasti (1917–1925): Sbornik dokumentov* (Leningrad, 1968), 41.

101 On Bryusova, see Viktor Belïy, 'Vïdayushchiysya deyatel' muzïkal'nogo
    prosveshcheniya', *Sovetskaya muzïka*, 9 (1951), 58–60. Smilga's reminiscences
    about his student years describe the growing number of Party and Komsomol
    activists at the conservatoire in the 1920s: 'Iz vospominaniy o Moskovskoy
    konservatorii dvadtsatïkh godov', in Yekaterina Alekseyeva *et al.* (ed.),
    Vospominaniya o Moskovskoy konservatorii (Moscow, 1966), 216–28.

102 Derzhanovsky to Myaskovsky, 17 July 1924, RGALI, 2040/1/114, ll. 11–12.

The following day, he sent a note to Yavorsky tendering his resignation. 'I have absolutely no aptitude for any kind of public service', he wrote, 'I lack the necessary qualities … I cannot get to grips with events and situations sufficiently quickly'.[103] Derzhanovsky, who delivered this missive by hand, reported that Yavorsky read it with visible amusement: he was clearly not taken in by these disclaimers. It would not be the last time that Myaskovsky had recourse to such excuses when he needed to extricate himself from difficult situations.

Myaskovsky's modesty and courtesy were unquestionably authentic character traits, but he also deployed them skilfully for self-protective purposes. The fact that his name did not feature amongst the list of staff members to be purged testifies to his shrewdness in dealing with colleagues and students, but also to his standing within the conservatoire. After the premiere of the Sixth Symphony, young composers increasingly sought him as a mentor. At the end of the 1924–5 academic year he had fifteen students in his class[104], a number that increased when he took on many of Catoire's pupils after the latter's death in May 1926.[105] By then, he was regarded as the conservatoire's leading composition teacher. Between 1924 and 1944, thirty-seven students would graduate under his supervision, and his class was attended by half as many again who for one reason or another did not take the composition diploma course in its entirety.[106] The conservatoire's patchy institutional records for the 1920s reveal little about his activities and conditions of employment[107], but a wage-book from 1928 preserved amongst his personal papers indicates that he was paid 140 roubles a month for 6 contact hours a week, which seems to have been his customary teaching load by the later 1920s.[108] He was evidently expected to undertake additional duties, such as sitting on examination and audition panels.

103 Myaskovsky to Yavorsky, 16 July 1924, RNNM, 146/2174.

104 Myaskovsky to Prokofiev, 28 June 1925, in Kozlova and Yatsenko, *Perepiska*, 215.

105 Vissarion Shebalin, 'Myaskovskiy-uchitel'', *Sovetskaya muzïka*, 4 (1941), 47.

106 Myaskovsky's list of his students between 1921 and 1944, RGALI, 2040/4/14, ll. 1–10b.

107 The materials in Myaskovsky's personnel file in the Moscow Conservatoire Archive (AMG, 1/23/84) date from after 1943. The records for the 1920s and 1930s in the portion of the conservatoire archive now housed in RGALI (fond 658) are very incomplete.

108 RGALI, 2040/1/167, ll. 11–120b. The account books recording his income and expenditure that the composer started to keep in 1927 show his average monthly income from the conservatoire after tax as 117 roubles that year ('Prikhodno-raskhodnïye tetradi', RGALI, 2040/1/67, ll. 1–6). Subsequent entries suggest that his workload remained at this level for the rest of the 1920s.

Several of Myaskovsky's pupils during the 1920s went on to make national and international reputations. Amongst them were Alexander Veprik (1899–1958), who graduated in 1924 and wrote works on Jewish subjects that received performances in Germany and in the United States; and Alexander Mosolov (1900–73), who graduated two years later, chiefly remembered now for his 'constructivist' piano and orchestral compositions of the 1920s. Other pupils of note included Vissarion Shebalin (1902–63), to whom Myaskovsky became particularly close, Dmitry Kabalevsky (1904–87), and Aram Khachaturian (1903–78), who would join his class in 1929. Like many of his colleagues, Myaskovsky often taught his students at home. As was customary at the time, they attended in small groups, so that each could learn from the discussions of work by others. Even when one makes due allowance for the idealising tendency frequently encountered in former students' reminiscences of their teachers, it is evident that Myaskovsky won admiration not only for his competence and erudition but also for his personal qualities. He set his charges high standards of professionalism and commitment: they were expected not only to be productive but to use their initiative in developing their craftsmanship and technique. He attached particular importance to acquiring a detailed knowledge of the musical literature and a breadth of general culture. When they played their work for him, they were impressed by the attentiveness of his listening: he seldom commented at length, but his observations were focussed and perspicacious. He was less interested in the finer details of a composition's workmanship than the quality of the musical material and its treatment. For the most part, he would concentrate on structural aspects – unsatisfactory proportions, climaxes that arrived too soon, ineffective tonal moves. He would hint at possible remedies, but without being proscriptive: not infrequently, he would take down scores from his library shelves to illustrate how other composers had dealt with similar technical problems. Students were encouraged to reflect on the underlying principles and to work out their own solutions independently. Members of his class repeatedly recalled his respect for their creative individuality: he never tried to force them to write in any particular way and was open-minded in matters of style and compositional idiom. Neither did he encourage them to experiment solely for experiment's sake: he disliked music that struck him as contrived.[109]

109 This account of Myaskovsky as teacher draws on the following reminiscences by composers who studied with him in the 1920s: Shebalin, 'Myaskovskiy-uchitel''; idem, 'Iz vospominaniy o Nikolaye Yakovleviche Myaskovskom,' in Shlifshteyn (ed.), *N. Ya. Myaskovskiy: Sobraniye materialo*, vol. 1, 276–97; Aram Khachaturyan, 'Iz vospominaniy', ibid., 298–306; Dmitriy Kabalevsky, 'O N. Ya. Myaskovskom', ibid., 307–33; Vladimir Fere, 'Nash uchitel' Nikolay Yakovlevich Myaskovskiy (stranitsï vospominaniya)', in Alekseyeva et al. (ed.), *Vospominaniya o Moskovskoy konservatorii*, 418–39.

FIGURE 7.2. Myaskovsky with his students
Vladimir Fere (left) and Dmitry Kabalevsky (right).

His reputation for unsociability notwithstanding, Myaskovsky's students found him kind and helpful. Unlike his own composition teacher
Lyadov, he always treated them with impeccable politeness and never
sought to humiliate them. If he had to express criticisms, he preferred to
do so obliquely: the pupil had to be alert to the implications of his delicately
phrased observations. When he taught at home, he would sometimes invite
students to stay for tea if he was not too busy: on these occasions, the conversation would broaden out into discussion of literature and other topics.
He was also supportive in practical ways – arranging performances of their
work, and later, assisting with its publication. Shebalin gratefully remembered Myaskovsky's intervention in his defence during the 1924 student
purge, when he was threatened with expulsion. More generally, his students
appreciated the stimulating environment that he helped to create and to
sustain – the ASM concerts, the musical evenings at Pavel Lamm's and the
Derzhanovskys'. His intense love of music made a deep impression, as did
the simplicity with which he lived and his complete lack of pretentiousness and self-importance: Kabalevsky's classmate Vladimir Fere noted his
reluctance to discuss his own compositions and his visible discomfiture on
receiving compliments. His manifest selflessness and unworldliness deepened the regard in which he was held – despite mounting complaints from

student activists about the apolitical atmosphere at the conservatoire. It is noteworthy that even one of the most vociferous of these, the young Ukrainian composer Alexander Davidenko (1899–1934), spoke of him with respect.[110] A number of Myaskovsky's students, including Kabalevsky, joined Prokoll[111], a 'production collective' set up by Davidenko to create a repertoire of agitprop works – principally choral music to political texts for performance by proletarian amateur music groups.[112] There is no evidence that they did so at Myaskovsky's suggestion, but their involvement probably helped to maintain amicable relations.

On the whole, he seems to have managed matters at the conservatoire adroitly, though he found teaching rather a strain, in spite of having capable students. His work for the state publishing house was a more taxing test of his diplomatic skills and reserves of patience. Once again, Muzsektor's records are too incomplete to enable his activities to be reconstructed in detail[113], but an employment contract for a three-month period in 1928 survives which gives an indication of his typical duties and the level of remuneration. In return for a monthly salary of two hundred roubles, he was required to report on the suitability for publication of new compositions submitted to the press, reviewing a minimum of three hundred pages of score per month, and to proofread publications of Russian music up to a limit of four hundred pages per month.[114] The work itself was straightforward: the job's more frustrating aspects arose from Muzsektor's lack of a coherent publishing strategy and the difficulties created by censorship. As Myaskovsky confided to Steinberg in January 1925, he found the situation so dispiriting that he was actively thinking of leaving. There was considerable opposition to publishing contemporary classical music at all: 'reforms' of Muzsektor's activities were regularly instituted in an attempt to halt it altogether. He could consequently never be sure that the works he recommended for acceptance would actually make their way into print.[115]

110 See Boris Shekhter, 'Godï tvorcheskogo obshcheniya', in Nikolay Martïnov (ed.), *Aleksander Davidenko: Vospominaniya, stat'i, materialï* (Leningrad, 1968), 45.

111 'Proizvodstvennïy kollektiv studentov-kompozitorov Moskovskoy konservatorii'.

112 Vladimir Fere, 'V Moskovskoy konservatorii dvadtsatïkh godov (po lichnïm vospominaniyam)', in Alekseyeva *et al.* (ed.), *Vospominaniya o Moskovskoy konservatorii*, 234–36.

113 The materials preserved in the State Music Publisher archive in RGALI (fond 653) mostly comprise musical manuscripts and published scores. The documentation of the press's operations is very fragmentary: there are no records from the 1920s.

114 RGALI, 2040/4/21. Myaskovsky's account books (see fn108 above) show that Muzsektor paid him at this rate from 1927 to 1930.

115 Myaskovsky to Steinberg, 29 January 1925, RIII, 28/1/487, l. 5.

He continued to work for the press, but the unsatisfactory state of affairs there led him to explore the possibility of publishing his work abroad. The problem was not merely that Muzsektor was inefficient: it did little to encourage performances of the music in its catalogue or even to distribute it. (During his visit to Russia in 1926, the Italian composer Alfredo Casella was surprised at how few scores by Soviet composers were stocked in music shops.[116]) As it was, Myaskovsky's compositions were infrequently performed at home; and although there were signs of interest in his work abroad – in June 1924 Prokofiev relayed the news that Siloti had drawn Leopold Stokowski's attention to the Fifth Symphony[117]– it would be slow to come to prominence outside Russia unless a foreign publisher helped to promote it. Myaskovsky was less concerned with his international reputation than his pressing need to earn more money so that he could secure better living conditions. Life in a communal apartment had become increasingly intolerable: apart from all the other inconveniences, the lack of privacy made it very difficult to compose. Steinberg marvelled that he managed to write anything at all under such circumstances[118]: the Eighth Symphony, which he completed in draft in September 1924, had mostly been sketched during snatched visits to the countryside earlier in the year.[119] Although the restrictions on living space were eased in 1925 to allow writers and artists avail of an additional room for use as a study, this was not always easy to arrange in practice. The right to single-family occupancy of an apartment was still mostly restricted to senior Party functionaries: most members of the artistic and intellectual elite did not yet enjoy this privilege, which only started to be extended more widely after 1932.[120] With the advent of NEP, however, the Central Committee promulgated a resolution permitting the formation of housing cooperatives to construct apartment buildings with private capital – a measure intended to alleviate the dire shortage of accommodation in major urban centres. In 1924 alone, over two hundred such cooperatives were set up in Moscow.[121] At the suggestion of Dmitry Melkikh, Myaskovsky joined one of them and began to make strenuous efforts to save sufficient money to place a deposit on an

---

116 'Il mio diario russo', in Alfredo Casella, *21 + 26* (Rome, 1931), 164–5.

117 Prokofiev to Myaskovsky, 1 June 1924, in Kozlova and Yatsenko, *Perepiska*, 196.

118 Steinberg to Myaskovsky, 8 December 1924, RGALI, 2040/2/281, l. 3.

119 'Vïpiski', entries for 27 January and 20 April 1924, RGALI, 2040/1/65, l. 40b; Myaskovsky to Asafiev, 30 March 1924, RGALI, 2658/2/50, ll. 8–80b.

120 See Mervyn Matthews, *Privilege in the Soviet Union: A Study of Elite Life-Styles under Communism* (London, 1978), 75–78; Nataliya Lebina, *Sovetskaya povsednevnost': Normï i anomalii*, 3rd ed. (Moscow, 2018), 106–13.

121 On the origins of Soviet housing cooperatives in the 1920s, see Mark Meyerovich, *Rozhdeniye i smert' zhilishchnoy kooperatsii: Zhilishchnaya politika v SSSR 1924–1937gg.* (Irkurtsk, 2004), 10–73.

apartment in a planned new development.[122] His anticipated initial outlay was eight thousand roubles, a sizeable sum that it would take him several years to accumulate.[123] He consequently had a strong practical incentive to try to maximise his earnings from composition.

Thanks to the foreign contacts that Derzhanovsky made through his work for the music section of International Books, an opportunity arose in 1924 to form a connection with Universal Edition. Under the directorship of Emil Hertzka, the Viennese firm became one of the leading international publishers of modern music: its catalogue included works by Schoenberg, Berg, Delius, Bartók, Szymanowski, and many other notable figures. By fortunate coincidence, Universal Edition had recently appointed a Russian-speaking staff member to its Vienna office – Abram Dzimitrovsky, a musician of Lithuanian-Jewish origin who had studied at the Vienna Conservatoire and worked for some time in Kiev before emigrating in 1922.[124] Derzhanovsky and he began to correspond in the spring of 1923. International Books undertook to act as Universal Edition's agent in Soviet Russia, and the firm in turn expressed interest in publishing Soviet music – starting with the work of Myaskovsky.[125] In May 1924, Derzhanovsky relayed its offer to sign him up. Myaskovsky was strongly tempted but objected to the terms, which he described to Prokofiev as 'shark-like'.[126] To his disappointment, Universal Edition did not immediately commit to publishing the Sixth Symphony: instead, it proposed to issue some of his smaller-scale works – *Silence*, the song-cycle *Madrigal* – and offered him a contract affording it the right of first refusal for any songs, piano works, and chamber works that he might write for the next five years in return for 15 percent of the profits from sales of any scores accepted for publication.[127] Prokofiev

122 Lamm, *Stranitsï*, 15. The year in which Myaskovsky joined the cooperative is not known, but a diary entry records that he began to save his earnings from composition to accumulate the deposit 'starting with the Eighth Symphony and even earlier': 'Vïpiski', 21 July 1930, RGALI, 2040/1/65, l. 7.

123 Myaskovsky to Prokofiev, 25 June 1929, in Kozlova and Yatsenko, *Perepiska*, 314.

124 Inna Barsova, 'Sotrudnichestvo i perepiska dvukh izdatel'stv: Universal Edition i Muzsektora Gosizdata v 20–30-ye godï: Vzglyad iz Venï', in Larissa Ivanova (ed.), *Muzïkal'noye prinosheniye: Sbornik statey k 75-letiyu Ye. A. Ruch'yevskoy* (St Petersburg, 1998), 255.

125 See Olesya Bobrik, *Venskoye izdatel'stvo 'Universal Edition' i muzïkantï iz sovetskoy Rossii* (St Petersburg, 2011), 86–93.

126 Myaskovsky to Prokofiev, 11 May and 24 October 1924, in Kozlova and Yatsenko, *Perepiska*, 193, 202.

127 A copy of the contract has not come to light either amongst Myaskovsky's papers or in what survives of the archive of Universal Edition's Viennese office (uncatalogued collection, WR), much of which was destroyed in the 1930s. Its terms can be discerned from Myaskovsky's letter to Prokofiev of 24 October

assured him that the terms were not disadvantageous and emphasised the benefits of being represented by an enterprising and energetic publisher which was well-placed to promote his music internationally.[128] He eventually signed the contract[129] and managed to conclude a separate agreement to publish miniature and full scores of the Sixth[130], but was deeply suspicious of Universal Edition's reluctance to pay an advance for major orchestral works – unlike Muzsektor, which adhered to the pre-Revolutionary practice of paying an advance for the first printing of a score, with any subsequent reprintings being reimbursed at a lower rate. (When he signed a contract with Muzsektor for the Fourth Symphony in January 1926, for example, he received 879 roubles and 40 kopeks for an estimated initial print run of 600 scores.[131]) This was not standard practice abroad: the revenues that publishers earned from orchestral works principally derived from the hire of materials rather than sales of scores.

Myaskovsky's mistrust of Universal Edition never dissipated fully, but his association with the firm was unquestionably beneficial. It would continue to publish his work until the early 1930s (at first independently and later in association with Muzsektor) and had considerable success in arranging performances in Europe and the United States. Dzimitrovsky kept up a voluminous correspondence with him throughout this period, reporting regularly on the firm's efforts on his behalf.[132] Universal Edition launched its publicity campaign for the new Russian works in its catalogue with a special issue of its house journal *Musikblätter des Anbruch* in March 1925[133] – an initiative prompted by Belyayev, who took an active role in developing ASM's foreign connections. The previous October, the association had sent him to Vienna to organise two concerts of modern Russian music as part of a festival in the Austrian capital (the second concert, which took place on 6 November, included a performance of Myaskovsky's Third Piano Sonata by Friedrich

---

1924 (see fn126 above) and a letter from Dzimitrovsky to Myaskovsky of 22 November 1924 (RGALI, 2040/2/140, ll. 2–30b).

128 Prokofiev to Myaskovsky, 1 June and 9 November 1924, in Kozlova and Yatsenko, *Perepiska*, 195, 205.

129 Myaskovsky to Prokofiev, 3 February 1925, ibid., 209.

130 Dzimitrovsky to Myaskovsky, 18 December 1924, RGALI, 2040/2/140, ll. 4–40b.

131 Muzsektor publication contract for Fourth Symphony (dated 26 January 1926), RGALI, 2040/2/323, ll. 7–70b.

132 Dzimitrovsky's letters to Myaskovsky between 1924 and 1940 are in RGALI, 2040/2/140–3. There are evident lacunae in the collection. Myaskovsky's letters to Dzimitrovsky and other Universal Edition personnel have all been lost except for two communications dating from 1929, both of which are preserved in the archive of Universal Edition's Vienna office (uncatalogued collection, WR).

133 *Russland: Sonderheft des Anbruch*, März 1925.

Wührer, a noted exponent of contemporary keyboard repertoire).[134] While there, he took the opportunity to meet Dzimitrovsky and his colleagues to explore possibilities for further promotional activities. Belyayev co-edited the special issue and helped to elicit contributions from his ASM associates. Myaskovsky was featured prominently as Soviet Russia's leading composer: his portrait photograph was used as the frontispiece, and he was the subject of two articles by Belyayev and Asafiev.

On the face of it, Myaskovsky had significantly greater cause for optimism about his circumstances in the spring of 1925 than a year previously. He seems to have taken surprisingly little pleasure in these encouraging developments, however, and remained in the grip of an ongoing depression: he complained of persistent exhaustion and low spirits, struggling to rouse himself to creative work. He escaped to the countryside for a fortnight's holiday in late June but returned unrefreshed. 'I did virtually nothing', he told Asafiev, 'but my nerves are as bad as ever – it seems that I've really gone to pieces'.[135] Derzhanovskaya confided to Asafiev that Myaskovsky 'looked awful' and worried that he was wearing himself out trying to earn extra money to support his relatives. There were also serious tensions in the background, she reported: ASM seemed on the verge of disintegrating; the director of Muzsektor, Alexander Yurovsky, had reacted furiously to the news that Myaskovsky signed a contract with Universal Edition and was making life difficult for Derzhanovsky as a result.[136] These strains would not have helped his mood, but the root causes of his depression lay deeper: perhaps the most important was a serious crisis of confidence in his abilities.

Prokofiev's scathing criticisms of the Fifth Symphony caused him to be assailed by fresh doubts about his creative direction. He had been particularly wounded by the insinuation, unjust though it was, that his work exemplified the dull academicism of the Rimsky-Korsakov school – stylistically *passé*, lacking in freshness and vitality. Having learned that Myaskovsky was planning another symphony, Prokofiev kept up the pressure on him to renovate his compositional idiom to make it respectably *à la mode*: he 'implored' him to make his orchestration more inventive and suggested that he think of writing for unconventional instrumental combinations, as Stravinsky and young French composers were now doing. He returned to the topic in subsequent missives, telling Myaskovsky that the lack of performances of new Western music in Soviet Russia did not excuse his failure to

134 Belyayev to Pavel Lamm, 18 October 1924, 2743/1/84 l. 20; Belyayev to
     Myaskovsky, 3 and 6 November 1924, RGALI, 2040/1/103, ll. 41, 42. The diary
     that Belyayev kept during his visit to Vienna is reproduced in Bobrik, *Venskoye
     izdatel'stvo Universal Edition*, 261–319.

135 Myaskovsky to Asafiev, 1 August 1925, RGALI, 2658/2/50, l. 30.

136 Derzhanovskaya to Asafiev, 9 September 1925, GABT, R-2252, KP3500/604, ll.
     1–20b.

be more stylistically innovative: he pointed out that his own *Scythian Suite* pre-dated the Revolution, but had proved capable of withstanding 'the most international of pressures'.[137]

'International pressures' were very much on Prokofiev's mind at the time, as he embarked on the Second Symphony, a self-consciously experimental score which he hoped would burnish his modernist credentials. Needless to say, his view of Myaskovsky's music cannot be accepted as a definitive judgement of its quality: like many artists, he found it difficult to engage sympathetically with work dissimilar to his own. Prokofiev consciously strove for vividness and arresting effect: he also coveted a reputation for daring and novelty. Myaskovsky's music reflects a very different sensibility, and he did not respond in the same way to the artistic ferment of the post-war era. Unlike Prokofiev, he had no ambition to lead international musical fashions or to style himself an iconoclast; nor does his work exhibit the reactions against Romanticism then prevalent. In seeking creative renewal, he was determined to pursue an independent path rather than imitate Western fashions. For the most part, his responses to contemporary Western music remained antipathetic, as they had been before the First World War – though there were a few notable exceptions, such as the work of Bartók, for which he had warm praise.[138] His dismissive comments about Western composers in his correspondence are sometimes of a startling vehemence – especially in view of his involvement in ASM. Writing to Prokofiev in August 1925, he remarked:

> I have formed a pretty dire picture of modern composition in Europe. The triviality and banality of the French and Italians (Ravel, Casella, Malipiero, Milhaud, Auric, Al[exander] Tcherepnin and so on; even Honegger seems more of a *petit maître* – look at [King] David); the unbelievable aridity and coarseness of the Germans (Hindemith, [Heinrich] Kaminski, even – Křenek, although he sometimes shows some personality) or the amorphously protoplasmic bloodlessness and beating-about-the-bush of Schoenberg and his litter – you simply do not know where to turn. And then there's Stravinsky, with his rubbish (has he lapsed into his second childhood?)![139]

A few months later, he commented *à propos* of the bewildering variety of contemporary musical fashions in Paris:

---

137 Prokofiev to Myaskovsky, 25 March and 1 June 1925, in Kozlova and Yatsenko, *Perepiska*, 188, 194.

138 In a letter to Asafiev of 19 December 1924, Myaskovsky had high praise for Bartók's first two string quartets: RGALI, 2658/2/50, l. 12.

139 Myaskovsky to Prokofiev, 16 August 1925, in Kozlova and Yatsenko, *Perepiska*, 219.

I am convinced that they have simply lost all sense in Paris – and not just common-sense. This war against Romanticism, the worship of the eighteenth century and simultaneously the adoration of Musorgsky, and in Germany of Mahler's vulgar sentimentality – all of this is such an absurdity, that it of itself is becoming Romantic. It is sickening to think of it. Sometimes I used to dream of taking a trip abroad, if only to feel the pulse of musical life and to hear you under proper conditions, but the thought of it makes my flesh creep [*beryot zhut'*] and induces something tantamount to revulsion.[140]

Extreme though these views were, Myaskovsky was by no means alone amongst his contemporaries in holding them. (Yavorsky, for example, considered the influence of Western modernism deeply harmful: in a letter of 1926, he excoriated Prokofiev and other young Russian composers for 'bowing down before the West' instead of 'creating what is innate in them'.[141]) It is also important to emphasise that his attitudes were not born of ignorance: he had an extensive selection of scores by Western modernists on his bookshelves and studied some of them closely.[142] They are most plausibly explained by the lingering influence of nineteenth-century Slavophile notions of Russian exceptionalism and concomitant suspicion of the West. Despite the official dominance of Marxism-Leninism, such outlooks persisted amongst the intelligentsia: in undated notes for a lecture delivered during the 1920s, the philosopher and literary critic Mikhail Bakhtin declared Slavophilism to be 'the most significant phenomenon in the history of Russian thought', deeming pro-Western intellectual currents a mere 'soap bubble that created nothing but chatter before bursting'.[143]

It is consequently unsurprising that the compositional idiom of the Eighth Symphony in A major, op. 26, owes little, if anything to contemporary Western modernist developments. In his 'Autobiographical Notes', Myaskovsky indicated that the symphony portrayed the deeds of the folk hero Stepan Razin, who led an uprising against the nobility and tsarist bureaucracy in 1670–1.[144] Although he elaborated on the details of this puta-

---

140 Myaskovsky to Prokofiev, 14 December 1925, ibid., 228–9.

141 Yavorsky to Sergey Protopopov, 16 May 1926, in Rabinovich, *Yavorskiy: stat'i, vospomianiya, perepiska*, 2nd ed. (Moscow, 1972), 343.

142 His diary entry for 2 September 1924, for example, reads: 'Studying Mahler and Schoenberg' (RGALI, 2040/1/65, l. 40b). The catalogue of his library prepared by Olga Lamm and his sister Valentina after his death (preserved in RGALI, 2040/4/4) lists over forty-five hundred scores that he accumulated over the course of his life, a sizeable proportion of which were works by contemporary Western composers.

143 Mikhail Bakhtin, *Sobranie sochineniy*, ed. Sergey Bocharov and Leontina Melikhova, vol. 2 (Moscow, 2000), 427.

144 Myaskovskiy, 'Avtobiograficheskiye zametki', 11.

tive programme for Alexey Ikonnikov in 1937[145], its authenticity is doubtful: the article on the Eighth published in *Modern Music* before the premiere makes no mention of it.[146] Razin had been a favoured subject for politically engaged artists since the Revolution[147] and one suspects Myaskovsky of inventing the programme *post hoc* to bestow some suitable 'ideological content' on the work. The results of his attempt to strike out in a new direction are disappointing: the symphony is one of the weakest in his output. Of its four movements, the first, a brisk sonata-allegro, is the most persuasive. The remaining movements are less so: the scherzo suffers from its monotonous phrase structure and unrelieved treatment of the 7/4 metre; the slow movement is excessively long for its material; and the diffuse finale seems merely to go through the motions. Although there are some good ideas (such as the opening modal cor anglais theme of the slow movement), much of the thematic material is undistinguished. On the whole, the symphony makes a curiously unfocused impression – a reflection, perhaps, of the difficult circumstances in which it was written. (Significantly, he took the best part of a year to orchestrate the work after finishing the sketch in September 1924.) There is little sense of a radically new approach – except, perhaps, in the orchestration, which shows a concern for greater transparency, and in the colourful employment of diatonic dissonance.

Before orchestrating the Eighth, Myaskovsky wrote another work, the Fourth Piano Sonata in C minor, op. 27, which he completed on 4 January 1925 and dedicated to Samuil Feinberg. It is an outstandingly fine score, composed under far higher pressure of inspiration. Like the Fourth and Sixth Symphonies, its psychological drama evokes a struggle to contain extreme disturbance. The first movement, *Allegro moderato, irato*, opens with a stentorian outburst that sets the tone for what is to follow (ex. 7.1): the ensuing sonata form juxtaposes a terse, repeated-note idea, subsequently subjected to intense contrapuntal development, with a wanly lyrical second subject, intoned against smouldering discords. The gestural violence and the dissonance of the harmonic language reach new extremes, powerfully evocative of anguish and desolation. While this kind of writing has clear precedents in Myaskovsky's earlier sonatas, the two remaining movements break significantly new ground, adumbrating the turn to classicism in his later work. The slow movement is a set of variations on an elegant sarabande-like theme: its gently plangent harmonisation retains a sense of unease, but the possibility of transcendence is glimpsed as the movement unfolds. The *maggiore* central variations attain a mood of radiant

145 Ikonnikov, *Khudozhnik nashikh dney*, 149–50.

146 'Myaskovskiy, Vos'maya simfoniya A-dur, soch. 26. Tematicheskiy ocherk', *Sovremennaya muzïka*, 15–16 (1926), 148–50.

147 See Boris Veymarn (ed.), *Istoriya sovetskogo iskusstva* (Moscow, 1965), 65.

EXAMPLE 7.1. Piano Sonata no. 4, first movement: opening.

serenity, their ethereal textures recalling the slow movements of the late Beethoven sonatas. The *moto perpetuo* finale also recalls Beethoven in its driving energy and brilliance, as it works through reminiscences of the first movement's disturbance and turbulence to conclude in a hard-won, but wholly persuasive C major.

Shortly after finishing the Eighth in late June 1925, Myaskovsky unsuccessfully attempted to resume work on sketches that he had made for a sinfonietta the previous autumn.[148] As it transpired, he would compose nothing until the summer of 1926 except *The Faded Garland* [*Venok poblekshiy*], op. 22, a cycle of settings of the early nineteenth-century poet Anton Delvig intended as a present for Derzhanovskaya. (In the event, she never performed them, having decided to retire from the concert platform because of her deteriorating vocal production.[149])

Teaching resumed at the conservatoire in September, and with it, his reviewing for Muzsektor. Although his day-to-day life was uneventful and

148 'Vipiski', 13 September 1925, RGALI, 2040/1/65, l. 5.

149 Koposova-Derzhanovskaya, 'Pamyati druga', 223.

followed its customary routine, the 1925–6 concert season saw a notable upsurge of interest in his work. Persimfans gave the Fifth Symphony on 26 October; two days later, he made a brief foray to Leningrad to hear the revised version of the Seventh performed by the Leningrad Philharmonic under Malko on 28 October – a concert that marked the beginning of Malko's increasingly active championship of his music. (Glazunov was present, and to Myaskovsky's amusement, complimented him on his orchestration and melodic inventiveness.[150]) After a lull in ASM's activities since the previous May, its committee members started to organise its third annual concert series. They initially hoped to hold six symphony concerts with the Theatre of the Revolution orchestra, including one with an all-Prokofiev programme[151] and a second at which the Eighth Symphony would be premiered, but these ambitious plans had to be scaled back drastically. In the end, only two concerts took place. The Prokofiev concert proved infeasible and Myaskovsky postponed the performance of the Eighth, preferring to feature music by others[152]: he invited Maximilian Steinberg to conduct a programme of his own compositions and works by Julia Weissberg, mindful that Steinberg was all but ignored in Leningrad and had few opportunities to hear anything that he wrote.[153] As it transpired, the premiere of the Eighth was not delayed for long: as part of a belated attempt to remedy its neglect of Soviet composers, Rosfil undertook to programme it during the summer of 1926.[154]

In the meantime, Prokofiev reported that Stokowski had given an excellent performance of the Fifth with the Philadelphia Orchestra in New York on 5 January 1926 – but did not let the opportunity pass to berate his correspondent once more for his 'Glazunovian, ridiculously textbookish approaches'.[155] Stokowski had already done the symphony twice (on 2 and 4 January[156]), conducting it from memory. It received laudatory reviews, including one in the *New York Times* from Olin Downes, who declared that Myaskovsky had

150   Myaskovsky to Pavel Lamm, 29 and 30 October 1925, RGALI, 2473/1/155, l. 3, 4.

151   Myaskovsky to Prokofiev, 14 December 1925, in Kozlova and Yatsenko, *Perepiska*, 229.

152   Myaskovsky to Asafiev, 26 February 1926, RGALI, 2658/1/641, l. 4.

153   Myaskovsky to Steinberg, 30 September 1925, RIII, 28/1/487, l. 130b.

154   Grigor'yev and Platek, *Moskovskaya gosudarstvennaya filarmoniya*, 71.

155   Prokofiev to Myaskovsky, 8 January 1926, in Kozlova and Yatsenko, *Perepiska*, 231.

156   Philadelphia Orchestra programme booklet, 2 and 4 January 1926, RGALI, 2040/2/359, ll. 51–20b.

'something real and big to say'.[157] Koussevitzky's nephew wrote to inform him of the Fifth's success and of Stokowski's desire to meet him.[158]

Three weeks later on 24 January, the Czech Philharmonic gave the Sixth and Seventh Symphonies in Prague under the direction of Konstantin Saradzhev; and on 1 March Saradzhev repeated the Sixth in Vienna.[159] These invitations had come about through the efforts of Belyayev, who had visited Prague in May 1925 to represent ASM at the International Society for Contemporary Music's annual festival before returning for a second visit to the Austrian capital.[160] The noted Czech historian and musicologist Zdeněk Nejedlý, a fervent communist and founder of the Czechoslovak Society for Economic and Cultural Alignment with the New Russia[161], played a major role in organising the Prague concert: during a visit to Moscow in September 1925 to attend the bicentenary celebrations of the Russian Academy of Sciences[162], he had heard Myaskovsky's Sixth performed at a musical evening in Pavel Lamm's apartment.[163] In his programme notes and subsequent review, Nejedlý pointedly contrasted the symphony's powerful authenticity of utterance with the 'conjuring tricks and circus humbug' of contemporary Western musical modernism, describing it as a moving monument to the 'human suffering through which the Revolution was born . . . viewed *sub specie aeternitatis*'.[164] Dzimitrovsky wrote on behalf of Universal Edition to congratulate him on a 'colossal' triumph: Saradzhev was called back onto the stage twelve times at the close.[165]

Both concerts had gone ahead with high-level approval and financial support from Narkompos[166]: in an article published in January 1926 Lunacharsky spoke of Myaskovsky as a major figure deserving of international recognition and expressed regret that the difficult conditions of the

157 'Music: Philadelphia Orchestra', *New York Times*, 6 January 1926.

158 Fabien Sevitzky [Faviy Kusevitskiy] to Myaskovsky, 4 April 1926, RGALI, 2040/2/169, ll. 1–4.

159 The orchestra for the Vienna performance is not identified on the concert poster (reproduced in Tigranov (ed.), *Saradzhev*, 38).

160 'Assotsiatsiya sovremennoy muzïki', *Sovremennaya muzïka*, 11 (1925), 29.

161 Společnosti pro hospodářské a kulturní sblížení s Novým Ruskem, founded in March 1925.

162 Jiří Křesťan, *Zdeněk Nejedlý: Politik a vědec v osamění* (Prague, 2013), 191–2.

163 Saradzhev to Lamm, 27 January 1926, RGALI, 2743/1/190, l. 23.

164 'První koncert nové ruské hudby', *Rudé právo*, 28 January 1926, in Zdeněk Nejedlý, *Kritiky II (Rudé právo 1923–1935)*, ed. Václav Pekárek (Prague, 1956), 152; Czech Philharmonic programme booklet, 24 January 1926, RNNM, 3/547, l. 3.

165 Dzimitrovsky to Myaskovsky, 27 January 1926, RGALI, 2040/2/140, l. 8; Saradzhev to Lamm, 21 January 1926, RGALI, 2743/1/190, l. 10.

166 'Assotsiatsiya sovremennoy muzïki', *Sovremennaya muzïka*, 13–14 (1926), 108.

post-Revolutionary period had limited the opportunities available to Soviet composers.[167] Once again, Myaskovsky's response to these signs of growing national and international renown was deeply curious. He remarked to Asafiev: 'I remain profoundly unsure of myself (in regard of the future) and disappointed (in respect of the past). I do not believe at all in the success of the Prague concert – it must have been for some other reason, and not because of the music. . . . No, I am not a composer, much less a musician. And the more they talk about me, the more ashamed I feel'.[168]

He continued to speak of his work in the most disparaging terms (describing his Fifth in the same letter as 'not a symphony, but a rattle-bag' [*pogremushka*]): his disinclination to make even a modest effort to promote it bordered on the perverse. Pierre Monteux expressed interest in meeting him when he visited Moscow in March 1926, but Myaskovsky let the opportunity pass, pleading low spirits, having previously told Prokofiev that he doubted whether his work would appeal to Monteux's Western tastes.[169] A few months earlier, he had an awkward encounter with Otto Klemperer, who came to Pavel Lamm's apartment one evening to hear a play-through of the Seventh Symphony: when Klemperer extolled the music of Mahler, Myaskovsky remarked with an uncharacteristic lack of diplomacy that Russian musicians found it banal, bringing the conversation to an abrupt end. It is difficult to interpret this puzzling behaviour: his proneness to serious depression may explain it in part, though one suspects that it was also prompted by a conviction that his music would not be understood by Western musicians.[170]

His low mood was not helped by the publication of Sabaneyev's book *Music Since the October Revolution*, which characterised his work as 'academic' and lacking originality[171], or the Bolshoi orchestra's rendition of the Seventh under Malko on 16 May and its premiere of the Eighth under Saradzhev a week later on 23 May. The poor quality of both performances plunged Myaskovsky into renewed doubts about his competence as an orchestrator, leading him to subject the Seventh to a second bout of revision and make substantial alterations to the Eighth.[172] The orchestra found the 7/4 metre of the Eighth's Scherzo particularly challenging. At the

---

167 Anatoliy Lunacharskiy, 'Odin iz sdvigov v iskusstvovedenii', *Vestnik Kommunisticheskoy akademii*, 15 (1926), 92.

168 Myaskovsky to Asafiev, 26 February 1926, RGALI, 2040/1/641, l. 4–40b.

169 Myaskovsky to Prokofiev, 16 March 1925 and 8 March 1926, in Kozlova and Yatsenko, *Perepiska*, 212–13, 235.

170 Lamm, 'Vospominaniya o N. Ya. Myaskovskom', 233–4.

171 Leonid Sabaneyev, *Muzïka posle Oktyabrya* (Moscow, 1926), 128–32; Myaskovsky to Prokofiev, 8 March 1926, in Kozlova and Yatsenko, *Perepiska*, 236.

172 Myaskovsky to Prokofiev, 27 May and 12 June 1926, ibid., 243–4, 245–6.

concert, the movement nearly fell apart when Saradzhev's shirt collar came undone: the conductor valiantly tried to continue beating time with his right hand alone while struggling to reattach the studs with his left.[173] (The previous year, the premiere of the Seventh had been disrupted by an even more unfortunate occurrence: Saradzhev's son suffered an epileptic fit during the performance and hurled himself with a shriek from the upstairs balcony – fortunately landing unhurt in the stalls below.[174])

Myaskovsky's faith in himself might have been restored if he had had the opportunity to hear some of the accounts of his music by musicians and ensembles of international calibre throughout this period. Hermann Scherchen conducted the Seventh Symphony in Winterthur in Switzerland on 24 March.[175] Frederick (Friedrich) Stock performed the Fifth Symphony with the Chicago Symphony Orchestra on 9 and 10 April. (Stock became a staunch advocate of Myaskovsky's music thereafter: between 1926 and his death in 1942 he conducted forty-nine performances of the nine Myaskovsky symphonies in his repertoire, including twenty-two of the Sixth alone.[176]) At an ISCM concert in Zurich on 23 June, Walter Gieseking gave a superb account of the Fourth Piano Sonata, which was very enthusiastically received.[177] Dzimitrovsky informed Myaskovsky that the Sixth Symphony would be given in Chicago, Philadelphia (by Stokowski), Minneapolis, London, Bochum, Dusseldorf, Frankfurt, Leipzig, and Leningrad during the 1926–7 season, which he deemed an exceptional level of attention for a new work.[178]

Even if his growing international reputation seems to have meant little to Myaskovsky, it increased Universal Edition's interest in him: negotiations commenced about publishing the Seventh and Eighth Symphonies.[179]

173 Myaskovsky to Asafiev, 23 May 1926, RGALI, 2658/1/641, l. 17; Mark Paverman, 'Dorogoy uchitel' i drug', Tigranov, *Saradzhev*, 106.

174 Shebalin, 'Iz vospominaniy', 279.

175 Werner Reinhart to Myaskovsky, 20 April 1926, RGALI, 2040/2/229, ll. 1–2.

176 I gratefully acknowledge the assistance of Frank Villella, director of the Rosenthal Archives of the Chicago Symphony Orchestra, and of Albrecht Gaub, both of whom provided information about Stock's performances of works by Myaskovsky. Dr Gaub's examination of the scores of Myaskovsky symphonies preserved in the Rosenthal Archives indicates that Stock habitually made extensive cuts: communication from Dr Gaub to the author, 21 January 2018.

177 Anton Haefeli, *Die Internationale Gesellschaft für Neue Musik (IGNM): Ihre Geschichte von 1922 bis zur Gegenwart* (Zurich, 1982), 484; Sergey Popov to Pavel Lamm, 4 July 1926, RGALI, 2040/2/213, l. 4.

178 Dzimitrovsky to Myaskovsky, 8 October 1926, RGALI, 2040/2/140, ll. 16–160b.

179 Myaskovsky to Prokofiev, 12 June 1926, in Kozlova and Yatsenko, *Perepiska*, 245; Dzimitrovsky to Myaskovsky, RGALI, 20 June 1926, RGALI, 2040/2/140, l. 11.

The circumstances are not entirely clear, but there was also serious talk of inviting Myaskovsky to spend a year in Vienna, where conditions would be more conductive to creative work. The subject is not raised in any of Dzimitrovsky's surviving letters to Myaskovsky (gaps in the collection suggest that items were destroyed), but Derzhanovsky alludes to it in his correspondence.[180] Myaskovsky did not pursue the idea, most likely for several reasons – his family commitments, a lack of interest in living abroad, and the necessity to continue saving to buy an apartment. As it happened, his creative block lifted unexpectedly during the summer: during a two-month sojourn in Mukhanovo, a former countryside estate ringed by woodland, situated about fifty miles west of Moscow, he felt sufficiently recovered to resume work on the sinfonietta – or the Ninth Symphony as it had now become – and to start planning other projects.[181] Despite his dislike of travelling, he even considered accepting an proposal to send him to Vienna to represent Soviet Russia at the Beethoven centenary celebrations the following year, thinking it might afford an opportunity to meet Prokofiev.[182]

In the event, he did not attend the Beethoven festivities, but he would see his conservatoire classmate before too much longer: after protracted discussions, plans were finally taking shape for Prokofiev to visit his homeland early in the New Year.[183] He did go to Vienna, however, but for a different reason – meetings with Universal Edition personnel. He travelled via Warsaw, arriving in time for the formal unveiling of Wacław Szymanowski's Chopin monument on 14 November in company with Yavorsky and other members of the Soviet delegation.[184] He subsequently spent about ten days in the Austrian capital before returning to Russia in early December. While there, he corrected the proofs of the Seventh and signed a publication contract for the Eighth and Ninth Symphonies, for which he managed to secure an advance of 750 dollars.[185] Virtually nothing else is known about his visit, except that he did not enjoy it very much. Alexander Kreyn's talented nephew Julian, who was studying in Vienna at the time, remembered being

180 Derzhanovsky to Myaskovsky, 27 June 1926, RGALI, 2040/1/114, l. 17.

181 Myaskovsky to Asafiev, 6 September 1926, RGALI, 2658/1/641, ll. 19–20; 'Vïpiski', 9 September 1926, RGALI, 2040/1/65, l. 5.

182 Myaskovsky to Prokofiev, 12 June and 11 July 1926, in Kozlova and Yatsenko, *Perepiska*, 246, 248.

183 Prokofiev to Myaskovsky, 1 September 1926, ibid., 249.

184 Rabinovich, *Yavorskiy: Stat'i, vospominaniya, perepiska*, 645. On the Chopin monument, see Hanna Kotkowska-Bareja, *Pomnik Chopina* (Warsaw, 1970).

185 'Vïpiski', 12 December 1926, RGALI, 2040/1/65, l. 50b; publication contract for Eighth and Ninth Symphonies, dated 26 November 1926, RGALI, 2040/2/140, l. 18.

struck by his extreme shyness and social awkwardness: he clearly could not wait to return home.[186]

Summing up his 'very hazy' impressions of the trip for Asafiev, Myaskovsky concluded:

> It was pleasant only in one respect: life there accommodates itself to the citizen, rather than the citizen being obliged to accommodate himself to everything, which obviously makes it possible to work in tranquillity. But I wouldn't want to 'live' there: the people are all so business-minded somehow and evidently preoccupied only with their own concerns, which is perhaps natural given the difficulties of musical life over there, but doesn't make them any more pleasant. . . . Musical affairs also made a humdrum, rather business-like impression.[187]

Although he acknowledged that he had been treated courteously and attentively, the visit only seems to have reinforced his prejudices about the artistic sterility and commercialism of Western musical life. He told Prokofiev that the people he met struck him as being preoccupied with 'trivialities' and had surprised him by their ignorance of anything 'outside their own swamp'.[188]

Shortly after his arrival home, Dzimitrovsky wrote to inform him of the Philadelphia Orchestra's highly successful performances of the Sixth under Stokowski and his assistant Artur Rodziński, adding that he hoped Myaskovsky might return to Vienna soon for a longer visit.[189] Myaskovsky never came back: this brief trip remained his sole excursion over the Soviet border. For better or worse, his fortunes would be entirely bound up with those of his homeland.

186 Yulian Kreyn, 'Stranitsï moyey muzïkal'noy zhizni: 1954–1990', RNNM, 482/32, l. 65.

187 Myaskovsky to Asafiev, 23 December 1926, RGALI, 2658/1/641, ll. 220b–3.

188 Myaskovsky to Prokofiev, 24 December 1926, in Kozlova and Yatsenko, *Perepiska*, 255.

189 Dzimitrovsky to Myaskovsky, 14 December 1926, RGALI, 2040/2/140, ll. 20–200b.

8

'Sheer Overcoming': 1927–31

Prokofiev arrived in Moscow by train on 20 January in company with his wife Carolina ('Lina'), *née* Codina, a soprano of Ukrainian-Spanish parentage whom he had met in America and married in 1923, shortly after leaving the United States to base himself in Europe. Before crossing the Soviet border, they stopped off in Riga to give a concert. An acquaintance from his student years invited the couple to his apartment for lunch. In the course of their conversation, their host produced a portrait photograph of Myaskovsky – almost certainly, the one which appeared on the frontispiece of the special 'Russia' issue of *Musikblätter des Anbruch* (and is also reproduced as the frontispiece of the present volume). 'I was amazed at the change', Prokofiev wrote in his diary later that day: 'the boring appearance, the stony stare'. His reaction to the image is revealing: the subject's haunted expression, the searching intensity of his gaze registered merely as uninteresting, and the photograph itself as a poorly posed shot.[1]

Myaskovsky came to his hotel to welcome him: Prokofiev found his former classmate charming and refined as of old and concluded that the photograph must have been taken at a bad moment. Although both were pleased to see one another, neither felt wholly at ease at this first encounter. The youthful prodigy who had left Russia in 1917 was returning as a figure of international renown: he felt a considerable weight of expectation and was anxious not to disappoint. Myaskovsky was also somewhat apprehensive, wondering how Prokofiev would be received and what he would make of musical life in Moscow.[2] The homecoming of someone whom he regarded as the greatest living composer had an enormous personal significance. Since their resumption of contact, he had avidly followed the younger man's career and written regularly to communicate his admiring responses to Prokofiev's recent work as he became acquainted with it. The tone of these letters is at times striking. After the premiere of the Second Symphony in Paris in June 1925, for example, he dispatched an impatient enquiry:

---

1 Prokof'yev, *Dnevnik 1919–1933*, 459. As Prokofiev remarked in the same diary entry, Myaskovsky disliked being photographed: the surviving photographs of him are not numerous, and this image was one of the very few to appear in print before the 1930s. Prokofiev does not specifically mention the *Musikblätter des Anbruch* issue, but his description of Myaskovsky's attire ('instead of a blazer [he was wearing] some kind of jacket buttoned up to the chin') would appear to confirm that this was the photograph in question.

2 Myaskovsky to Prokofiev, 24 December 1926, in Kozlova and Yatsenko, *Perepiska*, 254.

I am incapable of waiting any longer to receive your promised bulletin about the performance of the Second Symphony. I am writing to remind you. Almost a month has already gone by, after all! Can you really not understand that everything concerning you, especially when it comes to your new progeny [*chado*], is an exciting event for me – whatever it may be for others! I must insist on getting a report.[3]

On learning that the Second Symphony had been coldly received, he wrote immediately to inform Prokofiev of his desire to 'pour balm on [his] wounds', urging him not to be disheartened because 'idiots . . . completely failed to understand a work of genius'. He returned to the subject a few weeks later, assuring him that the symphony would elicit a very different response in Moscow.[4] 'It's impossible to rival the popularity of your music here!!', he observed proudly: 'Concerts of your compositions are packed to the rafters'.[5] He left unmentioned his own important role in helping to bring these concerts about. His concern that Prokofiev should not lose his Russian identity or his connection with his homeland was very apparent. At their second meeting, he expressed relief that younger man's Russian had not deteriorated during his lengthy residence abroad – rather to Prokofiev's discomfiture.[6]

Prokofiev's anxieties were quickly dispelled: his two-month tour was a personal triumph. It commenced with recitals and performances as soloist in his own concerti in Moscow and Leningrad, and concluded with concerts in Kharkov, Kiev, and Odessa. Even he, who was not given to displays of false modesty, was surprised by the acclaim with which he was greeted when he walked onstage at his first concert on 24 January to play the Third Piano Concerto with Persimfans, and the tumultuous applause that erupted at the close.[7] The rapturous audience receptions continued over the following weeks: he was fêted everywhere as an honoured guest. His visit was widely covered in the press, and ASM helped to generate additional publicity by bringing out two issues of *Modern Music* in close succession, both of which were largely devoted to his work.

Throughout his stay, Myaskovsky and his associates helped to smooth the way and to establish professional contacts that would strengthen Prokofiev's ties to Soviet Russia. But if it occurred to Prokofiev to wonder about his Russian acquaintances' personal circumstances, his reflections went unrecorded in the voluminous diary entries made during his visit. Myaskovsky's cramped living conditions in a communal apartment are

3   Myaskovsky to Prokofiev, 28 June 1925, ibid., 215.
4   Myaskovsky to Prokofiev, 16 August and 3 November 1925, ibid., 219, 226.
5   Myaskovsky to Prokofiev, 8 March 1926, ibid., 235.
6   Prokof'yev, *Dnevnik 1919–1933*, 468.
7   Ibid., 474.

noted virtually without comment, as are Asafiev's reports of the domestic tensions created by Valentina's daughter Marianna – now a headstrong young woman of twenty and a zealous member of the Communist Youth League, whose rude and offhand behaviour infuriated her mild-mannered uncle. ('Those are only your bourgeois theories', she would snap at her mother, brusquely cutting her off in mid-sentence.)[8] There is little indication that Prokofiev gave much thought to anyone else's affairs other than his own – or to other people's feelings. Anxious to introduce him to his friends and colleagues, Myaskovsky arranged for him to attend a musical evening in Pavel Lamm's apartment. The visit was not a success. Olga Lamm recalled that their guest seemed like a being from another world: even his elegant foreign clothes stood out in incongruous contrast against their shabby, motley attire. (Despite the advent of NEP, few Soviet citizens could afford to dress well: clothes and footwear were not only expensive, but in short supply.[9]) Although Prokofiev's social manner had become more polished during his years abroad, he had acquired the self-regarding air of the 'great artist' and lost nothing of his former abrasiveness.[10] His condescending attitude to the assembled company was all too evident:

> He reacted to the music that was played for him with polite indiffer-
> ence. After hearing Myaskovsky's latest symphony, his Eighth, played in
> an eight-hand arrangement, his sole comment was: 'No-one writes like
> that in Europe anymore'. An unpleasant silence descended on the room.
> Prokofiev struck everyone as behaving like a metropolitan sophisticate
> who had wound up in some provincial hole . . . Myaskovsky was deeply
> hurt by Prokofiev's dismissive comment. Afterwards, he said more than
> once with some bitterness: 'Serge is not interested in my music'.[11]

Whatever his personal feelings, Myaskovsky's admiration for Prokofiev as an artist remained undimmed. He commented to Kabalevsky and Fere that future music historians would distinguish two periods in the creativity of young Soviet composers – before and after Prokofiev's visit.[12]

As is evident from the high-flown praise that he repeatedly lavished on it, Myaskovsky regarded Prokofiev's music as the embodiment of an artistic ideal. (When the Quintet, op. 39, was performed at an ASM concert on 6

8   Ibid., 468, 479.

9   See Lebina, *Sovetskaya povsednevnost'*, 130–8; Yelena Osokina, *Za fasadom
    "Stalinskogo izobiliya": Raspredeleniye i rïnok v snabzhenii naseleniya v godï
    industrializatsii, 1927–1941* (Moscow, 1999), 39–40.

10 Lamm, 'Pavel Aleksandrovich Lamm: Opït biografii', RNMM, 192/361, l. 351.

11 Lamm, 'Druz'ya', 84. In his diary entry concerning this visit, Prokofiev
    recorded that the Seventh (rather than the Eighth) was performed and that he
    did not care for it very much. *Dnevnik: 1919–1933*, 528.

12 Fere, 'Nash uchitel'', 421.

March 1927, he sent Asafiev a rapturous report declaring 'full and unbridled admiration' for the score's 'incredible inventiveness' and 'Pushkinian profundity'.[13]) He also seems to have regarded it as embodying everything that he believed his own music to lack, especially the qualities of vividness and technical fluency. After Prokofiev's departure on 23 March, he complained of finding it difficult to settle back down to work: his low spirits returned, despite the unexpected award of a state honour, the title of Distinguished Artist of the Russian Soviet Federative Socialist Republic.[14] During Easter week, however, he managed to complete an outline sketch of a one-movement symphony, the Tenth, which he had commenced the previous December.[15] He commuted between Mukhanovo and Moscow for the much of the summer, working on the orchestration of the Ninth until 21 July.[16] On completion of this task, he revised six of the *Flofion* piano miniatures and assembled them into the set *Reminiscences* [*Vospominaniya*], op. 29, which he offered to Universal Edition.[17] The remainder of his vacation was spent correcting proofs of the Eighth Symphony and elaborating his draft of the Tenth. Orchestrating the Tenth occupied him until the end of the year.[18]

In their very different ways, the Ninth and the Tenth Symphonies are both remarkable achievements. The creative breakthrough which Myaskovsky had unsuccessfully sought in the Eighth was triumphantly realised in the Ninth Symphony in E minor, op. 28. Viewed in the context of Myaskovsky's output as a whole, it can be seen as inaugurating the turn to classicism in his later work, manifested as a concern to achieve greater cogency and economy of expressive means. A new poise and emotional restraint is in evidence, together with a greater clarity of formal outlines and transparency of texture. The harmonic language, though sometimes very dissonant, has a more diatonic basis, and the orchestration is both deft and colourful. In its fundamental conception the symphony is similar to the Fourth and Sixth, except that the struggle to contain disruption is not so strenuous and protracted: in writing his Ninth, Myaskovsky perhaps intentionally eschewed any impulse to monumentality. Like its predecessor, it is in four movements, but is more compact, lasting about thirty-five minutes in performance.

13   Myaskovsky to Asafiev, 6 March 1927, RGALI, 2658/2/50, l. 55.

14   Undated curriculum vitae [1943?], Myaskovsky's Moscow Conservatoire personnel file, AMK, 1/23/84, l. 36; Prokof'yev, *Dnevnik 1919–1933*, 535.

15   'Vïpiski', 29 December 1926, RGALI, 2040/1/65, l. 50b; Myaskovsky to Prokofiev, 12 May 1927, in Kozlova and Yatsenko, *Perepiska*, 236.

16   'Vïpiski', 21 July 1927, RGALI, 2040/1/65, l. 50b.

17   Myaskovsky to Prokofiev, 3 August 1927, in Kozlova and Yatsenko, *Perepiska*, 262.

18   'Vïpiski', 13 September and 29 December 1927, RGALI, 2040/1/65, ll. 50b, 6.

The large-scale ternary-form opening movement, marked *Moderato malinconico*, is prefaced by a slow introduction that adumbrates its principal thematic ideas – the wistful melody of the A section (ex. 8.1), the E minor tonality of which is continuously compromised, and the ardent contrasting idea of the B section, ingeniously constructed to permit varieties of canonic treatment (ex. 8.2). A transition theme in halting rhythms, first presented by the brass and strings in alternation (ex. 8.3), introduces a mood of anxious uncertainty and returns to make disruptive appearances in the slow movement and finale. The Scherzo is one of the most technically impressive stretches of music that Myaskovsky ever composed in its maintenance of an unflagging swift momentum. Its boisterous high spirits and glittering sonorities act as an effective foil to the subdued first movement and the exquisite *Lento molto* that follows. The sonata-rondo finale opens with a presentation of an elegant theme that attempts to preserve the tonality of E major in the face of destabilising chromatic incursions. Tonal lability becomes more pronounced in the course of the ensuing episodes and the task of restoring E major increasingly arduous: the second episode is largely taken up with a tense development of example 8.3 and other ideas from the first movement. The struggle to overcome the disruptive elements continues almost to the close, until the primacy of the tonic is affirmed definitively at the climax of the headlong coda.

The disruption that is subdued and contained in the Ninth erupts with unprecedented violence in the Tenth Symphony in F minor, op. 30, which marks the high point of the Expressionist tendencies in Myaskovsky's oeuvre to date. His diary reveals that the symphony was inspired by one of the most famous works of Russian literature, Alexander Pushkin's *The Bronze Horseman* (1833), and a celebrated set of illustrations of the poem that Diaghilev's associate Alexandre Benois produced between 1903 and 1916[19], published as a collection in 1923.[20] *The Bronze Horseman* relates the tale of Yevgeny, an impoverished clerk living in St Petersburg, who goes mad on learning that his fiancée Parasha has perished when the River Neva inundates the city in a catastrophic flood. After a year wandering the streets as a beggar, he chances to pass one of the capital's most notable landmarks, the equestrian statue of Peter the Great in Senate Square: he is suddenly struck by the thought that the ultimate responsibility for Parasha's death lies with Peter because he chose to found St Petersburg in such an inhospitable location. He upbraids the statue in fury – only to flee in terror as he

19   'Vïpiski', 20 April 1927, RGALI, 2040/1/65, l. 50b.

20   Aleksandr Pushkin, *Mednïy vsadnik: Peterburgskaya povest' (risunki Aleksandra Benua)* (Saint Petersburg, 1923). On Benois's illustrations, see Mikhail Seslavinskiy and Ol'ga Tarakanova, *Knigi dlya gurmanov: Bibliograficheskiye izdaniya kontsa XIX – nachala XX veka* (Moscow, 2010), 170–2.

EXAMPLE 8.1. Symphony no. 9, first movement: bars 25–8.

EXAMPLE 8.2. Symphony no. 9, first movement: bars 81–6.

imagines the bronze horseman coming to life and pursuing him implacably. The narrative concludes with the sombre discovery of Yevgeny's drowned body some months later.

The tale's richly suggestive symbolism permits a wealth of interpretations, but there is no mistaking *The Bronze Horseman*'s central concerns – the plight of the citizen under autocratic rule and the suffering caused by the grandiose schemes of despots. The resonance of such themes for contemporary Soviet readers need hardly be emphasised: in her memoirs, Olga Lamm explicitly described the Tenth Symphony as portraying 'the suppression of the individual through the diktat of state power'.[21] Although Myaskovsky inscribed the autograph score with a quotation from the

21   Lamm, 'Pavel Aleksandrovich Lamm: opït biografii', RNMM, 192/361, l. 366.

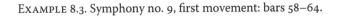

EXAMPLE 8.3. Symphony no. 9, first movement: bars 58–64.

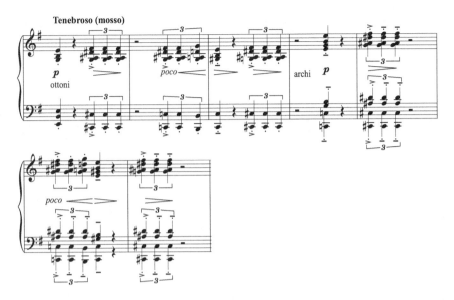

poem's closing section evoking Yevgeny's desperate attempt to escape ('In the light of a wan moon / with arm outstretched upwards / behind him hurtled . . .')[22], he did not disclose the literary inspiration of the work publically, fearing that it would only elicit obtuse comment from 'our clever critics', as he remarked wryly to Prokofiev.[23]

He was fully aware of having produced a score that was unlikely to meet with much understanding either at home or abroad. 'I fear that I've once again written redundant music . . . which no-one will want to hear!', he told Prokofiev, adding in a subsequent letter: 'I have absolutely no idea how I composed it'.[24] The Tenth certainly cannot be described as an appealing work in any conventional sense, but it is a powerfully compelling one. Its nightmarish, searingly intense atmosphere is without precedent in the Russian symphonic literature. Myaskovsky spoke ironically of its harmonic language as 'Schoenbergian', but the Tenth owes nothing to Austrian composer's post-tonal compositions. (At the time of writing it, Myaskovsky's knowledge of these was very limited: he acquired scores of the Second String Quartet and the opp. 11 and 19 piano pieces[25], but they seem to have made little impression on him. Moreover, there were few, if any opportunities to hear performances of Schoenberg's music in Moscow during the

22   RNMM, 71/5.

23   Myaskovsky to Prokofiev, 16 May 1930, in Kozlova and Yatsenko, *Perepiska*, 331.

24   Myaskovsky to Prokofiev, 12 May and 14 October 1927, ibid., 256, 266.

25   Catalogue of Myaskovsky's library, RGALI, 2040/4/4, ll. 187–8, 199.

FIGURE 8.1. A page of the compositional sketch of the Tenth Symphony.

1920s.[26]) The impulse to explore the expressive possibilities of extremes of dissonance seems to have arisen wholly independently, as a development of tendencies present in his earlier work.

The Tenth is noteworthy from a formal perspective, being the first of the three one-movement symphonies that Myaskovsky composed. Once again, there are few obvious Russian precedents for a one-movement symphony (with the possible exceptions of Skryabin's *Poem of Ecstasy* and *Prometheus* – though the status of these as symphonies is doubtful); and Myaskovsky only became acquainted with Sibelius's Seventh in 1935, ten years after it was published.[27] Lasting just over a quarter of an hour in performance, the Tenth is cast as a sonata structure. Myaskovsky did not attempt to depict the events of Pushkin's poem in programmatic fashion, but the music vividly captures its atmosphere. The brief introduction presents a stark unison statement of a six-bar idea that recurs throughout like a leitmotif: it conveys an unmistakable sense of menace, lurching ponderously upwards from the

26   Plans were announced to perform the Third String Quartet and *Pierrot Lunaire* during ASM's 1927–8 season, but it is unclear whether these concerts actually took place: see *Sovremennaya muzïka*, 23 (1927), 18; and 28 (1928), 107.

27   'Vïpiski', 20 September 1935, RGALI, 2040/1/65, l. 25.

FIGURE 8.2. Myaskovsky (1927).

deepest bass only to fade in a tense diminuendo on its climax note (ex. 8.4).
The first subject group, marked *Allegro tumultuoso*, comprises two ideas, a
writhing theme emerging out of hectic figurations suggestive of Yevgeny's
headlong flight, and a stentorian brass theme evocative of the bronze
horseman. The slower second subject group alternates a plaintive angular
melody, first heard on the oboe against a tremulous accompaniment in

EXAMPLE 8.4. Symphony no. 10: opening.

EXAMPLE 8.5. Symphony no. 10: bars 218–29.

the flutes and divided upper strings, and a more impassioned lyrical theme – respectively prompting associations with Yevgeny's madness and his anguish at the loss of Parasha. The development section is initially taken up with a furious treatment of the first subject group before breaking out in a strenuous fugato marked *Presto tempestuoso* (ex. 8.5): in its ferocious manic energy, this passage is amongst the most remarkable in the Russian symphonic literature, memorably conveying a mood of uncontrollable terror. A second wave of fugal development, this time of a motif from the exposition's codetta, rises to a forceful culmination. The recapitulation's curtailed presentation of the material of the exposition offers little respite from the foregoing tensions, which persist into the stormy coda. After an ethereal reminiscence of the first theme of the second subject group, the previous frenzied momentum resumes briefly before the symphony's arresting closing gesture – a low-lying chord surging violently to *fortissimo* and cut short by a brutal *sforzando*.

The Tenth's unrelievedly sombre mood epitomised everything that Party ideologues found objectionable in the work of the 'bourgeois individualists'. In a characteristic assessment, the composer's first biographer Tamara Livanova dismissed it as an 'almost pathological' manifestation of 'individualistic modernism' resulting from decadent Western influences, averring that its composition immediately following Myaskovsky's trip abroad the previous year was 'no accident'.[28] The premiere by Persimfans in the Great Hall of the Moscow Conservatoire on 2 April 1928 was not a success: the orchestral musicians disliked the symphony and found it very difficult.[29] The playing was tentative and the performance nearly fell apart during the fugato in the development section.[30] A repeat performance on 9 April was not much better: Myaskovsky recorded in his diary that the symphony was received 'with bewilderment' on both occasions[31], though it was reviewed respectfully.[32] Apart from an equally poor rendition by the Leningrad Philharmonic under Malko on 25 April 1928[33], the Tenth appears to have been given only once more in the Soviet Union during the composer's lifetime, at a Moscow symphony concert conducted by Grzegorz Fitelberg on 7 February 1934[34]. It did, however, receive several performances abroad – it was included in the programmes of three concerts given by the Philadelphia Orchestra under Stokowski in April 1930 and was done twice by Stock and the Chicago Symphony Orchestra in February 1931.[35]

The Tenth's covert literary basis would soon acquire a heightened contemporary relevance. Even as Myaskovsky was completing it, the political climate had begun to grow more oppressive, with significant consequences for cultural life. In the period following Lenin's death, the Bolshevik leadership was increasingly riven by tensions engendered by personal animosities

28 Livanova, *N. Ya. Myaskovskiy: Tvorcheskiy put'*, 119.

29 'Vïpiski', 30 March 1928, RGALI, 2040/1/65, l. 6.

30 Aleksandr Gol'denveyzer, *Dnevnik: Tetradi vtoraya-shestaya (1905–1929)* (Moscow, 1997), 214; Myaskovsky to Prokofiev, 12 April 1928, in Kozlova and Yatsenko, *Perepiska*, 274.

31 'Vïpiski', 12 April 1928, RGALI, 2040/1/65, l. 6.

32 Anatoliy Drozdov, 'Devyati kontsert Persimfansa', *Muzïka i revolyutsiya*, 4 (1928), 31.

33 Maximilian Steinberg recorded in his diary that the symphony was badly played and coldly received: see Ol'ga Dansker, 'Iz zapisnïkh knizhek M. O. Shteynberga 1919–1929 godov', in Galina Kopïtova (ed.), *Iz fondov Kabineta rukopisey Rossiyskogo instituta istorii iskusstv: Publikatsii i obzorï* (St Petersburg, 1998), 115–16.

34 'Vïpiski', 7 February 1934, RGALI, 2040/1/65, l. 120b.

35 Dzimitrovsky to Myaskovsky, 3 June 1930 and 21 March 1931, RGALI, 2040/2/141, ll. 20, 34.

and ideological disputes. These reached a climax in late 1927 with the defeat
of the so-called United Opposition faction and the expulsion of its leaders,
Trotsky, Kamenev and Zinoviev, from the Party – a development which
strengthened Stalin's dominance and facilitated his ascent to supreme
power. (Trotsky was eventually deported from the country in 1929, ridding
Stalin of his principal rival.) The same period also witnessed an escalation
of the conflicts over the New Economic Policy. In spite of a reasonably good
harvest in 1927, the collection of grain for the state stockpile fell sharply,
leaving an insufficient quantity for domestic needs (by the winter, food
shortages in the major cities once again became acute[36]) and forcing a deferral of purchases of industrial equipment.[37] These circumstances prompted
the government to reverse its previous policy of tolerance towards private
enterprise: ironically, Stalin now pressed for measures advocated by the
discredited opposition, including more aggressive regulation and taxation.
At the Fifteenth All-Union Communist Party Congress in December, delegates adopted a resolution that would have fateful repercussions over the
next few years: the 'transformation and unification of small peasant holdings into large collective farms' was declared a task of the utmost priority, as part of a renewed drive to liquidate 'capitalist elements' and raise
productivity.[38] The Politburo approved extraordinary measures to combat
'speculators' who were allegedly hoarding foodstuffs and driving up prices.
Early in the new year, Stalin personally oversaw grain collection in western
and southern Siberia, where his reintroduction of enforced requisitioning
led to outbreaks of violence. Such tactics heralded an assault on the private
sector that got underway in 1928. They dismayed Politburo colleagues such
as Bukharin, who favoured a more gradualist approach to economic development, but met with considerable support within the Party – many of
whose members persisted in regarding NEP as a betrayal of the Revolution.
Long-standing concerns about the Soviet Union's vulnerability to foreign
invasion, aggravated by crises in diplomatic relations with Britain and other
countries in 1927, heightened the perceived urgency of turning the Soviet
Union into a major industrial and military power.[39] In an abrupt volte-face,
the government abandoned the NEP model of a mixed economy in favour
of a centralised planned economy: October 1928 would see the inauguration
of the first Five Year Plan, an ambitious programme of intensive industrialisation and agricultural collectivisation that would not only transform

---

36   Osokina, *Za fasadom*, 47–9.

37   Gimpel'son, *NÈP*, 225.

38   'O rabote v derevne', in *XV s"ezd Vsesoyuznoy kommunisticheskoy partii (b):
     Stenograficheskiy otchyot* (Moscow, 1928), 1308.

39   See Nikolay Simonov, '"Krepit' oboronu Strani Sovetov" ("Voyennaya trevoga"
     1927 g. i yeyo posledstviya)', *Otechestvennaya istoriya*, 3 (1996), 155–61.

the country's infrastructure but also effect far-reaching demographic and social changes.

The shift in economic policy in 1927–8 was accompanied by a shift in attitudes towards fellow travellers. The hostility of Party members to Lenin's New Economic Policy extended to the prevailing climate of intellectual and cultural pluralism: by 1927, calls for more stringent ideological controls were growing insistent. A colloquium to discuss the state of Soviet theatre convened by the Central Committee's Agitation and Propaganda Department in May 1927 proved an important turning point. Lunacharsky, who was present, came under repeated attack from other attendees. Vladimir Blyum, a prominent theatre critic, declared it unacceptable that repertoire reflecting 'bourgeois' sensibilities continued to be staged and regarded as harmless entertainment.[40] The Party functionary Platon Kerzhentsev, Lunacharsky's most vocal opponent, instanced the entrenched 'reactionary' outlooks at the Bolshoi Theatre as further evidence of the undesirable tendencies encouraged by his *laisser-aller* policies. He went on to suggest that Lunacharsky's indulgence of fellow travellers revealed his fundamental misunderstanding of Lenin's directives: 'Lenin said that we should force these specialists to serve us. We should surround them with a comradely communist atmosphere and with the help of that comradely communist atmosphere – 'digest' them [*ikh perevarivat'*]. And what do we see? Have we surrounded them with that atmosphere, or are we 'digesting' them? Nothing of the kind'.[41]

The implications of Kerzhentsev's remarks were clear: fellow travellers had mostly proved recalcitrant to ideological re-education and were actively hindering the construction of an authentic proletarian culture. Friendly persuasion had failed, so more drastic measures were now necessary. These claims would soon constitute a central message of the relentless propaganda campaign that accompanied the Five-Year Plan. For the moment, Lunacharsky was in a sufficiently strong position to resist calls for a radical change in Narkompros's arts policy, but it is nonetheless indicative that the ministry moved to overhaul the administration of cultural life later in the year.[42] Up to now, responsibility for the arts had been dispersed across a number of government departments, an arrangement that proved cumbersome and inefficient. A new directorate, Glaviskusstvo[43], was set

40 *Puti razvitiya teatra: Stenograficheskiy otchyot i resheniya partiynogo soveshchaniya po voprosam teatra pri Agitprope TsK VKP(b) v maye 1927g.* (Moscow, 1927), 118–19.

41 Ibid., 97.

42 See Manin, *Iskusstvo v rezervatsii*, 125.

43 An acronym formed from 'Glavnoye upravleniye po delam khudozhestvennoy literaturï i iskusstva' – General Directorate of Literary and Artistic Affairs. On Glaviskusstvo, see Sheila Fitzpatrick, 'The Emergence of Glaviskusstvo. Class War on the Cultural Front, Moscow, 1928–29', *Soviet Studies*, 2 (1971), 236–53.

up under the aegis of Narkompros in April 1928 as 'a special organ for the implementation of ideological and organisational control in the domains of literature and art'.[44] Over the next eighteen months, official intervention in artistic affairs would grow steadily more invasive.

The effects of the changing climate were soon felt in musical life. Shortly after Prokofiev's departure in March 1927, new Narkompros directives obliged ASM to engage with proletarian audiences and leaven its programmes with standard classical and romantic repertoire.[45] While this new policy had much to commend it from a practical point of view, it fundamentally altered the Association's *raison d'être*, causing it to operate more like a regular concert agency rather than an organisation to foster the study and performance of modern music. The implementation of the new directives fell to Derzhanovsky, who returned to his former roles in the organisation earlier that year.[46]. He mooted ambitious plans to expand ASM's performance activities, but their feasibility was doubtful from the outset.[47] As he ruefully acknowledged in the November 1927 issue of *Modern Music*, which appeared after a seven month hiatus, not only was the association facing the perennial problem of exiguous financial resources, but it also had to contend with the antagonism of the government concert agency Rosfil, which regarded ASM as a threatening rival. (Having tried unsuccessfully to block ASM from engaging foreign artists, Rosfil resorted to obstructing its efforts to hire concert venues.) Although ASM had sought to reduce its overheads and discontinued its promotional activities abroad, it struggled to manage on its meagre annual stipend. Organising symphony concerts remained an enormous challenge, as ASM could not afford to hire professional ensembles. Attempts to involve the Bolshoi Orchestra in a projected series 'Beethoven and the Russian Symphony' came to nothing. In the end, ASM managed to secure the Moscow Conservatoire's student orchestra for the 1927–8 season – most likely with the help of Saradzhev, who ran the institution's conducting course.[48] Between November 1927 and May 1928, the association put on fifteen solo and chamber recitals and seven orchestral concerts, presenting a range of accessible classics alongside new

---

44 'Postanovleniye SNK RSFSR "Ob organizatsii v sostave Narodnogo komissariata prosveshcheniya RSFSR osobogo organa dlya osushchestvleniya ideologicheskogo i organizatsionnogo rukovodstva v oblasti literaturï i iskusstva"', *Sobraniye uzakoneniy i razporyazheniy Rabochego i krest'yanskogo pravitel'stva*, 41 (1928), 313.

45 'Khronika', *Sovremennaya muzïka*, 22 (1927), 287.

46 Derzhanovsky's name reappeared in the list of editors from *Modern Music*'s February 1927 issue onwards. It is not clear how his rapprochement with ASM came about.

47 Derzhanovsky to Asafiev, 30 April 1927, RGALI, 2658/1/542, ll. 12–120b.

48 'Assotsiatsiya sovremennoy muzïki', *Sovremennaya muzïka*, 23 (1927), 3–7.

Russian and foreign compositions: works by Mozart, Schubert, and Brahms provided a foil for scores by Bartók, Milhaud, and Hindemith. The first symphony concert on 4 December signalled the organisation's efforts at more active political engagement: designed to mark the tenth anniversary of the Revolution, the programme included Roslavets's cantata *October* and a new symphony, subtitled 'To October', by Maximilian Steinberg's brilliant student, the twenty-one-year-old Dmitri Shostakovich.

Myaskovsky's reaction to ASM's new programming policies and abandonment of its former apolitical stance is not recorded. One wonders what he made of Derzhanovsky's editorial in the December 1927 issue of *Modern Music*, which declared the need for a 'fundamental re-education of the old concert-going cadres of the intelligentsia'.[49] However, a perceptive piece in the same issue by Viktor Belyayev, 'Ten Years of Russian Symphonic Music', articulated concerns that were undoubtedly central to his preoccupations at this juncture.

Belyayev's essay returned to the issues that Asafiev had raised three years previously. He opened by acknowledging that composers everywhere, and not just in the USSR, faced 'a crisis of renewal': they could not but register the profound change in the prevailing *Zeitgeist* since the First World War, but many remained uncertain how to respond to it artistically. Soviet composers had been presented with this challenge in a particularly acute form: the Revolution had brought into being a 'new world with new ideals' which demanded a 'new language and a new art'. This imperative, he argued, could not be satisfied merely by imitating contemporary foreign artistic fashions. The artistic 'revolution' of Western musical modernism was primarily concerned with style rather than substance: at bottom, it was predicated on a rejection of Romanticism and the relentless pursuit of technical innovation. In the Soviet context, however, compositional idioms influenced by Romanticism persisted, being best suited to capturing the 'romanticism of the great Revolution, with its depth of feeling, its yearning for the sublime and the monumental'. Scores such as Gnesin's *Symphonic Monument* and Alexander Kreyn's *Funeral Ode for Lenin* exemplified this tendency, but the most significant achievements, he contended, had been in the domain of the symphony, that most 'perfect and profound' of forms. He instanced Myaskovsky's Sixth and Eighth as works that 'not only convey the general idea of our revolutionary modernity' but evoked 'the struggle, the victory, and the commemoration of the fallen':

> This romanticism, which is not formally revolutionary, possesses a strength of tragic and heroic feeling, which renders it suitable for our era and capable of embodying its vital ideas ... while Western European music is formally revolutionary, but not revolutionary in essence. This

49 'Oktyabr' i novaya muzïka', *Sovremennaya muzïka*, 24 (1927), 23.

circumstance makes possible mutually beneficial influences for the future development of world musical culture – which would be unthinkable, of course, without the participation of the USSR.[50]

In writing the piece, Belyayev evidently had several aims. First, he wished to counter perceptions that much Soviet music was stylistically retrogressive because it did not emulate 'advanced' European trends: he defended the right of native composers to pursue independent lines of exploration. Secondly, he attempted to combat the hostile portrayals of ASM's composer members as decadent, apolitical 'formalists', writing abstruse modern music that was incomprehensible to proletarian audiences and alien to them in sensibility. Finally, he sought to dispel simplistic understandings of what could constitute 'proletarian' music. The truly great composer, he argued, 'should stand at the head of the musical movement of his era . . . and point the way to new creative discoveries'. Crucially, he contended that was unnecessary for composers to engage explicitly with political subjects (either by setting texts or writing programme music) in order to reflect the spirit of the new epoch. Soviet composers should not seek merely to speak to their own era, but to future eras:

> A subject is only a means to express an underlying idea. And in order to be more universal and thus more capable of withstanding the passage of time, it should be a symbol that unites in itself the most salient traits of our era – in a manner transcending time and place . . .. The only truly contemporary music is that which reflects the influence of the living ideas of our contemporaneity in a profound and inward way.[51]

Belyayev concluded his essay on a combative note, declaring ASM's intention to fight for the right of such music to be heard.

Though Myaskovsky never discussed his views on these questions publicly, the standpoints articulated by Belyayev are demonstrably similar to his own: indeed, it is likely that the essay's contents were informed by Belyayev's first-hand knowledge of them. Belyayev remained an active propagandist for Myaskovsky's music throughout the 1920s: aside from his essays in *Modern Music*, he contributed articles on Myaskovsky to a range of foreign publications and wrote programme notes for the premieres of his new works.[52] The belief that Russian music should pursue its own path

---

50   'Desyat' let russkoy simfonicheskoy muzïki', *Sovremennaya muzïka*, 24 (1927), 29.

51   Ibid., 31.

52   See Yelena Dolinskaya, 'Stil' rannikh sochineniy N. Ya. Myaskovskogo v nauchnoy kontseptsii V. M. Belyayeva', in Anatoliy Belyayev and Irina Travina (ed.), *Viktor Mikhaylovich Belyayev: 1888–1968* (Moscow, 1990), 394–405. Earlier in the year, Belyayev had published the pamphlet *Nikolay Yakovlevich Myaskovskiy* (Moscow, 1927).

independently of the West was one that Myaskovsky had held for many years, like his conviction that artists should aspire to a universality of utterance which transcended national boundaries. His ambivalent responses to Western musical modernism had been long in evidence; as his letters to Prokofiev demonstrate, he was unsympathetic to the prevailing reaction against Romanticism and impatient with appraisals of works based solely on their degree of conformity to current stylistic fashions. In a letter of March 1928 to Maximilian Steinberg, he remarked waspishly à propos of the superior attitudes of young Leningrad composers towards music that they deemed insufficiently 'modern': 'In Moscow, we don't consider it necessary to give pieces titles such as *Rails*, *Submarines*, or *Skyscrapers* in order to write good music which is completely contemporary in spirit'.[53] (*Rails* was an allusion to Vladimir Deshevov's recently composed 'constructivist' piano piece of the same name, which had gained a certain notoriety.) Even more revealing are his humorous compliments to Steinberg on his recently completed Third Symphony:

> As far as being 'modern' is concerned, I think it has the main thing. You allow yourself to use all the means, but without exaggerating them (that is, without modernism – which in essence, for me at any rate, principally constitutes 'the conquest of new expressive means') . . .. Your symphony is . . . new in essence and is modern by virtue of that alone, though it's not 'industrial' (how nonsensical that word is!) and perhaps not even urbanistic. No, my dear Maximilian, you've written a wonderful and profoundly modern work.[54]

The viewpoint informing this response was entirely congruent with the position argued in Belyayev's essay: it was possible for a musical composition to be contemporary in sensibility without being self-consciously 'modern' in idiom. Composers' creative responses to the condition of modernity could be formulated entirely in musical terms, without recourse to descriptive titles and programmes – or burdening their work with crude political messages.

Whatever his misgivings about politicised art, he had warm praise for Shostakovich's Second Symphony, which he thought made a 'stunning' impression in ASM's first symphony concert of the season.[55] He had followed the young composer's development with keen interest since their first meeting three years previously, when Shostakovich auditioned for the Moscow Conservatoire, having enquired about studying with him. Myaskovsky recommended him for acceptance, but Shostakovich eventually

53   Myaskovsky to Steinberg, 29 March 1928, RIII, 28/3/487, l. 33.
54   Myaskovsky to Steinberg, 14 May 1928, RIII, 28/3/487, l. 340b.
55   Myaskovsky to Asafiev, 28 December 1927, RGALI, 2658/2/50, l. 640b.

decided to remain in Leningrad.[56] They met again in February 1926, when
Shostakovich called to show him his First Symphony.[57] Unbeknownst to
Shostakovich, only a few weeks previously, Myaskovsky had successfully
persuaded Muzsektor's editorial board to reconsider its initial refusal to
publish the symphony and the Two Pieces for String Octet, op. 11 (both
scores had aroused 'unanimous protest', as he reported to Steinberg).[58] On
learning that the young man was working as a cinema pianist, he urged
Asafiev to find him more suitable employment.[59] He remained supportive, though he did not care greatly for Shostakovich's music or warm to
him personally. As always, he did not allow these responses to interfere
with his objectivity. 'He's an unpleasant young lad', he remarked to Asafiev,
'but a really major talent'.[60] By contrast, Shostakovich's attitude towards
Myaskovsky grew more dismissive – probably under the influence of his
friend Ivan Sollertinsky.[61] (In a letter to Sollertinsky of 1931, he made sarcastic jibes about Myaskovsky's 'lackey-like physiognomy' and 'revolting'
music.[62]) In time, however, he grew to appreciate the older man's personal
qualities and spoke in a notably more respectful way about his work.

Two of Myaskovsky's own symphonies were given during ASM's 1927–8
season, the Third under the Hungarian conductor István Strasser on 15
April 1928 and the premiere of the Ninth under Saradzhev on 29 June. After
the debacle with the premiere of the Tenth a fortnight previously, Strasser's
fine reading of the Third came as a welcome relief, especially given the practical difficulties that had to be surmounted before the performance could
go ahead. Although the organisers managed to book the Great Hall of the
Moscow Conservatoire for the concert, they experienced acute difficulty
finding somewhere suitable to hold the rehearsals beforehand. The eminent
theatre director Vsevolod Meyerhold came to the rescue and offered the use

56 Shostakovich to Sof'ya Shostakovich, 8 April 1924, in Roza Sadïkhova and
    Dmitriy Frederiks, 'D. Shostakovich. Pis'ma k materi', *Neva*, 9 (1986), 170;
    Laurel E. Fay, *Shostakovich: A Life* (New York, 2000), 24–5.

57 Myaskovsky to Asafiev, 26 February 1926, RGALI, 2658/1/641, ll. 3–4.

58 Myaskovsky to Steinberg, 4 and 9 February 1926, RIII, 28/3/487, ll. 28–28 ob,
    23ob.

59 Myaskovsky to Asafiev, 28 February 1926, RGALI, 2658/1/641, ll. 60b–7.

60 Myaskovsky to Asafiev, 28 December 1927, RGALI, 2658/2/50, l. 64ob.

61 Shebalin recorded that Sollertinsky regarded Myaskovsky with hostility,
    even though he had never met him: Lyudmila Mikheyeva (ed.), *Pamyati I. I.
    Sollertinskogo: Vospominaniya, materialï, issledovaniya* (Leningrad, 1978),
    107. Comments in Shostakovich's letters of the 1920s indicate that he thought
    Myaskovsky's music gloomy and old-fashioned: see Miral'da Kozlova, '"Mne
    ispolnilos' vosemnadtsat' let. . .": Pis'ma D. D. Shostakovicha k L. N. Oborinu',
    in Natal'ya Volkova (ed.), *Vstrechi s proshlïm*, vol. 5 (Moscow, 1984), 247, 253.

62 Shostakovich to Sollertinsky, 13 December 1931, in Dmitriy Sollertinskiy *et al.*
    (ed.), *D. D. Shostakovich: Pis'ma I. I. Sollertinskomu* (St Petersburg, 2006), 99.

of his company's premises.[63] (Meyerhold held Myaskovsky in high regard and tried without success to persuade him to compose incidental music for his productions.[64]) The premiere of the Ninth, by contrast, was a lacklustre affair: the rehearsals went poorly and the performance, though respectable, was inartistic.[65] Mediocre renditions of this kind would scarcely have done much for Myaskovsky's morale, especially in a climate of mounting hostility towards modern music.

Attacks on ASM in the press were becoming more frequent. In his editorial for the April 1928 issue of *Modern Music*, Derzhanovsky felt obliged to respond to a recent article in the Moscow Conservatoire's journal *Music Education* which accused ASM of harming Soviet musical culture and acting as a conduit for decadent Western influences. Entitled 'Off with the Masks!' (a popular Soviet catchphrase), it was scathingly critical of Belyayev, whom it characterised as a class enemy, and of the views expressed in his essay of the previous December. The author, a student activist, took particular exception to Belyayev's praise of Myaskovsky: hinting darkly at the composer's non-proletarian social origins, he dismissed his music as a morbid manifestation of bourgeois individualism.[66] Derzhanovsky made a spirited rejoinder, pointing to official acknowledgements of ASM's important contribution to contemporary musical life.[67] But while a recent Narkompros resolution had indeed been broadly supportive of the organisation, it nonetheless sought to bring it more firmly under government control. The association was asked to clarify its 'artistic and ideological platform', to submit for approval its concert plan for the next season, to undertake a broader range of outreach activities, and to exercise greater vigilance over the articles published in *Modern Music*.[68] Its members did not yet realise it, but ASM's days were numbered. As with the other quasi-independent artistic organisations of the NEP years, there was no obvious rationale for its continued existence. From an official perspective, it was surplus to requirements, duplicating functions best assigned to a national concert agency that could reliably exercise the required degree of ideological and organisational oversight. (Such a body had already been created: in February 1928, local concert agencies in Moscow, Leningrad, and other centres were absorbed into a new administrative structure, 'Soviet Philharmonic' or 'Sofil'.[69])

63 Lamm, 'Vospominaniya', 234–5.

64 Shebalin, 'Iz vospominaniy', 286.

65 Myaskovsky to Prokofiev, 30 May 1928, in Kozlova and Yatsenko, *Perepiska*, 280.

66 Lev Kaltat, 'Maski doloy!', *Muzïkal'noye obrazovaniye*, 2 (1928), 13–21.

67 'Konservatorskiye nachyotniki', *Sovremennaya muzïka*, 27 (1928), 93–6

68 'Narkompros o rabote ASM', *Sovremennaya muzïka*, 27 (1928), 103–4.

69 See 'O Sofile', *Muzïka i revolyutsiya*, 10 (1928), 34–5.

As it proved, ASM's concert activities were severely curtailed following its 1927–8 season and the publication of *Modern Music* halted for ten months after its thirty-first issue of May 1928. If prospects for new music had started to look less favourable at home, interest in Myaskovsky's music abroad continued to grow. Dzimitrovsky, his contact at Universal Edition, reported forthcoming performances in major centres throughout the German-speaking world and in more distant locations such as London, New York, and Buenos Aires[70], as well as enquiries from conductors of the calibre of Wilhelm Furtwängler and Koussevitzky.[71] Nonetheless, Myaskovsky's attitude towards Universal Edition remained mistrustful. He was annoyed by its dilatoriness in publishing *Silence* and his Hippius settings, and especially by its failure to produce the score and parts of the Eighth by the agreed deadline – which resulted in the cancellation of performances that Koussevitzky had undertaken to give in Boston and New York in late 1927.[72] To his even greater vexation, Koussevitzky also had to cancel another projected performance of the symphony in Paris in May 1928: the set of parts had not only arrived too late but also turned out to be incomplete.[73] Dzimitrovsky was profusely apologetic and sought to dispel Myaskovsky's suspicion that the incident signalled the firm's lack of regard for him, but the damage was done.[74] When Emil Hertzka wrote shortly afterwards to enquire about publishing the Tenth, adding that Universal Edition was eager to represent him more extensively,[75] Myaskovsky took the opportunity to detail his dissatisfactions at length.[76] Universal Edition honoured its commitment to publish the Ninth and the other outstanding works, but the five-year contract that it had signed with Myaskovsky was broken by mutual agreement. His works from the Tenth Symphony onwards were issued by the Soviet state music publisher, but Universal Edition continued to promote them. In the long run, Myaskovsky's decision does not seem to have disadvantaged

70 Dzimitrovsky to Myaskovsky, 15 October 1927, RGALI, 2040/2/140, l. 37.

71 Furtwängler performed the Seventh Symphony in New York in 1927 and planned to give the Eighth in Berlin the following year: Dzimitrovsky to Myaskovsky, 24 May 1927, RGALI, 2040/2/140, l. 30.

72 See Bobrik, *Venskoye izdatel'stvo 'Universal Edition'*, 200–201. Correspondence between the librarian of the Boston Symphony Orchestra and Universal Edition's American agent Associated Music Publishers confirms Koussevitzky's intention to give the premiere of the Eighth in March 1928 and the cancellation of the performance because of delays in supplying the orchestral materials: Serge Koussevitzky Archive, LC, box-folder 43/18.

73 Prokofiev to Myaskovsky, 14 May 1928, in Kozlova and Yatsenko, *Perepiska*, 277.

74 Dzimitrovsky to Myaskovsky, 25 April 1928, RGALI, 2040/1/140, ll. 46–46ob.

75 Hertzka to Myaskovsky, 23 May 1928, RGALI, 2040/2/140, ll. 49–49ob.

76 Myaskovsky's letter has been lost: a draft, dated June 1928, is preserved amongst his personal papers: RGALI, 2040/2/32, ll. 1–2.

him – quite the contrary, in fact. By the mid-1930s, the state publishing house had become more efficient and was prepared to bring out virtually everything that he wrote; conversely, Universal Edition's operations were severely affected by the decade-long Great Depression (a recurrent theme of Dzimitrovsky's letters), which limited its appetite for risk. In any case, in the tense climate after Stalin's accession to supreme power, it is doubtful that he could have dealt directly with the firm for much longer. Muzsektor's director Alexander Yurovsky had been unhappy with the situation from the outset and threatened to lodge a formal complaint about Derzhanovsky for encouraging composers to approach foreign publishers.[77] And although foreign publication was never prohibited by law, the certain prospect of professional ostracism and accusations of 'anti-Soviet' conduct acted as powerful deterrents throughout the Stalinist era.

Myaskovsky's frustration with Universal Edition's dilatoriness in issuing his scores was heightened by his pressing need for additional income to pay for his new flat. The previous autumn, he had resorted to legal proceedings in an attempt to obtain a separate room in the communal apartment for Valentina's daughter, but was unsuccessful[78]: their living conditions remained as unsatisfactory as before. In September, he made a down payment of 1680 roubles to the housing co-operative – a sum comprising his entire annual salary from the conservatoire and representing roughly one-sixth of the anticipated total cost.[79] His summer vacation, which he spent as usual at Mukhanovo, passed quietly, but unproductively: he revised seven of the *Flofion* piano miniatures and assembled them into a set *Yellowed Pages*, which became his op. 31, but made little progress with a projected trio of light orchestral works. Writing to Pavel Lamm, who had gone abroad to study Musorgsky manuscripts (Lamm's pioneering new edition of *Boris Godunov*, which restored the composer's texts of the original and revised versions, had been performed in a highly successful Mariinsky production earlier in the year[80]), he complained of recurring depression and of being unable to work.[81] Lamm loyally remained in regular contact, sending accounts of his travels en route to Paris. After a detour to Geneva to see his brother Vladimir, who had emigrated earlier in the decade, he crossed the French border to Annemasse, where Prokofiev had rented a house. His visit coincided with that of Asafiev, who was also in France on business.[82]

77   Derzhanovsky to Myaskovsky, 14 July 1926, RGALI, 2040/1/114, ll. 16–160b.

78   'Vïpiski', 14 October 1927, RGALI, 2040/1/65, l. 6.

79   'Prikhodno-raskhodnoye tetradi', RGALI, 2040/1/67, l. 100b.

80   Lamm, 'Pavel Aleksandrovich Lamm: opït biografii', RNMM, 192/361, l. 356–7.

81   Myaskovsky to Pavel Lamm, 29 August 1928, RGALI, 2743/1/155, ll. 5–50b.

82   See Miral'da Kozlova, 'B. V. Asaf'yev: iz pisem k zhene, 1928 god', in Tamara Livanova (ed.), *Iz proshlogo sovetskoy muzïkal'noy kul'turi*, vol. 3 (Moscow,

Prokofiev took time off to bring his guests sightseeing.[83] Lamm's letters and postcards to Myaskovsky are poignant documents, recording a few weeks of unclouded enjoyment: he was never able to travel abroad to see Vladimir again and had to cease corresponding with him in the later 1930s when it became too dangerous.[84]

By the end of 1928, the sense of closing horizons had become too oppressive to ignore, as state ideology encroached inexorably on freedom of thought and expression. The indictment of fifty-three mining engineers and managers from the Donbass city of Shakhty on trumped-up charges of economic sabotage marked another turning point in the regime's treatment of fellow travellers. Their highly publicised trial, which took place in Moscow between 18 May and 6 June 1928, was held to demonstrate the dangers of continued reliance on 'bourgeois specialists'. Stalin declared the 'Shakhty affair' to have furnished irrefragable evidence of widespread 'wrecking activities' undertaken by 'class enemies', and urged 'the development and reinforcement of class vigilance by every means possible'.[85] On the opening day of the trial, *Pravda* carried an editorial calling for a 'cultural revolution' and 'the production of new loyal cultural cadres to construct the socialist economy': 'On every sector of the construction front we will tirelessly forge the vitally necessary armour of socialist culture which must shield us ... with an impenetrable wall from alien class influences, from bourgeois decadence, from petit bourgeois vacillations, and from the slackening of vigilance towards a more cultured class enemy'.[86]

The Cultural Revolution was presented as a vitally necessary concomitant of the economic revolution instituted by the Five-Year Plan. In addition to mobilising mass support for the programme of accelerated industrialisation and agricultural collectivisation, it enabled Stalin to strengthen his grip on power and weaken the last vestiges of resistance to Bolshevik rule. The initiative was welcomed not merely by those who had disdained the compromises of the NEP years. Many young people were enthused by a project that rekindled a spirit of revolutionary romanticism and promised to open up new professional opportunities as the old 'bourgeois specialists' were ousted from their positions.[87] Towards the end of 1929, Stalin would describe that year as having marked 'great turning point on all the fronts of

1982), 5–28.

83 Prokof'yev, *Dnevnik 1919–1933*, 639–42.

84 Lamm, 'Pavel Aleksandrovich Lamm: opït biografii', RNMM, 192/361, l. 415.

85 'O pravom uklone v VKP(b)', *I. V. Stalin: Sochineniya*, vol. 12 (Moscow, 1949), 12.

86 'Klassovïy protsess', *Pravda*, 18 May 1928.

87 For a seminal account of events, see Sheila Fitzpatrick, 'Cultural Revolution in Russia 1928–32', *Journal of Contemporary History*, 1 (1974), 33–52.

socialist construction' and called for a 'decisive offensive' against such 'capitalist elements' as remained.[88] Three weeks later, the last significant opposition to his policies within the Politburo collapsed when Bukharin and his associates publicly recanted their 'errors' – an event that was presented as a conclusive victory over the forces of ideological reaction. Stalin's ambitious campaign to transform not merely the country's economy but also the mentality of its citizens could now proceed unchecked.

The Cultural Revolution re-inflamed the class antagonisms of the Civil War years: the so-called 'bourgeois intelligentsia' was once more subjected to an aggressive campaign of harassment and intimidation. The campaign was largely driven by activists in the Communist Youth League and the Communist Academy who sought to seize control of intellectual and cultural life. Their militant attitudes were reflected in their routine recourse to military rhetoric: they spoke of their initiatives as 'engagements' intended to 'crush counterrevolution' on the 'cultural front'. Amongst their primary objectives were the expulsion of 'alien class elements' from educational institutions and the comprehensive reform of their curricula to 'socially useful' ends. They also pushed for all academic disciplines to be reconstituted on the supposedly 'scientific' basis of Marxist-Leninist philosophy and 'purged' of non-Marxist approaches. As part of this broad programme, the arts were to be firmly subordinated to the task of 'socialist construction' and the fulfilment of the Five Year Plan: in the words of Vladimir Friche, a notable literary critic of the period, their role was primarily envisioned as being to 'stimulate the activity and energy of the working class to the maximum extent'.[89]

The changed climate invigorated the proletarian artistic organisations, which quickly moved to assert their hegemony. Stalin was careful never to endorse their ideological platform outright or to indicate that they spoke on behalf of the Party, but he undoubtedly regarded their activities as useful in furthering his aims.[90] The largest of them, the Russian Association of Proletarian Writers (RAPP[91]), though nominally independent, apparently operated under the direct ideological and administrative supervision of the Central Committee.[92] Its cognates in the fields of music and the visual arts

88   'God velikogo pereloma: K XII godovshchine Oktyabrya', *Pravda*, 7 November 1929.

89   Vladimir Friche (ed.), *Iskusstvo v SSSR i zadachi khudozhnikov* (Moscow, 1928), 8.

90   See Yevgeniy Gromov, *Stalin: Iskusstvo i vlast'* (Moscow, 2003), 79–95.

91   Like the Association of Proletarian Musicians, this organisation changed its name periodically: it was styled 'RAPP' from the autumn of 1928.

92   See Galina Belaya, *Don Kikhotï revolyutsii: Opït pobed i porazheniy* (Moscow, 2004), 274.

were much smaller, and took their lead from RAPP in matters of policy and strategy.

This period saw a dramatic transformation in the fortunes of the All-Russian Association of Proletarian Musicians (VAPM), as it had been renamed in 1924.[93] During the intervening years, VAPM struggled to continue its operations and ceased to bring out its own journal due to budgetary constraints.[94] Its small membership (around forty in 1924) had been depleted when it split because of internal tensions, leading to the formation of a rival organisation, the Association of Revolutionary Composers and Musicians (ORKiMD) in 1925.[95] In the wake of the Shakhty trial, however, VAPM's leaders successfully petitioned for greater official recognition. Two Narkompros departments passed resolutions in support of the association, recommending that its subsidy be increased as a matter of priority and that it become more closely involved in 'institutions and organisations regulating the USSR's musical life'.[96] By the start of 1929, VAPM was able to launch a new journal, *The Proletarian Musician*, and became a much more assertive presence. No longer confined merely to organising amateur music-making in factories and workers' clubs, its leaders began to have a decisive say in the running of the country's conservatoires, opera houses, and orchestras.

VAPM's principal ideologue was Lev Lebedinsky (1904–92), an amateur composer and brother of the writer and prominent RAPP activist Yury Libedinsky.[97] Politically active from an early age, Lebedinsky joined the Party in 1919: he fought in the Civil War and subsequently worked as a secret police agent.[98] He had little, if any musical training prior to enrolling at the Moscow Conservatoire in 1923. After taking over as VAPM's

---

93　The first recorded use of the organisation's new title occurs in the article 'V proletarskikh muzikal'nïkh organizatsiyakh', *Muzïkal'naya nov'*, 12 (1924), 24–5. A comprehensive study of the association has yet to be written: Neil Edmund's monograph *The Soviet Proletarian Music Movement* (Bern, 2000) provides a serviceable account of its activities and discusses the music of some of its composer members, but relies predominantly on Soviet-era publications, leaving archival sources largely unexplored.

94　VAPM's second journal, *Music and October*, ceased production in 1926 after only four issues.

95　On ORKiMD, see Yelena Krivtsova, 'Iz istorii muzïkal'no-obshchestvennïkh organizatsiy: ORKiMD (1924–1932)', in Rakhmanova (ed.), *Al'manakh*, vol. 2, 268–90.

96　The departments in question were Glavnauka and Glavlitprosvet. The text of VAPM's submission and the relevant resolutions were published in the pamphlet *Vserossiyskaya assotsiatsiya proletarskikh muzïkantov* (Moscow, 1929), 12–21.

97　Libedinsky used a variant spelling of the family surname.

98　Little is known about Lebedinsky's early life beyond the brief summary provided in the article 'Kompozitor-komsomolets', *Muzïkal'naya nov'*, 8

chairman in 1925, his energies were largely directed into journalism: he produced a steady stream of polemical articles and brochures expounding the Association's views and wrote most of its major position statements. 'Social Groups of Musicians in Soviet Russia', published in 1928, identified some of the principal 'wreckers' on whom the association declared 'war' (to quote Lebedinsky's subsequent account of events[99]) – 'retrograde elements' in the Bolshoi Theatre and Sofil who resisted VAPM's policies; composers cultivating decadent modernist idioms; and teachers 'perverting' music education by foisting 'bourgeois' repertoire on their students.[100] VAPM's hostilities were also directed at religious music and various genres of popular music prevalent during the NEP years.[101]

The tensions in musical life escalated rapidly from the autumn of 1928. At a meeting of Party and Komsomol 'arts workers' in Moscow on 13 November, Kerzhentsev called for an immediate intensification of the struggle to combat 'alien ideologies' and 'bourgeois influences' in the arts. Lebedinsky, who was present, complained of 'harmful' staff members at the conservatoire who were promoting Prokofiev and other decadent composers.[102] Three days later, *Pravda* carried an article under the title 'All Is Not Well At the Conservatoire', condemning the activities of a 'reactionary' coterie of professors.[103] Alexander Goldenweiser, one of the professors concerned, was so worried by the attacks that he wrote to Lunacharsky beseeching his support.[104] In January 1929, a series of meetings were held at the conservatoire to discuss the allegations against the institution's staff.[105] The following month, Lunacharsky gave a speech in the conservatoire's Great Hall in which he acknowledged the soundness of many of the proletarian artistic organisations' aims but urged them to temper their zealotry. Presciently, he also warned of the temptation to exploit the climate of intensified 'class warfare' for cynical careerist motives.[106]

(1924), 21. See also Yekaterina Vlasova, *1948 god v sovetskoy muzïke* (Moscow, 2010), 25.

99 *Vosem' let bor'bï za proletarskuyu muzïku (1923–1931)* (Moscow, 1931), 121.

100 'Obshchestvennïye gruppirovki muzïkantov v RSFSR', *Revolyutsiya i kul'tura*, 15 (1928), 58–61.

101 See Amy Nelson, 'The Struggle for Proletarian Music: RAPM and the Cultural Revolution', *Slavic Review*, 1 (2000), 101–32.

102 'V ataku protiv vrazhdebnïkh vïlazok v iskusstve', *Komsomolskaya pravda*, 15 November 1928.

103 'V konservatorii neblagopoluchno', *Pravda*, 16 November 1928.

104 Goldenweiser to Lunacharsky, 16 November 1928, in Aleksandr Skryabin *et al.* (eds)., *Nash starik: Aleksandr Gol'denveyzer i Moskovskaya konservatoriya* (Moscow, 2015), 424–5.

105 Gol'denveyzer, *Dnevnik*, 266–7.

106 'Klassovaya bor'ba v iskusstve', *Iskusstvo*, 1–2 (1929), 7–24.

His intervention had little effect: VAPM's attacks continued. The first issue of *The Proletarian Musician* carried an essay by Yury Keldïsh, a student in the conservatoire's music theory division, which criticised the music of 'fellow traveller' composers and singled out Myaskovsky's Sixth as evincing a 'decadent and mystical worldview'.[107] (Keldïsh, subsequently a leading figure in Soviet musicology, became one of VAPM's most prominent polemicists.[108]) VAPM's 'ideological platform', published as a supplement to the same issue, declared its implacable hostility towards 'decadent' modern music influenced by the 'capitalist West' and organisations seeking to promote this repertory under the guise of conducting scholarship and research.[109] Though not mentioned by name, ASM was the obvious target of this diatribe. By this point, however, the association was effectively defunct, despite Derzhanovsky's attempt to run it on a different basis. (In October 1928 it had been renamed the All-Russian Society for Modern Music (VOSM) and provided with a new charter: Myaskovsky's name was conspicuously absent from the list of committee members.) As Derzhanovsky informed readers in what proved to be *Modern Music*'s last issue, his efforts to organise the 1928–9 season had run into insurmountable difficulties and it had only been possible to arrange a handful of chamber concerts.[110]

Archival documents explain what had been happening behind the scenes. The new state concert agency Sofil had agreed to put on eight symphony concerts in conjunction with VOSM, but reneged on its commitment at very short notice.[111] Myaskovsky told Steinberg that the proposed collaboration was a serious misjudgement on VOSM's part: predictably, Sofil used the opportunity to try to kill off its troublesome rival. It proceeded to give Derzhanovsky 'the run-around', claiming that 'there's no money or that they can't book halls'. Three weeks later, he informed his Leningrad colleague that the projected symphony concerts had fallen through – adding cryptically that Derzhanovsky had abandoned trying to organise anything else because of 'serious unpleasantness'.[112] The 'unpleasantness' in question was an anonymous denunciation of Derzhanovsky's activities at International Books. Soon afterwards, he came in to work one day to find that someone had broken into his office and ransacked his desk drawers. Though no

107 'Problema proletarskogo muzïkal'nogo tvorchestva i poputnichestvo', *Proletarskiy muzïkant*, 1 (1929), 14.

108 On Keldïsh's involvement in VAPM, see Nadezhda Teterina (ed.), *Yuriy Vsevolodovich Keldïsh: Vospominaniya, issledovaniya, materialï, dokumentï* (Moscow, 2015), 64–122.

109 *Vserossiyskaya assotsiatsiya proletarskikh muzïkantov*, 8–9.

110 'Na pereput'i', *Sovremennaya muzïka*, 32 (1929), 3–5. VOSM's charter is reproduced in the same issue on 6–7 (original in RNMM, 3/2128).

111 'Otchyot o deyatel'nosti ASM, 1929', RNMM, 3/3127.

112 Myaskovsky to Steinberg, 8 and 30 March 1929, RIII, 28/1/487, ll. 38, 390b.

formal allegations were made against him, Derzhanovsky resigned in disgust.[113] In the event, he tried to keep VOSM going for another year, but its concert activity never revived, despite expressions of support from the government's new arts directorate and further promises of collaboration from Sofil.[114] As Derzhanovsky quickly discovered, his colleagues showed little enthusiasm for engaging in outreach activities of the kind that Narkompros now expected; and understandably, given the increasingly fraught climate, some hesitated to have any further involvement in the VOSM's affairs.[115] (In the end, matters were taken out of their hands when the State Academy of Arts Studies, to which VOSM had remained affiliated, suffered an extensive staff purge later in the year.[116] The academy's new presidium regarded VOSM's activities with suspicion and formally dissolved the organisation in May 1930.[117]) VOSM's de facto demise in the spring of 1929 meant that the prospects for composers of contemporary classical music looked increasingly bleak, given the state concert agency's lack of interest in programming their work and VAPM's ideological hostility towards it. The performances of new Russian works at ASM's concerts may not have been of a high standard, but they were better than no performances at all.

VAPM'S influence over musical life intensified after a major national conference of musicians held in Leningrad between 14 and 19 June 1929. The conference formed part of a series of events convened to discuss aspects of Soviet culture, starting with an All-Union Congress of Proletarian Writers the previous year: having asserted more direct control over artistic affairs, the government was at last responding to calls to formulate an official arts policy. Like analogous congresses organised in other domains, its central purpose was to clarify which forms of artistic activity were most appropriate to the Soviet context, and to discuss strategy for the thoroughgoing 'proletarianisation' of artistic life.[118] In preparation for the conference, the Department of Agitation and Propaganda convened a smaller forum in Moscow shortly beforehand with the aim of 'uniting Party and social

113 Bobrik, *Venskoye izdatel'stvo 'Universal Edition'*, 164–7.

114 'Rezolyutsiya prinyata na soveshchanii v Glaviskusstve 18-go maya 1929 po dokladu Vserossiyskogo obshchestva sovremennoy muzïki, 13 iyunya 1929g.', RNMM, 3/2134.

115 Undated circular from Derzhanovsky to VOSM's members, early March 1930, RNMM, 3/3121.

116 "Korennaya reorganizatsiya GAKhN', *Rabochiy i iskusstvo*, 7–13 December 1929; see also: Yuliya Yakimenko, 'Iz istorii chistok apparata: Akademiya khudozhestvennïkh nauk v 1929–1932 gg.', *Novïy istoricheskiy vestnik*, 1 (2005), 150–61.

117 Extract from minutes of GAKhN presidium meeting, 24 May 1930, RNMM, 3/2135.

118 Semyon Korev (ed.), *Nash muzïkal'nïy front: Materialï Vserossiyskoy muzïkal'noy konferentsii, iyun' 1929g.* (Moscow, 1930), 3.

opinion' on policy. In his opening address, Kerzhentsev discussed the underdeveloped state of 'proletarian musical creativity' and the unacceptable preponderance of 'old specialists': he urged delegates to consider how music could be 'turned into a weapon of communist education and class struggle'.[119] Press coverage of the forum discussed the Party's concern to address the 'crisis' in Soviet musical life (echoing Asafiev's diagnosis four years previously) caused by the 'complete disconnection' of music and musicians from 'the living masses': one article warned 'petit bourgeois hyper-individualists' that the development of Soviet musical culture was 'inconceivable without being directly linked to our political and economic development'.[120]

The conference itself was attended by over 450 delegates engaged in a broad range of professional activities and ran conjunctly with a 'Soviet Russia Music Week', a programme of grandiose festivities featuring mass choirs and huge amateur instrumental ensembles formed of factory workers.[121] Although the Party resisted pressure from VAPM to grant it a dominant role in national musical affairs[122], the conference resolutions were in broad accord with its policies. Crucially, it was made clear that the artistic pluralism of the NEP years was at an end. Lunacharsky's speech at the conference was uncharacteristically muted: he even raised the possibility that 'collectives' of composers rather than 'individual creators' might produce symphonies, oratorios, and operas more suited to the new age.[123] On the eve of the event, however, the minister ventured into print one last time to urge moderation and remind readers that composers such as Myaskovsky and Glazunov were figures of 'world significance', even if their work did not obviously reflect 'Soviet modernity'[124]. By this point, Lunacharsky's position within the government had been seriously weakened by relentless criticisms of his policies: a month later, he resigned.[125] An honourable man, his diary records his deep misgivings about the regime that he had helped

119 *Puti razvitiya muzïki: Stenograficheskiy otchyot soveshchaniya po voprosam muzïki pri APPO TsK VKP(B)* (Moscow, 1930), 5–8.

120 'Muzïka v povestke dnya', *Rabochiy i teatr*, 9 June 1929.

121 See Valerian Bogdanov-Berezovskiy, *Dorogi iskusstva*, vol. 1 (Leningrad, 1971), 139–45.

122 *Puti razvitiya muzïki*, 54–5.

123 Korev, *Nash muzïkal'nïy front*, 27.

124 'Nakanune muzïkal'noy konferentsii', *Krasnaya gazeta* (evening edition), 8 June 1929.

125 See Irina Lunacharskaia, 'Why Did Commissar of Enlightenment A. V. Lunacharskii Resign? ', trans. Kurt S. Schultz, *The Russian Review*, 3 (1992), 319–42.

to bring into existence.[126] In the past, he had intervened publicly to defend Myaskovsky and his associates from attacks by Communist Party activists[127]: with his departure, the country's leading musicians lost an important patron and protector.

Myaskovsky did not attend the conference and refrained from public comment. His exiguous diary entries are uninformative about his responses to events, but it is evident that his circumstances were difficult. In a letter of October 1929 to Nicolai Malko, who was touring abroad and vacillating about returning to the USSR, Myaskovsky gave a cheerless summary of current conditions, telling his correspondent that performances of modern music had virtually ceased. 'Our musical life is starting to look like a rubbish dump (in all senses of the word)', he wrote. 'There's no chance that the air will clear any time soon. That you're abroad – I now envy you. . . . I'm feeling older every day'.[128] When Prokofiev saw him later that month during a three-week return visit to the USSR, he thought that Myaskovsky had indeed aged. Muzsektor's director Yurovsky told him that the time had come for Myaskovsky to emigrate because attitudes towards him were so hostile and he would soon find it impossible to make a living. Despite his awareness of his former classmate's plight, Prokofiev's diary entries show a curious lack of empathy. He responded in predictably condescending fashion to Myaskovsky's recently completed set of light orchestral works, *Divertissements*, op. 32, when he heard them played in a two-piano arrangement at Pavel Lamm's ('a tad provincial') and the subdued mood of Myaskovsky and his associates irritated him. ('One longs for some cheerfulness, but the milksops are weary'.) A recent convert to Christian Science, he had enthusiastically embraced the notion that prayer and a positive attitude rendered one proof against every misfortune: he observed sententiously that Myaskovsky's lack of religious faith was 'a great morbid void' in his life.[129]

Myaskovsky had little cause for cheerfulness: the threat to his livelihood was very real. After the premieres by Persimfans of the *Serenade*, op. 32/1 and the *Lyrical Concertino*, op. 32/3 in October 1929, his music was effectively banned. (None of his orchestral work would be played for over two years apart from a radio broadcast of the Sinfonietta, op. 32/2 in

126 See, for example, Lunacharsky's diary entry for 9 November 1930 in Viktor Yefimov, *Letopis' zhizni i deyatel'nosti A. V. Lunacharskogo*, vol. 3 (Dushanbe, 1992), 57–8.

127 'Pis'mo komsomol'tsev konservatorii tov. A. V. Lunacharskomu' and 'Otvet tov. A. V. Lunacharskogo', *Muzïka i Oktyabr'*, 4–5 (1926), 17–18.

128 Myaskovsky to Malko, 17 October 1929, RNMM, 71/782, l. 10b.

129 Prokofiev, *Dnevnik: 1919–1933*, 726, 730, 732.

May 1930.[130]) His position at the Moscow Conservatoire also became more vulnerable as increasing numbers of the institution's students enrolled in VAPM's ranks. Reconstructing this period in the conservatoire's history is difficult because of the patchiness of institutional records, and the surviving documentary evidence is comparatively uninformative about his professional interactions during VAPM's period of dominance. Nonetheless, the problems with which Myaskovsky had to contend are clear enough.

In May 1929, the conservatoire's director Konstantin Igumnov resigned.[131] Instead of replacing him with a musician of comparable stature, Narkompros appointed Bolesław Przybyszewski, a mid-ranking government functionary who was the son of the eminent Polish writer Stanisław Przybyszewski. Bolesław (1892–1937) had remained in Russia after being interned as an enemy alien during the First World War: he joined the Communist Party in 1920 and became a member of the Central Committee's Polish Bureau set up by Felix Dzerzhinsky, the head of the Soviet secret police. Thereafter, he taught at several educational institutions in Moscow, before taking a civil service post with Gosplan, the state agency responsible for central economic planning.[132] He had studied at the Warsaw Conservatoire but had little reputation to speak of as a musician: he probably owed his new appointment to the patronage of Dzerzhinsky's associate Felix Kon, another Polish revolutionary who had settled in Russia. (Though similarly lacking in relevant expertise, Kon took over as director of Glavisskusstvo in 1930 and promptly engaged Przybyszewski as his deputy.[133])

Przybyszewski initially made a positive impression (Goldenweiser thought the new director 'cultured' when he met him in early June[134]), but the rationale for his appointment became all too apparent when he published articles calling for the 'proletarianisation' of the conservatoire, purges of its staff and students, and the reform of its curriculum.[135] The nature of the proposed reforms were detailed soon afterwards in a resolution on the Moscow and Leningrad Conservatoires promulgated by Glavprofobr, the Narkompros department responsible for higher education.[136] They included

130 'Vïpiski', 18 October 1929 and 9 May 1930, RGALI, 2040/1/65, l. 7.

131 See Yakov Mil'shteyn, *Konstantin Nikolayevich Igumnov* (Moscow, 1975), 245–6.

132 Krystyna Kolińska, *Stachu: Jego kobiety, jego dzieci* (Kraków, 1978), 104–9.

133 On Kon's work for Narkompros, see Larisa Nagornaya, *Feliks Kon* (Kyiv, 1963), 128–35.

134 Gol'denveyzer, *Dnevnik*, 300.

135 'Puti reorganizatsiya Moskovskoy konservatorii', *Muzïkal'noye obrazovaniye*, 3–4 (1929), 11–15; 'Na muzïkal'nom fronte', *Rabochiy i iskusstvo*, 23 November 1929.

136 'Rezolyutsiya Glavprofobra po dokladam Moskovskoy i Leningradskoy konservatoriy', *Muzïkal'noye obrazovaniye*, 1 (1930), 44–7.

the introduction of compulsory quotas to boost the intake of proletarian applicants and making courses shorter and less demanding in content. The resolution also explicitly redefined the fundamental purpose of a conservatoire training: rather than nurturing highly skilled virtuosi and composers, their primary objective was now to turn out 'mass music specialists' and choral directors who could oversee amateur music-making in the provinces. These developments aroused widespread dismay: the reforms threatened to destroy the country's system of music education.

VAPM's leaders moved to remodel the conservatoires in accordance with their doctrines and to rid them of 'alien class elements'. The predictable result, as Yuri Keldïsh observed almost forty years later, was 'utter chaos': systematic teaching all but ceased as students were assigned to 'brigades' and sent out to organise musical activities at factories and collective farms.[137] Individual tuition was replaced with 'collective' instruction methods; most modern music and large swathes of the standard repertoire were expunged from the institution's syllabi because the association regarded much of the Western art music heritage as unsuitable for Soviet listeners.[138] As Myaskovsky reported to Steinberg in January 1930, VAPM seemed to approve of only three composers in the entire history of music – Bach, Beethoven, and Musorgsky – and of no modern composers other than its own members, who mostly confined themselves to writing part-songs on political themes for amateur choirs, seemingly regarding anything else as ideologically suspect. 'I have only one student – and the directorate is doing everything possible to force me out by means of various underhand slights to which I don't react, because I've decided to leave altogether in the spring'.[139] Myaskovsky did not specify the nature of these 'slights', but VAPM's leaders were undoubtedly aggressive. Like RAPP, VAPM attempted to harass rival organisations out of existence: it effectively absorbed ORKiMD and Davidenko's Prokoll group, having pressurised their members into joining.[140] Zara Levina, a migrant from Prokoll, recalled finding her interactions with VAPM's leadership so stressful that her health suffered: when she tried to distance herself from the group, she was subjected to bullying treatment and threatened with ostracism.[141] VAPM bore a distinct resemblance to a puritanical religious cult. The oppressive atmosphere that it engendered

137 Yuriy Keldïsh, *100 let Moskovskoy konservatorii: kratkiy istoricheskiy ocherk* (Moscow, 1966), 129.

138 See Lev Lededinskiy, 'Kontsertnaya rabota v rabochey auditorii', *Proletarskiy muzïkant*, 2 (1929), 9–12.

139 Myaskovsky to Steinberg, 10 January 1930, RIII, 28/1/487, l. 480b.

140 See Sergey Ryauzov, 'Vospominaniya o Prokolle', *Sovetskaya muzïka*, 7 (1949), 58.

141 Valentina Chemberdzhi, *V dome muzïka zhila* (Moscow, 2017), 252–3.

can be sensed from its members' writings – especially Lebedinsky's vitu-
perative exposés of perceived 'class enemies' and hostile diatribes about
musical repertories of which VAPM's leaders disapproved. Such fanatically
intolerant attitudes were very much a phenomenon of the period, at a time
when Party activists went so far as to insist that women's clothing be sewn
from fabrics featuring motifs of agricultural machinery and electric street
lights rather than 'petit bourgeois' polka dots and floral patterns.[142]

By early 1930, VAPM's most active members included several of
Myaskovsky's former students – amongst them, Viktor Bely (1904–83) and
Marian Koval (1907–71). The fact that his class dwindled to a single pupil
is a clear indication of the opprobrium in which he was held; and like other
fellow travellers and nonconformists, he came under pressure to 'reform'
his artistic and ideological orientation. However, he seems not to have been
harassed as much as other prominent musicians (Roslavets, for example,
was forced to issue a humiliating public retraction of his criticisms of the
organisation[143]) – and neither was he the subject of extensive hostile comment in VAPM's publications. In large part, this was probably due to the
way in which he dealt with the situation. From the outset, he avoided con-
frontations, recognising that they would be a waste of time and energy.
(He told Asafiev that he thought it best simply to ignore VAPM's attacks
because responding would be as futile as attempting to argue with 'the bark-
ing of dogs'.[144]) It would also seem that, in spite of their hostility, VAPM's
leaders regarded him with a grudging respect. When he tendered his resignation at the conservatoire in March 1930, Przybyszewski refused to accept
it, even though Myaskovsky no longer had any students in his class.[145] He
was not dismissed from the faculty during an ensuring staff purge and
Przybyszewski successfully prevailed on him to return for the 1930–1 academic year. Despite his misgivings about the new duties that were assigned
to him (he was expected to teach composition to students with little prior
musical training), he evidently thought it prudent to accept the offer.[146]

In spite of his remark to Malko, Myaskovsky never seriously considered
emigrating. (He was not prepared even to take a short trip aboard, let alone
leave the country for good: he repeatedly declined Prokofiev's invitations
to holiday with him in France in 1929, claiming that he could not face the

142 Lebina, *Sovetskaya povsednevnost'*, 152.

143 See K. Blagoveshchenskiy (ed.), *Dovesti do kontsa bor'bu s nêpmanskoy
     muzïkoy* (Moscow, 1931), 99–100.

144 Myaskovsky to Asafiev, 13 May 1929, RGALI, 2658/2/51, l. 150b.

145 Myaskovsky to Steinberg, 29 March 1930, RIII, 28/1/487, l. 55ob.

146 Myaskovsky to Steinberg, 10 October 1930, RIII, 28/1/487, l. 60.

ordeal of completing the necessary bureaucratic formalities.[147]) Although the atmosphere was unquestionably tense, Myaskovsky had dealt with far more stressful situations in the past: perhaps because of his army training and military experience, he reacted with a surprising degree of equanimity. The only thing that really worried him, he explained to Steinberg, was the prospect of being left without any source of income – especially in the event that he had to leave the conservatoire and the state publishing house, where VAPM also exerted an increasing degree of control. It would be impossible to survive solely on his earnings from composition if the restrictions on the publication and performance of modern repertoire persisted. However, he thought it unlikely that Soviet composers would be permanently constrained to write nothing but agitprop scores: 'serious, genuine music' would once again be in demand when the pressure to write for the 'man in the street' eased.[148] The challenge facing composers in the meantime, as he saw it, was to work out an accommodation to circumstances that would allow them to earn a livelihood from their music without an excessive compromise of artistic integrity.

This was not the only challenge, however: for many, it was a struggle even to summon the inner resources necessary to continue composing in such a hostile atmosphere. Despite Lebedinsky's indignant denials that VAPM was 'terrorising' the musical community[149], the prevailing climate was inhibiting, to say the least. Looking back on this period in old age, Anatoly Aleksandrov recalled becoming so demoralised by the demeaning treatment to which he and other members of the Myaskovsky-Lamm circle were subjected that he composed nothing for several years.[150] Accustomed to being treated with deference and respect, it was deeply humiliating for these eminent musicians to have to put up with disparaging dismissals of their work from student activists, some of whom could hardly read a score, yet did not hesitate 'to lay down the law for all and sundry with the utmost confidence', as Myaskovsky remarked mordantly to Steinberg. His archive contains not a few letters from colleagues describing their frustrating experiences of dealing with the gatekeepers that VAPM installed at the state publishing house and on committees in charge of programming, who zealously blocked compositions that failed to satisfy the association's exalted standards of ideological rectitude. Not infrequently, their vigilance was taken to absurd lengths. Gnesin's student Lyubov Streicher was bemused

---

147 Myaskovsky to Prokofiev, 13 August 1929, in Kozlova and Yatsenko, *Perepiska*, 318.

148 Myaskovsky to Steinberg, 24 February 1930, RIII, 28/1/487, ll. 500b–1.

149 See 'Politicheskiy smïsl' kampanii protiv Assotsiatsii proletarskikh muzïkantov', *Proletarskiy muzïkant*, 7 (1930), 1–5.

150 Blok and Polenova (ed.), *Anatoliy Nikolayevich Aleksandrov*, 124.

to discover that Muzsektor had refused to publish her setting of an innocuous poem about a 'dark-eyed youth' because listeners might think it a sympathetic portrayal of a Menshevik.[151] Steinberg submitted to the press an overture based on Russian folksongs only to find himself embroiled in an acrimonious dispute about their ideological suitability and the appropriateness of their musical treatment.[152] Myaskovsky relayed the eventual decision of the publications board:

> The business about your overture didn't end well: the entire communist faction ganged up against it. . . . [Viktor] Bely thought it was possible to use 'The Little Apple' [a popular urban song that became associated with the Russian revolutionary movement], but in some other context; and he criticised your handling of the themes as too perfunctory, that is, not sufficiently concerned with revealing their [ideological] substance. In short, the whole thing got so complicated that I couldn't follow it anymore. I really couldn't grasp what the point of it all was supposed to be.[153]

Compositions' fates – and composers' earnings – depended entirely on the outcome of these dubious hermeneutical exercises.

Aside from purging the literature of ideologically unsuitable repertoire, VAPM's oversight of musical creativity perfectly exemplified the 'pedagogical bent' of Soviet censorship, to quote a striking formulation from a government policy document: it aimed to encourage self-censorship and conformity to approved practices by 'bringing authors into contact with comrades who can really explain to them the reactionary elements of their work'.[154] Pressure mounted on composers to furnish evidence of their 'reformed' political outlook – compositions on overtly political themes couched in a broadly accessible musical idiom. Myaskovsky's frankest comments about these expectations are found in his letters to Steinberg, a colleague with whom his friendship deepened significantly in the late 1920s. Their correspondence is not only of interest for what it reveals about the circumstances of contemporary musical life but is also a moving record of their support of one another at a difficult and dispiriting time. Both men were sceptical that music could embody the 'ideological content' insistently demanded by Party activists. As Myaskovsky observed:

> Our Marxist 'ideologues' . . . miss the blindingly obvious. In stipulating various class criteria, they completely lose sight of the fact that music, being the most emotional of the arts, bears within itself the maximum number of elements that are biological and which transcend class. And

151 Streicher to Myaskovsky, 11 October 1929, RGALI, 2040/1/162, l. 10.

152 Steinberg to Myaskovsky, 1 November 1930, RGALI, 2040/2/282, l. 16.

153 Myaskovsky to Steinberg, 14 February 1931, RIII, 28/1/487, l. 68

154 Blyum, *Za kulisami "Ministerstva Pravdi"*, 87.

FIGURE 8.3. Maximilian Steinberg (late 1930s).

so, by overlooking what is common to all humanity, they end up talking absolute nonsense on this very point. . . . As far as the work of our 'leading' young composers is concerned – there are some talented people amongst them who write passable (though not very passable) music, but they try to enhance its effectiveness (which in reality isn't very great) by putting labels on it. Of course, if you and I were members of VAPM, then your Third Symphony and my Sixth Symphony would be regarded as excellent specimens of revolutionary music and exactly the kind of thing that's required.[155]

This passage merits closer scrutiny, because it demonstrates Myaskovsky's complete rejection of the premises on which VAPM's aesthetic platform rested. Attempting to extend the so-called 'sociological method' of Marxist literary criticism to music, VAPM's theorists claimed to be able to discern class characteristics in musical texts of the past and present, and proceeded to evaluate them positively or negatively according to the extent that they supposedly reflected a worldview consonant with Marxism. Myaskovsky regarded this enterprise as entirely misguided. Music, in his view, engaged with fundamental aspects of experience that were 'common to all humanity', irrespective of class origins or ideological outlook. Consequently, the very attributes that Marxist music critics sought to identify in music were almost entirely illusory, and their appraisals based on subjective imaginings and prejudices rather than anything objectively existent. The very fact that VAPM's composers had recourse to 'labels' – programmatic titles and descriptors such as 'proletarian' which sought to influence listeners' perceptions and responses – showed that the 'ideological content' did not and could not inhere in the stuff of the music itself, the notes, but had to be applied on the surface.

The ideological content of musical compositions would remain a central preoccupation of Soviet cultural policy on music and Soviet music criticism throughout the Stalinist era and beyond, but there is no evidence that Myaskovsky's views ever altered on these points. He continued to regard propagandistic art with disdain. In another letter of 1930 to Steinberg, he remarked that the subjects for symphonies and operas currently being foisted on composers made him 'sick to the stomach'. 'For some reason, they imagine it's impossible just to produce a strong piece and even one on a revolutionary topic but without naïve tendentiousness and agitprop placards'.[156] He came in for his own share of unwanted attention: later in the year, he informed Prokofiev that he was receiving offers of commissions 'right, left, and centre – chiefly for operas, of course . . . but the subjects

---

155   Myaskovsky to Steinberg, 24 February 1930, RIII, 28/1/487, l. 50, 51.
156   Myaskovsky to Steinberg, 10 January 1930, RIII, 28/1/487, ll. 49–490b.

being proposed are mostly an outrage on common sense'.[157] He was not exaggerating. The Bolshoi Theatre approached him to write an opera to a libretto by the RAPP dramatist Alexander Afinogenov about the construction of the Dnieper hydroelectric power station, one of the most ambitious engineering projects of the period. A draft scenario is preserved amongst Myaskovsky's papers. The wholly stereotypical plot portrayed communists' heroic efforts to build the enormous dam despite attempted sabotage by benighted local peasant 'wreckers'. After a pitched battle in the second act, the communists convert the peasants to the cause of technological progress: 'People do combat with machines, machines with people, machines with water. But out of the struggle, the defeats and the victories, a [new] rhythm is born [sic]: the machines are no longer enemies, but helpers. The artel peasants sign a socialist competition contract.[158] New songs about the new work, and a new organisational force are audible in the music of the third act'.

Myaskovsky skilfully extricated himself: he told the Bolshoi that he found the scenario 'interesting' but thought it more suited to a literary than an operatic treatment, adding that it was too similar in conception to Mosolov's recently completed opera *The Dam*.[159] He was wise to decline. Yavorsky accepted a Bolshoi commission for an opera entitled *The 'October' Oil Rig*, about Soviet initiatives to drill for oil in Azerbaijan: it was so severely criticised that it was taken off after its first and only performance on 6 November 1930.[160] Acceding to VAPM's demands by no means rendered one immune from attack.

'If I do write something', Myaskovsky told Steinberg, 'I will write what I feel the need to write: it seems to me that by remaining myself I will succeed in being understood by everybody'.[161] Myaskovsky's creative energies in late 1929 and early 1930 were expended not on writing a large-scale propagandistic score, but two string quartets, opp. 33/1 and 33/2. As he knew perfectly well, VAPM was particularly suspicious of chamber music, which it deemed largely redundant. Predictably, he was criticised when the second of the quartets was performed in December 1930 (by an ensemble of recent

---

157 Myaskovsky to Prokofiev, 1 August 1930, in Kozlova and Yatsenko, *Perepiska*, 338.

158 *Dogovor na sorevnovaniye.* These contracts, introduced during the Five Year Plan, obliged workers to compete at completing tasks as rapidly as possible. See Grigoriy Alekseyev (ed.), *Istoriya sotsialisticheskogo sorevnovaniya v SSSR* (Moscow, 1980), 85–6.

159 The Bolshoi's invitation, dated 19 October 1930, Afingenov's scenario, and a handwritten draft of Myaskovsky's response of 20 October 1930 are preserved in RGALI, 2040/2/87, ll. 1–5.

160 Yelena Grosheva, *Bol'shoy teatr Soyuza SSR* (Moscow, 1978), 136–7.

161 Myaskovsky to Steinberg, 24 February 1930, RIII, 28/1/487, l. 51.

conservatoire graduates who formed the renowned Komitas Quartet two years later). Even though it was warmly received, his former student Boris Shekhter, now an active VAPM member, bemoaned 'the tragedy of a great artist who cannot find a path to the masses and writes for the audience of the Small Hall of the [Moscow] Conservatoire'.[162]

It is not entirely clear what prompted Myaskovsky's return to the genre after an elapse of twenty years[163], but his decision certainly demonstrates a supreme disregard of external pressures. A possible explanation is that he deliberately chose the demanding medium of the string quartet as a self-imposed discipline. On completing the Tenth Symphony, he resolved that whatever he wrote next should be less 'ponderous' (*gromozdkiy*): he evidently recognised that it took certain aspects of his style to extremes, especially in its gestural violence and dense chromaticism. Rather than proceeding further in the same direction, he attempted something very different. The *Divertissements*, the three light orchestral works comprising op. 32 that he composed immediately before the quartets, were conceived as a compositional 'task', as he told Prokofiev: he wanted to write music that was more relaxed and melodious in character – 'cheerful, accessible, and uncomplicated'.[164] (It should be emphasised that his ideas for these scores had taken definite shape well before VAPM became dominant: a diary entry for September 1926 records that 'the themes and forms' were 'clear' by that point.)[165] The *Divertissements* continue the turn to classicism inaugurated in the Fourth Piano Sonata and Ninth Symphony, especially the Sinfonietta for string orchestra, op. 32/2, the finest of the set. Their transparency of sonority and spare harmonic language are in striking contrast to the Tenth's harmonic and textural complexity. Interestingly, Myaskovsky praised precisely these qualities in Prokofiev's recently completed ballet score *The Prodigal Son*[166], a work exemplifying the 'new simplicity' of style that Prokofiev espoused in the late 1920s. Quite independently, he was feeling his way towards a 'new simplicity' of his own.

---

162 Myaskovsky to Prokofiev, 11 January 1931, in Kozlova and Yatsenko, *Perepiska*, 350.

163 The quartets seem to have written for the Stradivarius Quartet, an ensemble attached to Narkompros – but it disbanded in 1930 before they could be performed. Myaskovsky to Malko, 31 May 1930, RNMM, 71/783, l. 1; Myaskovsky to Prokofiev, 15 November 1930, in Kozlova and Yatsenko, *Perepiska*, 348.

164 Myaskovsky to Prokofiev, 29 March 1928, 21 January and 12 February 1929, ibid., 272, 289–90, 292.

165 'Vïpiski', 9 September 1926, RGALI, 2040/1/65, l. 5.

166 Myaskovsky to Prokofiev, 22 May 1929, in Kozlova and Yatsenko, *Perepiska*, 309–10.

This 'simplicity' is also in evidence in the string quartets, both of which are indebted to classical rather than contemporary models – above all, the middle- and late-period Beethoven quartets. Although this influence is completely assimilated, it is nonetheless perceptible in the handling of texture and the driving energy of the fast music, especially in the finales. A homage to the Viennese classical tradition is also suggested by Myaskovsky's curious decision to group these quartets with the D-minor and F-minor quartets composed during his student years and assign them the collective opus number of 33. His decision seems almost whimsical when considers that the quartets are far from lightweight: both are substantial works (respectively, in four and three movements) and predominantly intense in mood. The intensity, however, is achieved in a very different way than in the Tenth – principally by contrapuntal means, rather than through harmonic and textural density. The quartets mark an important stage in the transition to the sparer, leaner style of Myaskovsky's later work and adumbrate traits that would come increasingly to the fore, such as his employment of a more pervasively diatonic and modal harmonic language. (That said, there are passages in both which are as strenuously dissonant as anything found in his earlier music: the restatement of the first subject in the exposition of the first movement of op. 33/1, shown in example 8.6, is an apt illustration in point.) In writing them, Myaskovsky took the opportunity to undertake a radical reappraisal of his compositional approach that not only brought an increased technical command but made possible a further broadening of expressive range. They contain music not only of an impressive sweep and brilliance but also of a haunted introspection and impassioned eloquence in their deeply felt slow movements.

It is difficult to imagine anything less akin to 'music for the masses' than these quartets, which explore an inward, intensely private realm of experience. If VAPM's leaders expected Myaskovsky to produce a major work demonstrating his acceptance of their aesthetic platform, they were to be disappointed. Myaskovsky's sole concession to circumstances was to compose two short marches for military band in the spring of 1930, seemingly as a sop to the association – though the circumstances are unclear. (A diary entry records that he was trying unsuccessfully to write music of 'broad appeal'.[167]) The marches are workmanlike, but undistinguished: Myaskovsky described them to Prokofiev as 'trash' and did not dignify them with an opus number.[168] They scarcely represent a substantial investment of time and energy: his student Shebalin, by contrast, undertook to write a *Lenin* Symphony for soloists, choir, and orchestra.

---

167 'Vipiski', 31 January 1931, RGALI, 2040/1/65, l. 7.

168 Myaskovsky to Prokofiev, 1 August 1930, in Kozlova and Yatsenko, *Perepiska*, 338.

EXAMPLE 8.6. String Quartet in A minor, op. 33/1, first movement: bars 23–37

As it transpired, Myaskovsky wrote very little for eighteen months after finishing the Second String Quartet in March 1930. His summer vacation was taken up with settling into his new flat, which was finally ready. At forty-nine years of age, after more than a decade of living in communal apartments, he at last had the domestic privacy that he craved. The flat itself, however, proved a great disappointment. The apartment building, a five-storey structure containing fifteen dwellings, was situated on Sivtsev Vrazhek Lane, a narrow side-street at the edge of the central Arbat District. The location was convenient, but noisy and dusty on account of major construction works nearby. The interior was meanly proportioned, with small rooms that received little direct sunlight, though the flat was on the fourth floor: as Myaskovsky described to Prokofiev, the windows on either side overlooked 'filthy courtyards filled with rubbish', in the midst of which a solitary scrawny poplar was 'eking out its unenviable existence'.[169] It is not difficult to see why the image made an impression on him.

Valentina moved with him (the siblings continued to live together until Myaskovsky's death, though Marianna took lodgings elsewhere), but her brother dispatched her to Leningrad for a holiday with Yevgeniya until the flat was in a habitable state. After moving in on 5 August, he spent an exhausting week transferring their belongings and the contents of his library, and cleaning up the worst of the grime from the construction work.[170] It soon became apparent that its quality left much to be desired: the walls in his study and bedroom were damp and quickly became covered in mould. Even in the hot summer, the flat felt cold. The electricity supply was intermittent and lengthy delays ensued before the gas supply was connected and the central heating started to function properly. After all his efforts, the move came as a dispiriting anticlimax. He once again found himself in the grip of depression and complained of feeling exhausted and unable to work. To add to his misfortunes, a painful furuncle erupted on his face: the infection spread to his neck, causing him great discomfort.[171]

When he returned to work in September, tired and in poor health, VAPM's stranglehold on musical life showed no signs of easing. Regular concert activity had more or less ceased in the capital: the organisation blocked performances of virtually all modern Western and Russian repertoire except compositions by its members. Apart from occasional chamber concerts at the conservatoire, the only other opportunities to hear new

169 Ibid., 339.

170 Myaskovsky to Valentina Menshikova, *circa* 10 August 1930, RGALI, 2040/1/74, ll. 18–200b; 'Vïpiski', 14 August 1930, RGALI, 2040/1/65, l. 7.

171 Myaskovsky to Malko, 7 September 1930, RNMM, 71/785; Myaskovsky to Prokofiev, 15 November 1930 and 11 January 1931, in Kozlova and Yatsenko, *Perepiska*, 347, 350.

music were provided by the Moscow Radio Symphony Orchestra – largely thanks to Derzhanovsky, who was now working for Narkompros's Radio Section, where attitudes to VAPM seem to have been more sceptical.[172] A return to the cultural isolation and stagnation of the Civil War years seemed imminent. Prokofiev was so dismayed by the persisting hostility towards his work since the cancellation of a Bolshoi production of his ballet *Le pas d'acier* in 1929 due to pressure from VAPM that he repeatedly deferred a third planned visit to the USSR. Demoralisation and anxiety about professional prospects became widespread as staff purges continued at the conservatoires and other institutions. Composers were by no means the only musicians affected: several of Myaskovsky's associates, including Lamm, Popov, and Asafiev, were forced out of jobs and struggled to find alternative employment. While no-one seems to have suffered more serious consequences because of VAPM's denunciations, such as being arraigned on charges of 'wrecking' and anti-Soviet activity, it was impossible to tell how the situation might develop. Pavel Lamm's arrest several years previously had graphically demonstrated that the authorities' interventions could be both unpredictable and ruthless. Myaskovsky knew at least one musician who came to grief at this period, though for reasons that had nothing to do with his professional activities – the young composer Mikhail Kvadri, a friend of Shebalin, who had been arrested with sixty others on fabricated charges of involvement in a terrorist youth organisation and shot in June 1929. Kvadri was forced by the secret police to draw up a comprehensive list of people with whom he came into contact: Myaskovsky was amongst those he named.[173] A keen admirer of the older man's work, Kvadri had consulted him periodically and dedicated his First Symphony to him. The manuscript score of the symphony only survived because Myaskovsky came into possession of it after Kvadri's death and preserved it amongst his own papers.[174]

Myaskovsky continued to work at Muzsektor and the conservatoire, though by the end of 1930 he doubted whether he could endure either for much longer. Earlier in the year, Muzsektor had been restructured, acquiring a new name ('Muzgiz'[175]) and a new director – Adolf Verkhotursky, a long-standing Party member. 'He supposedly studied music', Myaskovsky confided in Steinberg, 'which I think is probably worse than if he knew nothing at all'. His fears of intensified bureaucratic interference proved

---

172 Myaskovsky to Steinberg, 29 March 1930, RIII, 28/1/487, ll. 54–540b;
      Myaskovsky to Prokofiev, 16 May 1930, in Kozlova and Yatsenko, *Perepiska*,
      330.

173 See Izrail' Mazus (ed.), *Demokraticheskiy soyuz: Sledstvennoye delo 1928–1929
      gg.* (Moscow, 2010), 86–103.

174 Sof'ya Ovsyannikova, 'Mikhail Kvadri – Lider moskovskikh Six'ov', *Musicus*, 1
      (2018), 37.

175 Gosudarstvennoye muzïkal'noye izdatel'stvo – 'State Music Publisher'.

justified. Verkhotursky instituted a comprehensive overhaul of Muzgiz's publications policy: the output of serious music was drastically reduced in favour of 'mass music' and limited to works deemed 'most ideologically relevant or of historical value'. (It was even suggested that the publication of chamber music should cease altogether.) The press's efficiency plummeted once more after losing a large proportion of its personnel in a staff purge. Myaskovsky found himself putting in long, exhausting days, fulfilling tasks that he considered time-wasting and pointless.[176]

Matters were no better at the conservatoire. In February 1931, Narkompros announced that it was to be renamed the Felix Kon Higher Music School in honour of Kon's contribution to the revolutionary movement – an idea that presumably originated with his protégé Przybyszewski.[177] (Lenin would probably have been incredulous: he thought Kon 'an old nincompoop'.[178]) The announcement coincided with VAPM's proclamation of a 'new phase' in its 'struggle' to eradicate bourgeois influences and to 're-educate' fellow travellers.[179] The organisation pressed for even more radical reforms of music education and the conservatoire's change of name clearly reflected its intention to redefine the institution's fundamental purpose. Przybyszewski, incompetent and disorganised, readily allowed VAPM's leaders free rein. Myaskovsky told Steinberg that he had been overheard to remark: 'But does anyone really need music now?'[180] In a letter of April 1931, he gave a sombre summary of developments: 'The conservatoire is on the verge of falling apart. VAPM has taken over the management and wants to redirect all teaching and composing towards amateur musical activities. It's clear that anything aimed at turning out qualified people will get no support: in any case, more qualified teachers aren't even required, since under present conditions their jobs could be done by anyone at all'. He continued:

> The situation at Muzgiz is just as hopeless. . . . We haven't accepted a single new composition for publication since the start of the year! . . . I blame this on composers' complete lack of trust in Muzgiz's new management, and that mistrust is completely justified: I've concluded that the management has no interest in music whatsoever. . . . And we're still working out heaps of thematic plans [i.e., proposed ideological subjects for new commissioned works], but they're all so lacking in artistic and emotional appeal that they don't arouse the slightest desire to start work-

176 Myaskovsky to Steinberg, 10 October, 24 November, and 22 December 1930, RIII, 28/1/487, ll. 60–600b, 64–640b, 66–70b. On Muzgiz's new publications policy, see Adol'f Verkhoturskiy, *Muzgiz na stroyke* (Moscow, 1931).

177 'Khronika', *Khudozhestvennoye obrazovaniye*, 1 (1931), 41.

178 Yuriy Amiantov *et al.* (ed.), *V. I. Lenin: Neizvestnïye dokumentï, 1891–1922* (Moscow, 2000), 211.

179 See *Novïy ètap bor'bï na muzïkal'nom fronte* (Moscow, 1931), 67–72.

180 Myaskovsky to Steinberg, 19 May 1931, RIII, 28/1/487, l. 75.

ing on them. Because of that, I have absolutely no creative plans – all I want to do is to rest, rest, and distance myself from everything.[181]

On 22 April he turned fifty. Steinberg sent a warm note expressing deep appreciation of his friendship and admiration for his music. Myaskovsky replied:

> It means a lot to me that you value my own musical efforts, because I do not even consider myself to be fully a musician. Music for me is sheer overcoming. And I feel that particularly keenly now – as though I had never composed a note and never been a musician at all. Perhaps this is due to weariness or to being overwhelmed by all kinds of trivial day-to-day and musical matters – or perhaps it could really be that I've exhausted my entire store of creative powers. As you see, my passage over this threshold has been a sad one. And I do not really see any prospects ahead.[182]

By the start of the summer vacation, he felt exhausted. Leopold Stokowski met him at a reception in Moscow in mid-June and found him taciturn and withdrawn.[183] At the start of July he took his first extended summer holiday in several years. His customary lodgings at Mukhanovo were no longer available, so he stayed with Pavel Lamm and his family in Nikolina Gora, a small settlement situated on the Moskva River, thirty miles west of Moscow. The picturesque location delighted him, and he took advantage of the fine summer weather to explore the surrounding countryside on foot. He was clearly not well, however: he was troubled once more by a furuncle on his face which erupted into painful boils. In late July, he returned from a brief excursion to Moscow feeling seriously ill, scarcely able to drag himself home. A visiting cousin of the Lamms, Maria Petrovna, who was a surgical nurse, was alarmed to discover that his temperature had soared to 40°C. The underlying bacterial infection was on the point of developing into full-blown sepsis – a condition that was often fatal before the advent of antibiotics and could result in an agonising death from multiple organ failure. Myaskovsky was in danger of succumbing to the same fate as Skryabin.

He was saved through a stroke of good fortune that was nothing short of extraordinary, especially when one considers that he was in a remote village, far from emergency medical help. Maria Petrovna knew that an eminent Moscow surgeon, Aleksey Martïnov, happened to be holidaying nearby and ran to summon him. Martïnov was one of the Soviet pioneers of phage therapy, a technique of treating infections with preparations containing specially selected viruses ('bacteriophages') that kill the bacterial

181 Myaskovsky to Steinberg, 6 April 1931, RIII, 28/1/487, ll. 70–700b.
182 Myaskovsky to Steinberg, 27 April 1931, RIII, 28/1/487, ll. 72–720b.
183 Prokofiev to Myaskovsky, 7 July 1931, in Kozlova and Yatsenko, *Perepiska*, 359.

organisms responsible, but are harmless to the patient.[184] He immediately sent to Moscow for the necessary variety and began to treat Myaskovsky with injections and topical applications. The patient's life hung in the balance: there was a very real fear that he might not survive, but he slowly rallied. Treatment continued under Martïnov's assistant throughout August and he recovered sufficiently to be brought back to Moscow by 10 September. When she opened the apartment door, Valentina was so shocked at how ill he looked that she fainted: his friends scarcely recognised him, as he had been shorn of his beard and moustache to allow the abscess on his face to be dressed.[185] There was no question of returning to work: it would take him months to recuperate. As he did so, the crisis in Soviet musical life would reach its climax.

184　Viral phage therapy was extensively researched in the USSR and used in Soviet field hospitals during the Second World War. See David Shrayer, 'Felix d'Herelle in Russia', *Bulletin de l'Institut Pasteur* 94 (1996), 91–6; Richard Stone, 'Stalin's Forgotten Cure', *Science*, 5594 (2002), 728–31.

185　This account of Myaskovsky's illness draws on Lamm, 'Pavel Aleksandrovich Lamm: Opït biografii', RNMM, 192/361, ll. 388–9; eadem, *Stranitsï*, 16–17.

9

Time of Troubles: 1932–41

As he began his protracted convalescence, Myaskovsky's greatest worry, aside from his health, was how he would support himself. His weakened physical condition left him effectively housebound throughout the winter of 1931–2. At the insistence of his doctor, he took extended leave of absence from the conservatoire and relinquished most of his duties at Muzgiz, staying on only as an advisor to the editorial board.[1] He had been thinking of leaving both institutions for some time[2], but his illness decided matters. His overwhelming desire, he told Asafiev, was to distance himself from everything – the mere thought of having a conversation with Muzgiz's director Verkhotursky 'sickened' him.[3] Nonetheless, he needed to earn money somehow. For the time being, he had little choice but to try to eke out a living as a freelance composer. Although Myaskovsky's position was undoubtedly difficult, it was by no means hopeless. Over the previous two years he had successfully performed a delicate balancing act, managing to maintain good professional relations while making minimal concessions to circumstances. The reluctance of the senior management of the conservatoire and of Muzgiz to dispense with his services, notwithstanding the staff purges at both institutions, is noteworthy. Although his work was not being performed, he could not complain of any lack of willingness from Muzgiz to publish it, as he told Prokofiev.[4] He had also managed to avoid becoming the target of a campaign of public vilification by VAPM, even if the handful of mass songs and marches that he had produced hardly constituted persuasive evidence of thoroughgoing artistic and political 'reform'. VAPM's stranglehold on musical life persisted (the government concert agency seemed in a state of paralysis and even the radio ensembles had virtually ceased performing contemporary repertoire of any interest[5]), but

---

1   Myaskovsky to Steinberg, 5 October and 9 November 1931, RIII, 28/1/487, ll. 80–1, 83. In a letter to the director of the Felix Kon Higher Music School of 26 February 1932, Myaskovsky requested that his leave of absence be extended, adding that he wished to resign if this proved infeasible: RGALI, 2040/1/172, l. 1.

2   See Myaskovsky to Prokofiev, 11 January and 20 September 1931, in Kozlova and Yatsenko, *Perepiska*, 350–1, 365.

3   Myaskovsky to Asafiev, 5 October 1931, RGALI, 2658/1/641, l. 38.

4   Myaskovsky to Prokofiev, 11 January 1931, in Kozlova and Yatsenko, *Perepiska*, 350.

5   Myaskovsky to Steinberg, 5 October 1931, RIII, 28/1/487, l. 81.

there were grounds for cautious optimism that an improvement in conditions might be imminent.

In spite of the oppressive climate of the Cultural Revolution, state financial support for the arts had grown appreciably over the last two years. When the new arts directorate Glaviskusstvo was set up in 1929, it announced a range of initiatives – including competitions and prizes, subsidised exhibitions, and commissioning schemes – which significantly augmented artists' potential sources of income. These measures were prompted by the pragmatic acknowledgement that the arts could not thrive without state patronage, now that the last vestiges of private patronage had disappeared. (The government's motives were by no means disinterested, however: as a policy document explained, Glaviskusstvo aimed to exercise an 'intensified guiding influence' over artistic production, in contrast with the more 'passive oversight' of the NEP years.)[6] By the summer of 1931, commissioning schemes for dramatic and musical works had been introduced, administered by Vseroskomdram, the All-Russian Society of Soviet Dramatists and Composers[7] – a recently established division of Narkompros, formed by amalgamating two pre-Revolutionary performing rights societies that had survived into the NEP era. Vseroskomdram continued to collect authors' royalties but had a broader range of functions than its predecessors. In addition to awarding commissions, it promoted the ethos of the Cultural Revolution by encouraging its members to engage with political and ideological themes, fostering proletarian and peasant talent, and organising amateur performances at factories, collective farms, and workers' clubs.[8] A composers' commissioning scheme was a novel venture in Soviet musical life: previously, as in other countries, they had been solely reliant on income from publishing contracts and royalties. Insofar as it afforded composers greater material security, it was undoubtedly something to be welcomed – even if it also marked the beginning of the government's attempts to subject musical creativity to increasingly invasive bureaucratic controls.

In the autumn of 1931 Vseroskomdram commissioned new works to mark the impending fifteenth anniversary of the October Revolution from twenty-two composers –including Alexander Kreyn, Anatoly Aleksandrov, and Myaskovsky.[9] In Myaskovsky's case, the commission was for a symphony. The fact that Vseroskomdram was prepared to commission a symphony is

6   See Manin, *Iskusstvo v rezervatsii*, 128ff.

7   A contraction of 'Vserossiyskoye obshchestvo dramaturgov i kompozitorov'.

8   'Ustav Vserossiyskogo Obshchestva Sovetskikh dramaturgov, kompozitorov, avtorov kino, kluba i estradï', IMLI, 52/1/320, ll. 1–2. On Vseroskomdram, see Konstantin Plotnikov, 'Istoriya literaturnoy organizatsii Vseroskomdram (po materialam Otdela rukopisey IMLI RAN)', unpublished dissertation (Gorky Institute of World Literature/Russian Academy of Sciences, 2015).

9   'Kontraktatsiya kompozitorov', *Sovetskoye iskusstvo*, 25 November 1931.

significant: notwithstanding the pressures on composers to produce works on ideological subjects in styles calculated to appeal to uneducated listeners, it suggested that they would not be constrained merely to turning out agit-prop scores. Although members of the Russian Association of Proletarian Writers and the Association of Proletarian Musicians were strongly represented in Vseroskomdram's ranks, the organisation maintained its independence in matters of policy. Levon Atovmyan, the energetic young secretary general of Vseroskomdram's Composers' Section[10], did not share VAPM's doctrinaire outlook, despite being a Party member. On the whole, his attitude towards the 'fellow-traveller' composers was supportive: in the autumn of 1931 he started planning a series of symphony and chamber concerts at the Bolshoi Theatre in which their work featured prominently.[11] The programme for the first concert, scheduled for 12 December 1931, included Myaskovsky's Sinfonietta for string orchestra, op. 32/2, Kabalevsky's First Piano Concerto, and Shebalin's Second Symphony.[12]

Myaskovsky was initially wary of Atovmyan and expected little to come of his endeavours.[13] Nonetheless, these developments were encouraging: they seemed to confirm his belief that the disruption caused by VAPM would abate and that there would still be scope to compose in the genres central to his creative preoccupations. That said, accepting Vseroskomdram's commission necessitated a pragmatic compromise: as he informed Steinberg, Vseroskomdram stipulated that the symphony should have a programmatic basis and treat a Soviet topic.[14] A copy of the contract has not been preserved amongst his personal papers or in Vseroskomdram's archive, but in a diary entry, Myaskovsky noted that the work was to be 'about collective farms [*kolkhozi*[15]]'. The proposed subject was unsurprising: amongst the themes that Vseroskomdram recommended to its members in 1931 was 'the remoulding of the petit bourgeois proprietorial individualistic consciousness through the processes of socialist reconstruction of agriculture on the basis of thoroughgoing collectivisation'. (Other suggested topics included

---

10   The records of the Composers' Section have not been preserved with the remainder of the Vseroskomdram archive in IMLI (fond 52); if they still exist, their whereabouts is unknown.

11   See Levon Atovm'yan, 'Vospominaniya', in Nelli Kravets (ed.), *Ryadom s velikimi: Atovm'yan i yego vremya* (Moscow, 2012), 210–11.

12   The programme for the concert is preserved in RNMM, 336/1188.

13   Myaskovsky to Prokofiev, 20 October 1931, in Kozlova and Yatsenko, *Perepiska*, 366.

14   Myaskovsky to Steinberg, 9 November 1931, RIII, 28/1/487, l. 82.

15   Strictly speaking, the term *kolkhoz* (a contraction of *kollektivnoye khozyaystvo*, 'collective ownership') refers only to one variety of collective farm: unlike a *sovkhoz*, which was state-owned, a *kolkhoz* was an agricultural production co-operative which was supposedly formed voluntarily and notionally owned by its members.

'the cultural, economic, and political development of the peoples of the USSR on the basis of Lenin's nationalities policy' and 'the international education of the toiling masses by showing the organic connection between the successes of Soviet socialist construction and the international revolutionary workers' movement, and with the struggle of the international proletariat and oppressed colonies against exploiters and imperialists'.)[16] Novels, plays, and visual artworks offering idealised portrayals of life on collective farms proliferated during the Cultural Revolution, as did similar depictions of accelerated industrialisation.

Notwithstanding his profession of putative enthusiasm in his 'Autobiographical Notes'[17], Myaskovsky's private distaste for the project is abundantly manifest in his letters. Far from signalling the 'reform' of his political outlook, as Soviet commentators subsequently claimed[18], his acceptance of the commission was dictated by material necessity. There is no evidence to suggest that he viewed Stalin's collectivisation campaign in a positive light or had any desire to write a work lauding it. Despite glowing press accounts of the campaign's success and repeated promises of record agricultural yields, it was evident that collectivisation was proving highly disruptive and had precipitated a serious crisis in food production. The country was seething with discontent.[19] Rumours were rife of the authorities' brutal responses to manifestations of resistance from peasant farmers, who destroyed crops and slaughtered livestock rather than relinquish their holdings to the state.[20] And even before the catastrophic famines of 1932–3, which ravaged rural communities and caused millions of deaths, the inhabitants of Moscow and other large cities were going hungry once more. Rationing of bread, meat, potatoes, and other basic provisions was reintroduced in 1929 and remained in force for several years.[21] The composer Anatoly Dianov, a regular guest at Pavel Lamm's music evenings, recorded in his diary friends' reports from late 1931 onwards of food shortages, threatened famine, and epidemics in various regions of the USSR – as

---

16   Plotnikov, 'Istoriya', 85–6.

17   'When the first calls for the collectivisation of peasant agriculture were heard, I was very enthusiastic about the idea, which seemed to me particularly revolutionary in its consequences': Myaskovskiy, 'Avtobiograficheskiye zametki', 11.

18   See Livanova, *N. Ya. Myaskovskiy*, 122ff.

19   See Andrey Sokolov *et al.* (ed.), *Obshchestvo i vlast': 1930-ye gg. Povestvovaniye v dokumentakh* (Moscow, 1998), 13–73.

20   The diary of the Moscow historian Ivan Shitts [Schütz] repeatedly alludes to reports of executions, deportations, imprisonment in labour camps, and other harshly repressive measures: see *Dnevnik 'Velikogo Pereloma' (mart 1928–avgust 1931)* (Paris, 1986), 294–6, 309–10, 313–14.

21   See Osokina, *Za fasadom*, 71–88.

well as his own observations of hunger in the capital and lengthy queues for scarce commodities such as kerosene.[22] (The government's continued neglect of manufacturing at the expense of heavy industry also led to a renewed dearth of clothing and ordinary household goods.) Myaskovsky is unlikely to have been under any illusions about the true state of affairs: it is noteworthy that he asked Dzimitrovsky, his contact at Universal Edition's Vienna office, to send parcels of foodstuffs – salami, macaroni, rice, coffee – in lieu of royalty payments.[23]

One other important piece of evidence indicates that Myaskovsky's artistic outlook remained fundamentally unaltered by the Cultural Revolution, in spite of the pressures from VAPM. Prior to starting work on Vseroskomdram's commission in late October 1931, he sketched another symphony, the Eleventh, in B-flat minor, op. 34 – his first substantial creative project since the completion of the Second String Quartet in March 1930. He had composed virtually nothing in the intervening eighteen months apart from *Three Soviet Pilots' Songs*, a set of mass songs for two-part choir and piano evidently written as another sop to VAPM and to which he once again did not assign an opus number. (The opening of the first, 'The Wings of the Soviets', is shown in example 9.1: it is virtually indistinguishable from the trite productions of VAPM composers such as his former student Boris Shekhter.[24] For all the association's bellicose rhetoric, its members' notions of 'revolutionary music' were surprisingly tame: as Myaskovsky pointed out, their mass songs often display an incongruous resemblance to nineteenth-century 'bourgeois' salon music.[25]) As he informed Steinberg, the Eleventh was a three-movement symphony 'of the most ordinary variety', without a programme or political messages of any kind.[26] Neither did he make any stylistic concessions. The work is as complex in construction as any of the earlier symphonies and its harmonic language is at times bracingly astringent – most noticeably, in the dissonant fugato that comprises the brooding central section of the second movement (ex. 9.2). Though it lacks the tautness of the finest of Myaskovsky's symphonies, the Eleventh nonetheless contains some powerfully eloquent music and demonstrates a continued broadening of his expressive range. The serenely diatonic principal theme of the *Adagio ma non tanto* adumbrates the radiant tranquillity

---

22 'Dnevnik', RGALI, 2027/1/21, ll. 23–230b, 25.

23 Dzimitrovsky reported sending the first parcel in a letter of 26 October 1930 and others subsequently on 5 February and 17 April 1931: RGALI, 2040/2/141, ll. 260b, 32, 38.

24 Compare, for example, Shekhter's 'As Iron Reserves' ('Zheleznïmi rezervami'), reproduced in Edmunds, *The Soviet Proletarian Music Movement*, 251.

25 Myaskovsky to Steinberg, 10 January 1930, RIII, 28/1/487, l. 480b–9.

26 Myaskovsky to Steinberg, 9 November 1931, RIII, 28/1/487, l. 82.

EXAMPLE 9.1. 'The Wings of the Soviets' (opening).

The sparkle of polished wings. / Our planes ascend, / Our planes are a new era / Our planes ascend!

EXAMPLE 9.2. Symphony no. 11, second movement: bars 80–95.

of some of his later slow movements, while the finale, an interesting fusion of sonata and variation form, persuasively works through the residual tensions from the previous movements to end in a mood of high spirits.

Myaskovsky postponed orchestrating the Eleventh until he had written the symphony commissioned by Vseroskomdram, which became the Twelfth Symphony in G minor, op. 35. Unlike its predecessor, its composition cost him considerable difficulty: he complained to Steinberg that he had 'literally to squeeze' the ideas out of himself.[27] Under the circumstances, it was remarkable that he managed to write anything at all: as he commenced it, misfortune struck again. On 25 October, his sister Yevgeniya learned that her second husband Alexander Fedorovsky had been sentenced to five years in a labour camp subsequent to his and his father's arrest on fabricated charges of espionage.[28] As the wife of an 'enemy of the people', Yevgeniya faced the prospect of summary banishment from Leningrad, together with her five-year-old son, Nikita. The plight of spouses in Yevgeniya's position was unenviable: they were treated as outcasts and often experienced acute difficulty securing accommodation or employment. The family desperately sought to reverse the banishment order. It would appear that Myaskovsky approached Chekhov's widow, the famous actress and founder-member of the Moscow Arts Theatre Olga Knipper-Chekhova, whom he knew socially[29], and asked for her help. Knipper-Chekhova in turn availed of her contacts within the Political Red Cross, a Moscow-based charity set up to support political prisoners and their families, run by Gorky's first wife Yekaterina Peshkova. (Remarkably, this unique organisation was tolerated by the authorities and allowed to exist until 1938.[30]) After a nerve-wracking few weeks Yevgeniya learned that her appeal had been successful.[31]

The episode left Myaskovsky deeply shaken and nearly caused a relapse of the illness that he had suffered over the summer: work on the Twelfth was interrupted for three weeks while he recovered.[32] His brother-in-law's arrest potentially cast a cloud of suspicion over the entire family and was

---

27 Ibid., ll. 82–820b.

28 According to information provided to the Fedorovsky family by the Russian Federal Security Service in 2003, Pavel and Alexander Fedorovsky were arrested on 15 March and 19 November 1930, respectively. Both men were posthumously rehabilitated. I would like to thank Tatiana Fedorovskaya for allowing me to consult the document in question.

29 See Chemberdzhi, *V dome muzïka zhila*, 320.

30 See Maria Cristina Galmarini, 'Defending the Rights of Gulag Prisoners: The Story of the Political Red Cross, 1918–38', *Russian Review*, 1 (2012), 6–29.

31 The Political Red Cross's correspondence with Yevgeniya and Olga Knipper-Chekhova is preserved in GARF, 8409/1/574, ll. 168, 171, 172, 174.

32 Myaskovsky to Prokofiev, 24 December 1931, in Kozlova and Yatsenko, *Perepiska*, 370.

an unwelcome reminder of their vulnerability.[33] Writing to Steinberg, he reported that Yevgeniya had been reduced to selling items of furniture belonging to Valentina and himself (presumably to pay legal fees): fortunately, it did not prove necessary to part with his piano. 'Only when I received word that everything had concluded satisfactorily and that my sister wasn't going anywhere . . . did I return to the finale of the symphony, which was supposed to hymn the triumph of socialism – or collectivisation, to be more precise – in the countryside. You can imagine what the results were like! I have rarely been so dissatisfied with anything that I have written'. He added with heavy irony: 'I probably did not have a sufficiently deep appreciation of the ardour of the collective spirit and could not express it adequately in music'.[34]

This anxious period saw an escalation of the tensions in musical life – despite indications that the Party wished to curb the harassment of the 'old intelligentsia'. In a major speech to industrialists on 23 June 1931 entitled 'New Conditions, New Tasks', Stalin claimed that the attitudes of 'bourgeois specialists' to the regime had transformed sufficiently as to render them largely trustworthy: the Party could show them 'greater attention and solicitude', he suggested, and be 'bolder in engaging their services'.[35] The proletarian artistic organisations were reluctant to heed such signals. Having assumed control of key musical institutions, the Russian Association of Proletarian Musicians (as VAPM renamed itself in the autumn of 1931) would not cede it without a struggle. Its leaders' zealotry showed no signs of abating – as was demonstrated by their furious response to a spirited polemical campaign waged by Derzhanovsky, the theatre critic Vladimir Blyum, and others in the radio magazine *Moscow Speaking*, which poked fun at the overbearing behaviour of RAPM's leaders and the pretentious banality of the music written by its composers.[36] (One article naughtily pointed out melodic similarities between Davidenko's mass songs and 'bourgeois' salon music such as the Neapolitan ballad *Torna a Surriento*.[37]) Soon afterwards,

33 Suspicion attached to family members by association. Six years later, Shostakovich learned that he had not been elected to the directorate of the Leningrad branch of the Composers' Union because of the arrest of his sister's husband as an 'enemy of the people' and her banishment from the city. See Shostakovich to Platon Kerzhentsev, 11 June 1937, in Maksimenkov (ed.), *Muzïka vmesto sumbura*, 174–5.

34 Myaskovsky to Steinberg, 16 January 1932, RIII, 28/1/487, ll. 84–840b.

35 'Novaya obstanovka – Novïye zadachi khozyaystvennogo stroitel'stva', *Pravda*, 5 July 1931.

36 See Vlasova, *1948 god*, 114–16.

37 'Ėkskursiya na kukhnyu muzïki', *Govorit Moskva*, 23–4 (1931), 5.

Derzhanovsky was dismissed when Feliks Kon was put in charge of broadcasting and shut down the periodical in question.[38]

The brouhaha over the articles in *Moscow Speaking* may explain Myaskovsky's surprising decision to sign a statement published by a group of 'fellow-traveller' composers in the newspaper *Soviet Art* on 8 August 1931 declaring their intention to found a new 'creative association' similar in ethos to RAPM, but which would foster the composition of large-scale works such as symphonies and operas as well as smaller 'mass' genres.[39] Nothing is known about the circumstances which prompted this development, but it can safely be said that Myaskovsky's apparent endorsement of RAPM's policies cannot be taken at face value. An important clue to what might have happened is furnished by the references to Derzhanovsky and Blyum in writings by RAPM's chairman Lebedinsky around this time. Both men aroused Lebedinsky's deep hostility, not merely on account of their articles in *Moscow Speaking* but also because of their dogged efforts to reanimate ASM after it ceased operations in early 1929.[40] (Derzhanovsky found in Blyum an unlikely ally in this ultimately futile endeavour.) The possibility that ASM might revive became something of an *idée fixe* for Lebedinsky: he characterised the *Moscow Speaking* campaign as a conspiracy by former ASM personnel to sabotage RAPM's efforts to 'reform' fellow travellers. When the declaration signed by Myaskovsky was reprinted shortly afterwards in RAPM's journal *Proletarian Musician*, the facing page featured a statement from RAPM's secretariat condemning the articles in *Moscow Speaking* as wrecking activities by 'class enemies'.[41]

It is possible that Myaskovsky came under pressure in the summer of 1931 to make a statement distancing himself from his past involvement in ASM and confirming his intention to 'reform' – though there is no evidence to support this conjecture. If so, he perhaps signed the declaration simply in the hope of being left alone and forestalling further unpleasantness. However, it is suggestive that five of the nine signatories of the declaration were Myaskovsky's students, including Shebalin and Kabalevsky. Rather than being primarily concerned to protect himself, it may be that Myaskovsky signed it as a gesture of support for his young protégés as they attempted to come to an accommodation with RAPM while stopping short of actually joining the organisation. Whatever the reason, his action in no wise betokened a dramatic change of outlook, despite RAPM's attempt to

---

38 See Shostakovich to Ivan Sollertinsky, 14 October 1931, in *D. D. Shostakovich: Pis'ma I. I. Sollertinskomu*, 90–2.

39 'Za klassovuyu muzïkal'nuyu kul'turu', *Sovetskoye iskusstvo*, 8 August 1931.

40 See, for example, *Novïy étap bor'bï*, 57–75; *Vosem' let bor'bï*, 77–83; 'Bor'ba za perestroyku', *Proletarskiy muzïkant*, 10 (1931), 11–14.

41 'Ot sekretariata RAPMa', *Proletarskiy muzïkant*, 7 (1931), 48.

adduce the declaration as evidence of its success in winning over fellow travellers. The new 'creative organisation' had little more than a paper existence: no records of its activities have come to light after an initial meeting with RAPM's leaders to discuss how its members could apply themselves to the 'tasks of socialist construction'.[42] Myaskovsky's Eleventh Symphony, composed shortly afterwards, signally failed to demonstrate any such intention; and, as events would soon show, Shebalin's expression of support for RAPM was patently a ploy.

Though still powerful, RAPM was not invulnerable. In early October, Narkompros's collegium passed a resolution criticising the new RAPM-designed curricula at Moscow Conservatoire because of their neglect of technical training and canonical repertoire.[43] Around the same time, RAPM's more powerful sister organisation, the Russian Association of Proletarian Writers, began to find itself under attack from the Communist Youth League, which published articles in its newspaper *Komsomolskaya pravda* condemning RAPP's 'arrogance' and 'harmful sectarianism'[44] – charges subsequently reiterated in *Pravda*.[45] That such criticisms were starting to be voiced by the government and by Party-controlled organs put both organisations on the defensive.

Long-simmering resentments about RAPM finally boiled over at the start of October. With Atovmyan's support, Mikhail Gnesin, Shebalin, Shostakovich, and Aleksandrov pressed for a meeting with members of Vseroskomdram's presidium to discuss their grievances, but without having any RAPM personnel present.[46] The meeting duly took place on 2 October and was chaired by the RAPP leaders Leopold Averbakh and Alexander Afinogenov (the Bolshoi Theatre had proposed the latter as a potential opera librettist for Myaskovsky the previous year). Gnesin described the stultifying effects of RAPM's policies at the Moscow Conservatoire, while Shebalin discussed the organisation's inhibiting influence on composition and the venal behaviour of its leading representatives.[47] He pointed out that while fellow travellers found it impossible to get their work performed or published, Davidenko and Bely were having their mass songs issued by Muzgiz in 'colossal' quantities and earning large sums in royalties from

42 See 'Novoye tvorcheskoye ob"yedineniye', *Proletarskiy muzïkant*, 7 (1931), 49.

43 'Postanovleniye kollegii Narodnogo komissariata po prosveshcheniyu RSFSR', *Khudozhestvennoye obrazovaniye*, 9–10 (1931), 24–6.

44 See, for example, 'Starïye i novïye lozungi' and 'Novoye v tvorcheskoy diskussii (k itogam plenuma RAPP)', *Komsomol'skaya pravda*, 24 September and 16 October 1931.

45 See Aleksandr Dement'yev (ed.), *Ocherki istorii russkoy sovetskoy zhurnalistiki, 1933–1945* (Moscow, 1968), 264–5.

46 Atovm'yan, 'Vospominaniya', 198–9.

47 A transcript of Shebalin's speech is preserved in RGALI, 2012/1/137.

radio broadcasts – even though they were unable to orchestrate their own compositions and had to hire pupils of the very composers whom they reviled do it for them. He also described his frustrating experiences of trying to teach composition in the prevailing climate: 'My students ... bring me, say, three or four bars of some clumsy melody and a discussion starts about whether these three or four bars reflect some feelings or other of the proletariat during the Kronstadt uprising.[48] It's just idiotic word games'.[49]

Although Afinogenov and Averbakh listened courteously, the meeting had rather different consequences than the ones for which its instigators might have hoped. Copies of the stenographic transcript were circulated afterwards: whether by accident or design[50], RAPM's secretariat came into possession of one on 29 October. Outraged, Bely and his colleagues rushed out five thousand copies of a forty-page pamphlet entitled 'Facts and Figures Refuting the Constant Slander of RAPM' to counter what it described as the fellow travellers' 'lies and perversions of the facts'.[51] As Bely reported in an exultant postscript added just before the pamphlet went to press, the other members of the recently formed 'creative association' had passed a motion of censure against Shebalin and dissociated themselves from his criticisms of RAPM at a meeting on 20 November. The following day, Shebalin felt obliged to offer a humiliating apology at a meeting of RAPM's secretariat, the text of which Bely reproduced in full.[52] In a memoir, Anatoly Aleksandrov recalled that RAPM created 'a lot of unpleasantness' for Shebalin.[53] On meeting Dianov at a concert, Shebalin took him aside and whispered that 'the knives were out' for him. Trouble was brewing at Muzgiz, where Bely was a member of the board. Muzgiz's director Verkhotursky was incensed by Shebalin's suggestion that he was wasting resources printing worthless trash by RAPM's composers and threatened never to publish his work again.[54] Although his volte-face earned him a sharp rebuke from Shostakovich[55], it is not difficult to understand why Shebalin might have panicked as he contemplated the potential consequences for

---

48 The mutiny of the armed forces in the Kronstadt naval base in March 1921 – the last major revolt against the Bolshevik government on Russian territory during the Civil War.

49 RGALI, 2012/1/137, l. 13.

50 Afinogenov disclaimed responsibility: see Yekaterina Vlasova, 'Plenum Soveta Vseroskomdrama. Fragment stenogrammï, posvyashchyonnïy muzïkal'nïm voprosam (18–19 dekabrya 1931 goda)', *Muzïkal'naya akademiya*, 2 (1993), 175.

51 *Faktï i tsifrï protiv ocherednoy klevetï na RAPM* (Moscow, 1931), 37.

52 *Faktï i tsifrï*, 38–40.

53 Vladimir Blok (ed.), *A. N. Aleksandrov: Vospominaniya, stat'i, pis'ma* (Moscow, 1979), 92.

54 Dianov, 'Dnevnik', 23 November 1931, RGALI, 2027/1/20, ll. 10b–2.

55 Shostakovich to Shebalin, 29 December 1931, RGALI, 2012/1/188, 30b.

his career, especially now that he was a father with two small children. Myaskovsky regarded Shebalin's involvement in attempts to challenge RAPM's dominance as a waste of time. His attitude puzzled Dianov, who pointed out, not unreasonably, that Shebalin was attempting to improve the circumstances in which composers had to operate: Myaskovsky's quietism could be construed as an abdication of responsibility.[56] Given his poor health and the anxieties about his sister Yevgeniya, however, he had good reasons for wishing to remain aloof from events.

RAPM may have emerged victorious from the first round of the fray, but its opponents did not give up. Both sides confronted one another again at Vseroskomdram meetings on 18 and 19 December.[57] Bely, Keldïsh, and other members of RAPM's secretariat were present throughout, as well as Afinogenov; the meetings were chaired by Vseroskomdram's Secretary General, the dramatist and journalist Mikhail Rossovsky. Gnesin spoke once more. He showed remarkable courage, despite having been recently mauled in RAPM's journals[58], and reiterated the substance of his earlier criticisms. He was supported by Shostakovich and Atovmyan, both of whom forthrightly declared RAPM responsible for the unhealthy state of musical life. As Shostakovich pointed out, RAPM's bullying tactics had engendered a climate of fear and inhibition: many composers had retreated into writing film music and incidental music rather than risk more substantial creative undertakings. Atovmyan reinforced this point. Instead of feeling encouraged to engage constructively with the task of creating a proletarian musical culture, he observed that fellow travellers were simply feigning agreement with RAPM's views in the hope of being left alone. As cases in point, he instanced Shebalin's recent disingenuous apology and the declaration published by the members of the new 'creative association'. He also pointed out flagrant misrepresentations in Bely's recent pamphlet, especially in regard of the preferential treatment accorded RAPM's composers by Muzgiz. The stenographic transcript of the meeting reveals Bely and his associates in a very unflattering light: they emerge as self-righteous, arrogant, and contemptuous of those whom they regarded as enemies. Their customary tactics did not prevail this time, however. Afinogenov, conscious of the mounting public hostility towards RAPP, reminded RAPM's leaders of the need for humility and self-criticism: he castigated Bely for his comments about Gnesin, alluding to their distasteful anti-Semitic subtext,

56 Dianov, 'Dnevnik', 27 December 1931, ll. 17–170b.

57 The stenographic transcript of these meetings is partially reproduced in Vlasova, 'Plenum Soveta Vseroskomdrama'.

58 See Marina Lobanova, 'Michail Gnessin und die "proletarischen Musiker" (aus der Geschichte einer Konfrontation)', in Ernst Kuhn *et al.* (ed.), *'Samuel' Goldenberg und 'Schmuyle': Jüdisches und Antisemitisches in der russischen Musikkultur* (Berlin, 2003), 105–18.

and condemned Bely's recent pamphlet as an unhelpful and disproportionate response. Rossovsky echoed Afinogenov's comments about the need for self-criticism and pointedly emphasised the disparity between RAPM's self-aggrandising claims and its members' meagre creative achievements. He concluded by urging both sides to work together more productively.

RAPM's secretariat was in no mood to compromise. It dispatched a lengthy letter to Stalin's protégé Vyacheslav Molotov, the chairman of the Council of People's Commissars (the Soviet equivalent of a prime minister), demanding that the Party intervene in support of RAPM as a matter of urgency. Replete with emphatic underlinings, much of it was taken up with complaints about the continuous 'slander' directed against the association and lurid accounts of the supposed machinations of Gnesin, Atovmyan, and other 'opportunists' and 'class-hostile elements on the musical front'.[59] The government's increasingly unsympathetic response to such complaints was apparent from a high-profile speech given by Narkompros's deputy minister Moisey Epstein on 8 January at a conference of art workers in Moscow: Epstein singled out RAPM for sharp criticism, noting its intemperate treatment of fellow travellers.[60] There was little sign of any mellowing in attitudes when Boris Shekhter and other RAPM representatives attended a meeting of Vseroskomdram's Composers' Section on 31 January 1932, convened to discuss Myaskovsky's Sinfonietta, op. 32/2 and the other scores played at the Bolshoi Theatre symphony concert on 12 December. Prior to this event, none of Myaskovsky's orchestral compositions had been heard in over eighteen months.[61] The concert attracted a capacity audience and although the performances were lacklustre[62], it was generally accounted a success[63] – rather, one suspects, to RAPM's chagrin. Dianov, who was present at the Vseroskomdram meeting, noted that it was sparsely attended: Myaskovsky was ill (though it is doubtful that he would have come in any case) and others chose to stay away. The atmosphere was tense and sullen, and the two-hour discussion manifestly pointless. Shekhter and his colleagues complained that none of the music performed furnished evidence of the fellow travellers' intent to reform or to pursue the declared aims of their recently founded 'creative association'. The discussion descended into farce after it was pointed out that all the works had been written over two

---

59 Reproduced in Maksimenkov (ed.), *Muzïka vmesto sumbura*, 89–93. The letter is undated, but was evidently composed shortly after the Vseroskomdram plenum on 18–19 December.

60 'Stenogrammï zasedaniy VIII Vsesoyuznogo s"ezda rabotnikov iskusstv', GARF, 5508/1/1711, l. 326.

61 Myaskovsky to Prokofiev, 24 December 1931, in Kozlova and Yatsenko, *Perepiska*, 370.

62 Myaskovsky to Steinberg, 16 January 1932, RIII, 28/1/487, l. 85.

63 Atovm'yan, 'Vospominaniya', 211.

years previously. Atovmyan wound up the proceedings by counselling the need for patience and a gradualist approach, adding that attempts to force rapid change would be counterproductive.[64]

By this point, however, the demise of the proletarian artistic organisations was imminent. The exact sequence of events that led to this outcome remains unclear, but the most obvious explanation is probably the correct one: the Party leadership decided that they had served their purpose and that a change of policy was needed.[65] Criticisms of their deleterious influence on artistic life continued to mount. Gnesin outlined his concerns about RAPM in a lengthy report addressed to Stalin personally.[66] In his reminiscences, Atovmyan recalled his involvement in composing a collective letter of protest which was also sent to Stalin.[67] The document in question has not come to light, but Atovmyan's story would appear to be confirmed by an exchange of correspondence between Myaskovsky and Steinberg in February 1932 in which they allude to a letter to 'the authorities' that was being circulated for signatures.[68] Both men were disgusted by RAPM's harassment of Gnesin, which may have prompted this concerted action. A collective protest by a sizeable group of eminent musicians would have lent greater weight to complaints submitted by individuals: Myaskovsky's student Alexander Mosolov appealed directly to Stalin for assistance in March 1932, describing in his letter the various ways in which RAPM had made his professional life intolerable.[69] It would seem, however, that the complainants were already pushing against an open door.

The first clear indications of RAPM's impending downfall began with Narkompros's removal of Przybyszewski as director of the Felix Kon Higher Music School on 11 February.[70] (Three weeks previously it had been announced that he was taking 'temporary leave'.[71]) Przybyszewski's bungling incompetence had long been apparent, so his dismissal did not come as a surprise: Myaskovsky had predicted that he would not remain long in post, describing him to Steinberg as 'completely devoid of any organisational

64 Dianov, 'Dnevnik', RGALI, 2027/1/20, ll. 28–90b.

65 See Anthony Kemp-Welch, *Stalin and the Literary Intelligentsia, 1928–39* (Basingstoke, 1991), 114.

66 Reproduced in Vlasova, *1948 god*, 134–40.

67 Atovm'yan, 'Vospominaniya', 199.

68 Steinberg to Myaskovsky, 22 February 1932, RGALI, 2040/2/282, l. 330b; Myaskovsky to Steinberg, 24 February 1932, RIII, 28/1/487, ll. 89–890b.

69 See Mosolov to Stalin, undated letter [March 1932], in Inna Barsova, 'Iz neopublikovannogo arkhiva A. V. Mosolova [Part 1]', *Sovetskaya muzïka*, 7 (1989), 89–91.

70 See Vlasova, *1948 god*, 94–5.

71 'Tekushchiye dela', *Sovetskoye iskusstvo*, 20 January 1932.

abilities'.[72] More significant was the concomitant removal of Boris Shekhter and other RAPM personnel from the teaching staff under the pretext that they were taking 'creative leave' to concentrate on compositional projects. Przybyszewski's replacement Stanislav Shatsky, a notable expert on early childhood education, pressed Myaskovsky to return to the institution, but his continuing ill-health made this infeasible.[73] Later that month, Lebedinsky and Bely were summoned to a Narkompros meeting at which RAPM was reprimanded for its treatment of Gnesin and accused of alienating the majority of musicians.[74] On 8 March, the Politburo appointed a special commission, whose members included Stalin and Molotov, to investigate RAPP's activities.[75] Its purview extended to musical life, as Mosolov's letter was brought to its attention.[76] By mid-April, the fate of the proletarian artistic organisations was sealed. Derzhanovsky jubilantly related to Prokofiev: 'RAPM is now routed, their noxious *Proletarian Musician* has been taken away from them, and they're probably going to be removed from all positions of responsibility in concert life, publishing, and teaching'.[77] The *coup de grâce* was administered on 23 April, when the government promulgated a resolution entitled 'On the reform of literary and artistic organisations', which decreed the enforced dissolution of RAPP and its cognates because their narrow sectarianism was seriously hindering artistic creativity. In every artistic domain, they were to be replaced by a single state-run professional association uniting all its representatives. Membership would in principle be open to all artists who 'supported Soviet power and sought to participate in the construction of socialism'.[78]

The resolution gave no indication of how the new 'creative unions' might function, but it clearly conveyed the government's desire to effect a reconciliation with non-Party artists after the turmoil of the preceding three years. Despite newspaper headlines proclaiming that it was 'unanimously' hailed[79],

---

72 Myaskovsky to Steinberg, 10 October 1930, RIII, 28/1/487, l. 610b.

73 Myaskovsky to Steinberg, 24 February 1932, RIII, 28/1/487, l. 89; see also fn1 above.

74 See Marina Frolova-Walker and Jonathan Walker, *Music and Soviet Power, 1917–1932* (Woodbridge, 2012), 312, 314–15.

75 See 'Postanovleniye Politbyuro TsK VKP(b) ob organizatsii komissii Politbyuro po rassmotreniyu voprosov deyatel'nosti RAPPa', in Artizov and Naumov (ed.), *Vlast' i khudozhestvennaya intelligentsiya, Dokumentï TsK RKP(b), VChK-OGPU-NKVD o kul'turnoy politike 1917–1953 gg.* (Moscow, 1999), 168.

76 'Postanovleniye Politbyuro TsK VKP(b) o zayavlenii kompozitora A. V. Mosolova', Maksimenkov (ed.), *Muzïka vmesto sumbura*, 99.

77 Derzhanovsky to Prokofiev, 16 April 1932, RBML, SPA9569.

78 The text of the resolution is reproduced in Andrey Artizov and Oleg Naumov (ed.), *Vlast' i khudozhestvennaya intelligentsiya*, 172–3.

79 'Sovetskiye pisateli yedinodushno privetstvuyut resheniye TsK VKP(b)', *Literaturnaya gazeta*, 5 May 1932.

it met with mixed responses. The leaders of RAPP and its sister organisations were angry and resentful; the reactions of fellow travellers were understandably cautious.[80] The resolution would not resolve the tensions in Soviet artistic life – merely submerge them. But even if there was considerable uncertainty about what might happen next, many musicians greeted the disbandment of RAPM with unconcealed relief[81] – as was apparent when Andrey Bubnov, Lunacharsky's successor at Narkompros, held two days of meetings with prominent representatives of the musical community on 23 and 25 April. The composers present, who included Shostakovich, Steinberg, Gnesin, Mosolov, and Shebalin, took the opportunity to re-emphasise the damage that the organisation had wrought. Lebedinsky and the other RAPM leaders made no attempt to sound a conciliatory note: they were rebuked by Bubnov, who declared that their speeches showed them 'to have learned nothing and understood nothing'.[82] However, the government officials also upbraided the fellow travellers for not standing up to RAPM and preventing insufficiently qualified personnel such as Davidenko from being appointed to the teaching staff at the Moscow Conservatoire – an utterly disingenuous criticism, as Dianov observed in his diary.[83]

Myaskovsky did not attend these meetings: he had been continuously unwell throughout the spring, and in addition to his other ailments, developed a series of ear infections that affected his hearing for a time and caused him much anxiety.[84] Nevertheless, his absence did not prevent him from being referred to in flattering terms as one of the country's 'outstanding' composers in a front-page article in the newspaper *Soviet Art* published shortly after the resolution's promulgation.[85] Neither did he attend the premiere of the Twelfth Symphony on 1 June in the fourth of Vseroskomdram's symphony concerts, given by the Bolshoi Theatre orchestra under the English conductor Albert Coates. (The son of an English businessman who lived in Russia before the Revolution, Coates had previously worked at the Mariinsky Theatre and regularly returned to Russia for guest engagements.[86]) One suspects that his indisposition, while almost certainly genuine (a letter to his sister Valentina records that he was bedridden with

80 For a discussion, see Kemp-Welch, *Stalin and the Literary Intelligentsia*, 116–35.

81 See, for example, Bogdanov-Berezovskiy, *Dorogi iskusstva*, vol. 1, 180–1; Chemberdzhi, *V dome muzïka zhila*, 254.

82 'Kompozitorï u tov. A. S. Bubnova', *Sovetskoye iskusstvo*, 27 April 1932.

83 Dianov, 'Dnevnik', 18 May 1932, RGALI, 2027/1/21, l. 1.

84 Myaskovsky to Prokofiev, 18 May 1932, in Kozlova and Yatsenko, *Perepiska*, 382.

85 'Na muzïkal'nom fronte', *Sovetskoye iskusstvo*, 27 April 1932.

86 See Santie de Jongh, 'From St Petersburg to the Cape: Three Autobiographical Texts by Albert Coates', *Fontes artis musicae*, 3 (2007), 320–30.

influenza[87]), also proved convenient. It quickly became apparent at the rehearsals that the symphony would receive a mediocre performance, as Coates turned up inadequately prepared.[88] Myaskovsky felt uncomfortable about attending the event: he told Asafiev that he was 'ashamed' of the symphony as an artistic 'compromise' and disliked the fact that the organisers were trying to turn the premiere into 'an occasion'.[89]

Ultimately, however, he had compromised very little. Although the advance publicity for the concert alluded to the symphony's putative 'ideological content', it was simply styled 'Twelfth Symphony, op. 35' on the concert programme.[90] Myaskovsky never authorised the preposterous title '"Collective Farm" Symphony' or supplied a detailed programme note, even though there was evidently pressure on him to do so. (In an article published in *Soviet Art* shortly before the premiere, Muzgiz's director Verkhotursky lamented that Myaskovsky 'had not yet succeeded in providing an adequate literary formation of the ideas and thoughts that he has already expressed musically'.[91]) His sole public statement about the symphony's 'subject matter' is found in the brief autobiographical essay that he wrote for the journal *Soviet Music* in 1936, four years after the premiere, where he mentioned that its concept was suggested to him by one of his composition students, the RAPM activist Marian Koval.[92] Its three movements were supposed to depict the countryside before, during, and after the successful struggle to collectivise agriculture. He went on, however, to declare that the work 'did not quite turn out as I wished', as his realisation of the concept had proved 'insufficiently persuasive'.[93] To judge from a letter to Prokofiev, he resorted to this excuse to justify 'withdrawing' the symphony's presumably non-existent programme before it was published in 1932[94]: the printed score merely bears the subtitle 'To the Fifteenth Anniversary of the October Revolution'.

Myaskovsky clearly found the symphony's proposed programme embarrassing and jettisoned it at the first opportunity. Though he may not have devised a detailed programme himself, there were undoubtedly attempts to supply him with one. An outline of Koval's initial 'concept' survives – a

---

87 Myaskovsky to Valentina Menshikova, 13 June 1932, RGALI, 2040/1/74, l. 22.

88 Myaskovsky to Prokofiev, 18 June 1932, in Kozlova and Yatsenko, *Perepiska*, 386.

89 Myaskovsky to Asafiev, 6 April 1932, RGALI, 2658/1/642, l. 2.

90 RGALI, 2040/2/359, l. 221.

91 'Muzïka k XV godovshchine Oktyabrya', *Sovetskoye iskusstvo*, 9 May 1932.

92 'Marian' is a masculine first name of Polish origin.

93 Myaskovskiy, 'Avtobiograficheskiye zametki', 10–11.

94 Myaskovsky to Prokofiev, 18 June 1932, in Kozlova and Yatsenko, *Perepiska*, 386.

brief note that he passed to Myaskovsky during a Muzgiz meeting proposing that he write a symphony entitled 'The Sowing', depicting collectivised
peasants' transition from 'backbreaking individual toil to joyous, enthusiastic collective construction'.[95] Eager to supervise Myaskovsky's ideological
re-education, Koval subsequently wrote to provide detailed instructions
on how to go about composing the work. By his own admission, the twen-
ty-four-year-old Koval was still struggling to master elementary counterpoint[96], but he was wholly free of inhibitions when it came to dispensing
unwanted advice. He cautioned his teacher against his customary 'individualistic' compositional approaches and exhorted him to read 'Stalin's speech
at the Sixteenth Party Congress' and pertinent Marxist-Leninist theoretical
works to help orient himself to the task. Additionally, he advised that the
symphony should include choral settings of suitable texts to make its ideological content more explicit.[97] Myaskovsky's reply was a minor masterpiece of diplomatic evasion. He thanked Koval with exquisite courtesy but
explained that Koval's recommendations had arrived too late for him to act
on them because the symphony was virtually finished. With an ostentatious
show of self-deprecating modesty, he added that realising them would in
any case have 'exceeded his creative powers': despite his 'agonised' efforts,
he had felt 'quite unable to cope with the task as I would have wished'.[98] His
letter is an excellent illustration of the strategies that he employed to deal
with troublesome people and to minimise conflict.[99]

An attempt may even have been made to foist a programme on the symphony. Amongst Myaskovsky's papers is an undated German-language
summary of the 'content' of each movement, written in an unknown hand.
A possible explanation of its provenance is that it was a translation of a
Russian-language programme note, since lost, which was to be reproduced
in a bilingual preface to the full score published jointly by Muzgiz and
Universal Edition: Verkhotursky could have asked a Muzgiz staff member
to draft a text, since Myaskovsky was slow to oblige. The plausibility of this
explanation is strengthened by Myaskovsky's remark in a letter to Steinberg
that he had removed 'all prefaces about collective farms' from the score
before publication – which suggests that such a dual-language preface

95 Koval to Myaskovsky, undated note [autumn 1931?], RGALI, 2040/2/161, ll.
    2–20b.

96 Koval to Myaskovsky, 24 January 1932, RGALI, 2040/2/161, l. 6.

97 Koval to Myaskovsky, 6 December 1931, RGALI, 2040/2/161, ll. 3–4.

98 Myaskovsky to Koval, 16 January 1932, reproduced in Georgiy Polyanovskiy,
    Marian Koval' (Moscow, 1968), 14–15.

99 For a more extensive discussion of this exchange, see Patrick Zuk, 'Nikolay
    Myaskovsky and the "Regimentation" of Soviet Composition: A Reassessment',
    Journal of Musicology, 3 (2014), 354–93.

had already been written.[100] One can readily understand why Myaskovsky would have been unwilling to allow the text to go into circulation, and especially abroad, given passages such as the following:

> [The second movement] sets itself the task of portraying the class struggle that unfolds between the strata of the village that have liberated themselves from the yoke of landlord and peasant oppression and see all the hopelessness of individual labour – and the remnants of the forces of reaction. Only a close alliance with the working class under the leadership of the Party lends the driving forces of the village the necessary steadfastness and determination in this struggle. Moments of victory alternate with renewed angry resistance from the class enemy, whose downfall is inevitable.[101]

Even without Koval's advice, Myaskovsky was well aware of what was required to demonstrate his 'reform': a grandiose agitprop work in an accessible idiom, preferably involving amateur choristers (as representatives of 'the masses') and setting political texts. Davidenko and several other of RAPM's composer members had previously collaborated on a score that could have served as a model – the 'citizens' cantata' *The Path of October*, a montage of songs and choruses narrating the story of the Russian revolutionary movement. In the event, however, Myaskovsky ignored RAPM's expectations and produced another 'abstract' symphony. The Twelfth may not rank amongst Myaskovsky's finest achievements, but it contains some excellent music and displays his usual high level of craftsmanship. Listeners approaching it in anticipation of hearing a banal *pièce d'occasion* will be surprised to find that it is anything but blatant or overtly propagandistic, notwithstanding the finale's exuberant coda and major-key ending. Neither is the symphony noticeably different in its musical language and approach to the works that preceded it: there is nothing suggestive of an enforced stylistic simplification. Its atmosphere may be remote from the Expressionist *Angst* of the Tenth Symphony or the Third and Fourth Piano Sonatas, but it is important to remember that these works represent only one aspect of Myaskovsky's output during the 1920s. While its harmonic language mostly has a more diatonic basis, it still contains passages that are highly dissonant – especially in the central Scherzo, which has a similar driving energy as the Scherzo of the Ninth. On the whole, the Twelfth exemplifies the intensified concern for economy and clarity characteristic of Myaskovsky's music from the late 1920s onwards. The predominantly contrapuntal textural organisation, the pronounced modal inflexions, and the growing preference for individual rather than blended instrumental timbres continue

---

100 Myaskovsky to Steinberg, 26 September 1932, RIII, 28/1/487, l. 95.
101 RGALI, 2040/4/9, l. 11.

EXAMPLE 9.3. Symphony no. 12, first movement: bars 10–19.

EXAMPLE 9.4. *Concertino lirico*, second movement: bars 8–16.

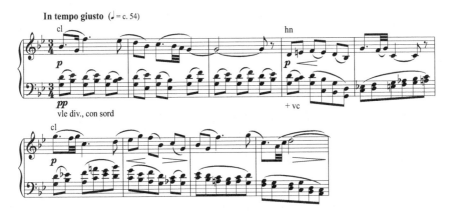

tendencies in evidence in the Eleventh Symphony and the *Divertissements*. These strong continuities with his earlier work can easily be demonstrated by textual comparisons. The plaintive main theme of the slow introduction to the first movement is strikingly similar to material from the slow movement of the *Concertino lirico*, op. 32/3, sketched in 1926: both ideas are presented by solo wind instruments against an ethereal undulating accompaniment played by muted divided strings; both ideas prominently feature the intervals of a perfect fourth and minor seventh (exx. 9.3 and 9.4). Even his employment of thematic material suggesting stylised evocations of folk music in the first and second movements has clear precedents in the Fifth Symphony of 1918 – down to the piquant chromatic harmonisations pervaded by sliding semitonal voice leading (exxs. 9.5 and 9.6). To anyone familiar with Myaskovsky's previous output, the Twelfth contains few surprises.

EXAMPLE 9.5. Symphony no. 12, first movement: bars 138–49.

EXAMPLE 9.6. Symphony no. 5, third movement: bars 129–42.

The Cultural Revolution was undoubtedly a turning point in Myaskovsky's life – though not in the ways that Soviet commentators claimed. The notion that the Twelfth Symphony signalled a decisive shift in his outlook – his abandonment of 'individualistic' modernism and his incipient transformation from fellow traveller to ideologically committed artist – was first mooted by his student Dmitry Kabalevsky in a newspaper article published shortly after the symphony's premiere.[102] Kabalevsky

102 'Simfoniya bor'bï', *Sovetskoye iskusstvo*, 15 June 1932.

elaborated this claim in several subsequent essays and memoirs in which he presented Myaskovsky's career as the edifying morality tale of a Soviet composer's arduous, but ultimately successful struggle to overcome decadent tendencies under the wise guidance of the Communist Party. His tendentious portrait, which informs the equally dubious productions of Myaskovsky's Soviet biographers, gives a highly misleading impression of his teacher's position. When reading Kabalevsky's reminiscences, it must be borne in mind that he was a loyal Party member of impeccably orthodox views. Olga Lamm recounted that he was distrusted and disliked by most members of Myaskovsky's circle: Kabalevsky was not above blocking performances of music of which he disapproved or hindering the careers of people whom he deemed insufficiently politically reliable. Myaskovsky took a similar attitude towards him as towards Prokofiev, telling his colleagues that they should not allow their feelings of personal antipathy to blind them to Kabalevsky's undoubted abilities as a musician.[103] Nevertheless, he was under no illusions: he noted waspishly in his diary that the ideological 'tendency' of a piece of music mattered more to Kabalevsky than its quality.[104] Consequently, when Kabalevsky recorded approvingly that copies of Marxist-Leninist classics started to appear on Myaskovsky's desk during the Cultural Revolution[105], it would be unwise to lend his statement too much weight: Kabalevsky's aim was not to give a dispassionate, searching analysis of his teacher's personality but to portray him as a model Soviet artist and citizen. Myaskovsky indisputably did read Marxist literature in the early 1930s, as two diary entries confirm, but we do not know what he made of Lenin's *Materialism and Empiriocriticism*, Engel's *Dialectics of Nature*, or the other works to which he alludes.[106] As Nadezhda Mandelstam points out, members of the intelligentsia quickly took to displaying such volumes in their bookshelves as a self-protective measure in the early 1930s.[107] The catalogue of Myaskovsky's personal library prepared after his death by Olga Lamm and his sister Valentina lists only a few Marxist texts.[108] There is nothing to suggest that he took more than a passing interest in political philosophy, and no evidence whatsoever of any impulse to active political engagement.

Neither is there any justification for adducing the Twelfth Symphony as a demonstration of Soviet composers' capitulation to ideological duress

103 Lamm, 'Pavel Aleksandrovich Lamm: Opït biografii', RNMM, 192/361, ll. 433–4.

104 'Vïpiski', 20 September 1933, RGALI, 2040/1/65, l. 90b.

105 Kabalevskiy, 'O N. Ya. Myaskovskom', 313.

106 'Vïpiski', 21 July 1930 and 17 August 1934, RGALI, 2040/1/65, ll. 7, 17.

107 Nadezhda Mandel'shtam, *Vospominaniya*, vol. 1 (Moscow, 1999), 364.

108 See RGALI, 2040/4/4, l. 2580b.

and enforced abjuration of modernist stylistic tendencies in the 1930s. Far from emerging a diminished figure from this difficult period, Myaskovsky's responses to events and the choices that he made reveal an impressive strength of character. Aside from the strains caused by his fraught professional environment, a near-fatal illness that left him seriously incapacitated, and Yevgeniya's distressing ordeal, he had to withstand a sustained assault on his artistic outlook and the belief in the value of individual selfhood on which it was predicated. In spite of all the pressures, he stood his ground: such concessions to circumstances as he felt obliged to make were ultimately insignificant.

In the months following the Party's resolution of 23 April, musical life slowly began to return to something resembling normality, even if RAPM did not cede control without a struggle. Unsurprisingly, Lebedinsky and his associates found the abrupt loss of their professional status deeply humiliating: Marian Koval became so depressed that he had to be admitted to a sanatorium.[109] Although some of RAPM's leaders may have acted out of sincere conviction (and allowance must also be made for their youth and inexperience[110]), their actions were not entirely free of self-interest: they clearly coveted the jobs of the senior personnel whom they had ousted – as Lunacharsky had warned. 'Privileged posts with good salaries habituate one to a certain way of life', Dianov remarked in a diary entry in which he reflected on RAPM's downfall. 'Having to make do with something more modest or give up these advantages altogether is difficult'.[111] Myaskovsky, by contrast, initially refused to resume teaching at the conservatoire at the start of the 1932–3 academic year and only did so after Shatsky, the new director, eventually asked Andrey Bubnov to intervene. He was similarly reluctant to return to Muzgiz, which he described to Steinberg as 'an absolute cesspit', though he eventually relented.[112] The directors of both institutions were manifestly unwilling to let him go: whatever reservations they may have harboured about him as a fellow traveller, they valued his abilities. Myaskovsky was perhaps reassured by signs of a decisive break with RAPM's policies at these and other institutions by the autumn of 1932 – the most conspicuous being a Narkompros decree of 16 October ordering the re-adoption of the historical name for the Moscow Conservatoire.[113]

109 Koval to Myaskovsky, 1 December 1932, RGALI, 2040/2/161, l. 8.

110 For an interesting discussion by a former RAPM member of his and his associates' attitudes and outlook at the period, see Daniėl' Zhitomirskiy, 'Mifologiya "klassovogo" iskusstva', *Muzïkal'naya akademiya*, 2 (1993), 144–54.

111 'Dnevnik', 18 May 1932, RGALI, 2027/1/21, l. 1.

112 Myaskovsky to Steinberg, 26 September 1932, RIII, 28/1/487, ll. 95–95ob.

113 See Vlasova, *1948 god*, 94.

Concert life began to revive, albeit slowly. Broadcast performances of orchestral and chamber works by Soviet composers resumed, if infrequently, due to financial constraints. The Moscow Philharmonic also grudgingly included a few Soviet works in its programmes – though its new artistic director had little interest in contemporary music.[114] Now that the oppressive atmosphere created by RAPM had dispelled, Prokofiev decided to risk a brief visit to the USSR to test the reception of his work. He arrived on 20 November and remained until 7 December, making several appearances as soloist and conductor. His impressions were sufficiently favourable as to encourage him to return the following year. (In the event, he came twice in 1933 – for a two-month sojourn in the late spring and early summer, and then for five weeks in October and November.) He was struck by a perceptible change in attitudes towards Myaskovsky, whom he described in his diary as 'rehabilitated' – though as before, he seems to have shown little interest in what had befallen him since their last meeting three years previously. He attended a musical evening in Shebalin's apartment at which he played his own Second Sonata before dutifully sitting through a performance of Pavel Lamm's eight-hand transcription of Myaskovsky's Eleventh Symphony. 'Lovely harmonies, lots of interesting things, but as always he cannot shrug off his provincialism', he recorded disapprovingly.[115] Before his next visit, he warned Myaskovsky of his intention to give him a stern lecture about his foursquare phrase structure – which was duly delivered, accompanied by the customary admonishments about the need for Myaskovsky to 'renew' his style.[116]

Prokofiev's characterisation of Myaskovsky as 'rehabilitated' is rather misleading: his authority and artistic standing had never been seriously questioned, even by RAPM's leaders. His centrality in national musical life was reaffirmed by his appointment, together with Glière, Aleksandrov, and other prominent musicians to the directorate of a Composers' Union for the Moscow region, which was established in the summer of 1932, pursuant to the April resolution. A fundamental aim of the new 'creative unions' was to transcend factional divisions by uniting representatives of all artistic tendencies in professional bodies subject to direct government oversight. As detailed in a Central Committee edict of 7 May, it was originally intended to create a single Union of Soviet Composers with branches around the country: the new organisation's title notwithstanding, its membership was to comprise 'the most authoritative practitioners of the art of

114 Myaskovsky to Steinberg, 28 March and 16 September 1933, RIII, 28/1/487, ll. 97–970b, 104.

115 Prokof'yev, *Dnevnik 1919–1933*, 813, 814.

116 Prokofiev to Myaskovsky, 28 March 1933, in Kozlova and Yatsenko, *Perepiska*, 398; Prokof'yev, *Dnevnik 1919–1933*, 823.

music (conductors and leading performers)' – and not merely composers.[117] Scant documentation has come to light about the Central Committee's initial attempts to realise this proposal, but it would seem that the arrangements were hastily improvised and then revised. By 7 June, the plan to create an overarching national administrative structure for the union – a so-called 'Organisational Committee' (*orgkomitet*) – had been declared 'impracticable'[118]: it was decided instead to set up local Composers' Unions in 'major musical centres' across the USSR before creating a superstructure that would integrate them into the national union.[119] The Moscow and Leningrad Composers' Unions were amongst the first to be founded: others were created elsewhere throughout the 1930s. A national Union of Soviet Composers came into being in 1934: curiously, it was constituted as a 'voluntary society' to which the local unions were affiliated.[120] An organisational committee was not formed until 1939, and for various reasons (including the disruption caused by the Second World War), it did not assume control of local unions until 1948. In the meantime, they operated to a considerable extent autonomously of one another, their activities being only loosely coordinated by the Moscow branch. It is also noteworthy that levels of Party membership in the Union of Soviet Composers remained low: throughout the 1930s, it even lacked a so-called *partorganizatsiya* ('Party organisation') of the members amongst its ranks – a ubiquitous feature of Soviet organisations and workplaces of any size. These circumstances had significant practical consequences, as they meant that Party oversight was laxer than in other artistic domains.[121] (The much larger Union of Soviet Writers, by contrast, was in a position to hold its first national congress as early as 1934 – fourteen years before the Union of Soviet Composers.) The fact that this state of affairs was allowed to persist for so long testifies to the low level of importance attached to music by the government.

Myaskovsky is known to have played a prominent role in the Moscow Composers' Union's affairs from the outset, though its institutional records for the 1930s are too fragmentary to permit an appraisal of his influence

117 'Postanovleniye Orgbyuro TsK VKP(b) o merepriyatiyakh po vïpolneniyu postanovleniya Politbyuro TsK VPK(b) "O perestroyke literaturno-khudozhestvennïkh organizatsiy"', in Artizov and Naumov (ed.), *Vlast' i khudozhestvennaya intelligentsiya*, 175. Performers were ultimately excluded from the Composers' Union: see Kiril Tomoff, *Creative Union: The Professional Organization of Soviet Composers, 1939–1953* (Ithaca, 2006), 30–3.

118 'Postanovleniye Orgbyuro TsK VKP(b) o netselesoobraznosti sozdaniya Orgkomkteta muzïkal'nïkh organizatsiy', in Maksimenkov (ed.), *Muzïka vmesto sumbura*, 103.

119 'Sozdan Soyuz sovetskikh kompozitorov', *Sovetskoye iskusstvo*, 3 July 1932.

120 The organisation is described as such in its charter, RGALI, 2077/1/1.

121 See Vlasova, *1948 god*, 146–54.

on policy or decision-making.[122] Neither is it clear to what extent he was involved in running the Union of Soviet Composers, but there was evidently some overlap. The Moscow union assumed many of the functions that had previously been performed by Vseroskomdram and other institutions: apart from supporting the professional activities of composers and writers on music, it also organised amateur music-making and outreach activities. Myaskovsky initially helped to run its so-called 'Creative Sector', which was chaired by Kabalevsky. The sector's responsibilities included the awarding of commissions, the formulation of 'thematic plans' for new works, and arranging consultations with composers about work-in-progress.[123]

It is interesting that Myaskovsky agreed to involve himself in the union to this extent, given his desire to distance himself from other institutions. Despite his introverted disposition, he had a very practical side to his nature, developed by his long years of military service and administrative experience: he evidently wished to ensure that satisfactory procedures were instituted and that composers were appropriately remunerated. He was probably also concerned to mitigate the influence of former RAPM members – several of whom held posts in the union's executive – and to guard against excessive bureaucratic interference in composers' affairs. These were causes of genuine concern, especially as the union's chairman Nikolay Chelyapov was not a musician, but a lawyer and career administrator unaverse to performing unsavoury tasks. In 1929, Chelyapov had chaired the government commission appointed to review postgraduate supervision at the State Academy of Arts Studies, the institution to which ASM had previously been affiliated. Its intentionally damning report set in motion a train of events that rapidly led to the institute being shut down.[124] Scattered remarks in Myaskovsky's diary suggest that his relationship with Chelyapov was uneasy, and hint at strong tensions within the union during the early years of its existence. The correspondence of Lev Knipper reveals an important cause of these tensions: Chelyapov's disrespectful attitude towards the older 'masters' amongst the fellow travellers.[125] Interestingly, Myaskovsky was by no means passive in his dealings with Chelyapov. He sent the union chairman an 'irate' letter when he attempted to step down in 1934 and foist 'an arrogant idiot' on the organisation as his successor. He also took exception to the behaviour of Atovmyan, who transferred to the union from Vseroskomdram, and moved to have him

122 What has survived of the Moscow union's archive is preserved in RGALI (fond 2077). The meagre contents of Myaskovsky's personnel file (2077/3/109) are uninformative about his work on the union's behalf.

123 'Struktura Soyuza sovetskikh kompozitorov', *Byulleten' soyuza sovetskikh kompozitorov*, 3–4 (1933), 6, 8.

124 See Yakimenko, 'Iz istorii chistok apparata'.

125 Knipper to Asafiev, 17 December 1934, GABT, KP3500/958, ll. 1–10b.

FIGURE 9.1. With colleagues and students from the Moscow Conservatoire (1934).
Front row (left to right): Vissarion Shebalin, Myaskovsky, Nikolay Zhilyayev,
Genrikh Litinsky. Standing (left to right): Yury Yatsevich, Aram Khachaturian,
Samuil Senderey, Yury Biryukov.

dismissed.[126] Such actions indicate a distinct confidence in his professional
standing. Kabalevsky was struck by Myaskovsky's remarkable self-possession in tense situations: he could be prickly and sarcastic, but never lost his
temper.[127]

By the start of 1933, Myaskovsky's life had settled back into its former
pattern. His health improved sufficiently to allow him to resume working as normal, though it remained delicate. The three years up the end of
1935 afforded welcome respite after the stressful period of the Cultural
Revolution, being largely uneventful by comparison – at least, as far as his
external life was concerned. His diary entries, which became much more
regular from this time, record a busy professional routine that varied little
until the outbreak of war between the USSR and Nazi Germany in 1941.
Aside from his teaching, reviewing and editing for Muzgiz, and his work

126 'Vïpiski', 22 March, 25, 28, and 29 April, and 6 May, RGALI, 2040/1/65, ll. 130b,
     140b, 15.
127 Kabalevskiy, 'O N. Ya. Myaskovskom', 307.

on behalf of the Composers' Union, he was increasingly asked to assume other responsibilities, such as acting as a jury member for competitions or sitting on committees of various kinds. He also received a steady stream of callers at home: composers wishing to show him their work; conductors requesting guidance on interpretative questions; former students and colleagues seeking his advice on professional matters. Requests of this kind grew so numerous that he eventually had to insist on only seeing visitors by appointment.[128] Notwithstanding his formality and reserve, which could produce an intimidating impression, Myaskovsky was very kind-natured. Shebalin recalled that he never refused anyone, even though these consultations tired him and often consumed valuable time that might have been better spent in other ways.[129] Yevgeny Golubev, who transferred into Myaskovsky's composition class in 1934, was struck by the aura of authority that his teacher radiated, despite his quiet and unassuming manner: 'Literally everybody wanted to show him their compositions, seek his opinion, get his advice – and not just Moscow composers'. Myaskovsky's collegial and supportive attitude earned him widespread respect: he diligently attended the premieres of major new works by his colleagues.[130]

A memoir of Myaskovsky by his sister Vera's daughter Tatyana Yakovleva provides an interesting glimpse of his domestic life during the 1930s.[131] Tatyana, who worked as a copyist, came into fairly frequent contact with him but found him something of an enigma. 'My uncle was very reticent and withdrawn by nature', she recalled. 'He lived an intense inner life and seemed to put up a barrier that he allowed no-one to get past – even the people who were close to him'. (This quality was also emphasised by Myaskovsky's sisters, who recorded his dislike of physical contact and overt displays of affection. He never confided in them about worries or problems – his only character trait that they found difficult.[132]) At the same time, he struck Tatyana as 'a very loving, decent, warm, and caring person, though he did not put these qualities on show'. He never forgot family members' birthdays and was thoughtful in choosing gifts for them. If he won a prize for his work, he generously distributed the proceeds amongst his relatives. Characteristically, he insisted on paying Tatyana at top professional rates for any copying assignments that she undertook for him. The punctiliousness that he displayed in personal relations extended to every other aspect

---

128 Men'shikova *et al.*, 'Pamyati brata', 182.

129 Shebalin, 'Iz vospominaniy', 286.

130 Golubev, 'Vospominaniya', RGALI, 2798/1/77, ll. 10b, 2–3.

131 Tat'yana Yakovleva, 'Moi vospominaniya o dyade Nikolaye Yakovleviche Myaskovskom', RGALI, 2040/4/28.

132 Men'shikova *et al.*, 'Pamyati brata', 192, 193.

of his behaviour – from his careful attentiveness to his dress and appearance to the meticulous preparation of his musical manuscripts.

Tatyana recalled that her uncle and her aunt Valentina adhered to a strict daily routine. Although Valentina now held a demanding civil service post at the People's Commissariat for Foreign Affairs, she insisted on doing all the housework herself: she was devoted to her brother and saw it as her responsibility to maintain a comfortable domestic environment for him. She was an excellent cook and kept the apartment spotlessly clean. Myaskovsky worked into the night, so rose late: his day began at eleven with his morning coffee, followed by a short session of piano practice. If he did not have to go out to the conservatoire, he settled down to work at home, writing reports on submissions for Muzgiz or attending to other tasks. He usually broke off at three to reheat the food that Valentina had prepared and eat his main meal of the day. After a short nap, he returned to his desk. His evenings were often spent at concerts (he seldom attended performances of opera or ballet), and he continued to frequent the musical evenings at the Lamms' and the Derzhanovskys'. On arriving home, he would resume work, or else read or study scores.

Like Mahler, Myaskovsky largely became a 'summer composer'. During the initial stages of creative work, and especially on a large-scale project, he needed to be completely free from distractions. Ideally, this meant removing himself to the countryside. With the exception of the war years, he spent his summer vacations from 1933 until his death in 1950 in Nikolina Gora, the picturesque hamlet outside Moscow that Pavel Lamm had discovered a few years before. Following the lead of Shebalin, Lamm joined an artists' building co-operative and had a *dacha* (summer home) constructed in the woods nearby.[133] The simple single-storied wooden structure comprised three rooms – one for Lamm's own use, a bedroom for Sofia and Olga, and a kitchen. (An upper storey was added in 1946.) Lamm arranged for a self-contained side-room to be built for Myaskovsky: it had a separate entrance off the covered terrace where meals were served, affording him maximal privacy. Its furnishings consisted merely of a bed, a writing desk, an armchair – and in later years, an upright piano.

Myaskovsky generally came to Nikolina Gora in mid- to late July, and remained there until the end of August, making brief return visits to Moscow as necessary. Although the number of summer residents at Nikolina Gora continued to grow as other artists acquired dachas there (amongst them, Prokofiev), it remained a peaceful location during his lifetime – largely because it was not served by public transport. The dacha was

133 On the history of the artists' colony at Nikolina Gora, see Aleksandr Yakovlev, 'Istoriya Nikolinoy', in Marina Gromova *et al.* (ed.), *Nasha Nikolina Gora*, vol. 1 (Moscow, 2008), 13–27.

FIGURE 9.2. Pavel Lamm's dacha at Nikolina Gora
(late 1940s, after construction of upper storey).

set on a fairly sizeable plot of land, which Lamm cleared and planted to create an attractive garden. The dense surrounding woods lent a sense of complete seclusion. On stepping outside the wicker gate, one could follow a number of woodland tracks for several miles, some of which offered lovely vistas over the Moskva River and environs. If he felt so inclined, it was easy for Myaskovsky to slip away for solitary walks to mull over compositions in progress, as was his habit. The Lamms understood his need to be alone and left him to work undisturbed, though he readily joined them for card games and conversation in the evenings. Nikolina Gora became a haven where he could escape from the demands of the outside world and concentrate on the activity that he regarded as central to his life. Additionally, it afforded a welcome refuge from the oppressive summer heat in Moscow, and the noise and dust caused by the vast construction works that were relentlessly transforming the city, as its old streets and historic buildings were torn down to be replaced with high-rise blocks and grandiose boulevards. Like Pavel Lamm, Myaskovsky found spending time in the countryside vitally necessary for his wellbeing. He delighted in observing birds and animals and was knowledgeable about trees and wildflowers. He took particular pleasure in the popular Russian pursuit of foraging for mushrooms, which grew in abundance in the area.[134]

For all his complaints about finding it difficult to compose, Myaskovsky generally wrote very quickly once he got down to work: many of his large-scale scores were sketched in only a few weeks. The remaining stages of the compositional process did not require such unbroken attention. After returning to Moscow for the start of the new academic year, he would refine his drafts and elaborate them into a final form throughout the winter. Perhaps the most striking feature of his output for the remainder of the decade was his intensified focus on the symphony. After completing the Eleventh and Twelfth in 1932, he wrote nine further symphonies over the eight ensuing years, which account for over half of the subsequent opus numbers up to the Twenty-First Symphony (1940), his op. 51. The symphonies between the Eleventh and the Sixteenth were written in immediate succession as op. 34 to op. 39. The remaining works, with the exception of the Violin Concerto (1938), op. 44 and the *Salutatory Overture* (1939), op. 48, were songs, keyboard works, and string quartets – the other genres to which he repeatedly returned throughout his career. The narrow range of Myaskovsky's creative interests set him apart from his contemporaries, whose outputs were generally more varied. Shebalin, Kabalevsky, Khachaturian, and Shostakovich contributed to the same genres as Myaskovsky but produced much else besides during the 1930s and 1940s, including stage works and considerable quantities of incidental music and film music. Myaskovsky, by contrast, declined all requests to compose 'applied music'[135], and although he occasionally spoke of writing an opera (he apparently mooted *King Lear* as a possible subject, and even more surprisingly, *Madame Bovary*[136]), the idea came to nothing. Writing film scores and music for the stage was much more lucrative than composing symphonies and string quartets, both in regard of commissioning fees and performing rights, so his eschewal of these genres meant that he earned significantly less than some of his colleagues. Data compiled by the Moscow branch of the Composers' Union in 1933 shows that his income from composing totalled 12,800 roubles that year, whereas Glière made 62,300 roubles, Mosolov 33,600 roubles,

---

134 This description of Myaskovsky's summers at Nikolina Gora draws on Ol'ga Lamm, 'Vospominaniya o N. Ya. Myaskovskom', 247–53; and eadem, 'Pavel Aleksandrovich Lamm: Opït biografii', RNMM, 192/361, ll. 403–8.

135 Amongst the invitations that he declined was a request to write a score for a cinematic adaption of Gogol's *Dead Souls*: he thought Mikhail Bulgakov's scenario 'exceedingly tasteless'. ('Vïpiski', 23 September 1934, RGALI, 2040/1/65, l. 170b.)

136 See Igor Bėlza, *O muzïkantakh XX veka: Izbrannïye ocherki* (Moscow, 1979), 67.

and Shebalin 25,000 roubles.[137] There is no indication that he was irked by this state of affairs: he had little interest in money beyond ensuring that he earned enough to meet his modest needs. He mostly wrote what he wanted to write, uninfluenced by financial or other external considerations.

Only one of Myaskovsky's symphonies, the Twenty-First, was written as a result of a commission from a specific orchestra and conductor. All the others were composed on his own initiative; and while most of those written after 1932 were paid for by state commissioning schemes, he nonetheless proposed the nature of the work to be written in each case – and, for the most part, without knowing in advance who would perform it. If he produced a large number of symphonies, it was simply because the orchestra and the challenges inherent in structuring lengthy spans of musical time were central to his creative preoccupations. In a letter to Steinberg of 1932, he lamented Soviet composers' neglect of the 'pure symphony' in favour of 'large-scale works of the kind I dislike, such as operas and choral-orchestral works', adding: 'I am incorrigibly old-fashioned: I love large forms'.[138] Concentrating on the 'pure symphony' was a far from unproblematic enterprise by this juncture, however.

Although the April 1932 resolution restored a measure of calm to Soviet musical life, the issues central to the conflicts of the preceding three years were by no means settled – first and foremost, the extent of composers' obligation to treat overt ideological and political themes, but also the permissible limits of technical and stylistic experimentation, and the degree to which music by Soviet composers should be accessible to a general listenership. Soon after its promulgation, there was talk of introducing an officially sanctioned policy to guide artistic production in accordance with Marxist-Leninist philosophy. Critics and theorists began to formulate the tenets of 'Socialist Realism', the creative aesthetic to which all Soviet artists would henceforth be expected to subscribe.[139] The impetus behind this initiative came chiefly from the Union of Soviet Writers: as before, literature remained the Party's paramount concern. The nascent doctrine's implications for literary practice soon became fairly clear. A cogent summary was provided in a *Pravda* article of June 1933 by the critic Valery Kirpotin,

---

137 'Zarabotok kompozitorov', *Byulleten' Soyuza sovetskikh kompozitorov*, 1–2 (1934), 7. Myaskovsky's records of his income and expenditure for the mid-1930s indicate that his income from all sources typically totalled around thirty thousand roubles *per annum*: RGALI: 2040/1/67, ll. 750b–85.

138 Myaskovsky to Steinberg, 26 September 1932, RIII, 28/1/487, ll. 94–940b.

139 The first recorded use of the term was in a speech by the journalist Ivan Gronsky at a meeting of Moscow writers on 20 May 1932: 'Obespechim vse usloviya tvorcheskoy raboti literaturnïkh kruzhkov', *Literaturnaya gazeta*, 23 May 1932.

the director of the Central Committee's Literature Sector.[140] Literature was ineluctably political in aim, Kirpotin explained: it was a weapon to defeat capitalism. Writers would help to build socialism by presenting a faithful picture of reality from the 'historical perspective of the proletarian revolution', freed from the distortions and mendacities of 'bourgeois ideology'. Only literature written from a working-class perspective could 'speak the full truth about the world': Soviet literature must consequently 'be for the masses ... and comprehensible to the masses'. Kirpotin favourably contrasted this politically engaged literature with 'reactionary' and 'degenerate' Western artistic tendencies, which he lumped together under the epithet 'formalism'.[141] These included abstraction, 'art for art's sake', and the deliberate elimination of 'national characteristics'. By its very nature, formalism was intrinsically harmful: 'Art cannot fulfil its political and educative role if it is incomprehensible to the masses and if its imagery does not truthfully portray reality. Bourgeois formalism fights to wrest art as a weapon of class struggle from the hand of the proletariat'. In other words, modernist art was a manifestation of 'mystification', to use Marx's term – another strategy by which capitalist society obfuscated reality in order to perpetuate itself.

The 'truthful portrayal of reality' meant anything but a dispassionate, unvarnished depiction – and especially of the Bolshevik regime's brutality, or of the hardships and privations experienced by Soviet citizens. Rather, as Lunacharsky clarified in a lecture of February 1933, the artist's task was to portray 'real reality' [*real'naya deystvitel'nost'*][142], 'truth' as revealed in the light of Marxist-Leninist philosophy – in effect, to produce tendentious, propagandistic representations of circumstances, whether past, present, or of an imagined 'bright future' under communism. It was not difficult to see what this might mean in practice, at least as far as literature and the visual arts were concerned: most obviously, idealised portrayals of workers and peasants' struggles to 'build socialism', in styles deriving from nineteenth-century realism. What was far less obvious, however, was the potential applicability of Socialist Realism to music, and especially to instrumental genres such as the 'pure symphony'.

140 'O sotsialisticheskom realizme', *Pravda*, 5 June 1933.

141 'Formalism' originally denoted a range of quasi-scientific Russian approaches to literary criticism that emerged during the 1910s and 1920s, and which were primarily concerned with technical aspects of poetic language. Its leading practitioners came under increasingly fierce attack from RAPP: by the early 1930s the so-called 'formalist school' had fallen into disrepute, and 'formalism' became a term of critical invective.

142 'Sotsialisticheskiy realizm', in Anatoliy Lunacharskiy, *Stat'i o teatre i dramaturgii* (Moscow, 1938), 18.

Although theoretical writings on Socialist Realism multiplied rapidly[143], comparatively few dealt specifically with music. The most noteworthy were by the young music critic and Party member Viktor Gorodinsky, who published three substantial essays on the subject in 1932–3. In the first[144], Gorodinsky warned that the resolution of 23 April did not portend a reversion to the *status quo ante*: ASM's 'Trotskyite-Menshevik' orientation and its promotion of decadent Western 'formalist' trends such as atonality and polytonality had been as inherently objectionable as RAPM's narrow dogmatism and indiscriminate rejection of the musical past. The new Composers' Union, he declared, would continue to combat manifestations of 'bourgeois individualism', which isolated composers from the masses and led them to produce esoteric works designed to gratify the *recherché* tastes of bourgeois aesthetes. Instead, composers would be expected to assist the construction of socialism by writing music 'under the guidance of the Party' in accordance with the tenets of Socialist Realism. More encouragingly, Gorodinsky was at pains to repudiate notions that composers should confine themselves to producing agitprop works and defended the continuing viability of large-scale instrumental forms. However, in the two lengthy essays on Socialist Realism that he subsequently contributed to the new Composers' Union journal *Soviet Music*, he had little enlightening to say about how instrumental music could depict 'reality' without recourse to textual or other adjuncts, except to insist that it could, though in ways that had yet to be fully understood. 'Music', he concluded rather helplessly, 'does not have the means at its disposal to reflect reality *directly* when not allied to words or choreographic movement'.[145] He mooted the possibility that composers could utilise a 'realistic musical speech' akin to language, capable of communicating concrete meanings that could be translated into words. One of the most pressing tasks facing Soviet musicology, he suggested, was to study this problem and the related issue of musical 'content'.[146] From the outset, Marxist critics were reluctant to accept that music's import might be intrinsically recalcitrant to verbal formulation. The import of all Soviet artworks had to be ideological first and foremost, and consequently amenable to elucidation and monitoring by the state's cultural gatekeepers.[147] The

143 See Nikolay Piksanov *et al.* (ed.), *Sotsialisticheskiy realizm: Bibliograficheskiy ukazatel'* (Moscow, 1934).

144 Viktor Gorodinskiy, 'Sovetskuyu muzïku – Na vïsshuyu stupen'', in Nikolay Chelyapov (ed.), *Muzïkal'nïy al'manakh: Sbornik statey* (Moscow, 1932), 5–18.

145 'Problema soderzhaniya i obraznosti v muzïke', *Sovetskaya muzïka*, 5 (1933), 20.

146 'K voprosu o sotsialisticheskom realizme v muzïke', *Sovetskaya muzïka*, 1 (1933), 16.

147 See Antoine Baudin and Leonid Heller, 'L'image prend la parole: Image, texte et littérature durant la période jdanovienne', in Wladimir Berelowitch and

attempt to evolve a Marxist-Leninist musical semantics would keep musicologists busy for several decades, resulting in the emergence of another
pseudo-discipline in which the research 'findings' were often every whit as
dubious as the 'discoveries' of Soviet linguistics, genetics, and sundry other
intellectual and scientific domains vitiated through political interference.

Theoretical deliberations such as Gorodinsky's provided scant assistance
to composers seeking to understand what was required of them – beyond
the expectations that they should engage with ideologically appropriate
subject matter, preferably made explicit by means of a text, and aim to write
in an accessible idiom, avoiding *outré* modernist tendencies. Myaskovsky
was unimpressed. Writing to Asafiev in the autumn of 1933, he remarked
that the 'vile stuff' published in *Soviet Music* depressed him: 'It's difficult
even to know whether it's intentionally vile or merely obtuseness and stu-
pidity. It's entirely characteristic of the tone of our musical life now that it's
run by Chelyapov, Gorodinsky . . . and such like parasitical nonentities'.[148]
Despite his involvement in running the union, Myaskovsky consistently
abstained from participating in discussions of Socialist Realism's application to music, whether in print or at the forums specially convened for that
purpose. As the USSR's foremost symphonist, his failure to attend a three-
day colloquium on the future of the Soviet symphony in February 1935 was
especially conspicuous: the reports on the proceedings make no allusion
to his presence.[149] His lack of engagement can hardly have escaped notice.
It is also noteworthy that the genuineness of Myaskovsky's 'reform' was
openly questioned – as is evident from an article by the musicologist Yury
Keldïsh on the Twelfth Symphony which had appeared in *Soviet Music* the
previous year. Although his account was respectful in tone, Keldïsh raised
some uncomfortable questions. It was hardly an accident, he suggested, that
the subtitle 'Collective Farm Symphony' did not appear on the published
score's title page or that Myaskovsky had not disclosed the symphony's
programme, leaving its details to be gathered at second hand from newspaper articles by his students Kabalevsky and Mikhail Cheryomukhin. 'If he
is to transform himself from an artist "sympathetic to socialist construction" into one whose creative work actively organises the masses to fulfil
the tasks imposed by the Party, he will have to subject a great deal more
of his ideological baggage to critical review', Keldïsh concluded. 'Whether

Laurent Gervereau (ed.), *Russie-URSS, 1914–1991: Changements de regards*
(Paris, 1991), 140–8.

148 Myaskovsky to Asafiev, 18 September 1933, RGALI, 2658/1/642, l. 5.

149 On this colloquium, see Pauline Fairclough, 'The "Perestroyka" of Soviet
Symphonism: Shostakovich in 1935', *Music and Letters*, 2 (2002), 259–73.

Myaskovsky will manage to do this and succeed in reforming himself completely – only the future course of his development will show'.[150]

Keldïsh's scepticism was not misplaced: Myaskovsky remained reluctant to make his work a vehicle for ideological propaganda. The Thirteenth Symphony in B-flat minor, op. 36, composed between February and May 1933, is a startlingly uncompromising score. Myaskovsky's second experiment in a one-movement form, the symphony comprises four linked sections which play without a break. The first, *Andante moderato*, presents the exposition and development of a sonata structure; the second, *Agitato molto e tenebroso*, and the third, *Andante nostalgico*, respectively have the character of a miniature scherzo and slow movement; and the fourth comprises a recapitulation of the material presented in the opening sonata exposition and a coda. The symphony is of unusual interest from a structural point of view, but its most striking features are its uncanny atmosphere and unrelentingly dissonant harmonic language. Proceeding mostly at hushed dynamic levels, its gaunt sonorities evoke an anguished desolation beyond assuagement or endurance – a dark night of the soul, passed in weary, fretful wakefulness awaiting a dawn that never breaks. Unquestionably one of Myaskovsky's most original and moving scores, the Thirteenth is also one of his most evocative. The music's searing eloquence is heightened by its extreme understatement: some of its most powerful expressive effects are achieved by the simplest of means – such as the ominous unaccompanied timpani motto that punctuates the opening woodwind threnody (ex. 9.7), or the symphony's remarkable closing bars, with faint oboe 'pips' sounded against an evanescent unresolved ninth chord in the upper strings, suggestive of a light flickering to extinction (ex. 9.8).

This deeply enigmatic work at once invites and eludes interpretation. Its position in Myaskovsky's output, coming directly after the Twelfth, is suggestive: it is difficult not to hear it as a studied negation of the 'life-affirming optimism' increasingly demanded of Soviet artists, mourning a past to which there can be no return. A few details of the score might support this reading – the curious marking *nostalgico* on the austere brass fugato that opens the third section, or the recurrent forlorn folk song–like theme reminiscent of Borodin or Glazunov (ex. 9.9). So too does Myaskovsky's discussion of the symphony in a letter to Asafiev, who wrote after hearing Myaskovsky play it to say what a deep impression its tragic atmosphere had made on him.[151] Myaskovsky was evidently disconcerted by Asafiev's reaction and became anxious about the constructions that might be placed on the score. Although he disavowed any conscious intent to write a tragic

150 Yuriy Keldïsh, '12-ya simfoniya Myaskovskogo i nekotorïye problemï sovetskogo simfonizma', *Sovetskaya muzïka*, 2 (1934), 8–23.

151 Asafiev to Myaskovsky, 5 November 1933, RGALI, 2040/1/98, ll. 4–40b.

EXAMPLE 9.7. Symphony no. 13: opening.

EXAMPLE 9.8. Symphony no. 13: ending.

work, the delicately poised ironic ambiguities of his remarks unmistakably suggest that its musical imagery evoked the dark spiritual void underlying the brave new world of 'socialist construction'. No matter how emphatically its existence was denied by materialist philosophy, that void would have to be confronted sooner or later:

> I still find the impression that Thirteenth Symphony made on you strange and incomprehensible . . . and also terrifying. . . . Does it mean that there

EXAMPLE 9.9. Symphony no. 13: bars 38–48.

is some force in us which acts contrary to our will and consciousness? For it is tragic if in our epoch – which in principle ought to be so radiant and joyous – works can appear that contradict the single-minded striving of their creator. Where does this foolish morbidity and canker come from . . .? What is it? An involuntary disclosure of the true inner essence, or merely a purgation, a self-purification from all the former dross? I am very struck that it affected you so strongly, whereas I myself adopted a most strange workmanlike approach to this piece – I 'fashioned' it on the basis of very strict postulates of an almost technical order . . . . All the same, the musical ideas themselves on which the work was based probably contained some kind of purulent poison that blighted the entire composition and lent it such a destructive and denunciatory tinge. And suddenly all our radiance and joy is merely an intoxication with achievements, and on achieving them, when we start to live 'the good life', most likely free from cares, this 'idealist' void will rise up before us, and that which now seems to me an eructation, a purgation, will be revealed to have a greater significance somehow. Although I am more inclined to think of myself as an obsolete, for whom all these heady achievements can only be an object of sympathetic observation rather than my life's concern.[152]

His claim to have written the Thirteenth without registering its emotional import is hardly credible: only a week after writing to Asafiev, he described the symphony to Prokofiev as 'solipsistic' and 'pessimistic'.[153] Neither can he have been unaware of the reactions that its compositional idiom was likely to provoke. Predictably, it met with incomprehension from the other members of the Composers' Union's Creative Sector when he showed them the score at a meeting in March 1934 – 'unwisely', as he noted subsequently.[154] The symphony's first and only performance in the USSR during Myaskovsky's lifetime was given by the radio orchestra under Leo Ginzburg

152 Myaskovsky to Asafiev, 24 December 1933, RGALI, 2658/1/642, ll. 7–70b.
153 Myaskovsky to Prokofiev, 1 January 1934, in Kozlova and Yatsenko, *Perepiska*, 411.
154 'Vïpiski', 15 March 1934, RGALI, 2040/1/65, l. 130b.

on 26 December 1934: the players' dislike of the music was evident at the rehearsals.[155] Although the symphony also received performances abroad under Stock (the work's dedicatee) and Scherchen, Myaskovsky withheld it from publication: he was eventually persuaded to allow it to be brought out by Muzgiz in 1944, only to try unsuccessfully to withdraw it at the last minute, fearing that its publication might have unpleasant consequences for his Muzgiz colleagues.[156]

After the Thirteenth, the Expressionist vein in Myaskovsky's output came to an end. The mid-1930s inaugurated a new phase of his creative development: during the last sixteen or so years of his life, the sound-world of his work changed appreciably, as did the realms of psychological experience that it explored. These changes were not abrupt, however, but continued tendencies that had been in evidence since the mid-1920s and even earlier. Certain features of his style, such as his intermittent employment of a densely chromatic harmonic language, receded into the background, and others came to the fore. The later music is more consistently diatonic; the textures are sparer and often organised contrapuntally; a new lyrical spontaneity and refinement of colouration are in evidence, and an avoidance of rhetorical and gestural extremes.

The question inevitably arises as to the extent to the stylistic turn in Myaskovsky's later work may have resulted from environmental pressures. Answering it definitively is clearly impossible, but a careful consideration of his position suggests that, on balance, external factors were less significant than has been assumed. There is no evidence to suggest that Myaskovsky would have composed very differently after 1932 had circumstances been otherwise. He had always held that Russian music should develop independently of foreign influences: as his diary entries and letters from the 1930s attest, he was firmly convinced that Western musical life was in decline. (His perusal of the scores that he continued to receive from Universal Edition and other sources did nothing to dispel this impression: he thought the work of Hindemith and Martinů 'ghastly', Ravel's recent compositions 'vulgar', and dismissed Schoenberg's *Variations for Orchestra* as 'scholasticism'.[157] Very little foreign music excited his admiration or praise.) Neither had he ever felt drawn to radical experimentation or to repudiate the musical past: if Myaskovsky can be regarded as a modernist at all, it is only in a very circumscribed sense. Notwithstanding the dissonance of his harmonic idiom in certain works, the music that he composed up to

155 'Vïpiski', 24 December 1934, RGALI, 2040/1/65, l. 20.

156 Bėlza, *O muzïkantakh XX veka*, 66.

157 Myaskovsky to Asafiev, 30 October 1931, RGALI, 2658/1/641, ll. 42–420b;
   Myaskovsky to Prokofiev, 30 January 1932, in Kozlova and Yatsenko, *Perepiska*,
   374–5; 'Vïpiski', 30 January 1935, RGALI, 2040/1/65, l. 21.

1932 remained firmly traditional in its approaches to formal organisation and its treatment of rhythm, sonority, and texture. While some Soviet composers undoubtedly felt obliged to rein in their stylistic adventurousness as the 1930s progressed (Shostakovich, Mosolov, and Gavriil Popov being notable cases in point), Myaskovsky's artistic orientation was very different from theirs.

This is not to suggest that he did not experience pressures to self-censorship: as the case of the Thirteenth Symphony shows, he was fully aware that music suggestive of 'pessimism' and 'bourgeois individualism' would incur criticism and was increasingly unlikely to be published or performed. The fact that he never wrote another work as unrelentingly dissonant and sombre as the Thirteenth does not justify viewing his subsequent output as an artistic capitulation, however: Sibelius never composed another symphony like his austere Fourth. While due weight must be given to the constraints and expectations to which Soviet composers were subject during the Stalinist era, there is a danger of exaggerating their inhibiting effects and appraising music in terms of reductive stereotypes. The causes of an artist's stylistic change are frequently intangible, and in appraising Myaskovsky's case, allowance must also be made for the possible role of other factors. Insofar as these changes are susceptible to elucidation at all, they often seem to be bound up with the transformations in artists' psychological outlook prompted by aging or personal crises.[158] The years between 1929 and 1932 unquestionably constituted a watershed in Myaskovsky's life, and the serenity and confidence of some of his later work may well derive from the discovery of his capacity for resilience in withstanding highly stressful life experiences: a close brush with death can dramatically alter one's perspective. Stylistic change can also result from a perceived need for creative self-renewal and a quest for new expressive means once a particular approach has come to feel limiting. The increasing transparency of Myaskovsky's later style and the replacement of the angst-ridden mood of some of his earlier music by a more relaxed and emotionally restrained atmosphere parallel developments in the work of notable contemporaries such as Hindemith and Bartók.

Myaskovsky's output after 1932 has often been regarded as exemplifying Socialist Realism – largely, it seems, because of its traditionalist cast. This view is fundamentally problematic, not least in its assumption that the application of Socialist Realism to musical composition was primarily a matter of remaining within officially approved stylistic parameters. But as one of its seminal theorists (the philosopher Pyotr Yudin) emphasised,

158 For a thought-provoking discussion of this issue, see the Canadian psychiatrist Henri Ellenberger's essay 'La notion de maladie créatrice', *Dialogue: Canadian Philosophical Review/Revue canadienne de philosophie*, 1 (1964), 25–41.

Socialist Realism was not a style, but a *method*, in the Marxist sense of a 'guide to action', that enabled artists to portray reality in the light of Marxist-Leninist philosophy and thereby participate in the construction of socialism.[159] A *Pravda* leading article explained that Socialist Realism was not 'a corpus of regulations limiting the scope of artistic creativity', and could accommodate 'the greatest possible variety of forms, genres, styles, and means' provided artists were willing to fulfil their political responsibilities.[160] Style was thus a matter of strictly secondary importance: first and foremost, the new doctrine aimed to ensure the thoroughgoing instrumentalisation of Soviet art to ideological ends. By avoiding being overly prescriptive and signalling its willingness to permit a degree of stylistic pluralism, the Party sought to quell the acrimonious factional disputes prevalent during the Cultural Revolution and to prevent their recurrence. For this reason, Socialist Realism was not codified into detailed directives on style or technique for every art form – which would have been impossible to do, in any case.[161] In practice, the demand that Soviet artworks should be accessible to mass audiences deterred artists from pursuing more overtly experimental tendencies, and they were increasingly encouraged to take favoured nineteenth-century models (and especially Russian ones) as a point of creative departure. However, Myaskovsky's self-alignment with nineteenth-century Russian musical traditions long pre-dated the advent of Socialist Realism: while this alignment persisted and even intensified during the 1930s, that of itself does not furnish incontrovertible evidence of a desire to adhere to the doctrine's tenets.

Viewed in an international context, the traditionalist orientation of Myaskovsky's later work was neither unusual nor especially remarkable at the period: much music written by notable contemporary figures based outside the USSR exhibits similar traits. (Bax and Vaughan Williams in England, Kodály in Hungary, Hugo Alfvén in Sweden, Joaquín Turina in Spain, or Joseph Haas in Germany furnish interesting comparisons.) This consequently begs the question as to what features, if any, mark it out as Socialist Realist. Judged in terms of the extent to which it demonstrated characteristics that Yudin and other theorists identified as crucially important – *ideynost'* (ideological commitment), *partiynost'* (Party spirit) – its conformity to the doctrine was very doubtful. Socialist Realism may have been nebulous, but its tenets were not so vaguely defined as to allow

159 See Kemp-Welch, *Stalin and the Literary Intelligentsia*, 170.

160 'Sotsialisticheskiy realizm – Osnovnoy metod sovetskoy literaturï', *Pravda*, 8 May 1934.

161 There is no evidence, incidentally, to support claims that the doctrine was intentionally left ill-defined so that its vagueness could be exploited to repressive ends: see, for example, Richard Taruskin, *Cursed Questions: On Music and Its Social Practices* (Oakland, 2020), 414.

much doubt on these fundamental requirements. The paucity of compositions on ideological themes in Myaskovsky's output was very conspicuous, as was his disinclination to set political texts (a few songs apart) or to write programme music. He was palpably reluctant to talk about his work (unlike Shostakovich and Prokofiev, he avoided giving interviews and making public statements) or to enter into discussions of its import. His programme notes were laconic and blandly non-committal, offering only the vaguest indications of scores' 'content'.[162] Myaskovsky's music similarly failed to evince other desirable traits, such as *klassovost'* (proletarian class consciousness) and *massovost'* (mass appeal). He continued to concentrate on serious, weighty instrumental genres, showing little inclination to write anything else.

Far from being a straightforward exemplification of Socialist Realism, his output was regarded as distinctly problematic by his politically engaged colleagues, who believed him to be exerting a harmful influence on younger composers. In a letter of November 1934, Lev Knipper informed Asafiev that he had been trying 'with all his might' to persuade Myaskovsky to abandon his apolitical stance and attachment to an ideal of an 'exalted, pure art', and encouraging Shebalin to distance himself from his former teacher.[163] (Knipper was a secret police agent, so one wonders whether he was acting entirely on his own initiative.[164]) Whatever pressures were brought to bear on Myaskovsky, however, he ignored them – and persisted in turning out one 'pure symphony' after another. It is noteworthy that the Composers' Union management did not hinder him from doing so. Like everyone else, Myaskovsky would have been expected to discuss work-in-progress and his plans for new projects with colleagues in the union's Creative Sector. If Chelyapov had been so minded, he could have refused to authorise further commissions unless Myaskovsky diversified his output and made more of an effort to treat ideological subjects. Chelyapov could also have sought to block his work from being published or performed. The fact that this did not happen exposes the dubiousness of Cold War–era claims that Soviet composition was subjected to thoroughgoing regimentation after 1932. In reality, composers retained a large measure of autonomy when it came to deciding what and how they would write, notwithstanding official monitions against 'formalism'. The comparatively lax government oversight of musical life meant that the extent of their compliance with Socialist Realism

---

162 His programme note for the Seventeenth Symphony (1937) is an excellent illustration in point: he commented merely that the symphony portrayed 'the opening-up and flowering of personality in our great epoch . . . with motifs of struggle and overcoming'. RNMM, 71/503, l. 1.

163 Knipper to Asafiev, 18 November 1934, GABT, KP-3500/957, ll. 1–10b.

164 See Antony Beevor, *The Mystery of Olga Chekhova* (London, 2004), 93–6, 135.

was to a considerable degree a matter of personal choice, even if all felt it necessary to make at least a show of conformity. Most, however, made more of an effort than Myaskovsky, whose compliance was minimal.

A comparison of his choices and actions with the behaviour of some of his colleagues is revealing – Asafiev being a particularly telling case in point. Asafiev embraced Socialist Realism with notable enthusiasm, hoping to emerge from under the cloud of opprobrium that had overshadowed him during the Cultural Revolution. Asafiev's professional ambitions had led him to try to straddle fundamentally incompatible positions throughout the 1920s: he sought to burnish his credentials as a champion of 'progressive' Western trends, though his private attitudes to Western musical modernism were very ambivalent; simultaneously, he presented himself as a committed Marxist, a staunch supporter of the regime's efforts to build a new proletarian artistic culture, and a trenchant critic of Western 'bourgeois' decadence. In seeking to advance his career, he did not scruple to have MUZO colleagues of dissenting views sacked under the pretext of combatting 'formalism' and 'academicism'.[165] With the rise of RAPM, however, he found himself on the receiving end of treatment that he had happily meted out to others: a highly strung, nervous man[166], he was so disconcerted when Party activists criticised his writings and lectures as being unacceptably at variance with Marxism-Leninism that he resigned from his institutional posts and resolved to give up writing on music altogether.[167] His correspondence with Derzhanovsky reveals that he was deeply bitter about RAPM's attacks: taking a decidedly selective view of events, he portrayed himself as an innocent victim, making out that he had supported the

165 See Kseniya Kumpan, 'Institut istorii iskusstv na rubezhe 1920 – 1930-kh gg', in Mariya Malikova (ed.), *Konets institutsiy kul'turï dvadtsatïkh godov v Leningrade. Po arkhivnïm materialam* (Moscow, 2014), 30–2.

166 Asafiev's student Semyon Ginzburg recalled: 'By nature, Asafiev was extremely nervous and volatile. He reacted sharply to external stimuli and was easily discomfited by life's rough and tumble, which often meant that he reacted in an exaggerated way to real or imagined injuries'. ('Pamyati uchitelya', in Andrey Kryukov (ed.), *Vospominaniya o B. V. Asaf'yeve* [Leningrad, 1974], 93–4). Another former colleague observed: 'He was pliant and malleable. . . . He was unable to resist or to put up a fight. For that reason, people who were decisive, forceful, or who held powerful positions frightened him. He tried to avoid meeting them'. (Margarita Rittikh, 'B. Asaf'yev i nauchnïye sessii klinskogo Doma-muzeya', ibid., 261.)

167 This episode in Asafiev's career has yet to be investigated fully. His distress at RAPM's attacks is repeatedly recorded in his correspondence with Myaskovsky and others. When student activists began to disrupt his classes at the Leningrad Conservatoire, he felt so harassed that he implored the faculty dean Maximilian Steinberg to hire a specialist in dialectical materialism who could check the texts of his lectures for ideological deviations before he delivered them, telling Steinberg that 'his nerves were shot': Asafiev to Steinberg, 18 December 1929 and n.d. [1930?], RIII, 28/1/484, ll. 19–190b and l. 320b.

association's position all along although its leaders failed to acknowledge the fact. He blamed Myaskovsky and his associates for his predicament, claiming that RAPM's rise could have been prevented had they heeded his polemical articles of 1924.[168] Having inadvertently found himself on what seemed to be the losing side, he was determined not to make the same mistake again. He initially sought to ingratiate himself with RAPM, which he praised in his correspondence as 'the liveliest and most vivid phenomenon in our musical life'[169], only to hail the organisation's downfall after the promulgation of the April 1932 resolution, which he lauded for instituting 'a renaissance of musical creativity' in an effusive endorsement of Socialist Realism published the following year.[170] Eager to establish himself as a leader of this 'renaissance', Asafiev seized the opportunity to try to revive his stalled composing career, seeing it as a less risky way of making a living than as a writer.[171] His ballet *The Flames of Paris*, premiered in Leningrad in November 1932, became the first in a series of stage works exploring edifying historical themes, whose contemporary ideological resonance he dutifully expounded in programme notes. He circumvented the problem of compositional idiom through recourse to pastiches of eighteenth- and nineteenth-century styles, which he justified as a device ensuring musical 'realism'. In his public statements, he took good care to advertise the 'reform' of his artistic and political outlook, which he attributed to 'the study of dialectical and historical materialism ... and the creative state process of [socialist] construction in our country, led by the Communist Party and its leaders of genius'.[172] Now that Lunacharsky had departed from Narkompros, Asafiev began to cultivate

---

168 Asafiev to Derzhanovsky, 28 February 1931, RNMM, 3/858, ll. 1–10b.

169 Asafiev to Alexander Waulin, 4 February 1932, RNMM, 171/179, l. 10b.

170 'Istoricheskiy god', *Sovetskaya muzïka*, 3 (1933), 106–8.

171 According to Olga Lamm, an unfortunate contretemps between Asafiev and the Myaskovsky-Lamm circle played a fateful role in prompting this development. Aware that Asafiev was experiencing financial hardship, Pavel Lamm engaged him in 1930 to orchestrate his new edition of Musorgsky's unfinished opera *Khovanshchina*. Although Asafiev claimed to be a Musorgsky specialist, Lamm was dismayed to find his realisation so inept and stylistically inappropriate as to be unusable. Anxious to give Asafiev the benefit of the doubt, he referred the matter to a reading panel comprising Myaskovsky, Shebalin, Saradzhev, and Shenshin, who concurred with his criticisms. Lamm sought to relay their negative verdict as tactfully has he could, but Asafiev was mortally offended – and especially resentful of Myaskovsky. The incident revived long-standing tensions and caused relations to deteriorate. Asafiev claimed to have experienced a renewal of his creative inspiration while orchestrating *Khovanshchina* and was determined to prove to his Moscow colleagues that they had seriously underestimated his compositional abilities. Lamm, 'Pavel Aleksandrovich Lamm: Opï?t biografii', RNMM, 192/361, ll. 384–5.

172 'Moy put'', *Sovetskaya muzïka*, 8 (1934), 48.

contacts with other prominent Party officials – including Nikolay Bukharin, whom he notified of his resolve to become a politically engaged artist.[173]

As with Prokofiev and Kabalevsky, Myaskovsky tried to maintain a balanced attitude towards his old friend, not allowing his clear-eyed view of Asafiev's character weaknesses to interfere with his feelings of genuine affection and regard. However, in common with other musicians, he did not rate Asafiev's creative talent very highly. Olga Lamm recalled that while he tried his best to be supportive and to find positive things to say, he began to wonder whether Asafiev's ceaseless productivity might not be a manifestation of 'something morbid, like unbridled graphomania'.[174] As he noted in his diary, it baffled him that Asafiev was capable of perpetrating hair-raising crudities and banalities, and that his critical faculty seemed to desert him when he sat down to compose.[175] Although *The Flames of Paris* and his next ballet *The Fountain of Bakhchisarai* (1933) were popular successes, largely because of their virtuosic choreography and spectacular staging rather than any intrinsic musical merits, Asafiev soon ran into fresh difficulties: his subsequent stage works were much more coolly received, and some were never accepted for performance. Convinced that he was the victim of professional jealousy and intrigues, he became suspicious of colleagues and increasingly isolated himself: by the end of the 1930s, his contact with Myaskovsky had all but petered out.[176]

Asafiev was by no means the only composer whose work aroused ambivalent responses. Myaskovsky's diary contains not a few sharp remarks about music by other colleagues (amongst them, Kabalevsky, Khrennikov, and Yury Shaporin) which struck him as technically deficient, vapid, or in dubious taste.[177] At the same time, he was generous in his praise of achievements that he admired – such as Khachaturian's First Symphony, which he thought 'superb'.[178] His highest accolades, however, were reserved for Prokofiev and Shostakovich.

173 Asafiev's letter to Bukharin is discussed in Knipper to Asafiev, 18 November 1934, GABT, KP-3500/957, l. 10b.

174 Ol'ga Lamm, 'Vospominaniya (fragment: 1948–1951 godï)', in Rakhmanova (ed.), *Sergey Prokof'yev: Vospominaniya, pis'ma, stat'i*, 246.

175 'Vïpiski', 13 March 1938, RGALI, 2040/1/65, l. 41.

176 The unpublished ninth and tenth chapters of Asafiev's autobiography detail the vicissitudes of his compositional career in the later 1930s: 'O sebe', RGALI, 2658/1/351, ll. 1–440b. In a remarkable letter of 22 November 1937 to Platon Kerzhentsev, the chairman of the Committee for Artistic Affairs, he implored Kerzhentsev to ask Stalin to come to his assistance, claiming that he had been reduced to a state of 'despair' by his experiences of persecution and demeaning treatment at the hands of his colleagues: RGALI, 962/3/331, ll. 98–108.

177 See, for example, 'Vïpiski', 11 January, 17 May, and 16 September 1936, RGALI, 2040/1/65, ll. 270b, 30, 310b.

178 'Vïpiski', 22 October 1935, RGALI, 2040/1/65, l. 250b.

His responses to the furore that erupted over Shostakovich's *Lady Macbeth of the Mtsensk District* in January 1936 demonstrated a remarkable degree of personal and professional integrity as well as disdain for official aesthetic orthodoxies. Given his lack of interest in the theatre, it is noteworthy that he not only sat in on rehearsals before the opera's Moscow production opened in January 1934 but also came to several performances. Deeply impressed, he declared Shostakovich's score 'magnificent' and a 'work of genius'.[179] The opera made a very different impression on Stalin and his entourage when they attended a showing on 26 January 1936. Myaskovsky's diary entry for 28 January laconically records the mood of 'general fright' following the publication of an unsigned *Pravda* editorial entitled 'Muddle Instead of Music', which roundly condemned *Lady Macbeth* for 'formalist' decadence.[180] Penned by a hack journalist who regularly undertook dubious assignments on the government's behalf, this venomous diatribe did not come entirely out of the blue: it instigated a new and more aggressive phase in a campaign against modernist and Western-influenced artistic tendencies that had been gathering momentum for several years.[181] The Party took the opportunity to drive home the message that 'formalism' would no longer be tolerated. Special meetings to consider the implications of the *Pravda* editorial (and a follow-up piece attacking Shostakovich's ballet *The Limpid Stream*) were convened not only for musicians but also for artists working in other domains. As documentation preserved in government archives attests, the responses of the artistic community were closely monitored by the secret police.[182] The author of one report indignantly noted that Myaskovsky, 'the acknowledged leader of the so-called "Moscow school" of formalists . . . did not even turn up' to a three-day forum organised by the local branch of the Composers' Union, and adduced his failure to condemn Shostakovich as evidence of a 'silent pact' between 'formalist' composers who were attempting to 'sabotage' the Party's efforts. A police informant dutifully relayed Myaskovsky's private verdict that the *Pravda* articles could cause Soviet music to regress to a 'wretched and primitive' state.[183]

As usual, he refrained from making any public statement – unlike Asafiev, who published an essay declaring his previous praise of Shostakovich's

179 'Vipiski', 22 January 1934 and 8 January 1936, RGALI, 2040/1/65, ll. 12, 27.

180 'Vipiski', RGALI, 2040/1/65, l. 28. On the background circumstances, see Yevgeniy Yefimov, *Sumbur vokrug "Sumbura" i odnogo malen'kogo zhurnalista: Stat'i i materialï* (Moscow, 2006).

181 See Anatoliy Morozov, *Konets utopii: Iz istorii iskusstva v SSSR 1930-kh godov* (Moscow, 1995), 27–58; Gromov, *Stalin: Iskusstvo i vlast'*, 271–81.

182 See Grigoriy Fayman, 'Lyudi i polozheniya', *Nezavisimaya gazeta*, 14 and 27 March 1996 (two-part article), and 'Dalyokoye. . .', *Nezavisimaya gazeta*, 5 December 1996.

183 Artizov and Naumov (ed.), *Vlast' i khudozhestvennaya intelligentsiya*, 295, 303.

opera to have been a serious lapse in judgement.[184] (On learning that Asafiev had been rewarded for his turncoatery by being appointed senior arts consultant to the government, Steinberg remarked mordantly in his diary: 'Poor Soviet music!'[185]) Asafiev was by no means alone in acting thus: Dianov came away from the Moscow meetings perturbed by the readiness of prominent composers and critics to join in the chorus of condemnation.[186] Even when put on the spot, Myaskovsky did not yield to peer pressure. Amongst his personal papers is his draft response to a request that he comment on the implications of the *Pravda* articles for composition teaching at the Moscow Conservatoire. He pointedly refrained from criticising Shostakovich, and although he acknowledged vaguely that the articles raised important issues, he stressed the need to discuss these in an 'objective and principled' manner. Of far greater concern than formalism itself, he suggested, were students' low levels of general culture and their reluctance to apply themselves seriously to mastering technical aspects of their craft out of a misplaced fear of being branded 'formalists'.[187]

Myaskovsky and his circle were also supportive of Shostakovich personally. On learning that he had finished a Fourth Symphony, Lamm promptly transcribed it for two pianos and arranged to have it played for the composer when he visited Moscow – a gesture that touched him greatly.[188] Myaskovsky thought the symphony made a 'stunning' impression and was dismayed to learn that Shostakovich had cancelled its premiere because of the attacks on his work, remarking in his diary: 'What a disgrace for us, his contemporaries'.[189] (He was less persuaded by the Fifth Symphony when he heard it two years later: he disliked its Mahlerian scherzo and the 'boiler-plate' (*otpiska*) of its closing peroration, but attended several performances in an attempt to get to grips with the score and 'hear it from the composer's point of view'.[190])

---

184 'Volnuyushchiye voprosï', *Sovetskaya muzïka* 5 (1936), 24–7. On Asafiev's volte-face, see Asaf'yev, Boris. 'D. D. Shostakovich', ed. Andrey Pavlov-Arbenin with an introduction and commentary by Lidiya Adėr, in Ol'ga Digonskaya and Lyudmila Kovnatskaya (ed.), *Dmitriy Shostakovich: Issledovaniya i materialï*, vol. 2 (Moscow, 2007), 38–44.

185 Entry for 26 February 1936, quoted in Lyudmila Kovnatskaya (ed.), *Shostakovich: Mezhdu mgnoveniyem i vechnost'yu. Dokumentï. Materialï. Stat'ï.* (St Peterburg, 2000), 116.

186 'Dnevnik', RGALI, 2027/1/22, 10–100b.

187 RGALI, 2040/1/64, ll. 1–10b. The document is untitled and dated 4 March 1936.

188 Lamm, 'Pavel Aleksandrovich Lamm: Opït biografii', RNMM, 192/361, ll. 417, 420.

189 'Vïpiski', 11 and 22 December 1936, RGALI, 2040/1/65, l. 33.

190 'Vïpiski', 23, 26, 28 January and 11 February 1938, RGALI, 2040/1/65, l. 400b.

It was not a coincidence that the intensification of the campaign against formalism followed moves to subject artistic life to greater centralised control. In late 1935, plans were finalised to transfer responsibility for the arts from Narkompros to a new ministry, the Committee for Artistic Affairs, which commenced operations in early 1936.[191] The committee had a very broad remit: in addition to maintaining oversight of the country's cultural infrastructure and personnel, it was also responsible for censorship of the arts and passing repertoire for performance. A distinct change was perceptible in the climate of artistic life. Music by contemporary Western modernists all but disappeared from concert programmes.[192] Even before Shostakovich's condemnation, other Soviet musicians of modernist sympathies experienced serious professional setbacks. The young Leningrad composer Gavriil Popov's First Symphony was banned immediately after its premiere in March 1935 because it supposedly reflected 'the ideology of classes hostile to the USSR'.[193] Later that year, Konstantin Saradzhev was forced to accept a conducting post at the opera house in Yerevan: he had increasingly struggled to find work in Moscow due to his former involvement in ASM.[194] This trend would continue, as Party officials moved to marginalise 'undesirable elements' in the arts world.

Emboldened by the Party's criticisms of Shostakovich, former RAPM members reasserted themselves: at the Moscow meetings in February 1936, Lebedinsky declared that Soviet music had no achievements to boast since the untimely death of his friend Davidenko two years previously.[195] Allegations about the pervasiveness of decadent artistic tendencies mounted, taking absurd forms. Not content with merely indicting living composers, including Myaskovsky and Steinberg, the author of an 'exposé' published in the leading daily *Leningradskaya pravda* in March 1936 posthumously 'unmasked' Lyadov and Taneyev as formalists also.[196] As Steinberg remarked mordantly, he and Myaskovsky found themselves 'in good company'.[197] 'I am delighted that we have been branded formalists', Myaskovsky replied: 'That is almost an accolade at present'. Responding to his Leningrad colleague's enquiry about conditions in Moscow, he reported

191 See Leonid Maksimenkov, *Sumbur vmesto muzïki: Stalinskaya kul'turnaya revolyutsiya, 1936–1938* (Moscow, 1997), 52–71.

192 See Pauline Fairclough, *Classics for the Masses: Shaping Soviet Musical Identity under Lenin and Stalin* (New Haven, 2016), 112–17.

193 Gavriil Popov, *Iz literaturnogo naslediya: Stranitsï biografii*, ed. Zarui Apetyan (Moscow, 1986), 260.

194 Lamm, 'Pavel Aleksandrovich Lamm: opït biografii', RNMM, 192/361, l. 412.

195 Artizov and Naumov, *Vlast' i khudozhestvennaya intelligentsiya*, 302–3.

196 'Protiv sumbura v muzïkal'noy uchyobe', *Leningradskaya pravda*, 16 March 1936.

197 Steinberg to Myaskovsky, 17 March 1936, RGALI, 2040/2/282, ll. 71–71ob.

that the ritualised 'self-flagellation' at the conservatoire had not got out of hand, thanks to the restraining influence of the new director, Heinrich Neuhaus, but the atmosphere in the Composers' Union was so unpleasant that he had actively sought to distance himself. Intrigue and denunciations were rife, and Chelyapov was throwing his weight about, attempting to subject composers to his 'ignorant tutelage'. 'The unhealthy interest that music has started to arouse somehow disinclines me to write for a "wide listenership"', Myaskovsky told Steinberg. 'I increasingly want to confine myself to more intimate genres (songs, chamber music) and stay away from the bazaar. The requirements that they are now imposing in regard of "music for the masses" don't attract me very much: I cannot write "happy music" and have absolutely no feeling for it. I hope that all this is only temporary and that interest in serious music will be allowed to revive'.[198]

In spite of his disdain for Chelyapov's attempts to meddle in his creative work, Myaskovsky had to be circumspect in dealing with him. When Chelyapov, in his capacity as editor of *Soviet Music*, contacted him shortly afterwards to request that he write an account of his career for publication, he found himself in a delicate position. The timing of this request, coming so soon after the censuring of Shostakovich, was unlikely to have been merely coincidental. Myaskovsky was well aware that anything he wrote would be closely scrutinised: it must also have occurred to him that the invitation could have been a trap. Writing about his compositions was a potentially hazardous undertaking, given his music's markedly apolitical character and his reputation as a 'formalist' with a dubious history of involvement in ASM. He tried to decline, but Chelyapov pressed him to agree, arguing that young composers would benefit from reading his autobiography.[199] Having evidently considered it inadvisable to refuse, he duly 'concocted' a text, as he noted ironically in his diary. The short essay 'Autobiographical Notes about My Creative Path', which appeared in *Soviet Music*'s June 1936 issue, was his first venture into print in over a decade. Myaskovsky adroitly circumvented the difficulties by means of a dual strategy. Most of the essay comprises a carefully pruned narrative of his early life which focusses on his struggles to pursue his artistic vocation – a suitably edifying topic for younger readers. Awkward subjects, such as his father's exalted rank in the tsarist army, are studiously avoided, and Myaskovsky played down his bourgeois social origins by repeatedly alluding to the family's very modest financial means. The concluding discussion of his output is brief and relentlessly self-critical. Notwithstanding his eminence, it seemed that the fifty-five-year-old composer could scarcely find a good word to say about anything he had written. His Sixth Symphony had reflected the 'neurasthenic' responses to

198 Myaskovsky to Steinberg, 19 March 1936, RIII, 28/1/487, ll. 115–115ob.

199 Kabalevskiy, 'O N. Ya. Myaskovskom', 309.

the Revolution prevalent amongst the old intelligentsia. He attempted to write music of a more 'objective' kind in the Eighth Symphony (which he retrospectively endowed with a vague programme portraying the folk hero Stepan Razin) but had only partially succeeded. The Tenth Symphony was a 'rather incoherent' response to Pushkin's *Bronze Horseman*; he had relapsed into 'subjectivism' in the Eleventh, and his attempt to treat a contemporary Soviet subject in the Twelfth proved disappointingly unsatisfactory. The 'pessimistic' Thirteenth originated from a misguided experiment; the Fourteenth was sounder in approach but lacked 'freshness'; and although the Fifteenth had won praise for its 'optimism and lyricism', its musical language did not yet allow him 'to feel fully an artist of our times'. He had planned to write a work to mark the twentieth anniversary of the October Revolution in 1937 but abandoned the project, feeling that his 'immature musical thinking' was as yet unequal to the task. Notwithstanding this lengthy litany of failure, he ended by assuring readers of his firm intention to persist in his quest for a 'Socialist Realist musical language' capable of depicting the 'feelings aroused by our great contemporaries ... who are reconstructing our life with the sagacity of genius'.[200]

As Yevgeny Golubev was at pains to emphasise in his reminiscences of his teacher, Myaskovsky's self-deprecating comments, here as elsewhere, should not be taken at face value and have given rise to serious misunderstandings. A person of his talent, intelligence, and keen critical acumen could hardly have been unaware of the quality of his finest compositions, but Myaskovsky was extremely careful never to do or say anything that might suggest an attitude of self-regard or provoke hostility. The ironic, disparaging manner in which he habitually referred to his work and his repeated 'confessions' of putative shortcomings were patently a self-protective strategy adopted by someone who was acutely aware of his potential vulnerability to attack. 'He never displayed his superiority', Golubev remarks. 'The conditions at that time obliged him to be very cautious in his behaviour'.[201] In writing the 'Autobiographical Notes', Myaskovsky adopted a similar technique as in his letter to Koval about the Twelfth Symphony, creating a smokescreen by means of an ostentatious display of modesty and rueful confessions of feelings of inadequacy in struggling to realise the lofty ideals of Socialist Realism. Even if his enemies suspected his sincerity, his essay gave them no purchase: his self-criticisms not only anticipated any criticisms that they were likely to voice, but echoed a received view of his career that had by now become standard – as is apparent if one compares his essay with the text of an article on the Fifteenth Symphony by

200 Myaskovskiy, 'Avtobiograficheskiye zametki', 9–11.

201 Golubev, 'Alogizmï', RGALI, 2798/2/23, ll. 36, 75–8.

the critic Georgy Khubov, published the previous year.[202] Although by no means hostile in tone, Khubov's discussion of Myaskovsky's artistic development reinforced the stereotype of the 'individualistic' composer who was striving to 'reform'. Following Asafiev, whom he cites, he characterised Myaskovsky's earlier compositions as depicting the 'tragedy of the doomed artist in the oppressive atmosphere of bourgeois reality' and noted that 'morbid echoes of the past' continued to be audible in more recent work. He commended the Fourteenth and Fifteenth Symphonies as marking a decisive turn towards 'healthy, vivid Soviet lyricism', and would subsequently hail the Sixteenth, completed in April 1936, as 'a major creative victory for Myaskovsky and Soviet music as a whole' which demonstrated that the composer had at last overcome his 'subjective' tendencies.[203] Myaskovsky's diary affords glimpses of his reactions to the constructions placed on his work. Khubov's article 'enraged' him: 'A load of rubbish. I prefer abuse – but intelligent abuse'.[204]

Khubov's claim that the Fourteenth, Fifteenth, and Sixteenth Symphonies inaugurated a new Socialist Realist phase in his development was entirely wishful thinking. All are 'pure symphonies', to use Myaskovsky's phrase, devoid of 'ideological content'. (Khubov made much of the fact that Myaskovsky used the melody of a 'mass song' written in 1931, 'Aeroplanes Are Flying', as a theme in the Sixteenth's finale, but his description of the score as being 'dedicated to the enthralling theme of Soviet aviation' is a journalistic fiction.[205]) They are, moreover, works of genuine substance, complex in import and evincing a highly refined craftsmanship: there is nothing blatant about them, or suggestive of an enforced stylistic simplification. Though markedly different to scores such as the Tenth and

---

202 'N. Ya. Myaskovskiy i XV simfoniya', *Sovetskoye iskusstvo*, 17 November 1935.

203 Georgiy Khubov, '16-ya simfoniya Myaskovskogo', *Sovetskaya muzïka*, 1 (1937), 19.

204 'Vïpiski', 15 February 1937, RGALI, 2040/1/65, l. 340b.

205 Kabalevsky drew attention to Myaskovsky's use of 'Aeroplanes Are Flying' in a newspaper article published before the Sixteenth's premiere ('Novaya simfoniya N. Ya. Myaskovskogo', *Muzïka*, 16 February 1937), which was subsequently adapted as a programme note. He pointed out, however, that this self-borrowing did not 'furnish sufficient grounds to assume that the symphony has a programme'. Myaskovsky apparently described the Sixteenth's slow movement to Alexey Ikonnikov as a funeral march commemorating the victims of a highly publicised Soviet aviation disaster – the crash of the Tupolev ANT-20 *Maxim Gorki*, then the largest aircraft in the world, on 18 May 1935. (See 'N. Ya. Myaskovskiy (biograficheskiy ocherk)', 29.) One suspects that this 'content' was bestowed on the movement retrospectively to provide a plausible justification for its sombre mood. There is no mention of the crash, or indeed, anything to do with aviation in Myaskovsky's own programme note for the Sixteenth, written for a performance in Paris in 1937 (RGALI, 2040/4/9, ll. 12–13).

Thirteenth Symphonies, they nonetheless display pronounced consistencies of style and approach with some of their predecessors, notably the Ninth and Eleventh. Like most of Myaskovsky's symphonies, their design follows nineteenth-century models: unlike Sibelius and Nielsen, he never felt the need for a radical rethinking of symphonic organisation. In general, they exemplify the growing classicism of his compositional idiom in the 1930s – manifested as a concern for greater formal cogency, textural clarity, and thematic definition, as well as the adoption of a harmonic language with a firmer tonal basis. In comparison with his earlier music, the focus is not so much on the expressive effects of local harmonic details as on filling larger expanses of tonal space and the attainment of long-range momentum. (The coruscating Scherzo of the Fourteenth affords an excellent illustration in point.) Interestingly, all three symphonies suggest a renewed engagement with the work of Tchaikovsky, a figure whom Myaskovsky had long admired and who was himself a composer of pronounced classicising tendencies. Tchaikovsky's influence is especially perceptible in the treatment of texture and orchestral sonority (notably, the writing for woodwinds), and in the cast of inner movements, such as the splendid waltz and the lovely intermezzo that respectively constitute the third and second movements of the Fifteenth and Sixteenth (exx. 9.10 and 9.11).

The turn to classicism is also noticeable in a tendency to greater emotional restraint and a marked broadening of expressive range. Although these symphonies are by no means without their sombre and strenuous moments, their atmosphere is on the whole more sunlit – in part, because of their more diatonic sound-world. This diatonicism, however, is by no means merely a regression to harmonic commonplaces. Myaskovsky's compositional idiom increasingly exhibits a piquant blending of modality and chromaticism, and a continuing penchant for highly elliptical progressions – a good example being the main theme of the Sixteenth's powerful slow movement (ex. 9.12). It also remains capable of considerable pungency: the first movement's vigorous opening idea, with its abrasive semitonal clashes (ex. 9.13), generates astringent polytonal sonorities when subjected to contrapuntal development (ex. 9.14).

All three symphonies were respectfully received, and the Sixteenth was performed several times after its Moscow premiere on 24 October 1936 under the Hungarian conductor Eugen Szenkar [Jenő Szenkár], its dedicatee.[206] There was clearly considerable eagerness to bestow a canonical status on the work and regard it as one of the first successful Socialist Realist

---

206 See Eugen Szenkar, *Mein Weg als Musiker: Erinnerungen eines Dirigenten*, ed. Sandra Szenkar (Berlin, 2014), 127–8. The dedication to Szenkar was omitted when the full score was published in 1939 – perhaps because association with foreigners had become dangerous.

EXAMPLE 9.10. Symphony no. 15, second movement: opening.

EXAMPLE 9.11. Symphony no. 16, second movement: opening.

symphonies: even Alexander Goldenweiser, who was generally antipathetic to Myaskovsky's music, declared that the Sixteenth should silence critics' reproaches about the paucity of 'monumental compositions in a "grand" style befitting our great epoch'.[207] To invoke comparisons between the compositional style of the Sixteenth and the vulgar, overbearing *bol'shoy stil'* prevalent in contemporary Soviet architecture, a Stalinist counterpart to the *style grand* associated with Louis Quatorze, would be entirely misplaced.[208] Notwithstanding the grandeur of its slow movement, much of the

207 '16-ya simfoniya Myaskovskogo', *Izvestiya*, 18 December 1936.

208 Such a comparison has been proposed: see Igor' Vorob'yov, *Sotsrealisticheskiy 'bol'shoy stil'' v sovetskoy muzïke (1930–1950-ye godï): Issledovaniye* (St

EXAMPLE 9.12. Symphony no. 16, third movement: opening.

EXAMPLE 9.13. Symphony no. 16, first movement: opening.

EXAMPLE 9.14. Symphony no. 16, first movement: bars 212–26.

Sixteenth is intimate and lyrical in nature: its finale eschews a bombastic conclusion for a quiet, serene ending. The symphony defines a psychological world far removed from that of artworks produced to reinforce Stalin's personality cult or to glorify Soviet power.

Myaskovsky's position in Soviet musical life of the mid 1930s was a curious one. Though by no means all his colleagues were well-disposed towards him, he undoubtedly won respect and admiration: he was customarily referred to as 'the artistic conscience of Soviet music' in acknowledgement of his integrity and concern to maintain high standards.[209] He was also widely liked: as contemporary reminiscences attest, those who came into contact with him found him courteous and helpful. Despite his uneasy relations with Soviet officialdom, there never seemed to be any question that he might be dismissed from his institutional posts. (Quite the contrary, in fact: he attempted to resign from Muzgiz on three occasions between 1934 and 1939, but the management refused to let him go.[210]) His position as one of the country's leading composers was unquestioned: his work had already started to attract the attention of young scholars, including his future biographer Alexey Ikonnikov.[211] At the same time, however, performances of it remained comparatively infrequent and much of his output was not performed at all.

Despite the revival of concert life after 1932, Myaskovsky's diary records only eleven performances of his compositions from the 1910s and 1920s in the period before January 1936, mostly given by foreign guest conductors. (The French-Hungarian conductor Georges Sébastian, for example, performed *Alastor*, the Third, Fourth, and Sixth Symphonies, and the Serenade, op. 32/1.) None of his symphonies were given with any regularity, and it appears that some, such as the Eleventh and Thirteenth, never received a second performance in the USSR during his lifetime.[212] Performances of his work outside Moscow, moreover, were rare. Myaskovsky was by no means alone in suffering such neglect: it is indicative that the Moscow Philharmonic only programmed three new Soviet works over the thirty-five concerts in its 1935–6 season.[213] However, the complex, predominantly serious nature of his output would not have made it very attractive to concert

Petersburg, 2013), 224–5.

209 Shlifshteyn (ed.), *N. Ya. Myaskovskiy: Sobraniye materialov*, vol. 1, 3.

210 'Vïpiski', 26 September 1934, 31 August 1937, and 13 February 1939, RGALI, 2040/1/65, ll. 170b, 37, 480b.

211 Myaskovsky's diary dates his first contact with Ikonnikov to 1 October 1935: 'Vïpiski', RGALI, 2040/1/65, l. 25.

212 The first performance of Eleventh Symphony was given by the radio orchestra under Saradzhev on 16 January 1933: 'Vïpiski', RGALI, 2040/1/65, l. 8.

213 'Vïpiski', 17 September 1935, RGALI, 2040/1/65, l. 8.

agencies tasked with introducing classical music to a new proletarian listenership. After 1936, very little of the music that he had written before 1933 was played – not even the Twelfth Symphony. There is no evidence to suggest that his earlier work was subject to informal ban, but the terms in which it was discussed by Soviet music critics, who emphasised its 'subjective' and 'gloomy' character, would have done little to encourage interest in it. Myaskovsky's status in the pantheon of Soviet composers remained highly ambiguous. Unlike Shostakovich, Prokofiev, or Khachaturian, he never composed anything that scored a widespread popular success, and while almost everything that he wrote was performed, his work did not establish itself in the regular Soviet concert repertoire. Matters were not helped by the generally mediocre quality of the renditions that it received, a recurrent complaint in his diary and letters. Although his new orchestral works were routinely entrusted to leading Soviet conductors of the day, he had a low opinion of their abilities. Diary entries for 1937 record his distress at Alexander Gauk's inept mangling of his Seventeenth and Eighteenth Symphonies: the rehearsals for the Eighteenth went so badly that he could not bring himself to attend the premiere.[214] He subsequently admitted to Asafiev that he no longer wanted to hear his music because it was 'so foully played'.[215]

By the mid-1930s, performances of Myaskovsky's music abroad had also become infrequent, so he was unable to console himself with the thought that it might be receiving superior renditions elsewhere. Although Dzimitrovsky, his Universal Edition contact in Vienna, loyally kept in touch, his efforts on Myaskovsky's behalf were hampered by the prevailing economic crisis and Hitler's accession to power in Germany, one of the firm's most important markets.[216] (Dzimitrovsky, who was Jewish, was forced to flee Austria after the Anschluss.[217]) The firm's interest in Soviet composers also waned because of its discouraging experiences of dealing with Soviet bureaucracy. To Dzimitrovsky's disappointment, International Books decided in 1932 not to renew its contract with Universal Edition and the Composers' Union rebuffed the publishing house's attempt to initiate a collaboration, leaving its letters unanswered.[218] Dzimitrovsky was also taken aback to discover that the All-Union Society for Cultural Relations

214 'Vipiski', 14 November and 10, 13, 14, 15, 16 December 1937, RGALI, 2040/1/65, ll. 38, 39–390b.

215 Myaskovsky to Asafiev, RGALI, 2658/2/51, l. 77.

216 Dzimitrovsky discussed these difficulties in his letters to Myaskovsky of 17 May and 12 November 1933, RGALI, 2040/2/142, ll. 15–150b, l. 270b.

217 His last communication to Myaskovsky was a postcard sent from New York, dated 10 September 1940: RGALI, 2040/2/143, l. 40.

218 Dzimitrovsky to Myaskovsky, 30 August 1932, 3 July and 12 November 1933, RGALI, 2040/2/141, 610b; 2040/2/142, ll. 17–180b, 270b.

with Foreign Countries (VOKS) had distributed the entire first print run of Myaskovsky's Twelfth Symphony as complimentary copies to institutions abroad – causing a potentially substantial loss of income in royalties.[219] The documentation that survives amongst Myaskovsky's personal papers and in Universal Edition's Vienna archive is too incomplete to yield much information about foreign performances of his work during the 1930s, but it is evident from Dzimitrovsky's correspondence that they dropped off sharply. The only notable foreign champion of Myaskovsky's music during the 1930s was Frederick Stock, who performed one of his symphonies with the Chicago Symphony Orchestra almost every year. Nicolai Malko, now an émigré, continued to conduct Myaskovsky's symphonies when circumstances allowed, but confirmed Dzimitrovsky's reports of a widespread disinclination to programme unfamiliar repertoire. In a letter of December 1936, he complained of experiencing acute difficulty in obtaining scores of Myaskovsky's more recent compositions – a further hindrance to the international dissemination of his work.[220]

Malko was understandably surprised at the Composers' Union's apparent lack of interest in promoting Soviet music abroad, but contact with the outside world and with foreigners in general was growing increasingly difficult as the domestic climate became more fraught. The assassination under mysterious circumstances of Sergey Kirov, the charismatic head of the Leningrad Party organisation, in December 1934 sparked a dramatic intensification of state repression that climaxed between 1936 and 1938. Its causes are still a matter of debate amongst historians, but an important factor was Stalin's continuing fear of counterrevolution and his anxiety that disaffected elements in Soviet society might collude with foreign powers to overthrow the regime.[221] Official attitudes to foreign visitors and residents grew increasingly suspicious, viewing them as potential threats and sources of ideological contagion. In March 1936, the government announced measures to combat 'spy, terrorist, and saboteur elements' – including more stringent visa regulations, moves to restrict the operation of international organisations on Soviet territory, and intensified surveillance of foreigners by the secret police.[222] The effects of the new policies were soon felt in musical life: Kirill Kondrashin, then at the start of his conducting career

219 Dzimitrovsky to Myaskovsky, 7 February 1933, RGALI, 2040/2/142, l. 9.

220 Malko to Myaskovsky, 13 December 1936, RGALI, 2040/2/181, ll. 49–50.

221 For a recent study focussing on this aspect, see James Harris, *The Great Fear: Stalin's Terror of the 1930s* (New York, 2016).

222 'O merakh, ograzhdayushchikh SSSR ot proniknoveniya shpionskikh, terroristicheskikh i diversionnïkh èlementov', 9 March 1936, in Vladimir Khaustov *et al.* (ed.), *Lubyanka. Stalin i VChK-GPU-OGPU-NKVD. Arkhiv Stalina. Dokumentï vïsshikh organov partiynoy i gosudarstvennoy vlasti. Yanvar' 1922 – dekabr' 1936* (Moscow, 2003), 738–41.

in Leningrad, noticed that foreign artists were no longer making appearances.[223] Before long, Soviet citizens would start avoiding foreigners and cease corresponding with relatives living abroad for fear of being accused of involvement in 'anti-Soviet activity'.

Given these circumstances, a communication from Malko presented Myaskovsky with a serious dilemma. Over the previous four years, Malko had been in intermittent contact with Myaskovsky's stepsister Varvara, who sought him out when he visited Brno for a conducting engagement in 1932. It is not clear how Varvara ended up in Brno or whether she had attempted previously to communicate with her half-siblings. Malko reported that she was experiencing great hardship: she had four children, was pregnant again, and her husband was unemployed. Malko and his wife did what they could to help, but their means were limited.[224] Myaskovsky's side of his correspondence with Malko is mostly lost, so it is not known whether he sought to assist Varvara financially. In 1932 Myaskovsky had little money to spare either, and Soviet restrictions on private citizens' access to foreign currency would have made it difficult, if not impossible, to send funds to a relative living abroad. In February 1936 Malko wrote to inform him that the family's plight had become desperate: Varvara's husband had abandoned her, and she was reduced to begging on the streets. Deeply distressed by the situation and his inability to help, Malko enquired whether her children could be sent to live in the USSR.[225] Myaskovsky's reply to this letter has not been preserved, but even if Varvara had been willing to agree to the plan, it would scarcely have been feasible to arrange for her five children, the youngest of whom was only three years old, to be brought to Moscow. Aside from the expense and the formidable bureaucratic and practical difficulties involved (not least, where the children would live and who would support them and look after them), it would have raised very awkward questions about Myaskovsky's father and his relationship with his émigré stepsister. He and his sisters were already in a vulnerable position since the imprisonment of Yevgeniya's husband on charges of espionage: one imagines that they would have been reluctant to risk attracting further unwanted attention from the authorities. Nothing more is known about the fate of Varvara and her family.

By the summer of 1936, Stalin had instituted a purge of the Communist Party, governmental officials, and the army which rapidly expanded to affect a wide cross-section of Soviet society. Zinoviev, Kamenev, Bukharin, and other former Party leaders were convicted in three highly publicised

223 Vladimir Razhnikov, *Kirill Kondrashin rasskazïvayet o muzïke i zhizni* (Moscow, 1989), 53.

224 Malko to Myaskovsky, 24 April 1932, RGALI, 2040/2/181, ll. 34–34ob.

225 Malko to Myaskovsky, 9 February 1936, RGALI, 2040/2/181, 48–48ob.

and elaborately stage-managed show trials held between August 1937 and March 1938. The accused confessed to a range of fantastic crimes – including plotting to kill Kirov and Stalin, organising large-scale 'wrecking' activities, and colluding with Trotsky and foreign governments to undermine Soviet power. Virtually all received the death penalty. Hundreds of thousands of others would be arraigned on similar fabricated charges in 1937–8, and after hasty secret trials were either summarily shot or sentenced to lengthy imprisonment in labour camps located in remote and inhospitable parts of the country. Widespread use was made of torture and aggressive interrogation techniques to extract 'confessions' and force the captives to name putative accomplices. The intelligentsia was not spared: the victims included many scientists, scholars, and artists.[226] Amongst them were prominent figures in the Writers' Union: the former RAPP leaders Leopold Averbakh and Vladimir Kirshon were executed for their supposed involvement in a counterrevolutionary terrorist organisation.[227]

The end of the 1930s is a sparsely documented period of Myaskovsky's career: his diary and what survives of his correspondence from these years reveal little of his inner life or his responses to events. He was undoubtedly affected by them, however: they impinged on him directly, though he was fortunate to escape arrest. It has been asserted that musicians were scarcely touched by the Great Purge[228], but this claim has come to seem increasingly dubious in the light of recent research.[229] Even before the massive escalation in state terror in 1937–8, a considerable number of musicians were indicted on trumped-up allegations, including singers and orchestral players attached to the Bolshoi Theatre. Almost certainly acting at the behest of the secret police, the Bolshoi management compiled covert lists of employees whose backgrounds or personal circumstances were considered 'compromising'. Common grounds for suspicion included having émigré relatives, being of aristocratic descent, or having a parent who had been a property owner, a member of the clergy, or a tsarist army officer.[230] A composition student of Myaskovsky's at the Moscow Conservatoire, Georgy Kirkor, was sentenced to five years hard labour in May 1935 under a recently introduced

---

226 See Robert Conquest, *The Great Terror: A Reassessment*, rev. ed. (London, 2008), 291–307.

227 For a discussion of the effects of the Great Purge on the literary community, see Kemp-Welch, *Stalin and the Literary Intelligentsia*, 205–39.

228 See, for example, Caroline Brooke, 'Soviet Musicians and the Great Terror', *Europe-Asia Studies*, 3 (2002), 397–413.

229 See especially Inna Klause, *Der Klang des Gulag: Musik und Musiker in den sowjetischen Zwangsarbeitslagern der 1920er- bis 1950er-Jahre* (Göttingen, 2014).

230 See Inna Klause, 'Composers in the Gulag: A Preliminary Survey', in Zuk and Frolova-Walker (ed.), *Russian Music since 1917*, 192–5.

law criminalising sodomy[231], which had come to be regarded as another manifestation of 'anti-Soviet tendencies': false allegations of homosexual activity often served as convenient pretext for arrest.[232] (The conservatoire's former director Bolesław Przybyszewski was apparently arrested for the same offence: he was released in 1936 only to be re-arrested the following year and shot after being convicted on charges of espionage.[233]) As the Great Purge took hold, Yevgeny Golubev, who was in the third year of his studies with Myaskovsky at the time, recalled the arrests of two other classmates and the suicide under mysterious circumstances of a friend who was taught by Shebalin. Golubev was not politically active and had left the Communist Youth League. On arriving to his lesson one day, Myaskovsky presented him with a slim volume entitled *Songs of the Peoples of the Far North*: 'It contained poems about the lives of the Laplanders. About their difficult past and joyful present [i.e., under socialism]. I understood Myaskovsky's hint. I was writing too much "textless" music. It was vital that I showed more patriotism and "loyalty to the cause of Lenin and Stalin" [a contemporary cant phrase]'. Myaskovsky was evidently concerned that Golubev might come to harm.[234]

The Purge claimed the lives of several people whom Myaskovsky knew well. His old acquaintance Viktor Naumov, who had run the farm at Mukhanovo where he holidayed throughout the 1920s, was arrested in the autumn of 1937 on the basis of a spurious denunciation. Like Myaskovsky, he came from the nobility and had served in the army.[235] His Muzgiz colleague Nikolay Zhilyayev was arrested in November 1937: a highly respected figure on the Moscow musical scene, Zhilyayev acted as mentor to Shostakovich and other notable young musicians.[236] The Terror struck closest, however, with the arrest of Sergey Popov, a long-standing participant in Lamm's musical evenings.

The tragic course of Popov's life graphically illustrates how potentially vulnerable Myaskovsky was because of his background and army career.

---

231 See Aleksandr Komarov, '"...zhivyom nadezhdoy na blizkoye vosvrashcheniye v Moskvu". Iz perepiski N. Ya. Myaskovskogo s G. V. Kirkorom 1942 goda', in Vlasova and Sorokina (ed.), *Naslediye*, 384.

232 See Healey, *Homosexual Desire in Revolutionary Russia*, 181–206; Aleksey Burleshin, 'Vskrïtaya povsednevnost", *Novoye literaturnoye obozreniye*, 2 (2010), 344–84.

233 Kolińska, *Stachu*, 113.

234 Golubev, 'Alogizmï', RGALI, 2798/2/23, ll. 45–6.

235 Lamm, 'Pavel Aleksandrovich Lamm: Opït biografii', RNMM, 192/361, l. 421.

236 See Inna Barsova, 'Opfer stalinistischen Terrors: Nikolaj Žiljaev', in Friedrich Geiger and Eckhard John (ed.), *Musik zwischen Emigration und Stalinismus. Russische Komponisten in den 1930-er und 1940-er Jahren* (Stuttgart/Weimar, 2004), 140–57.

FIGURE 9.3. Myaskovsky in 1937.

FIGURE 9.4. Myaskovsky's composition class (1939).
From left to right: Boris Shekhter, Igor Belorusets, Sergey Razoryonov,
Yevgeny Golubev (at the piano), Myaskovsky, Viktor Bely.

The scion of a wealthy merchant family whose property and businesses were expropriated after the Revolution, Popov fought in World War I and subsequently transferred into the Red Army: he and Myaskovsky had worked together in the naval headquarters in Petrograd. His army service did not spare him from repeated harassment by the authorities. After being arrested several times between 1917 and 1919 as a 'former tsarist army officer', he was arrested again in 1928 on false accusations of having been a White Army officer and engaging in 'anti-Soviet activity'. Though cleared of the charges, he was stripped of his voting rights in 1929, a common punitive action taken against 'former people' which made it difficult for them to find accommodation and work. His rights were restored after Myaskovsky and others made representations on his behalf, but misfortune struck again when he was sacked from Muzgiz in 1932 because of his class origins: in a further act of vindictiveness, the press's censor insisted on the removal of his name from forthcoming publications that he had helped to prepare. He managed to get work as a copyist in the Composers' Union, but his position remained precarious. Unsurprisingly, these events had a highly detrimental effect on Popov's mental state. He was arrested for the last time in September 1937 after being denounced by a neighbour and was condemned to death for 'counterrevolutionary activity and anti-Soviet agitation'. The sentence was carried out on 13 November 1937 at the Butovo Shooting Range, a notorious mass execution site located eighteen miles south of Moscow.[237]

Popov's family did not learn his fate at the time: they were merely informed that he had been 'imprisoned without the right of correspondence'. Officially, it was as though he had never existed. His library and personal effects disappeared without trace – including the manuscript of his reconstruction of Tchaikovsky's early opera *The Voyevoda*, on which he was still working at the time of his arrest. Like countless other victims of the Terror, Popov became a non-person: his former associates avoided mentioning him or talking about him. In her memoirs, Olga Lamm movingly described her uncle's distress at Popov's disappearance: he and Popov had been friends for over thirty years. The musical evenings in the Lamm's apartment became sporadic: Popov's absence from the two-piano ensemble was a constant distressing reminder of his loss. Evidently frightened by what had happened, some of their acquaintances stopped visiting them. The oppressive mood was heightened by the suspicion that the couple with whom they shared their communal apartment were acting as informers and reading their letters.[238]

The strain of living in such conditions need hardly be emphasised: no-one knew whether they themselves might be arrested next. Soviet newspapers and periodicals from 1937 and 1938 exude a deeply sinister atmosphere, with their strident headlines clamouring for intensified 'political vigilance' and savage punitive measures to combat counterrevolution. Specialist arts journals were no exception. 'UNMASK AND DESTROY ENEMIES OF THE PEOPLE, TRAITORS TO THE MOTHERLAND', demanded an editorial in the Artists' Union journal.[239] *Soviet Music* featured similar articles, with titles such as 'Death to the Vile Enemies of the People Seeking to Restore Capitalism' and 'Erase the Vile Traitors to the Motherland from the Face of the Earth'.[240] In such a context, acts of basic human decency stand out all the more strongly. After Alexander Mosolov was arrested in the autumn of 1937 and sentenced to eight years in a concentration camp for

237 On Popov, see Aleksandr Komarov, '"Prirozhdyonnïy arkhivist": Ocherk biografii S. S. Popova', in Marina Rakhmanova (ed.), *Al'manakh*, vol. 3, Trudï Gosudarstvennogo tsentral'nogo muzeya muzïkal'noy kul'turï imeni M. I. Glinki (Moscow, 2007), 769–800.

238 Lamm, 'Pavel Aleksandrovich Lamm: Opït biografii', RNMM, 192/361, ll. 414, 421–2.

239 'Vragov naroda, predateley rodinï razoblachat' i unichtozhat'', *Tvorchestvo*, 6 (1937), 2.

240 'Smert' podlïm vragam naroda, restavratoram kapitalizma' and 'Steret' s litsa zemli podlïkh izmennikov rodinï', *Sovetskaya muzïka*, 1 (1937), 5–7 and 8.

counterrevolutionary activity, his mother turned to Myaskovsky for help.[241] Jointly with Glière, Myaskovsky wrote a letter to Mikhail Kalinin, the chairman of the Presidium of the Supreme Soviet of the USSR, to request that Mosolov's case be reviewed. Their efforts may have helped to bring about his early release in October 1938, as the Great Purge wound down and a proportion of camp internees began to be released.[242] Myaskovsky was subsequently one of the signatories of a letter sent by a group of prominent musicians to Vyacheslav Molotov to enquire about the fate of Nikolay Zhilyayev, in which they emphasised Zhilyayev's outstanding contribution as an editor and teacher.[243]

The tensions created by the Terror were compounded by the mounting tensions in musical life. Party oversight intensified after the creation of the Committee for Artistic Affairs, resulting in stricter censorship and tighter bureaucratic controls. The committee's Music Section began to review the operation of performing groups and musical institutions, turning its attention to the Moscow Composers' Union in December 1936. Its report recommended a comprehensive overhaul, complaining of the organisation's inefficiency, mismanagement of financial resources, and failure to take the lead in directing the activities of the other union branches. The committee's Chairman Platon Kerzhentsev insisted on greater efforts to combat formalism and to encourage engagement with ideological themes. In the face of severe criticism, Chelyapov stepped down from his post in July 1937.[244] He was taken into custody soon afterwards. 'What a commonplace person! But he did a lot of damage', Myaskovsky commented in his diary on hearing of his arrest.[245] (Chelyapov was convicted of belonging to a counterrevolutionary terrorist organisation and shot on 8 January 1938.[246]) The committee's investigations of the union's affairs came at a time when the organisation was already riven with animosities and in-fighting, and former RAPM members such as Lebedinsky found themselves under attack because of their association with the recently arrested RAPP leader Leopold

---

241 Myaskovsky's diary records two visits from Mosolov's mother on 9 and 17 February 1938: 'Vïpiski', RGALI, 2040/1/65, ll. 400b, 41.

242 Glière and Myaskovsky's letter is reproduced in Inna Barsova, 'Iz neopublikovannogo arkhiva A. V. Mosolova [Part 2]', *Sovetskaya muzïka*, 8 (1989), 70–1.

243 See Inna Barsova (ed.), *Nikolay Sergeyevich Zhilyayev: Trudï, dni i gibel'* (Moscow, 2008), 39–40.

244 See Simo Mikkonen, '"Muddle Instead of Music" in 1936', in Pauline Fairclough (ed.), *Shostakovich Studies 2* (Cambridge, 2010), 236–45.

245 'Vïpiski', 30 August 1937, RGALI, 2040/1/65, l. 37.

246 Larisa Yeryomina and Arseniy Roginskiy (ed.), *Rasstrel'nïye spiski: Moskva 1937–1941, "Kommunarka", Butovo* (Moscow, 2000), 432.

Averbakh.[247] Writing to Myaskovsky in May 1937, Kabalevsky described the ceaseless 'nastiness and squabbling' as 'a nightmare'.[248]

The depths to which the nastiness could descend was graphically demonstrated later in the year when a denunciation of Myaskovsky's old acquaintance Vladimir Derzhanovsky appeared in the Committee for Artistic Affairs periodical *Music*. His 'crime' had been to submit an entry to a Composers' Union competition to write pieces for the Red Army ensembles. Prompted by a recent *Pravda* article that extolled Glinka's music as a model for Soviet composers[249], Derzhanovsky produced a potpourri for wind orchestra based on themes from *A Life for the Tsar*. The author of the denunciation seized on Derzhanovsky's use of the melody of the opera's most celebrated chorus (in the original version, set to a text beginning 'Hail to thee, our Russian Tsar!') as revealing covert monarchist sympathies – even though the *Pravda* article had approvingly quoted the nineteenth-century critic Vladimir Stasov's description of the same chorus as exemplifying Glinka's genius. Pointing to Derzhanovsky's 'doubtful past' promoting 'ultra-contemporary bourgeois modernist music' and his repeated 'slander' of Soviet musical life in ASM's journal, he declared Derzhanovsky's entry for the competition an 'anti-Soviet act' and an 'insult to our glorious Red Army'. He closed by asking: 'Is there a place for this person in the ranks of Soviet musicologists? Is it not time to disturb the "nests of cockroaches" in which the Derzhanovskys of this world have been hiding?'[250]

The piece was evidently published with the approval of the newspaper's editor, Viktor Gorodinsky. Gorodinsky loathed modernist music (he would subsequently write a book decrying the decadence of Western musical life[251]) and this attack on Derzhanovsky was almost certainly motivated by his desire to rid the Moscow Composers' Union of personnel sympathetic to 'formalism': the previous summer, while acting as director of the Arts Sector of the Central Committee's Cultural and Educational Department, Gorodinsky had arranged for Levon Atovmyan to be transferred to an administrative post in remote Turkmenistan.[252] (In late 1937 Atovmyan too was arrested and sentenced to ten years in a labour camp, but was fortunate to be released in 1939.) Coming at the height of the Terror, the public denunciation of Derzhanovsky was tantamount to calling for his arrest. Derzhanovsky did what he could do to defend himself in the face of

---

247 See 'Do kontsa likvidirovat' rapmovsko-averbakhovskoye "nasledstvo"', *Muzïka*, 26 May 1937.

248 Kabalevsky to Myaskovsky, 31 May 1937, RGALI, 2040/1/121, l. 2.

249 'Sozdatel' russkoy natsional'noy operï M. I. Glinka', *Pravda*, 15 January 1937.

250 'Chuzhak', *Muzïka*, 26 December 1937.

251 *Muzïka dushevnoy nishchetï* (Moscow, 1950).

252 Atovm'yan, 'Vospominaniya', 231.

demands for his expulsion from the Composers' Union.[253] That eventuality was averted, perhaps thanks to Myaskovsky's influence[254], but the episode took a serious toll on Derzhanovsky, who was by now nearly blind in one eye and in failing health. Professionally isolated, he struggled to find work: Myaskovsky helped him as best he could by arranging for him to be given assignments as a copyist, which he completed with the aid of his wife.[255]

Once again, this incident reveals Myaskovsky's potential vulnerability: as a fellow founder-member of ASM, he was part of the same 'nest of cockroaches'. The intensity of the antagonism towards the 'formalists' within the Soviet cultural administration was all too apparent. In a diary entry of the previous year, Myaskovsky noted 'difficult conversations' about Prokofiev, who had recently returned from emigration to live in the USSR as a permanent resident: the Committee for Artistic Affairs 'could not stand' him and Muzgiz was 'disdaining' his work.[256] Prokofiev's *Cantata for the Twentieth Anniversary of October* (1937), written in the hope of improving his standing in the eyes of the authorities, languished unperformed because Kerzhentsev objected to his musical treatments of texts by Marx, Lenin, and Stalin.[257] The failure of this major project proved an ominous portent of even more serious difficulties to come.

Up to 1936, Myaskovsky's strategies for dealing with his circumstances had served him well. By the end of 1936, however, his abstention from public comment on current events and continuing failure to produce politically engaged work risked being interpreted as 'anti-Soviet activity'. The effects of the dual pressures created by the Terror and the Committee for Artistic Affairs are evident from Composers' Union journal *Soviet Music*: throughout 1937 and 1938 it regularly carried pieces expounding the implications of Stalin's pronouncements for musical life and praising the dictator in effusive terms. The lead article for the April 1937 issue, for example, comprised a set of statements by Kabalevsky, Khachaturian, Goldenweiser, and other prominent musicians hailing Stalin's speech at the Central Committee plenum on 3 March, in which he reminded Soviet citizens of the ubiquity of 'wreckers, saboteurs, spies, and murderers' masquerading as Bolsheviks and

253 A copy of a submission to Kerzhentsev in which he rebutted the allegations is preserved in RNMM, 3/2957, ll. 1–6.

254 Myaskovsky's diary records attending a union meeting at which matters were resolved in Derzhanovsky's favour: 'Vipiski', 1 February 1938, RGALI, 2040/1/65, l. 400b.

255 Koposova-Derzhanovskaya, 'V. V. Derzhanovskiy po vospominaniyam zhenï i druga', RNMM, 3/3365, ll. 61–4.

256 'Vipiski', 23 September 1936, RGALI, 2040/1/65, l. 360b.

257 See Simon Morrison, *The People's Artist: Prokofiev's Soviet Years* (New York, 2009), 54–66.

called for redoubled efforts to 'liquidate Trotskyites and other double-dealers'.[258] Myaskovsky's name features amongst the signatories of a collective statement on behalf of the union in the June 1937 issue in support of the Supreme Court's decision to sentence Marshal Mikhail Tukhachevsky and other officers in the Red Army High Command to death for their supposed involvement in a Trotskyite underground terrorist organisation.[259] After the condemnation of Bukharin and other leaders in the final show trial of March 1938, *Soviet Music* once again published endorsements of the verdict by leading figures – amongst them, Myaskovsky, Shaporin, Asafiev, and Khachaturian. The text that appeared under Myaskovsky's name was typical of their tone and general tenor: 'The sentence pronounced by the Soviet judiciary on this gang of corrupt villains and murderers, who were tried as members of the 'Rightist-Trotskyite block', was a severe and just one. This trial aroused feelings of horror and revulsion. To what depths of moral degradation these people sank because of their bestial hatred for the free Soviet people and its great leaders, their insatiable rapacity, and base cowardice!'[260] It is not known how these statements came to be compiled: no documentation concerning them has come to light.[261] In consequence, it is impossible to establish whether the musicians involved actually had any part in writing them or consented to their appearance under their names. Boris Pasternak recounted that he came under strong pressure from the Secretary of the Writers' Union around this time to allow his name be attached to a similar published statement: he refused – only to find that his name was added anyway.[262] Myaskovsky may have been placed under similar duress. Even if he and other union members agreed to write statements or sign prepared texts, to speak of consent is scarcely meaningful in circumstances where a refusal might have had serious repercussions not only for these musicians themselves but also for their families and colleagues.

From late 1936 onwards, *Soviet Music* increasingly featured essays stressing the importance of producing compositions on ideological themes, abjuring formalism, and turning to the Russian classics and folk music

---

258 'Velikiy dokument ėpokhi: Sovetskiye muzïkantï dolzhnï ovladet' bol'shevizmom', *Sovetskaya muzïka*, 4 (1937), 5–10. The text of Stalin's speech was published in *Pravda* on 29 March 1937.

259 "Kompozitorï privetstvuyut resheniye Verkhovnogo Suda', *Sovetskaya muzïka*, 6 (1937), 5.

260 'Sovetskiye muzïkantï privetstvuyut prigovor Verkhovnogo Suda', *Sovetskaya muzïka*, 3 (1938), 7.

261 Printers' proofs of the June 1937 and March 1938 issues are preserved in the *Sovetskaya muzïka* archive: RGALI, 654/1/29 and 654/1/56.

262 See Ol'ga Ivinskaya, *Godï s Borisom Pasternakom: V plenu vremeni* (Moscow, 1992), 157–58.

for inspiration.[263] Several articles were devoted to discussing recently composed songs about Lenin and Stalin: one of these even reported on the spontaneous appearance of new folk songs extolling the Great Leader throughout the USSR.[264] Like several other composers, Myaskovsky evidently felt it would be prudent to contribute to the genre. In November 1936, he wrote 'With All My Heart' to words by the Kazakh folk singer Zhambyl Zhabayuly (1846–1945), a prominent literary figure of the period. (Zhabayuly's verse is thought to have been largely concocted by his Russian 'translators': the manufacture of pseudo-folklore became something of an industry throughout the USSR from the late 1930s onwards.[265]) The text was unlikely to inspire music of much distinction:

Я, столетний Джамбул-жирши,	I, the hundred-year-old bard Zhambyl
Восклицаю от всей души:	Exclaim with all my heart:
Для казаха в любой колхоз	It was Stalin who brought this happiness
Это счастье Сталин принёс.	For the Kazakh to each collective farm.
Это имя, как солнца свет,	This name, like the light of the sun,
Сталин – словно горный рассвет,	Stalin – like the mountain dawn,
Сталин – словно степной орёл,	Stalin – like the steppe eagle,
Счастье солнечное привёл.	Brought sunny joy.

Nonetheless, the song was the subject of a special review essay in *Soviet Music*, which enthusiastically welcomed it as further evidence of the composer's 'reform' but criticised its failure to convey the full extent of Stalin's heroic stature.[266] Writing in his diary, Myaskovsky dismissed this essay too as 'rubbish'.[267]

'With All My Heart' was the latest addition to the small number of songs and 'mass songs' to political texts (twelve in total) that he had turned out over the previous seven years. He dignified none of these scores with an opus number – an unambiguous indication that they were composed merely for form's sake. (Yevgeny Golubev records that he and his fellow students privately referred to 'With All My Heart' as 'With All My Might' – a cryptic acknowledgement of the effort it must have cost Myaskovsky

---

263 See, for example, the major position statement 'Na vïsokom pod'yome: Muzïkal'naya kul'tura Stranï Sovetov', *Sovetskaya muzïka*, 4 (1937), 11–20.

264 Amongst them: Georgiy Khubov, 'Pesnya o Staline', *Sovetskaya muzïka*, 12 (1936), 9–10; Viktor Belyayev, 'Shest' pesen o Lenine i Staline', *Sovetskaya muzïka*, 3 (1937), 5–8.

265 See Konstantin Bogdanov *et al.* (ed.), *Dzhambul Dzhabayev: Priklyucheniya kazakhskogo akïna v Sovetskoy strane: Stat'i i materialï* (Moscow, 2013).

266 Viktor Vinogradov, 'O pesnye "Ot vsey dushi" N. Myaskovskogo', *Sovetskaya muzïka*, 1 (1937), 31–4.

267 'Vïpiski', 15 February 1937, RGALI, 2040/1/65, l. 340b.

to overcome his aversion to writing pieces of this kind.[268]) Even during the tense closing years of the decade, however, he maintained his almost undeviating focus on 'pure' instrumental music. His sole concession to circumstances was his acceptance of a commission from the All-Union Radio Committee to compose a work for Stalin's sixtieth birthday celebrations in December 1939. (The resultant *Salutatory Overture*, op. 48 was a decidedly modest contribution to the proceedings and the only score not to set a text: like Prokofiev, whose produced the cantata *Zdravitsa* [*A Toast*], op. 85, Glière, Lyatoshinsky, Shekhter, and Myaskovsky's Georgian student Vano Muradeli all wrote vocal or choral works.[269])

Of Myaskovsky's compositions from this period, the finest is undoubtedly the Seventeenth Symphony in G-sharp minor, op. 41, written between October 1936 and June 1937. A generously proportioned work in four movements which lasts almost fifty minutes in performance, the Seventeenth demonstrates a remarkable creative self-renewal. On a technical level, that renewal is manifest in a significantly new approach to the construction of lengthy musical spans. The intense harmonic surface activity frequently encountered in Myaskovsky's earlier work tends to be replaced by a much slower underlying rate of harmonic movement: the music often unfolds in lengthy paragraphs of polyphonic development articulating large tonal expanses. This technique lends the music an imposing spaciousness far removed from the claustrophobic atmosphere of Myaskovsky's Expressionist works of the 1910s and 1920s. Its drama derives from the incursion of harmonically disruptive contrasting material and the working-through of the resultant tensions to achieve the restoration of stability.

The conflicts of the first movement culminate in a wave of powerful climaxes straining towards a breakthrough that is never achieved: an arresting presentation of the exposition's transition theme in imitation by the brass, sounded against a slow-moving, piercingly scored semitonal ascent in the winds and upper strings (ex. 9.15) collapses without decisive issue, forcing a postponement of a psychological resolution until later in the work. The slow movement is a remarkable inspiration: the serene, radiant mood of its outer sections evokes a realm of experience that seems wholly unimaginable in the circumstances of contemporary Soviet life (ex. 9.16). And yet, the authenticity of that experience and the eloquence with which it communicated cannot be gainsaid: the music movingly suggests a state of spiritual transcendence – the hard-won attainment of an inner refuge allowing the core of self to remain inviolate in the midst of brutality and degradation. Such music poses knotty aesthetic questions, especially when it comes to

268 Golubev, 'Alogizmï', RGALI, 2798/2/23, l. 49.

269 See Izrail' Nest'yev, 'Tret'ya dekada sovetskoy muzïki', *Sovetskaya muzïka*, 12 (1939), 46.

EXAMPLE 9.15. Symphony no. 17, first movement: bars 615–24.

Poco più pesante e sostenuto

EXAMPLE 9.16. Symphony no. 17, second movement: bars 57–70.

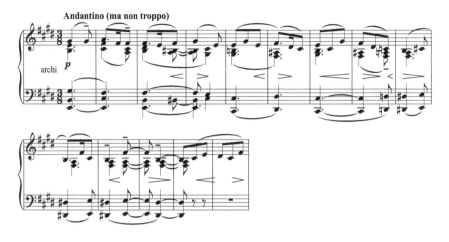

our assumptions about the nature of artworks originating under oppressive political regimes and our interpretations of them as affirming or critiquing prevailing social conditions. As Rilke reminds us in the *Sonnets to Orpheus*, artists have also understood their vocation as being to 'raise a lyre amongst the shadows', creating compensatory images of order and healing during times of destruction, and reminding us that these realms of experience continue to exist, if only as imaginative possibilities. Musical imagery evocative of stillness and serenity recurs in Myaskovsky's later symphonies as states that had continually to be regained.

Disruptive elements reassert themselves in the rugged Scherzo, which acts as an effective foil. The symphony's superb sonata-rondo finale shows Myaskovsky at the height of his creative powers and performs a remarkable compositional feat of integrating the disparate categories of musical material presented so far. Its main theme is a long-breathed suave melody in three-four time, largely consisting of an extended prolongation of the tonic major triad: its scoring is airborne, suggestive of flight (ex. 9.17). The episodes present highly contrasted material – a halting, dissonantly harmonised idea in two-four time that builds to a strenuous climax (ex. 9.18) and a boisterous idea outlining a chain of falling thirds (ex. 9.19), which is subjected to magnificently virtuosic fugal treatment. Over the movement's course, the three ideas are brought into conjunction with one another, acquiring each other's characteristics: the duple-time idea of the B section, for example, is subsequently developed against the flowing triple-time figurations associated with the A section. The development continues during the brilliant closing pages, which communicate an exhilarating sense of uplift.

EXAMPLE 9.17. Symphony no. 17, fourth movement: bars 68–79.

EXAMPLE 9.18. Symphony no. 17, fourth movement: bars 136–43.

EXAMPLE 9.19. Symphony no. 17, fourth movement: bars 270–9.

It would be several years before Myaskovsky composed another work under the same pressure of inspiration. His next two symphonies, while they contain good things, are less distinguished: they suggest a degree of adaption to the prevailing conditions. As Olga Lamm observed, the general atmosphere of anxiety and apprehension for the future meant that composers tended to play safe, writing works in more accessible styles and on ideological themes.[270] (The Pushkin centenary of 1937 proved a godsend, affording a convenient pretext to compose songs.[271]) Although Myaskovsky avoided burdening the symphonies with 'ideological content', he nonetheless took care to write music of a simpler and more lightweight nature. The Eighteenth Symphony in C major, op. 42, composed between June and September 1937, is a compact three-movement work lasting just over twenty minutes: it is interesting that Myaskovsky did not feel inclined to write something more substantial for the celebrations marking the twentieth anniversary of the October Revolution. He informed Asafiev that he had taken inspiration from Glinka's plans to write a 'Russian symphony'[272] – presumably the unfinished *Taras Bulba* Symphony, commenced in 1852, which Glinka abandoned because of his dissatisfaction with 'German' techniques of musical development.[273] The only conspicuously 'Russian' feature of the work, however, is the employment of themes reminiscent of folk songs – notably in the elegiac slow movement, which is framed by two determinedly cheerful movements in quick tempi.

The Nineteenth Symphony in F major, op. 46, for wind orchestra, came into being as a result of Myaskovsky's encounter with Ivan Petrov (1906–75), a recent Moscow Conservatoire graduate who went on to become one of the country's leading conductors of military bands.[274] After hearing the Eighteenth, Petrov was so taken with the score that he transcribed it for winds and invited Myaskovsky to hear the arrangement performed by a Red Army ensemble. To his dismay, Myaskovsky initially refused to attend, but he subsequently relented.[275] Impressed by Petrov's musicianship and the quality of the rendition, he decided to write a symphony specially for his

270 'Pavel Aleksandrovich Lamm: Opït biografii', RNMM, 192/361, l. 420.

271 See Philip Ross Bullock, 'The Pushkin Anniversary of 1937 and Russian Art-Song in the Soviet Union', *Slavonica*, 1 (2007), 39–56.

272 Myaskovsky to Asafiev, 24 September 1937, RGALI, 2658/2/51, l. 61.

273 See Marina Frolova-Walker, 'Against Germanic Reasoning: The Search for a Russian Style of Musical Argumentation', in Michael Murphy and Harry White (ed.), *Musical Constructions of Nationalism: Essays on the History and Ideology of European Musical Culture, 1800–1945* (Cork, 2001), 104–5.

274 On Petrov, see Valeriy Petrov (ed.), *Ivan Vasil'yevich Petrov: Stat'i, materialï, vospominaniya* (Moscow, 1983).

275 Ivan Petrov, 'Nastavnik i drug', in Shlifshteyn (ed.), *N. Ya. Myaskovskiy: Sobraniye materialov*, vol. 1, 334–5.

band – perhaps realising that fulfilling an assignment of this nature might help to avert adverse comment about his lack of political engagement. (In view of Myaskovsky's habitual reluctance to make public statements about his work, it seems noteworthy that he agreed to write an article explaining the genesis of the Nineteenth for the newspaper *Soviet Musician*.[276]) Given his own military background, he would almost certainly have been sympathetic to Petrov's efforts to improve the standards of the army ensembles. The Nineteenth, which is in four movements and lasts about twenty-five minutes, is very much in the nature of *Gebrauchsmusik*, though it is effectively written for the medium. Their collaboration led to a rapid deepening of the two men's friendship. Myaskovsky became very fond of Petrov: he even allowed the younger man to bring him to the cinema and the theatre and took to referring to him as 'my enlightener'.[277]

The two symphonies were interspersed with a number of smaller-scale opuses – the sets of easy piano miniatures comprising op. 43; and the *Three Sketches*, op. 45, settings of the Soviet poets Stepan Shchipachyov and Lev Kvitko composed at the request of the notable bass Alexander Okayomov. (Myaskovsky thought the texts 'dreadful'.[278]) Like the *Twelve Lermontov Songs*, op. 40, composed in 1935–6 between the Sixteenth and Seventeenth Symphonies, the *Three Sketches* are of a studied melodiousness and simplicity. The other major projects of this period were the Violin Concerto in D minor, op. 44, composed between March and July 1938, and the Fifth String Quartet, op. 47 (1939). It is not clear what prompted Myaskovsky to write his first concertante work: his diary and letters shed no light on the subject. When it was completed, he showed the score to David Oistrakh, a young violinist who had won first prize in the Queen Elizabeth Competition in Brussels the previous year – one of several notable successes by Soviet performers in international competitions around this time. Oistrakh agreed to give the premiere, which took place on 10 January 1939, with Gauk conducting. Although Myaskovsky's writing for the solo instrument is expert, employing the full panoply of brilliant virtuosic effects, it cannot be said that he solves the fundamental challenge inherent in writing a concerto – devising a satisfying distribution of roles between soloist and orchestra in presenting and developing the musical material. The first two movements are diffuse and overlong, and Oistrakh was justly critical of the very sectional finale.[279] The Fifth String Quartet, which he dedicated to Shebalin,

276 Nikolay Myaskovskiy, 'O svoyey novoy simfonii', *Sovetskiy muzïkant*, 22 February 1939.

277 'Vïpiski', 13 and 19 February 1939, RGALI, 2040/1/65, l. 490b.

278 Myaskovsky to Kabalevsky, 24 June 1938, RGALI, 2017/1/91, l. 4.

279 David Oistrakh, 'Skripichnïy kontsert N. Ya. Myaskovskogo (zametki ispolnitelya)', *Sovetskaya muzïka*, 12 (1938), 23.

FIGURE 9.5. With Ivan Petrov (late 1930s).

is a more distinguished score, exemplifying the classicism of Myaskovsky's later style at its most restrained and elegant.

It is hardly surprising that the quality of Myaskovsky's output between 1937 and 1939 was uneven. A communication to Asafiev in December 1937 affords a rare glimpse of his state of mind. By then, the two men's contact had attenuated. Asafiev's occasional letters exuded a mood of deep dejection: he complained of feeling very isolated, and was increasingly embittered by the lack of interest in his work and his colleagues' unwillingness to take him seriously as a composer – Prokofiev in particular.[280] The cooling of their friendship undoubtedly saddened Myaskovsky and he was sympathetic to Asafiev's plight. 'I have never felt such loneliness as I do now', he told Asafiev, 'and I do not know why, for I have loads of acquaintances and many "friends" – but not people as close to me in essence as you. Prokofiev remains an object of my admiration, devotion even, and he is also very well-disposed towards me, but he is a person of a completely different cast. To be genuinely intimate with him is completely impossible, especially as he merely tolerates my music'. Myaskovsky emphasised that this did not colour his attitude to Prokofiev, but it nonetheless created a barrier.[281]

280 Asafiev to Myaskovsky, 6 May and 8 December 1937, RGALI, 2040/1/98, l. 240b, 26.

281 Myaskovsky to Asafiev, 10 December 1937, RGALI, 2658/2/51, l. 65.

Ironically, a similar barrier now existed between Myaskovsky and Asafiev: as his diary attests, he did his utmost to give Asafiev's work its due but could not muster much enthusiasm for it either. Myaskovsky felt the loss of Asafiev's companionship very keenly: he evidently felt close to few other people.

By the end of the 1938, the Great Purge had abated: although the state's use of repressive measures persisted, Stalin seems finally to have recognised that continued recourse to mass murder and imprisonment on such an enormous scale would destabilise the country and jeopardise national security.[282] The disruption it had caused would be felt for a long time to come. Olga Lamm recalled that the atmosphere remained sombre: the outbreak of war on the continent subsequent to the invasion of Poland by Nazi Germany on 1 September 1939 darkened he general mood, as did the Winter War prompted by the Soviet invasion of Finland three months later.[283] The reorganisation of artistic life by the Committee for Artistic Affairs had continued throughout the Terror, but the Party leadership sacked Kerzhentsev as chairman in early 1938, deeming his discharge of his duties unsatisfactory.[284] He was replaced in May 1938 by Mikhail Khrapchenko, a young literary critic who was previously acting director of the Moscow Institute of Red Professors.[285] One of Khrapchenko's tasks in his first months of office was to propose candidates to sit on the Organisational Committee of a national composers' union, which would oversee the activities of local union branches throughout the USSR.[286] Preparations for the creation of this overarching body had commenced in March 1938.[287] When elections took place on 8 April, Myaskovsky found that he had been nominated: he duly attended the committee's first meeting on 10 April.[288] Glière was appointed chairman in recognition of his seniority, and Khachaturian as vice-chairman. The other twenty-one members included Shostakovich, Asafiev, and Kabalevsky, as well as notable musical figures from the other Soviet republics.

282　See Stephen Kotkin, *Stalin: Waiting for Hitler, 1929–1941* (London, 2018), 490–1.

283　Lamm, 'Pavel Aleksandrovich Lamm: opït biografii', RNMM, 192/361, ll. 429–30.

284　Maksimenkov, *Sumbur vmesto muzïki*, 282.

285　On Khrapchenko and his chairmanship of the Committee for Artistic Affairs, see Vladimir Perkhin, *Deyateli russkogo iskusstva i M. B. Khrapchenko, predsedatel' Vsesoyuznogo komiteta po delam iskusstv: Aprel' 1939–yanvar' 1948: Svod pisem* (Moscow, 2007), 7–124.

286　See Maksimenkov, *Muzïka vmesto sumbura*, 191–5.

287　Tomoff, *Creative Union*, 24–5.

288　'Vïpiski', 8 and 10 April 1938, RGALI, 2040/1/65, l. 42.

In the event, the Organisational Committee did not begin its work in earnest until May of the following year, when the national union was formally established by a Politburo decree.[289] It had two pressing tasks. The first was to organise an all-Union congress to bring the operations of the regional branches under firmer centralised control, but for a number of reasons, including the outbreak of the Second World War, another nine years would pass before the congress eventually took place. The second task, the establishment of a structure to administer the disbursement of government funds to the union's branches, was more swiftly realised. The USSR Music Fund (or 'Muzfond', as it came to be known) was established by September 1939[290]: its day-to-day running was largely overseen by Levon Atovmyan, who had recently been released and allowed to return to Moscow.[291] In addition to paying commissioning fees, Muzgiz provided material and practical support for the union's members, many of whom earned comparatively little. Amongst other things, it afforded access to medical treatment and to a network of special resorts where composers and musicologists could spend time completing major projects.[292]

Over the next two years, the union rapidly expanded its activities across the USSR. In the virtual absence of any documentary records for this period, it is difficult to tell how time-consuming Myaskovsky's duties as a committee member might have been. His diary entries from the second half of 1939 became increasingly intermittent, but it is evident that he was kept very busy. In addition to his other duties (he continued to teach at the conservatoire and work as a consultant for Muzgiz), he was appointed to the Artistic Council of the Committee for Artistic Affairs in April 1939, which in turn led to further professional responsibilities.[293] As part of the initiatives to mark Stalin's sixtieth birthday in December 1939, a government commission was established to oversee the annual award of state prizes for outstanding achievements in the arts.[294] In June 1940 Myaskovsky was invited to serve on the Stalin Prize Committee, which was chaired by the eminent theatre director Vladimir Nemirovich-Danchenko.[295] His membership of this

289 'Postanovleniye Politbyuro TsK VKP(b) ob organizatsii Soyuza sovetskikh kompozitorov SSSR. 3 maya 1939', in Maksimenkov (ed.), *Muzïka vmesto sumbura*, 200.

290 Muzfond's charter and other pertinent documentation is preserved in RGALI, 2077/1/21.

291 Atovm'yan, 'Vospominaniya', 254–5.

292 See Tomoff, *Creative Union*, 217–34.

293 'Vïpiski', 4 April 1939, RGALI, 2040/1/65, l. 490b.

294 For an account of this initiative, see Marina Frolova-Walker, *Stalin's Music Prize: Soviet Culture and Politics* (New Haven, 2016), 11–36.

295 Nemirovich-Danchenko to Myaskovsky, 29 June 1940, RGALI, 2040/2/237, ll. 1–30b.

elite body once again testifies to his standing in the Soviet artistic community, but it represented a very onerous commitment. As a jury member, he not only had to report on new musical compositions of note but also to take part in deliberations on recent work in other artistic domains: as a result, he spent a considerable amount of time attending theatre productions and showings of films, visiting art galleries, and reading recently published literature. In the first year, the assessors' task was made additionally burdensome by a last-minute government directive that they should not merely consider work produced in 1940, but everything that had appeared since 1935.[296] (Khrapchenko was probably discomfited to discover that the assessors had struggled to find anything worthy of nomination of a prize in some categories.[297])

Myaskovsky found his service on the prize committee a disillusioning experience – not on account of his fellow committee members, who were generally conscientious and approached their task in an idealistic spirit, but because the government shamelessly overrode the committee's decisions.[298] When the prizes were announced in March 1941, he was dismayed to discover that the committee's finalised list had been substantially altered: it particularly distressed him that Prokofiev was denied a prize for his cantata *Alexander Nevsky*.[299] And while he himself had received a Stalin Prize First Class for his recently completed Twenty-First Symphony, he could derive little satisfaction from the award because of the unpleasantness that the symphony's nomination had caused. Composed in June 1940, a few weeks after the completion of the Twentieth, the Twenty-First Symphony had been commissioned by Frederick Stock, who finally had an opportunity to meet Myaskovsky when he visited the USSR in the summer of 1939.[300] Myaskovsky did not publicise this circumstance, however, and no allusion was made to it in the programme note written for the symphony's Moscow premiere under Gauk on 16 November 1940.[301] The symphony was very warmly received on that occasion, so its nomination for a prize was not unexpected. The circumstances are not entirely clear, but it would seem that, unbeknownst to Myaskovsky, Shaporin notified other committee members that the symphony had been commissioned by a foreign orchestra, perhaps

296 Myaskovsky to Steinberg, 30 December 1940, RIII, 28/1/487, l. 121.

297 Frolova-Walker, *Stalin's Music Prize*, 44–6.

298 Frolova-Walker, *Stalin's Music Prize*, 57–62.

299 'Vïpiski', 15 May 1941, ll. 530b–4; Lamm, 'Pavel Aleksandrovich Lamm: Opït biografii', RNMM, 192/361, ll. 430–1, 433.

300 'Vïpiski', 2 July 1939, l. 500b. Henry Voegeli, the manager of Chicago Symphony Orchestra, wrote to Myaskovsky to confirm the commission on 2 August 1939: RGALI, 2040/2/283, l. 7.

301 Concert programme booklet, RGALI, 2040/2/359, l. 340.

FIGURE 9.6. With fellow Stalin Prize Committee members. From left to right: Yury Shaporin, Myaskovsky, Isaak Dunayevsky, Reinhold Glière.

hoping that this would jeopardise its candidacy. On being challenged, he denied responsibility and sought to deflect the blame onto Khachaturian and Prokofiev. Believing Khachaturian to be culpable, Myaskovsky broke off relations with his former student and attempted to withdraw his symphony from the list of nominated works. Khachaturian was deeply hurt and offended, but Atovmyan managed to effect a reconciliation: the misunderstanding was cleared up and Myaskovsky apologised to Khachaturian at a Composers' Union meeting on 25 January 1941. Nonetheless, he found the episode both disturbing and distasteful.[302]

Despite the award of a Stalin Prize, the Twenty-First Symphony in F-sharp minor, op. 51, is hardly an orthodox exemplar of Socialist Realism – any more than Shostakovich's Piano Quintet, another prize-winning work that year. A comparison with its predecessor, the three-movement Twentieth Symphony in E major, op. 50 is revealing. The Twentieth displays all of Myaskovsky's usual competence but strikes one as rather routine; the Twenty-First shows him at the height of his powers, both technically and imaginatively. Like the Tenth and Thirteenth, the Twenty-First is in one movement, lasting about fifteen minutes, but there the similarities

302 Lamm, 'Pavel Aleksandrovich Lamm: Opït biografii', RNMM, 192/361, l. 435; Atovm'yan, 'Vospominaniya', 256–7; Frolova-Walker, *Stalin's Music Prize*, 140–1.

EXAMPLE 9.20. Symphony no. 21, opening.

end: it explores a very different psychological world to these Expressionist scores. The introduction strikes a distinctly new tone in Myaskovsky's work, its soaring string polyphony conveying a powerful sense of grief and loss (ex. 9.20). This elegiac meditation prefaces a sonata-form structure based on two sharply contrasted ideas – an energetic theme first presented in A minor, and a lyrical second subject. Much of the development section comprises an energetic fugato based on a transformation of the first theme: its climax presages an even more powerful culminating presentation of the second subject in the recapitulation, which leads seamlessly into a curtailed restatement of the introductory material. The elegiac mood returns: in the deeply moving closing bars, fragments of the opening polyphony in the upper strings fade slowly into silence against a F-sharp minor triad sustained in the lower strings. Myaskovsky's Moscow colleagues were not alone in considering the Twenty-First a superb achievement: it elicited an equally enthusiastic response from Stock[303], who performed it several times after its American premiere by the Chicago Symphony Orchestra on 26 December 1940.

As Myaskovsky approached his sixtieth birthday in April 1941, the strains of the last few years were increasingly beginning to tell. In the summer of 1939, his doctors had detected the first signs of a serious heart condition and insisted that he avoid strenuous physical exercise.[304] References to suffering protracted bouts of depression and ill health recur in his diary and correspondence. Writing to Asafiev in January 1940 after a combined bout of influenza and myocarditis (inflammation of the heart muscle), he complained of feeling 'in a terrible mood': 'Nothing gives me cheer and the last remnant of my creative powers has vanished'.[305] This mood of 'melancholic gloom'[306] finds memorable expression in the slow movement of the Sixth String Quartet, op. 49, completed later that month: subtitled 'Malinconia', its oppressive central section, which is virtually atonal, recalls the bleakest of his early Hippius settings. (The movement is a striking demonstration that the densely dissonant chromaticism characteristic of some of Myaskovsky's earlier work remained available as an expressive resource when occasion required, even if he employed it less frequently.) It did not help that he was overworked. Taking stock of his professional commitments at the start of the new academic year in September 1940, he noted that Sunday was his only free day in the week. In addition to his teaching at the conservatoire and his work for the Composers' Union and the Artistic Council of the Committee for Artistic Affairs, he had also agreed to serve on an expert commission and on the editorial board of *Soviet Music*.[307] His Stalin Prize Committee duties at the end of the year added to already heavy burden. One wonders why he felt it necessary to take on quite so much: perhaps he sought distraction from his darker moods by ensuring that he was kept constantly busy. The physical demands eventually became too great: in April 1941, he had to be admitted to a sanatorium for six weeks. Rather to his relief, his indisposition meant that he did not have to attend the festivities to mark his sixtieth birthday. In his absence, these were conducted on a modest scale. The Violin Concerto and the Fifth and Twenty-First Symphonies were performed at a symphony concert; Okayomov premiered a new set

303 Stock to Myaskovsky, 14 October 1940 and 13 January 1941, RGALI, 2040/2/283, ll. 2, 3.

304 'Vïpiski', 12 July 1939, RGALI, 2040/1/65, l. 500b.

305 Myaskovsky to Asafiev, 8 January 1940, RGALI, 2658/2/51, l. 740b.

306 'Vïpiski', 12 January 1940, RGALI, 2040/1/65, l. 510b.

307 'Vïpiski', 11 September 1940, RGALI, 2040/1/65, l. 53.

of songs, the *Ten Shchipachyov Lyrics*, op. 52, that Myaskovsky had written for him earlier in the year.[308] The April 1941 issue of *Soviet Music* carried an encomium by Shebalin as well as essays by Ikonnikov and the musicologist Daniel Zhitomirsky that discussed his life and work in predictably sententious fashion, extolling his supposed artistic reform. Pavel Lamm had hoped to arrange a special tribute of a more unorthodox kind – a concert of his friend's Hippius settings by singers from the Soviet Opera Ensemble, for which he worked as a *répétiteur* and coach. To Lamm's dismay, Kabalevsky stopped the concert from going ahead, claiming that it would harm Myaskovsky professionally.[309] Kabalevsky's anxieties were by no means unfounded, but his intervention was also self-serving and indicative of his puritanical attitude to his teacher's 'decadent' past.

Shortly after being discharged in mid-May, Myaskovsky went to Nikolina Gora to recuperate. He could clearly have benefitted from an extended stay in the countryside, but it was not to be: only a few weeks later, the country was plunged into renewed turmoil.

308 'Vïpiski', 15 May 1941, RGALI, 2040/1/65, l. 54.

309 Lamm, 'Pavel Aleksandrovich Lamm: opït biografii', RNMM, 192/361, ll. 432–4.

10

Endurance: 1941–5

Shortly after midday on 22 June 1941, the Soviet Commissar for Foreign Affairs Vyacheslav Molotov took to the airwaves to inform a stunned population that an attempted invasion of the country was imminent. Like many of her fellow citizens, Olga Lamm heard the announcement at work, broadcast from loudspeakers in the street.[1] Without making a formal declaration of war, Germany had violated its non-aggression pact with the USSR and initiated a large-scale military offensive, code-named Operation Barbarossa, along the Soviet Union's entire western frontier. Three million soldiers stormed over the border as air raids were conducted on Kiev, Sevastopol, Kaunas, and other cities. Stalin initially reacted with disbelief and for several days apparently failed to grasp the magnitude of the unfolding catastrophe as the Wehrmacht penetrated deeper into Belorussia and Ukraine. Vissarion Shebalin had been examining at the conservatoire in Minsk when the city was bombed on 24 June: he was lucky to make it home safely after a long and hazardous journey, some of it undertaken on foot.[2] Soviet efforts to repulse the attack were at first disorganised and ineffectual. By the end of the month, German forces were advancing on Smolensk, placing Moscow itself under threat. The mood in the capital turned to panic: the government was compelled to issue a directive on 29 June threatening swift reprisals against 'fearmongering and cowardice'.[3]

Aerial bombardment of Moscow commenced on 22 July. Myaskovsky and Pavel Lamm were forced to cut short their holiday in Nikolina Gora, as it lay in the Luftwaffe's flight path. A few days later, a bomb landed not far from the apartment building in which Myaskovsky lived. As in other western Soviet cities, plans were hastily drawn up to evacuate staff members of major scientific and cultural institutions – part of a broader initiative to safeguard specialists whose services were considered vital to the war effort. The Committee for Artistic Affairs assumed responsibility for arrangements pertaining to the arts sector.[4] On 27 July, Myaskovsky learned that

1   Lamm, 'Pavel Aleksandrovich Lamm: Opït biografii', RNMM, 192/361, l. 436.

2   Vissarion Shebalin, 'Vospominaniya', in Valeriya Razheva (ed.), *V. Ya. Shebalin: Zhizn' i tvorchestvo* (Moscow, 2003), 73–6.

3   'O mobilizatsii vsekh sil i sredstv na razgrom fashistkikh zakhvatchikov', Klavdiy Bogolyubov and Nikolay Savinkin (ed.), *KPSS o vooruzhennïkh silakh Sovetskogo Soyuza: dokumentï, 1917–1981* (Moscow, 1981), 297–9.

4   For an informative general study, see Rebecca Manley, *To the Tashkent Station: Evacuation and Survival in the Soviet Union at War* (Ithaca, 2009). On the evacuation of the artistic intelligentsia, see Yevgeniya Vorozheykina, *Rossiyskaya khudozhestvennaya intelligentsiya v èvakuatsii v godï Velikoy*

he was to be dispatched to Sverdlovsk (Yekaterinburg), over a thousand miles east of Moscow, with a group from the Bolshoi Theatre. Not wishing to leave Valentina behind on her own, he persuaded her to resign from her civil service post so that she could accompany him.[5] They made hurried preparations – only to be notified that their departure had been postponed. Eager to have some respite from the continuous air raids, they accepted the Derzhanovskys' offer to stay with them at their dacha in Abramtsevo, forty-five miles to the north. Ten days later, they were called back to Moscow and on the evening of 8 August boarded a train bound for Nalchik, the capital of the Kabardino-Balkar Autonomous Soviet Socialist Republic, close to Russia's modern border with Georgia.[6] Their contingent comprised over two hundred people – other conservatoire professors and their families, artists and writers, and personnel attached to the Moscow Arts Theatre and the Maly Theatre. Headed by the eminent director Vladimir Nemirovich-Danchenko, it was an élite group comprising some of the most distinguished figures in national artistic life. Myaskovsky had been reluctant to leave, finding it difficult to credit that the capital was genuinely in danger, but was given little choice.[7] (A refusal could have had serious consequences: the pianist Heinrich Neuhaus declined evacuation to Nalchik only to be arrested on suspicions that he was 'waiting for the Germans'.[8]) The only consolation was that he was not cast entirely amongst strangers. His travelling companions included the Lamm, Aleksandrov, and Feinberg families – and also Prokofiev and his new partner Mira Mendelssohn. Prokofiev and Mendelssohn had first encountered one another three years previously: their relationship grew increasingly intimate and he eventually left his wife for her in the spring of 1941.[9] None of his colleagues had yet met Mendelssohn, who at twenty-six was considerably younger than him and clearly felt somewhat overawed by the assembled company. Valentina and Myaskovsky immediately sought to put her at her ease. Her

---

otechestvennoy voynï (Kostroma, 2004); and of Composers' Union personnel in particular: Tomoff, *Creative Union*, 65–73.

5   'Vïpiski', 27 July 1941, RGALI, 2040/1/65, l. 54.

6   The destination was stipulated in an Evacuation Council directive of 3 August, 'O napravlenii stareyshikh masterov iskusstv iz g. Moskvï v g. Nal'chik': see Konstantin Bukov and Anatoliy Ponomaryov (ed.), *Moskva voyennaya 1941–1945* (Moscow, 1995), 362.

7   Koposova-Derzhanovskaya, 'V. V. Derzhanovskiy po vospominaniyam zhenï i druga', RNMM, 3/3365, l. 65.

8   See Militsa Neugauz, *Istoriya aresta Genrikha Gustavovicha Neygauza* (Moscow, 2000), 5; Maria Razumovskaya, *Heinrich Neuhaus: A Life beyond Music* (Rochester, 2018), 70–5.

9   See Morrison, *The People's Artist*, 159.

simple, unaffected manner made a generally favourable impression: in time, Myaskovsky and his sister would grow very fond of her.[10]

As Nemirovich-Danchenko's assistant Igor Nezhny recalled in his memoirs, a subdued and anxious atmosphere prevailed: the camouflage netting covering the carriages was an ominous reminder of the perils that might await en route. A few hours after pulling out of Kazan station, the train halted unexpectedly. The sounds of distant explosions became audible – German aircraft were attempting to bomb a nearby railway junction. Fortunately, they were able to proceed after the all-clear was given.[11] The twelve-hundred-mile journey took over three days. When the party arrived on 10 August, it turned out that the local hotels could not accommodate all the evacuees. With a population of roughly fifty thousand, Nalchik was only the size of a large town. The Myaskovskys and the Lamms were put up in a rest home in the nearby village of Dolinsk: the two men were allocated a room in one building and the three women a room in another located across the street.[12]

In a letter to Shebalin, who had stayed behind to serve in the militia, Myaskovsky remarked that he was finding it difficult to settle in, although the climate was pleasant and the setting attractive. (The complex was ringed with orchards that provided fruit in abundance – an unaccustomed luxury for most Muscovites.) He was unused to being surrounded by so many people and initially unable to work because he had no piano.[13] The cost of living was high, despite Nalchik's provincial location: some of his colleagues were unable to afford the meals in the rest home's canteen. Nezhny claimed that all the evacuees continued to receive their institutional salaries[14], but the correspondence of Myaskovsky and his colleagues reveals that, in the case of the musicians at least, these fell far short of the funds required to support themselves and their dependents. Myaskovsky needed to earn money as a matter of urgency – and for the foreseeable future, he would be essentially reliant on income from composition. His predicament was no means unique. Given the scale and complexity of the evacuation operations (the total number of Soviet citizens displaced was probably in excess of sixteen million[15]), and the haste with which they had to be conducted, it

---

10 Ol'ga Lamm, 'Druz'ya Pavla Aleksandrovicha Lamma. V ėvakuatsii' (hereafter: 'V ėvakuatsii'), in Tamara Livanova (ed.), *Iz proshlogo sovetskoy muzïkal'noy kul'turï*, vol. 2 (Moscow, 1976), 99.

11 Igor' Nezhnïy, *Bïloye pered glazami. Teatral'nïye vospominaniya* (Moscow, 1963), 319–21.

12 Lamm, 'V ėvakuatsii', 100.

13 Myaskovsky to Shebalin, 23 August 1941, RGALI, 2012/1/173, l. 2.

14 Nezhnïy, *Bïloye pered glazami*, 322.

15 Manley, *To the Tashkent Station*, 50.

is not surprising that the plans were often sketchy in detail and haphazardly executed. Even in the case of a select group such as Myaskovsky's, little thought was often given to what would happen to evacuees on reaching their destination. It was not uncommon to find that important practicalities had been left unclarified – the extent of the host city's responsibilities towards them, where they would live, how they would support themselves, and whether they would be entitled to receive ration cards. Resolving these questions could involve protracted negotiations and time-consuming bureaucratic formalities. Much depended on the efficiency and good will of local officials, and the resources at their disposal.

Myaskovsky and his colleagues were initially fortunate. The director of the republic's Committee for Artistic Affairs, Khatu Temirkanov, was an energetic young man in his early thirties and keenly interested in his role.[16] Excited by the arrival of a group of eminent musicians, he promptly sought a meeting with the group's leader, Alexander Goldenweiser, and proposed commissioning a number of scores based on regional folk music.[17] Several composers readily acquiesced: Prokofiev undertook to write a string quartet, Feinberg a rhapsody, and Myaskovsky an orchestral work.[18] Levon Atovmyan had already arranged for Muzfond to commission Myaskovsky to write a symphony, so he now had two projects to fulfil. At the start of September, he managed to procure a piano (though in wretched condition, it was better than nothing) and could finally get down to composing. Pavel Lamm considerately left him on his own until lunchtime every day, allowing him to establish a working routine, to which he adhered strictly.[19] The next two months were remarkably productive considering his unsettled state of mind. The Twenty-Second Symphony in B minor, op. 54, was sketched between 10 and 24 September and the Seventh String Quartet in F major, op. 55, between 26 September and 8 October. By then, rumours had begun to circulate that the group would soon be transferred elsewhere because of

16 The committee's files have not been preserved in the Kabardino-Balkar Republic's archives. The present author's investigations turned up only a single record of Myaskovsky and his colleagues' sojourn in Nalchik – a collectively composed letter thanking local officials for their hospitality, dated 16 November 1941: TsDNI AS KBR, 45/1/1, l. 50. On Temirkanov, see Natal'ya Bal'zhatova, 'Pogib v rastsvete sil', *Kabardino-Balkarskaya Pravda*, 20 August 2019.

17 Goldenweiser's diary entry for 20 August 1941, in Skryabin *et al.* (ed.), *Nash starik*, 289.

18 Lamm, 'V ėvakuatsii', 101, 103. Myaskovsky received a commissioning fee of fifteen thousand roubles: RGALI, 2040/2/344, l. 13. See also Yevgeniy Khakuashev, *Kabardino-Balkarskaya ASSR v godï Velikoy otechestvennoy voynï (1941–1945)* (Nalchik, 1978), 63–4.

19 Myaskovsky to Shebalin, 18 September 1941, 2012/1/173, l. 3; 'Vïpiski', 24 September 1941, RGALI, 2040/1/65, ll. 54–540b.

the continuing Axis advance into Russian territory[20], which increased the pressure on him considerably. The Twenty-Third Symphony in A minor 'on themes from Kabardino-Balkar songs', op. 56, was drafted between 15 and 31 October; he also managed to complete the orchestration of the Twenty-Second before they were evacuated onwards to Tbilisi during the night of 23 November. By this point, Leningrad was under siege, Soviet forces were struggling to repel a massive attack on Moscow, and the Wehrmacht, having overrun Ukraine, was engaged in a pitched battle for Rostov-on-Don – a port city of major strategic importance affording access to the oil- and mineral-rich Caucasian region.

Although Tbilisi was only two hundred miles from Nalchik, the train journey took a circuitous eight-hundred-mile route south-eastward to Baku and then inland to the Georgian capital, a detour necessitated by the mountainous border territory between the two republics. Records of the local branch of the Committee for Artistic Affairs reveal the scale of the challenges confronting the Georgian authorities in dealing with the successive influxes of evacuees, as Myaskovsky's contingent was only one of fourteen such groups to arrive in the city from Moscow, Leningrad, Kharkov, Odessa, and elsewhere. The registers on which he and his sister are listed, which were repeatedly emended and augmented, contain information about some 350 displaced persons.[21] This time, the party was split up on arrival and mostly billeted in private homes around the city: the Myaskovskys were given a room in the apartment of a local engineer. The accommodation was of good quality and the family was pleasant, but he found the lack of privacy difficult to bear.[22] The winter was cold and there was little incentive to venture outside; Valentina left him alone as much as possible so that he could work, but had nowhere to go except the frigid apartment kitchen. She promptly fell ill, much to his dismay. Olga Lamm noticed that his spirits had plummeted: nonetheless, he dutifully put in the hours at his desk every day orchestrating the Twenty-Third Symphony and preparing piano transcriptions of the music composed in Nalchik for dispatch to Moscow.[23] Although the threat to the capital had receded by the New Year (Hitler, like Napoleon, failed to make due allowance for the severity of the Russian winter), the plight of Yevgeniya and her son Nikita, trapped in blockaded Leningrad, weighed heavily on his mind.

20   Pavel Lamm to Dmitry Melkikh, 8 October 1941, RNMM, 145/226.

21   'Spiski ėvakuirovannïkh v Gruzinskuyu SSSR rabotnikov iskusstv vo vremya otechestvennoy voinï', NAG, 2/2/579. The last register is dated 1 May 1942 (ll. 33–55).

22   'Vïpiski', 17 December 1941, RGALI, 2040/1/65, l. 540b.

23   Olga Lamm to Dmitry Melkikh, 26 December 1941, RNMM, 145/208.

In common with his colleagues, he was also worried by the rapidly spiralling prices of food and everyday necessities due to runaway inflation – a recurring theme of his letters during his time in Tbilisi. Black marketing and profiteering were rampant; across the country prices for potatoes, cabbage, and other staples rose to over ten times their pre-war value.[24] By the early summer of 1942, vendors in Tbilisi markets were charging 280 roubles for a litre of cooking oil[25] – and Myaskovsky's institutional stipend came to only 1500 roubles a month.[26] 'Absolutely everything of any value has disappeared from the market', he told Derzhanovsky. 'It's impossible to get butter or eggs or even milk or yoghurt, or potatoes (you have to queue half a day for those). Meat can only be got rarely and with difficulty. . . . Without "pull" in local nationalist circles, you can't even buy stuff for ready money'.[27] His rent alone cost six hundred roubles a month and heating fuel was prohibitively expensive, as he explained to Ivan Petrov, adding that the group would have been in dire straits without Temirkanov's commissions.[28] Several of his colleagues began to experience severe financial hardship shortly after arriving in Tbilisi. Unlike Temirkanov, the Georgian representatives of the Committee for Artistic Affairs made no attempt to assist the evacuees financially. As Tbilisi was a sizeable city with a reasonably well-developed musical infrastructure, the performers amongst the group could supplement their income by giving concerts, but opportunities of other kinds were scarce. At the start of February 1942, Anatoly Aleksandrov told a former student that he 'would be in a terrible fix' if he did not manage to earn some money soon, because 'Muzfond hasn't sent us a kopek'.[29] Writing to Dmitry Melkikh, who had remained in Moscow, Olga Lamm informed their friend that her stepfather's position was equally precarious, since copying scores of new works by Prokofiev, Myaskovsky, and others constituted his sole source of income, and his earnings scarcely covered their rent. In Nalchik Olga had been able to supplement the family finances by working as a librarian, but her lack of proficiency in Georgian hindered her efforts to secure new employment. Worst off of all, however, was Samuil Feinberg, whom she thought had aged terribly and was clearly going hungry. The strain was beginning to tell on everyone: Myaskovsky looked exhausted,

---

24 See Vitaliy Pushkaryov, '"Chyornïy rïnok" v SSSR v godï Velikoy otechestvennoy voynï i yego vliyaniye na sostoyaniye vnutrennego rïnka stranï', *Ėkonomicheskiy zhurnal*, 12 (2006), 212–26.

25 Myaskovsky to Dmitry Melkikh, 29 May 1942, RNMM, 145/243.

26 'RK profsoyuza Rabis. Spisok masterov iskusstv, pribïvshikh v g. Tbilisi, soglasno ukazaniyu SNK Soyuza SSR', NAG, 141/1/1543, l. 4.

27 Myaskovsky to Derzhanovsky, 27 April 1942, RNMM, 3/992–3

28 Myaskovsky to Ivan Petrov, 20 February 1942, RGALI, 2040/1/77, l. 13.

29 Aleksandrov to Vladimir Bunin, 1 February 1942, RGALI, 2748/1/171, l. 5–50b.

she added, and was complaining of insomnia and chest pains – an ominous sign of a deterioration in his heart condition.[30] The experiences that Lamm described were by no means unusual. Maximilian Steinberg gave similarly dispiriting accounts of conditions in Tashkent, where he had been evacuated with a contingent from the Leningrad Conservatoire just before the commencement of the blockade. He and four members of his family were living in a single room and cooking in an improvised kitchen in a hallway. Like Myaskovsky, he found it difficult to compose, as he could spend little time on his own.[31]

Myaskovsky did his best to assist colleagues in need and petitioned Atovmyan to issue contracts to Lamm, Goldenweiser, and others who were particularly hard-up.[32] Although Tbilisi was not without its compensations (its historic centre was attractive and, unlike Nalchik, it had an active cultural life), it was a struggle to maintain morale. The dispersal of the group's members in lodgings around the city meant that they saw much less of each other. They continued to meet for occasional musical evenings and games of *vint*, but the general shortage of funds made them reluctant to impose on one another's hospitality.[33] The only person unaffected by the general mood of despondency was Prokofiev, who seemed quite transformed by Mira's companionship. 'You wouldn't recognise Prokofiev', Olga Lamm wrote to Melkikh: 'He radiates happiness, is full of energy, and is remarkably unaffected and courteous to everyone'. Unlike Myaskovsky, who composed nothing for three months after completing the orchestration of the Twenty-Third Symphony in early December 1941, Prokofiev was also continuously productive, making swift progress with his new operatic project based on Tolstoy's *War and Peace*. (When Prokofiev played scenes for him as they were completed, Myaskovsky's reactions were ambivalent: he found that the continuous arioso palled and thought some of the music rather routine.[34])

The highlight of Myaskovsky's stay in Tbilisi was the performance of the Twenty-Second Symphony on 12 January 1942 by an ad hoc orchestra under the direction of the young conductor Abram Stasevich. Rather to his surprise, as he told Shebalin, it was warmly received – despite the 'mind-bogglingly' out-of-tune playing and the fact that his music was virtually

30 Olga Lamm to Dmitry Melkikh, 19 February 1942, RNMM, 145/211.

31 Steinberg to Myaskovsky, 27 January 1942, RGALI, 2040/2/282, l. 87.

32 Myaskovsky to Atovmyan, 2 February 1942, RNMM, 71/737.

33 Lamm, 'V ėvakuatsii', 104; eadem, 'Pavel Aleksandrovich Lamm: Opït biografii', RNMM, 192/361, ll. 438–9.

34 'Vïpiski', 17 December 1941 and 14 April 1942, RGALI, 2040/1/65, ll. 540b and 550b.

unknown in Georgia.[35] Whatever its inadequacies, the performance evidently managed to communicate something of the symphony's import. One of Myaskovsky's most engaging scores, the Twenty-Second is cast in three movements that play without a break –a lilting six-eight *Allegro non troppo*, prefaced by a slow introduction; a ternary-form *Andante con duolo*; and a concluding *Allegro energico*. Myaskovsky's discussion of the symphony in his correspondence confirms that his attitude to the vexed question of artworks' 'ideological content' had not changed. Under the circumstances, it was inevitable that artists would be expected to treat subject matter pertaining to 'The Great War for the Fatherland' (*Velikaya otechestvennaya voyna*), as the conflict quickly came to be called – and not merely popular songs and military music, but ambitious large-scale works. Myaskovsky initially subtitled the symphony 'Symphony-Ballade about the Great War for the Fatherland', which hinted at an underlying narrative – but much to the vexation of Aleksey Ikonnikov, he did not supply a programme. 'What connection does the music have with the war for the fatherland?', Ikonnikov enquired testily after the symphony's Moscow premiere under Golovanov on 19 April. 'If a composition speaks [*sic*] about the war, that means the listener is entitled to demand explanations from the author about what he wants to say about the war, and what aspects of this event are reflected in the composition, or perhaps prompted him to write it'. Ikonnikov also expressed dissatisfaction with the work's finale, which he found insufficiently 'powerful' and 'triumphant', and explained how the composer should have gone about matters differently.[36] To Ikonnikov's dismay, Myaskovsky responded that the work's connection with the war was too obvious to require detailed verbal elucidation, adding that he preferred to withdraw the subtitle rather than 'utter platitudes'.[37] In a draft programme note preserved amongst his personal papers, he took pains to emphasise that while the symphony's 'emotional content' was shaped by the war, he had not sought to evoke any 'concrete images'.[38]

Myaskovsky's refusal to concoct a spurious programme is noteworthy. In part, his decision was undoubtedly born of caution: a detailed exposition of the symphony's putative 'subject matter' would only provide critics with opportunities to find fault with his musical treatment of it. However, his reaction to Ikonnikov's letter and the symphony itself also demonstrate his continuing disinclination to produce the crassly propagandistic art

35   'Vïpiski', 13 January 1942, RGALI, 2040/1/65, l. 55; Myaskovsky to Shebalin, 22 January 1942, RGALI, 2012/1/173, l. 40b.

36   Ikonnikov to Myaskovsky, undated letter [late April 1942], RGALI, 2040/2/153, 14–150b.

37   Myaskovsky to Ikonnikov, 12 May 1942, in *Khudozhnik nashikh dney*, 269.

38   RGALI, 2040/4/9, l. 14.

demanded by Socialist Realism. One can readily understand why his experiences of combat in the previous World War might have deepened his distaste for stereotypical portrayals of the current one. If the Twenty-Second was genuinely conceived as an artistic response to contemporary events, that response took a highly mediated form: the symphony's most noteworthy features are its lyricism and avoidance of bombast. Powerful though some of the music is, especially in the deeply felt slow movement, it does not strive after monumentality. Imagery that might have prompted associations with the prevailing hostilities is entirely absent – with the possible exception, perhaps, of the distant fanfares heard during the brief transition from the slow movement to the finale, which subsequently form one of the latter's ancillary thematic ideas. It is noteworthy, however, that every time this material recurs and starts to develop, it is quickly interrupted by a playful repeated-note figure: the mood is mock-heroic rather than heroic, and the symphony's exultant closing pages are serene rather than triumphant.

Ikonnikov was not the only person to be disconcerted by symphony's failure to conform to expectations and its eschewal of brash musical rhetoric reminiscent of Tchaikovsky's *1812 Overture*. Derzhanovsky wrote to warn his friend that Viktor Bely and others had 'not lost any opportunity to get up to their dirty tricks' after the Moscow performance, and had impugned the work for not portraying the war.[39] 'For some reason they all think that one has to respond to a war of this kind with cannons and drums', Myaskovsky wrote exasperatedly to Ivan Petrov,

> whereas I see it as a colossal and tragic event for our society – and that, of course, acts on me more potently than the opportunity to represent individual acts of bravery and so on. I wrote the symphony as someone who feels the profound tragedy of what is taking place and believes that our nation will ultimately prove to have right on its side. This is the theme of my symphony – not battles![40]

He evidently had little difficulty ignoring Ikonnikov's attempts to guide his compositional practice, as he would also ignore the musicologist's attempts soon afterwards to cajole him into writing a ballet based on *War and Peace* because he thought it would do Myaskovsky good to write something other than symphonies.[41]

Although the Twenty-Third Symphony has been regarded as exemplifying the growing academic conservatism of Soviet music during the Stalinist period – because its use of folk music and its 'exotic' atmosphere are ostentatiously indebted to nineteenth-century Russian models – it is important

39   Derzhanovsky to Myaskovsky, 7 May 1942, RNMM, 71/479, l. 1.
40   Myaskovsky to Petrov, 12 June 1942, RGALI, 2040/1/77, l. 17.
41   Ikonnikov to Myaskovsky, 21 July 1942, RGALI, 2040/2/153, ll. 16–190b.

to bear in mind the very specific nature of Temirkanov's commission. The work is unique in Myaskovsky's output in being based entirely on borrowed material. His treatment of the Kabardino-Balkar folk melodies is very restrained: for the most part, he leaves them intact, and achieves variety by presenting them in different harmonisations and textural guises, after the manner of Glinka's *Kamarinskaya*. In doing this, he was almost certainly following stipulated guidelines. When Steinberg was asked to fulfil a similar commission for a symphony based on Uzbek folk music in October 1942, the local Committee for Artistic Affairs expressly requested that he leave the folk tunes unaltered to make the work maximally accessible to 'the broad mass of Uzbek listeners'[42]. (He was also instructed that the symphony should take the form of 'a letter from the happy Uzbek nation to the great leader of nations Joseph Vissarionovich Stalin' recounting the history of Uzbekistan 'from ancient times to the present day'[43]: as he remarked drily to Myaskovsky, he feared that this 'enticing task' might exceed his 'feeble powers'.[44]) Myaskovsky seems to have approached the assignment with genuine interest, although he found having to use themes that were not his own somewhat inhibiting and thought he could have been bolder in approach.[45] He was initially unsure whether to describe the work as a symphony or a suite, but eventually decided on the former designation, having concluded that the treatment of the ideas was genuinely symphonic in spite of the constraints.[46] While it is undoubtedly an external score, the Twenty-Third's craftsmanship cannot be faulted: the folk melodies are handled with sensitivity and tact, and their harmonisations and orchestral presentations are frequently ingenious. The last of the three movements, which is dominated by a vigorous 12/8 *lezginka* dance melody, rises to an exhilarating culmination and demonstrates a brilliant command of orchestral sonority. Temirkanov was delighted with the symphony when he heard it performed in a piano reduction in February 1942 during a visit to Tbilisi.[47] He pressed the musicians to return to Nalchik during the summer, but they never saw

---

42   See Maksimilian Shteynberg, 'Moya kompozitorskaya rabota nad uzbekskim fol'klorom', in Semyon Ginzburg (ed.), *Puti razvitiya uzbekskoy muziki* (Leningrad, 1946), 105.

43   The work's programme is detailed in Aleksandr Dolzhanskiy, 'Simfoniya-rapsodiya No. 5 Maksimiliana Shteynberga', in Ginzburg (ed.), *Puti razvitiya uzbekskoy muziki*, 126–8.

44   Steinberg to Myaskovsky, 14 October 1942, RGALI, 2040/2/282, ll. 56–56ob.

45   Myaskovsky to Shebalin, 22 January 1942, RGALI, 2012/1/173, l. 40b;
Myaskovsky to Steinberg, 29 July 1942, RIII, 28/1/487, l. 124ob.

46   'Vïpiski', 31 October 1941, RGALI, 2040/1/65, l. 540b; Myaskovsky to Melkikh, 25 June 1942, RNMM, 145/244.

47   Olga Lamm to Dmitry Melkikh, 19 February 1942, RNMM, 145/211;
Goldenweiser's diary entry for 10 February 1942, in Skryabin *et al.* (ed.), *Nash starik*, 339.

him again: Temirkanov was shot by the Gestapo on 29 November 1942 shortly after Nalchik's capture by Axis forces.

Myaskovsky would remain in Georgia until the end of August 1942. His letters indicate that he often felt physically unwell and in low spirits. Atovmyan invited him to propose new projects for which Muzfond could issue commissions, but he complained to Derzhanovsky of feeling disinclined to compose.[48] For the time being, he concentrated on smaller-scale tasks. In March, he completed two short piano works, the Sonatina, op. 57 and the *Song and Rhapsody*, op. 58[49]; the following month, he sketched another string quartet, the Eighth in F-sharp minor, op. 59, which he dedicated to the memory of the composer Zinovy Feldman, who died of a heart attack at the age of forty-nine on 9 April, a few days after returning to Moscow from evacuation.[50] Feldman was only one of many friends and acquaintances who would not survive the war. Around the same time, Steinberg wrote to tell him that Julia Weissberg had been committed to a psychiatric hospital in Leningrad after her son perished from starvation: she too died soon afterwards.[51] Heartrending stories such as these heightened his relief when Yevgeniya and Nikita eventually made it safely to Tbilisi, several weeks after being evacuated from Leningrad on 21 March over the so-called 'Road of Life' across frozen Lake Ladoga. Nikita arrived first on 19 April. His mother fell ill with dysentery in Baku and had to be hospitalised: she followed him a week later. Myaskovsky was shocked both by her appearance and her accounts of life in the besieged city, which were 'enough to disturb the equilibrium of even the soundest in mind', as he observed to Steinberg.[52]

The addition of his sister and nephew to his list of dependents placed considerable additional pressure on his finances, as he was also contributing to the upkeep of Vera and her family in Novosibirsk.[53] This circumstance explains his acceptance in early May of an uncongenial commission from the Committee for Artistic Affairs, which requested that he write a work for wind orchestra.[54] The *Dramatic Overture*, op. 60, seems to have

48   Atovmyan to Myaskovsky, 4 February 1942, RGALI, 2040/2/97, l. 1;
     Myaskovsky to Derzhanovsky, 22 March 1942, RNMM, 3/992.

49   'Vïpiski', 21 and 30 March 1942, RGALI, 2040/1/65, l. 55.

50   Atovmyan to Myaskovsky, 9 April 1942, RGALI, 2040/2/97, l. 20b.

51   Steinberg to Myaskovsky, 19 April 1942, RGALI, 2040/2/282, l. 89ob; Zivar
     Guseynova, 'M. O. Shteynberg: Pervïy god v Tashkente', *Opera musicologica*, 1
     (2011), 34–5.

52   'Vïpiski', 19 and 26 April 1942, RGALI, 2040/1/65, ll. 55ob, 56; Olga Lamm to
     Dmitry Melkikh, 21 April 1942, RNMM, 145/216; Myaskovsky to Steinberg, 2
     May 1942, RIII, 28/1/487, l. 125.

53   Atovmyan to Myaskovsky, 4 February 1942, RGALI, 2040/2/97, l. 1.

54   'Vïpiski', 2 May 1942, RGALI, 2040/1/65, l. 56.

been intended for Ivan Petrov, who repeatedly urged him to write a new piece for military band. As Myaskovsky admitted to Petrov, the overture cost him considerable effort[55]: though only ten minutes long, its composition occupied him from May until early July. The results were workmanlike, but the absence of inspiration is very apparent – as in most of the music that he composed in Tbilisi. 'My head is completely empty', he told Dmitry Melkikh. It is surprising that he managed to produce as much as he did. He continued to experience chest pains and severe discomfort from rheumatism[56], and summoning the mental energy for creative work became more difficult as the weather turned warmer: his diary entries repeatedly allude to the 'unbearable heat'.[57]

Myaskovsky led a fairly reclusive existence during his sojourn in Georgia. Despite being an avid walker all his life, he found the city's hilly terrain tiring[58] due to his increasingly poor health. He spent much of his spare time reading – amongst other things, Proust's *À la recherche du temps perdu*, which he came across by chance in a local bookshop.[59] His socialising was mostly limited to his Moscow colleagues, though he also enjoyed playing cards with the notable Soviet actress Varvara Massalitinova, with whom he and the Lamms had struck up a friendship. (The pair seem to have taken a great liking to one another, despite their very disparate personalities: the flamboyant Massalitinova was one of the few people capable of diverting Myaskovsky when he was in a downcast mood.) After Prokofiev left for Alma-Ata in late May to work on a film project and Massalitinova departed a few weeks later, their cheerful presences were sorely missed.[60] Apart from a few 'pointless' sessions at the Tbilisi Conservatoire with students of Andria Balanchivadze (the brother of the choreographer George Balanchine), he had little contact with local composers: they 'kept their distance', as he reported to Steinberg, adding that what he managed to hear of their work 'hadn't been particularly riveting'.[61]

Being in Tbilisi afforded an unexpected pleasure, however – a reunion with Konstantin Saradzhev, who made the 170-mile journey from Yerevan in mid-February specially to see him and Pavel Lamm. Although Saradzhev's customary high spirits and sense of humour were undimmed, Olga Lamm was struck by how tired he looked and much he had aged: now

55 Myaskovsky to Petrov, 12 June 1942, RGALI, 2040/1/77, ll. 17–170b.

56 Myaskovsky to Dmitry Melkikh, 29 May 1942, RNMM, 145/243.

57 'Vïpiski', 16 and 22 June and 1 July 1942, RGALI, 2040/1/65, ll. 560b, 57.

58 Myaskovsky to Gube, 20 May 1942, RGALI, 2012/2/208, l. 30b.

59 'Vïpiski', 16 April and 23 June 1942, RGALI, 2040/1/65, l. 550b, 57.

60 Lamm, 'V ėvakuatsii', 101–2, 105.

61 'Vïpiski', 21 March 1942, RGALI, 2040/1/65, l. 55; Myaskovsky to Steinberg, 2 May 1942, RIII, 28/1/487, l. 1250b.

FIGURE 10.1. A relaxed moment (1940s).

in his mid-sixties, he was still working twelve to fourteen hours a day to support his extended family.[62] He was delighted to have a chance to spend time with his friends and displayed a touching eagerness to hear the new works by Myaskovsky, Prokofiev, and the other visiting composers. After returning a second time in June, Saradzhev arranged for several students at the Yerevan Conservatoire to have consultations with Myaskovsky (amongst them Alexander Arutiunian) and even tried to persuade his old acquaintance to spend a year in the Armenian capital.[63] Myaskovsky was reluctant to part from his group, so the plan came to nothing. Nonetheless, he willingly took the opportunity to visit Yerevan in mid-July when he was invited to a specially arranged concert featuring Shostakovich's *Leningrad* Symphony – a score that had already become an iconic symbol of Soviet resistance to Nazism, though it had only been premiered a few months previously.

Surprisingly, given his dislike of travelling, his four-day stay proved a very pleasant experience: in between attending the orchestral rehearsals, he

---

62 Olga Lamm to Dmitry Melkikh, 19 February 1942, RNMM, 145/211; Ol'ga Lamm, 'K. S. Saradzhev i P. A. Lamm', in Tigranov (ed.), *Saradzhev*, 127–8.

63 Saradzhev to Myaskovsky, 3 August 1942, RGALI, 2040/2/240, ll. 13–130b.

fitted in trips to local museums and art galleries as well as an excursion to the beautiful environs of Lake Sevan. He was curious to hear how Shostakovich's symphony would work in concert, having had a chance to play through the score the previous February when Mikhail Khrapchenko and the musicologist Semyon Shlifshteyn made a flying visit to Tbilisi for a meeting with members of the Stalin Prize Committee and brought a copy with them.[64] Khrapchenko had evidently decided that the symphony would be nominated for a prize even though it had yet to be performed.[65] Myaskovsky informed Steinberg that the meeting had been a rather frustrating experience, as the committee members had been unable to obtain scores of several other works potentially worthy of nomination and Khrapchenko was clearly not interested in hearing any of his suggestions. Nonetheless, he thought the merits of the *Leningrad* Symphony beyond dispute, telling Steinberg that he had been 'amazed by the growth of Shostakovich's dramatic sense'.[66] With characteristic generosity, he promptly wrote to his younger colleague to congratulate him on his achievement. (Shostakovich sent a very cordial reply, expressing regret that Myaskovsky could not be present at the premiere and promising to visit him in Moscow at the earliest opportunity.[67]) It is also noteworthy that Myaskovsky asked Khrapchenko to remove his own Twenty-Second and Twenty-Third Symphonies from the list of works mooted for prizes.[68] When he eventually heard the *Leningrad* Symphony in Yerevan, however, his reactions were more ambivalent. Summarising his impressions for Steinberg, he reported finding the symphony rather dull and not up to the hyperbolic praise that had been lavished on it – though he acknowledged that the orchestral playing had been substandard.[69] The discussions of the symphony in the correspondence of Myaskovsky and his colleagues once again cast interesting light on their sceptical attitudes to Socialist Realism and the tendency to prize ideological content over artistic quality. On the whole, their evaluations tended to be negative, faulting Shostakovich's score for its agitprop blatancy and uneven quality of invention.[70] Writing to Myaskovsky, Dmitry Melkikh summed up a general

---

64   Myaskovsky to Alexander Kreyn, 7 April 1942, RGALI, 2435/2/163, ll. 3–30b. Ten of the committee's members assembled in Tbilisi; the other eleven had been evacuated to Kuibyshev (Samara).

65   See Frolova-Walker, *Stalin's Music Prize*, 91.

66   Myaskovsky to Steinberg, 11 March 1942, RIII, 28/1/487, l. 1240b.

67   Shostakovich to Myaskovsky, 27 February 1942, RGALI, 2040/2/279, ll. 2–20b. Myaskovsky's letter is lost.

68   Myaskovsky to Koposova-Derzhanovskaya, 27 February 1942, RNMM, 3/3292, l. 10b.

69   Myaskovsky to Steinberg, 29 July 1942, RIII, 28/1/487, ll. 127–1270b.

70   See Aleksandr Komarov, 'N. Ya. Myaskovskiy v godï Velikoy otechestvennoy voynï', in Vlasova and Sorokina (ed.), *Naslediye*, 377–80.

view that objective public discussion of the symphony's artistic merits was impossible for the time being, at least, because 'the scribblers have laid on the politics [i.e., explications of the symphony's 'content'] with a trowel'. He professed admiration for Shostakovich's craftsmanship but went on to pay a decidedly backhanded compliment: 'One marvels at what can be done with such shitty material as the German theme [i.e., the so-called 'invasion theme'] in the first movement'.[71] Pavel Lamm considered the increasingly insistent repetitions of the same theme mere empty noise, adding: 'They told me . . . it supposedly represents the Germans, but I hear a symphony, damn it – in other words, pure music; and I'm not obliged to take into account any programme, especially one that hasn't been indicated by the composer'.[72]

Myaskovsky would only remain in Tbilisi for another six weeks on returning from Yerevan. Over the summer, the Red Army suffered serious reverses. The important Black Sea port of Sevastopol was captured on 4 July after weeks of heavy bombardment; and having taken Rostov-on-Don on 23 July, Axis forces pushed relentlessly eastwards towards Stalingrad (Volgograd) and southwards towards the Caucasus Mountains. Although they ultimately did not manage to invade Georgia, that outcome was by no means a foregone conclusion. On 24 August, Myaskovsky and the other evacuated musicians met a visiting government official from the Committee for Artistic Affairs, Vladimir Surin, to learn where they would be sent next. They came away from the meeting none the wiser: confusion reigned, as he noted in his diary. Surin subsequently suggested transferring them to Tashkent, but others proposed alternative locations. Discussions dragged on for several days: Frunze (since 1991, Bishkek), the capital of the Kyrgyz Soviet Socialist Republic, emerged as the most popular choice – rather to Myaskovsky's puzzlement. On 31 August, almost thirteen months after leaving Moscow, he and his colleagues set off on the third lap of their travels, the longest and most arduous yet.[73] The fifty-strong party included the Aleksandrov, Lamm, Feinberg, Shaporin, and Goldenweiser families, as well as Myaskovsky, his sisters Valentina and Yevgeniya, and his nephew Nikita. They were also joined by Valentina's daughter Marianna, who had been in Stavropol with her husband but travelled to Tbilisi a fortnight previously to be with her mother as she was now several months pregnant.[74]

Although several members of the group subsequently published accounts of their wartime experiences, the exigencies of Soviet censorship led them to gloss over the details of their 2,500-mile journey to Central Asia. The

71 Melkikh to Myaskovsky, 4 April 1942, RGALI, 2040/2/188, ll. 6–60b.
72 Lamm to Myaskovsky, 19 May 1943, RGALI, 2040/2/172, ll.39–390b.
73 'Vïpiski', 24, 26 and 31 August 1942, RGALI, 2040/1/65, l. 580b.
74 'Vïpiski', 14 July and 16 August 1942, RGALI, 2040/1/65, ll. 570b, 58.

conditions of wartime rail travel necessitated lengthy detours: its first leg, which took three days, brought them southwards to Julfa in Azerbaijan via Yerevan, then along the border with Iran before heading northeast to Baku, from where they had to catch a ferry across the Caspian Sea to Krasnovodsk (now Türkmenbaşy in Turkmenistan). A bad storm delayed their departure for two days: no accommodation was available, so they had to wait on the jetty with their luggage.[75] Nightmarish scenes greeted them on arrival in Krasnovodsk, a busy port and important railway terminus. The city was thronged with contingents of half-starved convicts and refugees from Stalingrad, many of them children: they picked their way to the train station through the sick, the wounded, and the dying, assailed by desperate pleas for help from all sides.[76] Another three-day delay ensued before they could leave for Frunze: they camped on a slope by the train tracks in the baking heat, 'without shade, without water, without sanitation', as Myaskovsky recorded laconically in his diary.[77] The strain of travelling under such conditions can well be imagined, especially for a group of people who were mostly in their sixties. Their departure from Krasnovodsk was a disorganised shambles: unruly crowds of passengers mobbed the carriages, unceremoniously pushing past one another to board and to find seats. A further lengthy delay supervened as the train pulled into a siding to wait for an oncoming train to pass on the single-track line. The theatre director Savely Malyavin, who was also of the party, recalled that they seemed to progress across the vast expanses of desert at the sluggish tempo of a camel caravan.[78] Meals en route consisted of whatever they could manage to purchase from station vendors. On 18 September, they reached Tashkent, where some members of the party had asked to be settled instead, amongst them Goldenweiser and his family. Myaskovsky hoped to see Steinberg during their half-day layover but missed him due to a miscommunication, to both men's great disappointment.[79] Three days later, they at last pulled into Frunze.

The exhausted travellers' trials were by no means at an end. Many years later, Myaskovsky's former student Vladimir Fere, who had been based in Frunze since 1936, recalled that the news of their impending arrival had been greeted with consternation by local officials. The comparatively small city was already full to overflowing with evacuees: in addition to having to house the workforces of several factories transferred from western and southern Russia and the staff of various military and educational institutions, they had

---

75   'Vïpiski', 31 August 1942, RGALI, 2040/1/65, l. 580ob.

76   Lamm, 'Pavel Aleksandrovich Lamm: Opït biografii', RNMM, 192/361, l. 440.

77   'Vïpiski', 10 September 1942, RGALI, 2040/1/65, l. 580ob.

78   Saveliy Malyavin, 'Pamyati Nikolaya Yakovlevicha', in Shlifshteyn (ed.), *N. Ya. Myaskovskiy: Sobraniye materialov v dvukh tomakh*, vol. 1, 260.

79   Steinberg to Myaskovsky, 22 September 1942, RGALI, 2040/2/282, ll. 94–94ob.

also been required to accommodate the USSR State Symphony Orchestra and State Choir and a number of other musical ensembles. By this point, all the available accommodation was full to capacity. At a hastily convened meeting with Fere and other music personnel, the Kyrgyz Party Secretary Aleksey Vagov proposed sending the group on to Przhevalsk (now Karakol), a city located 250 miles further east near the border with China. Fortunately Fere and his colleagues were able to dissuade him from this plan: Przhevalsk was not connected to the railway network and in the virtual absence of any alternative means of transport (all the local cars had been requisitioned for use at the front), the group would have been stranded there, more or less cut off altogether from the outside world.[80]

The Party functionaries did not conceal their resentment at having to deal with a further influx of evacuees: the group met with a decidedly frosty welcome and was given to understand that the local authorities had not been expecting them. Rooms were eventually found for Shaporin and Myaskovsky when it emerged that they were recipients of Stalin Prizes, but turned out to be completely unfurnished. Fere ended up bringing Myaskovsky back to his already overcrowded apartment, and two days later, Shaporin and he were moved to a hotel.[81] The other members of the party were left on the train carriage and had to fend for themselves as best they could. As Myaskovsky informed Atovmyan, their position was 'catastrophic' – on top of everything else, all of them, himself included, were desperately short of money, and food prices proved as exorbitant as in Tbilisi. He urgently needed to make progress with his latest commission from the Committee for Artistic Affairs, a cantata to a text by the contemporary poet Nikolay Tikhonov, but his present circumstances made composing impossible.[82]

A week after their arrival, Myaskovsky was called to a meeting with Vagov: a message had eventually come from Moscow requesting that the rest of the group be provided with accommodation.[83] His sisters and his niece and nephew were given a room in the premises housing members of the USSR State Symphony Orchestra and State Choir. The building was unfurnished and unheated, without an electricity supply, running water, or bathroom facilities.[84] The latter amenities, as he informed Petrov, were a rarity in

80 Fere, 'Nash uchitel'', 434–5. Over 62,000 evacuees had to be accommodated in the Frunze region alone: on 12 September 1941, the maximum permitted allowance of living space throughout the Kyrgyz SSR was reduced from 8.25 to 5 square metres per person. See Suyun Kerimbayev, *Sovetskiy Kirgizstan v Velikoy otechestvennoy voyne, 1941–1945* (Frunze, 1985), 61–3.

81 'Vipiski', 21 and 23 September 1942, RGALI, 2040/1/65, l. 59.

82 Myaskovsky to Atovmyan, 24 September 1942, RNMM, 71/440.

83 'Vipiski', 29 September 1942, RGALI, 2040/1/65, l. 59.

84 Myaskovsky to Steinberg, 30 September 1942, RIII, 28/1/487, l. 130.

Frunze; the city was depressingly dirty and insanitary.[85] Three further unfurnished rooms were found in a half-built newsreel cinema, which had to be shared by the Lamms, Feinbergs, Aleksandrovs, and others – twenty people in total. The conditions there were even worse. The room allocated to the Aleksandrovs had no windows and was so small that Aleksandrov had to lie across it diagonally to sleep at night. Olga Lamm shared a room with her mother and uncle and five others: the limited floor space could only accommodate them all if everyone slept on their sides.[86] Meals were cooked outside in the street, where the air was thick with dust thrown up by passing camels and carts, over an improvised stove constructed from bricks and a metal girder. Maintaining even a semblance of hygiene was impossible. In these slum conditions, it was not long before they fell ill with colitis and graver ailments. Two members of the group came down with typhus. Sofia Lamm developed thrombophlebitis and a mysterious condition that caused her to become mentally disoriented: her life was only saved thanks to a chance encounter with a Moscow pathologist, a neighbour from Nikolina Gora, who arranged for her to be hospitalised.[87]

Myaskovsky's own living conditions, though better, were by no means luxurious: his tiny hotel room was dark and uncomfortably cold.[88] He too was far from well: he continued to experience chest pains and suspected that Frunze's high altitude at twenty-six hundred feet above sea level was exacerbating his heart condition.[89] Deeply concerned by the plight of his family, he made enquiries about renting a house for them – though this proved infeasible because of the acute shortage of accommodation and his lack of funds.[90] As he was their sole breadwinner, he had little choice but to focus all his energies on composing. He was unable to hire a piano, but at the end of September a pianist who worked for the local radio station agreed to allow him use her instrument for a few hours a day several times a week. Fere also invited him to work in his apartment.[91] These arrangements were less than ideal, as he found it difficult to compose when others were within earshot, but he had to manage as best he could.

The idea of writing a cantata had been suggested to him by Shlifshteyn, who wanted to commission a choral work to mark the twenty-fifth anniversary of the 1917 Revolution. Documentation preserved in the archives of the

85   Myaskovsky to Petrov, 22 October 1942, RGALI, 2040/1/77, l. 23.

86   Lamm, 'V ėvakuatsii', 105–6.

87   'Pavel Aleksandrovich Lamm: Opït biografii', RNMM, 192/361, l. 442.

88   Malyavin, 'Pamyati Nikolaya Yakovlevicha', 261.

89   Myaskovsky to Steinberg, 25 October 1942, RIII, 28/1/487, l. 121; Myaskovsky to Petrov, 1 November 1942, RGALI, 2040/1/77, l. 240b.

90   'Pavel Aleksandrovich Lamm: Opït biografii', RNMM, 192/361, l. 442.

91   Myaskovsky to Petrov, 1 November 1942, RGALI, 2040/1/77, ll. 24–240b.

Committee for Artistic Affairs indicates that the country's leading composers were regarded as failing in their duty to support the war effort, as they
were writing too few accessible works on ideological themes. At a meeting
of the Committee's Music Section in Tomsk in January 1942, Myaskovsky
was criticised for not writing more patriotic songs – especially as he had
been the recipient of a Stalin Prize.[92] It seems likely that these strictures
were relayed to him. When Shlifshteyn visited Tbilisi with Khrapchenko the
following month, Myaskovsky had tentatively proposed setting Tikhonov's
recently published poem *Kirov Is with Us*, which portrays the assassinated
Leningrad Party leader patrolling the streets of his native city as its *genius
loci*, overseeing efforts to resist the German blockade. Shlifshteyn seized
on the suggestion with alacrity, and forwarded a contract for the work
on 1 July.[93] Myaskovsky evidently regretted assenting to the idea when he
examined the poem more closely: he confided in Steinberg that he thought
Tikhonov's verses 'clumsy' and 'most unmusical', and ended up cutting
them fairly drastically.[94] Although he managed to draft several numbers
before leaving Tbilisi, his diary entries suggest a distinct lack of enthusiasm for the task; nonetheless, he dutifully resumed work on it at the first
opportunity. He completed the vocal score by the end of October and the
orchestration the following month. The cantata, which lasts about thirty
minutes in performance, is notable for its predominantly meditative mood
and abstention from grandiose gestures. It demonstrates Myaskovsky's customary professionalism but is not particularly memorable. Considering the
circumstances under which it was written, however, it is remarkable that he
managed to produce anything at all.

A spate of bad news about friends and colleagues intensified the prevailing atmosphere of gloom. On 19 October, he received word of Vladimir
Derzhanovsky's demise the previous month. As he subsequently discovered,
the last months of his friend's life had been exceedingly difficult. He and his
wife remained at Abramtsevo throughout the war but suffered great hardship on account of the shortages of food and fuel. Myaskovsky had tried to
assist them financially by asking Atovmyan to arrange for Derzhanovsky to

92 New musical repertoire was discussed at two meetings of the Committee's
    partorganizatsiya on 23 and 28 January 1942: TsDNI TO, 475/1/12, ll. 9–19
    (Myaskovsky is referred to on l. 160b). Similar complaints evidently reached
    the ears of the musicologist Mikhail Druskin, who told Sollertinsky that
    he feared Myaskovsky, Shostakovich, and others would end up in a 'very
    tricky position' because of their failure to write patriotic scores: Druskin to
    Sollertinsky, 1 August 1943, in Lyudmila Kovnatskaya *et al.* (ed.), *Pamyati
    Mikhaila Semyonovicha Druskina. Kniga II: Iz perepiski* (St Petersburg, 2009),
    54–5.
93 Shlifshteyn to Myaskovsky, 1 July 1942, RGALI, 2040/2/278, l. 2.
94 Myaskovsky to Steinberg, 25 October 1942, RIII, 28/1/487, l. 131.

proofread the scores of the Twenty-Second and Twenty-Third Symphonies[95], but the task proved beyond him because of his failing eyesight. He spent the last months of his life in a very depressed state of mind and in increasingly frail health: he began to complain of numbness in his legs and became unable to make the tiring journey to Moscow for provisions. He refused to seek medical attention and by the time the Composers' Union responded to his wife's requests to move him to Moscow, it was too late. Shebalin, who had tried to keep in touch with the couple, arrived to find him close to death from heart disease and malnutrition. Derzhanovskaya remained alone with his dead body at their dacha for four days while Shebalin sought assistance in Moscow. He returned with Mosolov and Cheryomukhin: the trio transported the corpse, precariously balanced in a cart, for several miles along potholed country roads to the nearest cemetery. They had to dig the grave themselves, assisted by a few local villagers whom they paid with vodka supplied by the Composers' Union.[96] Myaskovsky was grief-stricken and sent Derzhanovskaya a touching note. In one of his last letters to Myaskovsky, which he never got around to posting, Derzhanovsky exhorted his friend to compose a major work to celebrate the Red Army's inevitable defeat of Nazism, invoking Asafiev's essay 'Composers, Hurry Up!' as he reminded him of creative artists' obligation to put their art in the service of ideology. Despite all the humiliations that he had suffered, he had not lost faith that a great 'renewal of society' awaited under communism. Tellingly, however, he closed his letter with an acknowledgement that Myaskovsky was impervious to influence and would always do as he wished – like the obstinate 'Cat That Walked by Himself' from Kipling's *Just So Stories*.[97]

Myaskovsky's diary entry for 19 October also recorded the news that Dmitry Melkikh had suffered a stroke – apparently caused by the shock of Derzhanovsky's death. Four days later, he received a letter from Melkikh, who had been left paralysed down his left side: he had no illusions about the seriousness of his condition and expected to die soon.[98]

As October drew to a close, Myaskovsky felt increasingly unwell and faced the dismal prospect of remaining in Frunze for the winter. Atovmyan proposed trying to arrange for him to be recalled to Moscow[99], but he hesitated, knowing that conditions were also very difficult there and that he would most likely return to an unheated apartment because of the

95 Myaskovsky to Atovmyan, 27 February 1942, RNMM, 71/738, l. 1.

96 Koposova-Derzhanovskaya, 'V. V. Derzhanovskiy po vospominaniyam zhenï i druga', RNMM, 3/3365, l. 65–7; Shebalin, 'Vospominaniya', 77.

97 Koposova-Derzhanovskaya, 'Pamyati druga', 224–6.

98 'Vïpiski', 19 and 23 October 1942, RGALI, 2040/1/65, l. 590b; Melkikh to Myaskovsky, 8 October 1942, RGALI, 2040/2/188, 16–160b.

99 'Vïpiski', 19 October 1942, RGALI, 2040/1/65, l. 590b.

prevailing fuel shortages. He was also reluctant to leave behind his sister Yevgeniya, who as an inhabitant of Leningrad did not have a residence permit to live in Moscow. (Soviet citizens were prohibited by law from residing in a city other than the one in which they were registered.)[100] The circumstances of his conservatoire colleagues and their families remained dire. On 28 October, they dispatched a frantic collective telegram to Atovmyan in an attempt to obtain permission for them to return as a group: 'POSITION OF OVERWHELMING MAJORITY OF GROUP EXTEMELY SERIOUS NO ROOMS LAMMS SISTER SHURIK SHAPORIN GRAVELY ILL SENT TO HOSPITAL CREATIVE AND PROFESSIONAL WORK IMPOSSIBLE BECAUSE OF LACK OF PIANOS STAYING HERE ANY LONGER DANGEROUS DEMAND URGENT RECALL TO MOSCOW MYASKOVSKY ALEKSANDROV NECHAYEV SHAPORIN LAMM FEINBERG'.[101]

However sympathetic Atovmyan may have been to their plea, he was not in a position to grant it: due to wartime restrictions, travel permits were allocated to government agencies according to a strict quota system and the number available at any one time was limited. In the end, Myaskovsky decided that it would be best if he accepted Atovmyan's offer to procure passes for himself, Valentina, and the heavily pregnant Marianna, as Khrapchenko had pledged his assistance: he hoped to be in a better position to hasten the return of the others once he was on the spot in Moscow.[102] Documents confirming his and Valentina's recall came through on 5 November, but his request that Marianna be allowed to return with them was declined. It also transpired that Valentina's name had been misspelled, which made it impossible to proceed: a fortnight elapsed before Khrapchenko sent a telegram correcting the mistake. Further delays ensued before their travel permits and train tickets were issued. Thanks to Fere's connections with local Party officials, they eventually managed to book berths in a sleeper train leaving on 7 December.[103] They departed with very mixed feelings, having entrusted Marianna to Yevgeniya's care.

They arrived home eight days later, their route taking them through Uzbekistan and northward through Kazakhstan to Orenberg before proceeding westward to Moscow. To their great relief, they found their apartment undamaged and their belongings intact, as burglaries were far from uncommon during the war years. Myaskovsky spent the first few days doing the rounds of the Composers' Union, the conservatoire, Muzgiz, and the

100 Lamm, *Stranitsï*, 291.

101 RNMM, 71/763.

102 'Vïpiski', 1 November 1942, RGALI, 2040/1/65, l. 60.

103 'Vïpiski', 5, 10, and 20 November and 7 December, RGALI, 2040/1/65, ll. 60, 600b.

Committee for Artistic Affairs, trying to sort out his finances and various practicalities to do with his work duties, and also petitioning to bring the remaining evacuees home. As he reported to Pavel Lamm in a long letter of 25 December, life in the capital was very hard: the situation was reminiscent of the Civil War years. Apartment buildings were heated only to the extent necessary to keep water pipes from freezing, so Valentina and he had to wear their outdoor coats all the time. The Composers' Union agreed to provide him with some meals, but not his sister; little was on sale in the markets apart from potatoes, carrots, and pickled cabbage. Everyday commodities such as soap and sugar were unavailable. Gas was rationed, which made it difficult to cook, and so was electricity, which meant that one spent much of the time in darkness. Telephones in private dwellings had been disconnected, so he had no choice but to go out to conduct business. Public transport operated at reduced levels: buses no longer ran and the trams and metro were so packed that one could hardly get on board, making his long treks around the city in the freezing cold an exhausting ordeal.[104] By this point, some of the other evacuees had also been given permission to travel to Moscow, but it quickly became apparent that securing the return of the Lamms would not be straightforward. Aside from the constraints imposed by the travel quotas and the difficulties of dealing with Khrapchenko, who was not disposed to be helpful[105], the processing of these requests was often delayed by bureaucratic obstacles created by other government agencies. And as the conservatoire's functioning had yet to return to normal (a large proportion of its staff and students had been evacuated), bringing Lamm back was not seen as a priority.[106] Arranging for Yevgeniya and his niece and nephew to come to Moscow would be even more complicated. For the time being, Myaskovsky could only keep up his efforts and do what he could to assist his friends and relatives financially. At least their circumstances had improved somewhat, as they were able to move to better lodgings vacated by evacuees who had been allowed to go home.

In the lead-up to the New Year, he took the opportunity to catch up with friends and colleagues, including Yekaterina Derzhanovskaya, Prokofiev and Mira, who had returned briefly to Moscow from Alma-Ata, and Dmitry Melkikh, who had suffered a second stroke but had so far been unable to secure admittance to a hospital.[107] He also met Shebalin, who had been asked to take over as the conservatoire's rector in mid-November and was struggling to discharge his responsibilities in exceptionally challenging

---

104 Myaskovsky to Pavel Lamm, 25 December 1942, RGALI, 2743/1/155, ll. 17–18ob.

105 Myaskovsky to Pavel Lamm, 1 January 1943, RGALI, 2743/1/155, l. 20.

106 Myaskovsky to Gube, 25 December 1942, RGALI, 2012/2/208, l. 4.

107 'Vïpiski', 17, 25, and 30 December 1942, RGALI, 2040/1/65, l. 61, 61ob.

FIGURE 10.2. Pavel Lamm (1940s).

FIGURE 10.3. Olga Lamm, 1920s. Courtesy of Tatiana Fedorovskaya.

circumstances. Although the institution had reopened the previous March as some of the evacuated teachers and students began to return, it was still operating with a skeleton staff. The premises suffered significant damage during the Luftwaffe's air raids: many of its windows had been smashed and were still boarded up. In winter, the temperature inside remained barely above freezing point and classes could only be held on the lower floor and in the basement.[108] Shebalin had to contend with numerous practical difficulties, and his efforts to resolve them were hampered by internal intrigues and a lack of government support.[109] No doubt it was for this reason that Myaskovsky agreed to be appointed acting dean of the Faculty of Composition and Music Theory, a position that he held from January 1943 until May 1944.[110]

He and Valentina saw in the New Year at a small gathering in the Composers' Union, where they had to remain until 6 am because of the prevailing nocturnal curfew.[111] Their pleasure at being back in familiar surroundings was abruptly dispelled by the arrival of a telegram from Frunze on 6 January informing them that Marianna was in a critical condition after giving birth to a stillborn baby. By the time they received it, the worst had already come to pass: another message came the following day confirming her death from encephalitis on 4 January.[112] Valentina was disconsolate and wracked with guilt for having left her daughter, though Yevgeniya assured her that there was absolutely nothing she could have done even had she been there. 'It would only have compounded all her other sufferings with the torture of helplessness and despair that I remember having to endure', Yevgeniya wrote to her brother: 'I did not leave Marianna's side for a moment'.[113] The loss was not made any easier to bear by the knowledge that Marianna had been advised not to become pregnant on medical grounds, but her husband, a boorish military attorney, had insisted on her doing so because he wanted 'a real family'. Olga Lamm recalled having to help lower her body into the grave, as the local gravediggers refused to assist – presumably on religious grounds.[114]

108 Ginzburg (ed.), *Moskovskaya konservatoriya*, 353–5.

109 Myaskovsky to Pavel Lamm, 20 February 1943, RGALI, 2743/1/155, l. 24.

110 'Vïpiska iz prikaza No. 23 po Moskovskoy Gos. Konservatoriyi im. P. I. Chaykovskogo, 27 yanvarya 1943' and 'Prikaz No. 167, Glavnogo upravleniya uchebnïkh zavedeniy Komiteta po delam iskusstv pri SNK SSSR, 3 maya 1944g', AMK, 1/23/84, ll. 22, 24.

111 'Vïpiski', 31 December 1942 and 1 January 1943, RGALI, 2040/1/65, l. 61ob.

112 'Vïpiski', 6 and 7 January 1943, RGALI, 2040/1/65, l. 61ob.

113 Yevgeniya Fedorovskaya to Myaskovsky, 23 January 1943, RGALI, 2040/2/259, ll. 56–56ob.

114 'Pavel Aleksandrovich Lamm: opït biografii', RNMM, 192/361, l. 445.

Distressed though he was, Myaskovsky had no choice but to focus on his work, not least because Yevgeniya and Nikita were dependent on his financial support. Over the following months his letters and diary detail an onerous round of professional duties – teaching, administration, auditioning and examining, reviewing for Muzgiz, assessing new works for prospective performance, work on behalf of the Stalin Prize committee and the Composers' Union, sitting on advisory boards overseeing activities to commemorate various artistic figures – all of which had to be carried out amidst the privations and day-to-day inconveniences of life in wartime Moscow. He found it difficult to compose, and not merely due to lack of time but also to lack of light: although Massalitinova successfully petitioned for the restrictions on the electricity supply to his apartment to be eased, it nonetheless continued to be disconnected in the evenings.[115] The early months of the year were so cold that he and Valentina seldom went out unless absolutely necessary: they saw few people apart from occasional visitors such as Derzhanovskaya, who called to enjoy brief respite from hunger and hardship. Food shortages remained acute throughout the spring and prices rose relentlessly. As he told Yevgeniya, even had he been able to bring Nikita and herself to Moscow, he would have found it impossible to feed them.[116] Only the Red Army's recent victories provided some cause for cheer – the recapture of Stalingrad on 2 February 1943 after an epic struggle that left almost a million Russian soldiers dead and wounded; and the taking of Rostov, Kharkov, and Luhansk shortly afterwards. 'You're afraid to rejoice, as after a recovery from a serious illness', Myaskovsky wrote in his diary.[117] Only a few days later, however, he learned that Dmitry Melkikh had died: the neglect that Melkikh had suffered in his final years was a sad end to a career that had begun so promisingly.[118]

Concert life slowly began to resume in the spring, though the quality of the performance standards left much to be desired. In a letter to Gube, Myaskovsky unsparingly described the leading Soviet conductors of the period as uniformly mediocre.[119] His comments about much recent work by Soviet composers were equally unflattering: he thought scores by Glière and Chemberdzhi that he heard at a Composers' Union symphony concert on 19 April 'not up to much'; a concert of chamber music by Bely, Rakov, and Levina on 23 May left him 'cold'; and orchestral works by Zhelobinsky and

115 'Vïpiski', 15 January 1943, RGALI, 2040/1/65, l. 62; Myaskovsky to Pavel Lamm, 20 February 1943, RGALI, 2743/1/155, l. 230b–4.
116 Myaskovsky to Yevgeniya Fedorovskaya, 17 February and 12 March 1943, RGALI, 2040/1/80, ll. 26–70b and 28–280b.
117 'Vïpiski', 17 February 1943, RGALI, 2040/1/65, l. 620b.
118 'Vïpiski', 22 February 1943, RGALI, 2040/1/65, l. 63.
119 Myaskovsky to Gube, 4 June 1943, RGALI, 2012/2/208, ll. 8–80b.

Cheryomukhin performed five days later struck him as downright 'bad'.[120] There were some notable exceptions, however: he liked Khachaturian's ballet *Gayane* and was deeply impressed when he heard Shostakovich play his Second Piano Sonata at a private gathering in April.[121]

Myaskovsky had been issued with contracts for three new compositions – a violin sonata for David Oistrakh, a symphony, and a work for the twentieth anniversary celebrations of the Beethoven Quartet, which had recently premiered his Seventh and Eighth Quartets.[122] Although he complained to Prokofiev that his 'head was empty', he made swift progress on the second and third of these projects once he turned his attention to them from mid-April.[123] The Ninth String Quartet in D minor, op. 62 was completed on 4 June, and the Twenty-Fourth Symphony in F minor, op. 63, was sketched in eleven days between 10 and 20 June and orchestrated by 17 July. Both scores should undoubtedly be counted amongst his finest achievements.

Unlike its immediate predecessors, which are interesting works but not composed under the same pressure of inspiration, the three-movement Ninth Quartet exemplifies Myaskovsky's handling of the medium at its most accomplished. It also demonstrates his increasingly pared-down style (not only in its economical textures but also in its general tendency to understatement) and the highly individual harmonic language of his later music, with its intriguing blend of modality and chromaticism. The initial *Allegro inquieto* generates considerable dramatic tension, but the emotional centre of gravity of the quartet is its central movement, an ingenuous blend of slow movement and scherzo. Its searingly intense opening (ex. 10.1), with its plangent dissonances, is thrown into high relief by the ensuing *Allegro misterioso*, which is dominated by an idea that is more a texture than a theme – fleet semiquaver murmurings exchanged between the instruments playing *con sordino* (ex. 10.2). As the material develops contrapuntally, the opening lyrical theme is reintroduced against it, building to an impressive climax before a reprise of a subsidiary idea that brings the movement to a serene close. The ensuing *Allegro con brio* has an exhilarating buoyancy and forward momentum, and though it never sounds in the slightest like pastiche, it evinces a distinct indebtedness to music of the classical period in its employment of thematic ideas with highly contrasted components – such as the principal theme, with its arresting opening gesture and elegant continuation (ex. 10.3). The expansive mood in which the movement

120 'Vïpiski', RGALI, 2040/1/65, ll. 640b, 65.

121 'Vïpiski', 19 February and 8 April 1943, RGALI, 2040/1/65, ll. 63, 64.

122 The quartets had been performed on 26 December 1942 and 21 March 1943 respectively: 'Vïpiski', RGALI, 2040/1/65, ll. 610b, 630b.

123 Myaskovsky to Prokofiev, 24 April 1943, in Kozlova and Yatsenko, *Perepiska*, 469.

EXAMPLE 10.1. String Quartet no. 9, second movement: opening.

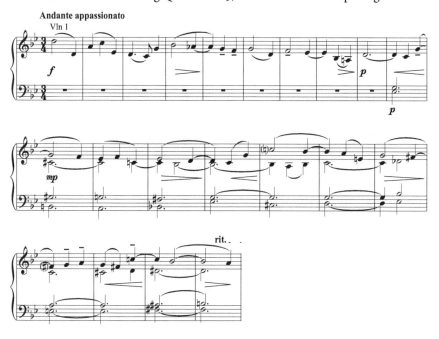

concludes conveys a sense of confident resilience, in spite of the turbulent times in the quartet was written. The work was very warmly received at its premiere on 30 October 1943 and would earn Myaskovsky his second Stalin Prize, first class.

The Twenty-Fourth Symphony, which Myaskovsky dedicated to the memory of Derzhanovsky, is also a deeply felt score. Despite the efforts of Soviet commentators to claim it as another 'war symphony', it is doubtful to what extent Myaskovsky envisaged it as a response to contemporary events – at least, in any obvious sense. The symphony explores a realm of inner spiritual experience that wholly transcends the impoverished psychological world of official Soviet art: it has no overt propagandistic 'content' and certainly in no way resembles the kind of celebratory homage to the Red Army that Derzhanovsky hoped he might write. Neither does it exhibit what Myaskovsky mordantly described as 'bureaucratic heroism'[124] – the clichéd depictions of struggle and triumph that were routinely expected of Soviet artists during the war years. Like much of Myaskovsky's late work, its style and musical language bears little obvious kinship to the work of his Russian contemporaries, especially in its extensive recourse to diatonic

124 Myaskovsky to Pavel Lamm, 16 January 1943, RGALI, 2743/1/155, l.210b.

EXAMPLE 10.2. String Quartet no. 9, second movement: bars 92–101.

EXAMPLE 10.3. String Quartet no. 9, third movement: bars 9–21.

modality. British listeners might find its sound-world surprisingly reminiscent of Vaughan Williams.

Cast in three movements, the Twenty-Fourth is a fairly compact work, lasting around thirty-five minutes in performance. The opening sonata-form *Allegro deciso* is complex in detail but presents a highly cogent formal argument dominated by three ideas – a first subject first enunciated on the bassoons against a pulsating pedal bass (ex. 10.4) and the two contrasting themes of the second subject group, one lyrical and inward, the other more impassioned. It affords an impressive demonstration of Myaskovsky's control of span and momentum, with its long paragraphs of polyphonic development rising to powerful culminations. Aside from its technical mastery, the music has an evocative, poetic quality that lingers in the memory: there are some marvellous moments, such as the coda's unexpected dramatic surge towards a subdominant seventh chord before fading mysteriously to silence. The slow movement is one of the most distinguished that Myaskovsky ever composed and offers an object lesson in the expressive gains made possible by his stylistic reorientation during the 1930s. Though its musical material looks deceptively simple on paper, such as the Dorian C-sharp minor theme first heard on strings (ex. 10.5), it has a remarkable emotional potency: the majestic restatements of this idea, presented as the outcome of two successive waves of development, movingly communicate a sense of desolation and loss. The finale too is very persuasive in its progressive transformation of the opening turbulence to end in a mood of radiant serenity on a diaphanous widely spaced F major triad in the strings, after distant echoes of motifs from the first movement.

Although he longed for a break in the countryside following this intense bout of creativity, wartime conditions made it impossible to take his usual holiday in Nikolina Gora. Khachaturian tried to persuade him to come to a Composers' Union 'creative residence' in Ivanovo, some two hundred miles to the north-east, but he was reluctant to make the long journey. He remained in Moscow and spent the summer months orchestrating the new symphony. In late July, he learned that he was to receive the Order of Lenin – rather to his surprise, as he told Yevgeniya, in view of his 'bad reputation' and Khrapchenko's antipathy to him.[125] The award was conferred at a ceremony in the Kremlin on 10 August.[126]

A week later, he had a touching reunion with the Lamms, who finally came back from Frunze – largely thanks to Shebalin's success in persuading Khrapchenko that Lamm's services would be indispensable for a new research institute that he proposed to set up under the conservatoire's

---

125 Myaskovsky to Yevgeniya Fedorovskaya, 9 August 1943, RGALI, 2040/1/80, l. 300b.

126 'Vipiski', 10 August 1942, RGALI, 2040/1/65, l. 67.

EXAMPLE 10.4. Symphony no. 24, first movement: bars 19–38.

EXAMPLE 10.5. Symphony no. 24, II, bars 44–54.

auspices.[127] Although Myaskovsky had done his best to help his friend by arranging commissions for piano transcriptions of various works, including Shostakovich's Seventh Symphony[128], the family's final months in Frunze were difficult. Lamm became seriously depressed and feared that he and his family would be never allowed to come home – an anxiety that was by no means unfounded, as he had been refused permission to visit Yerevan the previous year because of his half-German origins. Before their arrival, Myaskovsky saw to it that their apartment was cleaned and had the broken glass in the windows replaced: fortunately Lamm's library was unharmed, though some of the apartment fixtures had been stolen (amongst them, the stove and the toilet bowl – an item that was in particularly short supply).[129] On opening the door, the Lamms found the study table laden with flowers and presents. Pavel Lamm was eager to resume their regular musical evenings, but their first attempts were not very successful because the players were so out of practice.[130] It took another two months before Myaskovsky obtained the necessary permissions for Yevgeniya and Nikita to come to Moscow, using his connections in the Composers' Union. In the event, Nikita was called up before Yevgeniya eventually managed to secure a travel permit the following January.[131]

By the autumn of 1943, conditions in Moscow had improved sufficiently to permit the return of most of the evacuated musicians, amongst them, Prokofiev. Colleagues evacuated from other cities had longer to wait, however. Steinberg would remain in Tashkent for another year in circumstances of considerable hardship. (At the time of Myaskovsky's departure from Frunze, he was still sharing a room with four other people, trying to work by the light of a fifteen-watt bulb.[132]) His letters to Myaskovsky acquired an increasingly despondent tone, as he found it a struggle to compose and was disheartened by the lack of interest in his music. Myaskovsky did what he could to arrange a performance of Steinberg's Fifth Symphony in Moscow, but it had to be repeatedly postponed because Steinberg experienced acute difficulty procuring manuscript paper to copy out the score and parts. He also recommended the score for consideration for a Stalin Prize, but without success.[133]

---

127 Myaskovsky to Pavel Lamm, 24 April 1943, RGALI, 2743/1/156, l. 4.

128 Myaskovsky to Pavel Lamm, 31 March 1943, RGALI, 2743/1/155, l. 29.

129 Myaskovsky to Pavel Lamm, 5 March 1943, RGALI, 2743/1/155, l. 26

130 'Pavel Aleksandrovich Lamm: Opït biografii', RNMM, 192/361, ll. 443, 446.

131 Myaskovsky to Yevgeniya, 1 and 17 October 1943, RGALI, 2040/1/80, l. 31, 32; 'Vïpiski', 30 January 1944, RGALI, 2040/1/65, l. 71.

132 Myaskovsky to Steinberg, 17 December 1942, RGALI, 2040/2/282, l. 57.

133 Myaskovsky to Steinberg, 12 March 1943, RIII, 28/1/487, l. 135–1350b; Steinberg to Myaskovsky, 27 December 1943, RGALI, 2040/2/282, l. 109–1090b; 'N.

Myaskovsky commenced the new academic year feeling mentally and physically drained. The intensive labour on the new symphony and string quartet had 'worn him out', he confessed to Gube: he was suffering from dizzy spells and in a state of constant nervous exhaustion. Hearing the symphony performed in a piano transcription prepared by Lamm had not helped his spirits: he thought it a failure and was apprehensive about its forthcoming premiere under Yevgeny Mravinsky on 8 December – though as it transpired, the performance went well.[134] His diary entries and letters exude increasing frustration at the staleness of Soviet musical life and the tedium of his professional duties. The poor quality of many of the performances that he attended and the new music that he heard continued to irritate him; he was equally unimpressed by the productions of Soviet music critics and musicologists, which he regularly reviewed for Muzgiz and the Composers' Union journal *Soviet Music*. The standard of these writings was often low, and he was disquieted by their tendency to focus on the elucidation of compositions' supposed 'ideological content' to the virtual exclusion of everything else. ('It's all about the "subject matter", he complained of one essay: 'Music disappears from view'.[135]) Even the publications of his eminent contemporaries had started to disappoint. Essays by the recently deceased Boleslav Yavorsky left him baffled by their verbose obscurity.[136] A new article by Asafiev, 'Russian Music's Paths of Development', made a disagreeable impression: he was troubled by Asafiev's praise of 'assorted trash' for political reasons and by the article's 'ingratiating' tone, manifestly calculated to please Soviet officialdom.[137]

Asafiev had been brought to Moscow from Leningrad in February 1943[138]: he refused to be evacuated before the onset of the blockade[139] and was so apprehensive about the hazardous journey across Lake Ladoga that he could only be persuaded to leave with the greatest difficulty.[140] By then, he was in fragile health, having suffered a stroke the previous September, though the city authorities ensured that he received the best care possible.[141]

Ya. Myaskovskiy. Vïstupleniye na zasedanii muzïkal'noy sektsii Komiteta po gosudarstevennïm premiyam. 1943g.', RGALI, 2040/3/23, ll. 3, 5.

134 Myaskovsky to Gube, 22 November 1943, RGALI, 2012/2/208, ll. 10–100b.

135 'Vïpiski', 19 May 1943, RGALI, 2040/1/65, l. 65.

136 'Vïpiski', 11 March 1943, RGALI, 2040/1/65, l. 63.

137 'Vïpiski', 24 May 1943, RGALI, 2040/1/65, l. 65.

138 The theatre critic Vladimir Golubov, who was a secret police agent, was entrusted with assisting Asafiev, his wife, and his sister-in-law to evacuate: see Asafiev to Boris Zagursky, 28 January 1943, NLR, 1117/1698, ll. 1–10b.

139 Lyubov' Shaporina, *Dnevnik*, vol. 1 (Moscow, 2012), 407.

140 Anatoliy Dmitriyev, 'Moy dorogoy uchitel'', in Andrey Kryukov (ed.), *Vospominaniya o B. V. Asaf'yeve*, (Leningrad, 1974), 134.

141 Orest Yevlakhov, 'Iz vospominaniy', in Kryukov (ed.), *Vospominaniya o B. V. Asaf'yeve*, 36; Orlova and Kryukov (ed.), *Akademik Boris Vladimirovich*

Despite his reservations about Asafiev's work and the cooling of their friendship over the previous decade, these circumstances naturally disposed Myaskovsky to be sympathetic: he readily supported Asafiev's candidacy for a Stalin Prize in 1943 on the grounds of his service to Soviet musical life.[142] Although Asafiev would remain in Moscow until his death just under six years later, he and Myaskovsky saw little of one another. Their relations remained cordial on the surface, but Asafiev's envious and resentful attitude towards Myaskovsky persisted – in spite of all the flattering signs of official recognition that he received on arrival in Moscow. (In 1943 he became the first musicologist appointed to the Russian Academy of Sciences and a number of research and consultancy posts were specially created for him.) Myaskovsky's diary records only two occasions on which he met Asafiev over the next two years – at the celebrations to mark Asafiev's sixtieth birthday in July 1944, and the following March at a birthday party given for his wife and her twin sister.[143] The last recorded contact between them was a note that Myaskovsky sent Asafiev in July 1945 to congratulate him on a recent article on Tchaikovsky and to extend an invitation to visit during the summer.[144] It went unanswered. The likely explanation for Asafiev's silence is provided by Irina Asafieva's diary entry for 24 March 1945, in which she expressed outrage that her husband had not received a Stalin Prize for his latest ballet, blaming 'the scoundrels Shaporin and Myaskovsky'.[145] There is no evidence to support her perception of events or to suggest that Myaskovsky discharged his responsibilities as a member of the Prize Committee with anything other than scrupulous integrity. The two men never met again, but this incident would have fateful repercussions a few years later.

Myaskovsky's health deteriorated badly during the last eighteen months of the war. He fulfilled his professional duties conscientiously and continued to serve on the Stalin Prize Committee, but his creativity flagged. It is noteworthy that most of the scores he completed during this period were revisions or adaptations of unpublished works from his student years – the Fifth and Sixth Piano Sonatas, op. 64/1 and op. 64/2, the curiously titled orchestral suite *Zven'ya* (the plural form of *zveno*, a chain-link), op. 65, and the Tenth String Quartet, op. 67/1. None of these represents him at his best. The two-movement Concerto for Cello and Orchestra in C minor, op. 64, which was composed in late 1944, is more distinguished, though uneven: the introspective *Lento ma non troppo* has good ideas

---

Asaf'yev, 222.

142 'Vïpiski', 4 March 1943, RGALI, 2040/1/65, l. 63.

143 'Vïpiski', 26 and 31 July 1944, 11 May 1945, RGALI, 2040/1/65, ll. 73 and 77ob.

144 Myaskovsky to Asafiev, 20 July 1945, RGALI, 2658/1/642, l. 35.

145 RGALI, 2658/1/951, l. 180ob.

and is gratefully conceived for the solo instrument, but the concluding *Allegro vivace* is less persuasive. It is unclear what prompted Myaskovsky to compose the concerto, as it was not commissioned by or for a particular performer. When it was completed, Myaskovsky approached the Soviet cellist Svyatoslav Knushevitsky (1908–63), who played in a famous trio with David Oistrakh and Lev Oborin, to seek his advice on the solo part.[146] Knushevitsky premiered the concerto with the radio orchestra on 23 March the following year. Much to Myaskovsky's embarrassment, it too was awarded a Stalin Prize in 1946. Despite his attempts to withdraw it and his protests that it was time for prizes to be given to others, Shaporin insisted that it be included on the list of scores nominated by the committee's music section – an attempt, perhaps, to make amends for the unpleasantness caused by the nomination of the Twenty-First Symphony several years previously.[147] Nonetheless, his colleagues' reluctance to exclude his work from consideration says much for the respect in which he was held.

Myaskovsky's diary entries and letters from this period suggest that he was making valiant efforts to keep going despite increasingly frequent bouts of illness and depression. References to events from which he derived pleasure or artistic stimulus are infrequent, though not altogether absent. The most noteworthy instances, as usual, were connected with the work of Shostakovich and Prokofiev. Shostakovich's Eighth Symphony made a deep impression on him at its premiere in November 1943, though he had reservations about its formal organisation; and he enthusiastically praised Prokofiev's Fifth Symphony when he heard the composer play it in draft in the summer of 1944, describing it as 'a work of genius'.[148] Perhaps the most poignant of his diary entries records his delighted response to Eugene Ormandy's superb recent recording of his Twenty-First Symphony with the Philadelphia Orchestra, a performance that he described as 'magnificent in every respect'.[149] (This venture had resulted from the revival of cultural exchange between the USSR and the Allied powers during the war years.) It is only a pity he could not have heard such fine accounts of his compositions more often.

By the spring of 1945, the end of the war was at last in sight. On 30 April, the blackout in Moscow was lifted: he walked home that night

146 Svyatoslav Knushevitsky, 'Vstrechi s N. Ya. Myaskovskim', in Shlifshteyn (ed.), *N. Ya. Myaskovskiy: Sobraniye materialov*, vol. 1, 273.

147 See Frolova-Walker, *Stalin's Music Prize*, 143.

148 'Vïpiski', 4 November 1943, RGALI, 2040/1/65, l. 690b; Myaskovsky to Shlifshteyn, 27 August 1944, RNMM, 538/34 and 538/35.

149 'Vïpiski', 15 January 1945, RGALI, 2040/1/65, l. 750b.

through brightly lit streets for the first time in four years.[150] On 2 May
Berlin fell; a week later, hostilities ceased. Amidst the ensuing parades and
public celebrations, he attended a Kremlin reception in honour of the Red
Army and another hosted by Molotov in honour of victory.[151] He noted in
his diary that he 'felt dreadful': his colleagues were so concerned that the
Composers' Union arranged for him to be admitted to a sanatorium in
Barvikha, twenty miles west of Moscow.[152] He spent most of June and early
July there, but as he ruefully informed Steinberg, instead of alleviating his
ailments, the medical treatment 'conjured them forth, like the sorcerer's
apprentice'. Amongst the conditions that his doctors diagnosed was 'car-
diac sclerosis'.[153] His fellow patients included Varvara Massalitinova, now
terminally ill. There was little trace of her former gaiety: her mind was
clouded by dark forebodings prompted by dreams of Rachmaninoff, who
had died two years previously.[154] The list of friends and colleagues whom
he lost between 1942 and 1945 continued to lengthen.

Even after a long convalescence, he did not fully recover: it was becoming increasingly apparent just how heavy a toll the last few years had
exacted. He had the consolation of returning to Nikolina Gora in late July
and could at last enjoy a holiday in the countryside – his first since the
outbreak of the war.[155] (Although he had gone to the Composers' Union
rest home in Ivanovo the previous summer, he had been indisposed for
the duration of his stay with excruciatingly painful haemorrhoids that
made it impossible for him to walk and required prolonged treatment.[156])
To their relief, the Lamms had found their dacha still standing, but the
interior was in bad repair and required extensive renovation.[157] Rather
than trying to start a new work, Myaskovsky confined himself to tinker-
ing with the Tenth Quartet and transcribing for string orchestra the two
middle movements of the Nineteenth Symphony. Once back in Moscow,
he began to sketch another string quartet (the Eleventh, in E-Flat major,
op. 67/2) and to look for ideas for his next symphony, but made fitful
progress.[158] His lack of productively depressed him. 'I feel a lot better', he

150 'Vïpiski', 30 April 1945, RGALI, 2040/1/65, l. 77.
151 'Vïpiski', 24 and 31 May 1945, RGALI, 2040/1/65, l. 770b.
152 'Vïpiski', 19 May 1945, RGALI, 2040/1/65, l. 770b.
153 Myaskovsky to Steinberg, 31 January 1946, RIII, 28/1/487, l. 145.
154 'Vïpiski', 8 July 1945, RGALI, 2040/1/65, l. 78.
155 'Vïpiski', 13 September 1945, RGALI, 2040/1/65, l. 78.
156 Myaskovsky to Valentina Menshikova, 15 and 20 August 1944, RGALI,
     2040/1/74, ll. 27–270b, 29–290b.
157 'Pavel Aleksandrovich Lamm: opït biografii', RNMM, 192/361, l. 446.
158 'Vïpiski', 20 and 30 September 1945, RGALI, 2040/1/65, ll. 78, 780b.

wrote dejectedly to Kabalevsky, 'but . . . what use is my health to me if I cannot compose, which is all that I live for?'[159]

In what remained of his life, he would demonstrate that his creative powers and capacity for stoical endurance were by no means exhausted.

159 Myaskovsky to Kabalevsky, 6 October 1945, RGALI, 2017/1/91, l. 12.

11

Final Years: 1946–50

Breaking with tradition, Myaskovsky's friends saw in the New Year at his apartment rather than at Pavel Lamm's because he was still unwell. His lengthy illness the previous summer marked the onset of an accelerating decline in his health. From 1946 onwards, his diary entries make increasingly frequent allusions to persistent fatigue and indispositions that kept him housebound and hindered his work. He extricated himself from most of his teaching commitments, preferring to save his energies for composing, though he continued to act as consultant to the state music publisher and to sit on the Stalin Prize committee. Ideas for new creative projects were slow to take shape, so he turned to a less demanding task – fulfilling a request from the legislature of the Russian Soviet Federative Socialist Republic (the largest of the USSR's fifteen republics) to write an entry for a competition to compose its new anthem. Work advanced fitfully: he struggled to come up with anything interesting in response to Stepan Shchipachyov's wooden verses. The other participants evidently experienced even more acute difficulty, as his was the only entry to make it past the first round. A flurry of revision and re-composition ensued before the second round, which saw the sixty-eight submissions whittled down to eight, Myaskovsky's still amongst them. The conductor Nikolay Golovanov contacted him at the start of March to propose further 'improvements' to his anthem before the final round in April – 'which all came down to turning it into something commonplace', as he noted sourly in his diary. In the end, his efforts went for nothing: the jury was unenthusiastic about his score. The other finalists included Asafiev, whose anthem he found distastefully saccharine, and Shostakovich, whose entry he considered the best, if somewhat bland.[1]

On completing the first version of the anthem, he returned to the sketches he had made the previous year for two works, one of which would become the Sinfonietta in A minor for string orchestra, op. 68, and other, the Twenty-Fifth Symphony in D-flat major, op. 69; but finding himself unable to make much headway with either, he spent ten days revising settings of the symbolist poet Zinaida Hippius that he had made between 1904 and 1908, fashioning a new op. 4 from twelve previously published songs and a further six that had remained in manuscript. His decision to rework these early compositions indicates that he continued to regard them as

---

[1] 'Vipiski', 4 and 13 January; 13, 21, 22, and 24 February; 2 March; and 2 April 1946, RGALI, 2040/1/65, ll. 80–10b.

a significant achievement, especially as there was scant likelihood of the revised versions being published or performed. Hippius's poetry, like most work by Russian émigré writers, was effectively banned in the USSR by this point; moreover, the songs' sound-world conveyed an existential anguish far removed from the 'life-affirming optimism' and 'joy in socialist construction' expected of Soviet creative artists.

The sinfonietta and the new symphony made desultory progress until he left Moscow on 13 June to spend his summer holiday at Pavel Lamm's dacha: his work for the Stalin Prize committee occupied him throughout the spring and he was ill for several weeks in April and May. As usual, the congenial surroundings of Nikolina Gora exercised their beneficent effect: by the time he returned on 15 September, he had completed the sinfonietta in full score and the symphony in draft, as well as four other works – the Sonata in F major for violin and piano, op.70; the orchestral *Slavonic Rhapsody*, op. 71; the *Lyrical Notebook*, op. 72, six settings of poems by Mira Mendelson (including two of her translations of verse by the eighteenth-century Scottish poet Robert Burns); and a set of short piano pieces, *Stylisations*, op. 73.

Of these scores, the Sinfonietta, op. 68, is undoubtedly the finest. The majestic opening fugal fantasia, with its plangent dissonances, and the exhilarating impetus of the finale are effectively offset by the central movements, an elegant gavotte and a lyrical slow movement with a waltz-like central section: both pay affectionate homage to Tchaikovsky, but never degenerate into pastiche. The thematic material is of consistently high quality and deftly handled. Equally impressive is the writing for the medium, which is colourful and texturally inventive, with Myaskovsky's fluent contrapuntal technique abundantly in evidence. An excellent showpiece for a virtuoso string orchestra, the work would amply reward the attention of conductors.

The Twenty-Fifth Symphony, though it also contains very good things, is less persuasive. Here, Myaskovsky experimented with a three-movement design comprising a lengthy adagio, a brief scherzo in moderate tempo, and a sonata-allegro finale, with a combined duration of about thirty-five minutes. The serene first movement is well-sustained and has passages of affecting beauty, but neither it nor the ensuing scherzo engender much dramatic tension, being predominantly lyrical. The need for a strongly contrasting finale was self-evident, but the integration of that contrast with the proceeding music proved tricky. Myaskovsky's attempted solution was to cast the last movement as a turbulent sonata-allegro which culminates in a fortissimo apotheosis of the first movement's lyrical principal theme as a resolution of the preceding conflicts. The problem with postponing the first significant outbreak of conflict to such a late stage is that it seems psychologically unmotivated. Matters are not helped by the fact that the finale's thematic material is undistinguished and treated in rather formulaic

FIGURE 11.1. With Moscow Conservatoire colleagues (1946).
From left to right: Lev Oborin, Alexander Goedicke, Konstantin Igumnov,
Vissarion Shebalin, Myaskovsky, David Oistrakh.

fashion: the climactic return of the first movement theme strikes the listener as a clichéd gesture and does not form a persuasive conclusion to the
work as a whole. The symphony's fundamental flaw is that the first movement is too self-contained: there is no compelling necessity for anything to
follow.

The remaining scores are more routine, composed under a lower pressure of inspiration. The two-movement Violin Sonata, written for David
Oistrakh, makes a pallid impression in comparison to Prokofiev's First
Violin Sonata, completed the same year, for which Myaskovsky had lavish
praise ('a work of genius', he remarked in his diary).[2] The gently flowing
sonata-form first movement works well enough, though it suffers from a
lack of textural relief, but the same cannot be said of the second, a dull
set of variations on a folk song–like theme. The *Slavonic Rhapsody*, a single-movement work of overture length, is notable for featuring Polish liturgical chants that Myaskovsky had seen reproduced in a monograph on early
European musical culture by Asafiev's student Roman Gruber, a publication

2   'Vipiski', 29 October 1946, RGALI, 2040/1/65, ll. 820b–3.

FIGURE 11.2. In his study (1940s).

that appears to have sparked his interest in the origins of Slavic musical tra-ditions.[3] Myaskovsky told his future biographer Aleksey Ikonnikov that the rhapsody evoked a notable historical struggle of fellow Slavs against foreign oppressors – the fifteenth-century Hussite Wars, sparked by the Catholic Church's persecution of the Bohemian religious leader Jan Hus and his fol-lowers.[4] This putative 'content' was almost certainly a convenient fiction to pre-empt criticism of his use of melodies with religious associations.[5] The *Lyrical Notebook* realised a long-standing plan to compose a song cycle to texts by Mira Mendelson, an idea that had been suggested by Prokofiev. Myaskovsky set four lyrics that she had written in 1939–40, supplemented by her translations of Burns's 'My Heart's in the Highlands' and 'My Bonie [Bonny] Mary'.[6] Although she was appreciative of his gesture (Myaskovsky and she became very fond of one another), the songs are not amongst his best and make a rather monotonous impression as a group, as five of the

3   Roman Gruber, *Istoriya muzïkal'noy kul'turï*, vol. 1 (Moscow and Leningrad, 1941).

4   Ikonnikov, *Khudozhnik nashikh dney*, 304.

5   It is noteworthy that the *Slavonic Rhapsody*, like the Tenth and Thirteenth Symphonies, was considered unsuitable for inclusion in the posthumously published Selected Works: see Bèlza, *O muzïkantakh XX veka*, 68.

6   For an account of the cycle's genesis, see Mira Mendel'son-Prokof'yeva, *O Sergeye Sergeyeviche Prokof'yeve: Vospominaniya, dnevniki, 1938–1967*, ed. Yelena Krivtsova (Moscow, 2012), 280–1.

six are in a slow tempo. *Stylisations*, subtitled 'Nine Pieces in the Form of Old Dances', was the first of several piano works of moderate difficulty that Myaskovsky composed towards the end of his life, with young players in mind. The witty 'Galop', the eighth of the set, is particularly attractive and would make an excellent encore. Myaskovsky completed the orchestration of the *Slavonic Rhapsody* and the symphony in November, and characteristically, continued to polish during the winter what he had written the preceding summer.

Shortly after his return to Moscow, the local branch of the Composers' Union convened a conference which proved an ominous harbinger of impending difficulties. As the eminent writer Konstantin Simonov recalled in his reminiscences of the Stalinist period, many members of the intelligentsia hoped that the Soviet victory over the Nazis would bring about a relaxation of ideological restrictions and more extensive contact with the outside world – 'or at least those countries with whom we had fought against the enemy'.[7] These hopes were dashed with the onset of the Cold War: Stalin moved to strengthen the Party's control over Soviet cultural and intellectual life, fearing that Western influences might undermine loyalty to the regime. In 1946, Andrey Zhdanov, a senior Politburo member in charge of the Agitation and Propaganda Division, instigated a series of well-publicised investigations of alleged ideological deviations in various domains, starting with literature: on 15–16 August, he presided over two days of meetings in Leningrad with local party functionaries and members of the Writers' Union, at which he gave speeches condemning Mikhail Zoshchenko and Anna Akhmatova, two of the most significant literary figures of the period. On 21 August, *Pravda* published the text of a Central Committee resolution 'On the Journals *The Star* [*Zvezda*] and *Leningrad*', which condemned both leading periodicals for publishing 'vulgar' and unacceptably 'apolitical' writings by these and other authors. Zoshchenko and Akhmatova were unceremoniously ejected from the Writers' Union and publicly vilified, becoming the first prominent victims of a campaign that rapidly turned into a witch-hunt. *Leningrad* was closed down and the editorial board of *Star* reconstituted. Two further resolutions were promulgated in rapid succession – 'On Theatre Repertoire and Measures for Its Improvement' on 26 August, and 'On the Film *A Great Life*' on 4 September. The former reminded Soviet artists of their obligation to foster 'the best sides of Soviet man's character' and to educate Soviet youth to be 'of a vigorous and buoyant disposition, devoted to the Motherland and trusting in the victory of our cause, undaunted by obstacles and capable of surmounting

7   Konstantin Simonov, *Glazami cheloveka moyego pokoleniya* (Moscow, 1988), 109.

any difficulties'. All three resolutions signalled the government's intention to subordinate the arts more fully to ideological ends.

The Moscow Composers' Union conference, which took place over seven days from 2–8 October and was attended by representatives of union branches throughout the USSR, was expressly convened to consider the resolutions' implications for musical composition. The participants gathered in the knowledge that they would engage in ritual self-criticism and 'comradely' mutual criticism in conformity with these Party dicta. Predictably, the union's executive issued a statement lauding the resolutions' 'historic significance for the development of all Soviet culture' and welcoming the 'militant Bolshevik programme of action' that they afforded composers and musicologists alike.[8] Reflecting on Zhdanov's campaigns in old age, Tikhon Khrennikov rightly observed that this conference served as a dress rehearsal for events to come. In his keynote address, the union's de facto head Aram Khachaturian deplored composers' neglect of political themes and subject matter pertaining to contemporary Soviet life, their lack of interest in folk music, and their cultivation of 'pseudo-innovatory and abstract' compositional idioms rather than accessible styles developing the traditions of the great nineteenth-century Russian composers – in other words, their insufficient adherence to Socialist Realism. No doubt he was merely uttering the kinds of platitudes that he believed the occasion to require, but the fact remains that identical criticisms would subsequently be voiced by Party officials. In the course of the discussions, allegations were heard that would be reiterated two years later: that the union's executive neglected its duties and failed to maintain adequate oversight of musical affairs; that musicologists and critics were slow to point out shortcomings in the work of leading figures; and that insufficient attention was given to ideological questions during young composers' training. Resentments surfaced about the privileges enjoyed by prominent composers of 'serious' music and their condescending attitudes towards those working in more popular genres.[9]

It is not clear whether Myaskovsky actually attended the event: if he did, he maintained his habitual silence throughout, as the published transcripts make no allusion to his presence. Shortly after it concluded, he resumed his work on behalf of the Stalin Prize Committee. He spent several weeks perusing a mound of scores that included an operatic treatment of the Kyrgyz national epic *Manas*, co-authored by his former student Vladimir Fere, Vladimir Vlasov, and the tenor Aldïlas Maldïbayev ('not up to much'), and a violin concerto on Uzbek themes by Maximillian Steinberg ('rather

8   'Materiali plenuma Orgkomiteta SSK SSSR', *Sovetskaya muzïka*, 10 (1946), 12.

9   Khrennikov, *Tak èto bïlo*, 92–106. Khachaturian attempted to resign in the lead-up to the conference but was persuaded to remain in post: see Tomoff, *Creative Union*, 99–103.

boring'). On 8 December came the news that Steinberg had died. 'One of Rimsky-Korsakov's favourite pupils, but he had little luck as a composer', he observed in his diary, adding: 'Completely unfair'.[10] Although his contact with Steinberg had diminished in recent years, he retained a high regard for his Leningrad colleague: the two men had been very supportive of one another, especially during the difficult years of the Cultural Revolution. Myaskovsky had found in him a kindred spirit who, in spite of his central position in the northern capital's musical life, felt similarly isolated and beset by doubts about the social relevance of the high musical culture that they both strove to maintain. He understood only too well the setbacks that Steinberg had suffered and his disappointment at the lack of interest in his compositions.[11] Even at this late stage, such performances as Myaskovsky's own music received were often of mediocre quality. He declined to attend a concert featuring his Sixteenth Symphony conducted by Kirill Kondrashin on 21 November because of the 'abominable' playing at rehearsals and was similarly appalled by the radio orchestra's 'foul' account of his Sixth under Abram Stasevich the following month.[12] Renditions of this kind would scarcely have done his music much service or helped to dispel its reputation for being forbiddingly difficult.

There were compensations, such as the young Mstislav Rostropovich's enthusiastic advocacy of his Cello Concerto. 1946 also brought flattering signs of official recognition – two Stalin Prizes, first class, for the Ninth String Quartet and the Cello Concerto (the first of these prizes had been held over from the 1943–4 round), a State Laureate medal in July, and the bestowal of the title 'National Artist of the USSR' in December.[13] Nonetheless, his laconic diary entries continue to exude a mood of weariness and low spirits. The only other composition that he managed to complete in 1946 was *From the Past: Six Improvisations for Piano*, op. 74, reworkings of unpublished pieces written between 1906 and 1917. This set of atmospheric miniatures is much finer than the preceding opus: 'Outburst' [*Poriv*] and 'Chimes' [*Zvoni*] stand out for their harmonic piquancy and striking treatment of sonority.

1947 was notably less productive. He spent much of January and February ill with a series of infections, and complained of feeling 'worn out' from

10   'Vipiski', RGALI, 2040/1/65, l. 83.

11   In his last letter to Myaskovsky, dated 24 January 1946, Steinberg lamented the fact that Myaskovsky's music was so rarely performed in Leningrad, pointing out that some of his symphonies had never been given there: RGALI, 2040/2/282, l. 112.

12   'Vipiski', RGALI, 2040/1/65, l. 83, 830b.

13   Frolova-Walker, *Stalin's Music Prize*, 314, 316; 'Vipiski', 4 July and 29 December 1946, RGALI, 2040/1/65, ll. 82, 84.

reviewing articles for *Soviet Music*.[14] After hearing David Oistrakh play through the Violin Sonata in late February, he was so dissatisfied that he revised it drastically the following October.[15] Similarly, the Twenty-Fifth Symphony struck him as sounding disagreeably 'wizened' and 'geriatric'[16] when he attended the rehearsals, although it was well-received at its premiere under Alexander Gauk on 6 March. 'Feeling very tired: I'm clearly getting old', he confided to his diary later that month, as he faced into another round of work for the Stalin Prize committee. On this occasion, the discussions of the musical works proposed for nomination were tense because of Shostakovich's hostile attitudes towards a cantata by Myaskovsky's student Yevgeny Golubev and Anatoly Aleksandrov's opera *Béla*.[17] Myaskovsky also had reservations about Golubev's cantata, but admired *Béla*, and thought Shostakovich's dismissive comments tactless and unfair. To his disappointment, *Béla* did not feature amongst the prizewinning works when the results were announced, though he was gratified that Prokofiev's First Violin Sonata had made it onto the list.[18]

Creative work did not resume in earnest until he settled in Nikolina Gora for the summer. In spite of being ill initially, he managed to sketch a new choral and orchestral work – a project that had been suggested by Aleksey Ikonnikov, who was in fairly regular contact with Myaskovsky around this period while engaged in writing a study of his symphonies. Attempting to assume the role of Myaskovsky's ideological mentor, he continued to dispense unwanted advice on suitable subjects for musical works and how to go about composing them. Myaskovsky privately thought him a fool (a diary entry records that he found Ikonnikov's accounts of his symphonies to contain 'frightful quantities of drivel'[19]) but preferred to avoid alienating him: Ikonnikov was becoming an increasingly prominent figure in the Composers' Union, having previously held a senior position in the government's Committee for Artistic Affairs.[20] On 12 May, Ikonnikov sent him a newspaper clipping of a poem entitled 'The Kremlin at Night' [*Kreml' noch'yu*] by Sergey Vasilyev, a prominent young poet. In his covering note,

14   Myaskovsky joined the journal's editorial board in 1940 at the request of Kabalevsky, who acted as editor-in-chief from 1940–6: see Kabalevskiy, 'O N. Ya. Myaskovskom', 320.

15   'Vïpiski', 27 February and 13, 17, and 22 October 1947, RGALI, 2040/1/65, ll. 840b, 86, 860b.

16   Ibid., 2 March 1947, l. 840b.

17   Frolova-Walker, *Stalin's Music Prize*, 114–20.

18   'Vïpiski', 5 April and 8 June 1947, RGALI, 2040/1/65, ll. 85, 850b.

19   Ibid., 11 November 1947, l. 87.

20   A Party member, Ikonnikov held several posts within the Committee for Artistic Affairs between 1940 and 1946, including deputy director of the Musical Institutions section.

he proposed that Myaskovsky might make a choral setting or that the text could furnish the programmatic basis for an orchestral composition modelled on Tchaikovsky's *1812 Overture* (Ikonnikov obligingly provided a plan of its possible constituent sections and their general character).[21]

Ikonnikov's letter illustrates the role played by musicologists in shaping Soviet creative practices and the pressures that composers experienced by the late Stalinist period to produce work conforming to a narrow range of approved models drawn from the nineteenth-century Russian classics. One can safely guess Myaskovsky's reaction to the suggestion that he should write something akin to the *1812 Overture*, but his decision to act on Ikonnikov's idea of composing a choral work is interesting, given his marked disinclination to contribute to text-based 'democratic genres' – as programme music, operas, and cantatas were termed in the jargon of Soviet music criticism. In view of the strictures voiced at the previous year's Composers' Union conference about composers' neglect of ideological themes, he probably considered it prudent to be seen to respond to these criticisms, especially in the tense prevailing climate. Moreover, as 1947 marked the thirtieth anniversary of the October Revolution, it was expected that the country's leading composers would produce a substantial work to mark the occasion. Writing a cantata was consequently expedient from several points of view. He certainly was not drawn to Vasilyev's poem because of any literary merit. In his lexicon of twentieth-century Russian literature, the eminent Slavist Wolfgang Kasack dismissed Vasilyev's work as vapid and technically inept, noting his habit of padding out lines with superfluous words to maintain the metre or rhyming scheme.[22] These deficiencies proved no barrier to becoming one of the most successful and widely published poets of his era. By 1947, no fewer than fourteen collections of his work had appeared. 'The Kremlin at Night' was reprinted that year in a collection entitled *Soviet Moscow [Moskva sovetskaya]*, which mostly comprised verses about Stalin. These were frequently set by other composers at the period, so Myaskovsky could have been fairly confident that his chosen text would not raise objections on ideological grounds.[23]

'The Kremlin at Night' portrays the dictator's selfless labours on behalf of his countrymen, which regularly require him to work late into the night. Committed democrat that he is, he summons workers, farmers, and other representatives of Soviet society to a nocturnal meeting to seek their advice on important national affairs such as the development of industry and

21   Ikonnikov to Myaskovsky, 12 May 1947, RGALI, 2040/2/153, ll. 27–270b.

22   'Vasil'ev, Sergej Aleksandrovič', in Wolfgang Kasack, *Lexikon der russischen Literatur ab 1917* (Stuttgart, 1976), 419–20.

23   Konstantin Bogdanov, 'Pravo na son i uslovnïye refleksï: kolïbel'nïye pesni v sovetskoy kul'ture (1930–1950-ye godï)', in Nataliya Borisova *et al.* (ed.), *SSSR: Territoriya lyubvi* (Moscow, 2008), 125n197.

EXAMPLE 11.1. *The Kremlin at Night,* opening.

Someone [sic] somewhere clanked very faintly in the night. / It is the Old Woman of History taking out her keys.

EXAMPLE 11.2. *The Kremlin at Night,* bars 180–3.

agriculture. They depart towards sunrise, but Stalin remains at his desk. He is eventually persuaded to rest by a mysterious old woman who turns out to be the personification of History, and who chides him for overtaxing his strength. The poem ends with an evocation of the dawn breaking over Moscow as Stalin falls asleep. Its dismal quality can only be appreciated fully in the original Russian: Vasilyev's clumsy scansion, cacophonous rhymes, and infelicitous word choices produce an inadvertently comical impression and undermine the author's attempts to maintain an elevated stylistic register. There are some ludicrous moments of bathos, such as the account of farmers and workers bringing grain samples and machine parts to their meeting with the Great Leader, or the following description of the Kremlin telephones:[24]

А кремлёвские палаты	And the Kremlin halls
Чудеса таят,	house wonders:
Чудодеи-аппараты	miracle-working machines
На столах стоят.	stand on the tables.
По невиданной[25] проводке	Along an invisible wire
По путям прямым	by direct routes
Говорит с Кремлём Чукотка,	Chukotka[26] talks to the Kremlin
Отвечает Крым.	and the Crimea answers.

Pragmatic considerations aside, Vasilyev's poem had one distinct advantage from a compositional point of view: because the action takes place at night, it afforded the opportunity of composing a lyrical setting (Myaskovsky styled the work a 'cantata-nocturne') which could dispense with the kind of noisy bombast generally considered de rigueur in works of this nature. Cantatas on Soviet themes at this period tended to follow a standard pattern: a stirring opening, a slower lyrical central section, typically expressing pious aspirations for the future, and an affirmative conclusion that culminated in a rousing peroration. The general effect was mostly platitudinous

---

24   The version of the poem quoted is here is the one that Myaskovsky originally set. When the full score was published in 1968, the text was revised to eliminate catachreses and references to Stalin.

25   A typical example of Vasilyev's tendency to misuse words: the adjective *nevidanniy*, 'hitherto unseen' or 'unprecedented', is incongruous in this context. In the 1968 version, the similar-sounding *nevidimïy*, 'invisible', was substituted, which makes more sense. I have amended the English translation accordingly.

26   Chukotka is a region in the extreme far east of the Russian Federation. Vasilyev's image suggests that Stalin's paternal vigilance extended to the remotest parts of the USSR.

in the extreme, as Soviet music critics eventually came to acknowledge.[27] Myaskovsky was plainly reluctant to adopt this hackneyed formula.

While *The Kremlin at Night* cannot be described as being amongst his finest achievements, it displays his usual high level of technical competence and has some effective moments. Roughly twenty minutes in length, the cantata comprises five linked sections, the second and fourth of which respectively feature the solo tenor and soprano. Its harmonic language is firmly tonal, with pronounced modal inflexions, and at times evinces surprising stylistic similarities to the music of Vaughan Williams – the parallel triadic motion that accompanies the opening theme furnishing a good instance in point (ex. 11.1). Mindful of official strictures, Myaskovsky took care to ensure that the vocal writing was not only melodious, but 'Russian'-sounding: the soprano aria, for example, is cast as a folk song–like *kolïbel'naya pesnya*, or lullaby (ex. 11.2). The choral writing is carefully designed to allow the text to remain clearly intelligible throughout, and the orchestration, while uncomplicated, is effective and makes telling use of subtle colouristic effects. Although it rises at times to dramatic climaxes, the work is predominantly serene and meditative in mood, and ends with an atmospheric coda evoking the breaking dawn depicted at the end of Vasilyev's poem. Whatever Myaskovsky's feelings about writing a cantata in praise of Stalin, he somehow managed to come up with music that was not banal.

The other scores he sketched that summer suggest that weariness and ill health were preventing him from working at his best. The *Pathetic Overture*, op. 76, a sonata-form movement prefaced by a slow introduction, feels overlong for its thematic material. The Twelfth String Quartet, op. 77, has one excellent movement – a quirky Scherzo, dominated by energetic cross rhythms and striking bitonal clashes of superimposed perfect fifths – but the others are less cogent: the finale is especially problematic, as the opening fast momentum, necessary to provide contrast after the preceding lengthy Andante, is not sufficiently sustained, being twice interrupted by extended slow episodes. Myaskovsky returned from Nikolina Gora on 13 September and spent his spare time over the following weeks finalising the score of the new quartet and revising the Violin Sonata and *The Kremlin at Night*. The Moscow Conservatoire choir and orchestra began to rehearse the cantata in early October, and despite an unpromising start, gave an assured account of the work under the direction of Nikolay Anosov at the premiere on 15 November. The audience response was sufficiently enthusiastic for the piece to be encored.[28]

27 See, for example, Georgiy Khubov, 'Muzïka i sovremennost': O zadachakh razvitiya sovetskoy muzïki', *Sovetskaya muzïka*, 4 (1953), 16–22.

28 'Vïpiski', 15 November 1947, RGALI, 2040/1/65, l. 87.

On the face of it, musical life was continuing as normal, notwithstanding the disquieting discussions at the Composers' Union conference the previous year. Myaskovsky's diary records several other performances of his work around this time. The cantata's premiere clashed with a symphony concert featuring the Twenty-Fourth Symphony under Stasevich. On 18 November, Gauk gave a 'boring' account of the Twenty-Fifth Symphony and five days later performed the *Pathetic Overture*. The Twelfth String Quartet was premiered by the Beethoven Quartet in the Small Hall of the Moscow Conservatoire on November. In early November, the honorary title 'National Artist of the USSR' was conferred on Prokofiev, Shostakovich, Shaporin, Shebalin, and Khachaturian. Premieres of other major works composed for the celebrations to mark the thirtieth anniversary of the October Revolution continued to take place – including Prokofiev's cantata *Flourish, Mighty Land*, Khachaturian's Third Symphony, and, at the Bolshoi Theatre, a new opera *The Great Friendship*, by Myaskovsky's former student Vano Muradeli. The members of the Stalin Prize committee did their customary rounds of the concert halls, theatres, museums, and galleries. There were unmistakable signs, however, that trouble was brewing. On 24 November, a functionary of the Committee for Artistic Affairs notified Myaskovsky that *The Kremlin at Night* had been banned for 'mysticism' – an epithet that the composer noted in his diary with a bewildered accompanying exclamation mark.[29] A few weeks later, the newspaper *Soviet Art* carried a lengthy press release announcing the topics to be discussed at the forthcoming first national Composers' Union congress, the first in the union's history, which was planned to run from 26 February to 3 March. Though praising the 'great successes' achieved in some areas of Soviet composition, the anonymous author declared 'the struggle with modernist tendencies' to be far from over and underlined the pertinence to musical life of the Central Committee's recent 'historic' resolutions on literature and art. The piece called for a more thoroughgoing 'democratisation' of Soviet orchestral and chamber music, which, it alleged, were still found difficult of comprehension by 'even the musically trained masses amongst Soviet listeners', and suggested that critics had been negligent in pointing out composers' failings – especially their conspicuous disregard of genres with more widespread appeal. Accompanying the press release was a short piece by Asafiev entitled 'Music for the Millions', in which the eminent critic, echoing the rhetoric of his contributions to *Modern Music* over twenty years previously, exhorted composers 'to strive for a musical language that would be audible to the hearts of many millions' and warned those who sought to be original 'by speaking only in their own dialect, striving not to repeat themselves or to resemble anyone else' that the time had come 'to think

29   Ibid., 24 November 1947, l. 870b.

about the future of their creative development'.[30] With the publication of these articles, it was not difficult to surmise what lay in store.

Behind the scenes, preparations had been underway at the Department of Agitation and Propaganda for Zhdanov to instigate a large-scale enquiry into the state of musical life, along similar lines to his preceding interventions in other domains. The circumstances that directed the Party's attention to music, however, were rather more complex, even if the basic intention remained the same – to crush dissent amongst the intelligentsia.[31] Throughout 1947, this broader campaign continued apace, acquiring increased momentum after a manufactured scandal centring on the microbiologists Grigory Roskin and Nina Klyuyeva, who were denounced for publishing in the United States the findings of their joint research project on cancer treatment. The incident served as a pretext for the government to reinforce its repressive surveillance of intellectual and cultural life to eradicate 'kowtowing to the West' [*nizkopoklonstvo pered Zapadom*]. On 28 March 1947, the Politburo issued a resolution convening quasi-military 'courts of honour' to investigate 'antipatriotic, anti-state, and anti-Soviet' actions committed by managerial and scientific personnel in a range of government departments.[32] Forums (euphemistically described as 'creative discussions') were organised in philosophy and other fields to eradicate ideological heterodoxy and enforce adherence to xenophobic narratives of Russian intellectual and cultural supremacy.[33] It was probably only a matter of time before music came under the spotlight, but adventitious factors seem to have hastened the process.

The first was Zhdanov's decision to appoint a new deputy director at the Department of Agitation and Propaganda in September 1947 – the forty-one-year-old Dmitry Shepilov, who had previously headed the propaganda department of *Pravda* and was regarded as one of the Party's rising talents.[34]

---

30 'Muzïka dlya millionov', *Sovetskoye iskusstvo*, 20 December 1947.

31 A comprehensive account of the ideological campaigns of 1948–9 in Soviet music, drawing on documentary evidence available since *glasnost'*, has yet to be written. Yekaterina Vlasova's monograph *1948 god v sovetskoy muzïke* (Moscow, 2010) offers the most complete account to date.

32 'Postanovleniye Politburo TsK VKP(b) o sudakh chesti v ministerstvakh SSSR i tsentral'nïkh vedomstvakh', 28 March 1947, in Nikolay Sidorov, '"TsK vskrïl presmïkatel'stvo pered zagranitsey". Kak sozdavalis' "sudï chesti" v tsentral'nïkh organakh', *Istochnik*, 6 (1994), 68–9.

33 For an account of the 'creative discussions' in philosophy in 1947, see Ethan Pollock, *Stalin and the Soviet Science Wars* (Princeton and Oxford, 2006), 15–40.

34 For an outline of Shepilov's career, see Stephen Bittner's 'introduction' to Dmitriy Shepilov, *The Kremlin Scholar: A Memoir of Soviet Politics under Stalin and Khrushchev*, ed. Stephen V. Bittner, trans. Anthony Austin (New Haven and London, 2007), ix–xxvi.

A lawyer and economist by training, Shepilov hero-worshipped Zhdanov and carried out his new duties with zeal. He was keenly interested in music, had a pleasant baritone voice, and enjoyed singing Russian folk songs at musical evenings hosted by Tikhon Khrennikov, who would soon become his protégé.[35] His tastes did not extend to modern music, which he disliked intensely. According to an essay that Shepilov contributed as a supplement to Khrennikov's autobiography, the proposal to instigate a campaign for the ideological reform of musical life originated with him, prompted by his anxieties about 'harmful' and 'corrupting' artistic tendencies emanating from the West: he claimed that Zhdanov readily approved the idea and encouraged him to take the initiative, by-passing Mikhail Suslov, his rather inert superior.[36] Whether or not this is true (the reliability of Shepilov's reminiscences is open to question, as he gave conflicting accounts of events and sought to downplay the more dubious aspects of his behaviour), research has shown that he was indisputably the driving force behind the campaign's earlier stages.[37]

In early December, Shepilov submitted to the Central Committee a ten-page report on Soviet musical life, which he had drafted in consultation with a group of musicologists that included Asafiev's former student Boris Yarustovsky, a specialist advisor to Shepilov's department who also played a central role in events.[38] Although it opened with a brief acknowledgement of 'significant successes', Shepilov's account was overwhelmingly negative and reiterated in intensified form the criticisms voiced at the Composers' Union conference the previous year. The country's leading composers were deemed to be excessively preoccupied with the forms of abstract instrumental music to the detriment of 'democratic' genres, and their music held to exhibit 'formalistic and individualistic tendencies' of a kind which had been 'unmasked' in recent resolutions on literature and drama. Soviet

---

35   See Tikhon Khrennikov, 'Sud'ba chelovecheskaya', in Tamara Tolchanova and Mikhail Lozhnikov (ed.), *I primknuvshiy k nim Shepilov: Pravda o cheloveke, uchyonom, voine, politike* (Moscow, 1998), 146–51.

36   Dmitriy Shepilov, 'Post-scriptum: Ya skazal, chto nam nado gotovit' takoy dokument', in Khrennikov, *Tak èto bïlo*, 144–5.

37   In a second account, Shepilov claimed that Zhdanov was responsible for setting events in motion: 'Vospominaniya', *Voprosï istorii*, 5 (1998), 12–20. The editors of a major collection of documents pertaining to the ideological campaigns of the late Stalinist period point out that Shepilov's memoirs are demonstrably dishonest in their attempts to deflect responsibility for his actions, and that he played a crucial role in shaping and implementing the Party's repressive policies: Dzhakhangir Nadzhafov and Zinaida Belousova (ed.), *Stalin i kosmopolitizm: Dokumentï Agitpropa TsK KPSS, 1945–1953* (Moscow, 2005), 10–11.

38   'O nedostatkakh v razvitii sovetskoy muzïki', RGASPI, 17/125/571, ll. 103–12. The report was first published as an appendix to Khrennikov's autobiography *Tak èto bïlo* without explanation or accompanying commentary.

critics and musicologists, composition teachers at the conservatoires, and the senior management of the Composers' Union and the Committee for Artistic Affairs were all found to have been seriously negligent.

Interestingly, of the composers to whom Shepilov alludes, Myaskovsky, rather than Shostakovich or Prokofiev, is singled out for the most extensive adverse comment. Shepilov derided his work for its 'subjectivism', 'wilful complication of musical language', and 'formalistic gimmicks' and claimed that *The Kremlin at Night* demonstrated Myaskovsky's inability to compose in democratic genres 'which require the realistic representation of the life of the people, its thoughts and emotional experiences':

> This work should have aimed to give a realistic picture of the Kremlin at night, in which Comrade Stalin lives and works. Not only do the text and music of the composition fail to convey this image, but at times they actually pervert it . . . . The composer uses a feeble, melodically disjointed tune as the work's basic musical theme. There are many episodes of a deliberate, semi-mystical mysteriousness . . . . The climax is an episode depicting Stalin being visited by 'The Old Woman of History'. . . . The music of this episode, which is written in the form of a lullaby, is notable for its extremely gloomy colouring. In general, the cantata is consistently in the spirit of romantic tales of chivalry, which have nothing to do with reality. Curiously, this work was accepted by the Committee for Artistic Affairs and recommended for publication. The Composers' Union press issued 500 copies of the composition. It was only taken out of circulation after the intervention of the Department of Propaganda.

As this passage reveals, Myaskovsky's cantata had been banned on the instructions of Shepilov's department. Shepilov was evidently displeased because its portrayal of Stalin was unconventional. In contemporary novels and paintings, the Great Leader was typically represented as a paragon of the manly virtues.[39] Myaskovsky's introspective setting did not project these qualities. To judge from the ironical exclamation marks with which Shepilov peppered his quotations from Vasilyev's poem, he objected to its depiction of Stalin seeking advice from blacksmiths and country yokels and being summoned to bed by an elderly crone. There are, of course, multiple ironies attendant on his contention that the cantata failed to show Stalin in a sufficiently 'realistic' light, especially when one considers that in his declining years the dictator spent most nights at his suburban dachas rather than in his Kremlin apartment – often whiling them away in drinking bouts with members of his close circle.[40]

---

39   See Igor' Golomshtok, 'Sotsrealizm i izobrazitel'noye iskusstvo', in Khans Gyunter and Yevgeniy Dobrenko (ed.), *Sotsrealisticheskiy kanon* (St Petersburg, 2000), 134–45.

40   William Taubman, *Khrushchev: The Man and His Era* (New York, 2003), 211ff.

One of the chief criticisms to emerge from Shepilov's report was that Myaskovsky had conspicuously failed to conform to the tenets of Socialist Realism over a long period. Most fundamentally, and most seriously from an official point of view, his output demonstrated little evidence of active political engagement and 'Party spirit'. His persistent concentration on composing complex 'abstract' instrumental works devoid of popular appeal furnished damning evidence of his reluctance to fulfil the Party's expectations, as well as his lack of interest in writing music that mass audiences would find accessible. Shepilov's verdict, of course, was correct: Myaskovsky's supposed adherence to Socialist Realism had been entirely a matter of lip-service. Since 1932, he had maintained an undeviating focus on the handful of genres that interested him (principally, the symphony and the string quartet), making only occasional pragmatic concessions to circumstances. If he had genuinely embraced the doctrine, his output should have been very different, and would have contained a far higher concentration of tuneful vocal and choral works and compositions on explicitly ideological themes. It is vital to emphasise this point, especially in view of long-standing lazy assumptions that Myaskovsky's later work exemplifies Socialist Realist musical composition. In the view of a leading Party ideologue such as Shepilov, who was nothing if not well-versed in official cultural policy and in a position to pronounce authoritatively on the subject, Myaskovsky's music scarcely deserved to be described as Socialist Realist at all.

Shepilov's report boded ill in other respects. He accused the composition teachers at the Moscow Conservatoire of failing to foster enthusiasm for the 'democratic' genres of opera and vocal music, pointing out that the final-year students mostly submitted large-scale instrumental works as their graduation exercise: 'It ought to be remembered that the finest Russian composers chose to write as their graduation exercise works in popular genres which were accessible to the people. Thus, Tchaikovsky wrote a cantata in his final year while simultaneously working on an opera; Rachmaninoff's graduation exercise was the opera *Aleko*; and so on'. It was bad enough that Myaskovsky should write the kind of music that he did, but Shepilov regarded him as exerting a baneful influence on young composers, turning them away from the 'healthy' traditions of the Russian classics. His report ended with a call for action. As the threat to Soviet music had assumed such menacing proportions, he recommended that the issues he had raised should be discussed in depth at the forthcoming First All-USSR Congress of Soviet Composers.

While planning for the congress was in progress, circumstances conspired to draw further unwanted attention to musical affairs. The lavish Bolshoi Theatre production of Muradeli's opera *The Great Friendship* was the most imposing of the musical events planned to mark the anniversary celebrations of the October Revolution. Conceived as a fulsome tribute to the revolutionary hero Sergo Ordzhonikidze and to Stalin's native Georgia, the opera enjoyed considerable success at its premiere in Stalino (now Donetsk) on 28 September 1947 and went into production in about twenty other cities shortly thereafter.[41] However, permission was only granted for a lavish Bolshoi Theatre production after considerable vacillation on the part of Mikhail Khrapchenko, the chairman of the Committee for Artistic Affairs, who was clearly nervous about its reception.[42] The production eventually went ahead and opened on 7 November 1947[43], but Khrapchenko's anxieties proved well-founded. When Stalin and Zhdanov attended what appears to have been a private command performance on 5 January 1948, the dictator was not slow to make his displeasure known and to condemn the work on both musical and ideological grounds.[44] To make matters worse, enquiries made at Stalin's behest about the cost of the Bolshoi production revealed that not only had it considerably exceeded its budget but Muradeli had been paid commissioning fees for the opera by no fewer than seventeen different theatres.[45] These financial irregularities were a particularly sensitive matter, given the importance that Stalin attached to opera as a genre and the government's generous financial support of the Bolshoi's efforts to create a Socialist Realist operatic repertoire.[46]

The opera became the focus of a scandal that swiftly engulfed many of the leading figures in Soviet musical life, Myaskovsky included. The following day, on 6 January, Zhdanov summoned the hapless Muradeli and his librettist Georgy Mdivani to a meeting, which was also attended by members of the opera's cast and representatives of the Bolshoi management. The transcript of this meeting records that Zhdanov subjected *The Great Friendship* to scathing criticism for its feebleness of melodic invention,

---

41 See 'Proekt zapiski upravleniya propagandï i agitatsii TsK VKP(b) sekretariyu A. A. Zhdanovu o zapreshchenii postanovki operï V. I. Muradeli "Velikaya druzhba"', in Artizov and Naumov (ed.), *Vlast' i khudozhestvennaya intelligentsiya*, 627–8.

42 Tomoff, *Creative Union*, 131.

43 Valeriy Zarubin, *Bol'shoy teatr: Pervïye postanovki oper na russkoy stsene, 1825–1993* (Moscow, 1994), 252.

44 Leonid Maksimenkov, 'Partiya – Nash rulevoy', *Muzïkal'naya zhizn'*, 13–14 (1993), 6–8. After the performance, Stalin and his entourage went back to the dictator's Kremlin office, where they continued their discussion of the work: see Anatoliy Chernyayev *et al.*, 'Posetiteli kremlyovskogo kabineta I. V. Stalina: 1947–1949', *Istoricheskiy arkhiv*, 5–6 (1996), 25; and Kees Boterbloem, *The Life and Times of Andrei Zhdanov, 1896–1948* (Montreal, 2004), 318.

45 Tomoff, *Creative Union*, 137–9.

46 See Yekaterina Vlasova, 'The Stalinist Opera Project', in Patrick Zuk and Marina Frolova-Walker (ed.), *Russian Music since 1917: Reappraisal and Rediscovery* (Oxford, 2017), 164–87.

noisy orchestration, and strident dissonances, all of which he interpreted as symptomatic of modernist decadence. Anyone listening to the opera today is likely to be bewildered by Zhdanov's characterisation of the score, as it is strongly indebted to nineteenth-century models both in conception and in its musical language.[47] Muradeli attempted to shift the blame for the opera's shortcomings onto his composition teachers:

> When I enrolled at the Moscow Conservatoire, I loved folk music, and I also loved our Russian classical composers. But when I started to write my first small pieces, which I tried to base on folk music and the Russian classics, I was told they were unoriginal and that there was nothing new in them. . . . At the conservatoire, they forced us to study 'modern models' and poured scorn on 'traditionalism'.[48]

As everyone in the room would have been aware, Muradeli had studied under Myaskovsky. His contention that his talent had been forced to develop in an unnatural direction by his conservatoire training was backed up by Khrapchenko, who was eager to dissociate himself from the fiasco and deflect responsibility away from the Committee for Artistic Affairs: 'Our major musical figure is Myaskovsky – the teacher of a whole generation of young Soviet composers, amongst them Muradeli. In his time, Myaskovsky himself was under the influence of modern music and he has educated his students in its spirit. Eliminating these harmful enthusiasms is a very complex and protracted process'.[49]

The investigation gathered pace, as Zhdanov's department convened further meetings and elicited submissions from musical experts who could be relied on to support the general line that the Party proposed to take. On 10–13 January 1948, Zhdanov presided over a three-day forum attended by leading figures from the Soviet musical world. Its ostensible purpose was to discuss the fiasco of Muradeli's opera, but its scope quickly broadened to consider issues of a more general nature. In his second address, Zhdanov harshly castigated Myaskovsky, along with Shostakovich, Prokofiev, and other leading composers for the 'formalist' tendencies manifest in their 'false, vulgar, and frequently simply pathological' music and intimated that

47 The Soviet record label *Melodiya* issued a recording of excerpts from the opera in 1966 (Melodiya 33D-17647 and 33D-17648).

48 'Zapis′ soveshchaniya tov. Zhdanova s avtorami i ispolnitelyami operï *Velikaya druzhba*: 6 yanvarya 1948 g.', reproduced without identification of its source in Khrennikov, *Tak éto bïlo*, 198–9.

49 'Zapis′ soveshchaniya tov. Zhdanova', 201. In a note to Myaskovsky, Muradeli claimed – rather implausibly – that he had not intended to criticise his composition teachers, but the conservatoire 'environment': undated communication, RGALI, 2040/2/195, l. 3.

they had abused their positions of responsibility for personal gain.[50] Some of the participants were manifestly pleased at this turn of events – amongst them, the eminent pianist Alexander Goldenweiser, whose diary records his eagerness to 'seize the opportunity' to make his views heard.[51] His speech decried the 'harmonic chaos' and decadence of modernist music influenced by contemporary Western trends, and its corrupting effects on young Soviet musicians.[52] At its close, he sought permission to send Zhdanov a written statement about other matters that he had been unable to discuss in the time at his disposal – a request which was granted.

A copy of his submission was preserved in the Department of Agitation and Propaganda's archive, together with several others elicited around the same time.[53] Goldenweiser took full advantage of the opportunity to elaborate his criticisms and make them more explicit. He asserted that the country's leading composers disdained 'the great models of the Russian and Western classics' and encouraged the blind imitation of 'modernistic, formalistic' trends. As a result, the baneful effects of Western influences were ubiquitously apparent in composition teaching, music criticism, and programming practices. This dire situation, he claimed, was largely caused by the machinations of an élite group dominating the Composers' Union, whose members promoted their own work at the expense of everyone else's and blocked the performance and publication of music by those who did not share their decadent artistic outlook. In support of this contention, Goldenweiser described how his own compositions had been sidelined, instancing the union's refusal to fund the performance of a cantata that he had written to commemorate the thirtieth anniversary of the October Revolution.

A similar conspiracy theory was expounded by the musicologist and Party member Nikolay Sherman. Goldenweiser mostly refrained from naming names, but Sherman did not hesitate to identify the person he deemed chiefly responsible for the degeneracy of Soviet musical life – Myaskovsky, an account of whose purported vices occupies much of his submission of 13 January 1948. Sherman ascribed the unhealthy tendencies in Soviet composition to the baneful influence of Myaskovsky's 'musical

50 'Vïstupleniye A. A. Zhdanova', *Soveshchaniye deyateley sovetskoy muzïki v TsK VKP(b)* (Moscow, 1948), 135–6.

51 Gol'denveyzer, entry for 9 January 1948, *Dnevnik*, tetrad' 29, GMK.

52 'Rech' A. B. Gol'denveyzera', *Soveshchaniye deyateley sovetskoy muzïki*, 54–9.

53 A folder of some three hundred pages of documents pertaining to the department's intervention in musical life has been preserved in RGASPI, 17/125/636. The contents seem rather random and date from the period January–June 1948 only: other items could well have been lost or destroyed. Goldenweiser's submission, entitled 'Voprosï muzïkal'nogo fronta', comprises ll. 11–35 and is dated 19 January 1948.

intellectualism'. The composition courses at the Moscow Conservatoire were held to be a 'concentrated exposition' of all the fundamental principles of this 'intellectualism', 'elevated to the status of an incontestable dogma'. The students were forced to concentrate on writing complex 'formalist' instrumental compositions rather than in genres accessible to the masses. Though devoid of creative talent himself, Myaskovsky exerted a stranglehold over Soviet compositional affairs because he was the sinister *éminence grise* at the centre of a nexus of 'saboteurs' who obediently did his bidding:

> Myaskovsky is the most influential and authoritative composer in Soviet musical life. But his influence is not founded on the nationwide acceptance of his music. On the contrary, his music is only recognised by a very limited circle of musicians, who, if truth be told, exert a big influence on the activities of our musical institutions and our press. . . . Myaskovsky's influence is based on his outstanding organisational abilities, which have allowed him to gather around him the people he needs, maintain strict discipline amongst them, place them where he wants them and constantly direct their activities, while remaining in the background. . . . Myaskovsky's discipline and authority enable him to stifle dissenting opinions held by any of his students who have come to the conclusion that his pedagogical approach is very deeply flawed. Myaskovsky is the only Soviet composer whom no-one dares to criticise.[54]

Sherman accordingly recommended that the activities of Myaskovsky and his associates should be publicly exposed and condemned, and that politically reliable musicians (amongst whom he presumably counted himself) should be entrusted with overseeing the necessary root and branch reforms of musical life.

Like Goldenweiser's submission, Sherman's was prompted by his resentment at what he believed to be his marginalisation by Myaskovsky's circle.[55] Both furnish evidence of the extent to which the outcomes of the 1948 campaign were shaped by professional jealousies and rivalries. The claustrophobic atmosphere engendered by Stalin's isolationist foreign policies exacerbated these tensions, as musical life became increasingly insular and inward-looking. When one considers that Myaskovsky was known to be a friend of Prokofiev, and that his former students Khachaturian and Shebalin

---

54   'O sovetskom muzïkal'nom tvorchestve', RGASPI, 17/125/636, ll. 65–6. On Sherman, see Patrick Zuk, 'Nikolay Myaskovsky and the Events of 1948', *Music and Letters* 1 (2012), 61–85.

55   Goldenweiser particularly resented being replaced by Shebalin as director of the Moscow Conservatoire in 1942: see Vlasova, *1948 god*, 248–50. Goldenweiser and Sherman were acquainted and knew of one another's behind-the-scenes involvement in the 1948 campaign. Goldenweiser's diary entry for 26 January 1948 records a conversation 'about musical affairs' with Sherman: '[he] knows significantly more than he's willing to let on. I don't want to repeat what he said'. Gol'denveyzer, *Dnevnik*, tetrad' 29, GMK.

were respectively de facto head of the Composers' Union and rector of the Moscow Conservatoire, it is not difficult to see how perceptions might have formed that he was at the centre of a powerful clique whose members received a disproportionate number of high-profile commissions and official honours. Another submission authored by the head of the Music Broadcasting Commission, Moisey Grinberg, complained that undeserving figures were being awarded Stalin Prizes (he instanced Shebalin as a case in point) and asserted that critics lauded the music of 'formalist' composers to the skies rather than criticising its glaring defects.[56] The fact that Myaskovsky had been awarded three Stalin Prizes first class while serving on the Prize Committee doubtless set malicious tongues wagging: his detractors were not to know that he had tried to withdraw his own compositions from consideration on more than one occasion.

Zhdanov's department perused this expert 'testimony' carefully and drew such conclusions as suited its purposes: that Soviet music was dominated by 'wreckers' who were acting as a conduit for decadent Western influences, corrupting Russian musical traditions, and wasting the government's arts budget. The text of a Central Committee resolution on music was drawn up and went through three drafts before being submitted to Stalin, who made further emendations before it was published in *Pravda* on 11 February 1948.[57] Despite being entitled 'On the Opera *The Great Friendship* by V. Muradeli', Muradeli's score merely furnished a convenient pretext for the Party to make wide-ranging criticisms of contemporary Soviet composition and aspects of the country's musical life along lines adumbrated in the documents discussed above. The resolution upbraided the Composers' Union and the Committee for Artistic Affairs for extensive failures of oversight. It deplored the state of Soviet music criticism and declared the country's conservatoires (especially the Moscow Conservatoire) to be hotbeds of formalism. Together with Shostakovich, Prokofiev, Khachaturian, Shebalin, and Gavriil Popov, Myaskovsky was condemned as a composer whose work 'evinced to a particularly pronounced extent formalistic perversions and anti-democratic musical tendencies that are alien to the Soviet people and its artistic tastes'. Amongst these 'perversions' were 'atonality, dissonance, and disharmony' as an expression of putative artistic 'progress', the eschewal of melodiousness, and a preoccupation with 'muddled, neurasthenic sound-combinations that transform music into cacophony'.

From this lurid characterisation, one might imagine that the country's leading composers were vying with one another to emulate the most *outré* stylistic tendencies of Western musical modernism, subjecting Soviet concertgoers to a ceaseless aural assault of ear-splitting cacophony. Under

56   RGASPI, 17/125/636, ll. 92–105.
57   See Maksimenkov, *Muzïka vmesto sumbura*, 289–304.

normal circumstances, the allegations would have been regarded as preposterous – but the circumstances were far from normal. Heads began to roll even before the promulgation of the resolution: on 26 January, the Politburo issued a decree dismissing Khapchenko as Chairman of the Committee for Artistic Affairs and removing Khachaturian and Muradeli from their positions in the Composers' Union. The senior managerial committees of both institutions were dissolved and reconstituted afresh, as was the Stalin Prize committee.[58] Other sackings would follow. To Myaskovsky's dismay, his colleague Igor Boelza was dismissed from his editorial posts at Muzgiz and at the newspaper *Soviet Art* because he had written appreciative articles about the music of the proscribed composers.[59] The air thickened with rumours as everyone waited to see what would happen next.

Myaskovsky's diary records that he spent much of January and early February ill with influenza. There is no reason to doubt the genuineness of his indisposition, but one suspects that he welcomed having a convenient excuse not to attend the meetings on 10–13 January with Zhdanov, and the others that followed in their wake. As late as the mid-1980s, Soviet publications avoided discussion of the anti-formalism campaign's effects on the proscribed composers because the subject was considered too sensitive.[60] Notwithstanding recent claims that these have been greatly exaggerated and that the campaign was ultimately an affair of minor importance,[61] there can be no doubt that the musicians at the centre of the controversy experienced it as a degrading ordeal. Olga Lamm's memoirs movingly depict its toll on Myaskovsky and Prokofiev – both in rapidly deteriorating health, under severe strain, beset by money worries, and subjected to humiliating indignities.

From the outset, Myaskovsky behaved with remarkable composure. His student Grigory Frid, who met him on his way to the conservatoire on the day the resolution was promulgated, later recalled:

> In response to my salutation Myaskovsky doffed his cap and exchanged bows with me in a courtly fashion. ... When I subsequently remembered Myaskovsky's elegant figure with his doffed cap in his hand, I thought that his gesture had a metaphorical meaning – the final greeting,

---

58 Artizov and Naumov, *Vlast' i khudozhestvennaya intelligentsiya*, 628–9.

59 Grzegorz Wiśniewski, *Między Polską i Rosją: Igor i Swiatosław Bełzowie* (Warsaw, 2016), 40.

60 To take just one example: Gavriil Popov's wife Zarui Apetyan was forced by the censor to remove his diary entries about his condemnation in 1948 from the selection of Popov's writings that she published in 1986. See Vera Vasina-Grossman, 'Professiya – Istorik', *Muzïkal'naya zhizn'* 16 (1988), 8.

61 See Leonid Maksimenkov, 'Slovo o Khrennikove', in Andrey Kokarev (ed.), *Tikhon Nikolayevich Khrennikov: K 100-letiyu so dnya rozhdeniya* (Moscow, 2013), 135–8.

the final farewell to old illusions and hopes... and, at the same time, conveying that a man must preserve his dignity, no matter what the circumstances.[62]

Myaskovsky's gnomic diary entry about events presents a similarly imperturbable front to the reader: 'An interesting resolution of the Communist Party Central Committee in connection with Muradeli's opera. Positively correct, negatively inaccurate. [*Pozitivno vernoye, negativno netochnoye.*] I fear that it will do Soviet music more harm than good. All the mediocrities promptly rejoiced and have started to bestir themselves'.[63] He writes as though he were observing events with Olympian detachment: his employment of the bland epithet 'interesting' is surely ironic, though it is more difficult to know what to make of his puzzling characterisation of the resolution as 'positively correct' but 'negatively inaccurate'. In light of the numerous critical remarks in his diaries about other Soviet musicians (and not just composers, but also performers and writers on music), one possible interpretation suggests itself: he agreed with the Party's verdict that the state of Soviet musical life was far from satisfactory, but rejected the resolution's diagnosis of its shortcomings. His allusion to 'mediocrities' strongly suggests that he believed the problems to be caused by shoddy professional and artistic standards – a stance that would have been entirely consistent with views he had held since the very beginning of his career. In the short term, at least, his foreboding that the resolution would do little to help matters proved prescient.

Tellingly, his diary entry concludes with a description of his ongoing revisions to the Twenty-Fifth Symphony, as though to impress on the reader that the Party's damning indictment had not disrupted his creative routine in the slightest, but his mask of imperturbability concealed wholly predictable emotions of anger and disgust. Myaskovsky was outraged to discover that several notable figures in the musical community had agreed to assist Zhdanov, seeking to exploit the situation to their advantage. Goldenweiser greeted the publication of the resolution with unconcealed jubilation as marking the downfall of decadent modern art. Yury Shaporin hoped to profit from the discrediting of Myaskovsky, Shostakovich, and Shebalin to establish himself as the leading composition teacher at the Moscow Conservatoire. Most egregious of all was the conduct of Boris Asafiev, who consented to allow a keynote address endorsing the resolution to be delivered in his name at the forthcoming First Composers' Union Congress. (Asafiev was by then a chronic invalid and unable to leave his apartment, so it would have been infeasible for him to deliver it himself.) Relations

62 Grigoriy Frid, *Dorogoy ranenoy pamyati* (Moscow, 2009), 235.
63 'Vïpiski', 8 February 1948, RGALI, 2040/1/65, l. 880b.

with Asafiev had broken down altogether by that point, but Myaskovsky continued to make allowances for his behaviour. Despite Asafiev's suspicious responses to him, he preferred to try to understand rather than to condemn, as he told Kabalevsky in a letter of June 1948, and to believe that the sentiments expressed in Asafiev's keynote address were sincerely held, if seriously misguided. He acknowledged that he was virtually alone in taking such a charitable view of his former friend's actions, but as he explained in the same letter: 'I have a very strange nature: in order to wreck a friendship with me, I would have to be outwardly and inwardly persuaded that a person displayed a degree of dishonourableness exhibited only by inveterate gangsters, blackguards, and scoundrels, and for which I could find no mitigating explanations'.[64]

The circumstances are unclear, but his attitude to Asafiev's behaviour changed subsequently – perhaps on discovering the full extent of his behind-the-scenes involvement in events.[65] Far from being an unwilling accomplice, Asafiev eagerly seized the opportunity to avenge himself on colleagues whom he believed to have thwarted his career as a composer and failed to acknowledge his talent. As a reward for his cooperation with Zhdanov's department, he was appointed chairman of the reconstituted presidium of the Composers' Union. The musicologist Tamara Livanova, who came into regular professional contact with Asafiev around this time, recalled that his vanity was gratified 'as never before' by his new post: he saw it as a professional triumph and a belated compensation for years of humiliation and neglect. As she pointed out, the cynicism of the appointment was blatant. Asafiev passed his final years in an inebriated stupor: she often found him so drunk as to be incapable of forming a coherent sentence, let alone helping to direct one of the country's major artistic institutions.[66] Myaskovsky evidently regarded him as having finally crossed a line that made any attempt to revive their relationship impossible: according to Olga Lamm, he was unable to forgive what he regarded as a shameful betrayal by someone whom he had once counted amongst his closest friends.[67]

Asafiev was by no means alone in acting as he did. Reflecting on the anti-formalism campaign in old age, the eminent Soviet musicologist Daniel Zhitomirsky recalled finding it a sordid episode. Some of his colleagues displayed a nauseating servility, vying with one another to praise the

64 Myaskovsky to Kabalevsky, 18 June 1948, RGALI, 2017/1/91, l. 17.

65 For a discussion, see Patrick Zuk, 'Boris Asafiev in 1948', *Journal of the Royal Musical Association*, 1 (2019), 123–56.

66 Livanova, 'Vospominaniya', RNMM, 194/1754a, l. 550.

67 Lamm, 'Vospominaniya', 238–44.

resolution's 'wisdom' and 'historic significance'.[68] Olga Lamm was similarly repulsed by the 'well-wishers' who made a point of calling on Myaskovsky to relish his discomfiture and took visible pleasure in attempting to relay gossip. (Some of the stories circulating were not merely lurid, but quite fantastic: Goldenweiser recorded hearing from his student Grigory Ginzburg that Myaskovsky, Prokofiev, Shostakovich, Khachaturian, and other notable Moscow musicians attended private 'booze-ups' (*p'yanki*) hosted by a recently exposed American spy who had plied them liberally with alcohol to loosen their tongues about sensitive matters.[69]) Other colleagues were terrified of being compromised by association. Although Kabalevsky's name was not mentioned in the resolution, documents circulating in Zhdanov's department named him as one of the 'formalists': he had a narrow escape and was clearly unnerved by events.[70] Olga Lamm learned that he had called on Myaskovsky and, in a highly emotional scene, begged him on his knees to write a letter to Stalin recanting his errors – which Myaskovsky refused point-blank to do.[71] Prokofiev telephoned Myaskovsky to suggest that he make a statement expressing regret for his artistic failings, as he himself had done. Myaskovsky's sister Yevgeniya recalled that he met with a cold reception: 'That is your personal business', Myaskovsky told him, 'and you must act as you consider necessary. I have done nothing that requires me to justify myself'. He then replaced the receiver and terminated the conversation.[72]

Amidst all of this unpleasantness, however, there were occasional heartening indications that members of the general public were perfectly capable of making up their own minds about the Party's treatment of the condemned composers. Shortly after the resolution's promulgation, Myaskovsky received the following communication:

68 Daniėl' Zhitomirskiy, 'Na puti k istoricheskoy pravde', *Muzïkal'naya zhizn'*, 13 (1988), 4–5.

69 Gol'denveyzer, *Dnevnik*, tetrad' 30, GMK, entry for 18 April 1948.

70 Zarui Apetyan claimed that Popov's name was substituted for Kabalevsky's in the text of the resolution after an intervention by Kabalevsky's wife, who had good contacts in the security organs: see Lamm, 'Vospominaniya', 266, n4. This claim is not borne out by the surviving drafts of the resolution (see fn58 above), all of which mention Popov. Kabalevsky was described as a 'formalist' in at least one memorandum submitted to Zhdanov, however: Maksimenkov, *Muzïka vmesto sumbura*, 306.

71 Lamm, 'Vospominaniya', 244–5. In a letter to Myaskovsky of 10 June 1948, Kabalevsky wrote to express his hope that their 'difficult conversations' about the resolution would not result in their permanent estrangement: RGALI, 2040/1/121, ll. 109–12. The conductor Ivan Petrov recalled being present when a group of visitors (whom he does not identify) urged Myaskovsky to write a letter to the Composers' Union recanting his 'formalist errors', but similarly met with a point-blank refusal: Petrov, 'Nastavnik i drug', 341.

72 Ikonnikov, *Khudozhnik nashikh dney*, 291. A similar version of the story is given in Lamm, 'Vospominaniya', 245.

Dear Nikolay Yakovlevich,

I am not a musician, but merely someone who loves Russian music. We are not acquainted and I do not seek your acquaintance (though I would consider it a great honour). You may consequently trust all the more fully in the sincerity of this letter. Its purpose is to express my sympathy (perhaps unnecessarily) on learning of the unexpected and undeserved calumny to which you were recently subjected, together with almost all the other outstanding creators of modern Russian music. . . . Our children and grandchildren will smile in surprise to learn that their art was once deemed 'alien to the people'. . . . The names of Myaskovsky, Shostakovich, and Prokofiev already form part of the golden treasury of Russian and world music. There is no power on this earth that can alter their standing. I cordially wish you long life and fresh achievements. History will assure your fame.[73]

Pressure to make a public statement of contrition mounted in the weeks preceding the First Composers' Union Congress, but Myaskovsky remained silent, adhering unwaveringly to the policy that he had followed since the mid-1920s. Shortly after the resolution was promulgated, Khrennikov called on Myaskovsky at home in his new official capacity as the union's General Secretary to request that he deliver a speech at a forthcoming series of meetings of Moscow composers to be held over six days between 17 and 25 February.[74] (Prokofiev's statement, which took the form of a letter addressed to Khrennikov and Khrapchenko's successor Polikarp Lebedev, was read out at this forum.[75]) Once again, Myaskovsky refused, telling Khrennikov: 'Deeds, not words, are what is expected of us now. That is our most important task, and we must fulfil it'. It would be implausible to interpret this ambiguous rejoinder as conveying Myaskovsky's burning desire to fulfil the creative responsibility that had been imposed on him by the Party, as Ikonnikov claimed in his biography.[76] If that had genuinely been the case, it is difficult to understand why he did not agree even to write a brief text that could have been read out on his behalf. Myaskovsky's remark permits of a very different interpretation – that the 'deeds' to which he referred were his refusals to demean himself by apologising. Far from making a show of compliance, he wished to resist in the only way that seemed feasible. By

73 S. Khramov to Myaskovsky, 20 February 1948, RGALI, 2040/2/302, l. 20.

74 Ikonnikov refers to Khrennikov's visit on page 292 of the first edition of his biography *Khudozhnik nashikh dney: N. Ya. Myaskovskiy* (Moscow, 1966) – but Khrennikov's name was deleted in the revised edition of 1982 (compare page 291 of the latter).

75 The text of the letter is reproduced in Mendel'son-Prokof'yeva, *O Sergeye Sergeyeviche Prokof'yeve*, 353–6.

76 Ikonnikov, *Khudozhnik nashikh dney*, 291–2.

remaining silent, he could convey his contempt for the resolution as a document that he refused to dignify with a single word of comment.

In the event, Myaskovsky did not attend the First Composers' Union Congress when it took place on the rescheduled dates of 19–25 April, as he was once again ill. That his absence was construed as a mute expression of defiance is confirmed by a report on the congress submitted by Shepilov to Zhdanov: Shepilov noted drily that although Myaskovsky, 'pleading indisposition, came to neither the meetings in the Composer's Union nor any meetings at the Congress', he was nonetheless well enough to celebrate his birthday with a large group of friends and colleagues who came to his apartment. His activities were evidently being monitored by informers in his circle – likely candidates being the composer Lev Knipper and his wife Masha. Interestingly, Shepilov's report reveals that many attendees at the congress made little attempt to hide their distaste for the proceedings. Of the condemned composers, only Shostakovich and Muradeli were present with any frequency: Khachaturian, Prokofiev, Popov, and Shebalin merely made fleeting appearances. Delegates spent much of the time talking in the corridors rather than attending sessions. A steady stream of anonymous notes made their way up to the podium, many containing derogatory remarks about the union's new secretariat or defending the proscribed composers.[77] Although Asafiev's keynote address (which was delivered by the composer Vladimir Vlasov) did not allude to Myaskovsky by name, he came in for sharp criticism in Khrennikov's speech. Surveying the development of Soviet music, the new head of the Composers' Union stressed Myaskovsky's close involvement in the 1920s with the Association for Modern Music, an organisation that he declared responsible for strengthening 'formalist tendencies' and encouraging 'grovelling' [*nizkopoklonstvo*] to the West. He alleged that Myaskovsky had been instrumental in fostering a 'modernist craze' [*sovremennichestvo*] and characterised his music as decadent and embodying a world view at odds with Soviet reality, instancing his Hippius settings and Sixth Symphony.[78]

The transcripts of the other sessions at the week-long conference make for monotonous reading, as the participants largely couched their criticisms of the 'formalists' in the same ritualised stock phrases of opprobrium. On the whole, Myaskovsky got off more lightly than Shostakovich and Prokofiev, though he is unlikely to have derived much comfort from

77 Shepilov to Zhdanov *et al.*, 21 April 1948, RGASPI, 17/125/636, ll. 229–32. See also Tomoff, *Creative Union*, 146–50.

78 Viktor Gorodinskiy *et al.* (ed.), *Pervïy vsesoyuznïy s"ezd sovetskikh kompozitorov 1948: Stenografcheskiy otchyot* (Moscow, 1948), 26–7, 31. Khrennikov recalled that his speech was drafted for him by a group of musicologists headed by Boris Yarustovsky, who also oversaw the preparation of Asafiev's keynote address: *Tak èto bïlo*, 130.

the fact: to Olga Lamm he remarked that the campaign revealed the 'igno-rance and lack of personal integrity' pervasive in Soviet musical life.[79] His overriding response to events seems to have been a desire to distance him-self as much as possible. He kept himself busy throughout the spring with mechanical tasks – reworking fugues dating from his conservatoire years into a set of pieces for young pianists, *Polyphonic sketches*, op. 78; revising his early symphonic poem *Silence* and an unpublished Overture in G major, written in 1907–11; and preparing piano reductions and correcting proofs of other works. His health continued to give cause for concern: he devel-oped pleurisy shortly before the congress and began to experience severe pain in his side. X-rays did not disclose any abnormalities and the diagnosis was inconclusive, though intercostal neuralgia was suggested as a possible cause.

Throughout these difficult months, friends such as Shebalin, Khachaturian and his wife Nina Makarova, and the conductor Ivan Petrov were steadfast in their support. Pavel Lamm devotedly tried to shield Myaskovsky from as much unpleasantness as he could. When May arrived and the weather became warmer, he encouraged him to take up residence at Nikolina Gora, hoping that his removal to the countryside, away from the tense atmosphere in Moscow, would lift his spirits and help to re-establish his creative rou-tine. Myaskovsky's sisters Yevgeniya and Valentina took turns to stay with him and did their best to dispel the oppressive mood. Even here, however, there were intrusive reminders of present difficulties. His former student Alexander Lokshin was summarily sacked from the conservatoire staff: his only misdemeanour had been to compose settings of the 'decadent' verse of Charles Baudelaire. Myaskovsky's efforts to intervene proved unavailing: like other casualties of the 1948 campaign, Lokshin subsequently experi-enced acute difficulty in finding alternative employment.[80] Myaskovsky's diary also alludes to the machinations of the musicologist Yury Keldïsh 'and other musical parasites', and the arrival of a 'stupid' letter from Ikonnikov, once again dispensing unsolicited advice.[81] Having informed Myaskovsky that the Committee for Artistic Affairs intended to commission either a 'Slavonic symphony' or a cantata, Ikonnikov urged him to pay particular attention to 'themes connected with the reflection of our people's gigantic battles for a happy life':

> What is needed is radiant, life-affirming music with clearly and distinctly expressed emotions. ... Write simply, and, if expedient, banally, but expressively. No-one will criticise you now for sounding like Tchaikovsky,

79   Lamm,'Vospominaniya', 245.
80   See Aleksandr Lokshin (ed.), *A. L. Lokshin – Kompozitor i pedagog* (Moscow, 2005), 11, 72–3.
81   'Vïpiski', 23 and 30 May 1948, RGALI, 2040/1/65, l. 890b, 90.

Borodin, Glinka – what is more, they will approve of it and praise you for it. And they will rightly praise you, because you need to write music not for yourself and people like you, but for unsophisticated people. Forget about 'your lot's' conventional criteria. They've done their shameful work, or, in any case, were unable to satisfy society's demands – which means that you've got to discard them.[82]

One could scarcely find a franker acknowledgement of the stylistic and expressive constraints resulting from the Party's insistence on stricter adherence to Socialist Realism. After fudging the issue for over a decade, cultural bureaucrats finally made explicit what was required: uncomplicated, tuneful music conveying uplifting, positive emotions and dealing with suitable political themes, modelled on the nineteenth-century Russian classics and designed for the tastes of mass audiences. Anything else was considered intrinsically anti-Soviet. The composer's task was to write mood music evocative of the 'happy life' of the collective, rather than seek to communicate in artistic form truthful individual responses to existence and to the human condition. There is no reason to think that Ikonnikov's advice was offered cynically: he presumably saw it as his duty to encourage Myaskovsky's ideological 'reform' and help him to understand what the Party required of him.

As Glière reported to Boris Lyatoshinsky around the same time, the 'formalists' were being placed under pressure to write 'at least one large-scale work in a simple musical language'.[83] Such expectations were scarcely conducive to creativity, but Myaskovsky, like the other censured composers, had little choice but to keep writing – not least, for financial reasons. Shortly after the promulgation of the February resolution, the Committee for Artistic Affairs prohibited the performance of selected works by the 'formalists'.[84] Although not a blanket ban, performers and managers of concert venues were understandably nervous about including their music in programmes, or offering new commissions. Its immediate effect was a sharp drop in their incomes. Myaskovsky had savings to cushion the blow, including the income from his recent Stalin Prizes, but the drastic currency reform of December 1947 had halved their value.[85] Prokofiev's finances were in a dire state: he was unable to keep up the repayments on the 180,000-rouble loan from the Composers' Union that Levon Atovmyan

82 Ikonnikov to Myaskovsky, 21 May 1948, RGALI, 2040/1/153, ll. 32–30b.

83 Glière to Lyatoshinsky, 15 May 1948, in Ol'ha Holins'ka, *Boris Lyatoshyns'kyy: Epistolyarna spadshchina*, vol. 1 (Kyiv, 2002), 358.

84 'Prikaz No. 17 Glavnogo upravleniya po kontrolyu za zrelishchami i repertuarom Komiteta po delam iskusstv pri Sovete Ministrov SSSR, 14 fevralya 1948', in Irina Bobïkina (ed.), *Dmitriy Shostakovich v pis'makh i dokumentakh* (Moscow, 2000), 543–4.

85 'Vïpiski', 15 December 1947, RGALI, 2040/1/65, l. 88.

had arranged on his behalf to enable him to purchase a dacha in Nikolina Gora. Avtomyan became another casualty of the anti-formalism campaign and dismissed from his post. An investigation of the union's financial affairs ensued, and in mid-August Prokofiev was presented with a demand for immediate repayment in full.[86] Like Shostakovich and Myaskovsky, he was also asked to sign a declaration confirming the size of the commissioning fees that Atovmyan had paid him, and agreeing to reimburse the union if the auditors considered them excessive.[87] Coming in the wake of his condemnation in the February resolution and the arrest of his first wife Lina on fabricated charges of espionage shortly afterwards, these developments placed him under enormous strain, which Myaskovsky feared might prove too great for his increasingly fragile health. (Prokofiev suffered from severe hypertension and was by now a semi-invalid.) Myaskovsky was also apprehensive about the reception of the new opera that Prokofiev was composing in an attempt to redeem himself in the eyes of the authorities. *The Story of a Real Man* was based on a recently published novella by Boris Polevoy which portrayed in semi-fictionalised form the wartime exploits of the Soviet fighter pilot Alexey Maresyev (1916–2001). Maresyev's lower legs had to be amputated after his plane was shot down in combat, but he insisted on resuming flying after being equipped with artificial limbs. On the face of it, this tale of indomitable heroism was a judicious choice, as composers were expected to make a greater effort to treat subjects with strong ideological resonance. While Myaskovsky was genuinely enthusiastic about some of the music, he had serious reservations about Mira's libretto, and tried unsuccessfully to persuade Prokofiev to omit scenes that struck him as dramatically unviable – including one in which the wounded hero sings while crawling about the stage, having emerged from the wreckage of his crash-landed plane. Prokofiev stubbornly refused to alter his score, but as it transpired, Myaskovsky's forebodings about its reception were justified.[88]

In view of Myaskovsky's concerns about Prokofiev's new operatic project, the 'Slavonic' Twenty-Sixth Symphony, op. 79, on which he commenced work after arriving in Nikolina Gora strikes one as a curious undertaking. Like the *Slavonic Rhapsody*, the work was partially based on liturgical chants – in this instance, three Russian chants dating from the eleventh and twelfth centuries that had been deciphered by his old acquaintance Viktor Belyayev, who since their ASM days had become a

86 'Vïpiski', 18 August 1948, RGALI, 2040/1/65, l. 900b; Morrison, *The People's Artist*, 314–15.

87 Atovm'yan, *Ryadom s velikimi*, 287–8.

88 'Vïpiski', 14 May 1948, RGALI, 2040/1/65, l. 890b; Lamm, 'Vospominaniya', 246.

noted ethnomusicologist and specialist on early Russian music.[89] The first and second movements had been partially sketched the previous autumn, but he complained to Kabalevsky that he was finding it difficult to make further headway.[90] Kabalevsky's attitude to the project was sceptical: he wondered why Myaskovsky was bothering with these 'antediluvian' melodies and urged him to write instead 'a real song-symphony' based on folk music 'with alternating instrumental and vocal-choral themes'.[91]

Myaskovsky persisted with his original plan and the symphony was completed in draft by the beginning of July. He immediately started to sketch another orchestral work of a lighter nature, the three-movement *Divertissement*, op. 80, which he finished within a fortnight. On 21 July he returned to Moscow for three days. His schedule included a meeting to discuss his work in progress with Khrennikov and Ikonnikov, who were anxious to ensure that local composers, and especially the 'formalists', would complete a sufficiently large number of scores demonstrating stricter conformity to Socialist Realism in time to be performed at the forthcoming plenum of the Composers' Union's Moscow branch in December. He confided to his diary: 'Khrennikov and Ikonnikov are expecting compositions from the "formalists" so that they'll have something to tear to pieces at the plenum, but nobody wants to show anything. They're urging me to get a move on with orchestrating the symphony. They weren't even interested in the music!'[92] The remainder of summer was spent elaborating the sketches of the new orchestral works into four-hand piano reductions and sketching a sonata for cello and piano. On 22 August came the news that Shebalin had been sacked as rector of the Moscow Conservatoire. Four days later, Myaskovsky was summoned back to Moscow for meetings with Shebalin's replacement, the choral conductor Alexander Sveshnikov, who pressed him to take a class of composition students. This development suggests a thaw in official attitudes towards him, and also, perhaps, a pragmatic recognition that the institution was in danger of losing one of its most respected and experienced composition teachers.[93] Myaskovsky reluctantly

89 Belyayev became actively involved in research on early Russian music in the early 1940s, but most of his writings on the topic remained unpublished. I have been unable to identify the source of the chants used by Myaskovsky. For an overview of Belyayev's scholarly activity, see Yuriy Kholopov, 'V. M. Belyayev-uchyonïy', in Belyayev and Travina (ed.), *Viktor Mikhaylovich Belyayev*, 386–93.

90 Myaskovsky to Kabalevsky, 18 June 1948, RGALI, 2017/1/91, l. 18.

91 Kabalevsky to Myaskovsky, 26 June 1948, RGALI, 2040/1/121, ll. 60–600b.

92 'Vïpiski', 23 July 1948, RGALI, 2040/1/65, l. 900b.

93 The documents in Myaskovsky's Moscow Conservatoire personnel file (MGK, 1/23/84) do not shed any light on what prompted Sveshnikov to invite him to return.

agreed to teach for four hours a week. Amongst his new students were Boris Tchaikovsky and Khachaturian's nephew Karen Khachaturian, both of whom impressed him as talented.[94]

Khrennikov kept up the pressure on him to finish orchestrating the symphony after his return from Nikolina Gora on 9 September. In spite of another bout of ill health, he managed to do so on 2 October, and a fortnight later, completed scoring the *Divertissement*. A play-through of the symphony in a piano-duet reduction was duly arranged in the Composers' Union on 20 November. Amongst those present were Khrennikov and two other members of the union's new secretariat – Myaskovsky's former student Marian Koval and the popular song composer Vladimir Zakharov, who had been particularly vocal in his criticisms of the 'formalists'. Myaskovsky's laconic diary entry about the proceedings reads: 'At first – bewilderment, and then condescending praise and stupid criticisms. Got nothing useful from it'.[95] The composer Mieczysław Weinberg, who was one of the pianists, recalled that Zakharov remarked to Myaskovsky: 'Well, you're doing alright, but you still have some more work to do on your musical language'. Weinberg suspected Zakharov of being so poorly educated as to be ignorant of how an orchestral score was laid out: such was the calibre of some of the union's new senior personnel responsible for vetting works by their eminent colleagues. In private, Myaskovsky made little effort to conceal his attitude to the circumstances in which he found himself. When Weinberg made a quip about the 'historic' nature of the February resolution, ironically echoing the overblown language used at the April congress, Myaskovsky shot back: 'Not historical, but hysterical!'[96]

One of the most intriguing of his diary entries from this period concerns a visit from Shostakovich, who called on 30 November to show him his recently composed First Violin Concerto, op. 77 and the song cycle *From Jewish Folk Poetry*, op. 79 – both of which aroused Myaskovsky's warm enthusiasm.[97] Documentary evidence of contact between the two composers at this period is very sparse, but this visit suggests a desire on Shostakovich's part to show solidarity with his older colleague and a mellowing of his dismissive attitude towards him in the past. The fact that Shostakovich trusted Myaskovsky sufficiently to show him these scores, neither of which could be performed publicly until 1955, also seems significant. His trust was repaid. When Shostakovich's *Song of the Forests*, op. 81 was performed the following year, Myaskovsky was at pains to counter

94　'Vïpiski', 26 August and 17 September 1948, RGALI, 2040/1/65, l. 91.

95　Ibid., 20 November 1948, l. 92.

96　Lyudmila Nikitina, '"Pochti lyuboy mig zhizni – rabota." Stranitsï biografii i tvorchestva Mechislava Vaynberga', *Muzïkal'naya akademiya*, 5 (1994), 21.

97　'Vïpiski', 30 November 1948, RGALI, 2040/1/65, l. 92.

accusations that the cantata was an artistic compromise and mere hackwork cynically calculated to please the authorities: he warmly praised the younger man's consummate technical mastery and the vividness of the score's musical invention.[98]

Myaskovsky's defence of *Song of the Forests* was prompted not only by genuine admiration but also by his understanding of the pressure that Shostakovich was under and the difficulty of composing anything at all under the circumstances. Neither of the scores that he completed in 1948 represents him at his best. The three-movement *Divertissement*, op. 80, comprising a Waltz, Nocturne, and Tarantella, is the more engaging of the two: the outer movements are skilfully written and attractive, if overlong for their material. The Twenty-Sixth Symphony is not without its advocates: it has been argued that it is a score of comparable stature to the Sixth Symphony, expressive of the composer's spiritual resistance to an oppressive political regime.[99] In the opinion of the present writer, such claims are unpersuasive. The work lacks both formal cogency and thematic distinction and has little by way of vital content to communicate: Myaskovsky merely seems to be repeating himself. The determinedly upbeat first movement harks back to the sound-world of the Twelfth Symphony's finale, with a second subject idea recalling the corresponding theme in the first movement of the Ninth. The second movement conflates slow movement and scherzo, with outer sections in a serene F major flanking a quick central section – a set of *Kamarinskaya*-style variations on a chant melody associated with Christmas. This dutiful display of deference to nineteenth-century Russian musical traditions sounds tired and anachronistic. The finale struggles to maintain its momentum and repeatedly lapses into slower tempi, making an excessively sectional impression; meanwhile, the noisy concluding peroration descends into note-spinning. In assessing the Twenty-Sixth Symphony, it goes without saying that every allowance must be made for it, given the circumstances, both personal and professional, under which it was written – but the score nonetheless reminds one of the challenges inherent in sustaining interest over a lengthy time span of forty-five minutes.

The symphony's premiere under Alexander Gauk took place on 27 December in a concert scheduled during a nine-day forum organised by the Composers' Union from 21–29 December to review progress on implementing the recommendations of the February resolution. Over a hundred new compositions were performed, interspersed with talks by composers and musicologists.[100] Myaskovsky's diary entries drily record his impres-

---

98 Lamm, 'Vospominaniya', 259–60.

99 Mikhail Segel'man, "'Plach stranstvuyushchego' (ocherk o Dvadtsat' shestoy simfonii N. Myaskovskogo)," *Muzïkal'naya akademiya*, 3–4 (1998), 55–63.

100 *Sovetskoye iskusstvo*, 1 January 1949.

sions of the rehearsals: 'Gauk at sea'. 'Gauk forgot everything. Not a single correct tempo'. Unsurprisingly, things were not much better at the concert. Khrennikov and the other members of the secretariat pronounced the symphony 'very gloomy'.[101] Myaskovsky's sister Vera, who had attended the performance, sent him a letter afterwards which was as ill-timed as it was tactless, criticising the score as incomprehensible to untutored listeners.[102] The mediocre quality of much of the music heard at the forum did little to alleviate the dismal atmosphere. Myaskovsky attended Khrennikov's closing address in company with Prokofiev and Mira – almost certainly as a gesture of support for his beleaguered colleague, whose new opera had been savagely criticised after a private run-through before an invited audience in Leningrad on 5 December. The debacle effectively sealed the work's fate and it was not permitted to be staged.[103] Khrennikov took evident pleasure in this turn of events and made barbed comments about Prokofiev's opera in his speech, which struck Myaskovsky as gratingly condescending in tone.[104] One wonders whether Prokofiev rued his refusal to allow Khrennikov to graduate *summa cum laude* when he had acted as external examiner for the Moscow Conservatoire composition finalists twelve years previously.[105]

Myaskovsky's health continued to deteriorate. In January 1949, tests revealed abnormalities in his blood count and a polyp in his bowel. The director of the Kremlin Hospital's surgical unit Aleksey Ochkin recommended an urgent operation, but Myaskovsky insisted on postponing it until he finished the cello sonata that he had partially drafted the previous summer, and which Rostropovich had undertaken to perform. When the latter played through the score on 23 January, Myaskovsky thought it had turned out well, though he made some minor revisions at Rostropovich's suggestion.[106] On 28 January came the news of Asafiev's death, an event which marked the end of 'an entire epoch in my life', as he noted in his diary. Unlike Prokofiev and Pavel Lamm, Myaskovsky did not visit Asafiev before he died or attend his funeral: from his sister Yevgeniya, who kept in contact with Asafiev's wife Irina, he learned that his old friend had been so overcome by guilt at his actions that he summoned a priest to his deathbed.[107]

101 'Vïpiski', 15, 20, and 24 December 1948, RGALI, 2040/1/65, l. 92.

102 Vera Yakovleva to Myaskovsky, RGALI, 2040/2/294, ll. 25–6.

103 Mendel'son-Prokof'yeva, *O Sergeye Sergeyeviche Prokof'yeve*, 370–7, 389–93; Morrison, *The People's Artist*, 328–33.

104 'Vïpiski', 27 December 1948, RGALI, 2040/1/65, l. 920b.

105 Khrennikov, *Tak éto bïlo*, 23–35, 43–4.

106 'Vïpiski', 23 January 1949, RGALI, 2040/1/65, l. 920b; Lamm, 'Vospominaniya', 254–5.

107 Lamm, 'Vospominaniya', 255–6.

FIGURE 11.3. At Nikolina Gora (1949).

Myaskovsky duly underwent surgery and spent three weeks in hospital. He went to Nikolina Gora as usual for the summer, but was so ill when he arrived that he could barely walk: during the intervening period, he developed pleurisy once more (after another bout of influenza) and started to experience problems with his digestion. Notwithstanding his weakened state, he was remarkably productive, sketching in swift succession three small-scale piano sonatas of moderate difficulty and a new symphony and string quartet. Prokofiev's state of health, both physical and mental, continued to weigh on his mind, especially after a distressing incident when Prokofiev turned up at Lamm's dacha seemingly on the verge of a nervous breakdown. Prokofiev's doctors suspected that he had suffered a stroke and forbade him to work. The strains caused by money worries and tensions in the relationship with his sons were exacerbated by anxieties for the future. In his darkest moments, he feared his music was coming to be regarded as superfluous and that none of his recent work would ever be performed. Loyal as ever, Myaskovsky did what he could to be of support – correcting the proofs of the Third Suite from *Romeo and Juliet* and making representations to the Composers' Union and the Committee for Artistic Affairs to see if ways could be found to alleviate Prokofiev's financial predicament.[108]

Myaskovsky's own financial affairs were also in a far from satisfactory state. As Valentina confided to Mira, he was now earning considerably less than Pavel Lamm – a circumstance that undoubtedly explains the pressure he placed on himself to keep producing new work.[109] After returning from Nikolina Gora on 27 August, he finalised the new Thirteenth String Quartet. Working up the draft of the Twenty-Seventh Symphony took considerably longer: the orchestration was completed in mid-December, and he continued to tinker with the score into the New Year. In spite of his poor health and dispiriting professional circumstances, the works that he completed in 1949 demonstrate a remarkable late upsurge of inspiration.

The Second Sonata for Cello and Piano, op. 81, has justifiably entered the repertoire and been issued in numerous commercial recordings – including a fine reading by its dedicatee Rostropovich, whose courageous advocacy of Myaskovsky and Prokofiev's music at this difficult period earned him the gratitude of both composers. It is a superior work in every respect to the Violin Sonata, structurally taut and with thematic material of genuine distinction throughout. The lyrical, introspective first movement at times recalls Fauré in its wistfulness of mood and blending of modality and chromaticism. The slow movement is excellently sustained, building to a powerful climax, while the finale, an exhilarating *moto perpetuo*, brings the sonata to an arresting close with much brilliant virtuosic display for both instruments. The three piano sonatas comprising opp. 82, 83, and 84 are slighter works, all modestly proportioned and designed for younger players, but contain very attractive music – especially the last, in F major.

The Thirteenth String Quartet, op. 86, completed next, is also an excellent score and undoubtedly amongst the finest of Myaskovsky's contributions to the genre. Like the Second Cello Sonata, it exemplifies the increasing classicism of Myaskovsky's later style, reminding one just how far his artistic trajectory had taken him from his Expressionist explorations of the 1920s. During the intervening years, he had learned that intensity can be achieved without exaggerated striving after effect: the textual overload and densely dissonant chromaticism characteristic of his earlier music disappeared. The apparent simplicity of these late scores is deceptive, belying their remarkable subtlety and sophistication of compositional technique. Three gains are notable in particular. The more diatonic harmonic language facilitates

108 'Vïpiski', 27 August 1949, RGALI, 2040/1/65, l. 93–930b; Lamm, 'Vospominaniya', 257–9; Mendel'son-Prokof'yeva, *O Sergeye Sergeyeviche Prokof'yeve*, 416–18.

109 Mendel'son-Prokof'yeva, *O Sergeye Sergeyeviche Prokof'yeve*, 412.

the attainment of faster speeds and long-range momentum. The textual transparency makes possible a more telling and varied treatment of instrumental colour, especially in the orchestral works. Finally, there is a remarkable expansion of emotional range beyond the oppressive, claustrophobic atmosphere characteristic of much of Myaskovsky's earlier music. Although these later works are by no means without passages of disturbance, the disruption is contained and transcended. One's predominant impression is of a remarkable poise and control (the Thirteenth Quartet's exquisite opening movement is an excellent instance in point), and a new-found capacity for humour. Paradoxically, Myaskovsky discovered an increased expressive freedom at a time when circumstances seemed highly inimical to such a possibility.

The Twenty-Seventh Symphony in C minor, op. 85, ranks with the Sixth, Thirteenth, and Twenty-First Symphonies as one of Myaskovsky's supreme achievements, though one that is very different in nature. The thematic material of the Twenty-Seventh is exceptionally distinguished and memorable, and it is a work of compelling structural cogency. The flaws that mar Myaskovsky's less persuasive scores – diffuse tonal organisation, sectionality, longueurs, a tendency to overstate and overdevelop material – are altogether absent: the ideal advocated in his youthful essay 'Tchaikovsky and Beethoven' of an intimate correlation between a symphony's 'external form' and the 'inner form' of its psychological content is splendidly realised. The proportions of the thematic statements are perfectly judged, and their restatements and developments are never mechanical, but have a clear expressive point and serve to advance a tightly controlled unfolding drama. The symphony's emotional immediacy is heightened by its vivid orchestration, which is notable especially for the imaginative writing for solo wind instruments. In every respect, it demonstrates a consummate technical mastery that could scarcely have been foreseen from the First Symphony, composed over forty years before.

The Twenty-Seventh Symphony is in three movements – a quick sonata-allegro, a central slow movement, and a rondo finale. The first movement's slow introduction presents a pregnant motif, first heard on the bassoon, which outlines an arpeggiated C minor triad with the interpolated pitch of the supertonic – a contour that subtly unifies the musical material across all three movements and forms the basis of the allegro's impetuous first subject (ex. 11.3a and b).[110] For a demonstration of Myaskovsky's skill, one need look no further than the opening paragraph comprising the initial statement and restatements of this idea, which creates a powerful upsurge

---

110 For a discussion of these motivic relationships, see Nikolay Peyko, '27-ya simfoniya N. Ya. Myaskovskogo', in Shlifshteyn (ed.), *N. Ya. Myaskovskiy: Sobraniye materialov*, vol. 1 (Moscow, 1964), 78–95.

EXAMPLE 11.3. Symphony no. 27, first movement,
bars 25–31: (a) first subject; (b) motivic contour.

of irrepressible energy and sets the scene for the movement's subsequent dramatic conflicts. The lyrical second subject, first heard on the cor anglais, is one of Myaskovsky's finest melodic inspirations (ex. 11.4). These two ideas enter into fierce contention during a highly compressed development section – tensions that re-erupt in the movement's stormy coda. The slow movement, a large-scale ternary structure, constitutes the symphony's emotional centre of gravity. The return of the opening E major idea (ex. 11.5) is deeply moving after the turbulent central section and rises to a climax of great nobility, conveying a sense of serene acceptance. The rondo finale is especially impressive for its effortlessly sustained fast momentum, illustrating how the more diatonic harmonic language of Myaskovsky's late works facilitated sustained quick tempi. Its technique is essentially Beethovenian: for all the movement's dynamism, the rate of harmonic change is often extremely slow – the fleet principal theme is essentially an extended prolongation of the tonic triad (ex. 11.6). Its earnest purposefulness is effectively offset by a playful subsidiary theme with the character of a toy march, whose prototypes are undoubtedly the elegant marches from Tchaikovsky's *Sleeping Beauty* and *Nutcracker*, with their witty chromatic divagations and perky fanfares (ex. 11.7). Though completely unexpected, the change of tone

EXAMPLE 11.4. Symphony no. 27, first movement: bars 74–83.

EXAMPLE 11.5. Symphony no. 27, second movement: bars 23–31.

at this juncture feels wholly apt, signalling a transformation of the preceding atmosphere of tragedy and lofty seriousness after a hard-won transcendence of conflict. (The theme, incidentally, is a further transformation of the work's basic idea, motif *a*). The symphony ends in a mood of ebullient high spirits – testifying to a capacity for resilience that not even acute physical suffering and the indignities of 1948 could sap. Of the 'deeds' in response to the February resolution of which Myaskovsky spoke to Khrennikov, this is undoubtedly the most impressive.

Myaskovsky's accomplishment seems all the more remarkable given the tense state of Soviet musical life at the period. In mid-December,

EXAMPLE 11.6. Symphony no. 27, third movement: bars 29–36.

EXAMPLE 11.7. Symphony no. 27, third movement: bars 180–7.

the Composers' Union organised another congress to review progress. Myaskovsky managed to attend some of the concerts and listened to others on the radio. He noted in his diary that most of the music made a 'wretched' impression: 'One would almost think that composers had forgotten how to compose. Heaps of cantatas, one worse than the other. . . . Only Shostakovich's [*Song of the Forests*] was any good . . . .. Only one symphony was of a professional standard . . . .. The songs were disgraceful. The [symphonic] poems – hackwork and clichés. . . . The 'bigwigs' (Khrennikov and Kabalevsky) wiggled out of showing anything [i.e., having any of their own work performed]'.[111]

He was in persistently poor health during the winter, but despite feeling very unwell, saw in the New Year at Pavel Lamm's, who had transcribed the Twenty-Seventh Symphony for the occasion. The guests responded enthusiastically after the play-through but found it difficult to conceal their anxiety about his well-being. In mid-December, his gall bladder became

---

111 'Vïpiski', 15 December 1949, RGALI, 2040/1/65, l. 95.

inflamed: despite being put on a special diet, he continued to lose weight.[112] There were, however, further encouraging signs of a thaw in official attitudes towards him: on 18 January, he learned that the Stalin Prize Committee had overridden the objections of the Composers' Union and nominated his Second Cello Sonata for an award. It remained to be seen whether the nomination would be endorsed by the Ministerial Council: Myaskovsky anticipated that it would be blocked because of the hostility towards him in official quarters. When it was announced on 8 March that the sonata has been awarded a Stalin Prize second class, his friends greeted the news as a 'triumph of justice'. Though cheered by the stream of visitors who called to congratulate him, he was so unwell that he found the day exhausting. The prize money was welcome, and his finances soon received another boost when Muzgiz accepted the Thirteenth Quartet for publication on very favourable terms. These developments were also a reassuring indication that the new head of the Composers' Union did not necessarily have the final word in musical affairs. When Myaskovsky attended a dress rehearsal of Khrennikov's opera *Frol Skobeyev* on 4 March, he made no effort to conceal his contempt: outraged by the score's vulgarity and shoddy workmanship, he walked out during one of the entr'actes, remarking loudly, 'You'd think Glinka had never existed and that we're all still amateurs!' Nor did he hold back from criticising Khrennikov when Moisey Grinberg met him the following month to discuss the situation in the Composer's Union.[113]

Myaskovsky felt too unwell to compose during the spring, so busied himself by revising some of his songs for publication in a new collection. He also put his music library in order and prepared a compilation of extracts from his diaries before destroying the originals – actions which suggest a suspicion that a serious deterioration in his health was imminent. On 20 April, he celebrated his sixty-ninth birthday, and once again endured an exhausting day entertaining visitors. By the end of the month he underwent further tests which finally determined the underlying cause of his recent ailments: stomach cancer. He was admitted to the Kremlin clinic on 8 May and operated on by Alexander Bakulev, one of the foremost Soviet surgeons of his generation. Bakulev discovered that the disease was far advanced and the tumour inoperable, but this hopeless prognosis was concealed from Myaskovsky: only his sisters and a few close friends, including Pavel Lamm and Shebalin, knew the true state of affairs. He remained in hospital until 20 June, his discharge delayed by painful inflammation of the veins in his left leg due to a blood clot. When he returned home, he was so weak that he

---

112 Ibid., 18 December 1949 and 22 February 1950, ll. 950b, 97; Lamm, 'Vospominaniya', 260.

113 'Vïpiski', 5 March and 2 April 1950, RGALI, 2040/1/65, ll. 102, 1020b; Lamm, 'Vospominaniya', 260.

could hardly walk: he complained of excruciating pain in his stomach and a nauseous aversion to food. Pavel Lamm arranged for him to be brought to Nikolina Gora, but he was so ill that he scarcely left his room.[114]

When Mira called to see him, he put on a brave face, but admitted to feeling depressed at his inability to work. Though easier in his mind about the state of his finances, he continued to worry that his sisters would be evicted from his apartment if anything happened to him. The encounter made a deep impression on her:

> On the way home, I felt a keen pang at the powerlessness of the doctors, the powerlessness of all of us who were ready to do anything for Nikolay Yakovlevich but were helpless to avert his suffering . . .. His physical weakness at that time only intensified rather than diminished his spiritual fortitude and beauty, the clarity of his mind, and his courage. (Valentina told me that he turned away when he was in excruciating pain, not wanting his loved ones to see the distress on his face.) This spiritual fortitude and clarity were so great, that at times it seemed as though they would conquer his illness and one longed for a miracle. Declining to alter his habits, he sleeps alone in his room, not wishing to disturb anyone – remaining alone with his thoughts during the long, dark hours of the night.[115]

Myaskovsky remained at Nikolina Gora only a few weeks before returning to Moscow on 28 July. Mira called to say goodbye before he left:

> I went around to the Lamms. Mournful preparations for departure. Nikolay Yakovlevich is lying down in his room, Valentina packs the last few small things, repeating from time to time 'It's awful – awful', with tears in her eyes. . . . Our 'Moskvich' car pulls up, stopping not at the far gates as usual, but at the wicket gates, closer to the house. We are all out on the terrace. N[ikolay] Ya[kovlevich] comes out of his room dressed in his city clothes – a brightly coloured felt hat, his summer coat, woollen socks, brown leather boots. He says goodbye . . . Everyone goes down the stairs. Nikolay Yakovlevich holds himself upright. He sits into the car. Valentina says her goodbyes and gets in beside Volodya, the driver. Nikolay Yakovlevich says to me: 'Give my regards to Seryozhenka'. 'Seryozha is looking forward to seeing you again. We all are'. 'When . . . I can . . . get a little . . . strength back', N. Ya. replies, breathing with difficulty. Valentina turns towards me, her eyes full of tears and suffering. She nods to us for the last time and the car slowly pulls away. We all

114 'Vipiski', 12, 15, 20, 28, and 29 April 1950, RGALI, 2040/1/65, ll. 98–980b; Lamm, 'Vospominaniya', 260–1.
115 Mendel'son-Prokof'yeva, *O Sergeye Sergeyeviche Prokof'yeve*, 464.

Figure 11.4. Khrennikov and Kabalevsky at Myaskovsky's funeral service.

follow it for a while; it outdistances us, turns the corner, and is hidden from view.[116]

When the car reached his apartment building, it was met by a group of friends, who were shocked to find Myaskovsky so emaciated as to be almost unrecognisable. Ivan Petrov helped to carry him up to his fourth-floor apartment on a chair, as he could not manage the stairs.[117] His subsequent deterioration was swift. His sisters cared for him at home with the aid of a nurse rather than have him readmitted to hospital. By the time Mira and Pavel Lamm came to visit a week later, he was confined to bed, slipping in and out of consciousness, hallucinating and muttering incoherently. The events of the last few years continued to torment him. Amongst the last words that his sisters managed to make out were: 'I tried and tried all my life, but to no avail, it turned out' and 'Human dignity must be respected'.[118]

He died on 8 August.

116 Ibid., 465. 'Seryozhenka' and 'Seryozha' are both affectionate diminutive forms of 'Sergey'.

117 Petrov, 'Nastavnik i drug', 342.

118 Mendel'son-Prokof'yeva, '*O Sergeye Sergeyeviche Prokof'yeve*', 468.

Appendix I: A Note on Recordings

Readers curious to explore Myaskovsky's output may appreciate some suggestions on where to start. Rather than providing a comprehensive discography, I have confined myself to mentioning recorded performances that are easily accessible (most can be found on the internet) and of particular note. Commercial recordings of Myaskovsky's compositions are becoming more abundant: in addition to reissues of Soviet-era releases, quite a few new recordings have come out in recent years. Welcome though this has been, especially as concert performances remain infrequent, it must be said that the quality of these recordings is very variable. Myaskovsky's work presents taxing technical and interpretative challenges: it will not survive thoughtless, superficial readings and requires scrupulous attention to the fine details of phrasing, nuance, and textural balance if it is to make its effect. (In this respect, it is akin to the work of his English contemporary Arnold Bax, a composer with whom Myaskovsky had much in common.) But if some of the available recorded performances do Myaskovky's music little service, it has also attracted the attention of sympathetic advocates capable of revealing its artistic stature.

Of these, the Russian conductor Yevgeny Svetlanov (1928–2002) deserves special mention. A conductor of exceptional talent, Svetlanov had a deep affinity with Myaskovsky's music and made a sustained effort to rescue it from the neglect into which it had fallen after the composer's death.[1] By the end of his life, Svetlanov had managed to record all of Myaskovsky's symphonies, many of them for the Soviet label *Melodiya*. A compilation box set of sixteen compact discs entitled *Miaskovsky: Intégrale des symphonies*, which includes Myaskovsky's other orchestral works, was issued in the Warner Classics Svetlanov Edition in 2008. The playing of the USSR Symphony Orchestra and its successor the Russian Federation Symphony Orchestra is not always of the highest standard, and by all accounts, the recordings were sometimes made under less-than-ideal conditions. Nonetheless, one is deeply grateful for Svetlanov's enterprise, especially as his are still the only recordings available of some of these scores. At their best, the performances are very good – those of the Third and Twenty-Seventh Symphonies stand out especially. Other notable recordings of Myaskovsky symphonies include the wonderful readings of the Fifth and Ninth by the BBC Philharmonic under Edward Downes (Marco Polo 8.223499); the incandescent live performance of the Sixth given by Kirill

---

1   See the essay 'Nikolay Myaskovskiy (1881–1950)', in Yevgeniy Svetlanov, *Muzïka segodnya: Stat'i, retsenzii, ocherki* (Moscow, 1985), 100–104.

Kondrashin and the Moscow State Philharmonic Orchestra at a concert in 1978 (Melodiya 1000841); and the splendid version of the Twenty-First by Eugene Ormandy and the Philadelphia Orchestra that Myaskovsky so admired (reissued as Sony Classical 886447899533). Also worthy of mention is the recording of the Thirteenth Symphony by Alexander Rudin and the Ural Youth Symphony Orchestra (Naxos 8573988). One of Myaskovsky's most uncompromising scores, the Thirteenth is very difficult to bring off successfully, but this realisation comes close. Alexander Titov's lively rendition of the Twenty-Third Symphony with the St Petersburg State Academic Symphonic Orchestra (Northern Flowers NF/PMA9966) makes the most of this attractive work. David Oistrakh's account of the Violin Concerto and Mstislav Rostropovich's of the Cello Concerto have both been reissued in Brilliant Classics' *Historical Russian Archives* series (in box sets 92609 and 92771 respectively).

The best introductions to Myaskovsky's string quartets are the compelling readings of the First by the Renoir Quartet (AR20101) and the Thirteenth by the Borodin String Quartet (ONYX4051). The remaining quartets can be heard in renditions by the Taneyev Quartet, whose recordings of the complete Myaskovsky quartets have been reissued as a box set on the Northern Flowers label (NFPMA98005). While one is glad to have them in the virtual absence of any others, the playing is rather undistinguished and not always very well in tune. Sviatoslav Richter's tremendous live performance of the Third Piano Sonata is available on compact disc (*Richter Archives*, volume 9: Doremi DHR7806). Of the other available accounts of Myaskovsky's piano sonatas, those of Murray McLachlan are the most impressive, displaying a high level of imagination and intelligence (*Myaskovsky: Complete Piano Sonatas*, Musical Concepts 2506). Several fine recordings of both Myaskovsky cello sonatas have been released – including one of Cello Sonata no. 2 by Rostropovich and Alexander Dedyukhin (reissued on Warner Classics, 9029587196).

Little of Myaskovsky's vocal music is currently available on commercial recordings. Record buffs might be fortunate enough to come across the *Melodiya* LP made by the eminent Soviet soprano Nataliya Shpiller on which she sings the charming short cycle *Madrigal*, op. 7 (M10 46733 003). The *Three Sketches to Words by Vyacheslav Ivanov*, op. 8 have been recorded by mezzo-soprano Mila Shkirtil and Yuri Serov for the Northern Flowers label (NF/PMA 99103). Myaskovsky's Hippius settings, his finest achievement in this domain, still await the attention of enterprising singers and pianists equal to the demands of this formidably difficult, but rewarding, music.

Appendix II: List of Published Works

Myaskovsky's work was principally published by the Soviet state music publisher (Gosmuzizdat and its successors) and the Austrian firm Universal Edition. Virtually everything that he wrote made its way into print, apart from some juvenilia and a small number of scores which were lost or destroyed. Over the course of his life, he reworked many youthful compositional efforts that he had previously withheld from publication: the three string quartets produced during his period of study at the St Petersburg Conservatoire, for example, were eventually issued years later as String Quartets nos. 3, 4, and 10; and a large proportion of the early *Flofion* miniatures (see p. 17) went to make up the sets of short piano pieces that he published from the early 1920s onwards. Even during his lifetime, however, scores of his work were often difficult to obtain. The twelve-volume *Selected Works* (*Izbrannïye sochineniya*),[1] issued posthumously in 1953–6 under the general editorship of a committee comprising Glière, Shebalin, and others, is notable as much for what it excludes as for what it includes. The cantata *Kirov Is with Us* was featured, for example – but not 'decadent' scores such as the Tenth and Thirteenth Symphonies. (Only eleven of the twenty-seven symphonies were reissued.)

The brief worklist provided here is simply intended to afford a convenient overview of Myaskovsky's creative activity. More detailed information about individual compositions can be found in Semyon Shlifshteyn, *N. Ya. Myaskovskiy: Notograficheskiy spravochnik* (Moscow, 1962) and the appendices to the second volume of Shlifshteyn (ed.), *N. Ya. Myaskovskiy: Sobraniye materialov v dvukh tomakh*, 2nd ed. (Moscow, 1964).

Compiling a comprehensive *catalogue raisonné* of Myaskovsky's output would be an involved and time-consuming task. Some of his compositions were revised several times; not infrequently, he made further alterations after works had been republished in a revised form, inserting emendations in conductors' scores or in his personal copies. Researching these revisions exceeded the scope of the present study.

WITH OPUS NUMBER

Op. 1   *Razmïshleniya* [*Meditations*] (1907), seven songs for voice and piano. Texts: Yevgeny Baratïnsky

---

1   On this edition, see Aleksey Ikonnikov, 'Izbrannïye sochineniya N. Myaskovskogo', *Sovetskaya muzïka* 5 (1957), 169–73.

Op. 2   *Iz yunoshikh let [From My Youth]* (1903–06, rev. 1945], twelve
         songs for voice and piano. Texts: Konstantin Balmont

Op. 3   Symphony no. 1 in C minor (1908, rev. 1921)

Op. 4   *Na grani [On the Brink]* (1904–08), eighteen songs for voice
         and piano. Texts: Zinaida Hippius

Op. 5   *Iz Z. Gippius [From Z. Hippius]*, three songs for voice and piano
         (1905–08)

Op. 6   Piano Sonata no. 1 in D minor (1907–09)

Op. 7   *Madrigal* (1908–09, rev. 1925), suite for voice and piano. Texts:
         Konstantin Balmont

Op. 8   *Tri nabroska [Three Sketches]* (1908), three songs for voice and
         piano. Texts: Vyacheslav Ivanov

Op. 9   *Molchaniye [Silence]* (1909–10), symphonic poem for large
         orchestra after Edgar Allan Poe

Op. 10   Sinfonietta in A major (1910–11, rev. 1943), for small orchestra

Op. 11   Symphony no. 2 in C-sharp minor (1910–11)

Op. 12   Sonata no. 1 for Cello and Piano in D major (1911–13)

Op. 13   Piano Sonata no. 2 in F-sharp minor (1912)

Op. 14   *Alastor* (1912–13), symphonic poem for large orchestra after
         Percy Bysshe Shelley

Op. 15   Symphony no. 3 in A minor (1913–14)

Op. 16   *Predchuvstviya [Presentiments]* (1913–14), six songs for voice
         and piano. Texts: Zinaida Hippius[2]

Op. 17   Symphony no. 4 in E minor (1917–18)

Op. 18   Symphony no. 5 in D major (1918)

Op. 19   Piano Sonata no. 3 in C minor (1920)

Op. 20   *Six Songs for Voice and Piano to Words by Alexander Blok*
         (1920)

Op. 21   *Na sklonye dnya [At the Decline of Day]* (1922), three songs for
         voice and piano. Texts: Fyodor Tyutchev

Op. 22   *Venok poblekshiy [The Faded Garland]*, eight songs for voice
         and piano. Texts: Anton Delvig

Op. 23   Symphony no. 6 in E-flat minor (1921–3, rev. 1947–8)

Op. 24   Symphony no. 7 in B minor (1922)

Op. 25   *Prichudï [Capricii]* (1917–22), six pieces for piano

Op. 26   Symphony no. 8 in A major (1923–5)

Op. 27   Piano Sonata no. 4 in C minor (1924–5)

Op. 28   Symphony no. 9 in E minor (1926–7)

Op. 29   *Vospominaniya [Reminiscences]* (1927), six pieces for piano

---

2   This opus was originally titled *From Z. N. Hippius. Eight Sketches for Voice
     and Piano*. When he republished it in 1928, Myaskovsky changed the title and
     omitted two of the songs.

Op. 30   Symphony no. 10 in F minor (1926–7)

Op. 31   *Pozheltevshiye stranitsï [Yellowed Pages]*, seven pieces for piano (1906–28)

Op. 32   no. 1   *Serenata* (1928–9), for small orchestra
          no. 2   *Sinfonietta* (1928–9), for string orchestra
          no. 3   *Concertino lirico* (1929), for small orchestra

Op. 33   no. 1   String Quartet no. 1 in A minor (1929–30)
          no. 2   String Quartet no. 2 in C minor (1930)
          no. 3   String Quartet no. 3 in D minor (1910)
          no. 4   String Quartet no. 4 in F minor (1909–10, rev. 1936–7)

Op. 34   Symphony no. 11 in B-flat minor (1931–2)

Op. 35   Symphony no. 12 in G minor (1931–2)

Op. 36   Symphony no. 13 in B-flat minor (1933)

Op. 37   Symphony no. 14 in C major (1933)

Op. 38   Symphony no. 15 in D minor (1933–4)

Op. 39   Symphony no. 16 in F major (1935–6)

Op. 40   *Twelve Songs for Voice and Piano to Words by Mikhail Lermontov* (1935–6)

Op. 41   Symphony no. 17 in G-sharp minor (1935–6)

Op. 42   Symphony no. 18 in C major (1937)

Op. 43   no. 1   *Ten Easy Pieces for Piano* (1907–38)
          no. 2   *Four Easy Pieces for Piano* (1907–38)
          no. 3   *Simple Variations: Lyrical Suite for Piano* (1908–37)

Op. 44   Concerto for Violin and Orchestra in D minor (1938)

Op. 45   *Three Sketches for Voice and Piano to Words by Stepan Shchipachyov and Lev Kvitko* (1938)

Op. 46   Symphony no. 19 in E-flat major (1939) for wind orchestra

Op. 46bis *Two Pieces for String Orchestra* (1945) [transcriptions of second and third movements of Symphony No. 19]

Op. 47   String Quartet no. 5 in E minor (1938–9)

Op. 48   *Privetstvennaya uvertyura [Salutatory Overture]* (1939), for orchestra

Op. 49   String Quartet no. 6 in G minor (1939–40)

Op. 50   Symphony no. 20 in E major (1940)

Op. 51   Symphony no. 21 in F-sharp minor (1940)

Op. 52   *Iz liriki Stepana Shchipachyova* [From the lyric poetry of Stepan Shchipachyov] (1940), ten songs for voice and piano

Op. 53   no. 1   *Marsh geroicheskiy [Heroic March]*, for wind orchestra (1941)
          no. 2   *Marsh vesyoliy [Merry March]*, for wind orchestra (1941)

Op. 54   Symphony no. 22 (Symphony-Ballade) in B minor (1941)

Op. 55   String Quartet no. 7 in F major (1941)

Op. 56   Symphony no. 23 in A minor (1941)

Op. 57   Sonatina for Piano in E minor (1943)

Op. 58   *Pesnya i rapsodiya* [*Song and Rhapsody*] (1942), for piano
Op. 59   String Quartet no. 8 in F-sharp minor (1942)
Op. 60   *Dramaticheskaya uvertyura* [Dramatic overture] (1942), for
         wind orchestra
Op. 61   *Kirov s nami* [*Kirov Is with Us*] (1942), poem-cantata for solo-
         ists, mixed choir, and orchestra. Text: Nikolay Tikhonov
Op. 62   String Quartet no. 9 in D minor (1943)
Op. 63   Symphony no. 24 in F minor (1943)
Op. 64   no. 1   Piano Sonata no. 5 in B major (1907–08, rev. 1917 and 1944)
         no. 2   Piano Sonata no. 6 in A-flat major (1908, rev. 1925 and 1944)
Op. 65   *Zven'ya*³ [*Links*] (1944), suite for orchestra
Op. 66   Concerto for Cello and Orchestra in C minor (1944)
Op. 67   no. 1   String Quartet no. 10 in F major (1907?, rev. 1945)
         no. 2   String Quartet no. 11 in E-flat major, '*Vospominaniya*'
                 ['Reminiscences'] (1945)
Op. 68   Sinfonietta in A minor (1945–6), for string orchestra
Op. 69   Symphony no. 25 in D-flat major (1947)
Op. 70   Sonata for Violin and Piano in F major (1946–7)
Op. 72   *Tetrad' liriki* [*A Notebook of Lyric Poetry*] (1946), six songs for
         voice and piano. Texts: Mira Mendel'son and Robert Burns
         (trans. Mira Mendel'son)
Op. 73   *Stilizatsii: 9 p'es dlya fortepiano v forme starinnïkh tantsev*
         [*Stylisations: Nine Pieces for Piano in the Form of Old Dances*]
         (1946)
Op. 74   *Iz proshlogo: 6 improvizatsii dlya fortepiano* [*From the Past: Six
         Improvisations for Piano*] (1906, 1917, 1946)
Op. 75   *Kreml' noch'yu* [*The Kremlin at Night*] (1947), cantata for solo-
         ists, mixed choir, and orchestra. Text: Sergey Vasil'yev.
Op. 76   *Pateticheskaya uvertyura* [*Pathetic Overture*] (1947), for
         orchestra
Op. 77   String Quartet no. 12 in G major (1947)
Op. 78   *Polifonicheskiye nabroski* [*Polyphonic Sketches*] (1907–08, 1948),
         for piano
Op. 79   Symphony no. 26 in C major (1948–9)
Op. 80   *Divertisment* [*Divertimento*] (1948), for orchestra
Op. 81   Sonata no. 2 for Cello and Piano in A minor (1948–9)
Op. 82   Piano Sonata no. 7 in C major (1949)
Op. 83   Piano Sonata no. 8 in D minor (1949)
Op. 84   Piano Sonata no. 9 in F major (1949)
Op. 85   Symphony no. 27 in C minor (1947–9)
Op. 86   String Quartet no. 13 in A minor (1949)

3   For an explanation of this title, see p. 414.

Op. 87   *Za mnogiye godï* [*Of Many Years*] (1901–36, 1950), fifteen songs
           for voice and piano to texts by various authors.

WITHOUT OPUS NUMBER

ORCHESTRAL

Overture in G major (1907–11, rev. 1949)
Torzhestvennïy marsh [*Triumphal March*] (1930), for wind orchestra
Dramaticheskiy marsh [*Dramatic March*] (1930), for wind orchestra

VOCAL

'Zapevka' ['Folk ditty']⁴ (1930), for high voice and piano. Text: Vasily Nasedkin
'Krïl'ya Sovetov' ['The Wings of the Soviets'] (1931), for two-part mass
           choir and piano. Text: Nikolay Asayev
'Delo doblesti' ['A Matter of Courage'] (1931), for two-part mass choir.
           Text: Il'ya Frenkel'
'Letyat samolyotï' ['Airplanes are Flying'] (1931), for two-part mass choir.
           Text: I. Stroganov
'Leninskaya' ['Song of Lenin'] (1932–33), for unison mass choir and piano.
           Text: Aleksey Surkov
'Pesnya o Karle Markse' ['Song of Karl Marx'], for two-part choir and
           piano. Text: Semyon Kirsanov
Tri boevïye komsomolskiye pesni [*Three Komsomol Fighting Songs*] (1934),
           for unison mass choir and piano. Texts: Sergey Ostrovoy,
           Aleksey Surkov, and Viktor Vinnikov
'Slava sovetskim pilotam' ['Hail to Soviet Pilots'] (1934), for unaccompa-
           nied mixed choir. Text: Aleksey Surkov
'Kolkhoznaya osen'' ['The Collective Farm in Autumn'] (1935), for high
           voice and piano. Text: Äxmät Yerikäy [Akhmed Yerikeyev],
           trans. Semyon Lipkin
Chetïre pesni polyarnikov [*Four Songs of Polar Explorers*] (1939), for voice
           and piano. Texts: unknown author, Mikhail Svetlov, and Yuliy
           Zel'venskiy
'Pokhodnaya pesnya' ['Marching Song'] (1941), for unaccompanied two-
           part choir. Text: Mikhail Isakovsky

---

4   *Zapevka* is a diminutive form of *zapev*, an opening section found in many
     Russian folksongs: a *zapev* ranges in length from a short motif to a couplet
     and is sung by a solo singer (or small group of singers) before the remainder of
     the choir joins in with the *pripev* (chorus). The poem is an idealised evocation
     of a collective farm: Nasedkin presumably used the title to suggest a stylised
     imitation of folk poetry.

'Boyets molodoy' ['The Young Soldier'] (1941), for voice and piano. Text: Mikhail Svetlov

'Boyevoy prikaz' ['Combat Order'] (1941), for voice and choir with piano. Text: Viktor Vinnikov

Bibliography

Note: For a list of archives consulted, please see the list of abbreviations

PERIODICALS

RUSSIAN

Bor'ba
Byulleten' Soyuza sovetskikh kompozitorov
Byulleten' GAKhN
Golos Moskvï
Govorit Moskva
Inzhenernïy zhurnal
Iskusstvo
Izvestiya TsK KPSS
Khudozhestvennoye obrazovaniye
K novïm beregam muzïkal'nogo iskusstva
Komsomolskaya pravda
Krasnaya gazeta
Leningradskaya pravda
Literaturnaya gazeta
Mir iskusstva
Moskovskiye vedomosti
*Muzïka (órgan Vsesoyuznogo komiteta po delam iskusstv pri Sovnarkome
     SSSR)*
Muzïka (yezhenedel'nik)
Muzïka i Oktyabr'
Muzïka i revolyutsiya
Muzïkal'naya kul'tura
Muzïkal'naya letopis'
Muzïkal'naya nov'
Muzïkal'naya zhizn'
Muzïkal'nïy al'manakh
Muzïkal'nïy sovremennik
Muzïkal'noye obrazovaniye
Novaya muzïka
Pedagogicheskiy sbornik
Pravda
Proletarskiy muzïkant

Rabochiy i iskusstvo
Rabochiy i teatr
Radioslushatel'
Rech'
Revolyutsiya i kul'tura
Russkaya muzïkal'naya gazeta
Russkiye vedomosti
Severnïye zapiski
Sovetskaya muzïka
Sovetskiy muzïkant
Sovetskoye iskusstvo
Sovremennaya muzïka
Tvorchestvo
Utro Rossii
Vestnik Kommunisticheskoy akademii
Zhizn' iskusstva

UKRAINIAN

Muzika [Музика]

BOOKS, DOCUMENTARY COLLECTIONS,
ESSAYS, AND JOURNAL ARTICLES

——. *XV s'ezd Vsesoyuznoy kommunisticheskoy partii (b): Stenograficheskiy otchyot* (Moscow, 1928)
——. *Dekretï Sovetskoy vlasti: 25 oktyabrya 1917 g.–16 marta 1918 g.* (Moscow, 1957)
——. *Faktï i tsifrï protiv ocherednoy kletveï na RAPM* (Moscow, 1931)
——. *Moskva i Moskovskaya oblast' 1926/27–1928/29. Statistiko-èkonomicheskiy spravochnik po okrugam* (Moscow, 1930)
——. *Novïy ètap bor'bï na muzïkal'nom fronte* (Moscow, 1931)
——. *Polozheniye o kadetskikh korpusakh, vïsochayshe utverzhdyonnoye 14 fevralya 1886 g.*, vol. 6, *Polnoye sobraniye zakonov Rossiyskoy Imperii*, series 3 (St Petersburg, 1888)
——. *Programmï spetsialnïkh i obyazatel'nïkh muzïkal'nïkh predmetov i nauchnïkh klassov S.-Peterburgskoy konservatorii* (St Peterburg, 1909)
——. *Puti razvitiya muzïki: Stenograficheskiy otchyot Soveshchaniya po voprosam muzïki pri APPO TsK VKP(b)* (Moscow, 1930)
——. *Puti razvitiya teatra: Stenograficheskiy otchyot i resheniya partiynogo Soveshchaniya po voprosam teatra pri Agitprope TsK VKP(b) v maye 1927 g.* (Moscow, 1927)

——. *Pyat' let raboti Tsentral'noy komissii po uluchsheniyu bita uchyonïkh pri Sovete narodnïkh komissarov RSFSR (TsEKUBU), 1921–1926* (Moscow, 1927)

——. *Sobraniye uzakoneniy i razporyazheniy Rabochego i krest'yanskogo pravitel'stva*, 41 (1928)

——. *Soveshchaniye deyateley sovetskoy muziki v TsK VKP(b)* (Moscow, 1948)

——. *Trinadtsatïy s'ezd RKP(b): Stenografichskiy otchyot* (Moscow, 1963)

——. *Vserossiyskaya assotsiatsiya proletarskikh muzïkantov* (Moscow, 1929)

—— ['W']. *N. Ya. Myaskovskiy. K ispolneniyu yego simfoniy v Bol'shom teatre v Moskve* (Moscow, 1924)

Akhonen, Aleksandra. 'Prokof'yev v klasse Lyadova', in Tat'yana Zaytseva (ed)., *Nepoznannïy A. K. Lyadov* (Chelyabinsk, 2009), 278–91

——. *Prokof'yev v Peterburgskoy konservatorii* (St Petersburg, 2016)

Aksamitowski, Andrzej, ed. *200 lat Twierdzy Modlin (1806–2006)* (Modlin, 2006)

Aksyonenko, Nikolay, *et al.*, ed. *Istoriya zheleznodorozhnogo transporta Rossii i Sovetskogo Soyuza* (St Petersburg, 1997)

Aleksandrov, Anatoliy. 'O 6-y simfonii N. Ya. Myaskovskogo', *Muzïkal'naya kul'tura*, 1 (1924), 62–63

Alekseyev, Aleksandr, *et al.*, ed. *Russkaya khudozhestvennaya kul'tura kontsa XIX – nachala XX veka (1908–1917). Kniga tret'ya: Zrelishchnïye iskusstva, muzïka* (Moscow, 1977)

Alekseyev, Grigoriy, ed. *Istoriya sotsialisticheskogo sorevnovaniya v SSSR* (Moscow, 1980)

Alekseyeva, Yekaterina, *et al.*, ed. *Vospominaniya o Moskovskoy konservatorii* (Moscow, 1966)

Alexopoulos, Golfo. *Stalin's Outcasts: Aliens, Citizens, and the Soviet State, 1926–1936* (Ithaca and London, 2003)

Amiantov, Yuriy, *et al.*, ed. *V. I. Lenin: Neizvestnïye dokumentï, 1891–1922* (Moscow, 2000)

Amirkhanov, Leonid. *Morskaya krepost' imperatora Petra Velikogo* (St Petersburg, 1995)

Andreyev, V., *et al.* 'O tak nazïvayemom "Kremlyovskom dele"', *Izvestiya TsK KPSS*, 7 (1989), 86–93

Angert, G., and Ye. Shor, ed. 'Obzor muzïkal'noy zhizni za 1913 god', in *Muzïkal'nïy al'manakh*, (Moscow, 1914), 7–27

Annenkov, Yuriy. *Dnevnik moikh vstrech: Tsikl tragediy*, 2 vols. (Moscow, 1991)

Arkhangel'skiy, Igor'. *Annenshule. Skvoz' tri stoletiya* (St Petersburg, 2004)

Artizov, Andrey, and Oleg Naumov, ed. *Vlast' i khudozhestvennaya intelligentsiya: Dokumenti TsK RKP(b), VChK-OGPU-NKVD o kul'turnoy politike 1917–1953 gg.* (Moscow, 1999)

Asaf'yev, Boris. 'D. D. Shostakovich', ed. Andrey Pavlov-Arbenin with an introduction and commentary by Lidiya Adér, in Ol'ga Digonskaya and Lyudmila Kovnatskaya (ed.), *Dmitriy Shostakovich: Issledovaniya i materiali* (Moscow, 2007), vol. 2, 33–54

——. 'Istoricheskiy god', *Sovetskaya muzïka*, 3 (1933), 106–8

——. 'Moy put'', *Sovetskaya muzïka*, 8 (1934), 47–50

——. 'O sebe', in Andrey Kryukov (ed.), *Vospominaniya o B. V. Asaf'yeve* (Leningrad, 1974), 317–508

——. 'Volnuyushchiye voprosï', *Sovetskaya muzïka*, 5 (1936), 24–7

—— [Glebov, Igor']. 'Dvi techïï – dvi otsinky', *Muzïka [Музика]*, 11–12 (1925), 379–82

—— [Glebov, Igor']. 'Kompozitorï, pospeshite!', *Sovremennaya muzïka*, 6 (1924), 146–9

—— [Glebov, Igor']. 'Krizis lichnogo tvorchestva', *Sovremennaya muzïka*, 4 (1924), 99–106

—— [Glebov, Igor']. 'Krizis muzïki (nabroski nablyudatelya leningradskoy muzïkal'noy deystvitel'nosti)', *Muzïkal'naya kul'tura*, 2 (1924), 99–120

—— [Glebov, Igor']. 'O tvorcheskom puti N. Myaskovskogo', *Muzïka*, 18 April 1915, 257–62

Atovm'yan, Levon. 'Vospominaniya', in Nelli Kravets (ed.), *Ryadom s velikimi: Atovm'yan i yego vremya* (Moscow, 2012), 189–294

Augustine. *Confessions*, ed. James J. O'Donnell (Oxford, 1992)

Aver'yanov, Konstantin, ed. *Istoriya moskovskikh rayonov: Éntsiklopediya* (Moscow, 2005)

Bakhtin, Mikhail. *Sobranie sochineniy*, ed. Sergey Bocharov and Leontina Melikhova, 7 vols. (Moscow, 1997–2012)

Ball, Alan M. *Russia's Last Capitalists: The Nepmen, 1921–1929* (Berlekey and Los Angeles, 1987)

Barber, Charles F. *Lost in the Stars: The Forgotten Musical Life of Alexander Siloti* (Lanham, Maryland, 2002)

Barenboim, Lev, ed. *Iz istorii sovetskogo muzïkal'nogo obrazovaniya: Sbornik materialov i dokumentov, 1917–1927* (Leningrad, 1969)

Barry, Donald D. 'Nikolai Vasil'evich Krylenko: A Re-Evaluation', *Review of Socialist Law*, 15 (1989), 131–47

Barsova, Inna. 'Iz neopublikovannogo arkhiva A. V. Mosolova' [part 1], *Sovetskaya muzïka*, 7 (1989), 80–92

——. 'Iz neopublikovannogo arkhiva A. V. Mosolova' [part 2], *Sovetskaya muzïka*, 8 (1989), 69–75

——, ed. *Nikolay Sergeyevich Zhilyayev: Trudï, dni i gibel'* (Moscow, 2008)

——. 'Opfer stalinistischen Terrors: Nikolaj Žiljaev', in Friedrich Geiger and Eckhard John (ed.), *Musik zwischen Emigration und Stalinismus. Russische Komponisten in den 1930-er und 1940-er Jahren* (Stuttgart/ Weimar, 2004), 140–57

——. 'Sotrudnichestvo i perepiska dvukh izdatel'stv: Universal Edition i Muzsektora Gosizdata v 20–30-ye godï: vzglyad iz Venï', in Larissa Ivanova (ed.), *Muzïkal'noye prinosheniye: Sbornik statey k 75-letiyu Ye. A. Ruch'yevskoy* (St Petersburg, 1998)

Bator, Juliusz. *Wojna galicyjska: Działania armii austro-węgierskiej na froncie północnym (galicyjskim) w latach 1914–1915* (Kraków, 2005)

Baudin, Antoine, and Leonid Heller. 'L'image prend la parole: Image, texte et littérature durant la période Jdanovienne', in Wladimir Berelowitch and Laurent Gervereau (ed.), *Russie-URSS, 1914–1991: Changements de regards* (Paris, 1991), 140–8

Baumann, Robert F. 'Universal Service Reform: Conception to Implementation, 1873–1883', in David Schimmelpennick van der Oye and Bruce W. Menning (ed.), *Reforming the Tsar's Army* (Cambridge, 2004), 11–33

Bazilev, Boris. 'Pamyati odnogo iz nemnogikh', *Pedagogicheskiy sbornik*, 6 (1906), 497–517

Beevor, Antony. *The Mystery of Olga Chekhova* (London, 2004)

Bekman-Shcherbina, Yelena. *Moi vospominaniya* (Moscow, 1982)

Belaya, Galina. *Don Kikhotï Revolyutsii: Opït pobed i porazheniy* (Moscow, 2004)

Belïy, Viktor. 'Vïdayushchiysya deyatel' muzïkal'nogo prosveshcheniya', *Sovetskaya muzïka*, 9 (1951), 58–60

Belogrudov, Oleg. *N. Ya. Myaskovskiy-kritik* (Moscow, 1989)

Belyayev, Aleksandr. *Kadetskiye korpusa Rossii: Istoriya i sovremennost'* (Stavropol, 2008)

Belyayev, Viktor. *Nikolay Yakovlevich Myaskovskiy* (Moscow, 1927)

Belyayev, Viktor, ed. *Uchebnïye planï muzïkal'no-uchebnïkh zavedeniy RSFSR* (Moscow, 1924)

Belyayev, Viktor, and Yulia Veysberg. 'I. I. Krïzhanovskiy', *Sovremennaya muzïka*, 13–14 (1926), 97–100

Bèlza, Igor'. *O muzïkantakh XX veka: Izbrannïye ocherki* (Moscow, 1979)

Bèlza, Igor'. 'O T. I. Livanovoy – Uchyonom i cheleveke', in Devil' Arutyunov and Vladimir Protopopov (ed.), *T. I. Livanova: Stat'i, vospominaniya*, (Moscow, 1989), 287–300

Berlin, Isaiah. *Russian Thinkers*, ed. Henry Hardy and Aileen Kelly (London, 1978)

Beskrovnïy, Lyubomir. *Armiya i flot Rossii v nachale XX veka: Ocherki voyenno-èkonomicheskogo potentsiala* (Moscow, 1986)

Blagoveshchenskiy, K., ed. *Dovesti do kontsa bor'bu s nėpmanskoy muzïkoy* (Moscow, 1931)

Blok, Vladimir, ed. *A. N. Aleksandrov: Vospominaniya, stat'i, pis'ma* (Moscow, 1979)

Blok, Vladimir, and Yelena Polenova, ed. *Anatoliy Nikolayevich Aleksandrov: Stranitsï zhizni i tvorchestva* (Moscow, 1990)

Blyum, Arlen. *Sovetskaya tsenzura v ėpokhu total'nogo terrora, 1929–1953* (St Petersburg, 2000)

——. *Za kulisami "Ministerstva Pravdi": Taynaya istoriya sovetskoy tsenzurï, 1917–1929* (St Peterburg, 1994)

Bobïkina, Irina, ed. *Dmitriy Shostakovich v pis'makh i dokumentakh* (Moscow, 2000)

Bobïlyov, Leonid. *Istoriya i printsipï kompozitorskogo obrazovaniya v pervïkh russkikh konservatoriyakh* (Moscow, 1992)

——. *Russkaya kompozitorskaya pedagogika: Traditsii, lichnosti, shkolï* (Moscow, 2013)

Bobrik, Olesya. 'Arthur Lourié: A Biographical Sketch', in Klára Móricz and Simon Morrison (ed.), *Funeral Games in Honor of Arthur Vincent Lourié* (New York, 2014), 28–62

——. *Venskoye izdatel'stvo 'Universal Edition' i muzïkantï iz Sovetskoy Rossii* (St Petersburg, 2011)

Bochenek, Ryszard. *Twierdza Modlin* (Warsaw, 2003)

Bogdanov, Konstantin. 'Pravo na son i uslovnïye refleksï: Kolïbel'nïye pesni v sovetskoy kul'ture (1930–1950-ye godï)', in Nataliya Borisova *et al.* (ed.), *SSSR: Territoriya lyubvi* (Moscow, 2008), 79–127

Bogdanov, Konstantin, *et al.*, ed. *Dzhambul Dzhabayev: Priklyucheniya kazakhskogo akïna v sovetskoy strane. Stat'i i materialï* (Moscow, 2013)

Bogdanov-Berezovskiy, Valerian. *Dorogi iskusstva*, 2 vols. (Leningrad, 1971)

——. 'Leningradskaya Assotsiatsiya sovremennoy muzïki', in Igor' Glebov [Boris Asaf'yev] and Semyon Ginzburg (ed.), *Pyat' let novoy muzïki: Stat'i i materialï* (Leningrad, 1926), 37–41

——, ed. *Reyngol'd Moritsevich Gliėr: Stat'i, vospominaniya, materialï*, 2 vols. (Moscow, 1965)

Bogolyubov, Klavdiy, and Nikolay Savinkin, ed. *KPSS o Vooruzhyonnïkh Silakh Sovetskogo Soyuza: Dokumentï, 1917–1981* (Moscow, 1981)

Bogomolov, Nikolay, and Sergey Shumikhin, ed. *M. Kuzmin. Dnevnik, 1905–1907* (St Petersburg, 2000)

Bondarenko, Il'ya. 'V gostyakh u P. I. Chaykovskogo', *Moskovskiy zhurnal*, 10 (2005), 24–9

Boterbloem, Kees. *The Life and Times of Andrei Zhdanov, 1896–1948* (Montreal, 2004)

Bourdieu, Pierre. 'L'illusion biographique', *Actes de la Recherche en sciences sociales*, 62–3 (1986), 69–72

Boy-Żeleński, Tadeusz. *Ludzie żywi* (Warsaw, 1956)

Brooke, Caroline, 'Soviet Musicians and the Great Terror', *Europe-Asia Studies*, 3 (2002), 397–413

Bücher, Karl. 'August von Miaskowski', *Allgemeine Deutsche Biographie*, vol. 52 (Leipzig, 1906), 372–4

Bücher, Karl. 'Nekrolog auf August von Miaskowski', *Berichte über die Verhandlungen der königliche sächsischen Akademie der Wissenschaft zu Leipzig, Philologisch-Historische Klasse*, 52 (1900), 351–8

Bukov, Konstantin, and Anatoliy Ponomaryov, ed. *Moskva voyennaya, 1941–1945* (Moscow, 1995)

Bulat, Tamara. 'Pis'ma N. Ya. Myaskovskogo k Ya. S. Stepovomu', *Sovetskaya muzïka*, 12 (1979), 106–10

Bullock, Philip Ross. 'The Pushkin Anniversary of 1937 and Russian Art-Song in the Soviet Union', *Slavonica*, 1 (2007), 39–56

Burleshin, Aleksey, 'Vskrïtaya povsednevnost'', *Novoe literaturnoye obozreniye*, 2 (2010), 344–84

Bykova, Tetyana. *Stvorennya Kryms'koï ASRR (1917–1921 rr.)* (Kyiv, 2011)

Carpenter, Ellon DeGrief. 'The Theory of Music in Russia and the Soviet Union, ca. 1650–1950', unpublished dissertation (University of Pennsylvania, 1988).

Casella, Alfredo. *21 + 26* (Rome, 1931)

Cavalheiro, Edgard. *Biografias e biógrafos* (São Paulo, 1943)

Chemberdzhi, Valentina. *V dome muzïka zhila* (Moscow, 2017)

Chernïkh, Anna. 'Zhilishchnïy peredel: Politika 20-kh godov v sfere zhil'ya', *Sotsiologicheskiye issledovaniya*, 10 (1998), 71–8

Chernyayev, Anatoliy, Anatoliy Chernobayev, and Aleksandr Korotkov. 'Posetiteli kremlyovskogo kabineta I. V. Stalina: 1947–1949', *Istoricheskiy arkhiv*, 5–6 (1996)

Chernyayev, Vladimir. 'K izucheniyu ėpistolyarnïkh istochnikov nachala XX v. (kontrol' pochtovoy perepiski)', in Arkadiy Man'kov *et al.* (ed.), *Problemï otechestvennoy istorii* (Moscow and Leningrad, 1976), vol. 1, 134–55

Conquest, Robert. *The Great Terror: A Reassessment*, revised ed. (London, 2008)

Corobca, Liliana. *Controlul cărții: Cenzura literaturii în regimul comunist din România* (Bucharest, 2014)

Danchenko, Vladimir, and Gleb Kalashnikov. *Kadetskiy korpus: Shkola russkoy voennoy ėlitï* (Moscow, 2007)

Dansker, Ol'ga. 'Iz zapisnïkh knizhek M. O. Shteynberga 1919–1929 godov', in Galina Kopïtova (ed.), *Iz fondov Kabineta rukopisey Rossiyskogo instituta istorii iskusstv: Publikatsii i obzorï* (St Petersburg, 1998), 88–131

——, ed. *N. A. Mal'ko: Vospominaniya, stat'i, pis'ma* (Moscow, 1972)

——, ed. *V. G. Karatïgin: Izbrannïye stat'i* (Moscow and Leningrad, 1965)

Davïdova, Kseniya, *et al. Gosudarstvennïy dom-muzey P. I. Chaykovskogo v Klinu: Putevoditel'*, 4th ed. (Moscow, 1980)

de Jongh, Santie, 'From St Petersburg to The Cape: Three Autobiographical Texts by Albert Coates', *Fontes artis musicae*, 3 (2007), 320–30

Deklerk, Yuliya. '"Dolgaya doroga v rodnïye kraya". Iz perepiski S. S. Prokof'yeva s rossiyskimi druz'yami', in Marina Rakhmanova (ed.), *Sergey Prokof'yev. K 110-letiyu so dnya rozhdeniya. Pis'ma, vospominaniya, stat'i.*, 2nd ed. (Moscow, 2006), 5–120

Deklerk, Yuliya, *et al.*, ed. *Dernier cri, ili Posledniy krik modï v iskusstve nachala XX veka: Moskva, Parizh, Peterburg*, 5 vols. (Moscow, 2013)

Dement'yev, Aleksandr, ed. *Ocherki istorii russkoy sovetskoy zhurnalistiki, 1933–1945* (Moscow, 1968)

DiNardo, Richard L. *Breakthrough: The Gorlice-Tarnow Campaign, 1915* (Santa Barbara, 2010)

Dmitrenko, Vladimir. *Torgovaya politika sovetskogo gosudarstva posle perekhoda k NÈPu: 1921–1924 gg.* (Moscow, 1971)

Dmitriyev, Anatoliy. 'Moy dorogoy uchitel'', in Andrey Kryukov (ed.), *Vospominaniya o B. V. Asaf'yeve* (Leningrad, 1974), 113–34

Dolinskaya, Yelena. *Fortepiannoye tvorchestvo N. Ya. Myaskovskogo* (Moscow, 1980)

——. 'Stil' rannikh sochineniy N. Ya. Myaskovskogo v nauchnoy kontseptsii V. M. Belyayeva', in Anatoliy Belyayev and Irina Travina (ed.), *Viktor Mikhaylovich Belyayev: 1888–1968* (Moscow, 1990), 394–405

Dolzhanskiy, Aleksandr. 'Simfoniya-rapsodiya No. 5 Maksimiliana Shteynberga', in Semyon Ginzburg (ed.), *Puti razvitiya uzbekskoy muzïki* (Leningrad, 1946), 125–32

Dosse, François. *Le pari biographique* (Paris, 2011)

Drenski, Ivan. *General Radko Dimitriev: Biografichen ocherk* (Sofia, 1962)

Druskin, Mikhail. 'Deyatel'nost' LASM', in Igor' Glebov [Boris Asaf'yev] and Semyon Ginzburg ed., *Oktyabr' i novaya muzïka* (Leningrad, 1927), 53–56

——. *Issledovaniya, vospominaniya* (Leningrad, 1977)

Duz', Pyotr. *Istoriya vozdukhoplavaniya i aviatsii v Rossii.* 2nd ed. (Moscow, 1981)

Edmunds, Neil. *The Soviet Proletarian Music Movement* (Bern, 2000)

Ellenberger, Henri. 'La notion de maladie créatrice', *Dialogue: Canadian Philosophical Review/Revue canadienne de philosophie*, 1 (1964), 25–41

Èngel', Yuriy. 'A. N. Skryabin: Biograficheskiy ocherk', *Muzïkal'nïy sovremennik*, 4–5 (1916), 90–5

Èrenburg, Il'ya. *Lyudi, godï, zhizn'*, 3 vols. (Moscow, 1990)

Fairclough, Pauline. *Classics for the Masses: Shaping Soviet Musical Identity under Lenin and Stalin* (New Haven, 2016)

——. 'The "Perestroyka" of Soviet Symphonism: Shostakovich in 1935', *Music and Letters*, 2 (2002), 259–73

Fanning, David. 'The Symphony in the Soviet Union (1917–91)', in Robert Layton (ed.), *A Companion to the Symphony* (London, 1993), 292–326

Fay, Laurel E. *Shostakovich: A Life* (New York, 2000)

Feofanov, Yuri, and Donald D. Barry. *Politics and Justice in Russia: Major Trials of the Post-Stalin Era* (New York, 1996)

Fere, Vladimir. 'Nash uchitel' Nikolay Yakovlevich Myaskovskiy (stranitsï vospominaniy)', in Yekaterina Alekseyeva *et al.* (ed.), *Vospominaniya o Moskovskoy konservatorii* (Moscow, 1966), 418–39

——. 'V Moskovskoy konservatorii dvadtsatïkh godov (po lichnïm vospominaniyam)', in Yekaterina Alekseyeva *et al.* (ed.), *Vospominaniya o Moskovskoy konservatorii* (Moscow, 1966), 229–36

Fitzpatrick, Sheila. 'Cultural Revolution in Russia, 1928–32', *Journal of Contemporary History*, 1 (1974), 33–52

——. *Education and Social Mobility in the Soviet Union, 1921–1934* (Cambridge, 1979)

——. *The Commissariat of Enlightenment: Soviet Organization of Education and the Arts under Lunacharsky, October 1917–1921* (Cambridge, 1970)

——. 'The Emergence of Glaviskusstvo. Class War on the Cultural Front, Moscow, 1928–29', *Soviet Studies*, 2 (1971), 236–53

——. 'The Problem of Class Identity in NEP Society', in Sheila Fitzpatrick, Alexander Rabinowitch, and Richard Stites (ed.), *Russia in the Era of NEP: Explorations in Soviet Society and Culture* (Bloomington, 1991), 12–33

Friche, Vladimir, ed. *Iskusstvo v SSSR i zadachi khudozhnikov* (Moscow, 1928)

Frid, Grigoriy. *Dorógoy ranenoy pamyati* (Moscow, 2009)

Frid, Yakov. *Ėmil' Verkharn: Tvorcheskiy put' poėta* (Moscow, 1985)

Frolova-Walker, Marina. 'Against Germanic Reasoning: The Search for a Russian Style of Musical Argumentation', in Michael Murphy and Harry White (ed.), *Musical Constructions of Nationalism: Essays on the History and Ideology of European Musical Culture, 1800–1945* (Cork, 2001), 104–22

——. '"Music Is Obscure": Textless Soviet Works and Their Phantom Programmes', in Joshua S. Walden (ed.), *Representation in Western Music* (Cambridge, 2013), 47–63

——. *Stalin's Music Prize: Soviet Culture and Politics* (New Haven, 2016)

Frolova-Walker, Marina, and Jonathan Walker. *Music and Soviet Power, 1917–1932* (Woodbridge, 2012)

Fuglewicz, Stefan. 'Rozbudowa Twierdzy Modlin w XIX i XX wieku', in Andrzej Aksamitowski (ed.), *200 lat Twierdzy Modlin (1806–2006)* (Modlin, 2006), 47–55

Fülöp-Miller, René. *Geist und Gesicht des Bolschewismus: Darstellung und Kritik des kulturellen Lebens in Sowjet-Russland* (Vienna, 1926)

Galmarini, Maria Cristina. 'Defending the Rights of Gulag Prisoners: The Story of the Political Red Cross, 1918–38', *Russian Review*, 1 (2012), 6–29

Gatrell, Peter. *A Whole Empire Walking: Refugees in Russia during World War I* (Bloomington, 1999)

——. *Russia's First World War: A Social and Economic History* (Abingdon and New York, 2014)

Gimpel'son, Yefim. *NÈP i sovetskaya politicheskaya sistema v 20-ye godï* (Moscow, 2000)

Ginzburg, Lev, ed. *Moskovskaya konservatoriya, 1866–1966* (Moscow, 1966)

Ginzburg, Semyon. 'Pamyati uchitelya', in Andrey Kryukov (ed.), *Vospominaniya o B. V. Asaf'yeve* (Leningrad, 1974), 84–99

Glezer, Raisa, ed. *M. F. Gnesin: Stat'i, vospominaniya, materialï* (Moscow, 1961)

Gliėr, Reyngol'd. 'O professii kompozitora i vospitanii molodyozhi', *Sovetskaya muzïka*, 8 (1954), 5–11

Gofman, Modest. 'Peterburgskiye vospominaniya', in Vadim Kreyd (ed.), *Vospominaniya o Serebryanom veke* (Moscow, 1993), 367–78

——. *Poėtï simvolizma* (St Petersburg, 1908)

——. *Sobornïy individualizm* (St Petersburg, 1907)

Gojowy, Detlef. 'Sinowi Borissowitsch im Keller entdeckt: Sowjetische Musikwissenschaft in der Perestrojka', *Das Orchester*, 11 (1991), 1242–5

Gol'denveyzer, Aleksandr. *Dnevnik: Tetradi vtoraya-shestaya (1905–1929)* (Moscow, 1997)

——. 'O Myaskovskom-cheloveke', in Semyon Shlifshteyn (ed.), *N. Ya. Myaskovskiy: Sobraniye materialov v dvukh tomakh*, 2nd edn. (Moscow, 1964), vol. 1, 254–5

Golomshtok, Igor'. 'Sotsrealizm i izobrazitel'noye iskusstvo', in Khans Gyunter and Yevgeniy Dobrenko, *Sotsrealisticheskiy kanon* (St Petersburg, 2000)

Gor'kiy, Maksim. 'Razrusheniye lichnosti', in *Stat'i. 1905–1916 gg.*, 2nd ed. (Petrograd, 1918), 8–60

Gorodinskiy, Viktor. 'K voprosu o sotsialisticheskom realizme v muzïke', *Sovetskaya muzïka*, 1 (1933), 6–18

——. *Muzïka dushevnoy nishchetï* (Moscow, 1950)

——. 'Problema soderzhaniya i obraznosti v muzïke', *Sovetskaya muzïka*, 5 (1933), 2–22

——. 'Sovetskuyu muzïku – Na vïsshuyu stupen'', in Nikolay Chelyapov (ed.), *Muzïkal'nïy al'manakh: Sbornik statey* (Moscow, 1932), 5–18

Gorodinskiy, Viktor, *et al.*, ed. *Pervïy Vsesoyuznïy s"ezd sovetskikh kompozitorov: Stenograficheskiy otchyot* (Moscow, 1948)

Goryayeva, Tat'yana. 'Odna iz original'neyshikh i zamechatel'nïkh realizatsiy, osushchestvlennaya v SSSR. (K 70-letiyu RGALI)', *Otechestvennïye arkhivï*, 2 (2011), 27–39

Grechaninov, Aleksandr. *Moya zhizn'* (New York, 1952)

Grekov, F. B. *Kratkiy istoricheskiy ocherk voyenno-uchebnïkh zavedeniy, 1700–1910* (Moscow, 1910)

Grigor'yev, Lev, and Yakov Platek. *Moskovskaya gosudarstvennaya filarmoniya* (Moscow, 1973)

Gromov, Yevgeniy. *Stalin: Iskusstvo i vlast'* (Moscow, 2003)

Grosheva, Yelena. *Bol'shoy teatr Soyuza SSR* (Moscow, 1978)

Grossman, Joan Delaney. *Edgar Allan Poe in Russia: A Study in Legend and Literary Influence* (Würzburg, 1973)

Gruber, Roman. *Istoriya muzïkal'noy kul'turï. Tom 1. S drevneyshikh vremyon do kontsa XVI veka* (Moscow and Leningrad, 1941)

Gur, Golan. 'Music and *Weltanschauung*: Franz Brendel and the Claims of Universal History', *Music and Letters*, 3 (2012), 350–73

Gurkina, Nina. *Istoriya obrazovaniya v Rossii (X–XX veka)* (St Petersburg, 2001)

Guseynova, Zivar. 'M. O. Shteynberg: Pervïy god v Tashkente', *Opera Musicologica*, 1 (2011), 24–39

Gusin, Izrail'. 'Sovetskoye gosudarstvennoye muzïkal'noye stroitel'stvo', in Valerian Bogdanov-Berezovskiy and Izrail' Gusin (ed.), *V pervïye godï sovetskogo muzïkal'nogo stroitel'stva: Stat'i, vospominaniya, materialï* (Leningrad, 1959), 62–157

Haefeli, Anton. *Die Internationale Gesellschaft für neue Musik (IGNM): Ihre Geschichte von 1922 bis zur Gegenwart* (Zurich, 1982)

Harris, James. *The Great Fear: Stalin's Terror of the 1930s* (New York, 2017)

Healey, Dan. *Homosexual Desire in Revolutionary Russia* (Chicago and London, 2001)

Hellbeck, Jochen. *Revolution on My Mind: Writing a Diary under Stalin* (Cambridge, Masschusetts and London, 2006)

Henriksson, Anders. *The Tsar's Loyal Germans. The Riga German Community: Social Change and the Nationality Question, 1855–1905* (New York, 1983)

Holins'ka, Ol'ha, *et al.*, ed. *Boris Lyatoshyns'kyy: Epistolyarna spadshchina* (Kyiv, 2002), vol. 1

Holmes, Richard. *Shelley: The Pursuit* (London, 1994)

Hoshulyak, Ivan. 'Pro prychynu porazky Tsentral'noï Rady', *Ukraïn'skiy istorychnyy zhurnal*, 1 (1994), 31–44

Idzikowski, Tomasz. *Twierdza Przemyśl: Powstanie, rozwój, technologia* (Krosno, 2014)

Ikonnikov, Aleksey. 'Izbrannïye sochineniya N. Myaskovskogo', *Sovetskaya muzïka* 5 (1957), 169–73

——. *Khudozhnik nashikh dney: N. Ya. Myaskovskiy*, 2nd ed. (Moscow, 1982)

——. *N. Myaskovskiy* (Moscow, 1944)

——. 'N. Ya. Myaskovskiy (biograficheskiy ocherk)', *Sovetskaya muzïka*, 4 (1941), 21–31

Ikonnikov, Alexei [Aleksey]. *Myaskovsky: His Life and Work* (New York, 1946)

Il'yukhov, Aleksandr. *Kak platili bol'sheviki: Politika sovetskoy vlasti v sfere oplatï truda v 1917–1941 gg.* (Moscow, 2010)

——. *Zhizn' v ėpokhu peremen: Material'noye polozheniye gorodskikh zhiteley v godï revolyutsii i Grazhdanskoy voynï* (Moscow, 2007)

Ivanov, Dmitriy, and Ol'ga Deschartes, ed. *Vyacheslav Ivanov: Sobraniye sochineniy*, 4 vols. (Brussels, 1971–87)

Ivanova, Lidiya. *Vospominaniya: Kniga ob ottse* (Paris, 1990)

Ivinskaya, Ol'ga. *Godï s Borisom Pasternakom: V plenu vremeni* (Moscow, 1992)

Ivkov, Dmitriy. *Istoricheskiy ocherk Glavnogo inzhenernogo upravleniya* (Petrograd, 1915)

Jones, Edgar, and Simon Wessely. *Shell Shock to PTSD: Military Psychiatry from 1900 to the Gulf War*, Maudsley Monographs (Hove and New York, 2015)

Kabalevskiy, Dmitriy. 'O N. Ya. Myaskovskom', in Semyon Shlifshteyn (ed.), *N. Ya. Myaskovskiy: Sobraniye materialov v dvukh tomakh*, 2nd ed. (Moscow, 1964), vol. 1, 307–33

Kabalevskiy, Dmitriy, *et al.*, ed. *Akademik B. V. Asaf'yev: Izbrannïye trudï*, 5 vols. (Moscow, 1952–57)

Kabalevskiy, Dmitriy, and Dmitriy Shostakovich. 'Kniga o N. Ya. Myaskovskom', *Sovetskaya muzïka*, 7 (1954), 99–108

Kahan, Arcadius. *Russian Economic History: The Nineteenth Century*, ed. Roger Weiss (Chicago and London, 1989)

Karasik, Theodore. *The Post-Soviet Archives: Organization, Access and Declassification* (Santa Monica, 1993)

Karatïgin, Vyacheslav. 'N. Myaskovskiy. Sonata No. 2 fis-moll dlya f[orte]-p[iano]', *Muzïkal'nïy sovremennik*, 2 (1916), 117–20

——. 'Noveyshiye tendentsii v russkoy muzïke', *Severnïye zapiski*, 2 (1915), 99–109

Kartsov, Pavel. *Istoricheskiy ocherk Novgorodskogo grafa Arakcheyeva kadetskogo korpusa i Nizhegorodskoy voyennoy gimnazii* (St Petersburg, 1884)

Kasack, Wolfgang. *Lexikon der russischen Literatur ab 1917* (Stuttgart, 1976)

Keldïsh, Yuriy. '12-ya simfoniya Myaskovskogo i nekotorïye problemï sovetskogo simfonizma', *Sovetskaya muzïka*, 2 (1934), 8–23

——. *100 let Moskovskoy konservatorii: Kratkiy istoricheskiy ocherk* (Moscow, 1966)

Keldïsh, Yuriy *et al.*, ed. *Glazunov: Issledovaniya, materialï, publikatsii, pis'ma*, 2 vols. (Leningrad, n.d.)

—— *et al.*, ed. *Istoriya muzïki narodov SSSR*, 3 vols. (Moscow, 1970–72)

—— *et al.*, ed. *Muzïkal'naya ėntsiklopediya*, 6 vols. (Moscow, 1973–82)

Kelle, Valida. 'Ob otdel'nïkh faktakh tvorcheskoy biografii N. Myaskovskogo', in Yelena Dolinskaya (ed.), *Neizvestnïy Nikolay Myaskovskiy: Vzglyad iz XXI veka* (Moscow, 2006), 41–50

Kemp-Welch, Anthony. *Stalin and the Literary Intelligentsia, 1928–39* (Basingstoke, 1991)

Kerimbayev, Suyun. *Sovetskiy Kirgizstan v Velikoy otechestvennoy voyne, 1941–1945* (Frunze, 1985)

Khachaturyan, Aram. 'Iz vospominaniy', in Semyon Shlifshteyn (ed.), *N. Ya. Myaskovskiy: Sobraniye materialov v dvukh tomakh*, 2nd ed. (Moscow, 1964), vol. 2, 298–306

Khakuashev, Yevgeniy. *Kabardino-Balkarskaya ASSR v godï Velikoy otechestvennoy voynï (1941–1945)* (Nalchik, 1978)

Kharkhordin, Oleg. *The Collective and the Individual in Russia: A Study of Practices* (Berkeley, 1999)

Khaustov, Vladimir, *et al.*, ed. *Lubyanka. Stalin i VChK-GPU-OGPU-NKVD. Arkhiv Stalina. Dokumentï vïsshikh organov partiynoy i gosudarstvennoy vlasti. Yanvar' 1922 – dekabr' 1936* (Moscow, 2003)

Khodasevich, Vladislav. *Sobraniye sochineniy v chetïryokh tomakh. Tom chetvyortïy: Nekropol', vospominaniya, pis'ma*, ed. Inna Andreyeva *et al.* (Moscow, 1996)

Kholopov, Yuriy. 'V. M. Belyayev-uchyonïy', in Anatoliy Belyayev and Irina Travina (ed.), *Viktor Mikhaylovich Belyayev: 1888–1968* (Moscow, 1990), 386–93

Khrennikov, Tikhon. 'O neterpimom otstavanii muzïkal'noy kritiki i muzïkovedeniya', *Sovetskaya muzïka*, 2 (1949), 7–15

——. 'Sud'ba chelovecheskaya', in Tamara Tolchanova and Mikhail Lozhnikov (ed.), *I primknuvshiy k nim Shepilov: Pravda o cheloveke, uchyonom, voine, politike* (Moscow, 1998), 146–51

——. *Tak ėto bïlo: Tikhon Khrennikov o vremeni i o sebe*, ed. Valentina Rubtsova (Moscow, 1994)

Khubov, Georgiy. '16-ya simfoniya Myaskovskogo', *Sovetskaya muzïka*, 1 (1937), 17–30

——. 'Muzïka i sovremennost': O zadachakh razvitiya sovetskoy muzïki', *Sovetskaya muzïka*, 4 (1953), 16–22

Klause, Inna. 'Composers in the Gulag: A Preliminary Survey', in Patrick Zuk and Marina Frolova-Walker (ed.), *Russian Music since 1917: Reappraisal and Rediscovery* (Oxford, 2017), 188–217

——. *Der Klang des Gulag: Musik und Musiker in den sowjetischen Zwangsarbeitslagern der 1920er- bis 1950er-Jahre* (Göttingen, 2014)

Klimovitskiy, Arkadiy. "'Lyudi dolzhnï znat', chtó ya khochu skazat'!!": Arnol'd Shyonberg v Peterburge' [part 1], *Muzïkal'naya akademiya*, 4–5 (1995), 166–74

Kolińska, Krystyna. *Stachu: Jego kobiety, jego dzieci* (Kraków, 1978)

Kollerov, Aleksandr, and Andrey Samoylov. *Nezabïtaya voyna – nezabïtïye sud'bï. Kovrovskiy, Gorbatovskiy, Klyaz'minskiy pekhotnïye polki: Boyevoy put', lyudi i podvigi* (Vladimir, 2014)

Komarov, Aleksandr. "'. . .zhivyom nadezhdoy na blizkoye vosvrashcheniye v Moskvu". Iz perepiski N. Ya. Myaskovskogo s G. V. Kirkorom 1942 goda', in Yekaterina Vlasova and Yelena Sorokina (ed.), *Naslediye: Russkaya muzïka – Mirovaya kul'tura* (Moscow, 2009), 384–91

——. 'N. Ya. Myaskovskiy v godï Velikoy otechestvennoy voynï', in Yekaterina Vlasova and Yelena Sorokina (ed.), *Naslediye: Russkaya muzïka – Mirovaya kul'tura* (Moscow, 2009), 370–83

——. "'Prirozhdyonnïy arkhivist": Ocherk biografii S. S. Popova', in Marina Rakhmanova ed., *Al'manakh*, trudï Gosudarstvennogo tsentral'nogo muzeya muzïkal'noy kul'turï imeni M. I. Glinki (Moscow, 2007), vol. 3, 769–800

Konecny, Peter. 'Chaos on Campus: The 1924 Student *Proverka* in Leningrad', *Europe-Asia Studies*, 4 (1994), 617–35

Koposova-Derzhanovskaya, Yekaterina. 'Pamyati druga', in Semyon Shlifshteyn (ed.), *N. Ya. Myaskovskiy: Sobraniye materialov v dvukh tomakh*, 2nd ed. (Moscow, 1964), vol. 1, 201–26

Korev, Semyon, ed. *Nash muzïkal'nïy front: Materialï Vserossiyskoy muzïkal'noy konferentsii, iyun' 1929 g.* (Moscow, 1930)

Kotkin, Stephen. *Magnetic Mountain: Stalinism as a Civilization*, new ed. (Berkeley and Los Angeles, 1997)

——. *Stalin: Waiting for Hitler, 1929–1941* (London, 2018)

Kotkowska-Bareja, Hanna. *Pomnik Chopina* (Warsaw, 1970)

Kovnatskaya, Lyudmila ed. *Shostakovich: Mezhdu mgnoveniyem i vechnost'yu. Dokumentï. Materialï. Stat'i* (St Peterburg, 2000), 116

Kovnatskaya, Lyudmila, *et al.*, ed. *Pamyati Mikhaila Semyonovicha Druskina. Kniga II: Iz perepiski* (St Petersburg, 2009)

Kozlova, Miral'da, ed. 'B. V. Asaf'yev: Iz pisem k zhene, 1928 god', in Tamara Livanova (ed.), *Iz proshlogo sovetskoy muzïkal'noy kul'turï* (Moscow, 1982), vol. 3, 5–28

——, ed. "'Chuvstvuya polnotu oshchushcheniya i rost soznaniya": Iz perepiski Asaf'yeva s Myaskovskim 1914–1916 gg.' [part 1], *Sovetskaya muzïka*, 9 (1984), 45–55

——, ed. "'Chuvstvuya polnotu oshchushcheniya i rost soznaniya": Iz perepiski Asaf'yeva s Myaskovskim 1914–1916gg.' [part 2], *Sovetskaya muzïka*, 12 (1984), 88–94

——, ed. 'Iz perepiski B. V. Asaf'yeva i N. Ya. Myaskovskogo' [part 1], *Sovetskaya muzïka*, 11 (1979), 118–26

——, ed. 'Iz perepiski B. V. Asaf'yeva i N. Ya. Myaskovskogo' [part 2], *Sovetskaya muzïka*, 12 (1979), 95–105

——, ed. "'Mne ispolnilos' vosemnadtsat' let. . .": Pis'ma D. D. Shostakovicha k L. N. Oborinu', in Natal'ya Volkova (ed.), *Vstrechi s proshlïm*, vol. 5 (Moscow, 1984)

——, ed. 'Myaskovskiy pishet Asaf'yevu', *Muzïkal'naya zhizn'*, 20 (1975), 15

——, ed. 'Pis'ma S. S. Prokof'yeva B. V. Asaf'yevu (1920–1944)', in Tamara Livanova (ed.), *Iz proshlogo sovetskoy muzïkal'noy kulturï*, vol. 2 (Moscow, 1976), 4–54

——, ed. "'Teper vse troye – opredelivshiyesya velichinï. . .": Iz nenapechatannogo', *Sovetskaya muzïka*, 5 (1977), 93–9

Kozlova, Miral'da, and Nina Yatsenko, ed. *S. S. Prokof'yev i N. Ya. Myaskovskiy: Perepiska* (Moscow, 1977)

Krasnoborod'ko, Tat'yana. 'Pis'ma M. L. Gofmana k B. L. Modzalevskomu: chast' 1 (1904–1921)', in *Yezhegodnik Rukopisnogo otdela Pushkinskogo Doma na 2000 god* (St Petersburg, 2004), 180–238

——. 'Pis'ma M. L. Gofmana k B. L. Modzalevskomu: chast' 2 (1922–1926)', in *Yezhegodnik Rukopisnogo otdela Pushkinskogo doma na 2005–2006 godï* (St Petersburg, 2009), 797–943

Kravets, Nelli, ed. *Ryadom s velikimi: Atovm'yan i yego vremya* (Moscow, 2012)

Krebs, Stanley Dale. *Soviet Composers and the Development of Soviet Music* (London, 1970)

Křesťan, Jiří. *Zdeněk Nejedlý: Politik a vědec v osamění* (Prague, 2013)

Krïlov, Valeriy. *Kadetskiye korpusa i rossiyskiye kadetï* (St Petersburg, 1998)

Krïlov, Valeriy, and Vitaliy Semichev. *Zvan'ye skromnoye i gordoye kadet: Istoricheskiye i kul'turnïye traditsii kadetskikh korpusov Rossii* (St Petersburg, 2004)

Krivtsova, Yelena, 'Iz istorii muzïkal'no-obshchestvennïkh organizatsiy: ORKiMD (1924–1932)', in Marina Rakhmanova (ed.), *Al'manakh*, trudï Gosudarstvennogo tsentral'nogo muzeya muzïkal'noy kul'turï imeni M. I. Glinki (Moscow, 2003), vol. 2, 268–90

Kryukov, Andrey, ed. *Materialï k biografii B. Asaf'yeva* (Leningrad, 1981)

——. *Vospominaniya o B. V. Asaf'yeve* (Leningrad, 1974)

Kryzhanovsky, Ivan. *The Biological Bases of the Evolution of Music*, trans. Samuel Pring (London, 1928)

Kumpan, Kseniya. 'Institut istorii iskusstv na rubezhe 1920–1930-kh gg.', in Mariya Malikova (ed.), *Konets institutsiy kul'turï dvadtsatïkh godov v Leningrade. Po arkhivnïm materialam* (Moscow, 2014), 30–2

Kunin, Iosif, ed. *N. Ya. Myaskovskiy: Zhizn' i tvorchestvo v pis'makh, vospominaniyakh, kriticheskikh otzïvakh*, 2nd ed. (Moscow, 1981)

Kutateladze, Larisa, ed. *Artur Nikish i russkaya muzïkal'naya kul'tura* (Leningrad, 1975)

Kuznetsov, Anatoliy. '"Dorogoy Pyotr Petrovich…": Dva pis'ma S. S. Prokof'yeva k P. P. Suvchinskomu', *Muzïkal'naya zhizn'*, 15–16 (1991), 24–5

Kuznetsova, Tat'yana. 'K voprosu o putyakh resheniya zhilishchnoy problemï v SSSR (revolyutsionnïy zhilishchnïy peredel v Moskve, 1918–1921 gg.'), *Istoriya SSSR*, 5 (1963), 140–7

Lamm, Ol'ga. 'Druz'ya Pavla Aleksandrovicha Lamma i uchastniki muzïkal'nikh vecherov v yego dome (20-ye godï XX veka)', in Tamara Livanova (ed.), *Iz proshlogo sovetskoy muzïkal'noy kul'turï* (Moscow, 1975), vol. 1, 72–103

——. 'Druz'ya Pavla Aleksandrovicha Lamma. V évakuatsii', in Tamara Livanova (ed.), *Iz proshlogo sovetskoy muzïkal'noy kul'turï* (Moscow, 1976), vol. 2, 99–109

——. 'Pervïye godï rabotï Gosudarstvennogo muzïkal'nogo izdatel'stva: Dela i lyudi', in Dina Daragan (ed.), *Sovetskaya muzïkal'naya kul'tura: Istoriya, traditsii, sovremennost'* (Moscow, 1980), 190–206

——. *Stranitsï tvorcheskoy biografii Myaskovskogo* (Moscow, 1989)

——. 'Vospominaniya (fragment: 1948–1951 godï)', in Marina Rakhmanova (ed.), *Sergey Prokof'yev: Vospominaniya, pis'ma, stat'i* (Moscow, 2004), 227–73

——. 'Vospominaniya o N. Ya. Myaskovskom', in Semyon Shlifshteyn (ed.), *N. Ya. Myaskovskiy: Sobraniye materialov v dvukh tomakh*, 2nd ed. (Moscow, 1964), vol. 1, 227–53

——. 'Vospominaniya ob A. F. Gedike', in Konstantin Adzhemov (ed.), *A. F. Gedike: Sbornik statey i vospominaniy* (Moscow, 1960), 119–32

Lamm, Viktor, 'P. A. i O. P. Lamm v moikh vospominaniyakh', in Marina Rakhmanova (ed.), *Al'manakh: Sbornik nauchnïkh trudov* (Moscow, 2013), vol. 4, 537–43

Lebedinskiy, Lev. *Vosem' let bor'bï za proletarskuyu muzïku (1923–1931)* (Moscow, 1931)

Lebina, Nataliya. *Sovetskaya povsednevnost': Normï i anomalii*, 3rd ed. (Moscow, 2018)

Liddell, Henry George, and Robert Scott. *A Greek-English Lexicon*, new ed. (Oxford, 1940)

Lih, Lars T., *Bread and Authority in Russia, 1914–1921* (Berlekey and Los Angeles, 1990)

Lindeberg, Aleksandr, ed. *Istoricheskiy ocherk 2-go kadetskogo korpusa, 1712–1912* (St Petersburg, 1912)

Livanova, Tamara. *N. Ya. Myaskovskiy: Tvorcheskiy put'* (Moscow, 1953)

——. 'Spor o Myaskovskom', *Sovetskaya muzïka*, 9 (1948), 23–7

Lobanova, Marina. 'Michail Gnessin und die "Proletarischen Musiker" (aus der Geschichte einer Konfrontation)', in Ernst Kuhn *et al.* (ed.), *'Samuel' Goldenberg und 'Schmuyle': Jüdisches und Antisemitisches in der russischen Musikkultur* (Berlin, 2003), 105–18

Lokshin, Aleksandr, ed. *A. L. Lokshin – Kompozitor i pedagog* (Moscow, 2005)

Lunacharskaia, Irina. 'Why Did Commissar of Enlightenment A. V. Lunacharskii Resign?', trans. Kurt S. Schultz, *The Russian Review*, 3 (1992), 319–42

Lunacharskiy, Anatoliy. *Stat'i o teatre i dramaturgii* (Moscow, 1938)

——. 'Odin iz sdvigov v iskusstvovedenii', *Vestnik Kommunisticheskoy akademii*, 15 (1926), 85–107

——. '"Velikomuchenik individualizma" Avgust Strindberg', in *Meshchanstvo i individualizm* (Moscow and Petrograd, 1923), 224–9

——. 'Verkharn, Émil", in Vladimir Friche (ed.), *Literaturnaya éntsiklopediya*, (Moscow, 1929), vol. 2, 189–93

Mabbett, Thomas Ollive, ed. *The Collected Works of Edgar Allan Poe. Volume II: Tales and Sketches, 1831–1842* (Cambridge, Masschusetts, and London, 1978)

Madelénat, Daniel. *La biographie* (Paris, 1984)

Maksimenkov, Leonid, ed. *Muzïka vmesto sumbura: Kompozitorï i muzïkantï v strane Sovetov* (Moscow, 2013)

——. 'Partiya – nash rulevoy' [part 1], *Muzïkal'naya zhizn'*, 13–14 (1993), 6–8

——. 'Slovo o Khrennikove', in Andrey Kokarev (ed.), *Tikhon Nikolayevich Khrennikov: K 100-letiyu so dnya rozhdeniya* (Moscow, 2013), 122–55

——. *Sumbur vmesto muzïki: Stalinskaya kul'turnaya revolyutsiya, 1936–1938* (Moscow, 1997)

Malle, Silvana. *The Economic Organization of War Communism, 1918–1921* (Cambridge, 1985)

Mally, Lynn. *Culture of the Future: The Proletkult Movement in Revolutionary Russia* (Berkeley, 1990)

Malmstad, John E., and Nikolay Bogomolov. *Mikhail Kuzmin: A Life in Art* (Cambridge, Masschusetts and London, 1999)

Malyavin, Saveliy. 'Pamyati Nikolaya Yakovlevicha', in Semyon Shlifshteyn (ed.), *N. Ya. Myaskovskiy: Sobraniye materialov v dvukh tomakh*, 2nd edn. (Moscow, 1964), vol. 1, 258–68

Mandel'shtam, Nadezhda. *Vospominaniya* (Moscow, 1999)

——. *Vtoraya kniga* (Moscow, 1999)

Manin, Vitaliy. *Iskusstvo v rezervatsii: Khudozhestvennaya zhizn' Rossii 1917–1941 gg.* (Moscow, 1999)

Manley, Rebecca. *To the Tashkent Station: Evacuation and Survival in the Soviet Union at War* (Ithaca, 2009)

Markevich, Andrey, and Mark Harrison. 'Great War, Civil War, and Recovery: Russia's National Income, 1913 to 1928', *Journal of Economic History*, 3 (2011), 672–703

Markov, Anatoliy. *Kadetï i yunkera* (San Francisco, 1961)

Marks, Stephen. 'The Russian Experience of Money, 1914–1924', in Murray Frame *et al.* (ed.), *Russian Culture in War and Revolution, 1914–22* (Bloomington, 2014), vol. 2, 121–48

Martïnov, Nikolay, ed. *Aleksandr Davidenko: Vospominaniya, stat'i, materiali* (Leningrad, 1968)

Marx, Jacques. *Verhaeren: Biographie d'une œuvre* (Brussels, 1996)

Mason, Laura. *Singing the French Revolution: Popular Culture and Politics, 1787–1799* (Ithaca and London, 1996)

Matthews, Mervyn. *Privilege in the Soviet Union: A Study of Elite Life-Styles under Communism* (London, 1978)

Mazur, Marina. 'Perepiska Yu. Veyzberg s N. Myaskovskim', *Vestnik Akademii russkogo baleta imeni A. Ya. Vaganovoy*, 2 (2018), 104–12

Mazus, Izrail', ed. *Demokraticheskiy Soyuz: Sledstvennoye delo 1928–1929 gg.* (Moscow, 2010)

McQuere, Gordon Daniel, ed. *Russian Theoretical Thought in Music* (Ann Arbor, Michigan, 1983)

Melik-Khaspabov, Valentin. *Sbornik zakonov i postanovleniy (partiynïkh, profsoyuznïkh i sovetskikh) o trude rabotnikov iskusstv i khudozhestvennom proizvodstve* (Moscow, 1925)

Mendel'son-Prokof'yeva, Mira. *O Sergeye Sergeyeviche Prokof'yeve: Vospominaniya, dnevniki (1938–1967)*, ed. Yelena Krivtsova (Moscow, 2012)

Men'shikova, Valentina, Vera Yakovleva, and Yevgeniya Fedorovskaya. 'Pamyati brata', in Semyon Shlifshteyn (ed.), *N. Ya. Myaskovskiy: Sobraniye materialov v dvukh tomakh*, 2nd ed. (Moscow, 1964), vol. 1, 163–93

Merridale, Catherine. *Red Fortress: History and Illusion in the Kremlin* (London, 2013)

Meyerhold, Vsevolod. *Meyerhold on Theatre*, ed. & trans. by Edward Braun (London, 1978)

Meyerovich, Mark. *Rozhdeniye i smert' zhilishchnoy kooperatsii: Zhilishchnaya politika v SSSR 1924–1937 gg.* (Irkurtsk, 2004)

Mikhaylov, Andrey. *Rukovodstvo voyennïm obrazovaniyem v Rossii vo vtoroy polovine XIX – nachale XX veka* (Pskov, 1999)

Mikhaylov, Mikhail. *A. K. Lyadov: Ocherk zhizni i tvorchestva*, 2nd ed. (Leningrad, 1985)

Mikheyeva, Lyudmila, ed. *Pamyati I. I. Sollertinskogo: Vospominaniya, materialï, issledovaniya* (Leningrad, 1978)

Mikhutina, Irina. *Ukrainskiy Brestskiy mir* (Moscow, 2007)

Mikkonen, Simo, '"Muddle Instead of Music" in 1936', in Pauline Fairclough (ed.), *Shostakovich Studies 2* (Cambridge, 2010), 231–48

Milovanova, Ol'ga. *Ranneye tvorchestvo N. Ya. Myaskovskogo: Vzglyad sovremennikov. Materialï. Stat'i. Personalii* (Moscow, 2017)

Mil'shteyn, Yakov. *Konstantin Nikolayevich Igumnov* (Moscow, 1975)

Milstein, Nathan, and Solomon Volkov. *From Russia to the West: The Musical Memoirs and Reminiscences of Nathan Milstein*, trans. Antonina W. Bouis (London, 1990)

Milyutin, Dmitriy. *Dnevnik general-fel'dmarshala grafa Dmitriya Alekseyevicha Milyutina, 1873–1875*, ed. Larisa Zakharova, 2nd ed. (Moscow, 2008)

Mnukhin, Lev *et al.*, ed. *Rossiyskoye zarubezh'ye vo Frantsii 1919–2000 gg.: Biograficheskiy slovar'*, 3 vols. (Moscow, 2008)

Morozov, Aleksandr. *Konets utopii: Iz istorii iskusstva v SSSR 1930-kh godov* (Moscow, 1995)

Morrison, Simon. *The People's Artist: Prokofiev's Soviet Years* (New York, 2009)

Myaskovskiy, Nikolay. 'Avtobiograficheskiye zametki o tvorcheskom puti', *Sovetskaya muzïka*, 6 (1936), 3–11

Myaskovskiy, Yakov. 'Vopros o sovremennom znachenii krepostnogo forta', *Inzhenernïy zhurnal*, 12 (1889), 1351–80

Myers, Jeffrey. *Edgar Allan Poe: His Life and Legacy* (New York, 1992)

Nadzhafov, Dzhakhangir, and Zinaid Belousova, ed. *Stalin i kosmopolitizm: Dokumentï Agitpropa TsK KPSS, 1945–1953* (Moscow, 2005)

Nagornaya, Larisa. *Feliks Kon* (Kyiv, 1963)

Nazarenko, Kirill. *Flot, revolyutsiya i vlast' v Rossii, 1917–1921* (Moscow, 2011)

Nazarov, Aleksandr. *Tsezar' Antonovich Kyui* (Moscow, 1989)

Nejedlý, Zdeněk. *Kritiky II (Rudé Právo, 1923–1935)*, ed. Václav Pekárek (Prague, 1956)

Nelson, Amy. *Music for the Revolution: Musicians and Power in Early Soviet Russia* (University Park, Pennsylvania, 2004)

——. 'The Struggle for Proletarian Music: RAPM and the Cultural Revolution', *Slavic Review*, 1 (2000), 101–32

Nemirovskiy, Yevgeniy, *et al. Istoriya knigi v SSSR: 1917–1921*, 3 vols. (Moscow, 1983–86)

Nest'yev, Izrail'. 'Iz istorii russkogo muzïkal'nogo avangarda', *Sovetskaya muzïka*, 1 (1991), 75–87

——. 'Muzïkal'nïye kruzhki', in Aleksandr Alekseyev (ed.), *Russkaya khudozhestvannaya kul'tura kontsa XIX – nachala XX veka*, vol. 3 (Moscow, 1977), 474–82

——. *Zhizn' Sergeya Prokof'yeva* (Moscow, 1973)

Neygauz, Militsa. *Istoriya aresta Genrikha Gustavovicha Neygauza* (Moscow, 2000)

Nezhnïy, Igor'. *Bïloye pered glazami. Teatral'nïye vospominaniya* (Moscow, 1963)

Nice, David. *Prokofiev: From Russia to the West, 1891–1935* (New Haven and London, 2003)

Nikitina, Lyudmila. '"Pochti lyuboy mig zhizni – rabota". Stranitsï biografii i tvorchestva Mechislava Vaynberga', *Muzïkal'naya akademiya*, 5 (1994), 17–24

[Nurok, Al'fred], 'A. N.' 'O nekotorïkh muzïkal'nïkh novinkakh', *Mir iskusstva*, 11 (1902), 51–2

Orlov, Genrikh. *Russkiy sovetskiy simfonizm* (Moscow, 1966)

Orlova, Yelena, and Andrey Kryukov. *Akademik Boris Vladimirovich Asaf'yev: Monografiya* (Leningrad, 1984)

Osokina, Yelena. *Za fasadom "Stalinskogo izobiliya": Raspredeleniye i rïnok v snabzhenii naseleniya v godï industrializatsii, 1927–1941* (Moscow, 1999)

Ossovskiy, Aleksandr. 'V. G. Karatïgin', *Muzïkal'naya letopis'*, 3 (1926), 161–4

Ostrovityanov, Konstantin, *et al.*, ed. *Organizatsiya nauki v pervïye godï sovetskoy vlasti (1917–1925): Sbornik dokumentov* (Leningrad, 1968)

Ovsyannikova, Sof'ya. 'Mikhail Kvadri – Lider moskovskikh Six'ov', *Musicus*, 1 (2018), 35–9

Pachmuss, Temira. *Zinaida Hippius: An Intellectual Profile* (Carbondale and Edwardsville, 1971)

Patenaude, Bertrand M. *The Big Show in Bololand: The American Relief Expedition to Soviet Russia in the Famine of 1921* (Stanford, 2002)

Perkhin, Vladimir. *Deyateli russkogo iskusstva i M. B. Khrapchenko, predsedatel' Vsesoyuznogo komiteta po delam iskusstv (aprel' 1939 – yanvar' 1948): Svod pisem* (Moscow, 2007)

Petrov, Ivan. 'Nastavnik i drug', in Semyon Shlifshteyn (ed.), *N. Ya. Myaskovskiy: Sobraniye materialov v dvukh tomakh*, 2nd edn. (Moscow, 1964), vol. 1, 334–42

Petrov, Valeriy, ed. *Ivan Vasil'yevich Petrov: Stat'i, materialï, vospominaniya* (Moscow, 1983)

Petrovskiy, Boris, ed. *Bol'shaya meditsinskaya ėntsiklopediya*, 3rd ed., 30 vols. (Moscow, 1974–89)

Petrukhintsev, Nikolay. *Tsarstvovaniye Annï Ioannovnï: Formirovaniye vnutripoliticheskogo kursa i sud'bï armii i flota, 1730–1735 g.* (St Petersburg, 2001)

Peyko, Nikolay. '27-ya simfoniya N. Ya. Myaskovskogo', in Semyon Shlifshteyn (ed.), *N. Ya. Myaskovskiy: Sobraniye materialov v dvukh tomakh*, 2nd edn. (Moscow, 1964), vol. 1, 78–95

Pierre, Constant. *Hymnes et chansons de la Révolution: Aperçu général et catalogue avec notices historiques, analytiques et bibliographiques* (Paris, 1904)

Piksanov, Nikolay, *et al.*, ed. *Sotsialisticheskiy realizm: Bibliograficheskiy ukazatel'* (Moscow, 1934)

Plotnikov, Konstantin. 'Istoriya literaturnoy organizatsii Vseroskomdram (po materialam Otdela rukopisey IMLI RAN' (unpublished dissertation, Gorky Institute of World Literature/Russian Academy of Sciences, 2015)

Plotnikov, Nikolay, and Nadezhda Podzemskaya, ed. *Iskusstvo kak yazïk – Yazïki iskusstva: Gosudarstvennaya akademiya khudozhestvennïkh nauk i ėsteticheskaya teoriya 1920-kh godov*, 2 vols. (Moscow, 2017)

Pol'dyayeva, Yelena. '"Ya chasto s nim ne soglashalsya . . .": iz perepiski S. S. Prokof'yeva i P. P. Suvchinskogo', in Alla Bretanitskaya (ed.), *Pyotr Suvchinskiy i yego vremya* (Moscow, 1999), 56–104

Pollock, Ethan. *Stalin and the Soviet Science Wars* (Princeton and Oxford, 2006)

Polyakova, Lyudmila. *Soviet Music* (Moscow, n.d.)

Polyanovskiy, Georgiy. *Marian Koval'* (Moscow, 1968)

Ponyatovskiy, Stanislav. *Persimfans – Orkestr bez dirizhyora* (Moscow, 2003)

Popov, Gavriil. *Iz literaturnogo naslediya: Stranitsï biografii*, ed. Zarui Apetyan (Moscow, 1986)

Prokof'yev, Sergey. *Avtobiografiya*. 2nd ed. (Moscow, 1982)

——. *Dnevnik 1907–1918*, ed. Svyatoslav Prokof'yev (Paris, 2002)

——. *Dnevnik: 1919–1933*, ed. Svyatoslav Prokof'yev (Paris, 2002)

Protopopov, Vladimir. 'O tematizme i melodike S. I. Taneyeva', *Sovetskaya muzïka*, 7 (1940), 49–60

Pushkaryov, Vitaliy. 'Chyornïy rïnok v SSSR v godï Velikoy otechestvennoy voynï i yego vliyaniye na sostoyaniye vnutrennego rïnka stranï', *Ėkonomicheskiy zhurnal*, 12 (2006), 212–26

Pushkin, Aleksandr. *Mednïy vsadnik: Peterburgskaya povest' (risunki: Aleksandra Benua)* (Petrograd, 1923)

Pyatnitskiy, Mitrofan, *et al. Kontsertï M. Ye. Pyatnitskogo s krest'yanami (starinnïye pesni Voronezhskoy gubernii v narodnoy garmonizatsiyi, zapisannïye M. Ye. Pyatnitskim)* (Moscow, 1914)

Pyman, Avril. *A History of Russian Symbolism* (Cambridge, 1994)

Rabinovich, Izrail', ed. *B. Yavorskiy: Vospominaniya, stat'i i pis'ma* (Moscow, 1964)

——, ed. *B. Yavorskiy: Vospominaniya, stat'i i pis'ma*, rev. ed. (Moscow, 1972)

Ramming, Nikolai. *Die St.-Annen-Schule in St. Petersburg* (Berlin, 1936)

Rayskin, Iosif. 'Artisticheskiy vostorg i issledovatel'skaya glubina: N. Myaskovskiy o Chaykovskom-simfoniste', in Oleg Kolovskiy (ed.), *Kritika i muzïkoznaniye: Sbornik statey* (Leningrad, 1980), vol. 2, 207–16

Razhnikov, Vladimir. *Kirill Kondrashin rasskazïvayet o muzïke i zhizni* (Moscow, 1989)

Razumovskaya, Maria. *Heinrich Neuhaus: A Life beyond Music* (Rochester, 2018)

Rimskiy-Korsakov, Andrey, *et al.*, ed. *V. G. Karatïgin: Zhizn', deyatel'nost', stat'i, materialï* (Leningrad, 1927)

Rimskiy-Korsakov, Nikolay. *Letopis' moey muzïkal'noy zhizni*, ed. Nadezhda Rimskaya-Korsakova (St Petersburg, 1909)

Rittikh, Margarita. 'B. Asaf'yev i nauchnïye sessii klinskogo Doma-muzeya', in Andrey Kryukov (ed.), *Vospominaniya o B. V. Asaf'yeve*, (Leningrad, 1974), 254–68

Rosenthal, Bernice Glatzer. 'The Transmutation of the Symbolist Ethos: Mystical Anarchism and the Revolution of 1905', *Slavic Review*, 4 (1977), 608–27

Rossikhina, Vera. 'N. G. Aleksandrova i ritmika Dal'kroza v nashey strane', in Tamara Livanova (ed.), *Iz proshlogo sovetskoy muzïkal'noy kul'turï* (Moscow, 1982), vol. 3, 238–70

Rozanov, Aleksandr. *Muzïkal'nïy Pavlovsk* (Leningrad, 1978)

Rudakov, Vasiliy. 'Real'nïye uchilishcha', in Konstantin Arsen'yev and Fyodor Petrushevskiy (ed.), *Éntsiklopedicheskiy slovar' Brokgauza i Yefrona* (St Petersburg, 1899), vol. 26, 408–13

Ryauzov, Sergey. 'Vospominaniya o Prokolle', *Sovetskaya muzïka*, 7 (1949), 54–8

Sabaneyev, Leonid. *Muzïka posle Oktyabrya* (Moscow, 1926)

Sadïkhova, Roza, and Dmitriy Frederiks, Dmitriy. 'D. Shostakovich. Pis'ma k materi', *Neva*, 9 (1986), 166–75

Salu, Bart, ed. *Emile Verhaeren en Rusland* (Sint-Amands aan de Schelde, 1990)

Sargeant, Lynn. 'Kashchei the Immortal: Liberal Politics, Cultural Memory, and the Rimsky-Korsakov Scandal of 1905', *Russian Review* 1 (2005), 22–43

Savyolov, Leonid. *Vospominaniya* (Moscow, 2015)

Scheijen, Sjeng. *Diaghilev: A Life*, trans. Jane Hedley-Prôle and S. J. Leinbach (Oxford, 2009)

Scherchen, Hermann. *Aus meinem Leben. Rußland in jenen Jahren* (Berlin, 1984)

Schwarz, Boris. *Music and Musical Life in Soviet Russia, 1917–1981*, expanded ed. (Bloomington, 1983)

Segel'man, Mikhail. "'Plach stranstvuyushchego" (ocherk o Dvadtsat' shestoy simfonii N. Myaskovskogo)', *Muzïkal'naya akademiya*, 3–4 (1998), 55–63

Servaes, Paul. *Emile Verhaeren: Vlaams dichter voor Europa* (Berchem-Antwerpen, 2013)

Seslavinskiy, Mikhail, and Ol'ga Tarakanova. *Knigi dlya gurmanov: Bibliograficheskiye izdaniya kontsa XIX – nachala XX veka* (Moscow, 2010)

Shaporina, Lyubov'. *Dnevnik*, 2 vols. (Moscow, 2012)

Shebalin, Vissarion. 'Iz vospominaniy o Nikolaye Yakovleviche Myaskovskom', in Semyon Shlifshteyn (ed.), *N. Ya. Myaskovskiy: Sobraniye materialov v dvukh tomakh*, 2nd ed. (Moscow, 1964), vol. 1, 276–97

——. 'Myaskovskiy-uchitel'', *Sovetskaya muzïka*, 4 (1941), 47–51

——. 'O proydennom puti', *Sovetskaya muzïka*, 2 (1959), 74–84

——. 'Vospominaniya', in Valeriya Razheva (ed.), *V. Ya. Shebalin: Zhizn' i tvorchestvo* (Moscow, 2003), 13–88

[Shelley, Percy Bysshe], *Shelli. Polnoye sobraniye sochineniy v perevode K. D. Bal'monta*. 3 vols. (Moscow, 1903–7)

Shepilov, Dmitriy. *The Kremlin Scholar: A Memoir of Soviet Politics under Stalin and Khrushchev*, ed. Stephen V. Bittner, trans. by Anthony Austin (New Haven and London, 2007)

——. 'Vospominaniya', *Voprosï istorii*, 5 (1998), 12–20

Shitts [Schütz], Ivan. *Dnevnik 'Velikogo pereloma' (mart 1928 – avgust 1931)* (Paris, 1986)

Shlifshteyn, Semyon, ed. 'Iz neopublikovannoy perepiski N. Ya. Myaskovskogo', *Sovetskaya muzïka*, 8 (1960), 3–22

——. 'Myaskovskiy i opernoye tvorchestvo', *Sovetskaya muzïka*, 5 (1959), 41–6

——. *N. Ya. Myaskovskiy: Notograficheskiy spravochnik* (Moscow, 1962)

——, ed. *N. Ya. Myaskovskiy: Sobraniye materialov v dvukh tomakh*, 2nd ed. 2 vols. (Moscow, 1964)

——, ed. *S. S. Prokof'yev: Materialï, dokumentï, vospominaniya*. 2nd ed. (Moscow, 1961)

Shrayer, David. 'Felix d'Herelle in Russia', *Bulletin de l'Institut Pasteur*, 94 (1996), 91–6

Shteynberg, Maksimilian. 'Moya kompozitorskaya rabota nad uzbekskim fol'klorom', in Semyon Ginzburg (ed.), *Puti razvitiya uzbekskoy muzïki* (Leningrad, 1946), 103–6

Sidorina, Tat'yana, and Igor' Karpinskiy. 'Revolyutsiya i yeyo vïrazheniye v simfonicheskoy muzïke: N. Myaskovsky i D. Shostakovich', *Voprosï filosofii*, 12 (2017), 55–63

Sidorov, Nikolay. '"TsK vskrïl presmïkatel'stvo pered zagranitsey". Kak sozdavalis' "sudï chesti" v tsentral'nïkh organakh', *Istochnik*, 6 (1994), 68–81

Simonov, Konstantin. *Glazami cheloveka moyego pokoleniya* (Moscow, 1988)

Simonov, Nikolay. '"Krepit' oboronu stranï Sovetov" ("voyennaya trevoga" 1927 g. i yeyo posledstviya)', *Otechestvennaya istoriya*, 3 (1996), 155–61

Sitsky, Larry. *Music of the Repressed Russian Avant-Garde, 1900–1929* (Westport, Connecticut, 1994)

Skryabin, Aleksandr Serafimovich, *et al.*, ed. *Nash starik: Aleksandr Gol'denveyzer i Moskovskaya konservatoriya* (Moscow and St Petersburg, 2015)

——, *et al.*, ed. *Nastavnik: Aleksandr Gol'denveyzer glazami sovremennikov* (Moscow and St Petersburg, 2014)

Smilga, Pyotr. 'Iz vospominaniy o Moskovskoy konservatorii dvadtsatïkh godov', in Yekaterina Alekseyeva *et al.* (ed.), *Vospominaniya o Moskovskoy konservatorii* (Moscow, 1966), 216–28

Smirnova, Tat'yana. *'Bïvshiye lyudi' Sovetskoy Rossii: Strategii vïzhivaniya i puti integratsii, 1917–1936 godï* (Moscow, 2003)

Sokolov, Andrey, *et al.*, ed. *Obshchestvo i vlast': 1930-ye gg. Povestvovaniye v dokumentakh* (Moscow, 1998)

Sollertinskiy, Dmitriy, Lyudmila Kovnatskaya, and Ol'ga Dansker, ed. *D. D. Shostakovich: Pis'ma I. I. Sollertinskomu* (St Petersburg, 2006)

Sorokin, Pitirim. *A Long Journey: The Autobiography of Pitirim A. Sorokin* (New Haven, 1963)

Spiridovich, Aleksandr. *Zapiski zhandarma* (Kharkov, 1928)

Stalin, Iosif. *Sochineniya*, 13 vols. (Moscow, 1946–51)

Stasova, Yelena, ed. *V. V. Stasov: Pis'ma k rodnïm*, 3 vols. (Moscow, 1953–62)

Steinberg, John W. *All the Tsar's Men: Russia's General Staff and the Fate of the Empire, 1898–1914* (Baltimore and Washington, 2010)

Stepanova, Svetlana. *Muzïkal'naya zhizn' Moskvï v pervïye godï posle Oktyabrya* (Moscow, 1972)

——. 'Novïy Rastin'yak, ili Kak Kovalyov zavoyovïval Moskvu', *Muzïkal'naya akademiya*, 3–4 (1998), 306–15

Stone, Norman. *The Eastern Front: 1914–1917* (London, 1998)

Stone, Richard. 'Stalin's Forgotten Cure', *Science*, 5594 (2002), 728–31

Stravinsky, Igor. *Chroniques de ma vie* (Paris, 1935)

Stupel', Aleksandr. *Russkaya mïsl' o muzïke, 1895–1917: Ocherk istorii russkoy muzïkal'noy kritiki* (Leningrad, 1980)

Stupnicki, Hipolit. *Herbarz Polski i imionospis zasłużonych w Polsce ludzi wszystkich stanów i czasów*, 3 vols. (Lwów, 1855)

Svetlanov, Yevgeniy. *Muzïka segodnya: Stat'i, retsenzii, ocherki* (Moscow, 1985), 100–104

Svetlanova, Martina, ed. 'Pavel Lamm v tyur'makh i ssïlkakh: Po stranitsam vospominaniy O. P. Lamm', in Marina Rakhmanova ed., *Al'manakh*, Trudï Gosudarstvennogo tsentral'nogo muzeya muzïkal'noy kul'turï imeni M. I. Glinki (Moscow, 2003), vol. 2, 73–120

Szabó, László. *A nagy temető (Przemysl ostroma 1914–1915)* (Budapest, 1982)

Szenkar, Eugen. *Mein Weg als Musiker: Erinnerungen eines Dirigenten*, ed. Sandra Szenkar (Berlin, 2014)

Taruskin, Richard. *Cursed Questions: On Music and Its Social Practices* (Oakland, 2020)

——. *Defining Russia Musically: Historical and Hermeneutical Essays* (Princeton and Oxford, 1997)

——. *On Russian Music* (Berlekey and Los Angeles, 2009)

——. *Stravinsky and the Russian Traditions: A Biography of the Works through Mavra*, 2 vols. (Oxford, 1996)

Taubman, William. *Khrushchev: The Man and His Era* (New York, 2003)

Tassie, Gregor. *Nikolay Myaskovsky: The Conscience of Russian Music* (Lanham, Maryland, 2014)

Teterina, Nadezhda, ed. *Yuriy Vsevolodovich Keldïsh: Vospominaniya, issledovaniya, materialï, dokumentï* (Moscow, 2015)

Tigranov, Georgiy, ed. *K. S. Saradzhev: Stat'i, vospominaniya* (Moscow, 1962)

Tomoff, Kiril. *Creative Union: The Professional Organization of Soviet Composers, 1939–1953* (Ithaca, NY, 2006)

Tomozov, Valeriy. 'K yubileyu V. L. Modzalevskogo', in *Izvestiya Russkogo genealogicheskogo obshchestva*, 4 (1995), 45–51

——. 'Modzalevs'kyy, Vadim L'vovich', in Valeriy Smoliy *et al.* (ed.), *Entsiklopediya istorii Ukraïni*, 2010), vol. 7, 20–1

Topornin, Sh. *Novogeorgiyevsk (sine loco*, 1884)

Trotskiy, Lev. *Literatura i revolyutsiya* (Moscow, 1991)

Tschöpl, Carin. *Vjačeslav Ivanov: Dichtung und Dichtungstheorie* (Munich, 1968)

Tsukker, Arnol'd. *Pyat' let Persimfansa* (Moscow, 1927)

Tumanov, Alexander. *The Life and Artistry of Maria Olenina-d'Alheim*, trans. Christopher Barnes (Edmonton, 2000)

Tumarkin, Nina. *'Lenin Lives!' The Lenin Cult in Soviet Russia*, enlarged ed. (Cambridge, Masschusetts and London, 1997)

Tunstall, Graydon A. *Written in Blood: The Battles for Fortress Przemyśl in WW1* (Bloomington, 2016) van der Kolk, Bessel A., Alexander C. McFarlane, and Lars Weisaeth, ed. *Traumatic Stress: The Effects of Overwhelming Experience on Mind, Body, and Society* (New York, 2007)

Varunts, Viktor, ed. *I. F. Stravinskiy: Perepiska s russkimi korrespondentami. Materialï k biografii.* 3 vols. (Moscow, 1998–2003)

Vasilenko, Sergey. *Vospominaniya*, ed. Tamara Livanova (Moscow, 1979)

Vasina-Grossman, Vera. 'Professiya – istorik', *Muzïkal'naya zhizn'*, 16 (1988), 8

Velichko, Konstantin, *et al. Voyenno-inzhenernïy sbornik: Materialï po istorii voynï 1914–1918 gg.* (Moscow, 1918)

Verhaeren, Émile. *Hélène de Sparte – Les aubes*, 2nd ed. (Paris, 1920)

Verkhoturskiy, Adol'f. *Muzgiz na stroyke* (Moscow, 1931)

Veymarn, Boris, ed. *Istoriya sovetskogo iskusstva* (Moscow, 1965)

Viana Filho, Luis. *A verdade na biografia* (Rio de Janeiro, 1945)

Vinogradov, Viktor. *Spravochnik-putevoditel' po simfoniyam N. Ya. Myaskovskogo* (Moscow, 1954)

Vlasova, Natal'ya. 'A. Shyonberg v Rossii: Iz istorii vospriyatiya', in Yekaterina Vlasova and Yelena Sorokina (ed.), *Naslediye: Russkaya muzïka – Mirovaya kul'tura* (Moscow, 2009), 56–96

Vlasova, Yekaterina. *1948 god v sovetskoy muzïke* (Moscow, 2010)

——. 'N. Ya. Myaskovsky v perepiske s B. V. Asaf'yevïm', *Nauchnïy vestnik Moskovskoy konservatorii*, 4 (2017), 93–107

——. 'Plenum Soveta Vseroskomdrama. Fragment stenogrammï, posvyashchyonnïy muzïkal'nïm voprosam (18–19 dekabrya 1931 goda)', *Muzïkal'naya akademiya*, 2 (1993), 160–77

——. 'The Stalinist Opera Project', in Patrick Zuk and Marina Frolova-Walker (ed.), *Russian Music Since 1917: Reappraisal and Rediscovery*, Proceedings of the British Academy (Oxford, 2017), 164–87

——. '"Vï zhdyote Verdi. No ya ne uveren, chto éto yedinstvenno verno": Iz perepiski B.V. Asaf'yeva i N. Ya. Myaskovskogo', *Muzïkal'naya akademiya*, 3 (2018), 13–25

Volkov, Sergey. *Generalitet Rossiyskoy imperii: Éntsiklopedicheskiy slovar' generalov i admiralov ot Petra I do Nikolaya II* (Moscow, 2009)

——. *Russkiy ofitserskiy korpus* (Moscow, 2003)

von Crousaz, Adolf Friedrich Johannes. *Geschichte des königlich preussischen Kadetten-Corps, nach seiner Entstehung, seinem Entwickelungsgange und seinen Resultaten* (Berlin, 1857)

von Miaskowski, Kurt. 'Basler Jugenderinnerungen', *Basler Jahrbuch* (1929), 78–137

von Wistinghausen, Henning. *Zwischen Reval und St. Petersburg: Erinnerungen von Estländern aus zwei Jahrhunderten* (Weissenhorn, 1993)

Vorob'yov, Igor'. *Sotsrealisticheskiy 'bol'shoy stil'' v sovetskoy muzïke (1930– 1950-ye godï): Issledovaniye* (St Petersburg, 2013)

Vorozheykina, Yevgeniya. *Rossiyskaya khudozhestvennaya intelligentsiya v évakuatsii v godï Velikoy otechestvennoy voynï* (Kostroma, 2004)

Weisser, Albert. 'Lazare Saminsky's Years in Russia and Palestine: Excerpts from an Unpublished Autobiography', *Musica Judaica* 1 (1977–8), 1–20

Weissman, Benjamin M., 'Herbert Hoover's "Treaty" with Soviet Russia: August 20, 1921', *Slavic Review* 2 (1969), 276–88

——. *Herbert Hoover and Famine Relief to Soviet Russia 1921–23* (Stanford, California, 1974)

Wellens, Ian. *Music on the Frontline: Nicolas Nabokov's Struggle against Communism and Middlebrow Culture* (Aldershot, 2002)

Yakimenko, Yuliya. 'Iz istorii chistok apparata: Akademiya khudozhestvennïkh nauk v 1929–1932 gg.', *Novïy istoricheskiy vestnik*, 1 (2005), 150–61

Yakovlev [Trifonov-Yakovlev], Aleksandr. 'Istoriya Nikolinoy', in Marina Gromova *et al.* (ed.), *Nasha Nikolina Gora* (Moscow, 2008), vol. 1, 13–27

Yakovlev, Vasiliy. 'V yunïye godï', in Semyon Shlifshteyn (ed.), *N. Ya. Myaskovskiy: Sobraniye materialov v dvukh tomakh*, 2nd ed. (Moscow, 1964), vol. 1, 194–200

Yakovlev, Viktor. *Istoriya krepostey: Èvolyutsiya dolgovremennoy fortifikatsii* (Moscow, 1931)

Yarustovskiy, Boris. *Simfonii o voyne i mire* (Moscow, 1966)

Yastrebtsev, Vasiliy. *Nikolay Andreyevich Rimsky-Korsakov: Vospominaniya, 1886–1908*, 2 vols. (Leningrad, 1959–60)

Yavorskiy, Boleslav. *Stroyeniye muzïkal'noy rechi. Materialï i zametki* (Moscow, 1908)

Yefimov, Viktor. *Letopis' zhizni i deyatel'nosti A. V. Lunacharskogo*, 3 vols. (Dushanbe, 1992)

Yefimov, Yevgeniy. *Sumbur vokrug "Sumbura" i odnogo malen'kogo zhurnalista: Stat'i i materialï* (Moscow, 2006)

Yekelchyk, Serhy. *Ukraine: Birth of a Modern Nation* (Oxford, 2007)

Yeryomina, Larisa, and Arseniy Roginskiy, ed. *Rasstrel'nïye spiski: Moskva 1937–1941. "Kommunarka", Butovo* (Moscow, 2000)

Yevlakhov, Orest. 'Iz vospominaniy', in Andrey Kryukov (ed.), *Vospominaniya o B. V. Asaf'yeve* (Leningrad, 1974), 33–8

Yuzefovich, Viktor. *Sergey Kusevitskiy. Tom pervïy: Russkiye godï* (Moscow, 2004)

Zaretskiy, Yury. 'Confessing to Leviathan: The Mass Practice of Writing Autobiographies in the USSR', *Slavic Review*, 4 (2017), 1027–47

Zarubin, Valeriy. *Bol'shoy teatr: Pervïye postanovki oper na russkoy stsene, 1825–1993* (Moscow, 1994)

Zassimova, Anna. *Georges Catoire: Seine Musik, sein Leben, seine Ausstrahlung* (Berlin, 2011)

Zayonchkovskiy, Andrey. *Voyennïye reformï 1860–1870-kh godov v Rossii* (Moscow, 1952)

Żernicki-Szeliga, Emilian. *Der polnische Adel und die demselben hinzugetretenen andersländischen Adelsfamilien*, 2 vols. (Hamburg, 1900)

Zhitomirskiy, Danièl'. 'Mifologiya "klassovogo" iskusstva', *Muzïkal'naya akademiya*, 2 (1993), 144–54

——. 'Na puti k istoricheskoy pravde', *Muzïkal'naya zhizn'*, 13 (1988), 3–5

——. 'Vasiliy Vasil'yevich Yakovlev: ocherk zhizni i deyatel'nosti', in Yelena Grosheva *et al.* (ed.), *Vasiliy Yakovlev. Izbrannïye trudï o muzïke* (Moscow, 1964), vol. 1, 7–36

Zuk, Patrick. 'Boris Asafiev in 1948', *Journal of the Royal Musical Association*, 1 (2019), 123–56

——. 'Nikolay Myaskovsky and the Events of 1948', *Music and Letters*, 1 (2012), 61–85

——. 'Nikolay Myaskovsky and the "Regimentation" of Soviet Composition: A Reassessment', *Journal of Musicology*, 3 (2014), 354–93

——. 'Romansï N. Myaskovskogo na slova Z. Gippius', in Natal'ya Degtyaryova and Nataliya Braginskaya (ed.), *Sankt-Peterburgskaya konservatoriya v mirovom muzïkal'nom prostranstve: Kompozitorskiye, ispolnitel'skiye, nauchnïye shkolï 1862–2012* (St Petersburg, 2013), 218–23

Index of Myaskovsky's Works

General Index